Immigrant Identity and the Politics of Citizenship

A collection of articles from the
JOURNAL OF AMERICAN ETHNIC HISTORY

Edited by John J. Bukowczyk

COMMON THREADS

An anthology from the
University of Illinois Press

T0369786

Library of Congress Control Number: 2016938750
ISBN 978-0-252-08229-0 (paperback)
ISBN 978-0-252-09923-6 (e-book)

Contents

1

Introduction

JOHN J. BUKOWCZYK

Wayne State University
Editor, *Journal of American Ethnic History*

> Once I thought to write a history of the
> immigrants in America. Then I discovered that
> the immigrants *were* American history.[1]
> —Oscar Handlin

THE MASTER NARRATIVE OF AMERICAN HISTORY of a generation or two ago portrayed America as "a nation of immigrants,"[2] a place of refuge where Europe's "wretched refuse" (to quote the inscription on the base of the Statue of Liberty) melted together to form the American people. The image of the magnetic pull of America as land of opportunity and freedom long since has given way to more pointedly transnational approaches that stress the interconnectedness of the "push" and "pull" factors that caused population movements, that probe migrant subjectivities, and that follow the ongoing connections—and often movements—between and among the migrants and the peoples and places they left behind. In a more recent era of speedy transportation and communications, today's "immigrants," more so than ever before, really are migrants, transient participants in an increasingly global society and economy.

Both of these differently hopeful narratives, and the perspectives from which they derived, may suggest a story of uprooting but also one of mobility and progress, which, taken together, accurately represent two enduringly compelling versions of immigration history. But after the changes that roiled American society—and other so-called "receiver countries"—since the Second World War and, with that, transformed the practice of history, harsh national realities and darker interpretive themes now have intruded on these optimistic narratives. All along, for example, the America that immigrants were entering was, in fact, a society of sharp racial divisions, most graphically illustrated in America's "peculiar institution,"[3] the antebellum Southern

5

euphemism for black chattel slavery. Immigrants may have been, as historian Thomas Guglielmo has argued, "white on arrival" when they landed upon these metaphorical shores,[4] but this fact in no way alters the nineteenth-century racial order in which the "races of Europe," as nationality groups were then described, were arranged in a racial hierarchy—with southern, central, and eastern Europeans ranked as racially inferior to persons of putatively superior northwestern European racial stock—and America was divided between "white men and foreigners."[5]

Then there were immigrants of darker hue and what native-born European Americans have regarded as "stranger" and "more exotic" cultures (which is to say, cultures more unfamiliar to them), immigrants from the Middle East, Latin America, Asia, and Africa whom racialist pseudoscience defined as permanent racial Others. Not even the "nonwhite" native-born of these groups could escape from these irreducible racial categories of Otherness. Even as some of these were cast as "model minorities," for their seeming emulation of the values of self-discipline, education, hard work, and upward mobility as extolled by members of the native-born white, Protestant middle class, their ascribed racial identities remained. Meanwhile, in the American racial order, Mexicans and Indians, who had not migrated to the United States, but (via colonial conquest and territorial expansion) America had, so to speak, migrated to them, also were racialized by white Americans who considered them their racial inferiors.

If the central theme of American history, as historian Oscar Handlin wrote, has been immigration, the central problem of American history, since slavery days, arguably has been the problem of race. Although "race" may be a social construct, the concept has been used to order a system of "racial" subordination and domination. Race has molded immigrant identity and structured the politics of citizenship. It has shaped U.S. immigration policy, but it also has informed the ways in which immigrants and their children have been incorporated into American society; how they have related to each other and to the native-born; and how the native-born have reacted to them. As the interplay between immigration and race extends to such topics, it reveals how the study of immigration naturally opens onto, and connects to, the broader study of *ethnic* history—how immigrants are assimilated, incorporated, and integrated into the society of the country to which they have migrated, how and why they maintain transnational connections to friends and family abroad, and how they build new migrant and ethnic institutions and identities. Historians and sociologists variously have described some of these processes by which immigrants become ethnics as ethnicization or ethnogenesis, but it must be understood that these transformations do not take place in a social vacuum. Rather, immigrants and ethnics are shaped—even sometimes remade—by the societies they enter; and they also interact with, shape, and change these host societies in profound ways. Implicated in these various interactions is a changing discourse on how we understand immigration and migration; how we define race and nation; and how we think about social justice when persons of different cultural backgrounds mingle. No less involved is whether there is a "we" or instead many different and conflicting "we's."

The articles gathered together in *Immigrant Identity and the Politics of Citizenship* take readers through many of these themes. It is perhaps the case that, after historians like Francis Parkman and Frederick Jackson Turner, white Americans have idealized an American identity whose imagined essence derived from the heroic encounter of settlers of Anglo-Saxon stock with the American frontier, but Gunlög Fur's article, "Indians and Immigrants—Entangled Histories," the first in the collection, undermines this triumphalist, racialized narrative of the West. Fur usefully shows that western history was immigrant history and that contact between settlers and Indians on the western frontier often involved an ethnic encounter between Native Americans and the foreign-born. Next, articles by Hidetaka Hirota, "'The Great Entrepot for Mendicants': Foreign Poverty and Immigration Control in New York State to 1882"; Douglas C. Baynton, "Defectives in the Land: Disability and American Immigration Policy, 1882–1924"; and Lara Putnam, "Sentiment and the Restrictionist State: Evidence from the British Caribbean Experience, ca. 1925" examine the development and operation of American immigration policy in the nineteenth century, with its roots in the early regulation of immigration at the state level and then, in the federal government, of the ways immigrants came to be defined as desirable or undesirable and their entry into the United Sates controlled and policed. From there, James R. Barrett and David Roediger's now classic article, "Inbetween Peoples: Race, Nationality and the 'New Immigrant' Working Class," and Mark Overmyer-Velázquez's article, "Good Neighbors and White Mexicans: Constructing Race and Nation on the Mexico–U.S. Border," examine some of the ways that immigrants from Europe and both foreign-born and native-born Mexicans variously were racialized in the United States, showing race to have been both a formative and a malleable identity. Robert Fleegler's article, "'Forget All Differences until the Forces of Freedom Are Triumphant': The World War II–Era Quest for Ethnic and Religious Tolerance," meanwhile shows how the exigencies of World War

II and America's fight against racialist ideology abroad laid the groundwork for a more inclusive American civic identity and citizenship, while Allison Varzally's article, "Romantic Crossings: Making Love, Family, and Non-Whiteness in California, 1925–1950," examines the evolution of nonwhiteness as an American social category.

It is here in the collection that we come to David Reimers's pivotal essay, "An Unintended Reform: The 1965 Immigration Act and Third World Immigration to the United States," which investigates the great turning point in post–World War II American immigration policy, when many of the racialist restrictions on entry fell away and whose unintended consequence was the sweeping demographic—and racial—remaking of the American people. Putnam, Varzally, Julio Capó, Jr., and Vibha Bhalla explore ways that, as part of that remaking, sexuality and gender have complicated immigration and ethnic history themes. Capó's article, "Queering Mariel: Mediating Cold War Foreign Policy and U.S. Citizenship among Cuba's Homosexual Exile Community, 1978–1994," examines homosexuality as a category of immigrant undesirability, which now has fallen away, while Bhalla's article, "'Couch Potatoes and Super-Women': Gender, Migration and the Emerging Discourse on Housework among Asian Indian Immigrants," looks at how integration into American society affected gender and household relations between Asian Indian women and Asian Indian men. Immigrant integration into American society also entailed newcomers finding—or building—a place in the American economy. Willow Lung-Amam's article, "Malls of Meaning: Building Asian America in Silicon Valley Suburbia," explores how Asian immigrant entrepreneurs in California developed ethnic business establishments that anchored the burgeoning Asian communities in that Pacific state. The late Raymond A. Mohl's article, "The Politics of Expulsion: A Short History of Alabama's Anti-Immigrant Law, HB 56," recounts the resurgence of a racialist anti-immigrant policy in Alabama in response to what Mohl elsewhere described as the Latinization of the South in recent decades.[6] The final article in this collection, Karen Leonard's "American Muslims and Authority: Competing Discourses in a Non-Muslim State," broaches a subject of much current interest, the integration of Muslim immigrants into the American polity, in which Leonard dispels the notion that the Muslim community in America is a monolith.

The rich sampling of content from the *Journal of American Ethnic History* should prompt lively discussion of contemporary issues involving immigrant and ethnic identity and the politics of the citizenship and incorporation of the foreign-born into an ever-changing American society. Ironically, although the immigration and ethnic history field and, with it, the *JAEH* focus on cultural differences and the mixing and mingling of diverse peoples, the subtext throughout involves, so to speak, the other side of the coin. On the flip side of American coins reads the inscription *E Pluribus Unum*—"From Many, One." In our own times, as in the past, this motto raises questions that still beg for answers today. What is an America? What should it be? Ultimately, it is these two questions that have inspired the publication of the *JAEH* and that continue to animate scholarship in the immigration and ethnic history field.[7]

NOTES

The articles by David Reimers, Allison Varzally, and James R. Barrett and David Roediger appeared in print during the editorship of Ronald H. Bayor. His contributions to the journal are greatly appreciated and here duly acknowledged.

1. Oscar Handlin, *The Uprooted: The Epic Story of the Great Migrations That Made the American People* (Boston: Little, Brown, 1951), 3.

2. See, for example, John F. Kennedy, *A Nation of Immigrants* (New York: Anti-Defamation League of B'nai B'rith, 1959).

3. Kenneth M. Stampp, *The Peculiar Institution: Slavery in the Ante-Bellum South* (New York: Vintage Books, 1956), 3.

4. Thomas A. Guglielmo, *White on Arrival: Italians, Race, Color, and Power in Chicago, 1890–1945* (New York: Oxford University Press, 2003).

5. John J. Bukowczyk, "The Transformation of Working-Class Ethnicity: Corporate Control, Americanization, and the Polish Immigrant Middle Class in Bayonne, N.J., 1915–1925," *Labor History* 25 (Winter 1984): 69.

6. See Raymond A. Mohl, "Globalization, Latinization, and the Nuevo New South," *Journal of American Ethnic History* 22, no. 4 (Summer 2003): 31–66.

7. For a recent overview of the immigration and ethnic history field, see John J. Bukowczyk, "New Approaches in Teaching of Immigration and Ethnic History," in *Handbook of American Immigration and Ethnicity*, ed. Ronald H. Bayor (New York: Oxford University Press, 2016), 489–506.

2

Indians and Immigrants— Entangled Histories

GUNLÖG FUR

FROM THE MIDDLE of the nineteenth century until the end of the 1920s, almost 2.5 million people from the three Scandinavian countries Denmark, Norway, and Sweden migrated to North America.[1] Fredrika Bremer, on her visit to America in 1849–1851, wrote about Minnesota that it was "rightly a country for Nordic emigrants, rightly a country for a New Scandinavia."[2] But for centuries this country had been home to several different Indian nations, and in the mid-nineteenth century, they dominated this territory. Very rarely does this fact enter into descriptions of Scandinavian emigration to, and settlement in, North America. Countless books and articles have been written on the topic of Scandinavian emigration, yet not even a handful deal with interactions—voluntary or not—between Scandinavian immigrants and American Indians. Instead, the history of the "peopling of America" by immigrants coming from across the oceans, and the history of indigenous peoples of America have been, and largely remain, discussed in two different fields: immigration and migration history, and American Indian history.

This article examines the theme of concurrent Indian and immigrant histories in the American Midwest, to argue that a separation of the two is detrimental to an understanding of the processes of migration, ethnicity, and colonialism. It suggests possible reasons for this lack of convergence, identifies consequences of such separate histories, and discusses ways in which these histories may be brought together. With the aim of inspiring new research, this article alludes both to early colonial encounters and to the more sustained interaction in the regions of heavy Scandinavian immigration from the second half of the nineteenth century.

When Scandinavians arrived from across the ocean, Indians were forced to vacate lands that became conveniently empty for occupation. Beginning in the 1840s and at least continuing until the 1930s, Scandinavian immigrants settled on Indian land or near Indian reservations.[3] That Scandinavian immigrants and American Indians met and that Scandinavian settlement in America depended upon appropriation of Indian land is obvious, but settlement and removal are rarely discussed in the same context, and in most immigration history, these processes remain unconnected.[4] Most often when the question is raised, the response is that by the time Scandinavians settled in the Midwest, the Indians had already left. However, a cursory glance at the existing research on American Indian history demonstrates clearly that this was not the case.

It is not just immigrants who seemed oblivious to the existence of some of their neighbors—histories written concerning different American Indian peoples perform a similar feat of excision. Immigrants are rarely part of accounts of Indian experiences, whether they are tribal histories or interpretations of relations with colonists. Instead, in histories of American Indians, the preferred counterpart is the representatives of American or Canadian governments, even though immigrant settlers constituted the vehicle for colonial westward expansion. When immigrants enter into the picture, they are most often lumped together as "white settlers."[5]

For good reasons, specialization has been necessary, yet the two fields often concern themselves with the same territory at the same time, but move in unconnected categories, each field with its own sources, methods, theoretical and ideological underpinnings, and traditions. The separation of American Indian and immigrant histories depends on their relation to the dominant construction of national history and on the fictive notion that indigenous Americans and newcomers inhabited different times and different places. Paul Spickard suggests that American Indians have been treated as an issue apart from all other ethnic relations, obscuring that "immigration (by Europeans, Asians, and Latin Americans) to the newly colonized territories was partly a colonial story as well as a migrant story. Immigration and ethnic identity in U.S. history have been intimately tied to race and slavery, on the one hand, and to colonial expansion across the continent on the other." He argues that the colonial period has not ended and that this has profound consequences for the fields of migration and ethnic studies. "The first fact of the history of American immigration is genocide: the displacement and destruction of the Native peoples of North America. That is part of the story of *immigration*; it is not some other, parallel history."[6]

American Indian history was long dominated by the history of "Indian policy," and this led to a predominant focus on Indian-U.S. (or Indian-colonist) relations. Much more rarely, and recently, have studies emerged on Indian-immigrant, Indian-African, or Indian-Hispanic interaction.[7] As a historian working outside the United States with colonial cultural encounters and gender, I have noticed at least two recent trends in American Indian history. The first is a move toward indigenous perspectives on distinct ethnic communities, and toward more modern, even contemporary, history. The second trend is toward internationalization of indigenous histories.[8] While breaking away from the clutches of an earlier focus on colonial and federal "Indian policy," these moves still neglect encounters between indigenous peoples and non-Anglo American settlers. Instead of studying contacts between Indians and immigrants, the histories of both go through the federal government and its authorized bodies, naturalizing Anglo-normativity, as Spickard suggests.[9]

American Indian, immigration, and ethnic history are all fields that grew out of the movement toward "history from below." They are, to some extent, marginalized and often seen as subfields of social history. They also serve as an important means of contemporary identification. They are important for people's sense of belonging. From a decolonizing perspective, writing American Indian histories from within, privileging Indian sources and worldviews, is a necessary challenge to Western academic hegemony. Nonetheless, there are reasons why the entanglement between these subfields should be explored. I believe the separation is not only untruthful, but it is also detrimental. It denies the entanglements that are and always have been between people—whether they or their descendants wish to see it or not. It conceals and confounds any understanding of the power imbalance and the consequences of the process of massive transfer of land from American Indians to settlers, it ignores the significance of hybrid lives and culture, and it produces histories that confirm conventional national narratives of exceptionalism and progress, in America as well as in the Nordic countries.

While this article argues for the need to bridge the gulf between immigration history and American Indian history, it is written primarily from the perspective of Swedish, and Scandinavian, immigration history. It is done so for two reasons. Firstly, in order to dispel the notion that Scandinavians arrived in a country devoid of previous owners, I have begun to investigate immigrant sources. Secondly, I do not have sufficient knowledge of Dakota or Ojibwa history or language to enter the entanglement from those perspectives. Indeed, a primary observation is that this proposed bridge between perspectives requires active collaboration among historians with different skills and backgrounds.

The history and historiography of Scandinavians in America provide an illustrative case study for the arguments of this article. It is not unique to the Midwest, or to the relationship between Scandinavian immigrants and Native peoples, but it is useful as a starting point to discussing parallel but concurrent histories. In this article, an investigation of the concurrent claims of different Indian nations and primarily Swedish settlers on land in the Midwest and their continued co-presence in the region provide a good test case for a study of what Betty A. Bergland aptly calls "the temporal and spatial continuity and simultaneity of immigration and removal."[10]

FICTIONS

Fictions bookend the concurrent histories of Native peoples and newcomers in America. The first is the fiction of the American empire, the idea that destiny determined that the American nation should grow and the Indians vanish. This notion was touted in literature and visionary pamphlets almost from the beginning of nationhood, and it spread across the Atlantic through the enormous popularity of works such as those by James Fenimore Cooper. The second fiction is one of friendly relations that deny not only conflicts over land and resources and various and ongoing interactions, but also the erasure of indigenous Americans in the history of the continent.

In her description of a new Scandinavian land, Fredrika Bremer's generous inclusion of not only Minnesota but also the country all the way west across the Rocky Mountains reveals her attunement with the expansionist notions of the young American nation, but belies the reality of the situation. When Bremer traveled across the United States, both the Midwest and the Far West of the continent were Indian country. And it was precisely at the moment when she waxed lyrical about the possibilities of a New Scandinavia that she first encountered Indians. On October 25, 1850, she arrived in St. Paul and noted that the "city is thronged with Indians." She then offered a description of the country beyond. "Here the Indians come with their furs from that immense country lying between the Mississippi and the Missouri. . . . [T]he forests still unspoiled of their primeval wealth and the rivers and lakes abounding in fish offer their inexhaustible resources, while the great Mississippi affords the means of their conveyance to the commercial markets of the world" on its way down to New Orleans. "Floating down this great river" took her "between Indian camps, fires, boats, Indians standing or leaping, and shouting, or rather yelling, upon the shores; funeral erections on the heights; between vineclad islands, and Indian canoes paddling among them."[11] Indian country indeed! The fiction of empty land available for cultivation required an active denial of an Indian presence, even when they were everywhere, as in Bremer's description. It also served to deny the integral role of violence in the expansion of white settlement across the

North American continent.[12] Bremer's popularity as a writer on both sides of the Atlantic ensured that her observations reached a large audience.[13]

Relegating Indians to the margins of the account of progress equaled the very way in which the American nation was imagined in historical scholarship. Recently historian Ned Blackhawk commented on the strains inherent in teaching American Indian history and American history to undergraduates at a major U.S. university: "Indian history appears increasingly critical to nearly all epochs of the nation's past, while in the classroom reconciling commonplace assumptions about America with the traumatic histories of the continent's indigenous peoples can be an exceedingly turbulent endeavor."[14] Early American historian Joyce Chaplin described ethnohistory and the *new Indian history* as "two of the most important developments in early American history," which afforded the historical experiences of Native Americans a place alongside African American history, women's history, and Latino/a history, as radical challenges to the hegemony of an Anglo-Saxon, Protestant, manifest destiny understanding of America's past. Yet, in spite of the significance of these new fields, they had not led to "radical assessments of the Indian place in American history."[15] Thus, in spite of more than forty years of *new* Indian history, American Indians remain largely ignored in the envisioning of the genesis and evolution of the United States as a nation, leading to perceptions that Indians were not participants in or central to the shaping of the paths of history.[16] Instead, as literary scholar Kate Shanley has argued, American Indians are "a permanent 'present absence' in U.S. colonial imagination, an 'absence' that reinforces at every turn the conviction that Native peoples are indeed vanishing and that the conquest of Native lands is justified."[17]

Literary imagination played a significant part in this conjuring trick, and scholars have identified the significance of works such as those by James Fenimore Cooper. His depiction of fictional characters Chingachgook and Uncas immensely impressed generations of readers on both sides of the Atlantic. Jean O'Brien, in her study of how Indians were written out of New England existence, identifies in the region's print culture an enormously influential literary production that attempted to efface Indians from history through a strategy of "firsting and lasting." These works posited Indians as "prefatory to what they assert as their own authentic histories and institutions," and "as the last Indian who lived in places," thereby neatly excluding Indians from history proper and its modern manifestation.[18] Cooper's books were translated into Swedish and, already published in the 1820s, they became readily available for a reading audience. Fredrika Bremer regarded him as one of "the first to make us in Sweden somewhat at home in America."[19] Norwegian Ole Munch Raeder published travel letters in the Oslo newspapers in 1847 and 1848. He, too, was reminded of Cooper as he traveled through the Mississippi Valley. He imagined encountering "some stray Indian that night, fully equipped with tomahawk and other paraphernalia, and of course on watch for someone to scalp."[20]

American Indian histories thus struggle against overwhelming odds in their insistence on relevance and inclusion, but so do histories of various immigrant entities. Studies on inter-ethnic relations between various European immigrant groups, between white and non-white immigrants, and on the construction of whiteness offer a challenge to the dominant narrative of U.S. history. However, what this means for relationships, contacts, and conflicts between different groups of immigrants and American Indians remains under-studied. Perhaps that is, as Orm Øverland has demonstrated, because immigration histories often serve to strengthen the national focus as immigrant groups seek to outperform one another to illustrate their own specific links to the nation's past.[21]

There also may be contemporary reasons for this separation of histories. Scholars who wish to discuss the agency of non-white Americans may feel leery about returning to a focus on white people. The debate within studies of critical whiteness and settler colonialism demonstrates that there is a legitimate concern that a focus on whiteness again suggests that agency and history belong to white people, who attract interest even when they are at their worst.[22] On the other hand, conflating all settlers into one category of "white" offers non-Anglo immigrants and their chroniclers a convenient means of distancing themselves from any part in the displacement of Native peoples. In 1873, the monthly periodical *Svenska Familj-Journalen* published an article for Swedish readers on the extinction of the Mandan tribe. The article argued that Indians brought destruction upon themselves as a consequence of their refusal to "civilize," yet the reasons for the war against them lay in white behavior. White people "take everything without concerning themselves with either common human or judicial laws." Then it continued: *"Here is a race-war, which never rests. The Anglo-Saxons in America annihilate all other races, with whom they come in contact."*[23] Swedes in America did not immediately identify with Anglo-Americans, nor were they initially viewed as such.[24] The place of Swedes was unclear, in relation to the race war that the journal claimed occurred, and it offered an opportunity for creating a distance between them and the abhorrent practices of the Anglo-Saxon race.

ENTANGLEMENTS

It was the land itself that brought Indians and immigrants into contact and conflict. All concurrent histories begin there, and the significance of land cannot be overstated.[25] The physical space of American Indian land gave rise to other forms of entanglements, such as exchanges of food, sex, family-making, and impersonations. Yet, although land is a paramount concern in both novels and historical studies of migration and removal, the historiography of Scandinavian and Indian entanglements remains shackled by the two fictions of empty lands and friendly relations. A common assumption in scholarship as well as in schoolbooks is that by the time Scandinavians arrived in Minnesota and Wisconsin, the Indians had left (and how their departure came about is not cause for rumination).[26] However, when interactions emerge as a topic for discussion, it is cloaked in an aura of friendly and peaceful relations. Stories of special relationships between Swedes and Indians abound in reminiscences and commemorations of the Swedish presence in North America.[27] Such stories emerged in remembrances of the New Sweden colony along the banks of the Delaware River during a brief period in the seventeenth century, and they often accompany descriptions of Swedes in the Midwest as well. While celebratory pamphlets and speeches (but also scholarly publications) hold the Swedes responsible for peaceful relations in the Delaware Valley as a consequence of Swedish innate "qualities of integrity and strength of character,"[28] geographers Terry G. Jordan and Matti Kaups in 1989 attempted to identify more structural reasons for the assumed affinity between Indians and Swedish and Finnish immigrants. They argued that Finnish colonists in particular arrived in America armed with experiences of association with another indigenous people, the Sámis in Northern Sweden/Finland. These Finns also practiced a culture of forest shamanism that allowed them to establish an accord with Lenapes in the Delaware region. The encounter between Lenapes and Finnish colonists was, in Jordan's and Kaups's words, "a confrontation of two like peoples" leading to associations where "local Delaware Indians called the Finns and Swedes *akoores* or *nittappi* ('friend,' 'fellow tribesmen,' or 'those who are like us'), acknowledging the similarity, and they had a different collective word, *senaares*, for the English, Germans, and Dutch, whom they regarded as alien."[29] Their work deserves note because of its attempt to deal with the notion of "special friendship" that I suggest haunts so much of the imagination surrounding the expansion of white settlement in North America.[30]

While New Sweden continues to engage scholars and inspire commemorations, historical investigations of immigrant and Indian contacts from the mid-nineteenth century and onward rarely form the focus of study. In the 1960s, Albin Widén, writing mostly for a non-academic audience, included in his wide range of topics relating to Swedes in America a book on Swedish-Indian relations in Minnesota and the Midwest.[31] Contemporary scholarship has begun to probe the issue, particularly the relationships between Norwegian immigrants and Dakota Indians.[32]

This scarcity of historical scholarship would seem to indicate that Swedes were ignorant of Indians. That, however, was not the case. Ulf Jonas Björk has pointed to the early and extensive success in Sweden of dime novels, magazines, and later television shows depicting classic confrontations between white settlers and Indians, and a perfunctory survey of Swedish travel writing from America confirms that Swedes were by no means unaware of the existence of Indian peoples. Characterizations of American Indians were framed within a context of civilization and its opposite.[33] Thus, Bremer tried to temper the critique against the United States for dispossessing American Indians when she commented: "North America is not altogether to blame with regard to her Indians. If the Indian had been more susceptible to higher culture, violence and arms would not have been used against him, as is now the case."[34]

Not all travelers and immigrants were unaware of the conflicts surrounding settlement. Their observations are not representative of the majority of writings, but they did reach a reading audience in Sweden, both private and public, through letters and publications. Hugo Nisbeth was one of many visitors during the second half of the nineteenth century. Although fully conforming to the ideas of social evolution, he was nonetheless capable of understanding the trauma of dispossession. He described how American Indians always related to white people with great shyness, "bordering on suspicion. It will almost seem as if he can never be made to forget, that the land that the whites have encroached upon once was his, and the glowing strength of this sentiment, flows to not a small degree from the fact that the white man has not always behaved in a manner that has inspired in the red man a particularly elevated belief in white civilization."[35] Likewise, letters from railroad engineer Harald Fegraeus demonstrate that he remained aware of Indian anger at European encroachment, and his empathy was greatest at the point where he could identify the most, which was in their struggle to protect their land.[36] Louis Ahlström clearly sought to understand the despair of Ojibwa Indians on whose Wisconsin land his family settled. It was, he stated, white people's "unconscionable invasion of Indian home territories" that precipitated violent conflict. He related how, in 1869, he stood outside the family cabin between Round Lake and Little Trade Lake in Burnett County in Wisconsin, watching a woman trying to maneuver her canoe down the river. Timber from logging further upriver had clogged the passage and the woman, together with her many children and dogs, had to carry the bark canoe on her head several times to pass the logjam in the water. Ahlström concluded that this river and the land surrounding it "had been her and her peoples' homeland for generations. We had taken possession of this land. She and hers were pushed away. But whereto? This was also the last fully loaded Indian canoe to pass by our new home."[37]

Perhaps the most influential encounter between American Indians and Scandinavian immigrants in the Midwest occurred around the year 1862. Dakota Indians, forced onto a reservation after treaties at Traverse de Sioux and Mendota in 1851, took to arms when annuities did not come, causing starvation. Under the reluctant leadership of Little Crow, Dakota forces took up arms against the United States. The first act of open violence, in what was to become a frightful conflict, occurred in Acton on August 17, 1862, when four young Dakota men shot five white settlers. More than five hundred settlers were killed during the following month, and an unknown number of Dakotas, before they were forced to surrender to the U.S. army at the end of September. A military commission condemned over three hundred Dakotas to death, but the president pardoned all but thirty-eight of them. The rest were imprisoned at Camp McClellan in Davenport, Iowa, under gruesome conditions, until they were sent to the newly established Santee Reservation in western Nebraska in 1866. One year later, they were forced to move again, to Dakota Territory, after Nebraska citizens refused their presence in the state.[38]

The conflict had its epicenter in southwestern Minnesota, and some of the settlers killed were Swedes and Norwegians. The violence descended upon the Scandinavian settlers in Kandiyohi county "like lightning from a clear sky" on August 20, 1862. On a sunny afternoon at the Broberg and Lundborg homesteads, Indians arrived and greeted the families as usual. But suddenly they opened fire and killed five men, then pursued a wagon and shot the driver and killed his wife and newborn child with vicious blows from their axes. Others fled in terror, gathering toward nightfall on an island in Norway Lake, and in the next couple of days, they buried thirteen bodies in a common grave.[39] Their memories filled with horror, precisely because Indians presumed friendly had taken part in the massacres of white settlers. Swedish-language papers reported on the conflict, and correspondents charged both Sioux (Dakota) and Chippewa (Ojibwa) warriors with "raging like wild animals, burning, pillaging and murdering all in their path."[40] Twenty-four Swedish and Norwegian settlers died in the fighting, and Victor Lawson, who wrote extensively about Scandinavian settlements in the Kandiyohi region, was adamant that they "had given the Indians no just cause for complaint or revenge. These immigrants were absolutely innocent of any wrong done to the red man."[41]

At the time, others expressed awareness that there may have been legitimate reasons for the Indians' frustration. Eric Norelius, an Augustana Synod pastor, admonished Christians to "take pity on these poor heathens, who do not know any better. A melancholy thought possesses you as you see how this race will be swept off the face of the earth. . . . [H]ave the white men, who call themselves Christian and civilized, discharged their duty toward them? We have reason to dread the day when the reckoning will be made."[42] But just as Lawson distanced the Swedes from any responsibility for the tragedy, later writers acquit Nordic settlers of blame. Larry Lundblad claims that the Scandinavians'

> only guilt was that they were a part of the vast numbers of settlers who were moving into areas recently taken from the Native American Indians. The real villains in the story appear to be the traders and the agents of the U.S. Government, who, through their mistreatment of the Indians, precipitated a strong reaction by many of them. This reaction cost the lives of numerous innocent and decent people who were trying to establish a better life for their families and themselves.[43]

For the Dakotas, the war and the memories of it spelled unmitigated disaster. The conflict tore at the community from inside, as some Dakotas saw no other way than war, while others refrained from taking up arms. It meant exile from the tribe's homeland and devastation. What did they think of the immigrants? Gary Anderson, in his biography of the Dakota leader Little Crow, notes Indian displeasure with German and Scandinavian settlers: "The members of the Mdewakanton soldiers' lodge particularly disliked the German and Scandinavian settlers, who shared very little with them."[44] Stingy, not sharing, food in particular—was that how Dakota and Ojibway indigenous owners of the land viewed the waves of Scandinavian settlers? Anderson writes that, by the early 1860s, relations between Dakotas and white settlers were severely strained as a consequence of the sheer numbers of newcomers, and the cultural perceptions they brought with them did not help the situation. "Most newcomers were from Germany or Scandinavia and carried a cultural baggage into Minnesota that was of necessity thrifty, so they saw no reason to share resources with Indians."[45] Anderson notes that the Dakotas had little to barter with and mostly viewed the influx of settlers with hostility.

Yet, sharing of food is a staple of immigrant stories. Settlers who reminisced about the early days of homesteading often remarked on food exchanges with neighboring Indians. "Indians roamed around and often visited them in their sodhouse. They asked for food and often brought food as well," reported one from Kasota, Minnesota, and O. E. Olson recalled from Maple Ridge that they "traded with them, receiving venison in exchange for bread and potatoes" and described how, despite no common language, an old Indian man had asked him to dig up potatoes.[46] Swedish stories frequently comment on food sharing, but they also often frame Indians as beggars, and in doing so, reveal their lack of understanding of Indian norms of sharing and giving, and of the situation where not sharing food meant condemning someone else to starvation and death.[47]

The Dakota conflict itself clearly had no winners. Newly arrived homesteaders were caught in a situation not of their own making, but for which they had become vehicles through their very presence, and cultural differences exacerbated the conflict. Desperate Dakotas faced destruction in every direction, and found no allies among the new arrivals. The aftermath spelled an even greater distance between Indians and immigrants and ensured that Swedes and Norwegians supported policies to have all Dakotas removed from the state. The Swedish-language newspaper *Hemlandet* noted that banishing the Dakotas from Minnesota would mean more free land for settlers.[48] Indeed, as Karen Hansen demonstrates, the Spirit Lake Dakota Reservation in North Dakota became a space "where dispossession and immigration faced off," and the "convergence of federal policy and economic opportunity positioned Scandinavian immigrants and their children to gain from the expropriation of Indian land."[49]

DONNING INDIAN GEAR

Several scholars have identified the allure in what Phil Deloria calls "playing Indian." On both sides of the Atlantic, white people desired to tap the reservoir of connections to land, culture, and manliness through romantic notions of American Indians.[50] One strong motivation for this performance lay in a desire to belong to the new land. Orm Øverland argues that "[v]irtually all immigrant groups from Europe have stories that claim that a group was a founding group, that it fought harder and sacrificed more for American freedom and independence than any others, and that it was the foremost bearer of traditional American values." Homemaking myths, as he calls them, are typical of the immigrant condition.[51] Jennifer Attebery, in her study of Swedish immigrant letters from the far West, cites Øverland's exploration of ethnic foundation myths to argue that "immigrants lay claim to the place where they find themselves by saying, in essence, 'we were here first or at least as early as you were.'" With this reference, she analyzes the words of Swedish westerners and finds that some of them imagine themselves "as 'going native,' and through association with American Indians lay claim to being not just an American but an indigenous Westerner, transformed by the region into a rugged individual who is at home in the new region." Attebery provides an argument for electing to study Swedish immigrants' fascination with Native America when she notes that while "[t]he myth of the West . . . portrays the region as a frontier, a border at which those coming into the region from the East met the wilderness . . . a liminal place, where civilization meets the wild and primitive and is transformed or renewed," it is nonetheless almost always told from a perspective of the Anglo-American role. Ironically, she states, in spite of the significance of immigration for westward expansion, the "non-Anglophone European immigrants' participation in the history of the West and in the framing of a Western myth has received less attention."[52] My addition to this argument would be that by "firsting," by "seizing indigeneity . . . as their birthright," as Jean O'Brien describes, European immigrants participated in the process of American Indian erasure.[53]

For young Swedish men, as for many other white men growing up in the West, an attachment to the land and to their new home could take the form of Indian play and enactment.[54] For some, the connection to Indian America offered a platform from which to establish themselves as true Americans. Oscar B. Jacobson arrived at the age of eight to Lindsborg, Kansas, with his parents and siblings. He grew up on the prairie, where he developed a love of art and eventually went to art school at Yale. There he participated in the student play *Sunset*, where he played the Pawnee chief "Mistonkah." A review in the Yale newspaper described his performance: "He is a wonderful Indian impersonator and his Indian effects were all obtained by himself from an Indian reservation near his home. His chief's head gear is the genuine article and was obtained under great danger."[55]

After finishing his studies at Yale and in Paris, Jacobson went on to secure a position as Professor of Fine Arts at the University of Oklahoma with the task to establish a new department. He enthusiastically embraced western art and promoted American Indian art as a genuine and significant American art form, becoming well known around the country and in the world for encouraging and supporting American Indian artists such as "the Kiowa Five." As a consequence, and in an evocative twist, Jacobson once again became an Indian chief. Kiowas honored him at a powwow near Anadarko and named him "Naquo" and chief of the tribe "in recognition of his interest in three Kiowa youths, students in the university's art department, and his service in perpetuating tribal art."[56]

Historian Elliott West, in interpreting westward expansion and American Indian experiences, discusses the constraints and expectations that circumscribe all historical actors. He gives as an example that a "Swedish homesteader in the Dakotas was free to wake up one day in 1870 and choose to become a blackface minstrel entertainer, and nobody was stopping a nearby Sioux man from riding to Bismarck to try to open a mortuary. Given each man's accumulated past and culture, however, neither was likely to behave in these ways."[57] Swedish homesteaders did on occasion don Indian costume, and it is likely that it aided them in establishing themselves, not as Indians, but as white Americans because it is the strange nature of white privilege that it allows those deemed to be white the leeway to incorporate, pass through, and speak for all other races and ethnicities. It seems that because Indians were construed as primitive, men like Oscar Jacobson became properly modern through impersonations of them.

ERASURE

Paradoxically, when white settlers played Indians or lamented the deterioration of previously friendly relations, they participated in a politics of erasing Indians from the land. Louis Ahlström concluded his description of his childhood in western Wisconsin by citing "the kind Chippewa chief Gis-Kil-a-Way" who had told the incoming immigrants that the Indians feared that they would take away their land. "And now we," Ahlström ended, "the whitest of the white had proved that the chief's fears were well founded."[58] Nisbeth, who had expressed an awareness of what encroachment on Indian land led to, nonetheless described the opportunities for emigration as "an almost unthinkable amount of fertile soil as yet untaken."[59] Scholars perpetuated this eradication. Geographer Helge Nelson asserted in the 1940s, in an exhaustive study of the Swedish settlements in North America, that at "the time when the modern Swedish settling activity was starting in the 1840s, only the eastern part of the actual United States was in the main taken possession of by man." He emphasized how the Swedes were indeed spearheads in the westward drive across the uncultivated Native American land since "they became frequently with or against their will pioneers in the drier western parts of the prairies, where in the 1860s the prospects of colonization were considered doubtful."[60]

The paucity of records on Scandinavian and American Indian interaction, and the silence in them, may be a consequence of subconscious erasure. Sven Delblanc, a Swedish novelist who grew up on a farmstead in western Canada in the 1930s, reminisced about his childhood, and the good relationship among neighbors: "However, Indians were not a part of this spirit of community. One did not see them; I think one repressed the fact of their existence. I was surprised myself when I returned in my 50s and found them everywhere. As a child and a young man I had not seen them."[61] Norwegian literary scholar Orm Øverland pondered the question of why there were so few references to Indians in the letters of Norwegian immigrants, and concluded "[i]t may be that the silence of the letters reflects the invisibility of people who were uncomfortable reminders of the ethical ambiguities of immigrant homemaking."[62]

These are valid points, but I would like to warn against too much emphasis on the paucity of records, as I believe that idea itself contributes to an erasure of American Indian presence—now and in the past. There is frequently a resounding silence in historical records, particularly from the nineteenth and twentieth centuries, regarding interactions between immigrants and Indians. This forces scholars to look beyond traditional written sources, as well as looking long and hard at what there is. However, as the previous pages demonstrate, there are records, and so far, scholars have only begun to scratch the surface. There is likely to be much more in local histories, reminiscences, letters, diaries, and oral history collections. The lack of concurrent histories also may follow from a contemporary trend in historical work. The link between history and identity has become so entrenched today that they appear almost identical. The notion of historians working to excavate some kind of exact meaning or experience adhering to past lives has been discredited, and it is only with the greatest caution that a historian can claim to access the past through the sources that remain today. The very necessary criticism of a positivist and universalist empiricism also has led to a denial of consequences—that actions lead to consequences that take shape not only in the form of identities. History as a narrative of identity stresses that which keeps immigrants and American Indians apart. Fields of research then become self-referential histories that focus on perseverance and victory or survival and risk neglecting interactions—conflicts as well as collaboration.

History as materiality places entanglements and their consequences in focus. Interactions had consequences both in the shape of good relations, beneficial exchanges, and not least in children, who prove that the separation of Indian and immigrant histories runs straight through individual human beings. Countless homesteads belonged to both worlds, and their offspring are as much part of American history as any other. "And here I may as well remark, *en passant*," writes Bremer with characteristic hauteur,

> that the children of Indian women by white men commonly attach them-
> selves to the white race. They are most frequently fine specimens of human-
> ity, although not of a remarkably elevated kind. They are praised for their
> acuteness of eye and the keenness of their perceptive faculties generally.
> I have heard that the greater number of the steersmen of the Mississippi
> boats belong to this half-breed race.[63]

In Bremer's world, "half-breeds" may have attempted to become white, but the legacy of these entanglements created new worlds, new allegiances, and complications. Surely, the history of the Ojibwa people and Swedish immigration is mirrored in the descendants of Kahjiji, an Ojibwa woman, and Ozaawandib, also known as Jacob Fahlström ("the first Swede in Minnesota"). Their seven children and many offspring represent the entanglements of origins, ethnicities, and cultures in what was to become the state of Minnesota.[64]

History has a way of emerging as memory and in struggles that involve claims for inclusion in the nation or for the right to self-determination. In the relation between a nation's majority and minorities, the "question as to whose narrative it is, and under whose control it lies, is ever-present."[65] Realizing this, constitutive groups within nation-states and sometimes their governments have initiated attempts to bring reconciliation for past injuries. Indigenous peoples have an urgent need to confront and seek healing from the history of colonial violence, but so do non-indigenous people. "To be sure," writes philosopher Charles L. Griswold, "each party is defined by the history of wrong-doing . . . in the sense that the history shaped a phase of their existence." But political apologies, and the new narratives of history that they may entail, offer the possibility for a future that is not "determined by the injuries and resentments of the past" and that our identities and communities are not "immune to revision, and therefore . . . not immune to emendation."[66] American historian Sherry L. Smith writes about three prominent examples in the American West where collective apologies have been offered that have had an impact on the historical narrative in several significant ways.[67] The recent sesquicentennial of the Dakota Conflict motivated a number of initiatives to view the conflict from many different perspectives and to recognize the continuing plight but also resilience of Dakota Indians.[68]

In the late 1980s, a poem entitled "A Freedom Song" attracted my attention. The author, Tala Sanning, described himself as "of the Oglala Sioux with almost an equal part of me Swedish." This mixture caused him tension, and "beyond these emotions lay the ancestral chantings of the 'Freedom Song' my pale grandfather never quite understood from the lips of my Oglala grandmother who was once raped by a white settler."[69] Though briefly presented, the anguish of this historical entanglement was apparent, but what struck me the most was his name. *Tala sanning* means "speak the truth" in Swedish. Did the "pale grandfather" choose this name for an Oglala grandson, or did the man take the name himself as a reference to a Swedish ancestry? I do not know, but I have carried this brief encounter with me for years, building in me a desire to "speak the truth" about Swedish and American Indian relations.

To do so will require cooperation and exchange among practitioners of American Indian, immigration, and ethnic history, each bringing their expertise, methodologies, and knowledge to the encounter. The challenge in concurrent histories is to keep a double vision in view, to make it possible to listen to complementary or conflicting occurrences at the same time and in the same place, and to communicate this plurality in one and the same narrative, in order to account for the complexity of lived experience. Any viable response requires cross-disciplinary fertilization and widespread collaborative efforts. It requires developing methodological and theoretical foundations for empirical studies that seek to map forms of simultaneous, concurring claims of reality, experience, and meaning. This essay has contributed to that effort by investigating the entangled histories of Scandinavian immigrants and American Indians in the upper Midwest.

NOTES

The author wishes to thank Karen V. Hansen, Betty A. Bergland, Diana Brydon, and my anonymous readers for their invaluable help in the preparation of this article. Funding for research provided by Linnaeus University Centre: Concurrences in Colonial and Postcolonial Studies.

1. United States Department of Homeland Security, *Yearbook of Immigration Statistics: 2011* (Washington, DC, 2012), 6–7; K. G. Basavarajappa and Bali Ram, *Statistics Canada,* Section A: "Population and Migration," http://www.statcan.gc.ca/pub/11–516–x/sectiona /4147436–eng.htm (accessed May 17, 2013).

2. Fredrika Bremer, *Hemmen i den nya Verlden,* Vol. 2 (Stockholm, Sweden, 1853), 350–51 (my translation). Bremer's description of the New World has been translated and edited by Adolph B. Benson, *America of the Fifties: Letters of Fredrika Bremer* (New York, 1924). Further quotations are from the English translation.

3. See, for example, Karen V. Hansen, *Encounter on the Great Plains: Scandinavian Settlers and the Dispossession of Dakota Indians, 1890–1930* (New York, 2013); Karen V. Hansen and Duffy Mignon, "Mapping the Dispossession: Scandinavian Homesteading at Fort Totten, 1900–1930," *Great Plains Research* 18, no. 1 (Spring 2008): 67–80. Accounts of reminiscences of Swedish immigrants attest to how they took up homesteads on or near reservations. See accounts of Erick P. Erickson (1897), Mrs. Swan Nelson (1890s), Carl Johnson (around 1900), and Amy K. Mattsson (1910s), in "Emigranters självbiografier," 15:7:10–12, Albin Widén's *samling,* Svenska Emigrantinstitutet; Nils Johansson, letter August 31, 1879, from Pawnee Agency, Kansas. Nils Johansson's *nordskånska amerikabrevsamling* 22:17, Vol. 14, Svenska Emigrantinstitutet.

4. Betty Bergland made a similar observation in an article from 2000, dealing with Norwegian immigrants and Indians. I am much indebted to her for discussions on the subject over the years. Betty Ann Bergland, "Norwegian Immigrants and 'Indianerne' in the Landtaking, 1838–1862," *Norwegian American Studies* 35 (2000): 320–22.

5. While fully cognizant of immigrants as a vehicle for expansion, several excellent studies nonetheless conflate all immigrant experiences into one, with expressions such as "chaotic storms of European expansion," or "influx of whites." Examples from Ned Blackhawk, *Violence over the Land: Indians and Empires in the Early American West* (Cambridge, MA, 2006), 265; and Michael L. Tate, *Indians and Emigrants: Encounters on the Overland Trails* (Norman, OK, 2006), 229. While being admirably sensitive to the complexities of American Indian and African American identities and ethnic formation, the constitution of the category "white American" requires no further elaboration in David A. Chang's *The Color of the Land: Race, Nation, and the Politics of Landownership in Oklahoma, 1832–1929* (Chapel Hill, NC, 2010). I want to make absolutely clear that I do not view this as a shortcoming on the part of the named works; rather, my purpose is to identify one perspective that could augment the necessary revisioning of the history of expansion.

6. Paul Spickard, *Almost All Aliens: Immigration, Race, and Colonialism in American History and Identity* (New York, 2007), 23, 25 (emphasis in original); evidence of the separation of histories can be found in how book catalogs and lists of recent scholarship divide categories. *The Journal of American History* lists recent scholarships under three separate headings: Immigration, Ethnic, and American Indian. During the years 2006–2013, five articles listed under "Immigration history" referred to relationships between immigrants and Indians; eleven articles listed within the field of "American Indians" dealt with various immigrant groups, while no article under "Ethnic history" made such references. See also the definition of the fields in David Gerber and Alan M. Kraut, eds., *American Immigration and Ethnicity: A Reader* (New York, 2005).

7. See Chang, *Color of the Land*; Eric V. Meeks, *Border Citizens: The Making of Indians, Mexicans, and Anglos in Arizona* (Austin, TX, 2007); Fay A. Yarbrough, *Race and the Cherokee Nation: Sovereignty in the Nineteenth Century* (Philadelphia, 2008).

8. See the creation of the Native American and Indigenous Studies Association (NAISA) and the Newberry Consortium in American Indian Studies, http://www.naisa.org; and http://www.newberry.org/mcnickle/ncais.html.

9. Spickard, *Almost All Aliens*, 6.

10. Betty Bergland, e-mail conversation, January 16, 2010.

11. Bremer, *America of the Fifties*, 228, 237; for another description of multitudes of Indians in the land where the first Swedish settlers arrived, see Louis John Ahlström, *Femtiofem år i vestra Wisconsin. Historiska skildringar* (Minneapolis, 1924), 51–69, 296–307.

12. Michael Witgen demonstrates in his magisterial counternarrative how rhetorical assumptions of empire faltered on real conditions in the interior of the continent when white travelers could not go anywhere without the guidance and permission of Indian nations. Witgen, *An Infinity of Nations* (Philadephia, 2012). Violence has certainly been discussed in relation to American history, ever since Richard Slotkin's now classic study *Regeneration through Violence: The Mythology of the American Frontier 1600–1860* (Norman, OK, 1973). What I argue here is that it has not been incorporated into the study of immigration and its impact on Native American nations. See Blackhawk, *Violence over the Land*, 3–10; see also the thought-provoking analysis in Steven T. Newcomb, *Pagans of the Promised Land: Decoding the Doctrine of Christian Discovery* (Golden, CO, 2008).

13. Bremer, *America of the Fifties*, trans. and ed. Benson, xvii.

14. Ned Blackhawk, "Recasting the Narrative of America: The Rewards and Challenges of Teaching American Indian History," *Journal of American History* 93, no. 4 (March 2007): 1165.

15. Joyce E. Chaplin, "Expansion and Exceptionalism in Early American History," *Journal of American History* 89, no. 4 (March 2003): 1432, 1447–48.

16. A symposium held at the McNickle Center at the Newberry Library, Chicago, May 3–4, 2013, bears the title "Why You Can't Teach U.S. History without American Indians." The aim of the symposium was to challenge the view that Indians vanished shortly after the initial encounter and to change how U.S. history is taught by offering new and expanding resources for college-level faculty. http://www.newberry.org/why-you-cant-teach.

17. Quoted in Andrea Smith, *Conquest: Sexual Violence and American Indian Genocide* (Cambridge, MA, 2005), 9.

18. Jean M. O'Brien, *Firsting and Lasting: Writing Indians Out of Existence in New England* (Minneapolis, 2010), xxiii–xxiv.

19. Ulf Jonas Björk, "Stories of America: The Rise of the 'Indian Book' in Sweden 1862–1895," *Scandinavian Studies* 75, no. 4 (2003): 510–15; Bremer, *America of the Fifties*, 10. "Indian books" were immensely popular in Sweden from the second half of the nineteenth century until the late twentieth. See Yvonne Pålsson, *I Skinnstrumpas spår. Svenska barn-och ungdomsböcker om indianer, 1860–2008* (Umeå, Sweden, 2013).

20. Quoted in Bergland, "Norwegian Immigrants," 333.

21. Orm Øverland, *Immigrant Minds, American Identities: Making the United States Home, 1870–1930* (Urbana, IL, 2000); see also Spickard, *Almost All Aliens*, xix–xx; Bergland, "Norwegian Immigrants," 321–22.

22. On the problem with focusing on whiteness, see Richard Dyer, *White* (New York, 2010), 10–13.

23. "En utdöd folkstam," *Svenska Familj-Journalen* 6 (1873): 178–80; and 8 (1873): 232–34. Quotation is from 178 (emphasis in original).

24. See articles by Brøndal and Blanck in this issue of the journal, and ongoing dissertation work by Jens Björk Andersson at Linnaeus University (available at http://lnu.se/personal/jens.bjork.andersson). Nineteenth-century commentators noted what they described as a deteriorating influence of Indian "contagion" on Swedes, usually as a part of political argumentation; see, for example, Gustaf Thyreen, *Skall jag resa till Amerika? Kortfattad skildring af Förenta Staterna vid 20de århundradets början* (Stockholm, Sweden, 1911), 145.

25. For highly pertinent demonstrations of this, see Karen V. Hansen, "Land Taking at Spirit Lake: The Competing and Converging Logics of Norwegian and Dakota Women, 1900–1930," in *Norwegian American Women: Migration, Communities, and Identities*, ed. Betty A. Bergland and Lori Ann Lahlum (St. Paul, MN, 2011), 211–45; Hansen, *Encounter on the Great Plains*; Bergland, "Norwegian Immigrants."

26. Ulf Beijbom, *Mot löftets land. Den svenska utvandringen* (Stockholm, Sweden, 1995), 99–100; Helge Nelson, *The Swedes and the Swedish Settlements in North America* (Lund, Sweden, 1943), 180, 182, 183; Robert C. Ostergren, *A Community Transplanted: The Trans-Atlantic Experience of a Swedish Immigrant Settlement in the Upper Middle West, 1835–1915* (Uppsala, Sweden, 1988), 155, 166–76; Ulf Beijbom, "Svenskar och indianer. Efterskrift," in *Lansens folk*, ed. Henrik Larsson (Växjö, Sweden, 1996); Indians are entirely absent in Lars Ljungmark, *For Sale—Minnesota: Organized Promotion of Scandinavian Immigration 1866–1873* (Göteborg, Sweden, 1971); in Hans Norman, *Från Bergslagen till Nordamerika. Studier i migrationsmönster, social rörlighet och demografisk struktur med utgångspunkt från Örebro län 1851–1915* (Uppsala, Sweden, 1974); and in Jimmy Engren, *Railroading and Labor Migration: Class and Ethnicity in Expanding Capitalism in Northern Minnesota, the 1880s to the mid 1920s* (Växjö, Sweden, 2007); but see brief mention in Carina Rönnqvist, *Svea folk i Babels land. Svensk identitet i Kanada under 1900–talets första hälft* (Umeå, Sweden, 2004), 154–55. For similar findings regarding Norwegian immigration history, see Bergland, "Norwegian Immigrants," 319.

27. Gunlög Fur, "Romantic Relations: Swedish Attitudes towards Indians during the Twentieth Century," *Swedish-American Historical Quarterly* 3, no. 55 (July 2004): 145–64.

28. *Observance of the Three Hundredth Anniversary of the First Permanent Settlement in the Delaware River Valley 1938* (Washington, DC, 1940).

29. Terry G. Jordan and Matti Kaups, *The American Backwoods Frontier: An Ethnic and Ecological Interpretation* (Baltimore, MD, 1989), 89, 90. Finns continued to be connected with Indians in popular imagination in the new American nation, in particular, the politically radical Finnish immigrants in the upper Midwest. David R. Roediger, *Working Toward Whiteness: How America's Immigrants Became White* (New York, 2006), 61–64.

30. For comparison regarding this trope, see Colin G. Galloway, Gerd Gemunden, and Susanne Zantop, eds., *Germans and Indians: Fantasies, Encounters, Projections* (Lincoln, NE, 2002). See also Adam Hjorthén's ongoing dissertation project on Swedish commemorations, Stockholm University (available at http://www.fokult.su.se/doktorand/vara-doktorander/adam-hjorthen-1.36832).

31. Albin Widén, *Svenskarna och Siouxupproret* (Stockholm, Sweden, 1965).

32. In addition to previously cited works by Betty Bergland and Karen Hansen, see Betty Ann Bergland, "Settler Colonists, 'Christian Citizenship,' and the Women's Missionary Federation at the Bethany Indian Mission in Wittenberg, Wisconsin, 1884–1934," in *Competing Kingdoms. Women, Mission, Nation, and the American Protestant Empire, 1812–1960*, ed. Barbara Reeves-Ellington, Kathryn Kish Sklar, and Connie A. Shemo (Durham, NC, 2010), 167–94; Orm Øverland, "Norwegian Americans Meet Native Americans: Exclusion and Inclusion in Immigrant Homemaking in America," in *Postcolonial Dislocations: Travel, History, and the Ironies of Narrative*, ed. Charles I. Armstrong and Øyunn Hestetun (Oslo, Norway, 2006), 109–22; Maria Erling, "Wrestling with the Mission Mantle: Matthias Wahlstrom, Failed Missionary to the Comanche, and the Relation between the Augustana Synod and the Covenant Church," *Swedish-American Historical Quarterly* 63 (April–July 2012): 135–57; Joy Lintelman and Betty Bergland, "Scandinavian Immigrants and Indigenous Peoples: Ethnicity, Gender, and Colonial Encounters in Midwestern Regions of the United States, 1830–1930," unpublished paper, conference presentation at International Federation of Research in Women's History (IFRWH), Oslo, Norway, August, 10, 2000.

33. Ulf Jonas Björk, "The Dangerous Prairies of Texas: The Western Dime Novel in Sweden, 1900–1908," *Swedish-American Historical Quarterly* 3, no. 60 (July 2004): 165–78; Stefan Eldevall, "'Naturbarn begåfvade med många goda och många dåliga egenskaper.' Synen på den nordamerikanska urbefolkningen i svenska reseskildringar och memoarer från 1853–1891" (Senior thesis in history, Lund University, 2003); Julia Köpsén, "Fredrika Bremers syn på indianerna" (Senior thesis in history, Uppsala University, 1996); for examples of romanticized stories of American Indians available to a Swedish audience at the time of mass emigration, see *Helsingfors Morgonblad* 2, no. 73 (1833); *Nytt Sockenbibliothek* (1852), 2 (1864); *Svenska Familj-Journalen* 1 (1866), 6 (1868), 9, 10, 12 (1869), 5 (1870), 3, 7 (1872, 1873); *Illustrerad Tidning* (1857, 1861).

34. Bremer, *America of the Fifties*, 232; Norwegian newpaper man Johan Reinert Reiersen used the same logic when he argued that the United States' policy was "just and peaceful" because "[t]he red man was a monopolist. He took possession of more land than could be reconciled with the welfare of the human race. And he was a barbarian, hostile to the useful occupations and fair arts of a civilized life." Bergland, "Norwegian Immigrants," 331.

35. Hugo Nisbeth, "Indianerna i Nord-Amerika," *NU. Månadstidsskrift* 2 (April 1976): 139–43.

36. Johanna Hedenquist, "En klarsynt man? Möten mellan en svensk immigrant och nordamerikanska indianer under 1800-talets sista decennier" (Master's thesis in history, Växjö University, 1998).

37. Ahlström, *Femtiofem år*, 293, 297.

38. The Santee Sioux or Dakota people consisted of four related tribes. It was primarily members of the Mdewakanton and Wahpekute tribes who fought, while most of the Sisseton and Wahpeton tribes tried to stay out of the conflict. The war and its consequences are still mourned today in Dakota communities. Sarah-Eva Ellen Carlson, "They Tell Their Story: The Dakota Internment at Camp McClellan in Davenport, 1862–1866," *Annals of Iowa* 3, no. 63 (Summer 2004): 251–78. Historical scholarship on the conflict includes Gary Clayton Anderson, *Kinsmen of Another Kind: Dakota-White Relations in the Upper Mississippi Valley, 1650–1862* (St. Paul, MN, 1984); Gary Clayton Anderson, *Little Crow: Spokesman for the Sioux* (St. Paul, MN, 1986); and Gary C. Anderson and Alan R. Woolworth, eds., *Through Dakota Eyes: Narrative Accounts of the Minnesota Indian War of 1862* (St. Paul,

MN, 1988); Waziyatawin Angela Wilson, ed., *In the Footsteps of Our Ancestors: The Dakota Commemorative Marches of the 21st Century* (St. Paul, MN, 2006); Angela Cavender Wilson, "Decolonizing the 1862 Death Marches," *American Indian Quarterly* 28 (2004): 185–215; and Kathryn Zabelle Derounian-Stodola, *The War in Words: Reading the Dakota Conflict through the Captivity Literature* (Lincoln, NE, 2009).

39. Widén has described the events from Swedish perspectives in *Svenskarna och Siouxupproret*. His sources came from oral accounts, and he was heavily endebted to Victor E. Lawson's writings (see endnote 41 below).

40. Hans Mattson, *Minnen* (Lund, Sweden, 1890), 50; Report to *Hemlandet*, August 27, 1862: 2; quoted from Ulf Jonas Björk, "The Swedish-Americans and the Sioux: How an Immigrant Group Viewed One Particular Indian Tribe" (paper presented at Nordic Association for American Studies, Tampere, Finland, May 25, 2007).

41. Victor E. Lawson, "The First Settlements in the Kandiyohi Region and Their Fate in the Indian Outbreak," *Yearbook of the Swedish Historical Society of America* 10 (1925–1926): 31, 44. Lawson ended his account by proclaiming the Swedish and Norwegian settlers "innocent martyrs to the advance of civilization over barbarism."

42. Norelius, in *Hemlandet*, September 3, 1862: 3, cited in Björk, "The Swedish-Americans."

43. Larry Lundblad, "The Impact of Minnesota's Dakota Conflict of 1862 on the Swedish Settlers," *Swedish-American Historical Quarterly* 3, no. 51 (July 2000): 219–20; cf. Widén, *Svenskarna och Siouxupproret*, 66.

44. Anderson, *Little Crow*, 138.

45. Ibid., 130.

46. Mrs. Joe Gustafsson, account in "Emigranters självbiografier efter person A-H," 15:7:10; O. E. Olson, in "Emigranters självbiografier N-W," 15:7:12; see also accounts by Mrs. Victor Dahlman; Col. John Lundeen, in "Emigranters självbiografier J-H," 15:7:11; S. P Swedin, in K: Pionjärminnen, "nedtecknade och inskickade," 15:8:1, all in Albin Widéns *samling*, Swedish Emigrant Institute. Lawson, "First Settlements," 31; Widén, *Svenskarna och Siouxupproret*, 12, 19, 66, 67, 149; P. P. Waldenström, *Genom Canada. Reseskildringar från 1904* (Stockholm, Sweden, 1905), 85; Mattson, *Minnen*; Ahlström, *Femtiofem år*, 300–02, 303.

47. Widén suggests that Dakota Indians did not like Germans and viewed them as stingy, while "Scandinavians were in their eyes more decent and accessible." Widén, *Svenskarna och Siouxupproret*, 66.

48. *Hemlandet*, September 9, 1862.

49. Hansen, introduction to *Encounter on the Great Plains*.

50. Phil Deloria, *Playing Indian* (New Haven, CT, 1998); also Shari M. Huhndorf, *Going Native: Indians in the American Imagination* (Ithaca, NY, 2001).

51. Øverland, *Immigrant Minds*, 17.

52. Jennifer Eastman Attebery, *Up in the Rocky Mountains: Writing the Swedish Immigrant Experience* (Minneapolis, MN, 2007), 112, 114.

53. O'Brien, *Firsting and Lasting*, 51.

54. Carl Nelson remembers his sons around 1900 emulating both Daniel Boone and Kit Carson "and on more than one occasion three sheepish, hungry Indian fighters slunk home for a square meal." Carl Nelson, in "Emigranters självbiografier"; playing cowboys and Indians (or *indianer och cowboys* as the Swedish version is called) is, of course, a game

known throughout the world. In different contexts, it has served to express different kinds of gendered, ethnic, and political identities and hopes, often through particular attachment to American Indians. See Michael Dorris, "Indians on the Shelf," in *The American Indian and the Problem of History*, ed. Calvin Martin (New York, 1987), 99; Ann McGrath, "Playing Colonial: Cowgirls, Cowboys, and Indians in Australia and North America," *Journal of Colonialism and Colonial History* 1, no. 2 (Spring 2001): 1–19.

55. "Real Thing in These Costumes," *London*, January 2, 1908.

56. "Professor Jacobson Named Chief of Kiowa Tribe at Ceremony near Anadarko Friday," *Chickasha Daily Express*, July 28, 1928.

57. Elliott West, "The Nez Perce and Their Trials. Rethinking America's Indian Wars," *Montana: The Magazine of Western History* (Autumn 2010), 12.

58. Ahlström, *Femtiofem år*, 61, 308.

59. Hugo Nisbeth, "Amerika ur emigrationssynpunkt," *Svenska Familj-Journalen* 12 (1874): 12, 367.

60. Nelson, *Swedes*, 27, 56.

61. Sven Delblanc, *Livets Ax* (Falun, Sweden, 1992), 16.

62. Øverland, "Intruders on Native Ground: Troubling Silences and Memories of the Land-Taking in Norwegian Immigrant Letters," in *Transnational American Memories*, ed. Udo Hebel (Berlin, Germany, 2009), 84.

63. Bremer, *America of the Fifties*, 236–37; on families of mixed Scandinavian and Indian origin, see Ahlström, *Femtiofem år*, 52, 58, 61ff.

64. http://www.ojibwe.info/Ojibwe/HTML/people/p000015u.htm#I27975 (accessed May 17, 2013).

65. Charles L. Griswold, *Forgiveness. A Philosophical Exploration* (Cambridge, England, 2007), 139.

66. Ibid., 145, 191.

67. Sherry L. Smith, "Reconciliation and Restitution in the American West," *Western History Quarterly* 1, no. 40 (Winter 2010): 23.

68. See, for example, the website for the Minnesota Historical Society, http://usdakotawar.org/history/today/memory-commemoration.

69. Tala Sanning, "A Freedom Song," in *Living the Spirit. A Gay American Indian Anthology*, ed. Will Roscoe (New York, 1988), 195.

3

"The Great Entrepot for Mendicants": Foreign Poverty and Immigration Control in New York State to 1882

HIDETAKA HIROTA

IN SEPTEMBER 1880, members of the New York State Board of Chari-ties, a state agency supervising issues of poverty and welfare, received a report on an English immigrant family. The report stated that the family—husband, wife, and three children, who were "all feeble-minded, and entirely destitute"—had been deported from New York to Ontario, Canada. They had originally emigrated from London to Quebec with financial assistance from the Ladies' Emigrant Association in Quebec. The authorities in Quebec then sent the family to New York via London, Ontario. After their arrival in New York, the family members became destitute and entered an almshouse. Their removal was executed not under federal deportation law, which did not yet exist in 1880, but under a newly passed state law. Enacted in June 1880, the law authorized the Board of Charities to return to their places of origin "any crippled, blind, lunatic, or other infirm alien paupers" in charitable institutions in New York whose emigration had been financed by foreign governments, charitable organizations, or landlords. This deportation law was limited in scope, for it did not apply to those who crossed the Atlantic on their own, exempting most foreign inmates from removal. Yet it was a product of the state's century-long effort to restrict the immigration of people of undesirable character. In particular, it was a response to repeated calls by state immigration officials and citizens in New York since the antebellum period for the deportation of foreign paupers.[1]

In American historical scholarship, immigration control has long been dis-cussed on the basis of federal policy that developed from the 1870s onward. Historians have typically located the origins of this policy in legislation that emerged largely as a result of anti-Chinese sentiment in California. In 1875, Congress passed the Page Act, forbidding the entry of foreign convicts and laborers brought involuntarily from "China, Japan, or any Oriental country." The act also denied admission to women imported "for the purposes of prostitution," a stricture designed chiefly against Chinese women. In 1882,

Congress barred Chinese laborers from entering the United States for ten years with the Chinese Exclusion Act.[2]

The focus on the federal Chinese exclusion laws does not mean that historians have been unaware of prior immigration control that was conducted at the state level. From the colonial period onward, Atlantic seaboard states regulated immigration through state passenger laws. Previous generations of historians explored this legislation, but their analysis was usually limited to a few representative state laws and relevant court decisions, overlooking how immigration policies in states developed over time.[3] When historians began in the 1970s to rescue the Asian American experience from previous scholarly neglect, Chinese exclusion received extensive attention as the foundation of American immigration restriction. This put a halt to further inquiry into state laws, ironically creating a new form of neglect. Some recent immigration scholars have revisited state laws and analyzed the role of states in the emergence of the federal immigration legislation of the 1880s. Yet the same critique of the earlier studies of state laws about selective coverage can apply to their works. Also, these scholars' primary concerns were with legal doctrines and with theories of immigration policy, rather than the laws' enforcement and practical impact.[4] Consequently, how state control developed before the 1880s, how the laws were carried out, and the implications for federal restriction all remain unclear. As this article reveals, state policies were not simply piecemeal responses to local immigration situations. They laid tangible foundations for later federal laws. An examination of the development and implementation of state-level regulation allows for a better understanding of the roots of federal immigration restriction and a perspective that views earlier regional practices and federal policies as a single story, rather than separate accounts, of immigration control in the United States.

This article examines the evolution of immigration control in the state of New York, the busiest port of entry in nineteenth-century America, from the late eighteenth century through the introduction of federal immigration law in the 1880s. Since New York City was the place where the majority of immigrants to the state landed and where state immigration law was implemented most actively, this article pays particular attention to New York City. Like other coastal states, New York confronted the economic problem of supporting a large number of impoverished immigrants from Europe. To protect the state's treasury, the New York legislature developed exclusion policies for preventing the landing of destitute immigrants unless shipmasters provided bonds that would cover the expenses of maintaining them at charitable institutions. In 1847, the legislature placed the administration of state immigration law, which had hitherto been overseen by municipal officials, under the control of the state Board of Commissioners of Emigration, a body that included the mayor of New York City as well as state officials. In an effort to reduce the number of immigrants dependent on public charity, legislators also authorized the commissioners to assist the voluntary return of indigent foreigners to Europe.

Viewing the policies for exclusion and assisted return as insufficient to reduce foreign poverty, nativist state immigration officials and citizens in New York continually called for the deportation, or post-entry compulsory return, of foreign paupers. The demand for more extensive immigration restriction resulted in the expansion of the category of excludable passengers in 1849 and 1851; the empowerment of state poor law officials, in addition to immigration officials, to assist voluntary return in 1873; and the passage of the deportation act in 1880. This momentum for immigration control in New York was adopted on a national scale in the 1870s. When the Supreme Court declared the unconstitutionality of state passenger laws in 1876, immigration officials in New York organized a campaign with those in other states to nationalize state policies. The campaign was, in effect, a continuation of New York officials' effort to prevent pauper immigration. The result was the enactment of the Immigration Act of 1882, which provided for the exclusion of destitute immigrants as federal policy. Erika Lee has argued that Chinese exclusion triggered America's transformation into a "gatekeeping nation" and that the West was the major geographical arena of this transformation.[5] But the evolution of immigration policy in New York, and its influence on national legislation, demonstrates that the roots of this transformation can also be traced to state-level policies on the East Coast.

The development of immigration control in New York suggests that the legislature responded to two kinds of foreign poverty in different ways. Legislators regarded immigrants' poverty as a social and moral problem, but they saw the practical and humanitarian necessity of accommodating poor immigrants who came to the United States on their own. For this reason, the legislature authorized state immigration officials to provide protection and care to those immigrants who were allowed to land, and resisted deporting them, however poor they were, even if they became paupers after landing. This stance, however, did not apply to those who had already been paupers in their homeland and had migrated to New York with assistance from the local authorities in Europe. Policy makers were much less sympathetic to these assisted paupers because of their predetermined status as public charges and their seemingly low likelihood of becoming independent, productive American citizens. Resistance to imported pauperism shaped the course of restrictive policies in New York, leading to the 1880 deportation law, which specifically targeted assisted paupers. Long before the formation of federal regulatory policies, then, America's biggest immigrant-receiving state was firmly committed to regulating the quality of newcomers who would join American society.

New York state's first move toward immigration control was stimulated by the growth of pauperism in New York City due to urbanization and the influx of poor European immigrants after the American Revolution. In 1788, the state legislature passed a law that required shipmasters arriving in the port of New York to report to the mayor the names and occupations of the passengers they landed within twenty-four hours of arrival. If any passenger could not give "a good account of himself or herself" or appeared likely to become a pauper chargeable to New York City, shipmasters had to either bring the person back to the place of embarkation within one month or provide to the mayor or aldermen a bond of £100 with surety that the person would not become a public charge. Nine years later, the bonding policy was modified so that bonds should be provided *prior* to the landing of passengers. By compelling shipmasters to bring back destitute immigrants unless shippers prepaid the cost of supporting such aliens in the form of bonds, state legislators sought to check foreign poverty in New York.[6]

Comparison of New York's immigration law with those of other states helps locate New York's policy in a national context of state-level immigration control. New York regulated immigration through exclusion—prohibition of the landing of destitute immigrants through bonding and their subsequent return to the place of departure. An exclusion policy of this kind was adopted by most of the coastal states prior to the 1880s, including Pennsylvania, Louisiana, California, and the New England states, but New York and Massachusetts pursued pauper exclusion most rigorously by creating state agencies devoted to that purpose—the Commissioners of Emigration in New York in 1847 and the Commissioners of Alien Passengers and Foreign Paupers in Massachusetts in 1851. As E. P. Hutchinson has written, New York and Massachusetts "took the lead in this form of legislation," and no other states "approached the legislative effort made" by those two.[7]

There was nevertheless a significant distinction between New York and Massachusetts. In the eighteenth century, both states retained the colonial poor law policy of banishing indigent aliens from the state. In the early nineteenth century, however, New York retreated from pauper removal. In February 1824, responding to rising poor relief expenditures, the legislature authorized Secretary of State John Van Ness Yates to file a report on the state poor laws. In his report, Yates proposed to abolish pauper removal. Under the existing law, paupers had been expelled in a practice known as "passing on." Upon obtaining a court warrant for removal, officials in the town passed the pauper to officials in the adjacent town. This process was repeated until the pauper was conveyed to his or her last place of residence or driven from the state. Yates found that this practice was costly and caused unnecessary complications between town officials. In addition, Yates claimed that removal was cruel and humiliating, inconsistent with "principles of pure benevolence and humanity." Accepting Yates's argument, legislators abolished the practice in 1824 and decided to support all destitute people, including foreigners, at county almshouses instead.[8] By contrast, Massachusetts built upon its pauper removal law to develop policies for deporting immigrant paupers already in the state to their countries of origin, a move triggered by the immigration of impoverished Catholics from Ireland during the first half of the nineteenth century. The state's exceptionally strong anti-Catholic Anglo cultural tradition enabled nativist frustration with the Irish-born, who accounted for a disproportionately large share in the state's pauper population, to be easily converted into deportation policy. Unlike other states, including New York, Massachusetts thus conducted the deportation, as well as exclusion, of immigrants.[9] In New York, exclusion remained the chief device for immigration control for most of the nineteenth century.

During the 1830s, one particular form of immigrant poverty provoked outrage among native-born Americans in New York. The prevalence of poverty among immigrants in general raised nativist tension, but it was the practice known as assisted emigration that exasperated New Yorkers.[10] From the 1830s onward, governments, landlords, and parishes in Europe repeatedly financed the emigration to North America of paupers, and sometimes criminals, in order to avoid the long-term expense of supporting such people. The overall scale of assisted emigration remains unknown, pending additional research, but paupers were sent from various parts of Europe, including Britain, Ireland, Germany, and Switzerland.[11] In 1837, almshouse officials in New York City reported to the Common Council that "this metropolis [was] forced to be the recipient of the poor objects" sent from foreign countries.[12] Mayor Aaron Clark, a nativist sympathizer, complained in the same year that assisted emigrants "cannot fail to become an intolerable burden to us."[13] The voluntary arrival of penniless immigrants was irritating enough, but many New Yorkers viewed it as unjust and unacceptable to arrange shipment of people who were destined to become public charges from the moment of landing in the United States.

Antipathy to foreign pauperism, fostered by assisted emigration, appeared so intense that British officials anticipated the wholesale deportation of immigrant paupers from New York. Reporting to the Foreign Office in the fall of 1843, Anthony Barclay, the British consul in New York City, stated he had received information that municipal officials were "about to ship back to Liverpool, perhaps directly to Ireland . . . all such native British subjects" who were or would become charges upon the city. Referring to New York's pauper exclusion policy, Barclay reported that he had seen the rejection of the landing in New York of twenty-six passengers in one ship and their subsequent return to Liverpool "by the order and at the expense of the city authorities," and that "great numbers were being sent by other vessels at the same time by the same authority."[14] Barclay's fears about the prospect of deportation were exaggerated, as New York had abolished laws for removing paupers from the state almost twenty years earlier. Yet the growing tension over foreign paupers and the active enforcement of pauper exclusion in New York City raised the possibility that deportation laws might be revived.

The presence of needy foreigners revealed significant problems with the immigrant reception policy in the 1840s. Under New York's passenger law, the bonds that shipmasters paid upon arrival were to be spent on the maintenance of the bonded passengers if they entered public charitable institutions after landing. To retain the bond money, shipowners sent their former passengers, when they became destitute, to private poorhouses or hospitals instead of public almshouses. Filthy and overcrowded, these private facilities were often utterly ill-equipped for accommodating humans. Newcomers were also often vulnerable to frauds such as the imposition of arbitrary rents by avaricious boardinghouse keepers and their agents, or "runners." In addition, a municipal investigation of the bonding system in 1842 discovered that the mayor's clerk, who was in charge of keeping account of the bonds, had been pocketing the money collected from shipmasters, causing a significant drain in the city's treasury.[15]

Under these circumstances, private parties and municipal officials called for reform to state immigration law. Presidents of immigrant societies in New York City petitioned the state legislature through the Common Council for a better law to "secure the emigrants from the frauds now practiced upon them." Influential public figures who sympathized with the plight of immigrants, such as the Whig leader and newspaper editor Thurlow Weed and Irish-born Catholic Archbishop John Hughes, endorsed the protection of newcomers. These actions moved Mayor William V. Brady to call a public meeting of citizens "irrespective of party" to pressure the state legislature for immigration reform in March 1847. At the meeting, participants resolved to establish a body of nonpartisan commissioners who would be responsible for properly collecting bonds and using them for the support of immigrants. To develop their resolution into state policy, they also appointed a committee to deliver to the legislature a bill that provided for state immigration commissioners.[16] Thus, during the 1840s, there was a growing demand in New York for a better immigration law that would prevent pauper immigration more effectively and that would protect the welfare of immigrants who were admitted to the country.[17]

The legislature passed the bill for immigration reform in May 1847, establishing the Board of the Commissioners of Emigration of the State of New York. Friedrich Kapp, one of the commissioners in 1870, attributed the passage of the bill to the lobbying campaign inside and outside of the legislature by Thurlow Weed, who mobilized Whig members and his Democratic friends, and by Andrew Carrigan, a wealthy Irish American citizen who later became the president of the New York Irish Emigrant Society. The creation of the state board signified the enhancement of the state's authority over immigration. At the same time, however, municipal governments remained an integral part of immigration control in that the commissioners included the mayors of New York City and Brooklyn, in addition to six officials appointed by the governor. To ensure that the commissioners' activities would extend to the protection of immigrants, the presidents of the Irish Emigrant Society and the German Society were included as commissioners, giving the board ten members.[18]

The commissioners' principal task was twofold: immigrant protection and immigration regulation. The officials were authorized to "provide for the maintenance and support" of the persons for whom shipmasters had paid bonds and landing taxes upon arrival. The state-run marine hospital on Staten Island was placed under the commissioners' supervision for this purpose, and another immigrant hospital was established on Ward's Island in 1848. The commissioners also assisted newcomers in proceeding to other parts of New York or other states, where they could meet their relatives or friends or obtain employment by "writing and receiving letters for the uneducated" and by "providing the means of conveyance to distant places."[19] In this way, the commissioners provided social services to those who were permitted to land.

The other chief duty of the Commissioners of Emigration was the supervision of immigrant admission. The commissioners were authorized to board ships arriving in the port of New York and inspect the condition of passengers. If they found "any lunatic, idiot, deaf and dumb, blind or infirm persons, not members of emigrating families, and who . . . are likely to become permanently a public charge," the commissioners were to require shipmasters to provide a bond of $300, which would be effective for five years, for the landing of each of these passengers. Besides bonds for those who might become dependent on public charity, shipmasters had to pay a one-dollar capitation tax, or so-called "head money," for each healthy passenger. The aggregate of head money would cover the expense of the activities of the commissioners, including their management of charitable institutions.[20] Pauper exclusion through bonding was not a new policy, but legislators sought to tighten passenger inspection and admission regulation by creating a state agency devoted to the matters of immigration.

The creation of the state board did not solve the problem of imported pauperism in New York primarily because the volume and nature of Irish famine immigration in mid-century exceeded the commissioners' capacity to strictly regulate immigrant landing. Between 1846 and 1855, starvation and destitution in Ireland brought by the potato famine led to the emigration of about 1.5 million Irish men and women to the United States, and New York City was the principal port of arrival for these immigrants. Landlords and workhouse officials in Ireland intensively shipped their destitute tenants and inmates to New York during the famine period. From December 1850 to March 1851, for example, 1,700 tenants were sent to New York from the estate of the Marquis of Lansdowne in County Kerry.[21] The passenger reports at the quarantine station on Staten Island described with great frequency the figure of a destitute Irishman "sent out by his landlord." Many of the assisted emigrants were recorded as "cripple," "deformed," or "paralyzed."[22] Having been physically and mentally weakened as a result of malnutrition, famine-related diseases, and the unhygienic transatlantic voyage, many of the Irish immigrants quickly sought admission to public charitable institutions in the city.[23] "Ship-loads of these helpless and often vicious persons are sent here," the Commissioners of Emigration wrote, "and become a permanent burden and nuisance, from the moment of their arrival."[24] Voluntary agencies also noted the unmanageable burden placed on the city's resources by assisted emigration schemes. In 1851, the New York Association for Improving the Condition of the Poor, a private charitable society, complained about the "systematic invasion of our country by the indigent."[25]

The influx of assisted Irish paupers led legislators to expand the category of people who required bonds for landing. The Commissioners of Emigration had collected bonds for people unable to support themselves, such as those with disabilities and those likely to become public charges. In 1849, the legislature modified the bonding category to include persons "who *have been* paupers in any other country or who from sickness or disease, *existing at the time of departing from the foreign port* are or are likely soon to become a public charge."[26] Clearly, the explicit emphasis on pauper status and the state of dependency at the time of departure was targeted against assisted pauper passengers. Two years later, the legislature passed a new passenger act to extend the bonding category to "persons above the age of sixty years, or widow with a child or children, or any woman without a husband, and with a child or children."[27] Recent studies of Irish assisted emigration during the famine reveal that assisted emigrants were more likely to have been in their fifties or older than the average Irish immigrant, and that women with children were overrepresented among assisted emigrants sent from workhouses.[28] In light of these findings, the specification of particular passenger groups in the new bonding policy must have been designed to identify assisted paupers. By setting up detailed rules for bonds, legislators made it difficult for shipmasters to evade bonds for assisted paupers and may have been seeking to exert pressure on shipmasters to bring them back to Europe.

In addition to regulating admission, immigration officials sought ways to return immigrant paupers to Europe. New York state law did not permit the compulsory removal of aliens from the state, but it did allow the commissioners to transfer immigrants to other parts of the state or other states by helping them reach their final destinations. Beginning in 1850, New York officials used this power to send back destitute foreigners who expressed their wish to return home, by financing their passage to Europe. In 1853, for example, the commissioners sent 271 persons "back to Europe at [their] own request." When the commissioners found "inmates of foreign poor houses" in New York's almshouses, they "endeavored to trace such cases" and "aided to return them whence they came." By using "the power already given to them by the laws under which they act," the officials tried to reduce the number of foreign paupers in the state. Before the Civil War, the commissioners returned at least 2,505 persons back to Europe.[29]

Despite the commissioners' efforts to exclude and return destitute immigrants, it became clear during the 1850s that these policies were not extensive enough to curtail foreign pauperism in New York. The commissioners were convinced that it would be "most desirable" to deport assisted paupers regardless of their will. At the same time, however, the officials regretfully noted that "this direct power is not granted by the existing laws of this State." Reflecting on the effectiveness of their immigration regulation, the commissioners remarked in December 1854 that "if they have not done more, it has not been from negligence or want of disposition; but purely insufficiency of power."[30] The New York *Journal of Commerce* contrasted New York with Massachusetts, where state immigration officials were authorized to deport destitute aliens abroad. While Massachusetts had been expelling assisted paupers, "[w]e have no law in this State by which European paupers, idiots, &c., can be sent back, without their consent."[31] Proponents of immigration control in New York thus increasingly regarded deportation as imperative to protect the state from foreign pauperism.

A glance at federal passenger policy helps explain how New York officials viewed immigration control in their state. Aristide Zolberg has shown that antebellum federal passenger laws, which reduced the number of passengers one vessel could carry for the humanitarian purpose of securing sufficient space for each passenger, operated as a form of immigration regulation by raising fares and preventing the emigration of poor people from Europe.[32] It is nevertheless worth underscoring that Zolberg's study focuses on the *practical* function of federal legislation as immigration regulation, whereas most state officials did not recognize federal passenger laws in this way. In the state-level discourse on immigration control, few if any officials saw federal law as something that could supplement state pauper policies. The extent to which state officials were unaware of federal measures, or at least regarded them as inadequate, is clear from the repeated submission of petitions from Atlantic seaboard states for a federal law "which will effectually prevent the introduction" of foreign paupers to the United States.[33] From the perspective of officials in New York, federal regulation was virtually nonexistent until the 1880s. They viewed state law as the only tool to reduce pauper immigration.

The rise of Know-Nothingism in the mid-1850s invigorated anti-foreign pauper sentiment in New York. The unprecedented inflow of impoverished

Catholics from Ireland and Germany from 1845 to 1854 provoked intense nativism, resulting in the sweeping victories of nativist politicians, the so-called Know Nothings, in northern states in the elections of 1854. In New York state, the political power of immigrants, who accounted for about a quarter of the state's population, hampered Know Nothingism as a political force. The immense popularity of William H. Seward, the renowned Whig antislavery U.S. senator and former New York governor who was supportive of immigrants, also worked against the Know Nothings in state politics.[34] The nativists' political influence was thus limited, but their criticism of foreign pauperism, which they believed directly threatened the stability and morality of American society, echoed the anti-pauper language that had developed in the state. Thomas R. Whitney, a Know-Nothing congressman from New York, argued that "our hospitality is abused, and the moral atmosphere of society [is] contaminated" by the assisted emigration of paupers.[35] Nativist state senator Erastus Brooks regretted that America had made itself "the common Alms-House of the world" by keeping its gates wide open.[36] Hostility to immigrants' poverty was so central to Know-Nothing ideology that the *New York Times* called foreign pauperism "the great battle-cry" in the Know-Nothing movement.[37]

The "battle-cry" was shared not only by nativists but also by the Democratic mayor of New York City, Fernando Wood, who was otherwise sympathetic to immigrants. In January 1855, requesting federal assistance in preventing pauper immigration, Wood wrote to President Franklin Pierce that "[a]s it is its [the national government's] duty to protect us from foreign aggression, with ball and cannon, so it is its duty to protect us against an enemy more insidious and destructive, though coming in another form."[38] Claiming that "[t]his City has been made the great *entrepot* for the delivery of these outcasts and banished mendicants," Wood also asked that American consuls abroad furnish to him on a regular basis "evidence sufficient to fix the character" of emigrants who departed European ports, in order to strengthen vigilance over assisted pauper immigration.[39] Despite the absence of a deportation law, Wood declared that if an immigrant was found destitute in the city, "he is immediately ordered back—and, if necessary, transferred *forcibly* back."[40] The mayor was even reported to have stated on one occasion that "if it be necessary to call out the forces within the power of the city government to fire on and sink every emigrant vessel coming into this harbor with pauper and criminal emigrants, I shall do so."[41]

Wood did not go so far as to sink emigrant vessels, but he prohibited the landing of some passengers and ordered their return at his discretion.

In September 1855, four criminals who had been shipped from a prison in Germany were found among passengers on the *Deutschland* from Hamburg upon its arrival in New York. By order of the mayor, the criminals were removed from the ship and detained at "a place of security." Determined to "return all such forthwith, in every case known to me, by the same vessel," he ordered the return of the four men to Hamburg on the *Deutschland* in October.[42] Their criminal status might have been the decisive reason for their compulsory return, but Wood's bellicose statement on his wish to sink vessels carrying paupers and criminals transported from Europe implies that assisted paupers might be subject to similar treatment. In the nineteenth-century discourse on immigration restriction, paupers and criminals were often listed together as equal threats to public morality for their inability to hold gainful employment and the belief that idleness and criminality were both rooted in defects of character. The *New York Evening Express*, for example, described the *Deutschland* case as one of "a series of like imports from the *Prison and Pauper Houses* of the old World to the shores of the new." "We hope," the newspaper declared, "the example of sending back foreign paupers and criminals will at least abridge the number of that class of persons who have hitherto thronged to our shores."[43]

Mayor Wood's words and actions against foreign paupers and criminals deserve attention for two reasons. First, they represent what his biographer Jerome Mushkat calls Wood's "characteristic double game." From the early years of his political career, Wood was committed to establishing an immigrant constituency by supporting Ireland's nationalist struggle against Britain and contributing money to immigrant societies. At the same time, being opportunistic, Wood did not mind joining the nativists, accepting a position on the executive committee of the Know Nothing Party when it became strong in 1854. Given that the Know Nothings and Whigs were in control of the Common Council during his mayoral tenure, Wood's aggressive attitude toward undesirable foreigners might also have been calculated to appease his nativist opponents in municipal politics.[44]

More importantly, Wood's assertion of the city's right to protect itself from "foreign aggression" can be interpreted as precedent for the sovereignty argument based on police power that later became the backbone of federal exclusion policy. The period from the 1830s to the 1850s witnessed the expansion of the state's police power—a constitutional right to protect its citizens from outside physical and moral threats—in the form of state immigration policy. In *City of New York v. Miln* (1837), the United States Supreme Court upheld New York's pauper exclusion policy as an exercise of the state's right to "regulate their own internal police [power]" and to provide measures against the moral and physical "pestilence of paupers, vagabonds, and possibly convicts."[45] In his letter to President Pierce in 1855, Fernando Wood asserted that "[t]he inherent right of every community to protect itself from dangers arising from such [pauper] immigration, cannot be questioned."[46] This line of argument laid the rationale for Chinese exclusion decades later. Supporting the suspension of Chinese immigration, San Francisco lawyer H. N. Clement claimed in 1878 that "[a] nation has a right to do *everything* that can secure it from threatening danger."[47] Wood's words and actions suggest that the sovereignty argument in federal immigration restriction had some of its roots in the local, as well as state, articulation of police power on the eastern seaboard against Europeans in the antebellum period.

Meanwhile, the state's charitable policy toward immigrants met aggressive opposition from New Yorkers. In May 1855, the Commissioners of Emigration leased an old fort in lower Manhattan known as Castle Garden to build an immigrant landing station where the commissioners alone could supervise the landing process. By prohibiting the entry of unauthorized persons into the depot, the officials sought to strengthen the protection of newcomers from runners at the time of arrival.[48] The construction of the Castle Garden depot provoked fiery protests not only from the runners but also from residents and businessmen in lower Manhattan. New Yorkers believed that Castle Garden would become "a pest house" and draw poverty-stricken foreigners who would "certainly spread pestilential diseases of every kind among us." Fearing that such a contaminated institution would cause a decline in property values in the city's First Ward, wealthy New Yorkers and businessmen also opposed the depot.[49] Three years later, a mob of 1,000 angry residents and property holders on Staten Island, alarmed by the potential spread of contagious diseases from sick immigrants at the marine hospital on the island, burned the institution to the ground after repeatedly requesting the legislature to remove the hospital and threatening to destroy it if the requests were not met.[50]

This opposition to New York's immigrant-related institutions indicates the state's failure to secure public support for its immigration policy. In the mid-1850s, immigration officials in Massachusetts rigorously carried out deportation policy under the auspices of the Know-Nothing legislature and governor.[51] The criticism of immigrant pauperism was voiced as enthusiastically in New York as in Massachusetts, and nativist New Yorkers decidedly wanted harsh measures against foreign paupers such as deportation. The unpopularity of the state's policies for immigrant landing and sick foreigners, however, prevented the Commissioners of Emigration from securing public understanding, or political capital, necessary for the further expansion of their authorities, which could have allowed them to initiate the compulsory removal of foreign paupers. With New Yorkers' hostility to the administration of state immigration policy and immigrants' voting power against nativist force in state politics, deportation was not introduced in New York during the 1850s.

The decline of political nativism after 1860 did not signify the end of antipathy to foreign pauperism in northern states during the era of the Civil War and Reconstruction. In the middle of the Civil War, the New York Association for Improving the Condition of the Poor remarked that foreign immigration still "inflicts upon the community an abnormal amount of pauperism and crime."[52] The assisted emigration of paupers, including those with mental illness, continued to concern the Commissioners of Emigration. In 1870, the officials noted that "idiots and imbeciles are systematically sent to this country from Europe, by relatives or local authorities, in order to shift on this Commission the burden of their support."[53]

After the Civil War, the Commissioners of Emigration regulated the landing of pauper passengers in a more restrictive way than before. Technically, shipmasters could still land pauper passengers with the payment of bonds for them. Starting in the postbellum years, however, the commissioners routinely pressured shipmasters to bring destitute passengers back to the other side of the ocean without giving them the option for bonds. Paupers or criminals, the commissioners wrote, were to be detained on arrival so that "measures may be taken to cause their return to the port of embarkation." In June 1873, for instance, when the commissioners found a Swiss pauper named August Cruger among arriving passengers on the *Batavia* and confirmed his assisted status, the commissioners "required the steamship company to return him to his home in Switzerland."[54] The legal structure of passenger regulation remained the same as in the 1840s, but its practical operation increasingly became subject to officials' discretion.

The strict approach to destitute immigrants, especially assisted paupers, was part of a growing hostility toward a certain type of poor person during Reconstruction. One of the major social problems after the Civil War was the increase of vagrants, or "tramps," who survived through street begging even though they were physically able to work. The harsh realities of industrialization and the devastating effects of the war created a class of paupers who were temporarily unemployed despite their willingness to work or were disabled because of uncontrollable misfortune. While charity officials regarded these needy people as "deserving," vagrants were viewed as the "undeserving" whose chronic poverty stemmed from personal laziness and moral defects. More than being burdens on charity, vagrants posed an ideological threat to American society for violating what historian Eric Foner calls "free labor ideology," a dominant social thinking in the nineteenth century. It assumed that, in a free society, citizens would engage in productive work to achieve economic independence, and that this formula for success was available to everyone. Vagrants, who voluntarily placed themselves out of the world of wage labor and deliberately chose a life of dependency, appeared to threaten the integrity of a post-emancipation, free American society that was supposed to consist of industrious, self-sufficient workers. States responded to the problem of tramps by tightening the execution of vagrancy laws under which beggars were arrested and forced to perform compulsory labor at workhouses.[55] Assisted paupers, who had been dependent on private or public aid even before their emigration to the United States, fitted into the category of undeserving poor for their predestined unlikelihood to become ideal American citizens.

When the Panic of 1873 even further deteriorated immigrant destitution and vagrancy, the New York legislature decided to reform the state's charity, and consequently immigration, policies. In 1867, New York had established the Board of State Commissioners of Public Charities as a comprehensive state agency to deal with issues of poverty and relief arising from the Civil War. When the worst economic collapse Americans had yet experienced engulfed the nation in 1873, the New York legislature reorganized the state's public charity system to better handle mounting poverty. In that year, the legislature renamed the board the State Board of Charities and extended the number of officials from eight to eleven.[56]

One of the powers the New York State Board of Charities acquired in 1873 was the return of immigrants. The authority for assisting destitute immigrants' voluntary return to Europe had been vested in the Commissioners of Emigration. In order to facilitate the removal of foreign paupers from the state through this policy, the legislature extended the authority to the Board of Charities in 1873. In June, legislators passed a law providing that if any almshouse inmate expressed "a preference to be sent" to any state or country where the person had original residence or sources of support, the secretary of the Board of Charities could "cause the removal of such pauper to such state or country."[57] No state law of New York permitted the deportation of immigrants against their will, but the 1873 act expanded the mode of reducing the number of foreign paupers by empowering almshouse officials, along with the Commissioners of Emigration, to send voluntary returnees to Europe.

The expansion of the power to return alien paupers galvanized calls for deportation. While acknowledging the importance of the new law in reducing foreign pauperism in the state, Martin B. Anderson, a member of the Board of Charities, advocated a further step, namely the deportation of assisted emigrants: "Should we not be justified in sending back to Europe to be cared for by their own people, these *unnaturalized* paupers and convicts, who have been surreptitiously introduced into our country and made a burden to the tax payers of New York?"[58] Every "blind, idiotic, crippled, epileptic, lunatic, or other infirm foreign pauper, designedly thrust upon us," declared the charity board, "should immediately be sent back to the place whence he or she came."[59] The *New York Times* even suggested that the city of New York launch the deportation of paupers on its own and "return them where they belong."[60]

A sudden interruption of the implementation of state passenger law in 1876 strengthened the argument in favor of deportation in New York. Regarding the payment of head money as detrimental to their business, steamship companies had attempted for decades to remove the tax by challenging states' constitutional right to collect it. In 1849, the United States Supreme Court had declared in the *Passenger Cases* that the policies of New York and Massachusetts for collecting head money were unconstitutional, as they infringed upon Congress's exclusive authority over foreign commerce. To overcome the constitutional problem, New York legislators modified state passenger law three months after the ruling to require shipmasters to provide a bond of $300 for *every* passenger regardless of his or her condition or to pay a $1.50 fee for each non-pauper passenger in lieu of a bond. This arrangement practically coerced shipmasters into choosing head money over bonds, allowing New York to still collect head money not as a mandatory tax but as a voluntary payment by shipmasters.[61] In the spring of 1876, shippers won a decisive victory on the head-money question when the Supreme Court confirmed the unconstitutionality of New York's passenger policies in *Henderson v. Mayor of the City of New York*.[62] The Supreme Court decision paralyzed the activities of the Commissioners of Emigration in New York, as head money had been a critical financial resource for running immigrant hospitals and Castle Garden.

If New York could not secure money to support foreigners dependent on public charity through taxation, the remaining means of protecting the state's treasury was their removal. Yet the state still lacked a deportation law. In February 1879, the commissioners accommodated three "almost entirely penniless" Swiss immigrants who had been sent to New York by the local authorities in the Canton of Aargau, Switzerland. The *New York Times* lamented: "There is no law which empowers the Commissioners to send such persons back."[63] Six months later, when another group of assisted paupers arrived, the commissioners remarked that "[t]he law, as now in force, does not give power to compel the return of any pauper, lunatic or criminal that may be brought to this country."[64] Without head money, deportation began to appear as a necessary measure in New York.

It is crucial to note that the *Henderson* ruling did not deny states the right to control immigration entirely. The Supreme Court confirmed that the whole subject of passenger taxation belonged to the domain of Congress's power over foreign commerce, but the court did not deny, or even address, the right of states to exercise internal police power. Nor had this right been denied in the *Passenger Cases*. As Justice John McLean, one of the majority, explained in 1849, "[i]n giving the commercial power to Congress, the States did not part with that power of self-preservation."[65] In delivering the opinion of a unanimous court in the *Henderson* case, Justice Samuel Miller declared that "we do not decide" whether states could "protect themselves against actual paupers, vagrants, criminals, and diseased persons" from abroad.[66] In *Chy Lung v. Freeman*, in which the court struck down California's bond requirement on the same day as the *Henderson* case, Miller reconfirmed that the court would not "lay down the definite limit" of states' police power. The problem with the California law, the justice made it clear, was not its regulatory nature in itself but its "manifest purpose" to obtain money from passengers "far beyond" the appropriate application of police regulation, an invasion of congressional authority over foreign commerce.[67] Legal scholar Hiroshi Motomura has recently written that the Supreme Court "did not repudiate the state police power" in these decisions and "continued to acknowledge" its exercise.[68] Thus, while states' *exclusion* policies for regulating entry through taxation were invalidated, the court did not deprive states of the right to *deport* undesirable aliens. The *Henderson* decision endorsed federal superiority to states in the realm of immigration control only partially, leaving space for sustained state involvement.

The continual arrival of assisted paupers after the Supreme Court ruling convinced the New York legislature, which had been reluctant to resume pauper removal since its abolition in 1824, to introduce a new deportation law in 1880. In June, legislators passed an act authorizing the Board of Charities to return to their countries of origin "any crippled, blind, lunatic, or other infirm alien paupers" in any charitable institutions in the state, who had been sent "by cities or towns in the various governments of Europe, or by societies, relatives or friends."[69] The language of the law seemed to cover every immigrant pauper, since most immigrants came to the United States with some form of assistance from their families or friends. But the charity board's report reveals that the law was targeted at assisted paupers, who "do not come to our country as immigrants and prospective citizens, but as paupers born and bred," and who were shifted "from care and support in European alms-houses and hospitals to ours."[70] The act provided that the board would receive an annual appropriation from the state's treasury to fund deportation. The loss of head money forced the state to use its own treasury to cover the costs related to immigrants, including deportation. Charity officials found that removal would still help the state reduce the expense of pauper immigrants, as sending a pauper to Europe would cost less than $30, while the average annual expenditure for supporting the person was about $150.[71] The implementation of forcible removal was modest at best. During 1881, for example, forty-five paupers were banished from New York under the 1880 act.[72] Nevertheless, the 1880 act resurrected pauper removal in New York nearly half a century after its abolition.

The development of immigration control policy in New York in the 1870s and 1880s corresponded with immigrant exclusion sentiment at the national level. The anti-Chinese hostility that had grown in California since mid-century resulted in the passage of the Page Act in 1875 and the Chinese Exclusion Act in 1882. But the impetus for federal immigration control came from the other side of the continent as well. Immediately after the *Henderson* decision, the New York Commissioners of Emigration instigated a campaign with immigration officials in other states, particularly Massachusetts, to establish national immigration legislation that would allow states to collect head money. In early July, the Commissioners sent to Congress a draft bill, which they prepared after consulting with the state boards of charities in Massachusetts, Pennsylvania, Rhode Island, Michigan, Wisconsin, and Illinois. The bill proposed a capitation tax payable to the United States Treasury Secretary and prohibited the entry of criminals and paupers. Such passengers would be returned to their place of departure at the expense of the steamship company.[73] The Commissioners of Emigration

regarded the exclusion policy as "an absolute necessity" to check the shipment of paupers from Europe.[74]

Vehement protest from shippers and merchants against the bill delayed
its congressional proceedings. This slow progress of national immigration
legislation explains the enactment of state deportation law in 1880 in New
York, which desperately needed some device to trim the cost of foreign paupers in the absence of state passenger taxes. In August 1882, however, three
months after the immigration of Chinese laborers was suspended, Congress
passed the national Immigration Act, partly as a result of the New York
Emigration Commissioners' threat to shut down Castle Garden unless the
federal government moved for national legislation. The act, applying to all
immigrants, instituted a federal capitation tax of fifty cents on each alien
passenger and banned the landing of "any convict, lunatic, idiot, or any
person unable to take care of himself or herself without becoming a public
charge," with a deportation clause for criminals.[75] Together with the Chinese
exclusion laws, the Immigration Act set the groundwork for the system of
federal immigration control that would develop in the following decades.[76]

The introduction of federal immigration policy in 1882 did not end pauper deportation in New York. Due to the lack of a federal infrastructure,
the 1882 act authorized existing state immigration agencies, including the
Commissioners of Emigration in New York, to enforce its provisions. In
1891, a new federal immigration act, which made deportable all excludable
immigrants including paupers, placed the administration of immigration
policy under the federal Superintendent of Immigration in the Treasury
Department, replacing state agents with federal employees. In New York,
throughout these years of federal expansion in the sphere of immigration
control, the Board of Charities independently continued to expel assisted
paupers. The scale of removal remained modest, with the annual number
of deportees never exceeding one hundred, but the board was conducting
deportation as late as 1900, when seventy assisted paupers in the state's
charitable institutions were sent back. Similarly, in Massachusetts, neither
the *Henderson* decision nor the 1882 act disrupted the state's policy for
deporting destitute immigrants to Europe. That these states kept exercising
their internal police power against foreign paupers after the consolidation of
federal control illuminates the enduring significance of states in America's
policy for regulating the quality of people who would reside in the nation.[77]

In examining the development of immigration control in the United States,
it is essential to acknowledge its bi-coastal origins. The state of New York

had regulated the immigration of destitute Europeans since the eighteenth century, and both public officials and citizens kept calling for a more extensive state immigration policy, particularly the deportation of foreign paupers. State legislators responded by broadening the bonding category in state passenger law, expanding the power for assisting the voluntary return of indigent foreigners, and initiating pauper removal. After the *Henderson* decision, immigration control in New York developed in tandem with an interstate campaign for national legislation to restrict undesirable immigration from Europe, which led to the creation of the Immigration Act in 1882. While the Chinese Exclusion Act of 1882 can be regarded as class legislation for its focus on laborers, and its passage was nationally supported, it is fair to state that immigration scholars tend to attribute the establishment of federal immigration law to anti-Asian racial prejudice arising from the West. The evolution of New York's immigration policy, together with developments in Massachusetts, demonstrates that Atlantic seaboard states' economic nativism against destitute Europeans also contributed to the rise of national control. As much as racism on the West Coast guided America's transformation into a "gatekeeping nation," the transformation also began on the East Coast through state-level policy for imported poverty in the antebellum period.

New Yorkers had a special antipathy for the assisted emigration of paupers from European states. Poor immigrants who came on their own, and were subsequently admitted into American almshouses, were bad enough. But assisted paupers were even worse. New Yorkers felt foreign governments that provided assistance for emigration were simply dumping their poor on the United States. In 1876, Martin Anderson, one of the New York charity officials, argued that immigrant poverty in general was "an evil incidental to emigration" and should be "accepted as a matter of course." But it was "the imperative duty" of Americans, Anderson asserted, to take measures to prevent undesirable foreigners "from being sent to our country."[78] The frustration about assisted paupers, intensified by the loss of head money in the *Henderson* decision, caused the legislature to overcome its long hesitation about pauper removal and to launch the deportation of assisted paupers in 1880. Pauperism after entry still had to be grudgingly tolerated, but pauperism before entry, or the "undeserving" kind of immigrant poverty, was subject to strict punishment in the form of banishment. In 1885, the federal government passed the Foran Act, prohibiting the landing of unskilled workers under labor contract signed abroad whose emigration was assisted by their American employers. The act was a response to pressure from native-born workers who resented competition with cheap foreign contract labor.[79] The

Foran Act was not designed for paupers, but New York's distinction between voluntary and assisted immigrants suggests that the pre-1882 state policies shaped some of the ideological principles of federal contract labor law.

One of the features of immigration policy in New York is the state government's relatively moderate position on immigration control, including its reluctance to adopt deportation as state policy. The Commissioners of Emigration constantly returned immigrant paupers to Europe, but only at the paupers' own request. Despite repeated calls for the compulsory removal of foreign paupers since the 1850s, the legislature did not move for that specific purpose until 1880, when the four-year absence of the head money revenue since the *Henderson* decision and the sluggish progress of national immigration legislation forced the state to take direct action to reduce the burden of immigrant poverty. Furthermore, unlike deportation policy in Massachusetts, which applied to all destitute foreigners dependent on public charity, New York's 1880 deportation law was limited to assisted paupers.

The principal explanation for New York's moderate approach to immigration restriction is surely the sheer volume of immigration to New York. New York City alone received approximately seventy percent of all immigrants to the United States before the Civil War while only seven percent of immigrants arrived in Boston. In 1882, sixty-four percent of immigrants entered the United States through the port of New York.[80] In light of the magnitude of immigration, the rigid enforcement of immigration control through deportation would simply have been beyond the capacity of the state government. While deportation was much more manageable in Massachusetts, accommodating rather than removing newcomers was the realistic option in New York.

The substantial size of the immigrant population in New York—about a quarter of the state's population and half of New York City's population from the 1850s to the 1880s—also curbed the growth of restrictive policies by politically empowering the immigrants. Political scientist Daniel Tichenor has demonstrated that the recurrent failure of nativist attempts to restrict European immigration in the nineteenth century was due to the value of immigrants as a voting bloc that "Democratic leaders and other politicians had a compelling interest in winning over."[81] When an election day approached, as Robert Ernst has written, agents of political parties in New York even "made use of the inmates," many of whom were of Irish birth, by visiting almshouses and providing paupers with food and clothes.[82] Democratic politicians, who controlled state and city politics for much of the period between the 1850s and 1880s with immigrant support, and even

Whigs and Republicans, realized that the immigrant vote was too valuable to alienate by sponsoring, let alone rigorously executing, restrictive policies such as deportation.[83] Given the difficulty of pursuing immigration restriction in New York, the limited deportation law of 1880 can be interpreted as a compromise for policy makers that appeased the nativists without offending their immigrant constituencies.

Nonetheless, New York had been deeply engaged in the regulation of immigration by the time the national government assumed an active role in it. With the exception of Massachusetts, no state conducted immigration control more systematically than New York. Efforts in states such as Pennsylvania to construct a counterpart of Castle Garden ended in failure.[84] Massachusetts, to be sure, established the most rigid state policy for immigration restriction. Yet New York, the nation's biggest point of entry, also had a long-standing commitment to immigration regulation. Landing stations established after the 1880s and operated under federal supervision, such as Ellis Island and Angel Island, have come to symbolize the tradition of immigration control in America. Yet New York's ongoing efforts to reduce foreign pauperism reveal that restriction was an integral part of the American immigration experience long before the emergence of these historical icons.

NOTES

The author would like to thank Kevin Kenny, Heather Cox Richardson, Ian Delahanty, Gráinne McEvoy, Seth Meehan, and anonymous readers for their comments on early drafts of this article. Research for the article was supported by generous financial assistance from the American Historical Association, the Immigration and Ethnic History Society, the Gilder Lehrman Institute of American History, and the Boston College Clough Center for the Study of Constitutional Democracy.

1. Report on the English family dated September 15, 1880, Minutes of the Board's Meetings from February 5, 1878, to December 7, 1885, State Board of Charities, pp. 195–96, New York State Library; the newly passed state law was "[a]n Act making appropriations for certain expenses of government and supplying deficiencies in former appropriations" [hereafter, New York Law of 1880] (June 7, 1880), *Laws of New York*, chap. 549 (Albany, NY, 1880), Vol. 1: 795.

2. For recent representative works on Chinese exclusion laws, see Charles J. McClain, *In Search of Equality: The Chinese Struggle against Discrimination in Nineteenth-Century America* (Berkeley, CA, 1994); Lucy E. Salyer, *Laws Harsh as Tigers: Chinese Immigrants and the Shaping of Modern Immigration Law* (Chapel Hill, NC, 1995); Erika Lee, *At America's Gates: Chinese Immigration during the Exclusion Era, 1882–1943* (Chapel Hill, NC, 2003).

3. John Cummings, "Poor-Laws of Massachusetts and New York: With Appendices Containing the United States Immigration and Contract-Labor Laws," *Publications of the American Economic Association* 10, no. 4 (July 1895): 15–135; Roy L. Garis, *Immigration Restriction: A Study of the Opposition to and Regulation of Immigration into the United States* (New York, 1927); Richard J. Purcell, "The New York Commissioners of Emigration and Irish Immigrants: 1847–1860," *Studies: An Irish Quarterly Review* 37, no. 145 (March 1948): 29–42; Edward F. Tuerk, "The Supreme Court and Public Policy: The Regulation of Immigration, 1820–82" (master's thesis, University of Chicago, 1951); Benjamin J. Klebaner, "State and Local Immigration Regulation in the United States Before 1882," *International Review of Social History* 3, no. 2 (1958): 269–95; Marcus Lee Hansen, *The Atlantic Migration 1607–1860: A History of the Continuing Settlement of the United States* (1940; New York, 1961).

4. Gerald L. Neuman, *Strangers to the Constitution: Immigrants, Borders, and Fundamental Law* (Princeton, NJ, 1996); Mary Sarah Bilder, "The Struggle over Immigration: Indentured Servants, Slaves, and Articles of Commerce," *Missouri Law Review* 61, no. 4 (Fall 1996): 743–824; Kunal M. Parker, "State, Citizenship, and Territory: The Legal Construction of Immigrants in Antebellum Massachusetts," *Law and History Review* 19, no. 3 (2001): 583–643; Daniel J. Tichenor, *Dividing Lines: The Politics of Immigration Control in America* (Princeton, NJ, 2002); Aristide R. Zolberg, *A Nation by Design: Immigration Policy in the Fashioning of America* (Cambridge, MA, 2006).

5. Lee, *At America's Gates*.

6. "An Act for the Better Settlement and Relief of the Poor" (March 7, 1788), in *Immigration: Select Documents and Case Records*, ed. Edith Abbott (Chicago, 1924), 104–05. Neuman, *Strangers to the Constitution*, 27–28; Klebaner, "State and Local Immigration Regulation," 273. On the history of the port of New York, see Robert Greenhalgh Albion, *The Rise of New York Port, 1815–1860* (New York, 1939).

7. E. P. Hutchinson, *Legislative History of American Immigration Policy, 1798–1965* (Philadelphia, 1981), 400, 403; 396–404; Klebaner, "State and Local Immigration Regulation," 274, 276. For state immigration legislation, see also Senate, *Reports of the Immigration Commission: Immigration Legislation*, 61st Cong., 3d sess., 1911, S. Doc. 758.

8. Martha Branscombe, "The Courts and the Poor Laws in New York State, 1784–1929" (PhD diss., University of Chicago, 1943), 18, 26–36; David M. Schneider, *The History of Public Welfare in New York State, 1609–1866* (Chicago, 1938), 211–30; Raymond A. Mohl, *Poverty in New York, 1783–1825* (New York, 1971), 58, 62–65. Yates quoted in Branscombe, "Courts and the Poor Laws," 29.

9. Kunal M. Parker, "From Poor Law to Immigration Law: Changing Visions of Territorial Community in Antebellum Massachusetts," *Historical Geography* 28 (2000): 61–85.

10. For nativism in the 1830s, see David H. Bennett, *The Party of Fear: The American Far Right from Nativism to the Militia Movement*, rev. ed. (1988; New York, 1995), 27–47; Dale T. Knobel, *"America for the Americans": The Nativist Movement in the United States* (New York, 1996), 49–57; Leo Hershkowitz, "The Native American Democratic Association in New York City, 1835–1836," *New York Historical Society Quarterly* 66, no. 1 (January 1962): 41–59.

11. For assisted emigration from Europe, see Garis, *Immigration Restriction*, 37–42; Benjamin J. Klebaner, "The Myth of Foreign Pauper Dumping in the United States," *Social Service Review* 35, no. 3 (September 1961): 302–09; Gerard Moran, *Sending Out Ireland's Poor: Assisted Emigration to North America in the Nineteenth Century* (Dublin, Ireland, 2004); Wolfgang Helbich and Walter D. Kamphoefner, "The Hour of Your Liberation Is

Getting Closer and Closer . . . ," *Studia Migracyjne—Przeglad Polonijny* 35, no. 3 (2009): 43–58. Gerard Moran estimates that in Ireland, between 250,000 and 300,000 people received full or partial assistance from workhouses, landlords, or philanthropists to emigrate to North America in the nineteenth century. Moran, *Sending Out Ireland's Poor*, 14–15.

12. Schneider, *History of Public Welfare*, 299.

13. Rose May Pirraglia, "The Context of Urban Pauperism: Foreign Immigration and American Economic Growth, 1815–1855" (PhD diss., Columbia University, 1984), 133.

14. Two letters from Anthony Barclay to the Foreign Office, September 19, 1843, and December 30, 1843, Registered Papers, Home Office, HO45/478, National Archives (UK).

15. Friedrich Kapp, *Immigration and the Commissioners of Emigration of the State of New York* (New York, 1870), 41–84.

16. Ibid., 85–93. Immigration society presidents' petition quoted in ibid., 88. The call for a public meeting quoted in ibid., 91.

17. In 1843, the nativist American Republican Party, with the help of the Whigs, succeeded in electing its nominee, former Whig James Harper, mayor of New York City. The goal of the party focused on the restriction of officeholding to native-born citizens and the extension of the waiting period for naturalization, rather than immigration restriction. Without leaving any impact on state immigration policy, the American Republican Party disappeared by 1847. Tyler Anbinder, *Nativism & Slavery: The Northern Know Nothings & the Politics of the 1850s* (New York, 1992), 11–13; Bennett, *Party of Fear*, 53–60; Ira M. Leonard, "The Rise and Fall of the American Republican Party in New York City, 1843–1845," *New York Historical Society Quarterly* 50, no. 2 (April 1966): 151–92.

18. Kapp, *Immigration and the Commissioners of Emigration*, 94–95; Tuerk, "Supreme Court and Public Policy," 14–15; Marion R. Casey, "Refractive History: Memory and the Founders of the Emigrant Savings Bank," in *Making the Irish American: History and Heritage of the Irish in the United States*, ed. J. J. Lee and Marion R. Casey (New York, 2006), 313. For the Irish Emigrant Society, see Richard J. Purcell, "The Irish Emigrant Society of New York," *Studies: An Irish Quarterly Review* 27, no. 108 (December 1938): 583–99.

19. Kapp, *Immigration and the Commissioners of Emigration*, 125–27; Schneider, *History of Public Welfare*, 313. The officials' task quoted in *Annual Reports of the Commissioners of Emigration of the State of New York: From the Organization of Commission, May 5, 1847, to 1860, Inclusive: Together with Tables and Reports, and Other Official Documents* [hereafter, ARCESNY], Appendix, 3. The commissioners' activities quoted in ibid., 135.

20. ARCESNY, Appendix, 2.

21. Tyler Anbinder, "From Famine to Five Points: Lord Lansdowne's Irish Tenants Encounter North America's Most Notorious Slum," *American Historical Review* 107, no. 2 (April 2002): 365.

22. Records of the Office of the Mayor, Box 1202, Caleb S. Woodhull, 7, New York Municipal Archives.

23. For Irish famine immigration, see Kerby A. Miller, *Emigrants and Exiles: Ireland and the Irish Exodus to North America* (New York, 1985), 280–344; Robert James Scally, *The End of Hidden Ireland: Rebellion, Famine, and Emigration* (New York, 1995); Kevin Kenny, *The American Irish: A History* (New York, 2000), 89–130. Tyler Anbinder has recently demonstrated that New York's famine immigrants were eventually able to save a substantial amount of money, challenging the notion prevalent among historians that these immigrants rarely rose from poverty to wealth. Tyler Anbinder, "Moving beyond 'Rags to Riches': New

York's Irish Famine Immigrants and Their Surprising Savings Accounts," *Journal of American History* 99, no. 3 (December 2012): 741–70.

24. ARCESNY, 76–77.

25. *The Eighth Annual Report of the New York Association for Improving the Condition of the Poor, for the Year 1851* (New York, 1851), 24. On poverty and charity in antebellum New York, see Stephen Anthony Klips, "Institutionalizing the Poor: The New York City Alms-house, 1825–1860" (PhD diss., City University of New York, 1980); Maureen Fitzgerald, *Habits of Compassion: Irish Catholic Nuns and the Origins of New York's Welfare System, 1830–1920* (Urbana, IL, 2006); Gunja SenGupta, *From Slavery to Poverty: The Racial Origins of Welfare in New York, 1840–1918* (New York, 2009).

26. "An act to amend certain acts concerning passengers coming to the city of New York" (April 11, 1849), *Laws of the State of New York, Passed at the Seventy Second Session of the Legislature*, chap. 350 (Troy, NY, 1849), 506; emphasis added.

27. "An act to amend . . . acts concerning passengers coming to the city of New York, and the public health" (July 11, 1851), *Laws of the State of New York, Passed at the Seventy Fourth Session of the Legislature*, chap. 523 (Albany, NY, 1851), 971–72.

28. Anbinder, "From Famine to Five Points," 366; Moran, *Sending Out Ireland's Poor*, 139.

29. ARCESNY, 135, 157, 397; Raymond L. Cohn, *Mass Migration under Sail: European Immigration to the Antebellum United States* (New York, 2009), 163–65.

30. ARCESNY, 156, 397.

31. Cited in "Importation of Paupers and Convicts," *Charleston Mercury*, October 3, 1854.

32. Zolberg, *Nation by Design*, 110–13, 145–50, 156–58. Congress passed passenger laws in 1819, 1847, and 1855.

33. House, *Foreign Paupers and Naturalization Laws*, 25th Cong., 2nd sess., 1838, Report 1040, 1.

34. *Census of the State of New York, for 1855; Taken in Pursuance of Article Third of the Constitution of the State, and of Chapter Sixty-Four for the Laws of 1855* (Albany, NY, 1857), xl. For the Know Nothings in New York, see Anbinder, *Nativism & Slavery*, 75–87; Bennett, *Party of Fear*, 117–29; Thomas Joseph Curran, "Know Nothings of New York State," (PhD diss., Columbia University, 1963).

35. Thomas R. Whitney, *A Defence of the American Policy, as Opposed to the Encroach-ments of Foreign Influence, and Especially to the Interference of the Papacy in the Political Interests and Affairs of the United States* (New York, 1856), 180.

36. Erastus Brooks, *American Citizenship and the Progress of American Civilization: An Oration Delivered before the Order of United Americans, at the Academy of Music, February 22d, 1858* (New York, 1858), 17.

37. "Something to Be Done," *New York Times*, July 23, 1857.

38. House, *Foreign Criminals and Paupers*, 34th Cong., 1st sess., 1856, Report 359, 136–37.

39. "Emigrant Paupers," *New York Evening Express*, April 16, 1855.

40. "Immigrant Paupers and Convicts," *New York Evening Express*, February 27, 1855; emphasis added.

41. "The Mayor and Pauper Immigrants," *New York Herald*, February 16, 1855.

42. "More About Paupers and Criminals," *New York Evening Express*, October 16, 1855.

43. "Criminals to the United States," *New York Evening Express*, October 17, 1855; emphasis added. For the antebellum views of paupers and criminals, see William J. Novak, *The People's Welfare: Law and Regulation in Nineteenth-Century America* (Chapel Hill, NC, 1996); David J. Rothman, *The Discovery of the Asylum: Social Order and Disorder in the New Republic*, rev. ed. (1971; New York, 2002).

44. On Fernando Wood, see Florence E. Gibson, *The Attitudes of the New York Irish toward State and National Affairs, 1848–1992* (New York, 1951), 91–97; Jerome Mushkat, *Fernando Wood: A Political Biography* (Kent, OH, 1990); Oliver E. Allen, *The Tiger: The Rise and Fall of Tammany Hall* (New York, 1993), 51–79; "characteristic double game" quoted in Mushkat, *Fernando Wood*, 48.

45. *City of New York v. Miln*, 36 U.S. 102 (1837); Zolberg, *Nation by Design*, 141–44.

46. House, *Foreign Criminals and Paupers*, 137.

47. Lee, *At America's Gates*, 29; emphasis in the original.

48. Kapp, *Immigration and the Commissioners of Emigration*, 105–11; Vincent J. Cannato, *American Passage: The History of Ellis Island* (New York, 2009), 35–36.

49. "The Battery and the Emigrants," *New York Evening Express*, May 15, 1855; Cannato, *American Passage*, 30–36. For Castle Garden, see also George J. Svejda, *Castle Garden as an Immigrant Depot, 1855–1890* (Washington, DC, 1968).

50. Kathryn Stephenson, "The Quarantine War: The Burning of the New York Marine Hospital in 1858," *Public Health Reports* 119, no. 1 (2004): 79–92. For nativist perceptions of the sanitary threat of immigrants in nineteenth-century New York, see John Duffy, *A History of Public Health in New York City 1625–1866* (New York, 1968); Alan M. Kraut, *Silent Travelers: Germs, Genes, and the "Immigrant Menace"* (Baltimore, MD, 1994).

51. Parker, "State, Citizenship, and Territory," 627–35.

52. *The Twenty-First Annual Report of the New York Association for Improving the Condition of the Poor, for the Year 1864* (New York, 1864), 49.

53. *Annual Report of the Commissioners of Emigration, of the State of New York: For the Year Ending December 31, 1870* (New York, 1871), 34. On New York during the Civil War and Reconstruction, see Ernest A. McKay, *The Civil War and New York City* (Syracuse, NY, 1990); David Quigley, *Second Founding: New York City, Reconstruction, and the Making of American Democracy* (New York, 2004).

54. *Annual Report of the Commissioners of Emigration, of the State of New York: For the Year Ending December 31, 1873* (New York, 1874), 8, 72–73.

55. Amy Dru Stanley, *From Bondage to Contract: Wage Labor, Marriage, and the Market in the Age of Slave Emancipation* (New York, 1998), 98–137. For the concept of the undeserving poor, see Michael B. Katz, *The Undeserving Poor: From the War on Poverty to the War on Welfare* (New York, 1989). On free labor ideology, see Eric Foner, *Free Soil, Free Labor, Free Men: The Ideology of the Republican Party before the Civil War* (1970; New York, 1995); Jonathan A. Glickstein, *American Exceptionalism, American Anxiety: Wages, Competition, and Degraded Labor in the Antebellum United States* (Charlottesville, VA, 2002).

56. David M. Schneider and Albert Deutsch, *The History of Public Welfare in New York State, 1867–1940* (Chicago, 1938), 13–26. On the Panic of 1873, see Edwin G. Burrows and Mike Wallace, *Gotham: A History of New York City to 1898* (New York, 1999), 1020–38; Quigley, *Second Founding*, 104–08.

57. Montgomery H. Throop, ed., *The Revised Statutes of the State of New York* (Albany, NY, 1882), Vol. 3: 1888–91.

58. *Eighth Annual Report of the State Board of Charities of the State of New York* (Albany, NY, 1875), 139; emphasis in the original.

59. *Thirteenth Annual Report of the State Board of Charities of the State of New York* (Albany, NY, 1880), 42–43.

60. "A Cure for Mendicity," *New York Times*, November 24, 1874.

61. Zolberg, *Nation by Design*, 140–50; "An act to amend certain acts concerning passengers coming to the city of New York" (April 11, 1849), *Laws of the State of New York*, chap. 350, 505–06.

62. *Henderson v. Mayor of the City of New York*, 92 U.S. 259 (1875). The court also struck down similar statutes in Louisiana.

63. "Arrival of Foreign Paupers," *New York Times*, February 9, 1879.

64. New York, *Annual Report of the Commissioners of Emigration, of the State of New York: For the Year Ending December 31, 1879*, 1880, Assembly Doc. 14, 30–32.

65. *Passenger Cases*, 48 U.S. 283 (1849).

66. *Henderson v. Mayor of the City of New York*, 92 U.S. 259 (1875).

67. *Chy Lung v. Freeman*, 92 U.S. 275 (1875).

68. Hiroshi Motomura, *Americans in Waiting: The Lost Story of Immigration and Citizenship in the United States* (New York, 2006), 24.

69. New York Law of 1880.

70. *Fifteenth Annual Report of the State Board of Charities* (Albany, NY, 1882), 28.

71. New York Law of 1880; *Fourteenth Annual Report of the State Board of Charities*, (Albany, NY, 1881), 36.

72. *Fifteenth Annual Report of the State Board of Charities*, 35.

73. "The Immigrant Commission," *New York Irish-American*, July 29, 1876; Massachusetts, *Thirteenth Annual Report of the Board of State Charities of Massachusetts*, 1877, Public Doc. 17, xliii; New York, *Annual Report of the Commissioners of Emigration of the State of New York for the Year Ending December 31, 1876*, 1877, Senate Doc. 21, 74–78.

74. New York, *Annual Report of the Commissioners of Emigration of the State of New York for the Year Ending December 31, 1877*, 1878, Senate Doc. 18, 25.

75. An act to regulate Immigration, 22 Stat. 214 (1882). For the making of the 1882 act, see Edith Abbott, "Federal Immigration Policies, 1864–1924," *University Journal of Business* 2, no. 2 (March 1924): 133–56; John Higham, *Strangers in the Land: Patterns of American Nativism, 1860–1925* (1955; New York, 1970), 43–45; Tichenor, *Dividing Lines*, 67–69; Zolberg, *Nation by Design*, 185–93.

76. For the development of federal policy after 1882, see Keith Fitzgerald, *The Face of the Nation: Immigration, the State, and the National Identity* (Stanford, CA, 1996); Roger Daniels, *Guarding the Golden Door: American Immigration Policy and Immigrants since 1882* (New York, 2004); Erika Lee, "A Nation of Immigrants and a Gatekeeping Nation: American Immigration Law and Policy," in *A Companion to American Immigration*, ed. Reed Ueda (Malden, MA, 2006), 5–35; Torrie Hester, "'Protection, Not Punishment': Legislative and Judicial Formation of U.S. Deportation Policy, 1882–1904," *Journal of American Ethnic History* 30, no. 1 (Fall 2010): 11–36; Deirdre M. Moloney, *National Insecurities: Immigrants and U.S. Deportation Policy since 1882* (Chapel Hill, NC, 2012).

77. *Annual Report of the State Board of Charities for the Year 1900*, Vol. 1 (Albany, NY, 1901), 140. Recent research has demonstrated that state officials' sustained commitment to immigration control after 1882 affected the way federal policy was enforced. In particular,

the state-level harsh treatment of indigent Europeans prior to 1882 was inherited in federal control in the form of American officers' virtually unlimited power over the decision on exclusion and deportation, one of the characteristics of federal immigration policy from the late nineteenth century onward. For the gradual nature of the nationalization of immigration control and state officials' influence on federal policy, see Hidetaka Hirota, "The Moment of Transition: State Officials, the Federal Government, and the Formation of American Immigration Policy," *Journal of American History* 99, no. 4 (March 2013): 1092–1108.

78. *Proceedings of the Conference of Charities, Held in Connection with the General Meeting of the American Social Science Association, at Saratoga, September, 1876* (Albany, NY, 1876), 170, 183.

79. Higham, *Strangers in the Land*, 45–52; Zolberg, *Nation by Design*, 193–95.

80. U.S. Treasury, Bureau of Statistics, *Tables Showing Arrivals of Alien Passengers and Immigrants in the United States from 1820 to 1892* (Washington, DC, 1893), 86–87; Cohn, *Mass Migration under Sail*, 156.

81. Tichenor, *Dividing Lines*, 59. For an explanation of nineteenth-century nativists' failure, see also Kitty Calavita, *U.S. Immigration Law and the Contract of Labor: 1824–1924* (New York, 1984).

82. Robert Ernst, *Immigrant Life in New York City, 1825–1863* (1949; Syracuse, NY, 1994), 162.

83. On the political history of nineteenth-century New York, see Quigley, *Second Founding*; Allen, *Tiger*; Steven P. Erie, *Rainbow's End: Irish-Americans and the Dilemmas of Urban Machine Politics, 1840–1985* (Berkeley, CA, 1988).

84. J. Matthew Gallman, *Receiving Erin's Children: Philadelphia, Liverpool, and the Irish Famine Migration, 1845–1855* (Chapel Hill, NC, 2000), 42–45.

4

Defectives in the Land:
Disability and American Immigration Policy, 1882–1924

DOUGLAS C. BAYNTON

SOPHIE FUKO OF HUNGARY embarked from Hamburg aboard the SS *Kaiserin Auguste Victoria* in late November 1912, with her six-year-old son, Kalman. Fuko's husband had died four years earlier and now, at the age of 46, with no remaining relatives in her native land, she had decided to emigrate to the United States to join her two adult sons, Laszlo and Bela. She and Kalman arrived at Ellis Island December 4. They immediately encountered difficulties. The medical inspectors certified Sophie Fuko as "practically blind in right eye," her son as "afflicted with deaf mutism," and therefore both of them as "likely to become public charges."

When their hearing before the Board of Special Inquiry was held four days later, Fuko's adult sons were there to testify on her behalf. Fuko testified that she had $20 with her and had been self-supporting in Hungary as a housekeeper. Her sons Laszlo and Bela testified that they were employed and earning decent wages. They had spent $170 for a second-class cabin for their mother and brother and $100 to furnish a home for them, as well as paying for the passage from Hungary for Bela's wife and child who were due to arrive soon. Ordinarily, the family's finances would have been more than sufficient, but for the medical certificates. The Board ruled that Fuko and her son were "suffering from physical defects, the nature of which will affect their ability to earn a living" and were therefore "likely to become public charges." It ordered them deported, informing her of her right to appeal to the Secretary of the Department of Commerce and Labor.

Fuko did appeal. In her letter to the Secretary, she said that her sons were prepared to furnish bonds guaranteeing that she and her son would not become public charges. She added that while she had little cash, she owned a house in her native town that she would soon sell, "promisery [sic] notes" on which she would soon collect, and a substantial life insurance policy covering herself and her young son. In addition, she claimed that her son was neither deaf nor mute, but could hear when spoken to loudly and that "of late he begain [sic] to talk very nicely." He could also read and write. Finally, she appealed to the Secretary's sympathy by stressing that she had no one left in Hungary to return to, that her only family was here in the United States.

William Williams, the Commissioner of Immigration at Ellis Island, had built a reputation as a strict enforcer of the immigration laws, particularly those related to physical and mental defects. He urged the Secretary to dismiss Fuko's appeal, because "her child will always be physically defective, and it would be improper to admit merely because of the relatives here." The Commissioner General of the Bureau of Immigration agreed, saying that "the Bureau does not think the mere presence here of two sons affords any good ground for admitting these physically defective aliens." The Secretary, deferring as he usually did to the Commissioner of the station and the Commissioner General when they were in agreement, dismissed the appeal. Sophie Fuko and her son were put aboard the USS *Pennsylvania* on December 21 and returned to an unknown fate in Hungary.[1]

One of the driving forces behind early federal immigration law, beginning with the first major Immigration Act in 1882, was the exclusion of people with mental and physical defects (as well as those considered criminal or immoral, problems seen at the time as closely related to mental defect). Congressional legislation throughout this period repeatedly, and with ever increasing urgency, identified defective immigrants as a threat to the nation. The desire to keep out immigrants deemed defective was not an isolated development, but rather was one aspect of a trend toward the increasing segregation of disabled people into institutions and the sterilization of the "unfit" and "degenerate" under state eugenic laws.

While anti-immigrant sentiment in the United States has long been a significant area of scholarly research, disability has held a marginal place in that scholarship. John Higham's *Strangers in the Land* identified three main currents of anti-immigrant sentiment: anti-Catholicism, fear of foreign radicals, and racial nativism. Roger Daniels stated in *Coming to America* that "by 1917 the immigration policy of the United States had been restricted in seven major ways," with admission being denied to "Asians . . .; criminals; persons who failed to meet certain moral standards; persons with various diseases; paupers; assorted radicals; and illiterates." Alan Kraut's *Silent Travelers* and Amy Fairchild's recent book, *Science at the Borders,* brought a welcome focus to medical inspection, but did not examine communicable disease and disability as distinct issues, nor explore the cultural stigmatization of disability that formed the background to these laws.[2]

Sophie Fuko does not fit into any of the categories that historians of immigration policy have described as fundamental to anti-immigrant sentiment or the enactment of exclusionary immigration policies in the United States. Though she had little money at hand, she was by no definition a pauper. Neither she nor her son was a carrier of disease. The only charge against Fuko, and many other similar immigrants, was that they were defective. Countless other immigrants passed through Ellis Island with fewer financial resources, no family in the United States to turn to in case of difficulty, and certainly less poignant personal circumstances. Disability was a crucial factor in deciding whether an immigrant would be allowed to enter the United States.

The first major immigration law, the Act of 1882, prohibited entry to any "lunatic, idiot, or any person unable to take care of himself or herself without becoming a public charge." Those placed in the categories "lunatic" or "idiot" were automatically excluded. The "public charge" provision was intended to encompass individuals with disabilities more generally, and was left to the examining officer's discretion.[3] The criteria for excluding disabled persons were steadily tightened as the eugenics movement and popular fears about the decline of the national stock gathered strength. The Act of 1891 replaced the phrase "*unable* to take care of himself or herself without becoming a public charge," with *likely* to become a public charge." The 1907 law then required a medical certificate for anyone judged "mentally or physically defective, such mental or physical defect being of a nature which *may affect* the ability of such alien to earn a living." While nondisabled immigrants continued to be admitted unless found to be "likely to become a public charge," disabled people were subject to this more rigorous standard.[4]

Exclusions for mental defect were steadily expanded. In 1903 people with epilepsy were added, as well as "persons who have been insane within five years previous [or] who have had two or more attacks of insanity at any time previously." In 1907 "imbeciles" and "feeble-minded persons" had been barred, in addition to "idiots." In 1917 the classification of "constitutional psychopathic inferiority" was added, which inspection regulations described as including "various unstable individuals on the border line between sanity and insanity, such as . . . persons with abnormal sex instincts." Officials were instructed to exclude persons with "any mental abnormality whatever . . . which justifies the statement that the alien is mentally defective." This provision, the regulations explain, was intended "as a means of excluding aliens of a mentally inferior type, not comprehended in the other provisions of the law, without being under the necessity, as formerly, of showing that they have a defect which may affect their ability to earn a living."[5]

The rules governing exclusion for physical disabilities were equally vague and expansive. Regulations instructed inspectors that "each individual should be seen first at rest and then in motion," in order to detect "irregularities in movement" and "abnormalities of any description." It listed defects that could be cause for exclusion, a few examples of which were arthritis, asthma, bunions, deafness, deformities, flat feet, heart disease, hernia, hysteria, poor eyesight, poor physical development, spinal curvature, vascular disease of the heart, and varicose veins.[6] An Ellis Island medical inspector later wrote that his task was "to detect poorly built, defective or broken down human beings."[7] In short, the exclusion of disabled people was central to the laws governing immigration. As the Commissioner General of Immigration reported in 1907, "The exclusion from this country of the morally, mentally, and physically deficient is the principal object to be accomplished by the immigration laws."[8]

These laws were usually presented as simply a matter of economics. The issue, however, was rarely so straightforward. Many rejected immigrants had been self-supporting in their home countries. Others received job offers while awaiting their hearing, but still were deported as likely to become public charges. More importantly, to the extent that some people with disabilities might indeed encounter difficulties in finding employment, the public charge law also assumes that the unemployment or underemployment of disabled people is a problem centered in bodies rather than in the relationship between particular bodies and the constructed physical and social environments in which they live. This may have been the only practical assumption for immigration officials, but historians should put immigration restriction into context as one element in a larger system of discrimination that made it difficult for disabled people to live and move about independently. Leaving aside, however, complex questions of what factors made (and still make) it difficult for disabled people to find work, the economic explanation for exclusion remains an incomplete one. Two examples of the mixed motives and reasoning that went into these exclusions were the diagnoses "poor physique" and "lack of sexual development."

In his *Annual Report* of 1904, the Commissioner of Ellis Island, William Williams, suggested that the country was "receiving too many immigrants whose physical condition is poor." The only disabled persons specifically excluded under law at that time were idiots, insane persons, and epileptics (the category of "physical and mental defects" came in 1907). As Williams explained, to exclude immigrants certified with physical impairments required finding that they were likely to become public charges, "yet it is obviously impossible to exclude on this ground all persons whose physical condition is poor." He urged that the exclusion of immigrants certified as having "poor physique" be made mandatory in all cases.[9] Soon thereafter, Robert DeCourcey Ward of the Immigration Restriction League wrote to the Commissioner General of Immigration, Frank Sargent, urging him to take up Williams's cause before Congress.[10]

The specific diagnostic category was never embodied in law, but within a year "poor physique" was being widely used as a diagnosis by immigration officials to exclude immigrants on grounds of being "likely to become a public charge." The immigration service defined poor physique as covering individuals "who have frail frame, flat chest, and are generally deficient in muscular development," or who are "undersized—markedly of short stature—dwarf."[11] As one medical officer explained, the "immigrant of poor physique is not able to perform rough labor, and *even if he were able,* employers of labor would not hire him."[12] That is, the belief that an immigrant was unfit to work justified exclusion, but so did the belief that an immigrant was *likely to encounter discrimination* because of a disability.

Eugenic considerations also played an important role in both the creation and the application of immigration law. In a letter to the Commissioner General, the Ellis Island Commissioner wrote that the Bureau had "no more important work to perform than that of picking out all mentally defective immigrants, for these are not only likely to join the criminal classes and become public charges, but by leaving feebleminded descendents they start vicious strains which lead to misery and loss in future generations and influence unfavorably the character and lives of hundreds of persons."[13] This inter-generational "contagion" of defect worried the Commissioner General about immigrants with "poor physiques." In a 1905 memorandum, he explained that "a certificate of this nature implies that the alien concerned is afflicted with a body but illy adapted . . . to the work necessary to earn his bread," and further that the immigrant is "undersized, poorly developed [and] physically degenerate, and as such, not only unlikely to become a desirable citizen, but also very likely to transmit his undesirable qualities to his offspring, should he unfortunately for the country in which he is domiciled, have any."[14]

On January 30, 1906, Israel Bosak was certified at Ellis Island for "poor physique." He was not destitute, having $65 in his possession, a respectable sum for an immigrant at the time. Bosak testified that he had owned a tailor shop in Russia before it was destroyed by a mob during an anti-Jewish pogrom. He intended to send for his wife and children as soon as he had gotten himself established, explaining that he had "plenty of countrymen here who are just as good as relatives, to help me." After a brief hearing, the Board of Special Inquiry voted unanimously to exclude. Bosak had a second hearing when two distant relatives appeared to assure the Board that they would assist him in finding work and provide for him until he did so. Such testimony rarely changed a Board's decision, but this time the Board had a new member, Philip Cowen, who was not a regular member of the service but rather a political appointee of Theodore Roosevelt. Cowen proved to be a maverick in many cases. He questioned Bosak about his business in Russia and the pogrom in which it was destroyed, then made a short speech:

> The alien before the Board has come here because of the unsettled con-
> dition of affairs in his home; the rioters having despoiled him of the
> property which he held in his business, and prevented him from earning
> a livelihood; he is thus practically driven from his home by the mob; he
> comes to this country to establish a home for himself and family; a man
> who has once been possessed of a home and property seems to me to be
> valuable material for immigration and needs nothing more than a help-
> ing hand of friends to become self sustaining; these friends appear in the
> persons of the witnesses before the board; and it seems to me that there is
> no danger whatever of the man becoming a public charge. . . . I therefore
> move his admission.

Inspector Smiley, who had been on the previous Board and voted to exclude, was moved to change his vote: "From the excellent showing of the witnesses made in the alien's behalf, I second the motion to admit." Inspector Paul, however, voted to exclude which meant that the Secretary of Labor would have to decide the matter. In his letter to Washington, Inspector Paul noted that he wished to "particularly call attention to Department letter 48,462," the circular that had emphasized the danger to the eugenic health of the nation in admitting people "whose offspring will reproduce, often in an exaggerated degree, the physical degeneracy of their parents." The Commissioner at Ellis Island "strongly" recommended deportation, and he too called attention to the same Bureau circular on the eugenic dangers of admitting immigrants of poor physique. The Commissioner General concurred, and the Secretary ordered Israel Bosak returned to Russia.[15]

Since the screening of immigrants was mostly a matter of detecting visual abnormality, the appearance of immigrants played an important role.

Inspectors prided themselves on their ability to make a "snapshot diagnosis" as immigrants streamed past them single file. For most immigrants, a normal appearance usually meant an uneventful passage through the immigration station. An abnormal appearance, however, meant a chalked letter on the back. Once chalked, a closer inspection was required—"L for lameness, K for suspected hernia, G for goiter, X for suspected mental illness," and so on.[16] The inspection then would be general, not confined to the abnormality that set them apart, which meant that visibly different people—as well as those whose ethnic appearance was abnormal to the inspectors—were more likely to be set apart for close examination, and therefore more likely to have other problems discovered and to be excluded.

Donabet Mousekian had an abnormal appearance. On April 23, 1905, this Armenian Turk stood before the Board of Special Inquiry with an inspection certificate that read "feminism." In other instances the term used was "lack of sexual development." In this case, it meant an absence of male sexual organs, in others, insufficient development (now known to be caused by a hormonal deficiency). Mousekian's hearing was extraordinarily brief. No one mentioned the diagnosis or questioned him about it. After asking only the most basic questions concerning his identity and background, and noting that he brought $48 with him, the transcript reads as follows: "Mr. Rotz: In view of the Doctor's certificate I move to exclude him as likely to become a public charge. Mr. Ryan: Second motion. Mr. Smiley: Excluded." This was all the hearing that Mousekian received.

In his appeal, Mousekian explained that he had fled the violent oppression of Armenians in Turkey and had officially renounced his citizenship. Since he would never be permitted to return to Turkey and remain free, rather than send him back, "it would be much better that you kill me," he wrote. His relatives were all in America, including his two brothers who were citizens and well employed. He was a photographer by trade, as well as a skilled weaver and dyer of rugs and a cook, and could work at any of these trades. He wrote, "I am not ill, have no contagious disease; my eyes, feet, hands and ears are sound; only I am deprived of male organs; this is not a fault because it has come from God and my mother: what can I do? It won't do any harm to my working; or what harm can I do to the U.S. by my being deprived of male organs?" His brothers wrote letters in much the same vein, asking plaintively, "How is it his fault? Our father and mother are dead; he is our only brother . . .; we guarantee that he will not be a public charge; we are able to give the required guarantee; he can not return to Turkey; we are US citizens, hence we beg US government not to separate our brother from us." The Commissioner at Ellis supported the Board's decision, largely on the basis of an unfavorable appearance: "Appellant is devoid of every external evidence of desirability. He is weak . . ., repulsive in appearance, the doctor's certificate . . . furnishing sufficient indication of his physical defects." Mousekian was returned to Turkey where, if he remained and lived that long, he would be caught up in the Armenian genocide ten years later.[17]

In cases of lack of sexual development, the files rarely explained the reasons for exclusion. The Surgeon General, however, did explain in a memo the reasoning behind this exclusion: "These persons present bad economic risks . . . [T]heir chief failure to adjust is due to the fact that their abnormality soon becomes known to their associates who make them the butt of coarse jokes to their own despair, and to the impairment of the work in hand. Since this is recognized . . . among employers, it is difficult for these unfortunates to get or retain jobs, their facial and bodily appearance, at least in adult life, furnishing a patent advertisement of their condition."[18] The disability that justified exclusion in these cases was a matter of an abnormal appearance that might invite discrimination and therefore poverty. Thus it was an economic argument, but at two steps removed.

The justification given was not always economic, however, whether directly or indirectly. Nicolaos Xilomenos was refused entry in 1912 for "lack of sexual development." The Commissioner noted that while "the individual may appear strong and robust" and brought with him sufficient cash, his condition indicates the probability of "perversions or mental instability." In a similar case in 1908, Helena Bartnikowska was refused entry. The physician explained that "this supposed woman" was a hermaphrodite, who were "usually of perverted sexual instincts, and with lack of moral responsibility," adding significantly that her voice was masculine and that she had facial hair. Although her family was willing and able to guarantee her support, she was also deported.[19]

In March 1905, Domenico Rocco Vozzo, a 35-year-old Italian immigrant, was puzzled to find himself barred from entering the country at the port of Boston. Vozzo was a "bird of passage," a migrant worker who intended to earn some money and then return to Italy. This was his second trip to the United States, and he had encountered no difficulty his first time three years earlier. The medical inspector certified him for "debility," and he was excluded as likely to become a public charge. Vozzo retained an attorney who explained in his appeal that Vozzo was strong, robust, and healthy. In fact, he "looks perfectly healthy below the head," but has a "curiously shaped head, and his skin looks rather white, almost bleached, and his ears are quite thin." He had never been ill, had always worked, and during his recent two-year sojourn in the United States had fully supported himself while saving money. He brought with him twenty dollars in cash and had friends who filed affidavits on his behalf. The Commissioner at the Boston station, however, recommended against admission and sent to the Secretary this evidence: "I enclose his picture which I think will convince you that he is not a desirable acquisition." Vozzo was deported.[20]

The principle that persons of abnormal appearance were not "desirable acquisitions" was not universally held nor consistently applied. For example, when Abraham Hoffman, a twenty-five-year-old tailor with a prosperous brother working in the same trade in New York, was ruled likely to become a public charge by the immigration board because of his curved spine, his attorney labeled this assumption "ridiculous and absurd." "The axiom," he continued, "that one who is unfortunate enough to suffer from a certain infirmity, is likely for that reason alone, to become a public charge, is entirely new to us." Warming to the subject, the attorney asked, "Are we living in this enlightened Twentieth Century where everyone is supposed to be given a fair opportunity, or are we going back to the times of the Salem witch-craft, when, because a woman was old and afflicted with a high back (spinal curvature), she was considered and treated as a witch? . . . The immigrants affliction can in no wise affect his earning capacity as a tailor."

The Commissioner at Ellis was torn. The evidence on the basis of appear-ance was conflicting. On the one hand, visually "the spinal curvature for which he is certified is quite obvious." On the other, "I may state in appel-lant's behalf, that he is a man of considerable intelligence, is very well dressed, and came as a second cabin passenger." With appearance working both against and in favor of the immigrant, the Commissioner made the unusual decision to forward the case files to Washington without recom-mendation. In his summary for the Secretary, the Commissioner General re-emphasized the immigrant's appearance: "The Commissioner states that the alien is intelligent looking and is well dressed; he came in second cabin." In this case, the positive aspects of his appearance and his class status trumped the negative appearance of his disability. Hoffman was admitted on appeal.[21]

The precise number of those turned back for physical and mental defects each year is difficult to pin down. Until 1908, exclusions based on physical defects were mixed with nondefectives in the category of "likely to become a public charge." After 1908, rejected immigrants were counted in the cat-egory of "mental or physical defective" if they were deemed defective but not likely to become public charges, and counted in the "public charge" category if they were determined to be both defective and potential paupers.[22] In any case, taken together, exclusions in both categories grew considerably, if erratically, over the years. In 1895, 1,720 were excluded, or .6 percent of all immigrants. By 1905, the number excluded had increased to just over 8,000, or .7 percent of all immigrants. And in 1910, 16,000 or 1.6 percent were excluded. Due to wartime disruptions, the numbers during and just after World War One fluctuated widely, making useful comparisons difficult.[23]

These numbers are all likely to be just the tip of the iceberg, however. Those who arrived at American shores to be inspected had already been through several screens. First, many would be deterred by the general inaccessibility of transportation. Second, since American immigration laws were widely advertised and easily available to people interested in immigrating, a significant number must have decided not to risk the journey and the expense knowing they might be turned back. Third, American law required ship captains to examine all passengers and certify that none appeared to be mentally defective. The manifest was to describe "the immigrant's condition of health mentally and physically, and whether deformed or crippled, and if so, from what cause."[24] Fourth, ships were required to return rejected immigrants at no charge and pay a fine for each, and if the immigrant was admitted but later discovered to have an excludable disability that initially passed unnoticed, they could be deported up to three years later at the expense of the company. Shipping companies therefore had strong incentives to refuse passage to anyone they thought unlikely to get by the inspectors, and ship captains became, in effect, an unofficial arm of the immigration service.[25] Finally, ticket agents, who were stationed throughout inland Europe, also became inspectors, because they were fined by the shipping companies if they sold tickets to anyone who was rejected when they tried to board the ship. The superintendent of immigration in 1894 noted approvingly that steamship lines instructed their agents to refuse tickets to "the blind, deaf and dumb, and crippled persons." There is good reason, then, to suppose that those turned away at the borders were a small minority of those who would have emigrated to America but were deterred because of disability. A federal commission in 1911 estimated that about ten times as many were refused transportation for medical reasons as were barred at U.S. ports.[26]

In 1924, a new quota system was instituted, based on national origin, that severely limited immigration from southern and eastern Europe. In the debate leading up to this legislation, disability figured prominently. Quota advocates warned that particular nationalities were disproportionately prone to be mentally defective. Rhetoric about "the slow-witted Slav," the poor physique of Jews, the "neurotic condition of our Jewish immigrants," and the "degenerate and psychopathic types, which are so conspicuous and numerous among the immigrants," was pervasive.[27] Restrictionists emphasized the inferior appearance of recent immigrants. One avowed that "the physiognomy of certain groups unmistakably proclaims inferiority of type." When he observed immigrants, he saw that "in every face there was something wrong. . . . There were so many sugar-loaf heads, moon-faces, slit mouths, lantern-jaws, and goose-bill noses that one might imagine a malicious jinn had amused himself by casting human beings in a set of skew-molds discarded by the Creator." Most were physically inadequate in some way: "South Europeans run to low stature. A gang of Italian navvies filing along the street present, by their dwarfishness, a curious contrast to other people. The Portuguese, the Greeks, and the Syrians are, from our point of view, undersized. The Hebrew immigrants are very poor in physique . . . the polar opposite of our pioneer breed."[28] The issues of ethnicity and disability were inextricably intertwined.

While disability has been largely overlooked as a category of analysis in the literature on immigration, this is by no means unique to immigration studies. Disability is conspicuously absent from all fields of histories. In areas of study where disability is clearly central, such as the consequences of war, industrialization, and the rise of the automobile, even in the history of the eugenics movement, the literature has focused elsewhere, emphasizing better established categories of analysis such as race, gender, and class, and leaving disability unexamined at the periphery. When historians do take note of disability, they usually treat it merely as personal tragedy rather than a cultural construct to be questioned and explored.[29] In immigration historiography, as in so many other areas of historical inquiry, disability has long been present but rendered either invisible or insignificant. A disability analysis is essential, however, to making sense of the depth of anti-immigrant sentiment and the workings of immigration policy at the turn of the twentieth century. While it is certain that immigration restriction rested in good part on a fear of "strangers in the land," in John Higham's phrase, it was fueled at least as much by a fear of *defectives* in the land.

NOTES

1. National Archives, Record Group 85, Records of the Immigration and Naturalization Service, Accession 60A600, File no. 53,550/580.

2. John Higham, *Strangers in the Land: Patterns of American Nativism, 1860–1925* (1955; New York, 1963), 5; Roger Daniels, *Coming to America: A History of Immigration and Ethnicity in American Life* (New York, 1990), 279; Alan M. Kraut, *Silent Travelers* (New York, 1994), 55; Amy L. Fairchild, *Science at the Borders: Immigration Medical Inspection and the Shaping of the Modern Industrial Labor Force* (Baltimore, 2003).

3. An earlier immigration act, passed in 1875, excluded criminals and prostitutes (this also was a disability issue, as immorality was thought to be closely associated with mental defect). *United States Statutes at Large,* Vol. 22 (Washington, DC, 1883), 214.

4. Emphases added. *United States Statutes,* Vol. 26 (1891), 1084; *United States Statutes,* Vol. 34 (1907), 899.

5. *United States Statutes,* Vol. 32 (1903), 1213. *United States Statutes,* Vol. 34 (1907), 898. United States Public Health Service, *Regulations Governing the Medical Inspection of Aliens* (Washington, DC, 1917), 25–26, 28–29, 30–31.

6. *Regulations,* 16–19.

7. Victor Safford, *Immigration Problems: Personal Experiences of An Official* (New York, 1925), 244–45, 46.

8. U.S. Bureau of Immigration, *Annual Report of the Commissioner of Immigration* (Washington, DC, 1907), 62.

9. William Williams, "Ellis Island Station," in *Annual Report of the Commissioner General of Immigration, 1904* (Washington, DC, 1904), 105.

10. Robert DeCourcey Ward to Frank P. Sargent, Commissioner General of Immigration, Washington, DC, dated January 11, 1905, National Archives, Record Group 85, Records of the Immigration and Naturalization Service, Entry 9, File no. 51490/19.

11. Letter from George Stoner, Chief Medical Officer, Public Health and Marine Hospital Service, to Surgeon General of the Public Health and Marine Hospital, Nov. 29, 1912, National Archives, Record Group 90, Records of the Public Health Service, Entry 10, File no. 219.

12. Allan McLaughlin, "The Problem of Immigration," *Popular Science Monthly* 66 (April 1905): 532 (emphasis added).

13. Letter dated March 31, 1913, National Archives, Record Group 85, Records of the Immigration and Naturalization Service, Entry 9, File no. 51490/19.

14. Letter from F. P. Sargent, Commissioner General of the Bureau of Immigration, to the Commissioner of Immigration on Ellis Island, April 17, 1905, National Archives, Record Group 90, Records of the Public Health Service, Entry 10, File no. 219.

15. National Archives, Record Group 85, Records of the Immigration and Naturalization Service, Entry 7, File no. 49,968/4.

16. Alan M. Kraut, *Silent Travelers* (New York, 1994), 55.

17. National Archives, Record Group 85, Records of the Immigration and Naturalization Service, Entry 7, File no. 48,599/4.

18. Letter from W.W. Husband, Commissioner General, Bureau of Immigration, to H.S. Cumming, Surgeon General, United States Public Health Service, September 27, 1922; and reply from Cumming to Husband, September 29, 1922; National Archives, Record Group 90, Records of the Public Health Service, Entry 10, File no. 219.

19. National Archives, Record Group 85, Records of the Immigration and Naturalization Service, Accession No. 60A600, File No. 53542-952. National Archives, Record Group 85,

Records of the Immigration and Naturalization Service, Accession No. 60A600, File no. 51,806–16.

20. National Archives, Record Group 85, Records of the Immigration and Naturalization Service, Entry 7, File no. 48,462. Aside from several days beard growth and a scowl, it is hard to see to what the Commissioner was referring.

21. National Archives, Record Group 85, Records of the Immigration and Naturalization Service, Entry 7, File no. 49951-1 (the immigrant's name is rendered Abram Hofmann and Abram Hofman by immigration officials, Abraham Hoffman by his attorney). Spinal curvature was a common reason for rejection. A fifty-year study at the University of Iowa recently concluded that persons with late-onset scoliosis (occurring during puberty) "are productive and functional at a high level at 50-year follow-up" and experienced "little physical impairment," with "cosmetic concerns" being the only significant problem. This finding contradicts the common perception among physicians and the general public that this is a serious and debilitating condition. Stuart Weinstein, et al., "Health and Function of Patients With Untreated Idiopathic Scoliosis: A 50-Year Natural History Study," *Journal of the American Medical Association* 289 (February 5, 2003): 559–68.

22. The LPC or pauper category was always the largest category of exclusion, but the criteria used are not entirely clear. Lack of money in itself was not a primary factor, though it was taken into consideration. Disability appears to have been a major factor. The definition of "pauper" for the immigration service was "one who is actually dependent upon public funds for support and who, in addition, is unable to work by reason of mental or physical infirmity, or who is unwilling to work." The Dillingham Commission reported in 1911 that, "At the present time . . . pauperism among newly admitted immigrants is relatively at a minimum, owing to the fact that the present immigration law provides for the admission only of the able-bodied, or dependents whose support by relatives is assured." United States Government, *Abstracts of Reports of the Immigration Commission, Vol. I* (Washington, DC, 1911), 35. The Report of the Commissioner General of Immigration in 1912 states that while 3,055 were rejected as mentally or physically defective, 12,004 were rejected as "likely to become a public charge," and of those "a considerable portion . . . were excluded on the additional ground of being mentally or physically defective. . . . Where the exclusion occurs on both grounds, it is not an easy matter properly to classify the cases in the statistical reports; and the figures representing those 'LPC' and those 'mentally and physically defective' should be considered together." *Annual Report of the Commissioner General of Immigration, 1912* (Washington, DC, 1912), 125.

23. United States, *Abstracts of Reports of the Immigration Commission, Vol. I* (Washington, DC, 1911), also known as the Dillingham Report. In 1915, nearly 5% were excluded, probably because the reduced number of immigrants during the war allowed more careful inspection.

24. *United States Statutes,* Vol. 27 (1893), 569; *United States Statutes,* Vol. 34 (1907), 901–02.

25. The Act of 1882 required vessel owners to provide return passage and reimburse inspection costs. The 1891 Act added that immigrants could be deported up to one year after entry, at the cost of the shipping company, if discovered to have had a disability that initially passed unnoticed. In 1903, companies were made responsible for returning a deported immigrant for two years after landing, and in 1907, for three. Significant fines were added in 1907 for ships that carried immigrants deemed mentally defective.

26. E. Abbott, *Immigration: Select Documents and Case Records* (Chicago, 1924), 71; U.S. Bureau of Immigration, *Annual Report of the Commissioner of Immigration* (Washington, DC, 1907), 10; U.S. Immigration Service, *Annual Report of the Superintendent of Immigration* (Washington, DC, 1894), 12–13; Abstract of Reports of the Immigration Commission [Dillingham Commission], Vol. I (Washington, DC, 1911), 26; Amy Fairchild's *Science at the Borders* (56–63) gives an excellent account of the multiple inspections immigrants faced along the way.

27. James W. Trent Jr., *Inventing the Feeble Mind: A History of Mental Retardation in the United States* (Berkeley, 1994), 166–69; Thomas Wray Grayson, "The Effect of the Modern Immigrant on our Industrial Centers," in *Medical Problems of Immigration* (Easton, PA, 1913), 103, 107–09. I examine how disability has been used to deny citizenship rights to women and minority groups in "Disability and the Justification of Inequality in American History," in Paul Longmore and Lauri Umansky, eds., *The New Disability History: American Perspectives* (New York, 2001), 33–57.

28. Edward Alsworth Ross, *The Old World and the New: The Significance of Past and Present Immigration to the American People* (New York, 1914), 285–90. Disability scholars have emphasized the importance of appearance to the construction of disability. For example, Martin Pernick has described the importance of aesthetics in eugenics literature, how fitness was equated with beauty and disability with ugliness, and Lennard Davis has maintained that disability presents itself "through two main modalities—function and appearance." Martin Pernick, *The Black Stork: Eugenics and the Death of 'Defective' Babies in American Medicine and Motion Pictures Since 1915* (New York, 1996) 60–71; Lennard Davis, *Enforcing Normalcy: Disability, Deafness, and the Body* (London, 1995), 11–12. See also Harlan Hahn, "Antidiscrimination Laws and Social Research on Disability: The Minority Group Perspective," *Behavioral Sciences and the Law* 14 (1996): 54.

29. One of the first to point out the distorting effects of this omission on our understanding of history was Paul Longmore, in two review essays in the 1980s: 'The Life of Randolph Bourne and the Need for a History of Disabled People," *Reviews in American History* 13 (December 1985): 581–87; and "Uncovering the Hidden History of Disabled People," *Reviews in American History* 15 (September 1987): 355–64. Longmore and David Goldberger also demonstrated the importance of disability in the history of the Great Depression and the New Deal in "The League of the Physically Handicapped and the Great Depression: A Case Study in the New Disability History," *Journal of American History* 87 (December 2000): 888–922. A recent corrective to the lack of attention given to disability among war veterans is David A. Gerber, ed., *Disabled Veterans in History* (Ann Arbor, MI, 2000). For a review of recent work on disability in history, see Catherine J. Kudlick. "Disability History: Why We Need Another 'Other'," *The American Historical Review* 108 (June 2003): 763–93.

5

Sentiment and the Restrictionist State: Evidence from the British Caribbean Experience, ca. 1925

LARA PUTNAM

THE INTERNATIONAL MOBILITY CONTROL REGIME consolidated in the decade after World War I made intimate sentiment a systematic concern for states policing borders and rights. New U.S. immigration laws in the 1920s made family reunification one of the few routes through which migrants could enter the United States when their home society's quota was exhausted. (That is, the laws extended to much of the world both the exclusionary stance and the kin-based exceptions pioneered in regard to Asian migrants a generation before.[1]) Adjudicating the right to cross borders and work now required state agents to assess intimate bonds and the intentions they fostered: the sentimental as well as documentary dimensions of kinship. The impact of this shift was felt sharply in the British Caribbean, which was placed under quota restriction for the first time in 1924, cutting legal immigration from the islands from over ten thousand to under five hundred per year.

For migrants and would-be migrants, family acquired a contradictory relationship to state power. On the one hand, family ties became more important than ever in supporting mobility, providing not only resources and support (as had long been the case) but also—for a select few—formal entitlement to entry. On the other hand, kin practice became a key point of vulnerability for working-class migrants, as the U.S. government placed itself in the position of verifying the highly restricted set of family ties that could justify non-quota entry under the new law. Commonplace Caribbean practices like consensual unions, sibling reliance, and informal fostering created bonds given no protection under U.S. immigration law. Moreover, the new state interest created a new venue for intrafamily dispute. Raising the stakes of family ties, the restrictionist regime offered tempting leverage to those struggling with straying spouses, headstrong offspring, or scofflaw siblings. Men and women alike could and did seek to use this leverage, but it was a blunt instrument, unpredictable and often irreversible. Its power to harm was far more consistent than any power to help.

The importance of family to immigration restrictionism has been studied by scholars along three separate axes. Firstly, scholars have noted that fears surrounding sexual coupling drove the eugenicist case for restriction, centered on the supposed heritability of "feeblemindedness" and "criminality," the demographic consequences of differential fertility, and the "social traits of the hybrid" who resulted from "race crossing."[2] Secondly, scholars have called attention to the ways the immigration apparatus measured would-be migrants against middle-class, patriarchal, heterosexual norms and barred or expelled those found lacking.[3] Thirdly, scholars have analyzed the role of family reunification policy in shaping both opportunities for inclusion and patterns of exclusion.[4]

A different dimension of state enmeshment with intimate life—related to all of the preceding, but distinct from them—comes to the fore in documents generated by entry officials and consuls abroad as the 1924 Johnson-Reed Act came into operation. Written into the new regulatory instruments were myriad matters for which border-crossers' sentiments, and not merely their bodies, morals, documents, or acts, needed to be assessed. Had a permanent resident left the United States with the intention of return, or to follow her heart elsewhere? Which kinds of family ties made an islander's quick return to the islands a sure bet, justifying "bona fide non-immigrant" status? Which lures might induce a sojourner instead to stay? While family reunification rules remitted to the formalities of kinship—birth and marriage certificates above all—these ancillary questions turned state agents' eyes to kinship's informal dimensions instead. In doing so, the process offered wide scope for perceptions of race, class, and virtue to shape the extension of rights.

This essay uses micro-historical sources to evaluate the consequences of the sentimental interests of the restrictionist state. Because micro-level sources allow us to get at the actual functioning of law, it is through them that we can learn how it came to be that laws that were formally race-blind, class-neutral, and silent on gender brought results that were race- and class-biased and that created new burdens for women in particular. Judging merely by the letter of the law, the United States was the exception to an era of anti-black xenophobia, which saw immigrants of "Negro race" explicitly banned in Panama, Costa Rica, the Dominican Republic, Venezuela, and beyond, in the 1920s and 1930s. But when we look at results evidenced in entry statistics, we see that U.S. law was applied to function as a de facto ban on black entry.[5] Not so race-blind after all, and not so exceptional.

And when we shift our gaze to the micro-level processes that generated those results, we see that the new laws used family to police borders in ways that were anything but gender-neutral. With determination of sentimental intent now essential, state agents looked to testimony from family and friends to judge where sentiment lay. Ideas about proper female behavior, maternal feeling, and sexual virtue had a major impact on how cases were adjudicated: the ideas of state agents first and foremost, but the ideas of community and family members as well. That did not mean women were always kept out and men always let in: quite the contrary. But it meant gendered constructs shaped the gates to legal mobility.

It is also micro-level sources that show us that in practice, family testimony could work against claimants but rarely in their favor. At least for the migrants studied here—all literate, working-class, English-speaking, and "Negro"—state agents listened carefully for testimony that undercut claims to entry, and discounted testimony that supported those claims. In a sense, this was the functional counterpart, albeit spatial opposite, of the "remote control" policing via consulates abroad that Ari Zolberg identified.[6] The power to force territorial exclusion—but not the ability to countermand it—was placed in the heart of the family.

To what extent were these dynamics particular to Caribbean immigrants, and to what extent shared by other non-white, or non-Anglo-Saxon, or even all non-citizen claimants? These are questions for future research. Aspiring immigrants of many origins came under restrictive quotas by 1924. The U.S. consul in Havana, when asked in December 1924 how many "aliens now in your consular district . . . would proceed immediately to the United States if the quota restrictions were removed," offered a glimpse of the global chains interrupted by the new U.S. law. Six thousand Russian and Polish Jews, he reported, three thousand Spaniards, two thousand "Jamaican Negroes," and smaller numbers of others.[7] This glimpse of Havana jammed with desperate and polyglot would-be entrants suggests the potential reach of the processes explored below. From Brooklyn to Barbados and far beyond, the immigration regimes cemented in the interwar years both radically disrupted family practice and radically shifted the role of family in the allocation of rights to non-citizens.

SETTING THE STAGE:
CARIBBEAN FAMILIES AND NEW YORK STREETS

Ada C. and Samuel A. met in Panama, 1,500 miles away from the isle of Barbados where both had been born. They were married in the Canal Zone's Episcopal church in 1913. Things did not go well. Within a few years, Ada had returned to Barbados and, from there, ended up in Havana, perhaps after several years spent working in the United States (her sister Theresa was in Philadelphia and her cousin Mae, in Harlem).[8] For his part, Samuel left Panama in 1920, after fourteen years laboring there, to seek work in Cuba along with thousands of others like him. Over 27,000 British Caribbeans entered Cuba that year, thousands of them declaring a last place of residence other than their country of birth.[9] Samuel did not stay long. In August 1920, he took a boat from Havana for Key West, giving as his destination the home of his twenty-six-year-old cousin Beatrice Reed in Brooklyn, where she headed a household that included two other women and nine men, all in their twenties and thirties, all classified as black and all native English speakers: one born in Cuba, two in North Carolina, two in the "West Indies," five in Puerto Rico.[10]

Ada and Samuel had not always stayed in touch, and Ada would later say she "did not know when" Samuel left Panama for Cuba, or Cuba for the United States. But somehow, in Havana, they had reconnected. A month after Samuel's departure for Key West, Ada shipped out of Havana on a boat bound for New York, her husband and his new Brooklyn address her destination.[11]

The world she stepped into was one of rhythmic brownstone and cacophonous humanity: all-white blocks filled with Irish, Italian, Russian, and Swedish immigrants and their growing New York-born families; all-black buildings full of Barbadians, North Carolinians, Virginians, and more Barbadians: the men working as porters, elevator operators, and factory laborers, the women as housemaids in private homes.[12] Samuel worked at the YMCA and Ada at St. Christopher's Hospital. Soon they moved six blocks north to Cumberland Street, where landlady Edna James (herself the New York-born child of a British Caribbean father and a mother from Virginia) rented one floor of her fourteen-room house to tenants, who, in 1920, included her husband's brother-in-law and cousin, the cousin's wife, a Dutch Caribbean seaman and his Alabama-born wife, and another British Caribbean couple.[13]

What were they doing in Gotham, so many islanders far from home? The answer points to a multi-generational process through which labor migration and Caribbean life became inextricably linked. In the era after emancipation (1834–1838), the descendants of freedpeople faced a grim panorama. Plantation elites refused to pay the wages that would have drawn free workers into steady employ, instead using their political clout to demand subsidized indentured immigration from India, re-creating the unfree workforce they preferred. In response, Afro-West Indians sought opportunity overseas but

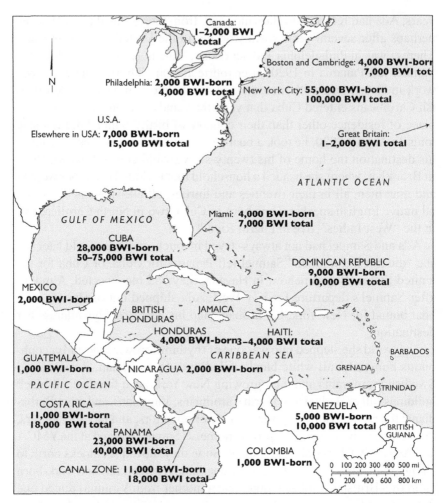

Figure 1: "First- and Second-Generation British West Indian Populations, ca. 1930."
Map drawn by Bill Nelson; data and design by Lara Putnam. Reprinted from Lara
Putnam, "Citizenship from the Margins: Vernacular Theories of Rights and the State
from the Interwar Caribbean," *Journal of British Studies* 53, no. 1 (2014): 162–91.

nearby, forming migratory circuits in the eastern Caribbean (with movement
from Barbados, Grenada, St. Vincent, and other Windwards southward to
Trinidad, Guiana, and Venezuela) and the western Caribbean (as Jamaicans
traveled to Colón, Bocas del Toro, Puerto Limón, Bluefields, and other litto-
ral settlements). The few Caribbeans whose families could afford multi-year

schooling found island careers blocked by unspoken rules preferring white Europeans to locals of color; increasingly, British Caribbeans of this class sought opportunity in the United States as ministers, publishers, doctors, or teachers.[14]

The expansion of U.S. investment at the start of the twentieth century drew on and accelerated these pre-existing circuits. Labor recruiting for Panama Canal construction after 1904 for the first time drew large numbers of eastern Caribbean migrants to the western rimlands, while intensified investment in sugar transformed the northern Antillean islands of Cuba and Santo Domingo into major destinations as well. As increased shipping brought down ticket prices, the relative ease of movement meant folks rarely moved only once. Families bootstrapped their way to collective advance as news, children, and earnings crisscrossed the region.[15]

While the initial migrant flow to any given destination was usually 75 to 80 percent male, at each, the portion of women among arrivals grew over time, as island women found a market for their skills in the booming ports their brothers and cousins helped build. Women ran boarding houses, laundered clothes, made pastries for sale. Cities offered women both high demand for their labor and supportive neighbors to cushion the risks that mobility (and men) brought, and by 1920, New York City had become the most important destination for women from across the Anglophone Caribbean.[16] Women made up 50 percent of the 35,000 black immigrants who entered the United States from 1918 to 1922, and 55 percent of the twenty thousand who did so from 1923 to 1924.[17] Indeed, by the time the Johnson-Reed Act brought entry to a halt, New York City had the largest population of British Caribbean women and girls on the planet: about forty thousand of them, including locally born daughters, topping Kingston's 37,000 and Port of Spain's 34,000 women and girls.[18] In total, by 1930, 42,000 foreign-born West Indians resided in Manhattan, thirteen thousand in Brooklyn, and six thousand elsewhere in New York City—along with 57,000 of their locally born children.[19]

Writing in 1943, pioneering journalist Roi Ottley marveled at the "bewildering array of clans, tribes, races, cultures, and colors" on Harlem's streets.[20] Yet the explosion of diversity reflected a prosaic pattern: social networks made migration happen. What could look like exotic fragmentation in fact indexed enduring connection, both among those arriving and between them and distant homes. Indeed, Ottley himself grew up in a household on West 136th Street in the 1920s that exemplified this reality. His parents had reached Harlem from Grenada in 1904, part of the early, small wave of arrivals from the British islands' middle classes of color. Circa 1900, these were the only Afro-Caribbeans with the resources to pay passage north out of pocket. The migrants who turned the United States-bound stream into a flood in the years after the Great War, in contrast, were more heavily drawn from the working classes, leveraging resources marshaled by kin from sojourns in the circum-Caribbean.

We see this in the trajectories of the thirteen lodgers, from Grenada, St. Vincent, Jamaica, and beyond, to whom Roi Ottley's mother and father, in 1920, sublet rooms.[21] Consider lodgers Vinette Hunter and Miriam Vaz, born in Jamaica in 1900 and 1898, respectively, who had entered the United States in 1917 and 1918 and now both worked as seamstresses in a dress factory. A working woman who relied on family earnings from the Spanish American republics to make it to Harlem, Vinette was typical of early 1920s arrivals, and her trajectory tells us much about the transnational ties of working-class Caribbeans in this era. Vinette sailed to New York from Panama in 1918, the "show money" she carried provided by her mother, who stayed behind in Colón. The big city awaiting was hardly anonymous: Vinette would join her Aunt Claire, a schoolteacher who had reached New York from Kingston in 1916 alongside her brother and his wife.[22] By 1930— ten years after we met her in Roi Ottley's household—Vinette had married George Vaz, a British Caribbean born in Panama in 1897 to Panama-born parents (and perhaps a relation of her 1920 roommate, Miriam Vaz). George had come to the United States in 1914 and now worked as a bellman in a hotel; his younger brother Clifford, who had moved to the United States at age nine, two years after George, now worked as a merchant seaman. Meanwhile, Vinette's mother had joined Vinette in New York in 1921, and, in 1930, resided with Vinette and George, doubtless minding three-year-old George, Jr., since Vinette still worked as a dressmaker in a factory. Eight lodgers hailing from Texas to Georgia to Long Island rounded out the household.[23]

Gazing up and down the street from the Vazes' Edgecombe Avenue stoop in 1930, we see that the Vazes' connections to the Spanish-speaking circum-Caribbean were not exceptional. The house next door was headed by Virginia-born William Ward and his Panama-born wife, Marie. Like George and Clifford Vaz, Marie was a native speaker of English whose parents were both of Panamanian birth. William and Marie had surely met in Panama, where their eldest daughter Cleopatra was born in 1916; they had relocated to New York in 1923. One of the Wards' eight lodgers was from the British Caribbean, the others from Virginia, West Virginia, North Carolina. On the Vazes' other side was a less international household: only one of the lodgers had been born abroad, in the Virgin Islands, although another was New York-born to British Guianese parents. Next door, a sixty-four-year-old widow from North Carolina rented rooms to six lodgers, including a couple from Bermuda, a man from South Carolina, a man born in Panama to British Caribbean parents, and British Honduran Thomas Martinez and his two-year-old New York-born son. All were Negro, according to census takers, just like every resident of this long block.[24]

People like Vinette, George, and Marie would have identified as British West Indian, although their degree of connection to the British colonies varied widely. More than simply islanders—indeed, sometimes not island-born at all—they were products of the circum-Caribbean migratory sphere, and this had patterned their life experiences in common ways. Their parents or grandparents had left their home islands to seek opportunity abroad, and they themselves had spent their youth on polyglot streets of tropical ports, finding commonality and difference with Spanish-speaking *mestizo* laborers, Chinese shopkeepers, Yankee bosses, and islanders from across the Caribbean. Each had negotiated the bureaucracies of at least three different political systems—the British colonies that issued his or her passport, the Spanish American republic where he or she had resided, and the United States to which he or she had gained entry—in many cases, before turning twenty.

The historiography of labor migration in the early twentieth-century Caribbean, disproportionately focused on male workers and employers like the United Fruit Company, has not wondered enough about the kinship structures undergirding this mobility.[25] As we have seen, most initial migrant flows were heavily male, but in receiving-society ports, British Caribbean populations were balanced or female-predominant, and New York-bound migration was the extreme version of this trend. Women outnumbered men among Caribbeans entering the United States from 1918 onward, and they headed to New York above all. Over 70 percent of them were single.[26] They worked as housemaids, dressmakers, cleaning staff; they were of what demographers call prime reproductive age. Was no one having sex? Was no one getting pregnant? And if they were, given that almost all these women worked all day—or all week—outside the home, who was minding the children? The answers are consistent with what we know about international migration and reproductive labor from the contemporary world. Family did the work of family—but family as understood by participants, which meant a much wider web than mother, father, and child.

Across the British Caribbean, post-emancipation women's roles encompassed own-account farming and marketing as well as daily reproductive labor in their own homes. Customary forms like "family land" emerged to spread among expansively reckoned kin the security that land access offered. Neither formal marriage nor nuclear family was a key building block of communal life for the majority of Caribbean people. Legal marriage was class-specific in its timing: for women of the region's elite and middle classes, marriage preceded sexual union, but for the rural and working-class majority, church marriage came as the culmination of a long reproductive life. For most women, that life included one or more early, non-residential partnerships as well as later enduring co-residential unions. As a result of these combined trends, across the nineteenth and twentieth centuries, roughly two-thirds of Caribbean children were born to unmarried mothers. Their siblings, half siblings, aunts, uncles, and grandmothers were critical sources of support.[27]

These kin forms proved extraordinarily well adapted to an era of intense long-distance labor mobility—indeed, they may have become entrenched in Caribbean family practice for precisely that reason.[28] The correspondence of U.S. consuls in Caribbean ports in the 1920s reveals a world of children and siblings in motion, as parents relied on kin back home to raise their children while they worked "in foreign." Vinette Vaz's mother traveled from Panama to Harlem to reside with her daughter and grandson, but, more commonly, children went to grandmothers rather than grandmothers to children. Indeed it was a recognized pattern at the time for British Caribbean women who became pregnant in New York to go home to the islands to give birth and return within the year, leaving the child behind in the care of female kin.[29]

Temporary child-shifting and serial reunion seem to have been nearly universal among British Caribbeans seeking advance in the North, whatever their class. Unitarian minister and Harlem civic leader Reverend Ethelred Brown wrote to the U.S. consul in Kingston in 1923 seeking visas for his "last two children," aged sixteen and eleven, "on the ground of coming over to join their parents who are able to take care of them."[30] Census returns show that the Browns' eldest son had preceded his parents to the United States in 1919, at age eighteen; one daughter had arrived a year after the couple, when she was eighteen; and the oldest and youngest daughters, then ages twenty-two and eight, followed the year after that. By 1924, the parents and six children lived reunited on St. Nicholas Avenue.[31] Arthur Barker waited until his son was sixteen before sending for the boy and his grandmother, who had been raising him, to join Arthur and his wife in New York. Arthur was a mail clerk and homeowner, a U.S. resident since 1907 and naturalized citizen since 1914—yet his mother was illiterate, confirming significant intergenerational mobility. There was no impediment to Arthur's mother's migration, the U.S. consul reassured.[32] (A year later, as we will see, the answer would be quite different.)

To make the most of the uneven opportunities the circum-Caribbean economy offered, families needed to be able to regroup and rejoin. Barbados-born Donald B. reached New York harbor in 1920 as a seaman, but chose—illegally, as it happens—to stay ashore. In 1922, he married Helen, a Barbadian woman he had met on arrival. Donald already had three children back in Barbados by his deceased first wife. Helen gave birth to his fourth, her first, in New York. Eight months later she was expecting her second and she and Donald returned to Barbados with their infant son. Months later, a former employer wrote from the Upper West Side to tell Donald he had work for him, and Donald re-embarked to stay with his brother in New York while Helen stayed in Barbados with the two little ones and their three older (half) siblings.[33] Donald could not read or write more than his name, and the doctors at Ellis Island discovered heart disease they thought would be incapacitating: he was barred from entry. But he had done all right for himself and his family so far, in good part because the two-way valve of New York's port had allowed Donald and Helen to redistribute wage earners and dependents across households in multiple countries, making the most of the non-economic resources they could muster.

REGIME CHANGE, 1921–1924: THE IMPOSITION OF QUOTAS AND THE ELEVATION OF CONJUGAL TIES

After June 1924, this would no longer be possible. From the point of view of European immigrants, the Johnson-Reed Act of 1924 intensified a process that had begun with the Emergency Quota Act of 1921, setting numerical caps by "national origins" that both lowered immigration overall, and drastically reduced the numbers of Southern and Eastern Europeans allowed entry. For British Caribbeans, the impact was even more momentous. Johnson-Reed placed the "non-self-governing" colonies of the Americas (e.g., the British West Indies but not British Canada) under quota control for the first time. Covered by the British quota that Johnson-Reed had expanded, British Caribbeans might have continued to travel north in strong numbers. But the State Department ensured otherwise, sending just three hundred of the

34,000 annual British quota numbers to be divided among all U.S. consulates in the British Caribbean. In practice, then, legal entry to the United States by British West Indians without claim to non-quota status had been brought to a halt.[34]

Overnight, "remote control" policing via U.S. consuls became a decisive factor in Caribbean family trajectories. Before 1924, the key issue that U.S. gatekeepers in the circum-Caribbean were asked to judge was whether intending emigrants had someone in the United States to rely on for support. Consuls clearly felt comfortable with the presumption that brothers, sisters, and cousins would be there for each other (as indeed they most always were). When Simeon Beckford of Brooklyn wrote to the U.S. consul in Kingston in 1923 to inquire about his sister Theresa Davies—

> Please send 'U' tell me what is the Enderance [illeg.] is it that she cannot get out of the country. I guest she must have not pay to you $10 ten dollars for the signing of the PassPort. Sir so doing Please Send and let know. So that I may Send the Money my self and Pay for the Passport are Stamp. So that she may be able to gut through for the Spring.

—the consul immediately reached out to Simeon's sister on the basis of this and an affidavit of support, with no need to question, much less document, their relationship. By April 6, Theresa's passport had been visaed and, the consul wrote to assure Simeon, she was free to travel any time.[35] Did Simeon and Theresa share two parents? Had their parents been legally married? Had they stayed together? Did Simeon have other sisters? Was Theresa his favorite? His only favorite? We don't know, of course, because the consul did not need to know and would not have imagined asking.

This presumption that the bonds on which visa applications hinged were strong and reliable, whatever their particulars, with state sanction or without, would two years later look like a quaint vestige of a bygone era. Under the new system, documentation of formal marriage was essential for those seeking family reunification, evidence of ongoing U.S. domicile was essential to claim returning resident status, and proof of permanent foreign domicile and the absence of economic need were essential for a non-immigrant (tourist) visa: and, in each case, the details of family sentiment became matters of explicit state interest.

The fact that legal marriage was rare and class-specific within British Caribbean societies now carried portentous consequences. The channels along which entry outside the quota queue would be permitted as "family reunification" were very narrow. Only legitimate spouses and minor legitimate children of U.S. citizens, and minor children of U.S. citizen mothers regardless of legitimacy, could claim non-quota status.[36]

Given that less than a quarter of Caribbean-born residents of the United States were naturalized as of 1930, for the great majority of long-distance parents, the answer was no before the question was even asked.[37] Mrs. Amy Cozier of Stamford, Connecticut, filed an affidavit of support in April 1924 to bring her son from Bridgetown. Under the law in force at the time, he could have joined her without question. By the time the U.S. consul processed the papers, however, unless Mrs. Cozier had acquired U.S. citizenship, the eleven-year-old was staying right where he was.[38]

Meanwhile, beyond the narrow realm of legal spouses and minor children, even citizens' kin ties opened no doors. An Anglican priest in Antigua wrote on behalf of his servant, "a black, woman, Felicia Charles, Married, but separated from her husband; aged 52 years, who is anxious to go to the USA to join and live with her daughter." Felicia Charles was an excellent cook, the priest assured, and "a woman who is sure to make good."[39] The testimonial was irrelevant. Even if her daughter became a naturalized citizen, Felicia could gain nothing more than preference status on a waiting list for a quota number that would never come. Anna Matthews, a respectable housekeeper "now and for many years past" employed in a Turtle Bay home, sought to bring her brother Joseph's one son and three daughters, ages six to nineteen, from St. Kitts to live with her, documenting her ability to pay for their schooling and support.[40] Like Amy Cozier and Felicia Charles, Anna Matthews sought a redoubtable (and, frankly, undoubtedly white) interlocutor for her first sally against state power, in her case, the vice president of the Long Island Railroad. Again: no matter what, ten months too late.

Nominally supportive of family reunification, in practice, the system imposed in 1924 cut a fierce breach through precisely the practices of shared childrearing and serial reunion that had made the mass expansion of British Caribbean migration possible in the first place. Even the consuls charged with applying the new rules struggled to wrap their minds around them. What of the hundreds of British Caribbean women, legally resident in New York, who returned to the islands to give birth? The women themselves would maintain non-quota status, as long as they could persuade consuls that their "intent" had always been to return and their Harlem households had remained their "bona fide domicile." But their newborns were non-citizen children of non-citizen mothers. The Kingston consul queried superiors in alarm. "I see nothing in the regulations and instructions whereby they would not come under the quota. If this is the case, a great many of the quota numbers will be used as this office is considering the status of some fifteen or twenty Jamaicans at this time under such circumstances."[41] By the time Johnson-Reed's new system was understood by those tasked with implementing it, waiting lists for quota numbers were five to twenty times longer than the annual supply at each of the region's consulates.[42]

SENTIMENT AS STATE BUSINESS:
THE INTERROGATION OF ADA A.

The state engagement with intimate life occasioned by the restrictionist era went far beyond family reunification constraints. Legal domicile had become key to determining what visa status or right of return a migrant might claim, and bona fide domicile was defined by intent. Agents were asked to judge travellers' hearts, an even harder business than reviewing documentation of birth, marriage, and conduct. New regulations explicitly instructed consuls to presume the possibility of deceit, and to not only redouble interrogation but "take any other actions which seems necessary or desirable, in order to ascertain the true facts."[43] Intent's place in the equation was explicit, for instance, in guidance to consuls on claims to ongoing U.S. residence. The burden of proof was on the "returning alien" to show "[t]hat he went abroad with the intention of returning to reside in the United States," "[t]hat he has an established domicile in the United States," and "[t]hat his stay abroad, if protracted, was caused by justifiable reasons over which he had little or no control."[44] In each case, determination rested on sentiment and perception rather than deed or document.

The mandate to assess intent almost ensured that government agents' presumptions about gender, sex, race, class, and virtue would shape the rulings that determined migrants' rights. To see how, let us return to Ada and Samuel A., whose travels from Barbados to Panama to Cuba to Brooklyn we traced at the start of this essay.

In fall 1922, Ada heard that her mother "had some trouble" back home. She left Cumberland Street for Barbados, where she lived with her sister and sister's husband while caring for her mother. She had "expected to stay only a few months" but then was "taken sick with fever" herself.[45] By the time she recovered, it was halfway through 1924 and, she later explained, "I could not get a quota then." Finally, in March 1925, she convinced the U.S. consul in Bridgetown to give her a non-quota visa as a returning resident. On the ship's passenger manifest, prepared for immigration officials in New

York, Ada declared that she was travelling to rejoin her husband, who had paid her passage, and that she planned to stay permanently; she showed $50 in her possession and reported that she had lived in the United States from 1917 to 1922. The receiving officer scrawled "non quota" across her entry.[46] So far, so good. However: "Practically every case of an alien returning from abroad from a protracted visit is made the subject of an investigation by the board of special inquiry at the port of entry and many are referred on appeal to the Secretary of Labor," State Department instructions informed the consuls responsible for remote control, and so it was in this case.[47]

After walking Ada through her account of her travels, officials started down a line of questioning that made it clear that a competing tale lay in wait. They asked about a particular man who had traveled on same boat as she to Barbados in 1922. Hadn't he deserted his wife when he left New York? Didn't he talk with Ada on the boat? The crescendo of innuendo was capped with the revelation of an affidavit filed by Ada's husband Samuel in New York two months after Ada's 1922 departure, an affidavit that declared, in officials' words, "that since your arrival in the US you have not been conducting yourself in the proper manner, that you were associating with companions of poor reputation, that on Oct. 11 1922 you left home and sailed to Barbados taking with you what money the two of you had saved and that you were accompanied by a man named Aubrey Sinclair S. who had abandoned his wife in NY City and had run away with you."

Ada denied all. Samuel must have filed the affidavit because he wanted to marry another woman, she insisted. At first, she had not believed the rumors that had reached her in Barbados that Samuel had taken another wife in her absence, she said, but a woman on the boat with her from Barbados just now had said "she witnessed the wedding" herself. This new plot twist developing, inspectors sent Ada out and summoned Samuel in. They asked him about his and Ada's marriage in Panama, his travels, Ada's arrival from Cuba, his employment history. Had the two any children? "No, but she had one since she went away"—eleven months after her departure, he added pointedly, somewhere in Trinidad where she had stayed with Aubrey S.'s mother. Where was S. now? "Still in Barbados begging his wife [in New York] to send for him." "Q. Have you ever had immoral relations with another woman besides your wife? A. Not while we lived together. Q. Since she went away did you have another woman? A. No." This was a remarkable response, given that by his own account, he had in fact *married* another woman—then-eighteen-year-old Myrtle C.—a year and three months after Ada left.

More fundamentally, let us pause to notice and marvel, if we can manage to denaturalize our knowledge of what states do around their borders today, at the interrogation underway. After all, neither Samuel's marital status nor his residence status was at stake in this inquiry (and indeed, neither would be affected by it: five years later, he and Myrtle and their four-and-a-half-year-old daughter resided on Atlantic Avenue, a block away from the lodging rooms he and Ada had shared).[48] The fact that Samuel had "committed bigamy" was noted by interrogators only in passing. Samuel's truculent reply distilled all resentment against Ada: "She was called Mistress S. in Trinidad." And if she were? Why did what she was called in Trinidad matter? Ada was not claiming non-quota status by virtue of her marriage to Samuel: she could not, for he was not a citizen. Theoretically, neither Samuel's morals nor Ada's were under examination; and yet, everything about their conjugal life was—and by law. The burden of proof fell to Ada to demonstrate that she had had "the intention of returning to reside in the United States" when she left; that she had "an established domicile in the United States"; and that her "stay abroad, if protracted, was caused by justifiable reasons over which [she] had little or no control."[49] This was about intentions and expectations and loyalties. It was about where home was.

Officials were asked to read backward from subjects' actions to their sentiments, and pass judgment on the sentiments themselves. So their questions burrowed in to intimate choices, and received radically different answers from these two former lovers. Ada had left her husband to stay with a sick mother (or had run away with another man), had visited an uncle in Trinidad (or had stayed with a new mother-in-law there), had lost a child to early death when she herself was a teen in Barbados (or had left a newborn in Trinidad just now to try her luck back in the United States). Samuel had sent letters and sometimes money to Ada in Barbados (or nothing at all); had been humiliated by her affairs and had reproached her for infidelity (or lived in harmony while hatching schemes to wed another). Each one of these allegations appeared in response to specific questions from review board members. This is what officials thought they had to know in order to decide whether Ada A. had a right to walk out onto the streets of New York. The hearing, like so many of its kind, hinged ultimately on the experience of family. For whose needs was the intending immigrant responsible? Who would take them in? Who must want to be with whom?

In light of our preceding discussion of U.S. immigration law's hyper-validation of the conjugal unit and disinterest in kin bonds that had greater

Caribbean importance, it is worth noting just how intensely the officials focused on conjugal comity and sexual fidelity. To Ada, they asked, "Did you know that [your husband] did not want you to come here, before you left Barbados?" "Did you have any idea that your husband was interested in another woman when you went away?" "Have you ever been intimate with any other man than your husband?" (She answered no in every case.) All the more so in questions to Samuel. Had Samuel complained to Ada about her conduct? "Do you know if she committed adultery?" Had Samuel had sufficient proof for divorce? It was not all about sex. What was the name of the Reverend who had married Samuel and Myrtle? Did they have any children? Had Ada come from Cuba alone in 1920, the inspectors inquired, even though nothing that either Samuel or Ada had said so far implied otherwise? "Alone so far as I know," Samuel responded, letting the new doubt linger. Had Ada had a child with her then? "Not that I know of." Doubt spread.

Apparently disjointed, Ada's concluding statement held up a mirror to the topography of legal concern, reflecting back exactly the issues that state agents had demonstrated, through their questioning, to be relevant. Her words made patent just how central intimate intention, conjugal practice, and reproduction had become to the adjudication of mobility rights under the new regime. Ada's concluding statement, in its entirety:

> I sailed in October 1922 and my husband took me to the dock, pier 24, Brooklyn, S/S Diana and when I got there, he presented me with a watch and he gave me $7. He knew this man S. went on the boat the time I did and he knew he was going away to visit his home and I to visit my home, but he wanted to be married again and that is the reason he said I went away with this man. He claims I had a baby but I did not have a baby because this Dr Wilson attended me for woman trouble and he said I could never have babies.

It was on facts such as these that her claim to domicile within the United States now hinged, on sentimental rather than documentary traces of kinship. Had her husband seen her off at the dock with gifts, expecting to welcome her home once her visit to her ailing mother concluded? Had she always intended to return to her home in Brooklyn, or only done so after a Port of Spain dalliance came to nought? Why had she no children to her name?

Such concerns not only preoccupied the Department of Labor inspectors on the review board at Ellis Island; under the remote control system of immigrant screening, interrogation of the domestic details and family lives of visa applicants occupied ever more of consular officials' time. (Again, this has become so routinely the case in all non-rich nations from which working folk seek to depart, that it is hard to remind ourselves just how unnatural such a system seemed at its start.) The transcript of Ada A.'s interrogation appears in Bridgetown consular records because it was forwarded to the consul, as were all transcripts of cases in which officials at Ellis Island reversed the consul's conclusion regarding the "admissibility" of "the alien." The returned transcripts were prefaced by an exhortation to "study the records of the hearings carefully with a view to correcting any errors in your visa practice which may be disclosed by them," with the ominous warning that supervisors in Washington proposed "to scan future performances carefully and to make appropriate notations" on the consul's "efficiency records . . . if similar mistakes occur."[50] Consuls who cared about their careers had best emulate the skeptical intimate inquiry that now guarded the golden door.

STATE POWER AND INTERNAL POLICING

The restrictionist regime asked officials to attend to the affections of a potentially huge number of people: to wit, all non-citizens seeking to cross U.S. borders. In practice, though, the trigger for investigation and intervention came more often from below than above. When agents of the state ended up in some family's business, it was usually because some family member had wanted them there. Working-class Caribbeans had long used letters and lawsuits, addressed to British officials on the islands or receiving society officials in the rimlands, to seek allies in their intimate conflicts.[51] As visa requirements created a new point of mandatory state contact, U.S. immigration officials became another looked-to lever.

This was true even before 1924. Mrs. Edward T. wrote to Bridgetown from Ozone Park, New Jersey, in 1923:

> To American Consul—
>
> Dear Sir—
>   If a party named Maud L. or [alternate spelling] should apply to you for a passport she is not entitled to one. My husband (a man unwilling to properly look after his own family) has been corresponding with her, and sending *registered mail*—Which undoubtedly will mean her coming to this country—and being received by him—Last winter my husband E.A.T. went to Barbados and left us *penniless*—he stayed there 5 months—we had no support—from him—but the children and I depended on charity until we got a going—This woman is the outcome of his visit there.[52]

Similar letters reached consuls from islands and mainland alike. Most often, the relatives whose movements the authors sought to control were spouses, but there were others as well. Samuel D. of Atlantic City went to the trouble of notarizing the letter in which he informed the consul at Bridgetown that he had brought his seventeen-year-old daughter from Barbados to New Jersey (following the life cycle pattern so common before 1924) "but she refused to go to school and became very disobedient to me, her father. Her misbehaviour compelled me to send her back Home and she became incorrigible and her conduct to me was such that I felt she would not become a good American Citizen; and that she would be better off home with her mother. I further ask that she never be allowed to come to America again."[53]

Clyde Austin H. wrote to the same consul in the same year about his wife, who had left him four months earlier at her mother's urging. "Dear Consul, I would like to know, if it is possible for my wife to leave the Colony, without my knowledge or consent. As I am much grieved over the attitude. To my mind, I don't think your country is desirous of having women who desert their husbands through the indifferent actions of mothers." Revealing an apparently common conviction, which resembled none of the specifics of U.S. law and yet captured how its fixation on specific documents of identity was experienced on the island, Clyde wrote that he had always heard a wife could not go to the United States without the consent of her husband "and she must have one of his photos." If Clyde's wife had a photo of him now, he insisted, it was an old one acquired surreptitiously: "she haven't got it since she has left me."[54]

As it happened, though, Clyde was out of luck. Although relatives' (or friends') support was, in 1923, a prerequisite for travel, relatives' opposition was not then enough to derail it. Lady Liberty was no more or less desirous of receiving "women who desert their husbands through the indifferent actions of mothers" than of receiving any other women from the islands. As the U.S. consul at Kingston explained to Robert B. (just back from Cuba in 1923 and convinced his wife, Eugenie, planned to depart Cuba for New York intending "never to return to her husband"), "lack of a husband's consent" was not "in itself sufficient to be a bar to entry." Unless the consul became convinced that Eugenie was ineligible for a visa—which, in 1923, meant incapable of supporting herself, illiterate, or medically unfit—he "would not be inclined" to pass Robert's allegations along to authorities in New York.[55]

Attempts to use the power of papers and borders as leverage in intrafamily struggles were, then, nothing new. But even as the Johnson-Reed Act made it radically more difficult for British Caribbeans to facilitate the movement of kin across U.S. borders, it also offered more purchase to those seeking to block it. Again, the interrogation of Ada A. offers confirmation. By his own account, Samuel A. had sought assistance from multiple authorities in his struggles against his wife. When, after her departure, he heard rumors from friends back home that Ada had spent only four days in Barbados before heading on to Trinidad with Aubrey S., "I wrote to the Colonial Secretary at the Port of Spain, Trinidad and explained to him about her going off with this man with my money and he replied she was living at the home of the mother of this Aubrey S." One might well be amazed that Samuel got a reply at all, much less such an informative one. But, at the end of the day, this attempt to pull the British colonial state into his conjugal conflict yielded no impact. Samuel also went to the British consul in New York to get a lawyer for a divorce, although he did not proceed with the process. Most effectively of all, two months after Ada's departure, Samuel lodged the affidavit alleging bad behavior and abandonment, which would success-fully trigger a Special Inquiry when Ada attempted, in 1925, to disembark at Ellis Island.

Little wonder that Ada's description of her plight to her friend Edna James was not about eugenicist legislation or anti-immigrant nationalism but about Samuel's ability to marshal state power against her. Edna recalled, "I asked [Ada] what she was doing on Ellis Island and she told me she was being detained because her husband said she ran away from America and he was trying to stop her from coming to America." And he did. In the end, the board unanimously determined that Ada had failed to establish non-quota status—that she had not intended to return when she left in 1922. They also unanimously judged her "likely to become a public charge." That is, weighing, on the one hand, the testimony of a husband who had remarried without divorcing her, had a child from a bigamous union on the way, had just quit his job for want of a raise, and when asked "Have you any savings?," responded, "I have $2 in my pocket"—and, on the other hand, a pledge of support from Ada's cousin Mae and a letter from Ada's sister's employer promising work in Philadelphia, the board had decided that this thirty-five-year-old woman, who had already made her way from Barbados to Panama to Barbados to Cuba to New York to Barbados to Trinidad to Barbados to New York, would find no way to support herself on northern soil.

April 1930 found Samuel A. in the heart of Barbadian Brooklyn with his wife, Myrtle, whom he had married six years before.[56] Like so many others of her generation, Myrtle had been raised by a grandmother in Barbados while her mother worked in Brooklyn; turning seventeen in 1923, she had left the island to join her mother in Gotham's working world.[57] Myrtle arrived just before the imposition of Johnson-Reed's divide. Two years later—and two months before Myrtle and Samuel's daughter Adeline was born—Samuel A. successfully placed his first wife on the other side of the international barrier that U.S. immigration law had built.

British Caribbean families adapted to the radical new strictures imposed in 1924, as people do. Jamaicans and Barbadians and other islanders continued to enter the United States as best they could, through means that were legal or not. And individuals continued to try to use the powerful but unpredictable leverage offered by state interest in transnational family matters to their advantage. Let us glance forward one decade, and check on popular awareness of state interest in family ties. In 1937, Thomas D. wrote from Harlem to the U.S. Department of Labor to denounce his brother Ebenezer, who "had entered the U.S. illegally." Such a move might seem to suggest the weight of sibling loyalty was waning among British Caribbeans. But, on the contrary, Thomas's letter attests to an enduring moral economy of family-of-origin ties that Ebenezer, putting conjugal needs first, had contravened. As a result of marrying a domineering New York wife, Ebenezer

> neglected sending any help to his Father and Mother who are 83 and 70 years old respectively, he also has a boy child left there at home with the old folks and I have several letters in my possession from them telling me that sometimes for more than a year and other times once a year he would send a suit of clothing or two and not even a dollar to pay the duty on them. The burden of feeding [Ebenezer's child] is bourne by father out of what little assistance I send every month or what one of my other bros. at home is able to give him.[58]

How to make Ebenezer step up? Thomas first sought to use the specter of state power "just to scare [Ebenezer] to give some kind of aid better than he was doing since he had a steady job": Thomas "approached [Ebenezer] on the matter of neglecting his duty to his parents and his child through a selfish woman who he has no a single child with and threaten[ed] to take the matter up with authorities here." But the selfish woman called his bluff. Ebenezer's wife, Ione, had replied, in Thomas's words: "[I]f I [Thomas] even have him deported I [Ione] will see that he comes back here, so she has sent him out to get himself freed from fear any report I or anyone may make against him." That is, she sent Ebenezer down to Jamaica to petition for legal entry to the United States on the basis of their marriage. His first feint thus countered, Thomas sought to mobilize a higher authority. "So my reason for writing this letter and explaining," he concluded to the U.S. Secretary of Labor, "is to ask you to notify the U.S. Consulate in Kingston, Jam., BWI not to vise his pass port in a hurry for many years that he may realize his responsibilities there."[59]

Just as Thomas expected, Department of Labor officials sent a careful transcript of his letter to the consul at Kingston to inform deliberations in Ebenezer's case. One is struck both by the knowledge of U.S. immigration law built into this kitchen-table argument, and by the particular points on which the confident and canny contenders at the table were wrong. Ione was right about which kin relations U.S. laws sanctioned and which they ignored, but not necessarily right that her marriage to Ebenezer would trump all as the wheels of state action ground forward. Meanwhile, Thomas was quite wrong about which kin ties would win support from U.S. immigration officials, but right that he could use his brother's vulnerability, as shaped by immigration restriction, to make Ebenezer's life difficult, and perhaps even push him out of ranks of residents and potential citizens entirely.

CONCLUSION

The rise of restrictionism in the interwar years is often figured as having been about bodies and blood, the physicality of human reproduction—and it was. But, for multiple reasons, it was also about hearts and minds, loyalty and desire. On the one hand, immigration incited concern precisely because of restrictionists' fears and fantasies about human desire: that sex across boundaries would dilute purities, that if one could not rely on "a feeling of caste or race reluctance as has served in the United States for a pronounced check upon white intermixture with black," the "extreme fecundity [of] the negro" would introduce indelible "black blood" into all other "stocks."[60] Meanwhile, immigration restrictions were crafted in response to the initiatives migrants took in order to sustain family as they knew it—a dense web of obligation, labor, and love between brothers and sisters and cousins; daughters sweating in Manhattan to support the grandmothers who were raising those daughters' daughters back home.

That is, the emergent border control regime was shaped both by elite concern over dysgenic reproduction and by members of complicated families seeking advancement wherever they could find it, which, for sons and daughters from Naples to Nevis, by 1920 had routinely come to mean overseas. In attempting to ensure state control over population composition, the

U.S. government put itself in the position of adjudicating family not only for its own citizens, not only for residents of its soil, but for the much larger universe of people seeking to become such. This meant not only policing bodies and acts but also assessing the dreams and desires that motivated them. That historical moment is nine decades gone, but the institutions it birthed guard our borders to this day.

NOTES

1. Lucy Salyer, *Laws Harsh as Tigers: Chinese Immigrants and the Shaping of Modern Immigration Law* (Chapel Hill, NC, 1995); Erika Lee, *At America's Gates: Chinese Immigration during the Exclusion Era, 1882–1943* (Chapel Hill, NC, 2003); Marilyn Lake and Henry Reynolds, *Drawing the Global Colour Line: White Men's Countries and the International Challenge of Racial Equality* (Cambridge, UK, 2008); Adam McKeown, *Melancholy Order: Asian Migration and the Globalization of Borders* (New York, 2008).

2. For example, Robert F. Foerster, *The Racial Problems Involved in Immigration from Latin America and the West Indies to the United States: Hearings of the Committee on Immigration and Naturalization, House of Representatives, March 3, 1925* (Washington, DC, 1925); Charles B. Davenport and Morris Steggerda, *Race Crossing in Jamaica* (Washington, DC, 1929); Alexandra Minna Stern, *Eugenic Nation: Faults and Frontiers of Better Breeding in Modern America* (Berkeley, CA, 2005).

3. Eithne Luibhéid, *Entry Denied: Controlling Sexuality at the Border* (Minneapolis, 2002); Martha Gardner, *The Qualities of a Citizen: Women, Immigration, and Citizenship, 1870–1965* (Princeton, NJ, 2005); Deirdre M. Moloney, "Women, Sexual Morality, and Economic Dependency in Early U.S. Deportation Policy," *Journal of Women's History* 18, no. 2 (2006): 95–122; Lorna Biddle Rinear, "Phyllis Ann Edmeade (1920s): Caribbean Migrant Worker Deported from the United States," in *The Human Tradition in the Black Atlantic, 1500–2000*, ed. Beatriz G. Mamigonian, Karen Racine, Aaron P. Althouse, and Alan Bloom (Lanham, MD, 2010), 103–22; Nayan Shah, *Stranger Intimacy: Contesting Race, Sexuality and the Law in the North American West* (Berkeley, CA, 2011).

4. Catherine Lee, *Fictive Kinship: Family Reunification and the Meaning of Race and Nation in American Immigration* (New York, 2013). See also Nancy Cott, *Public Vows: A History of Marriage and the Nation* (Cambridge, MA, 2002), 133–55; Lara Putnam, "The Ties Allowed to Bind: Kinship Legalities and Migration Restriction in the Interwar Americas," *International Labor and Working-Class History* 83 (Spring 2013): 191–209. On contemporary experience, see Seyla Benhabib and Judith Resnick, eds., *Migrations and Mobilities: Citizenship, Borders, and Gender* (New York, 2009); and Deborah A. Boehm, *Intimate Migrations: Gender, Family, and Illegality among Transnational Mexicans* (New York, 2012).

5. Lara Putnam, "Unspoken Exclusions: Race, Nation, and Empire in the Immigration Restrictions of the 1920s in North America and the Greater Caribbean," in *Workers across the Americas: The Transnational Turn in Labor History*, ed. Leon Fink (New York, 2011), 267–94; Putnam, *Radical Moves: Caribbean Migrants and the Politics of Race in the Jazz Age* (Chapel Hill, NC, 2013), chap. 3.

6. Aristide Zolberg, "The Archaeology of 'Remote Control,'" in *Migration Control in the North Atlantic World: The Evolution of State Practices in Europe and the United States from the French Revolution to the Inter-War Period*, ed. Andreas Fahrmeir, Olivier Faron, and Patrick Weil (New York, 2003), 195–222; Zolberg, *A Nation by Design: Immigration Policy in the Fashioning of America* (New York, 2006).

7. United States National Archive [henceforth, USNA], RG 84 Consular Posts, Havana, Cuba 523: Correspondence, American Consulate-General Havana Part XXI 1924, Classes 851–861.3: Cable from Department of State and reply from consul, Havana, December 15, 1924.

8. USNA, RG 84 Consular Posts, Bridgetown, Barbados, vol. 208 [henceforth, RG 84 vol. 208]: Correspondence, American Consulate, Barbados, 1925, vol. 3: Transcript, Board of Special Inquiry, Ellis Island, April 8, 1925: A——, Ada. (Note: Surnames are omitted for private individuals tracked from confidential entry hearings.) In later testimony, Ada claimed to have lived in New York from 1917 to 1923, with only a brief detour to Havana to accompany her U.S. employer, but when she entered the United States in 1920 from Havana, she reported that it was her first entry to the country. Passenger List, S.S. Mexico, November 30, 1920, List 7. All passenger lists and census sheets cited in this essay have been accessed as digital images through Ancestry.com.

9. Cuba, Secretaría de Hacienda, Sección de Estadística, *Informe y movimiento de pasajeros . . .* (Havana, 1917–1921).

10. Passenger List, S.S. Mascotte, August 24, 1920, List 164. U.S. Census 1920, Brooklyn Assembly District 1, Enumeration District 50, sheet 11B.

11. Passenger List, S.S. Mexico, November 30, 1920, List 7.

12. See U.S. Census of 1920, Brooklyn Assembly District 8, Enumeration District 435, Sheets 1A-XXB. (Sheet 17 A includes the home the couple would move into four months later.)

13. U.S. Census of 1920, New York, Brooklyn Assembly District 10, Enumeration District 588, Sheets 6A, 6B.

14. Elizabeth Mclean Petras, *Jamaican Labor Migration: White Capital and Black Labor, 1850–1930* (Boulder, CO, 1988); Elizabeth M. Thomas-Hope, "The Establishment of a Migration Tradition: British West Indian Movements to the Hispanic Caribbean in the Century after Emancipation," in *Caribbean Social Relations*, ed. Colin G. Clarke (Liverpool, 1978), 66–81; Putnam, *Radical Moves*, chap. 1.

15. Velma Newton, *The Silver Men: West Indian Labour Migration to Panama, 1850–1914* (Mona, Jamaica, 1984); Bonham Richardson, *Panama Money in Barbados, 1900–1920* (Knoxville, TN, 1985); Lara Putnam, *The Company They Kept: Migrants and the Politics of Gender in Caribbean Costa Rica, 1870–1960* (Chapel Hill, NC, 2002); Jorge L. Giovannetti, "Black British Subjects in Cuba: Race, Ethnicity, Nation, and Identity in the Migratory Experience, 1898–1938" (PhD diss., University of North London, 2001); Cadence Wynter, "Jamaican Labor Migration to Cuba, 1885–1930, in the Caribbean Context" (PhD diss., University of Illinois at Chicago, 2001); Audrey K. Charlton, "'Cat Born in Oven Is Not Bread': Jamaican and Barbadian Immigrants in Cuba between 1900 and 1959" (PhD diss., Columbia University, 2005).

16. See Irma Watkins-Owens, "Early Twentieth-Century Caribbean Women: Migration and Social Networks in New York City," in *Islands in the City: Caribbean Migration to New York*, ed. Nancy Foner (Berkeley, CA, 2001), 25–51. For region-wide sex ratio data,

see Lara Putnam, "Rewriting Ravenstein from the Greater Caribbean," paper presented at the Social Science History Association 39th Annual Conference, Toronto, November 6–9, 2014.

17. Ira de Augustine Reid, *The Negro Immigrant: His Background, Characteristics, and Social Adjustment, 1899–1937* (1939; New York, 1969), 243; Winston James, *Holding Aloft the Banner of Ethiopia: Caribbean Radicalism in Early Twentieth-Century America* (New York, 1998), 364.

18. Combining census data with annual entry data yields a estimated total of 89,600 black immigrants and their children in the city in 1925, who would have been at least 49 percent female, and the women among them overwhelmingly British West Indian. United States, Department of Commerce, Bureau of the Census, *Fifteenth Census of the United States: 1930*, Vol. 2 (Washington, DC, 1933), 70, 446; Trinidad, Registrar General, *Census of the Colony of Trinidad and Tobago, 1921* (Port of Spain, 1923), 59; George W. Roberts, *The Population of Jamaica* (Cambridge, UK, 1957), 51, 72.

19. United States, *Fifteenth Census of the United States*, Vol. 2, 33, 70, 231, 250. Census figures for foreign-born "West Indians" in New York include Cubans, French Caribbeans, and others (although not Puerto Ricans or U.S. Virgin Islanders). Combining the available census evidence on race, birthplace, and nationality suggests a total of 55,000 British Caribbean-born and 45,000 of their children citywide in 1930. Key scholarship on British Caribbeans in the early twentieth-century United States includes Irma Watkins-Owens, *Blood Relations: Caribbean Immigrants and the Harlem Community, 1900–1930* (Bloomington, IN, 1996); James, *Holding Aloft the Banner*; Joyce Moore Turner with W. Burghardt Turner, *Caribbean Crusaders and the Harlem Renaissance* (Urbana, IL, 2005); Louis J. Parascandola, ed., *Look for Me All around You: Anglophone Caribbean Immigrants in the Harlem Renaissance* (Detroit, 2005); Violet Showers Johnson, *The Other Black Bostonians: West Indians in Boston, 1900–1950* (Bloomington, IN, 2006). See also Ira Kasinitz, *Caribbean New York: Black Immigrants and the Politics of Race* (Ithaca, NY, 1992); and Nancy Foner, *In a New Land: A Comparative View of Immigration* (New York, 2005), both focused on a later era but offering key insights into the earlier wave.

20. Roi Ottley, *New World A'Coming* (Boston, 1943), 40–41. Ottley's book offers a vivid portrait of British Caribbean New York, as do Claude McKay's *Negro Metropolis* (New York, 1940); and Ira de Augustine Reid's *Negro Immigrant*. McKay was a Jamaican immigrant (arrived 1912); Reid was the U.S.-born son of a Jamaican minister (arrived 1892). Equally essential are works by the daughters of 1920s arrivals, including Paule Marshall, *Brown Girl, Brownstones* (1959; New York, 1981); Marshall, *Triangular Road: A Memoir* (New York, 2009); Audre Lorde, *Zami: A New Spelling of My Name* (Freedom, CA, 1982); June Jordan, *Soldier: A Poet's Childhood* (New York, 2001); and Yevette Richards, ed., *Conversations with Maida Springer: A Personal History of Labor, Race, and International Relations* (Pittsburgh, 2004).

21. U.S. Census of 1920, Borough of Manhattan, Enumeration District 1414, Sheet No. 1855.

22. Passenger list for S.S. Advance, sailing from Cristobal, June 10, 1918; passenger list for S.S. Almirante, sailing from Kingston, May 6, 1916.

23. U.S. Census of 1930, Borough of Manhattan, Enumeration District 31–1003, Sheet No. 8B.

24. Ibid.

25. But see Watkins-Owens, *Blood Relations*; Watkins-Owens, "Early Twentieth-Century Caribbean Women"; Putnam, "Ties Allowed to Bind." Gender and kinship have been prominent in research on post-World War II migration, including Constance Sutton and Elsa M. Chaney, eds., *Caribbean Life in New York City: Sociocultural Dimensions* (1987; New York, 1992); Mary Chamberlain, *Family Love in the Diaspora: Migration and the Anglo-Caribbean Experience* (New Brunswick, NJ, 2006); and Karen Fog Olwig, *Caribbean Journeys: An Ethnography of Migration and Home in Three Family Networks* (Durham, NC, 2007).

26. Reid, *Negro Immigrant*, 243.

27. Pioneering studies were Fernando Henriques, *Family and Colour in Jamaica* (London, 1953); Raymond T. Smith, *The Negro Family in British Guiana: Family Structure and Social Status in the Villages* (London, 1956); Roberts, *Population of Jamaica*; Edith Clarke, *My Mother Who Fathered Me: A Study of the Families in Three Selected Communities in Jamaica* (London, 1957); Michael G. Smith, *West Indian Family Structure* (Seattle, 1962). Not just the literature on Caribbean kinship, but the literature on that literature is quite large. See Raymond T. Smith, "Family, Social Change, and Social Policy in the West Indies," *Nieuwe West-Indische Gids: New West Indies Guide* 56, nos. 3–4 (1982): 111–42; Christine Barrow, *Family in the Caribbean: Themes and Perspectives* (Kingston, 1996); Mary Chamberlain, "Small Worlds: Childhood and Empire," *Journal of Family History* 27, no. 2 (2002): 186–200; D. Alissa Trotz, "Behind the Banner of Culture: Gender, 'Race,' and the Family in Guyana," *Nieuwe West-Indische Gids: New West Indies Guide* 77, nos. 1–2 (2003): 5–29; Lara Putnam, "Caribbean Kinship from Within and Without," *History Workshop Journal* 66, no. 1 (2008): 279–88; Barbara Bush, "Colonial Research and the Social Sciences at the End of Empire: The West Indian Social Survey, 1944–57," *Journal of Imperial and Commonwealth History* 41, no. 3 (2013): 451–74. Crucial recent contributions on nineteenth- and early twentieth-century family practice include Jean Besson, *Martha Brae's Two Histories: European Expansion and Caribbean Culture-Building in Jamaica* (Chapel Hill, NC, 2002); Brian L. Moore and Michele A. Johnson, *Neither Led nor Driven: Contesting British Cultural Imperialism in Jamaica, 1865–1920* (Mona, Jamaica, 2004); Henrice Altink, *Destined for a Life of Service: Defining African-Jamaican Womanhood, 1865–1938* (Manchester, UK, 2011).

28. Given the unevenness of information on kin forms before the nineteenth-century emergence of intense labor mobility, it is hard to establish chronology, much less causation.

29. USNA, RG 84 Consular Posts, Kingston, Jamaica, vol. 329 [henceforth, RG 84 vol. 329]: Correspondence, American Consulate, Kingston JA 1924 Part 8: Letter from U.S. consul, Kingston, to U.S. consulate, London, September 6, 1924. On child fostering, see also Watkins-Owens, "Early Twentieth-Century Caribbean Women," 39–42.

30. USNA, RG 84 Consular Posts, Kingston, Jamaica, vol. 321 [henceforth, RG 84 vol. 321]: Correspondence, American Consulate, Kingston JA 1923 Part 5: Letter to consul, February 13, 1923.

31. Note that all of the sons were in factory work, and Brown himself appears in 1925 as an elevator operator—underlining the narrowness of class hierarchies among British West Indian migrants. New York State Population Census Schedules, 1925; Election District: 27; Assembly District: 13; City: New York; County: New York; Page: 12.

32. RG 84 vol. 321: Correspondence, American Consulate, Kingston JA 1923 Part 5: Letter to consul, Jan. 1923. Parents of U.S. citizens were exempted from the literacy requirements instituted by the Immigration Act of 1917.

33. RG 84 vol. 208: Correspondence, American Consulate, Barbados, 1925, vol. 3: Transcript, Board of Special Inquiry, Ellis Island, October 8, 1924: B——, Donald.

34. See Mae Ngai, *Impossible Subjects: Illegal Immigrants and the Making of Modern America* (Princeton, NJ, 2004); Putnam, *Radical Moves*, chap. 3.

35. RG 84 vol. 321: Correspondence, American Consulate, Kingston JA 1923 Part 5: Letter to consul, March 22, 1923; letters from consul, January 16, 1923 and April 6, 1923.

36. For extended discussion, see Putnam, "Ties Allowed to Bind."

37. Reid, *Negro Immigrant*, 249. Wives and minor children of U.S. permanent residents were given second-rank priority (secondary to parents of U.S. citizens) for one-half of allocated quota visa numbers each year. But, in practice, with only a few hundred quota visas available annually for the entire British Caribbean, and waiting lists ten times longer than the annual supply at each of the region's consulates, this "preferred status" meant almost nothing.

38. RG 84 vol. 208: Correspondence, American Consulate, Barbados, 1925, vol. 3: Letter to consul, April 7, 1925.

39. RG 84 vol. 208: Correspondence, American Consulate, Barbados, 1925, vol. 3: Letter to consul, May 29, 1925.

40. RG 84 vol. 208: Correspondence, American Consulate, Barbados, 1925, vol. 3: Letter to consul, March 27, 1925; Letter from consul, April 14, 1925.

41. RG 84 vol. 329: Correspondence, American Consulate, Kingston JA 1924 Part 8: letter from consul, Kingston, to U.S. consulate, London, September 6, 1924.

42. For example, among many, USNA, RG 84 Consular Post Kingston, Jamaica, vol. 352: Consular Post Kingston, Jamaica, 1926, Correspondence 811.11: Letter from consul, November 16, 1926.

43. United States, Department of State, *Admission of Aliens into the United States: Notes to Section 361, Consular Regulations* (Washington, DC, 1932), 79.

44. Ibid., 89.

45. RG 84 vol. 208: Correspondence, American Consulate, Barbados, 1925, vol. 3: Transcript, Board of Special Inquiry, Ellis Island, April 8, 1925: A——, Ada. All information and quotes unattributed in the paragraphs that follow come from this eleven-page transcript.

46. Passenger List, S.S. Voltaire, April 4, 1925, List 31.

47. United States, Department of State, *Admission of Aliens*, 89.

48. U.S. Census of 1930, New York, Borough of Brooklyn, Assembly District 10, Enumeration District 24–1486, Sheet 6B.

49. United States, Department of State, *Admission of Aliens*, 89.

50. RG 84 vol. 208: Correspondence, American Consulate, Barbados, 1925, vol. 3: Letter to consul, March 17, 1925; cf. letter to consul, August 15, 1925.

51. See Putnam, *Company They Kept.*

52. USNA, RG 84 Consular Posts, Bridgetown, Barbados, vol. 201 [henceforth, RG 84 vol. 201]: Correspondence, American Consulate, Barbados, 1923, vol. 2: Letter to consul, July 28, 1923.

53. RG 84 vol. 201: Correspondence, American Consulate, Barbados, 1923, vol. 2: Letter to consul, June 5, 1923.

54. RG 84 vol. 201: Correspondence, American Consulate, Barbados, 1923, vol. 2: Letter to consul, November 20, 1923.

55. RG 84 vol. 321: Correspondence, American Consulate, Kingston JA 1923 Part 5: Letter to consul, May 7, 1923; letter from consul, May 9, 1923.

56. U.S. Census of 1930, New York, Borough of Brooklyn, Assembly District 10, Enumeration District 24–1486, Sheet 6B.

57. Passenger List, S.S. Hubert, July 16, 1923, List 2.

58. USNA, RG 84 Jamaica, Kingston Consulate, Consul Records, 1936–1952, Entry 2821, Box 2: c8.1 496 (1937, vol. 9. Classes 6–8): Letter to consul, May 18, 1937.

59. Ibid.

60. Foerster, *Racial Problems*, 321; Lothrop Stoddard, *The Rising Tide of Color against White World Supremacy* (New York, 1920), 90; Carleton Beals, "The Black Belt of the Caribbean," *Fortnightly Review*, September 1, 1931: 357–59, 366–67.

6

Inbetween Peoples: Race, Nationality and the "New Immigrant" Working Class

JAMES R. BARRETT AND DAVID ROEDIGER

> By the eastern European immigration the labor force has been cleft horizontally into two great divisions. The upper stratum includes what is known in mill parlance as the 'English-speaking' men; the lower contains the 'Hunkies' or 'Ginnies.' Or, if you prefer, the former are the 'white men,' the latter the 'foreigners.'
>
> —John Fitch, *The Steel Workers*

IN 1980, JOSEPH LOGUIDICE, an elderly Italian American from Chicago, sat down to give his life story to an interviewer. His first and most vivid childhood recollection was of a race riot that had occurred on the city's near north side. Wagons full of policemen with "peculiar hats" streamed into his neighborhood. But the "one thing that stood out in my mind," Loguidice remembered after six decades, was "a man running down the middle of the street hollering . . . 'I'm White, I'm White!'" After first taking him for an African American, Loguidice soon realized that the man was a white coal handler covered in dust. He was screaming for his life, fearing that "people would shoot him down." He had, Loguidice concluded, "got caught up in . . . this racial thing."[1]

Joseph Loguidice's tale might be taken as a metaphor for the situation of millions of Eastern and Southern European immigrants who arrived in the United States between the end of the nineteenth century and the early 1920s. The fact that this episode made such a profound impression is in itself significant, suggesting both that this was a strange, new situation and that thinking about race became an important part of the consciousness of immigrants like Loguidice. We are concerned here in part with the development of racial awareness and attitudes, and an increasingly racialized worldview among new immigrant workers themselves. Most did not arrive with conventional United States attitudes regarding "racial" difference, let alone its significance and implications in the context of industrial America. Yet most, it seems, "got caught up in . . . this racial thing." How did this happen? If race was indeed socially constructed, then what was the raw material that went into the process?

We are also concerned with how these immigrant workers were viewed in racial terms by others—employers, the state, reformers, and other workers. Like the coal handler in Loguidice's story, their own ascribed racial identity was not always clear. A whole range of evidence—laws; court cases; formal racial ideology; social conventions; popular culture in the form of slang, songs, films, cartoons, ethnic jokes, and popular theater—suggests that the native born and older immigrants often placed these newer immigrants not only *above* African and Asian Americans, for example, but also *below* "white" people. Indeed, many of the older immigrants and particularly the Irish had themselves been perceived as "nonwhite" just a generation earlier. As labor historians, we are interested in the ways in which Polish, Italian, and other European artisans and peasants became American workers, but we are equally concerned with the process by which they became "white." Indeed, in the United States the two identities intertwined and this explains a great deal of the persistent divisions within the working-class population. How did immigrant workers wind up "inbetween"?

Such questions are not typical of immigration history which has largely been the story of newcomers becoming American, of their holding out against becoming American or, at best, of their changing America in the process of discovering new identities. To the extent, and it is a very considerable extent, that theories of American exceptionalism intersect with the history of immigration, the emphasis falls on the difficulty of enlisting heterogeneous workers into class mobilizations or, alternatively, on the unique success of the United States as a multiethnic democracy.[2] But the immigration history Robert Orsi has recently called for, one which "puts the issues and contests of racial identity and difference at its center," has only begun to be written. Proponents of race as an explanation for American exceptionalism have not focused on European immigrants, at best regarding their racialization as a process completed by the 1890s.[3]

Even with the proliferation of scholarship on the social construction of race, we sometimes assume that such immigrants really were "white," in a way that they were not initially American. And, being white, largely poor, and self-consciously part of imagined communities with roots in Europe, they were therefore "ethnic." If social scientists referred to "national" groups as races (the "Italian race") and to Southern and East European pan-nationalities as races (Slavonic and Mediterranean "races"), they did so because they used race promiscuously to mean other things. If the classic work on American exceptionalism, Werner Sombart's 1906 *Why Is There No Socialism in The United States?* has a whole section on "racial" division with scarcely a mention of any group modem Americans would recognize as a racial minority, this is a matter of semantic confusion. If Robert Park centered his pioneering early twentieth-century sociological theory of assimilation on the "race relations cycle," with the initial expectation that it would apply to African Americans as well as European immigrants, he must not have sorted out the difference between race and ethnicity yet.[4] Indeed, so certain are some modem scholars of the ability of "ethnicity" to explain immigrant experiences which contemporaries described largely in terms of race and nationality that a substantial literature seeks to describe even the African-American and native American experiences as "ethnic."[5]

Racial identity was also clearly gendered in important ways, and historians are just beginning to understand this gendered quality of racial language, conventions, and identity. It is apparent even in the sorts of public spheres privileged here—citizenship, the state, the union, the workplace. But we are *most* apt to find the conjunctions between gender and race in places that are not probed here—at those points where more intimate relations intersected with the rule of law.

The taboo against interracial sex and marriage was one obvious boundary between low-status immigrant workers and people of color with whom they often came in contact. As Peggy Pascoe has noted, "although such marriages were infrequent throughout most of U.S. history, an enormous amount of time and energy was spent in trying to prevent them from taking place . . . the history of interracial marriage provides rich evidence of the formulation of race and gender and of the connections between the two." Yet we have little understanding of how this taboo was viewed by immigrant and African- or Asian-American workers. One obvious place to look is at laws governing interracial marriage and court cases aimed at enforcing such laws. Native-born women who became involved with immigrant men could lose their citizenship and, if the immigrant were categorized as non-white, they could be prosecuted for "race-mixup." "Race mixing" occurred in spite of all this, of course. Chinese men who lived under particularly oppressive conditions because of restrictions on the immigration of Chinese women, tended to develop relationships with either African Americans or Poles and other "new immigrant" women.[6] We have not attempted to unravel this fascinating and complex problem or the racial identity of immigrant women here. Except where clearly indicated, we are describing situations where racial identity was informed and shaped by, often even conflated with, notions of manhood.

Thus, we make no brief for the consistency with which "race" was used, by experts or popularly, to describe the "new immigrant" Southern and East Europeans who dominated the ranks of those coming to the United States between 1895 and 1924 and who "remade" the American working class in that period. We regard such inconsistency as important evidence of the "inbetween" racial status of such immigrants.[7] The story of Americanization is vital and compelling, but it took place in a nation also obsessed by race. For immigrant workers, the processes of "becoming white" and "becoming American" were intertwined at every turn. The "American standard of living," which labor organizers alternately and simultaneously accused new immigrants of undermining and encouraged them to defend via class organization, rested on "white men's wages." Political debate turned on whether new immigrants were fit to join the American nation and on whether they were fit to join the "American race." Nor do we argue that Eastern and Southern European immigrants were in the same situation as non-whites. Stark differences between the racialized status of African Americans and the racial inbetween-ness of these immigrants meant that the latter *eventually* "became ethnic" and that their trajectory was predictable. But their history was sloppier than their trajectory. From day to day they were, to borrow from E. P. Thompson, "proto-nothing," reacting and acting in a highly racialized nation.[8]

Overly ambitious, this essay is also deliberately disorderly. It aims to destabilize modem categories of race and ethnicity and to capture the confusion, inbetween-ness and flux in the minds of native-born Americans and the immigrants themselves. Entangling the processes of Americanization and of whitening, it treats a two-sided experience: new immigrants underwent racial categorizing at the same time they developed new identities, and the two sides of the process cannot be understood apart from one another. Similarly, the categories of state, class and immigrant self-activity, used here to explain how race is made and to structure the paper, can be separated at best arbitrarily and inconsistently. Expect therefore a bumpy ride, which begins at its bumpiest—with the vocabulary of race.

INBETWEEN IN THE POPULAR MIND

America's racial vocabulary had no agency of its own, but rather reflected material conditions and power relations—the situations that workers faced on a daily basis in their workplaces and communities. Yet the words themselves were important. They were not only the means by which native born and elite people marked new immigrants as inferiors, but also the means by which immigrant workers came to locate themselves and those about them in the nation's racial hierarchy. In beginning to analyze the vocabulary of race, it makes little sense for historians to invest the words themselves with an agency that could be exercised only by real historical actors, or meanings that derived only from the particular historical contexts in which the language was developed and employed.

The word *guinea*, for example, had long referred to African slaves, particularly those from the continent's northwest coast, and to their descendants. But from the late 1890s, the term was increasingly applied to southern European migrants, first and especially to Sicilians and southern Italians who often came as contract laborers. At various times and places in the United States, guinea has been applied to mark Greeks, Jews, Portuguese, Puerto Ricans and perhaps any new immigrant.[9]

Likewise, *hunky*, which began life, probably in the early twentieth century, as a corruption of "Hungarian," eventually became a pan-Slavic slur connected with perceived immigrant racial characteristics. By World War One the term was frequently used to describe any immigrant steelworker, as in *mill hunky.* Opponents of the Great 1919 Steel Strike, including some native-born skilled workers, derided the struggle as a "hunky strike." Yet Josef Barton's work suggests that for Poles, Croats, Slovenians, and other immigrants who often worked together in difficult, dangerous situations, the term embraced a remarkable, if fragile, sense of prideful identity across ethnic lines. In *Out of this Furnace,* Thomas Bell's 1941 epic novel based on the lives of Slavic steelworkers, he observed that the word hunky bespoke "unconcealed racial prejudice" and a "denial of social and racial equality." Yet as these workers built the industrial unions of the late 1930s and took greater control over their own lives, the meaning of the term began to change. The pride with which second- and third-generation Slavic-American steelworkers, now women as well as men, wore the label in the early 1970s seemed to have far more to do with class than with ethnic identity. At about the same time the word *honky,* possibly a corruption of hunky, came into common use as Black nationalism reemerged as a major ideological force in the African-American community.[10]

Words and phrases employed by social scientists to capture the inbetween identity of the new immigrants are a bit more descriptive, if a bit more cumbersome. As late as 1937, John Dollard wrote repeatedly of the immigrant working class as "our temporary Negroes." More precise, if less dramatic, is the designation "not-yet-white ethnics" offered by Barry Goldberg. The term not only reflects the popular perceptions and everyday experiences of such workers, but also conveys the dynamic quality of the process of racial formation.[11]

The examples of Greeks and Italians particularly underscore the new "immigrants'" ambiguous positions with regard to popular perceptions of race. When Greeks suffered as victims of an Omaha "race" riot in 1909 and when eleven Italians died at the hands of lynchers in Louisiana in 1891, their less-than-white racial status mattered alongside their nationalities. Indeed, as in the case of Loguidice's coal handler, their ambivalent racial status put their lives in jeopardy. As Gunther Peck shows in his fine study of copper miners in Bingham, Utah, the Greek and Italian immigrants were "nonwhite" before their tension-fraught cooperation with the Western Federation of Miners during a 1912 strike ensured that "the category of Caucasian worker changed and expanded." Indeed, the work of Dan Georgakas and Yvette Huginnie shows that Greeks and other Southern Europeans often "bivouacked" with other "nonwhite" workers in Western mining towns. Pocatello, Idaho, Jim-Crowed Greeks in the early twentieth century and in Arizona they were not welcomed by white workers in "white men's towns" or "white men's jobs." In Chicago during the Great Depression, a German-American wife expressed regret over marrying her "half-nigger," Greek-American husband. African-American slang in the 1920s in South Carolina counted those of mixed American Indian, African American and white heritage as *Greeks*. Greek Americans in the Midwest showed great anxieties about race, and were perceived not only as Puerto Rican, mulatto, Mexican or Arab, but also as non-white *because of* being Greek.[12]

Italians, involved in a spectacular international diaspora in the early twentieth century, were racialized as the "Chinese of Europe" in many lands.[13] But in the United States their racialization was pronounced and, as *guinea's* evolution suggests, more likely to connect Italians with Africans. During the debate at the Louisiana state constitutional convention of 1898, over how to disfranchise blacks, and over which whites might lose the vote, some acknowledged that the Italian's skin "happens to be white" even as they argued for his disfranchisement. But others held that "according to the spirit of our meaning when we speak of 'white man's government,' [the Italians] are as black as the blackest negro in existence."[14] More than metaphor intruded on this judgment. At the turn of the century, a West Coast construction boss was asked, "You don't call the Italian a white man?" The negative reply assured the questioner that the Italian was "a dago." Recent studies of Italian and Greek Americans make a strong case that racial, not just ethnic, oppression long plagued "nonwhite" immigrants from Southern Europe.[15]

The racialization of East Europeans was likewise striking. While racist jokes mocked the black servant who thought her child, fathered by a Chinese man, would be a Jew, racist folklore held that Jews, inside-out, were "niggers." In 1926 Serbo-Croatians ranked near the bottom of a list of forty "ethnic" groups whom "white American" respondents were asked to order according to the respondents' willingness to associate with members of each group. They placed just above Negroes, Filipinos, and Japanese. Just above them were Poles, who were near the middle of the list. One sociologist has recently written that "a good many groups on this color continuum [were] not considered white by a large number of Americans."[16] The literal inbetween-ness of new immigrants on such a list suggests what popular speech affirms: The state of whiteness was approached gradually and controversially. The authority of the state itself both smoothed and complicated that approach.

WHITE CITIZENSHIP AND INBETWEEN AMERICANS: THE STATE OF RACE

The power of the national state gave recent immigrants both their firmest claims to whiteness and their strongest leverage for enforcing those claims. The courts consistently allowed "new immigrants," whose racial status was ambiguous in the larger culture, to be naturalized as "white" citizens and almost as consistently turned down non-European applicants as "nonwhite." Political reformers therefore discussed the fitness for citizenship of recent European immigrants from two distinct angles. They produced, through the beginning of World War One, a largely benign and hopeful discourse on how to Americanize (and win the votes of) those already here. But this period also saw a debate on fertility rates and immigration restriction which conjured up threats of "race suicide" if this flow of migrants were not checked and the fertility of the native-born increased. A figure like Theodore Roosevelt could stand as both the Horatio warning of the imminent swamping of the "old stock" racial elements in the United States and as the optimistic Americanizer to whom the play which originated the assimilationist image of the "melting pot" was dedicated.[17]

Such anomalies rested not only on a political economy, which at times needed and at times shunned immigrant labor, but also on peculiarities of United States naturalization law. If the "state apparatus" both told new immigrants that they were and were not white, it was clearly the judiciary which produced the most affirmative responses. Thus United States law made citizenship racial as well as civil. Even when much of the citizenry doubted the racial status of European migrants, the courts almost always granted their whiteness in naturalization cases. Thus, the often racially based campaigns against Irish naturalization in the 1840s and 1850s and against Italian naturalization in the early twentieth century aimed to delay, not deny, citizenship. The lone case which appears exceptional in this regard is one in which United States naturalization attorneys in Minnesota attempted unsuccessfully to bar radical Finns from naturalization on the ethnological grounds that they were not "caucasian" and therefore not white.[18]

The legal equation of whiteness with fitness for citizenship significantly shaped the process by which race was made in the United States. If Southern and Eastern European immigrants remained "inbetween people" because of broad cultural perceptions, Asians were in case after case declared unambiguously non-white and therefore unfit for citizenship. This sustained pattern of denial of citizenship provides, as the sociologist Richard Williams argues, the best guide to who would be racialized in an ongoing way in the twentieth-century United States. It applies, of course, in the case of Native Americans. Migrants from Africa, though nominally an exception in that Congress in 1870 allowed their naturalization (with the full expectation that they would not be coming), of course experienced sweeping denials of civil status both in slavery and in Jim Crow. Nor were migrants from Mexico truly exceptional. Despite the naturalizability of such migrants by treaty and later court decisions, widespread denials of citizenship rights took place almost immediately—in one 1855 instance in California as a result of the "Greaser Bill"—as the Vagrancy Act was termed.[19]

Likewise, the equation between legal whiteness and fitness for naturalizable citizenship helps to predict which groups would *not* be made non-white in an ongoing way. Not only did the Irish, whose whiteness was under sharp question in the 1840s and 1850s, and later the "new immigrants" gain the powerful symbolic argument that the law declared them white and fit, but they also had the power of significant numbers of votes, although naturalization rates for new immigrants were not always high. During Louisiana's disfranchising constitutional convention of 1898, for example, the bitter debate over Italian whiteness ended with a provision passed extending to new immigrants protections comparable, even superior, to those which the "grandfather clause" gave to native white voters. New Orleans' powerful

Choctaw Club machine, already the beneficiary of Italian votes, led the campaign for the plank.[20] When Thomas Hart Benton and Stephen Douglas argued against Anglo-Saxon superiority and for a pan-white "American race" in the 1850s, they did so before huge blocs of Irish voters. When Theodore Roosevelt extolled the "mixture of blood" making the American race, a "new ethnic type in this melting pot of the nations," he emphasized to new immigrant *voters* his conviction that each of their nationalities would enrich America by adding "its blood to the life of the nation." When Woodrow Wilson also tailored his thinking about racial desirability of the new European immigrants, he did so in the context of an electoral campaign in which the "foreign" vote counted heavily.[21] In such a situation, Roosevelt's almost laughable proliferation of uses of the word *race* served him well, according to his various needs as reformer, imperialist, debunker and romanticizer of the history of the West, and political candidate. He sincerely undertook seemingly contradictory embraces of Darwin and of Lamarck's insistence on the hereditability of acquired characteristics, of melting pots and of race suicide, of an adoring belief in Anglo-Saxon and Teutonic superiority and in the grandeur of a "mixed" American race. Roosevelt, like the census bureau, thought in terms of the nation's biological "stock"—the term by now called forth images of Wall Street as well as the farm. That stock was directly threatened by low birth rates among the nation's "English-speaking race." But races could also progress over time and the very experience of mixing and of clashing with other races would bring out, and improve, the best of the "racestock." The "American race" could absorb and permanently improve the less desirable stock of "*all* white immigrants," perhaps in two generations, but only if its most desirable "English-speaking" racial elements were not swamped in an un-Americanized Slavic and Southern European culture and biology.[22]

The neo-Lamarckianism which allowed Roosevelt to use such terms as "English-speaking race" ran through much of Progressive racial thinking, though it was sometimes underpinned by appeals to other authorities.[23] We likely regard choosing between eating pasta or meat, between speaking English or Italian, between living in ill-ventilated or healthy housing, between taking off religious holidays or coming to work, between voting Republican or Socialist as decisions based on environment, opportunity and choice. But language loyalty, incidence of dying in epidemics, and radicalism often defined *race* for late nineteenth- and early twentieth-century thinkers, making distinctions between racial, religious and anti-radical varieties of nativism messy. For many, Americanization was not simply a cultural process but an index of racial change which could fail if the concentration of "lower" races kept the "alchemy" of racial transformation from occurring.[24] From its very start, the campaign for immigration restriction directed against "new" Europeans carried a strong implication that even something as ineluctable as "moral tone" could be inherited. In deriding "ignorant, brutal Italians and Hungarian laborers" during the 1885 debate over the Contract Labor Law, its sponsor framed his environmentalist arguments in terms of color, holding that "the introduction into a community of any considerable number of persons of a lower moral tone will cause general moral deterioration as sure as night follows day." He added, "The intermarriage of a lower with a higher type certainly does not improve the latter any more than does the breeding of cattle by blooded and common stock improve the blooded stock generally." The restrictionist cause came to feature writings that saw mixing as always and everywhere disastrous. Madison Grant's *The Passing of the Great Race* (1916), a racist attack on recent immigrants which defended the purity of "Nordic" stock, the race of the "white man par excellence," against "Alpine," "Mediterranean" and Semitic invaders, is a classic example.[25]

Professional Americanizers and national politicians appealing to immigrant constituencies for a time seemed able to marginalize those who racialized new immigrants. Corporate America generally gave firm support to relatively open immigration. Settlement house reformers and others taught and witnessed Americanization. The best of them, Jane Addams, for example, learned from immigrants as well and extolled not only assimilation but the virtues of ongoing cultural differences among immigrant groups. Even progressive politicians showed potential to rein in their own most racially charged tendencies. As a Southern academic, Woodrow Wilson wrote of the dire threat to "our Saxon habits of government" by "corruption of foreign blood" and characterized Italian and Polish immigrants as "sordid and hapless." But as a presidential candidate in 1912, he reassured immigrant leaders that "We are all Americans," offered to rewrite sections on Polish Americans in his *History of the American People* and found Italian Americans "one of the most interesting and admirable elements in our American life."[26]

Yet Progressive Era assimilationism, and even its flirtations with cultural pluralism, could not save new immigrants from racial attacks. If racial prejudice against new immigrants was far more provisional and nuanced than anti-Irish bias in the antebellum period, political leaders also defended *hunkies* and *guineas* far more provisionally. Meanwhile the Progressive project of imperialism and the Progressive non-project of capitulation to Jim Crow ensured that race thinking would retain and increase its potency. If corporate leaders backed immigration and funded Americanization projects, the corporate model emphasized standardization, efficiency and immediate results. This led many Progressives to support reforms that called immigrant political power and voting rights into question, at least in the short run.[27] In the longer term, big business proved by the early 1920s an unreliable supporter of the melting pot. Worried about unemployment and about the possibility that new immigrants were proving "revolutionary and communistic races," they equivocated on the openness of immigration, turned Americanizing agencies into labor spy networks, and stopped funding for the corporate-sponsored umbrella group of professional Americanizers and conservative new immigrant leaders, the *Inter-Racial Council.*[28]

Reformers, too, lost heart. Since mixing was never regarded as an unmitigated good but as a matter of proportion with a number of possible outcomes, the new immigrants' record was constantly under scrutiny. The failure of Americanization to deliver total loyalty during World War One and during the postwar "immigrant rebellion" within United States labor made that record one of failure. The "virility," "manhood" and "vigor" that reformers predicted race mixture would inject into the American stock had long coexisted with the emphasis on obedience and docility in Americanization curricula.[29] At their most vigorous, in the 1919–1920 strike wave, new immigrants were most suspect. Nationalists, and many Progressive reformers among them, were, according to John Higham, sure that they had done "their best to bring the great mass of newcomers into the fold." The failure was not theirs, but a reflection of the "incorrigibly unassimilable nature of the material on which they had worked."[30]

The triumph of immigration restriction in the 1920s was in large measure a triumph of *racism* against new immigrants. Congress and the Ku Klux Klan, the media and popular opinion all reinforced the inbetween, and even non-white, racial status of Eastern and Southern Europeans. Grant's *Passing of the Great Race* suddenly enjoyed a vogue which had eluded it in 1916. The best-selling United States magazine, *Saturday Evening Post,* praised Grant and sponsored Kenneth Roberts's massively mounted fears that continued immigration would produce "a hybrid race of people as worthless and futile as the good-for-nothing mongrels of Central America and Southeastern Europe." When the National Industrial Conference Board met in 1923, its director allowed that restriction was "essentially a race question." Congress was deluged with letters of concern for preservation of a "distinct American type" and of support for stopping the "swamping" of the Nordic race. In basing itself on the first fear and setting quotas pegged squarely on the (alleged) origins of the current population, the 1924 restriction act also addressed the second fear, since the United States population as a whole came from the northern and western parts of Europe to a vastly greater extent than had the immigrant population for the last three decades. At virtually the same time that the courts carefully drew a color line between European new immigrants and non-white others, the Congress and reformers reaffirmed the racial inbetween-ness of Southern and Eastern Europeans.[31]

Americanization therefore was never just about nation but always about race and nation. This truth stood out most clearly in the Americanizing influences of popular culture, in which mass market films socialized new immigrants into a "gunfighter nation" of Westerns and a vaudeville nation of blackface; in which popular music was both "incontestably mulatto" and freighted with the hierarchical racial heritage of minstrelsy; in which the most advertised lures of Americanized mass consumption turned on the opportunity to harness the energies of black servants like the Gold Dust twins, Aunt Jemina and Rastus, the Cream of Wheat chef, to household labor. Drawing on a range of anti-immigrant stereotypes as well, popular entertainments and advertisements cast newcomers as nationally particular and racially inbetween, while teaching the all-important lesson that immigrants were never so white as when they wore blackface before audiences and cameras.[32]

Occasionally, professional Americanizers taught the same lesson. In a Polish and Bohemian neighborhood on Chicago's lower west side, for example, social workers at Gads Hill Center counted their 1915 minstrel show a "great success." Organized by the Center's Young Men's Club, the event drew 350 people, many of whom at that point knew so little English that they could only "enjoy the music" and "appreciate the really attractive costumes." Young performers with names like Kraszewski, Pletcha and Chimielewski sang "Clare' De Kitchen" and "Gideon's Band." Settlement houses generally practiced Jim Crow, even in the North. Some of their leading theorists invoked a racial continuum which ended "farthest in the rear" with African Americans even as they goaded new immigrants toward giving up particular Old World cultures by branding the retention of such cultures as an atavistic clinging on to "racial consciousness."[33]

"INBETWEEN" JOBS: CAPITAL, CLASS AND THE NEW IMMIGRANT

Joseph Loguidice's reminiscence of the temporarily "colored" coal hauler compresses and dramatizes a process that went on in far more workaday settings as well. Often while themselves begrimed by the nation's dirtiest jobs, new immigrants and their children quickly learned that "the worst thing one could be in this Promised Land was 'colored.'"[34] But if the world of work taught the importance of being "not black," it also exposed new immigrants to frequent comparisons and close competition with African Americans. The results of such clashes in the labor market did not instantly propel new immigrants into either the category or the consciousness of whiteness. Instead management created an economics of racial inbetween-ness which taught new immigrants the importance of racial hierarchy while leaving open their place in that hierarchy. At the same time the struggle for "inbetween jobs" further emphasized the importance of national and religious ties among immigrants by giving those ties an important economic dimension.

The bitterness of job competition between new immigrants and African Americans has rightly received emphasis in accounting for racial hostility, but that bitterness must be *historically* investigated. Before 1915, new immigrants competed with relatively small numbers of African Americans for northern urban jobs. The new immigrants tended to be more recent arrivals than the black workers, and they came in such great numbers that, demographically speaking, they competed far more often with each other than with African Americans. Moreover, given the much greater "human capital" of black workers in terms of literacy, education and English language skills, immigrants fared well in this competition.[35] After 1915, the decline of immigration resulting from World War One and restrictive legislation in the 1920s combined with the Great Migration of Afro-Southerners to northern cities to create a situation in which a growing and newly arrived black working-class provided massive competition for a more settled but struggling immigrant population. Again, the results were not of a sort that would necessarily have brought bitter disappointment to those whom the economic historians term SCEs (Southern and Central Europeans).[36] The Sicilian immigrant, for example, certainly was at times locked in competition with African Americans. But was that competition more bitter and meaningful than competition with, for example, northern Italian immigrants, "hunkies," or white native-born workers, all of whom were at times said to be *racially* different from Sicilians?

The ways in which capital structured workplaces and labor markets contributed to the idea that competition should be both cutthroat and racialized. New immigrants suffered wage discrimination when compared to the white native born. African Americans were paid less for the same jobs than the immigrants. In the early twentieth century, employers preferred a labor force divided by race and national origins. As the radical cartoonist Ernest Riebe understood at the time, and as the labor economists Richard Edwards, Michael Reich and David Gordon have recently reaffirmed, work gangs segregated by nationality as well as by race could be and were made to compete against each other in a strategy designed not only to undermine labor unity and depress wages in the long run but to spur competition and productivity every day.[37]

On the other hand, management made broader hiring and promotion distinctions which brought pan-national and sometimes racial categories into play. In some workplaces and areas, the blast furnace was a "Mexican job"; in others, it was a pan-Slavic "hunky" job. "Only hunkies," a steel industry investigator was told, worked blast furnace jobs which were "too damn dirty and too damn hot for a white man." Management at the nation's best-studied early twentieth-century factory divided the employees into "white men" and "kikes." Such bizarre notions about the genetic *"fit"* between immigrants and certain types of work were buttressed by the "scientific" judgments of scholars like the sociologist E. A. Ross, who observed that Slavs were "immune to certain kinds of dirt . . . that would kill a white man." "Scientific" managers in steel and in other industries designed elaborate ethnic classification systems to guide their hiring. In 1915 the personnel manager at one Pittsburgh plant analyzed what he called the "racial adaptability" of thirty-six different ethnic groups to twenty-four different kinds of work and twelve sets of conditions and plotted them all on a chart. Lumber companies in Louisiana built what they called "the Quarters" for black workers and (separately) for Italians, using language very recently associated with African-American slavery. For white workers they built company housing and towns. The distinction between "white" native-born workers and "non-white" new immigrants, Mexicans and African Americans in parts of the West rested in large part on the presence of "white man's camps" or "white man's towns" in company housing in lumbering and mining. Native-born residents interviewed in the wake of a bitter 1915 strike by Polish oil refinery workers recognized only two classes of people in Bayonne, New Jersey: "foreigners" and "white men." In generalizing about early twentieth-century nativism, John Higham concludes: "In all sections native-born and Northern European laborers called themselves 'white men' to distinguish themselves from Southern Europeans whom they worked beside." As late as World War Two, new immigrants and their children, lumped together as "racials," suffered employment discrimination in the defense industry.[38]

There was also substantial management interest in the specific comparison of new immigrants with African Americans as workers. More concrete in the North and abstract in the South, these complex comparisons generally, but not always, favored the former group. African-Americans' supposed undependability "especially on Mondays," intolerance for cold, and incapacity of fast-paced work were all noted. But the comparisons were often nuanced. New immigrants, as Herbert Gutman long ago showed, were themselves counted as unreliable, "especially on Mondays." Some employers counted black workers as more apt and skillful "in certain occupations" and cleaner and happier than "the alien white races." An occasional blanket preference for African Americans over immigrants surfaced, as at Packard in Detroit in 1922. Moreover, comparisons carried a provisional quality, since ongoing competition was often desired. In 1905 the superintendent of Illinois Steel, threatening to fire all Slavic workers, reassured the immigrants that no "race hatred" [against Slavs!] motivated the proposed decision, which was instead driven by a factor that the workers could change: their tardiness in adopting the English language.[39]

The fact that recent immigrants were relatively inexperienced *vis-à-vis* African-American workers in the North in 1900 and relatively experienced by 1930 makes it difficult for economic historians to measure the extent to which immigrant economic mobility in this period derived from employer discrimination. Clearly, timing and demographic change mattered alongside racism in a situation in which the immigrant SCEs came to occupy spaces on the job ladder between African Americans below and those who were fed into the economic historians' computers as NWNPs (native-born whites with native-born parents). Stanley Lieberson uses the image of a "queue" to help explain the role of discrimination against African Americans in leading to such results.[40] In the line-up of workers ordered by employer preference, as in so much else, new immigrants were inbetween.

In a society in which workers did in fact shape up in lines to seek jobs, the image of a queue is wonderfully apt. However, the Polish worker next to an African American on one side and an Italian American on the other as an NWNP manager hired unskilled labor did not know the statistics of current job competition, let alone what the results would be by the time of the 1930 census. Even if the Polish worker had known them, the patterns of mobility for his group would likely have differed as much from those of the Italian Americans as from those of the African Americans (who in some cities actually out-distanced Polish immigrants in intra-working-class mobility to better jobs from 1900 to 1930).[41] Racialized struggles over jobs were fed by the general experience of brutal, group-based competition, and by the knowledge that black workers were especially vulnerable competitors who fared far less well in the labor market than any other native-born American group. The young Croatian immigrant Stephan Mesaros was so struck by the abuse of a black coworker that he asked a Serbian laborer for an explanation. "You'll soon learn something about this country," came the reply, "Negroes never get a fair chance." The exchange initiated a series of conversations which contributed to Mesaros becoming Steve Nelson, an influential radical organizer and an anti-racist. But for most immigrants, caught in a world of dog-eat-dog competition, the lesson would likely have been that African Americans were among the eaten.[42]

If immigrants did not know the precise contours of the job queue, nor their prospects in it, they did have their own ideas about how to get on line, their own strategies about how to get ahead in it, and their own dreams for getting out of it. These tended to reinforce a sense of the advantage of being "not nonwhite" but to also emphasize specific national and religious identifications rather than generalized white identity. Because of the presence of a small employing (or subcontracting) class in their communities, new immigrants were far more likely than African Americans to work for one of "their own" as an immediate boss. In New York City, in 1910, for example, almost half of the sample of Jewish workers studied by Suzanne Model had Jewish supervisors, as did about one Italian immigrant in seven. Meanwhile, "the study sample unearthed only one industrial match between laborers and supervisors among Blacks."[43]

In shrugging at being called *hunky*, Thomas Bell writes, Slovak immigrants took solace that they "had come to America to find work and save money, not to make friends with the Irish." But getting work and "making friends with" Irish-American foremen, skilled workers, union leaders and politicians were often very much connected, and the relationships were hardly smooth. Petty bosses could always rearrange the queue.[44] But over the long run, a common Catholicism (and sometimes common political machine affiliations) gave new immigrant groups access to the fragile favor of Irish Americans in positions to influence hiring which African Americans could not achieve. Sometimes such favor was organized, as through the Knights of Columbus in Kansas City packinghouses. Over time, as second-generation marriages across national lines but within the Catholic religion became a pattern, kin joined religion in shaping hiring in ways largely excluding African Americans.[45]

Many of the new immigrant groups also had distinctive plans to move out of the United States wage labor queue altogether. From 1880 to 1930, fully one-third of all Italian immigrants were "birds of passage" who in many cases never intended to stay. This pattern likewise applied to 46 percent of Greeks entering between 1908 and 1923 and to 40 percent of Hungarians entering between 1899 and 1913.[46] Strong national (and sub-national) loyalties obviously persisted in such cases, with saving money to send or take home probably a far higher priority than sorting out the complexities of racial identity in the United States. Similarly, those many new immigrants (especially among the Greeks, Italians and Jews) who hoped to (and did) leave the working class by opening small businesses, set great store in saving, and often catered to a clientele composed mainly of their own group.

But immigrant saving itself proved highly racialized, as did immigrant small business in many instances. Within United States culture, African Americans symbolized prodigal lack of savings as the Chinese, Italians and Jews did fanatical obsession with saving. Popular racist mythology held that, if paid a dollar and a quarter, Italians would spend only the quarter while African Americans would spend a dollar and a half. Characteristically, racial common sense cast both patterns as pathological.[47]

Moreover, in many cases Jewish and Italian merchants sold to African-American customers. Their "middleman minority" status revealingly identifies an inbetween position which, as aggrieved Southern "white" merchants complained, rested on a more humane attitude toward black customers and on such cultural affinities as an eagerness to participate in bargaining over prices. Chinese merchants have traditionally and Korean merchants more recently occupied a similar position. Yet, as an 1897 New York City correspondent for *Harper's Weekly* captured in an article remarkable for its precise balancing of anti-black and anti-Semitic racism, the middleman's day-to-day position in the marketplace reinforced specific Jewish identity and distance from blacks. "For a student of race characteristics," the reporter wrote, "nothing could be more striking than to observe the stoic scorn of the Hebrew when he is made a disapproving witness of the happy-go-lucky joyousness of his dusky neighbor."[48]

Other immigrants, especially Slovaks and Poles, banked on hard labor, homeownership and slow intergenerational mobility for success. They too navigated in very tricky racial cross-currents. Coming from areas in which the dignity of hard, physical labor was established, both in the countryside and in cities, they arrived in the United States eager to work, even if in jobs which did not take advantage of their skills. They often found, however, that in the Taylorizing industries of the United States, hard work was more driven and alienating.[49] It was, moreover, often typed and despised as "nigger work"—or as "dago work" or "hunky work" in settings in which such categories had been freighted with the prior meaning of "nigger work." The new immigrants' reputation for hard work and their unfamiliarity with English and with American culture generally tended to lead to their being hired as an almost abstract source of labor. *Hunky* was abbreviated to *hunk* and Slavic laborers in particular treated as mere pieces of work. This had its advantages, especially in comparison to black workers; Slavs could more often get hired in groups while skilled workers and petty bosses favored individual "good Negroes" with unskilled jobs, often requiring a familiarity and subservience from them not expected of new immigrants. But being seen as brute force also involved Eastern Europeans in particularly brutal social relations on the shopfloor.[50]

Hard work, especially when closely bossed, was likewise not a badge of manliness in the United States in the way that it had been in Eastern Europe. Racialized, it was also demasculinized, especially since its extremely low pay and sporadic nature ensured that new immigrant males could not be breadwinners for a family. The idea of becoming a "white man," unsullied by racially typed labor and capable of earning a family wage, was therefore extremely attractive in many ways, and the imperative of not letting one's job become "nigger work" was swiftly learned.[51] Yet, no clear route ran from inbetweenness to white manhood. "White men's unions" often seemed the best path, but they also erected some of the most significant obstacles.

WHITE MEN'S UNIONS AND
NEW IMMIGRANT TRIAL MEMBERS

While organized labor exercised little control over hiring outside of a few organized crafts during most of the years from 1895 until 1924 and beyond, its racialized opposition to new immigrants did reinforce their inbetweenness, both on the job and in politics. Yet the American Federation of Labor also provided an important venue in which "old immigrant" workers interacted with new immigrants, teaching important lessons in both whiteness and Americanization.

As an organization devoted to closing skilled trades to any new competition, the craft union's reflex was to oppose outsiders. In this sense, most of the AFL unions were "exclusionary by definition" and marshaled economic, and to a lesser extent political, arguments to exclude women, Chinese, Japanese, African Americans, the illiterate, the non-citizen, and the new immigrants from organized workplaces, and, whenever possible, from the shores of the United States. So clear was the craft logic of AFL restriction-ism that historians are apt to regard it as simply materialistic and to note its racism only when direct assaults were made on groups traditionally regarded as non-white. John Higham argues that only in the last moments of the major 1924 debates over whom to restrict did Gompers, in this view, reluctantly embrace "the idea that European immigration endangered America's racial foundations."[52]

Yet Gwendolyn Mink and Andrew Neather demonstrate that it is far more difficult than Higham implies to separate appeals based on craft or race in AFL campaigns to restrict European immigration. A great deal of trade unions' racist opposition to the Chinese stressed the connection between their "slave-like" subservience and their status as coolie laborers, schooled and trapped in the Chinese social system and willing to settle for being "cheap men."[53] Dietary practices (rice and rats rather than meat) symbolized Chinese failure to seek the "American standard of living." All of these are cultural, historical and environmental matters. Yet none of them prevented the craft unions from declaring the Chinese "race" unassimilable nor from supporting exclusionary legislation premised largely on racial grounds. The environmentalist possibility that over generations Asian "cheap men" might improve was simply irrelevant. By that time the Chinese race would have polluted America.[54]

Much of anti-Chinese rhetoric was applied as well to Hungarians in the 1880s and was taken over in AFL anti-new immigration campaigns after 1890. Pasta, as Mink implies, joined rice as an "un-American" and racial-ized food. Far from abjuring arguments based on "stock," assimilability and homogeneity, the AFL's leaders supported literacy tests designed specifically "to reduce the numbers of Slavic and Mediterranean immigrants." They sup-ported the nativist racism of the anti-labor Sen. Henry Cabot Lodge, hoped anti-Japanese agitation could be made to contribute to anti-new immigrant restrictions, emphasized "the incompatibility of the new immigrants with the very nature of American civilization," and both praised and reprinted works on "race suicide."[55] They opposed entry of "the scum" from "the least civilized countries of Europe" and "the replacing of the independent and intelligent coal miners of Pennsylvania by the Huns and Slavs." They feared that an "American" miner in Pennsylvania could thrive only if he "Latinizes" his name. They explicitly asked, well before World War One:

"How much more [new] immigration can this country absorb and retain its homogeneity?" (Those wanting to know the dire answer were advised to study the "racial history" of cities.)[56]

Robert Asher is undoubtedly correct in arguing both that labor movement reaction to new immigrants was "qualitatively different from the response to Orientals" *and* that AFL rhetoric was "redolent of a belief in racial inferiority" of Southern and Eastern Europeans. Neather is likewise on the mark in speaking of "semi-racial" union arguments for restriction directed against new immigrants.[57] Gompers' characterization of new immigrants as "beaten men of beaten races" perfectly captures the tension between fearing that Southern and Eastern Europe was dumping its "vomit" and "scum" in the United States and believing that Slavic and Mediterranean people were scummy. Labor sometimes cast its ideal as an "Anglo–Saxon race . . . true to itself." Gompers was more open, but equivocal. He found that the wonderful "peculiarities of temperament such as patriotism, sympathy, etc.," which made labor unionism possible, were themselves "peculiar to most of the Caucasian race." In backing literacy tests for immigrants in 1902, he was more explicit. They would leave British, German, Irish, French and Scandinavian immigration intact but "shut out a considerable number of Slavs and other[s] equally or more undesirable and injurious."[58]

Such "semi-racial" nativism shaped the AFL's politics and led to exclusion of new immigrants from many unions. When iron puddlers' poet Michael McGovern envisioned an ideal celebration for his union, he wrote,

> There were no men invited such as Slavs and "Tally Annes," Hungarians
> and Chinamen with pigtail cues and fans.

The situation in the building trades was complicated. Some craft unions excluded Italians, Jews and other new immigrants. Among laborers, organization often began on an ethnic basis, though such immigrant locals were often eventually integrated into a national union. Even among craftsmen, separate organizations emerged among Jewish carpenters and painters and other recent immigrants. The hod carriers union, according to Asher, "appears to have been created to protect the jobs of native construction workers against competing foreigners." The shoeworkers, pianomakers, barbers, hotel and restaurant workers and United Textile Workers likewise kept out new immigrants, whose lack of literacy, citizenship, English-language skills, apprenticeship opportunities and initiation fees also effectively barred them from many other craft locals. This "internal protectionism" apparently had lasting results. Lieberson's research through 1950 shows new immigrants and their children having far less access to craft jobs in unionized sectors than did whites of northwestern European origin.[59]

Yet Southern and Eastern European immigrants had more access to unionized work than African Americans and unions never supported outright bans on their migration, as they did with Asians. Organized labor's opposition to the Italians as the "white Chinese," or to recent immigrants generally as "white coolies" usually acknowledged and questioned whiteness at the same time, associating whites with non-whites while leaving open the possibility that contracted labor, and not race, was at issue. A strong emphasis on the "brotherhood" of labor also complicated matters. Paeans to the "International Fraternity of Labor" ran in the *American Federationist* within fifteen pages of anti-immigrant hysteria such as A. A. Graham's "The un-Americanizing of America." Reports from Italian labor leaders and poems like "Brotherhood of Man" ran hard by fearful predictions of race suicide.[60]

Moreover, the very things that the AFL warned about in its anti-immigrant campaigns encouraged the unions to make tactical decisions to enroll Southern and Eastern Europeans as members. Able to legally enter the country in large numbers, secure work, and become voters, *hunkies* and *guineas* had social power which could be used to attack the craft unionism of the AFL from the right or, as was often feared, from the left. To restrict immigration, however desirable from Gompers' point of view, did not answer what to do about the majority of the working class which was by 1910 already of immigrant origins. Nor did it speak to what to do about the many new immigrants already joining unions, in the AFL, in language and national federations or under socialist auspices. If these new immigrants were not going to undermine the AFL's appeals to corporate leaders as an effective moderating force within the working class, the American Federation of Labor would have to consider becoming the Americanizing Federation of Labor.[61]

Most importantly, changes in machinery and Taylorizing relations of production made real the threat that crafts could be undermined by expedited training of unskilled and semi-skilled immigrant labor. While this threat gave force to labor's nativist calls for immigration restriction, it also strengthened initiatives toward a "new unionism" which crossed skill lines to organize recent immigrants. Prodded by independent, dual-unionist initiatives like those by Italian socialists and the United Hebrew Trades, by the example of existing industrial unions in its own ranks, and by the left-wing multinational, multi-racial unionism of the Industrial Workers of the World, the AFL increasingly got into the business of organizing and Americanizing new immigrant workers in the early twentieth century. The logic, caught perfectly by a Lithuanian-American packinghouse worker in Chicago, was often quite utilitarian:

> because those sharp foremen are inventing new machines and the work is easier to learn, and so these slow Lithuanians and even green girls can learn to do it, and the Americans and Germans and Irish are put out and the employer saves money. . . . This was why the American labor unions began to organize us all.

Even so, especially in those where new immigrant women were the potential union members and skill dilution threatened mainly immigrant men, the Gompers' leadership at times refused either to incorporate dual unions or to initiate meaningful organizing efforts under AFL auspices.[62]

However self-interested, wary and incomplete the AFL's increasing opening to new immigrant workers remained, it initiated a process which much transformed "semi-racial" typing of recently arrived immigrants. Unions and their supporters at times treasured labor organization as the most meaningful agent of democratic "Americanization from the bottom up," what John R. Commons called "The only effective Americanizing force for the southeastern European."[63] In struggles, native-born unionists came to observe not only the common humanity, but also the heroism of new immigrants. Never quite giving up on biological/cultural explanations, labor leaders wondered which "race" made the best strikers, with some comparisons favoring the recent arrivals over Anglo-Saxons. Industrial Workers of the World leader Covington Hall's reports from Louisiana remind us that we know little about how unionists, and workers generally, conceived of race. Hall took seriously the idea of a "Latin race," including Italians, other Southern Europeans *and Mexicans*, all of whom put Southern whites to shame with their militancy.[64] In the rural west, a "white man," labor investigator Peter Speek wrote, "is an extreme individualist, busy with himself," a "native or old-time immigrant" laborer, boarded by employers. "A foreigner," he added, "is more sociable and has a higher sense of comradeship" and of nationality. Embracing the very racial vocabulary to which he objected, one socialist plasterer criticized native-born unionists who described Italians as *guineas*. He pointed out that Italians' ancestors "were the best and unsurpassable in manhood's glories; at a time when our dads were running about in paint and loincloth as ignorant savages." To bring the argument up to the present, he added that Italian Americans "are as manly for trade union conditions as the best of us; and that while handicapped by our prejudice."[65]

While such questioning of whiteness was rare, the "new unionism" provided an economic logic for progressive unionists wishing to unite workers
across ethnic and racial lines. With their own race less open to question, new
immigrants were at times brought into class conscious coalitions, as whites
and with African Americans. The great success of the packinghouse unions
in forging such unity during World War One ended in a shining victory and
vastly improved conditions. The diverse new immigrants and black workers
at the victory celebration heard Chicago Federation of Labor leader John
Fitzpatrick hail them as "black and white together under God's sunshine." If
the Irish-American unionists had often been bearers of "race hatred" against
both new immigrants and blacks, they and other old immigrants also could
convey the lesson that class unity transcended race and semi-race.[66]

But even at the height of openings toward new unionism and new immigrants, labor organizations taught very complex lessons regarding race. At
times, overtures toward new immigrants coincided with renewed exclusion
of nonwhite workers, underlining W.E.B. DuBois's point that the former
were mobbed to make them join unions and the latter to keep them out.
Western Federation of Miners (WFM) activists, whose episodic radicalism
coexisted with nativism and a consistent anti-Chinese and anti-Mexican racism, gradually developed a will and a strategy to organize Greek immigrants,
but they reaffirmed exclusion of Japanese mine workers and undermined
impressive existing solidarities between Greeks and Japanese, who often
worked similar jobs.[67] The fear of immigrant "green hands," which the
perceptive Lithuanian immigrant quoted above credited with first sparking
the Butcher Workmen to organize recent immigrants in 1904 was also a fear
of black hands, so that one historian has suggested that the desire to limit
black employment generated the willingness to organize new immigrants.[68]

In 1905, Gompers promised that "caucasians are not going to let their
standard of living be destroyed by negroes, Chinamen, Japs, or any others."[69] Hearing this, new immigrant unionists might have reflected on what
they as "caucasians" had to learn regarding their newfound superiority to
non-whites. Or they might have fretted that *guineas* and *hunkies* would be
classified along with "any others" undermining white standards. Either
way, learning about race was an important part of new immigrants' labor
education.

Teaching Americanism, the labor movement also taught whiteness. The
scattered racist jokes in the labor and socialist press could not, of course,
rival blackface entertainments or the "coon songs" in the Sunday comics
in teaching new immigrants the racial ropes of the United States, but the

movement did provide a large literature of popularized racist ethnology, editorial attacks on "nigger equality" and in Jack London, a major cultural figure who taught that it was possible and desirable to be "first of all a white man and only then a socialist."[70]

But the influence of organized labor and the left on race thinking was far more focused on language than on literature, on picket lines than lines on a page. Unions which opened to new immigrants more readily than to "nonwhites" not only reinforced the "inbetween" position of Southern and Eastern Europeans but attempted to teach immigrants intricate and spurious associations of race, strikebreaking and lack of manly pride. Even as AFL exclusionism ensured that there would be black strikebreakers and black suspicion of unions, the language of labor equated scabbing with "turning nigger." The unions organized much of their critique around a notion of "slavish" behavior which could be employed against ex-slaves or against Slavs, but indicted the former more often than the latter.[71] Warning all union men against "slave-like" behavior, unions familiarized new workers with the ways race and slavery had gone together to define a standard of unmanned servility. In objectively confusing situations, with scabs coming from the African-American, immigrant and native-born working classes (and with craft unions routinely breaking each others' strikes), Booker T. Washington identified one firm rule of thumb: "Strikers seem to consider it a much greater crime for a Negro who had been denied the opportunity to work at his trade to take the place of a striking employee than for a white man to do the same thing."[72]

In such situations, whiteness had its definite appeals. But the left and labor movements could abruptly remind new immigrants that their whiteness was anything but secure. Jack London could turn from denunciations of the "yellow peril" or of African Americans to excoriations of "the dark-pigmented things" coming in from Europe. The 1912 Socialist party campaign book connected European immigration with "race annihilation" and the "possible degeneration of even the succeeding American type." The prominence of black strikebreakers in several of the most important mass strikes after World War One strengthened the grip of racism, perhaps even among recent immigrants, but the same years also brought renewed racial attacks on the immigrants themselves. In the wake of these failed strikes, the *American Federationist* featured disquisitions on "Americanism and Immigration" by John Quinn, the National Commander of the nativist and anti-labor American Legion. New immigrants had unarguably proven the most loyal unionists in the most important of the strikes, yet the AFL now supported exclusion based on "racial" quotas. Quinn brought together biology, environment and the racialized history of the United States, defending American stock against Italian "industrial slaves" particularly and the "indigestion of immigration" generally.[73]

INBETWEEN AND INDIFFERENT:
NEW IMMIGRANT RACIAL CONSCIOUSNESS

One Italian-American informant interviewed by a Louisiana scholar remembered the early twentieth century as a time when "he and his family had been badly mistreated by a French plantation owner near New Roads where he and his family were made to live among the Negroes and were treated in the same manner. At first he did not mind because he did not know any difference, but when he learned the position that the Negroes occupied in this country, he demanded that his family be moved to a different house and be given better treatment." In denouncing all theories of white supremacy, the Polish language Chicago-based newspaper *Dziennik Chicagoski* editorialized, "if the words 'superior race' are replaced by the words 'Anglo-Saxon' and instead of 'inferior races' such terms as Polish, Italian, Russian and Slavs in general—not to mention the Negro, the Chinese, and the Japanese—are applied, then we shall see the political side of the racial problems in the United States in stark nakedness."[74] In the first instance, consciousness of an inbetween racial status leads to a desire for literal distance from non-whites. In the second, inbetweenness leads to a sense of grievances shared in common with non-whites.

In moving from the racial categorization of new immigrants to their own racial consciousness, it is important to realize that "Europeans were hardly likely to have found racist ideologies an astounding new encounter when they arrived in the U.S.," though the salience of whiteness as a social category in the United States was exceptional. "Civilized" Northern Italians derided those darker ones from Sicily and the *mezzogiorno* as "Turks" and "Africans" long before arriving in Brooklyn or Chicago. And once arrived, if they spoke of "little dark fellows," they were far more likely to be describing Southern Italians than African Americans. The strength of anti-Semitism, firmly ingrained in Poland and other parts of Eastern Europe meant that many immigrants from these regions were accustomed to looking at a whole "race" of people as devious, degraded, and dangerous. In the United States, both Jews and Poles spoke of riots involving attacks on African Americans as "pogroms." In an era of imperialist expansion and sometimes strident nationalism, a preoccupation with race was characteristic not only of the United States but also of many European regions experiencing heavy emigration to the United States.[75]

Both eager embraces of whiteness and, more rarely, flirtations with non-whiteness characterized these immigrants' racial identity. But to assume that new immigrants as a mass clearly saw their identity with non-whites or clearly fastened on their differences is to miss the confusion of inbetweenness. The discussion of whiteness was an uncomfortable terrain for many reasons and even in separating themselves from African Americans and Asian Americans, immigrants did not necessarily become white. Indeed, often they were curiously indifferent to whiteness.

Models that fix on one extreme or the other of immigrant racial consciousness—the quick choice of whiteness amidst brutal competition or the solidarity with non-white working people based on common oppression—capture parts of the new immigrant experience.[76] At times Southern and Eastern Europeans were exceedingly apt, and not very critical, students of American racism. Greeks admitted to the Western Federation of Miners saw the advantage of their membership and did not rock the boat by demanding admission for the Japanese American mine workers with whom they had previously allied. Greek Americans sometimes battled for racial status fully within the terms of white supremacy, arguing that classical civilization had established them as "the highest type of the caucasian race." In the company town of Pullman and adjacent neighborhoods, immigrants who sharply divided on national and religious lines coalesced impressively as whites in 1928 to keep out African-American residents.[77] Recently arrived Jewish immigrants on New York City's Lower East Side resented reformers who encouraged them to make a common cause with the "schwartzes." In New Bedford, "white Portuguese" angrily reacted to perceived racial slights and sharply drew the color line against "black Portuguese" Cape Verdeans, especially when preference in jobs and housing hung in the balance.[78] Polish workers may have developed their very self-image and honed their reputation in more or less conscious counterpoint to the stereotypical *niggerscab*. Theodore Radzialowski reasons that "Poles who had so little going for them (except their white skin—certainly no mean advantage but more important later than earlier in their American experience), may have grasped this image of themselves as honest, honorable, non-scabbing workers and stressed the image of the black scab in order to distinguish themselves from . . . the blacks with whom they shared the bottom of American society."[79]

Many new immigrants learned to deploy and manipulate white supremacist images from the vaudeville stage and the screens of Hollywood films
where they saw "their own kind" stepping out of conventional racial and
gender roles through blackface and other forms of cross-dress. "Facing
nativist pressure that would assign them to the dark side of the racial divide,"
Michael Ragin argues provocatively, immigrant entertainers like Al Jolson,
Sophie Tucker and Rudolph Valentino, "Americanized themselves by crossing and recrossing the racial line."[80]

At the same time, immigrants sometimes hesitated to embrace a white
identity. Houston's Greek Americans developed, and retained, a language
setting themselves apart from *i mavri* (the blacks), from *i aspri* (the whites)
and from Mexican Americans. In New England, Greeks worked in coalitions with Armenians, whom the courts were worriedly accepting as white,
and Syrians, whom the courts found non-white. The large Greek-American
sponge fishing industry based in Tarpon Springs, Florida, fought the Ku
Klux Klan and employed black workers on an equal, share-the-catch system. Nor did Tarpon Springs practice Jim Crow in public transportation.
In Louisiana and Mississippi, southern Italians learned Jim Crow tardily,
even when legally accepted as whites, so much so that native whites fretted
and black Southerners "made unabashed distinctions between Dagoes and
white folks," treating the former with a "friendly, first name familiarity."
In constructing an anti-Nordic supremacist history series based on "gifts"
of various peoples, the Knights of Columbus quickly and fully included
African Americans. Italian and Italian-American radicals "consistently
expressed horror at the barbaric treatment of blacks," in part because "Italians were also regarded as an inferior race." Denouncing not only lynchings
but "the republic of lynchings" and branding the rulers of the United States
as "savages of the blue eyes," *Il Proletario* asked: "What do they think they
are as a race, these arrogant whites?" and ruthlessly wondered, "and how
many kisses have their women asked for from the strong and virile black
servants?" Italian radicals knew exactly how to go for the jugular vein in
United States race relations. The Jewish press at times identified with both
the suffering and the aspirations of African Americans. In 1912, Chicago's
Daily Jewish Courier concluded that "In this world . . . the Jew is treated
as a Negro and Negro as a Jew" and that the "lynching of the Negroes in
the South is similar to massacres on Jews in Russia."[81]

Examples could, and should, be piled higher on both sides of the new
immigrants' racial consciousness. But to see the matter largely in terms of

which stack is higher misses the extent to which the exposed position of racial inbetweenness could generate both positions at once, and sometimes a desire to avoid the issue of race entirely. The best frame of comparison for discussing new immigrant racial consciousness is that of the Irish Americans in the mid-nineteenth century. Especially when not broadly accepted as such, Irish Americans insisted that politicians acknowledge them as part of the dominant race. Changing the political subject from American-ness and religion to race whenever possible, they challenged anti-Celtic Anglo-Saxonism by becoming leaders in the cause of white supremacy.[82] New immigrant leaders never approximated that path. With a large segment of both parties willing to vouch for the possibility of speedy, orderly Americanization and with neither party willing to vouch unequivocally for their racial character, Southern and Eastern Europeans generally tried to change the subject from whiteness to nationality and loyalty to American ideals.

One factor in such a desire not to be drawn into debates about whiteness was a strong national/cultural identification as Jews, Italians, Poles and so on. At times, the strongest tie might even be to a specific Sicilian or Slova-kian village, but the first sustained contact between African Americans and "new immigrants" occurred during World War One when many of these immigrants were mesmerized by the emergence of Poland and other new states throughout eastern and southeastern Europe. Perhaps this is why new immigrants in Chicago and other riot-torn cities seem to have abstained from early twentieth-century race riots, to a far greater extent than theories connecting racial violence and job competition at "the bottom" of society would predict. Important Polish spokespersons and newspapers empha-sized that Chicago riots were between the "whites" and "Negroes." Polish immigrants had, and should have, no part in them. What might be termed an *abstention from whiteness* also characterized the practice of rank-and-file East Europeans. Slavic immigrants played little role in the racial violence which was spread by Irish-American gangs.[83]

Throughout the Chicago riot, so vital to the future of Slavic packinghouse workers and their union, Polish-American coverage was sparse and occurred only when editors "could tear their attention away from their fascination with the momentous events attending the birth of the new Polish state." And even then, comparisons with pogroms against Jews in Poland framed the discussion. That the defense of Poland was as important as analyzing the realities in Chicago emerges starkly in the convoluted expression of sympathy for riot victims in the organ of the progressive, pro-labor Alliance of Polish Women, *Glos Polek*:

> The American Press has written at length about the alleged pogroms of Jews in Poland for over two months. Now it is writing about pogroms against Blacks in America. It wrote about the Jews in words full of sorrow and sympathy, why does it not show the same today to Negroes being burnt and killed without mercy?[84]

Both "becoming American" and "becoming white" could imply coercive threats to European national identities. The 1906 remarks of Luigi Villari, an Italian government official investigating Sicilian sharecroppers in Louisiana, illustrate the gravity and inter-relation of both processes. Villari found that "a majority of plantation owners cannot comprehend that . . . Italians are white," and instead considered the Sicilian migrant "a white-skinned negro who is a better worker than the black-skinned negro." He patiently explained the "commonly held distinction . . . between 'negroes,' 'Italians' and 'whites' (that is, Americans)." In the South, he added, the "American will not engage in agricultural, manual labor, rather he leaves it to the negroes. Seeing that the Italians will do this work, naturally he concludes that Italians lack dignity. The only way an Italian can emancipate himself from this inferior state is to abandon all sense of national pride and to identify completely with the Americans."[85]

One hundred percent whiteness and one hundred percent Americanism carried overlapping and confusing imperatives for new immigrants in and out of the South, but in several ways the former was even more uncomfortable terrain than the latter. The pursuit of white identity, so tied to competition for wage labor and to political citizenship, greatly privileged male perceptions. But identity formation, as Americanizers and immigrant leaders realized, rested in great part on the activities of immigrant mothers, who entered discussions of nationality and Americanization more easily than those of race.[86] More cast in determinism, the discourse of race produced fewer openings to inject class demands, freedom and cultural pluralism than did the discourse of Americanism. The modest strength of herrenvolk democracy, weakened even in the South at a time when huge numbers of the white poor were disfranchised, paled in comparison to the opportunities to try to give progressive spin to the idea of a particularly freedom-loving "American race."

In a fascinating quantified sociological study of Poles in Buffalo in the mid-1920s, Niles Carpenter and Daniel Katz concluded that their interviewees had been "Americanized" without being "de-Polandized." Their data led to the conclusion that Polish immigrants displayed "an absence of strong feeling so far as the Negro is concerned," a pattern "certainly in contrast to the results which would be sure to follow the putting of similar questions to a typically American group." The authors therefore argued for "the inference that so-called race feeling in this country is much more a product of tensions and quasi-psychoses born of our own national experience than of any factors inherent in the relations of race to race." Their intriguing characterization of Buffalo's Polish community did not attempt to cast its racial views as "pro-Negro" but instead pointed out that "the bulk of its members express indifference towards him." Such indifference, noted also by other scholars, was the product not of unfamiliarity with, or distance from, the United States racial system, but of nationalism compounded by intense, harrowing and contradictory experiences inbetween whiteness and non-whiteness.[87] Only after the racial threat of new immigration was defused by the racial restriction of the Johnson-Reed Act would new immigrants haltingly find a place in the ethnic wing of the white race.

This brief treatment of a particularly complicated issue necessarily leaves out a number of key episodes especially in the latter stages of the story. One is a resolution of sorts in the ambiguous status of inbetween immigrant workers which came in the late 1930s and the World War II era. In some settings these years brought not only a greater emphasis on cultural pluralism and a new, broader language of Americanism that embraced working-class ethnics, but also a momentary lull in racial conflict. With the creation of strong, interracial industrial unions, African-American local officials and shop stewards fought for civil rights at the same time they led white "ethnic" workers in important industrial struggles.[88] Yet in other settings, sometimes even in the same cities, the war years and the period immediately following brought riots and hate strikes over the racial integration of workplaces and, particularly, neighborhoods. Most second-generation ethnics embraced their Americanness, but, as Gary Gerstle suggests, this "may well have intensified their prejudice against Blacks, for many conceived of Americanization in racial terms: becoming American meant becoming white."[89]

During the 1970s a later generation of white ethnics rediscovered their ethnic identities in the midst of a severe backlash against civil rights legislation and new movements for African-American liberation.[90] The relationship between this defensive mentality and more recent attacks on affirmative action programs and civil rights legislation underscores the contemporary importance in understanding how and why these once inbetween immigrant workers became white.

NOTES

1. The epigraph is from John A. Fitch, *The Steel Workers* (New York, 1910), p. 147. Joe Sauris, Interview with Joseph Loguidice, 25 July 1980, Italians in Chicago Project, copy of transcript, Box 6, Immigration History Research Center, University of Minnesota, St. Paul, Minn. Such a sprawling essay would be impossible without help from students and colleagues, especially regarding sources. Thanks go to David Montgomery, Steven Rosswurm, Susan Porter Benson, Randy McBee, Neil Gotanda, Peter Rachleff, Noel Ignatiev, the late Peter Tamony, Louise Edwards, Susan Hirsch, Isaiah McCaffery, Rudolph Vecoli, Hyman Berman, Sal Salerno, Louise O'Brien, Liz Pleck, Mark Leff, Toby Higbie, Micaela di Leonardo, Dana Frank, and the Social History Group at the University of Illinois.

2. See, for example, Gerald Rosenblum, *Immigrant Workers: Their Impact On American Labor Radicalism* (New York, 1973); C.T. Husbands, "Editor's Introductory Essay," to Werner Sombart, *Why Is There No Socialism In The United States?* (White Plains, New York, 1976), p. xxix.

3. Robert Orsi, "The Religious Boundaries of an Inbetween People: Street *Feste* and the Problem of the Dark-Skinned 'Other' in Italian Harlem, 1920–1990," *American Quarterly,* 44 (September 1992): 335. Michael Omi and Howard Winant, *Racial Formation In The United States: From The 1960s To The 1980s* (New York and London, 1986), pp. 64–65; Gary Gerstle, "Working Class Racism: Broaden the Focus," *International Labor And Working Class History* 44 (1993): 38–39.

4. Sombart, *No Socialism,* pp. 27–28; Stanford M. Lyman, "Race Relations as Social Process: Sociology's Resistance to a Civil Rights Orientation," in Herbert Hill and James E. Jones, Jr., *Race In America: The Struggle For Equality* (Madison, Wisc. 1993), pp. 374–83; cf. Omi and Winant, *Racial Formation,* pp. 15–17, for useful complications on this score; Thomas F. Gossett, *Race: The History Of An Idea in America* (Dallas, 1963); Barbara Solomon, *Ancestors And Immigrants* (Cambridge, Mass., 1956); Gloria A. Marshall, "Racial Classification: Popular and Scientific," in *The "Racial" Economy Of Science,* ed. Sandra Harding (Bloomington and Indianapolis, Ind., 1993), pp. 123–24. On Park, race and ethnicity, see also Omi and Winant, *Racial Formation,* pp. 15–17; Stow Persons, *Ethnic Studies at Chicago, 1905–1945* (Urbana, Ill., 1987), p. 602.

5. For historical invocations of "ethnicity" to explain situations experienced at the time as racial, in otherwise brilliant works, see Mary C. Waters, *Ethnic Options: Choosing Identities In America* (Berkeley, 1990), p. 79, and Werner Sollors, *Beyond Ethnicity; Consent And Descent In American Culture* (New York, 1986), pp. 38–39. See also Michael Banton, *Racial Theories* (Cambridge, 1988), and David Theo Goldberg, "The Semantics of Race," *Ethnic And Racial Studies,* 15 (October 1992): esp. 554–55. The most devastating critique of the "cult of ethnicity" remains Alexander Saxton's review essay on Nathan Glazer's *Affirmative Discrimination* in *Amerasia Journal,* 4 (1977): 141–50. See also Gwendolyn Mink, *Old Labor And New Immigrants In American Political Development* (Ithaca, N.Y., 1986), esp. p. 46, n. 1.

6. Peggy Pascoe, "Miscegenation Law, Court Cases, and Ideologies of 'Race' in Twentieth
Century America," *Journal of American History,* 83 (June 1996): 44–69; Peggy Pascoe,
"Race, Gender, and Intercultural Relations: The Case of Interracial Marriage," *Frontiers: A
Journal of Women's Studies,* 12 (1991): 5–17, quotes); Paul Spickard, *Mixed Blood,* Appendix
A, pp. 374–75; see Paul Siu, *The Chinese Laundryman: A Study Of Social Isolation* (New
York, 1987), pp. 143, 250–271.

7. We borrow "inbetween" from Orsi, "Religious Boundaries of an Inbetween People,"
passim and also from John Higham, *Strangers In The Land: Patterns Of American Nativism,
1860–1925* (New York, 1974), p. 169. Herbert Gutman with Ira Berlin, "Class Composition and the Development of the American Working Class, 1840–1890," in Gutman, *Power
And Culture: Essays On The American Working Class,* ed. Ira Berlin, (New York, 1987),
pp. 380–94, initiates vital debate on immigration and the "remaking" of the United States
working class over time. We occasionally use the phrase "new immigrants," the same one
contemporaries sometimes employed to distinguish more recent—and "less desirable"—from
earlier immigrant peoples, but we do so critically. To use the term indiscriminately tends
not only to render Asian, Latin, and other non-European immigrants invisible, but also to
normalize a racialized language we are trying to explicate.

8. Lawrence Glickman, "Inventing the 'American Standard of Living': Gender, Race and
Working-class Identity, 1880–1925," *Labor History,* 34 (Spring–Summer, 1993): 221–35;
David Montgomery, *Beyond Equality: Labor And The Radical Republicans, 1862–1872*
(Urbana, Ill., 1981), p. 254. Richard Williams, *Hierarchical Structures And Social Value: The
Creation Of Black And Irish Identities In The United States* (New York, 1990); Thompson,
Customs In Common: Studies In Traditional Popular Culture (New York, 1993), p. 320.

9. On *guinea's* history, see Roediger, "*Guineas, Wiggers* and the Dramas of Racialized
Culture," *American Literary History,* 7 (Winter 1995): 654–68. On post-1890 usages, see
William Harlen Gilbert, Jr., "Memorandum Concerning the Characteristics of the Larger
Mixed-Blood Islands of the United States," *Social Forces,* 24 (March 1946): 442; *Oxford
English Dictionary,* 2d ed. (Oxford, 1989), 6: 937–38; Frederic G. Cassidy and Joan Houston
Hall, eds., *Dictionary Of American Regional English* (Cambridge and London, 1991), 2:
838; Harold Wentworth and Stuart Berg Flexner, *Dictionary of American Slang* (New York,
1975), p. 234 and Peter J. Tamony, research notes on *guinea,* Tamony Collection, Western
Historical Manuscripts Collection, University of Missouri, Columbia.

10. Tamony's notes on *hunky* (or *hunkie*) speculate on links to *hankie* (or *hanky*) and
refer to the former as an "old labor term." By no means did Hun refer unambiguously to
Germans before World War I. See, e.g., Henry White, "Immigration Restriction as a Necessity," *American Federationist,* 4 (June 1897): 67; Paul Krause, *The Battle For Homestead,
1880–1892: Politics, Culture And Steel* (Pittsburgh, 1992), pp. 216–17; Stan Kemp, *Boss
Tom: The Annals Of An Anthracite Mining Village* (Akron, Ohio: 1904), p. 258; Thames Wil-
liamson, *Hunky* (New York, 1929), slipcover; Thomas Bell's *Out Of This Furnace* (Pittsburgh,
1976; originally 1941), pp. 124–25; David Brody, *Steelworkers In America* (New York,
1969), pp. 120–121; Josef Barton, *Peasants And Strangers* (Cambridge, Mass., 1975), p.
20. Theodore Radzialowski, "The Competition for Jobs and Racial Stereotypes: Poles and
Blacks in Chicago," *Polish American Studies,* 22 (Autumn 1976): n. 7. Sinclair, *Singing
Jailbirds* (Pasadena, 1924). Remarks regarding *mill hunky* in the 1970s are based on Barrett's anecdotal observations in and around Pittsburgh at the time. See also the *Mill Hunk
Herald,* published in Pittsburgh throughout the late 1970s.

11. Dollard, *Caste And Class In A Southern Town* (Garden City, N.Y., 1949), p. 93; Barry Goldberg, "Historical Reflections on Transnationalism, Race, and the American Immigrant Saga" (unpublished paper delivered at the Rethinking Migration, Race, Ethnicity, and Nationalism in Historical Perspective Conferences, New York Academy of the Sciences, May, 1990). Confusion regarding citations has in the past led David Roediger to attribute "not yet white ethnic" to immigration historian John Bukowczyk rather than Goldberg.

12. Albert S. Broussard, "George Albert Flippin and Race Relations in a Western Rural Community," *The Midwest Review,* 12 (1990): 15, n. 42; J. Alexander Karlin, "The Halo-American Incident of 1891 and the Road to Reunion," *Journal Of Southern History,* 8 (1942); Gunther Peck, "Padrones and Protest: 'Old' Radicals and 'New' Immigrants in Bingham, Utah, 1905–1912," *Western Historical Quarterly,* (May 1993): 177; Georgakas, *Greek America At Work* (New York, 1992), pp. 12 and 16–47; Huginnie, *Strikitos: Race, Class, And Work In The Arizona Copper Industry, 1870–1920,* forthcoming; Ruth Shonle Cavan and Katherine Howland Ranck, *The Family And The Depression: A Study Of One Hundred Chicago Families* (Chicago, 1938), pp. 38–39; Isaiah McCaffery, "An Esteemed Minority? Greek Americans and Interethnic Relations in the Plains Region" (unpublished paper, University of Kansas, 1993); see also Donna Misner Collins, *Ethnic Identification: The Greek Americans Of Houston, Texas* (New York, 1991), pp. 201–11. For the African-American slang, Clarence Major, ed., *From Juba To Jive: A Dictionary Of African-American Slang* (New York, 1994), p. 213.

13. Donna Gabaccia, "The 'Yellow Peril' and the 'Chinese of Europe': Italian and Chinese Laborers in an International Labor Market" (unpublished paper, University of North Carolina at Charlotte, c. 1993).

14. George E. Cunningham, "The Italian: A Hindrance to White Solidarity in Louisiana, 1890–1898," *Journal Of Negro History,* 50 (January 1965): 34, includes the quotes.

15. Higham, *Strangers In The Land,* p. 66; Gary R. Mormino and George E. Pozzetta, *The Immigrant World Of Ybor City: Italians And Their Latin Neighbors In Tampa, 1885–1985,* (Urbana, Ill., 1987), p. 241; Micaela DiLeonardo, *The Varieties Of Ethnic Experience* (Ithaca, N.Y., 1984), p. 24, n. 16; Georgakas, *Greek Americans At Work,* p. 16. See also Karen Brodkin Sacks' superb, "How Did Jews Become White Folks?" in *Race,* ed. Steven Gregory and Roger Sanjek forthcoming from Rutgers University Press.

16. Quoted in Brody, *Steelworkers,* p. 120; W. Lloyd Warner and J. O. Low, *The Social System Of The Modern Factory, The Strike* (New Haven, 1947), p. 140; Gershon Legman, *The Horn Book* (New York, 1964), pp. 486–87; *Anecdota Americana: Five Hundred Stories For The Amusement Of Five Hundred Nations That Comprise America* (New York, 1933), p. 98; Nathan Hurvitz, "Blacks and Jews in American Folklore," *Western Folklore,* 33 (October, 1974): 304–07; Emory S. Borgardus, "Comparing Racial Distance in Ethiopia, South Africa, and the United States," *Sociology And Social Research,* 52 (January, 1968): 149–56; F. James Davis, *Who Is Black? One Nation's Definition* (University Park, Pa., 1991), p. 161.

17. Thomas G. Dyer, *Theodore Roosevelt And The Idea Of Race* (Baton Rouge, La., 1980), pp. 131 and 143–44; Mirian King and Steven Ruggles, "American Immigration, Fertility and Race Suicide at the Turn of the Century," *Journal Of Interdisciplinary History,* 20 (Winter, 1990): 347–69. On "stock," see M. G. Smith's "Ethnicity and Ethnic Groups in America: The View from Harvard," *Ethnic And Racial Studies,* 5 (January 1982): 17–18.

18. On race and naturalization law, see David Roediger, "Any Alien Being a Free White Person': Naturalization, the State and Racial Formation in the U.S., 1790–1952," forthcoming

in Ramon D. Gutierrez, ed., *The State And The Construction Of Citizenship In The Americas*; D. O. McGovney, "Race Discrimination in Naturalization, Parts I–III" *Iowa Law Bulletin,* 8 (March 1923); and "Race Discrimination in Naturalization, Part IV," *Iowa Law Bulletin,* 8 (May 1923): 211–44; Charles Gordon, "The Race Barrier to American Citizenship," *University Of Pennsylvania Law Review,* 93 (March 1945): 237–58; Stanford Lyman, "The Race Question and Liberalism," *International Journal Of Politics, Culture, And Society,* 5 (Winter 1991): 203–25. On the racial status of Finns, A. William Hoglund, *Finnish Immigrants In America, 1908–1920* (Madison, Wisc. 1960), pp. 112–14; Peter Kivisto, *Immigrant Socialists In The United States; The Case Of Finns And The Left* (Rutherford, N.J., 1984), pp. 127–28. The whiteness of Armenians was also sometimes at issue, even if they lived on "the west side of the Bosphorus." See *In Re Halladjian Et Al,* C.C., D. mass., 174 Fed. 834 (1909), and *U.S. v. Cartozian,* 6 Fed. (2nd), (1925), 919.

19. *U.S. v. Bhagat Singh Thind,* 261 U.S. 204; Joan M. Jensen, *Passage From India: Asian Indian Immigrants In North America* (New Haven, 1988), pp. 246–69. On the non-white status of Asians, see ibid., and *In Re Ah Yup,* 1 Fed. Cas. 223 (1878); *In Re Saito,* C.C.D. Mass., 62 Fed. 126 (1894); *Ozawa v. U.S.,* 260 U. S. 178 (1922). Williams, *Hierarchical Structures,* David Montejano, *Anglos And Mexicans In The Making Of Texas, 1836–1986* (Austin, 1987); Sharon M. Lee, "Racial Classifications in the U.S. Census, 1890–1990," *Ethnic And Racial Studies,* 16 (January 1993): 79: Almaguer, *Racial Faultlines,* pp. 55–57; George Sanchez, *Becoming Mexican American; Ethnicity, Culture And Identity In Chicano Los Angeles, 1900–1945* (New York, 1993), pp. 29–30.

20. Oscar Handlin, *Race And Nationality In American Life* (Boston, 1957), p. 205; Cunningham. "Hindrance to White Solidarity," pp. 33–35, and esp. Jean Scarpaci, "A Tale of Selective Accommodation: Sicilians and Native Whites in Louisiana," *Journal of Ethnic Studies,* 3 (1977): 44–45, notes the use of "dago clause" to describe the provision. For the Irish, see Roediger, *The Wages Of Whiteness: Race And The Making Of The American Working Class* (New York and London, 1991), pp. 140–43, and Steven P. Erie, *Rainbow's End: Irish-Americans And The Dilemmas Of Urban Machine Politics, 1840–1985* (Berkeley, 1988) pp. 25–66 and 96, table 10.

21. Reginald Horsman, *Race And Manifest Destiny: The Origins Of American Racial Anglo-Saxonism* (Cambridge, Mass., 1981), pp. 250–53. Dyer, *Idea of Race,* p. 131; Mink, *Old Labor And New Immigrants,* pp. 224–27.

22. Dyer, *Idea of Race,* pp. 29–30 and 10–44, *passim.* Stephen Thernstrom, Ann Orlov and Oscar Handlin, eds., *Harvard Encyclopedia Of Ethnic Groups* (Cambridge, Mass., 1980), p. 379; quotations, Dyer, *Idea of Race,* pp. 55, 66, 132.

23. Dyer, *Idea of Race,* p. 132; and for Roosevelt's revealing exchanges with Madison Grant, p. 17.

24. Higham, *Strangers In The Land,* pp. 238–62.

25. Quoted in Mink, *Old Labor Immigrants,* pp. 71–112, 109–10; Grant quote, Higham, *Strangers In The Land,* pp. 156–57. In his *The Old World And The New* (New York, 1914), the reformer and sociologist E. A. Ross maintained that "ethical endowment" was innate, and that southern Europeans lacked it.

26. Jane Addams, *Twenty Years At Hull House* (New York, 1910); Mink, *Old Labor And New Immigrants,* pp. 223 and 226 for the quotes.

27. James Weinstein, *The Corporate Ideal In The Liberal State, 1900–1918* (Boston, 1968).

28. Stephen Meyer III, *The Five-Dollar Day: Labor Management And Social Control In The Ford Motor Company, 1908–1921* (Albany, 1981), pp. 176–85; Higham, *Strangers In The Land,* pp. 138, 261–62, and 316–17.

29. Cf. Dyer, *Idea of Race,* pp. 42–44, 63, 130–31; Higham, *Strangers In The Land,* p. 317; John F. McClymer, "The Americanization Movement and the Education of the Foreign-Born Adult, 1914–1925," in *American Education And The European Immigrant, 1840–1940,* ed. Bernard J. Weiss (Urbana, 1982), pp. 96–116; Herbert Gutman, *Work, Culture And Society In Industrializing America: Essays In Working-Class And Social History* (New York, 1976), pp. 7–8 and 22–25. On the curricula in factory-based Americanization programs, see Gerd Korman, "Americanization at the Factory Gate," *Labor And Industrial Relations Review,* 18 (1965): 396–419.

30. Higham, *Strangers In The Land,* p. 263.

31. Quotes from ibid., pp. 273 and 321. See also pp. 300–330 *passim.* On the triumph of terror and exclusion and the consequent turn by leading liberal intellectuals to a defeatism regarding "race and ethnicity," see Gary Gerstle, "The Protean Character of American Liberalism," *American Historical Review,* 99 (October 1994): 1055–67.

32. Richard Slotkin, *Gunfighter Nation: The Myth Of The Frontier In Twentieth-Century America* (New York, 1992); Michael Rogin, "'The Sword Became a Flashing Vision': D. W. Griffith's *The Birth Of A Nation,"* in *"Ronald Reagan": The Movie And Other Essays In Political Demonology* (Berkeley, 1987), pp. 190–235. "Incontestably mulatto" comes from Albert Murray, *The Omni-Americans* (New York, 1983), p. 22; Zena Pearlstone, ed., *Seeds Of Prejudice: Racial And Ethnic Stereotypes In American Popular Lithography, 1830–1918,* forthcoming. See esp. Michael Rogin, "Blackface, White Noise: The Jewish Jazz Singer Finds His Voice," *Critical Inquiry,* 18 (Spring 1992): 417–53; Rogin, "Making America Home: Racial Masquerade and Ethnic Assimilation in the Transition to Talking Pictures," *Journal Of American History,* 79 (December 1992): 1050–77.

33. Gads Hill Center, "May Report" (1915) and "Minstrel Concert" flyer. Thanks to Steven Rosswurm for identifying this source. See also Elisabeth Lasch-Quinn, *Black Neighbors: Race And The Limits Of Reform In The American Settlement House Movement, 1890–1945* (Chapel Hill, N.C., 1993), esp. pp. 14–30, quote 22; Lyman, "Assimilation-Pluralism Debate," p. 191; Krause, *Battle For Homestead,* p. 218.

34. Kathleen Neils Conzen, David A. Gerber, Ewa Morawska, George E. Pozzetta, and Rudolph J. Vecoli, "The Invention of Ethnicity: A Perspective from the U.S.A.," *Journal Of American Ethnic History,* 12 (Fall 1992): 27.

35. Stanley Lieberson, *A Piece Of The Pie; Black And White Immigrants Since 1880* (Berkeley, 1980), pp. 301–59; Bodnar, Simon and Weber, *Lives Of Their Own,* pp. 141–49; Suzanne Model, "The Effects of Ethnicity in the Workplace on Blacks, Italians, and Jews in 1910 New York," *Journal Of Urban History,* 16 (November 1989): 33–39.

36. Ibid. See also Sterling D. Spero and Abram L. Harris, *The Black Worker* (New York, 1969; originally 1931), pp. 149–81 and 221; and David Ward, *Poverty, Ethnicity And The American City, 1840–1925* (Cambridge, 1989), p. 211.

37. Harold M. Baron, *The Demand For Black Labor* (Cambridge, Mass., n.d.), pp. 21–23; Spero and Harris, *Black Worker,* pp. 174–77; Edward Greer, "Racism and U.S. Steel," *Radical America,* 10 (September-October 1976): 45–68; Paul F. McGouldrick and Michael Tannen, "Did American Manufacturers Discriminate Against Immigrants Before 1914?" *Journal Of Economic History,* 37 (September 1977): 723–46; Allan Kent Powell, *The Next Time We*

Strike: Labor In Utah's Coal Fields, 1900–1933 (Logan, Utah 1985), p. 92; John R. Commons, "Introduction to Volumes III and IV," Commons and others, *History Of Labor In The United States,* 4 vols. (New York, 1966; originally 1935), 3: xxv. Bodnar, Simon and Weber, *Lives Of Their Own,* p. 5; quote, Montgomery, *Fall,* p. 243. For the cartoon, see Ernest Riebe, *Mr. Block* (Chicago, 1984; originally 1913); unpaginated. See also Gordon, Edwards and Reich, *Segmented Work, Divided Workers: The Historical Transformations Of Labor In The United States* (Cambridge, 1982), pp. 141–43.

38. Ross, as quoted in Lieberson, *A Piece Of The Pie,* p. 25; Brody, *Steelworkers In America,* p. 120. Peter Speek, "Report on Psychological Aspect of the Problem of Floating Laborers," United States Commission on Industrial Relations Papers (25 June 1915): 31. Thanks to Tobias Higbie for the citation. Huginnie, *Strikitos,* forthcoming; Georgakas, *Greek Americans At Work,* p. 17; John Bukowczyk, "The Transformation of Working-Class Ethnicity: Corporate Control, Americanization, and the Polish Immigrant Middle Class in Bayonne, New Jersey, 1915–1925," in *Labor Divided: Race And Ethnicity In United States Labor Struggles, 1835–1960,* ed. Robert Acher and Charles Stephenson (Albany, N.Y., 1990), p. 291; Higham, *Strangers In The Land,* p. 173. See also, Saxton, *Indispensable Enemy,* p. 281; Richard W. Steele, "No Racials: Discrimination Against Ethnics in American Defense Industry, 1940–42," *Labor History,* 32 (Winter 1991): 66–90.

39. Jean Scarpaci, "Immigrants in the New South: Italians in Louisiana's Sugar Parishes, 1880–1910," *Labor History,* 16 (Spring 1975); Lieberson, *Piece Of The Pie,* pp. 346–50. The judgment changed briefly in African-Americans' favor in the early 1920s. See Peter Gottlieb, *Making Their Own Way: Southern Blacks' Migration To Pittsburgh, 1916–30* (Urbana, Ill., 1987), pp. 126 and 162; Baron, *Demand For Black Labor,* p. 22; quotes from Lieberson, *Piece Of The Pie,* p. 348; Thaddeus Radzialowski, "The Competition for Jobs and Racial Stereotypes: Poles and Blacks in Chicago," *Polish American Studies,* 33 (Autumn 1976): 16.

40. Lieberson, *Piece Of The Pie,* pp. 299–327; John Bodnar, Roger Simon, Michael Weber, "Blacks and Poles in Pittsburgh, 1900–1930," *Journal Of American History,* 66:3 (1979): 554.

41. Bodnar, Simon and Weber, *Lives Of Their Own,* p. 141, table 16.

42. Steve Nelson, James R. Barrett and Rob Ruck, *Steve Nelson, American Radical* (Pittsburgh, 1981), p. 16.

43. Model, "Effects of Ethnicity," pp. 41–42. Cf. Bodnar, Simon and Weber, *Lives Of Their Own,* p. 141.

44. Bell, *Out Of This Furnace,* p. 124; Attaway, *Blood On The Forge* (New York, 1941, reprint 1987), pp. 122–23.

45. Roger Horowitz, "'Without a Union, We're All Lost': Ethnicity, Race and Unionism Among Kansas City Packinghouse Workers, 1930–1941" (unpublished paper given at the "Reworking American Labor History" conference, State Historical Society of Wisconsin, April 1992), p. 4. On marriage between Catholics but across "ethnic" lines, see Paul Spickard, *Mixed Blood,* pp. 8, 450, n. 70.

46. Mark Wyman, *Round Trip To America: The Immigrants Return To Europe, 1880–1930* (Ithaca, N.Y., 1993), pp. 10–12; see also Michael J. Piore, *Birds Of Passage; Migrant Labor And Industrial Societies* (Ann Arbor, Mich., 1978), *passim.*

47. See Arnold Shankman, "This Menacing Influx: Afro-Americans on Italian Immigration to the South," *Mississippi Quarterly,* 31 (Winter 1977–78): 82 and 79–87 *passim;* Scarpaci, "Immigrants in the New South," p. 175; Robert Asher, "Union Nativism and

Immigrant Response," *Labor History,* 23 (Summer 1982): p. 328; Gabaccia, "'Chinese of Europe,'" 16–18; Scarpaci, "Sicilians and Native Whites," p. 14.

48. Ibid., and, for the quotation, Harold David Brackman, "The Ebb and Flow of Race Relations: A History of Black-Jewish Relations Through 1900" (Ph.D. diss. University of California, Los Angeles, 1977), p. 450. See Loewen, *Mississippi Chinese,* pp. 58–72; Youn-Jin Kim, "From Immigrants to Ethnics: The Life Worlds of Korean Immigrants in Chicago," (Ph.D. diss., University of Illinois at Urbana-Champaign, 1991).

49. Adam Walaszek, "'For in America Poles Work Like Cattle': Polish Peasant Immigrants and Work in America, 1880–1921," in *In The Shadow Of The Statue Of Liberty: Immigrants, Workers And Citizens In The American Republic, 1880–1920,* ed. Marianne Debouzy (Urbana, 1992), pp. 86–88 and 90–91; Bodnar, Simon and Weber, *Lives Of Their Own,* pp. 5 and 60.

50. Ibid.; Roediger, *Towards The Abolition Of Whiteness: Essays On Race, Politics, And Working-Class History* (London and New York, 1994), p. 163; Tamony Papers, on *hunkie,* excerpting *American Tramp And Underworld Slang*; Scarpaci, "Immigrants in the New South," p. 174; Andrew Neather, "Popular Republicanism, Americanism and the Roots of Anti-Communism, 1890–1925" (Ph.D. diss., Duke University, 1993), p. 242; Model, "Effects of Ethnicity," p. 33; Bodnar, Simon and Weber, *Lives Of Their Own,* p. 60.

51. Ibid.; Neather, "Roots of Anti-Communism," pp. 138–223; James Barrett, "Americanization from the Bottom Up: Immigration and the Remaking of the Working Class in the United States, 1880–1930," *Journal Of American History,* 79 (December 1992): 1009.

52. Barrett, "From the Bottom Up," p. 1002. The classic recognition of this reality is found in DuBois, *The Philadelphia Negro,* 332–33. Higham, *Strangers In The Land,* pp. 305 and 321–22.

53. Neather, "Roots of Anti-Communism," pp. 235–40; Mink, *Old Labor And New Immigrants,* pp. 71–112; Messer-Kruse, "Chinese Exclusion and the Eight-Hour Day": Ira Steward's "Political Economy of Cheap Labor" (unpublished paper, University of Wisconsin, Madison, 1994), pp. 13 and *passim.* The classic expression of both the biological and cultural racism and much else is Samuel Gompers and Herman Guttstadt, "Meat vs. Rice: American Manhood Against Asiatic Coolieism: Which Shall Service?" (San Francisco, 1902). On the distinction between opposition to coolies and to the Chinese "race," see Andrew Gyory, "Rolling in the Dirt: The Origins of the Chinese Exclusion Act and the Politics of Racism, 1870–1882" (Ph.D. diss., University of Massachusetts at Amherst, 1991), esp. ch. 4–6.

54. Gyory, "Rolling"; and Glickman, "American Standard," pp. 221–35.

55. Krause, *Homestead,* p. 216.

56. Collomp, "Unions, Civics, and National Identity: Organized Labor's reaction to Immigration, 1881–1897," in *Shadow Of The Statue Of Liberty,* pp. 240, 242 and 246.

57. Neather, "Roots of Anti-Communism," p. 242; White, "Immigration Restriction as a Necessity," pp. 67–69; A. A. Graham, "The Un-Americanization of America," *American Federationist,* 17 (April 1910): 302, 303 and 304.

58. Asher, "Union Nativism," p. 328; Neather, "Roots of Anti-Communism," pp. 242 and 267; Gompers as in Arthur Mann, "Gompers and the Irony of Racism," *Antioch Review,* 13 (1953): 212; in Mink, *Old Labor And New Immigrants,* p. 97; and in David Brody, *In Labor's Cause: Main Themes On The History Of The American Worker* (New York, 1993), p. 117. Cf. Prescott F. Hall, "Immigration and the Education Test," *North American Review,* 165 (1897): 395; cf., Lydia Kingsmill Commander, "Evil Effects of Immigration," *American Federationist,* 12 (October 1905).

59. McGovern, quoted in David Montgomery, *The Fall Of The House Of Labor: The Workplace, The State And American Labor Activism, 1865–1925* (Cambridge, Mass., 1987), p. 25; Asher, "Union Nativism," 339 and 338–42. "Internal protectionism" is Mink's term, from *Old Labor And New Immigrants,* p. 203; Lieberson, *Piece Of The Pie,* pp. 341–44. Cf. the explicit Anglo-Saxonism of *Railroad Trainmen's Journal,* discussed in Neather, "Roots of Anti-Communism," pp. 267–68.

60. Lieberson, *Piece Of The Pie,* pp. 342–43; Gabaccia, "Chinese of Europe," pp. 17–19; Mink, *Old Labor And New Immigrants,* p. 108. See also Lane, *Solidarity Or Survival.* Graham, "The Un-Americanizing of America," pp. 302–04, runs in the same 1910 issue of the *American Federationist* as "Where Yanks Meet Orientals" and "The International Fraternity of Labor." J. A. Edgerton's "Brotherhood of Man," *American Federationist,* 12 (April 1905): 213, runs an issue before Augusta H. Pio's "Exclude Japanese Labor." On "race suicide" see Lizzie M. Holmes review of *The American Idea* in *American Federationist,* 14 (December 1907): 998.

61. Asher, "Union Nativism," *passim;* Mink, *Old Labor And New Immigrants,* pp. 198–203.

62. Philip S. Foner, *History Of The Labor Movement In The United States,* 3 vols. (New York, 1964), 3: 256–81; Asher, "Union Nativism," p. 345, for the quote.

63. Barrett, "From the Bottom Up," pp. 1010 and *passim;* cf. Brody, *In Labor's Cause,* p. 128.

64. Asher, "Union Nativism," p. 330; Covington Hall, "Labor Struggles in the Deep South" (unpublished ms., Labadie Collection, University of Michigan, 1951), pp. 122, 138, 147–48 and 183; *Voice Of The People* (5 March 1914); Roediger, *Towards The Abolition Of Whiteness,* pp. 149, 150 and 175, n. 75. See also Peck, "Padrones and Protest," p. 172.

65. Speek, "Floating Laborers," pp. 31, 34 and 36; plasterer quoted in Asher, "Nativism," p. 330.

66. *New Majority,* 22 November 1919, p. 11. See John Howard Keiser, "John Fitzpatrick and Progressive Unionism, 1915–1925" (Ph.D. diss., Northwestern University, 1965), pp. 38–41; William D. Haywood, *Big Bill Haywood's Book* (New York, 1929), pp. 241–42; James R. Barrett, *Work And Community In The Jungle: Chicago's Packinghouse Workers, 1894–1922* (Urbana, Ill., 1987), pp. 138–142.

67. DuBois, as quoted in Thomas Holt, "The Political Uses of Alienation: W.E.B. DuBois on Politics, Race and Culture," *American Quarterly,* 42 (June 1990): 313; Peck, "Padrones and Protest," p. 173.

68. Dominic A. Pacyga, *Polish Immigrants And Industrial Chicago: Workers On The South Side, 1880–1930* (Columbus, Ohio, 1991), p. 172; Barrett, *Work And Community In The Jungle,* pp. 172–74. If newly organized Poles read John Roach's "Packingtown Conditions," *American Federationist,* 13 (August 1906): 534, they would have seen strikebreaking described as an activity in which "the illiterate southern negro has held high carnival" and have wrongly learned that the stockyards strike was broken simply by black strikebreakers, "ignorant and vicious, whose predominating trait was animalism."

69. Gompers, "Talks on Labor," *American Federationist,* 12 (September 1905): 636–37.

70. Quoted in Allen with Allen, *Reluctant Reformers,* p. 213; Mark Pittenger, *American Socialists And Evolutionary Thought, 1870–1920* (Madison, Wisc., 1993); Higham, *Strangers In The Land,* p. 172; London's animus was characteristically directed against both 'racial' and 'semi-racial' groups, against 'Dagoes and Japs.' See his *The Valley Of The Moon* (New York, 1913), pp. 21–22.

71. Roediger, *Towards The Abolition Of Whiteness,* pp. 158–69; Powell, *Next Time We Strike,* p. 436, n. 11; Barry Goldberg, "'Wage Slaves'" and "'White Niggers,'" *New Politics* (Summer 1991): 64–83.

72. Warren C. Whatley, "African-American Strikebreaking from the Civil War to the New Deal," *Social Science History* 17:4 (1993): pp. 525–58; Allen with Allen, *Reluctant Reformers,* p. 183; Roach, "Packingtown Conditions," p. 534; Radzialowski, "Competition for Jobs," p. 8, n. 7, and *passim*; Leslie Fishel, "The North and the Negro, 1865–1900: A Study in Race Discrimination" (Ph.D. diss., Harvard University, 1953), pp. 454–71; Ray Ginger, "Were Negroes Strikebreakers?" *Negro History Bulletin* (January 1952): 73–74; on the *niggerscab* image, see Roediger, *Towards The Abolition Of Whiteness,* pp. 150–53.

73. Higham, *Strangers In The Land,* pp. 172 and 321–22; Mink, *Old Labor And New Immigrants,* p. 234; James R. Barrett, "Defeat and Decline: Long Term Factors and Historical Conjunctures in the Decline of a Local Labor Movement, Chicago, 1900–1922," unpublished manuscript in Barrett's possession; Quinn, "Americanism and Immigration," *American Federationist,* 31 (April 1924): 295; Gompers linked support for the 1924 restrictions to "maintenance of racial purity and strength." See Brody, *In Labor's Cause,* p. 117.

74. Scarpaci, "Immigrants in the New South," p. 177; Radzialowski, "Competition for Jobs" p. 17.

75. The first quote is from David Montgomery to Jim Barrett, 30 May 1995. On old world prejudices, see Orsi, "Inbetween People," p. 315; Mormino, *Immigrants On The Hill: Italian-Americans In St. Louis,* (Urbana, Ill., 1986). For popular antisemitism in Poland in the era of massive Polish and East European Jewish immigration to the United States, see Celia S. Heller, *On The Edge Of Destruction: Jews Of Poland Between The Two World Wars* (New York, 1977), pp. 38–76.

76. Ronald L. Lewis, *Black Coal Miners In America: Race, Class, And Community Conflict, 1780–1900* (Lexington, Ky., 1987), p. 110; Allen and Allen, *Reluctant Reformers,* p. 180. For a recent expression of the common oppression argument, see Paul Berman, "The Other and the Almost the Same," introducing Berman, ed., *Blacks And Jews* (New York, 1994), pp. 11–30.

77. Peck, "Padrones and Protest," pp. 172–73; "The Greatness of the Greek Spirit," (Chicago) *Saloniki* (15 January 1919); Georgakas, *Greek American At Work,* p. 17; Kivisto, *Immigrant Socialists,* pp. 127–28; Thomas Lee Philpott, *The Slum And The Ghetto: Neighborhood Deterioration And Middle Class Reform, Chicago, 1880–1930* (New York, 1978), p. 195.

78. Brackman, "Ebb and Flow of Conflict," pp. 461–64; Marilyn Halter, *Between Race And Ethnicity: Cape Verdean American Immigrants, 1860–1965* (Urbana, Ill., 1993), pp. 146–49; Mormino and Pozzetta, *Ybor City,* p. 241.

79. Radzialowski, "Competition for Jobs," p. 14, n. 20.

80. Rogin, "Making America Home," p. 1053; Robert W. Snyder, *The Voice Of The City: Vaudeville And Popular Culture In New York* (New York, 1989), p. 120; Lewis Erenberg, *Steppin' Out: New York Nightlife And The Transformations Of American Culture, 1890–1930* (Chicago, 1981), p. 195; Rogin, "Blackface, White Noise," pp. 420, 437–48; Brackman, "Ebb and Flow of Conflict," p. 486.

81. Collins, *Ethnic Identification,* pp. 210–11; Georgakas, *Greek Americans At Work,* pp. 9–12. Hodding Carter, *Southern Legacy,* p. 106; John B. Kennedy, "The Knights of Columbus History Movement," *Current History,* 15 (December 1921): 441–43; Herbert Aptheker,

"Introduction" to W.E.B. DuBois, *The Gift Of Black Folk* (Millwood, N.Y., 1975; originally 1924), pp. 7–8; Rudolph J. Vecoli, 'Free Country': The American Republic Viewed by the Italian Left, 1880–1920," in *Shadow Of The Statue Of Liberty,* pp. 38, 33 and 34, for the quotes from the Italian-American press; and (Chicago) *Daily Jewish Courier* (August 1912).

82. See Noel Ignatiev, *How The Irish Became White* (New York, 1996).

83. Barrett, *Work And Community In The Jungle,* pp. 219–223; cf. William M. Tuttle, Jr., *Race Riot: Chicago In The Red Summer Of 1919* (New York, 1984); cf. Roberta Senechal, *The Sociogenesis Of A Race Riot* (Urbana, Ill., 1990). On the highpoint for Polish- and Lithuanian-American nationalism in the World War One era, see Victor Greene, *For God and Country: The Rise of Polish and Lithuanian Ethnic Consciousness in America, 1860–1910* (Madison, Wisc., 1975), chapters 7–9.

84. Radzialowski, "Competition for Jobs," p. 16; *Glos Polek* (31 July 1919); cf. *Daily Jewish Courier* (22 April 1914), and *Narod Polski* (6 August 1919).

85. Luigi Villari, "Relazione dell dott. Luigi Villari gugli Italiani nel Distretto Consolare di New Orleans," *Bolletino Dell Emigrazione* (Italian Ministry of Foreign Affairs, Royal Commission on Emigration, Pg 1907), pp. 2439, 2499, and 2532. Thanks to Louise Edwards for the source and the translations.

86. Barrett, "From the Bottom Up," esp. pp. 1012–1013; John McClymer, "Gender and the 'American Way of Life': Women in the Americanization Movement," *Journal Of American Ethnic History* 11 (Spring 1991): 5–6.

87. Niles Carpenter with Daniel Katz, "The Cultural Adjustment of the Polish Group in the City of Buffalo: An Experiment in the Technique of Social Investigation," *Social Forces* 6 (September 1927): 80–82. For further evidence of such "indifference," see Scarpaci, "Immigrants in the New South," p. 175, and Edward R. Kantowicz, *Polish American Politics In Chicago, 1888–1940* (Chicago, 1975), p. 149.

88. Gary Gerstle, *Working Class Americanism: The Politics Of Labor In A Textile City, 1914–1960* (Cambridge, Mass., 1989); Roger Horowitz, *Organizing The Makers Of Meat: Shopfloor Bargaining And Industrial Unionism In Meat Packing, 1930–1990,* forthcoming, University of Illinois Press, 1997; Rick Halpern, *"Down On The Killing Floor": Black And White Workers In Chicago's Packinghouses, 1904–1954,* forthcoming, University of Illinois Press, 1997; Michael Goldfield, "Race and the CIO: The Possibilities for Racial Egalitarianism in the 1930s and 1940s," *International Labor And Working Class History* 44 (1993): 1–32.

89. Dominic Capeci, *Race Relations In Wartime Detroit* (Philadelphia, 1984); Gerstle, *Working-Class Americanism,* p. 290; Arnold Hirsch, *Second Ghetto*; see also Thomas Sugrue, "The Structures of Poverty: The Reorganization of Space and Work in Three Periods of American History," in *The Underclass Debate: The View From History,* ed. Michael B. Katz, (Princeton, 1993), pp. 85–117. Russell A. Kazal, "Revisiting Assimilation: The Rise, Fall, and Reappraisal of a Concept in American Ethnic History," *American Historical Review* 100:2 (1995): 468–70. The little information we have on hate strikes suggests that they more likely involved recent Southern white migrants than "ethnics." See Nelson Lichtenstein, *Labor's War At Home: The CIO In World War II* (Cambridge, 1982), pp. 1251–26; Joshua Freeman, "Delivering the Goods: Industrial Unionism in World War II," in *The Labor History Reader,* ed. Daniel J. Leab (Urbana, Ill., 1985), pp. 398–400.

90. David R. Colburn and George E. Pozzetta, "Race, Ethnicity, and the Evolution of Political Legitimacy," in *The Sixties: From Memory To History,* ed. David Farber (Chapel Hill, N.C., 1994), pp. 130–138.

7

Good Neighbors and White Mexicans: Constructing Race and Nation on the Mexico-U.S. Border

MARK OVERMYER-VELÁZQUEZ

ON OCTOBER 5, 1936, the city registrar of El Paso, Texas, Alex K. Powell, announced that from that date onward, government officials would register Mexican Americans as "colored" in birth and death records, a radical departure from the previous racial categorization of "white."[1] The proclamation sparked impassioned official and popular political debate and mobilization in the United States and Mexico around the racial and legal status of Mexican migrants and their descendants. Working in the context of a détente in foreign relations, Mexican and U.S. officials scrambled to minimize the damage done by the El Paso announcement. Existing within histories of racialization that emerged from similar imperial and liberal origins, but ultimately diverged in the process of each nation's formation, Mexicans on both sides of the border took offense at the reclassification.[2] Both groups of ethnic Mexicans deemed the use of the term "colored" anathema to their attempts to situate themselves in positions of power and legitimacy. Framed by the decennial federal censuses of 1930 and 1940, the confrontation was part of larger legal debates at local and national levels around whiteness and the citizenship status of ethnic Mexicans in the United States. The El Paso incident and the responses it engendered underscored how issues of migration and historical constructions of race were intimately linked to the definition of the two nations.

Whereas at the time of the El Paso incident the predominant U.S. model of white supremacy excluded and separated perceived non-white races, in Mexico, for the most part, elites worked to incorporate, albeit in a limited and paternalistic fashion, the country's indigenous and other "non-white" populations into a national narrative of *mestizaje*, or a mixture of Spanish and Indian blood. Despite the different racial categories and hierarchical orders developed in each country (and the varying abilities of individuals to transcend those categories), both nations prioritized white supremacy.[3] It was in this historical context of bi-national racial claims that ethnic Mexicans in places like El Paso fought to be categorized as white and thus asserted their rights as citizens. "Faced with an intensifying territorial encroachment by white Americans on the one hand and by a pervasive atmosphere of racial and cultural hostility on the other," historian David Gutiérrez explains, "ethnic Mexicans were increasingly forced to devise defensive strategies of adaptation and survival in an intermediate, 'third' social space that was located in the interstices between the dominant national and cultural systems of both the United States and Mexico."[4]

This article expands upon nation-bound studies by utilizing broad, transnational historical perspectives to examine the mutually constitutive racial formation of Mexicans in Mexico and the United States. Chicana/o historians and historians of Mexico have either scrutinized the arrival and adaptation of Mexican citizens to the United States (the only significant destination for Mexican migrants) or focused largely on the history of the people confined to Mexico's national territory. In particular, this article builds on studies of the nineteenth-century borderlands[5] and further complicates the research of scholars such as Neil Foley, George J. Sánchez, and David G. Gutiérrez that examines the ethno-racial construction of Mexicans in the United States during the twentieth century. The work of these and other historians also analyzes the historical formation of whiteness as the simultaneous construction and negation of a non-white Other and helps to "bridge the chasm" dividing commonplace historical narratives and historiographies in the United States. However, while these authors acknowledge the sustained influence of Mexican migration and migrants on identity formation, politics, and other areas of life north of the border, their twentieth-century narratives and research are almost entirely focused on U.S.-bounded histories and sources.[6] The migrants' departure from Mexico (up to ten percent of its citizens left, comprising the world's largest sustained movement of migratory workers in the twentieth century) and the transnational dynamics of race formation have been largely neglected and require historical studies using Mexican archives.[7] My examination of the El Paso episode takes into consideration the transnational experience of migrants, challenges us to confront questions that stake claim to the epistemological importance of utilizing bi-national source material, and contributes to the hemispheric and global reorientation of Latin American and U.S. history, respectively.[8] I draw on the concept of "border thinking" in the work of scholars such as Walter Mignolo and José Saldívar, to "re-imagine the nation as a site within many 'cognitive maps' in which the nation-state is not congruent with cultural identity."[9] Far from ignoring national histories and the unique experiences of Mexicans in the United States, my approach builds upon country-specific narratives that examine the economic and social dimensions of Mexican migration from either side of the border and thus complicates and reframes our understanding of this mutually constitutive transnational story.

Taking a transnational perspective of racial formation, this essay examines how the reclassification of Mexicans from white to colored in El Paso was part of a larger struggle over the whiteness and citizenship status of Mexicans in comparative relationship to blacks and Chinese in Mexico *and* the United States. This wider transnational conceptualization of the 1936 dispute explains how policies and racial ideologies emerging from Mexico and the United States influenced the complex and intersecting relationships among Mexican American, Mexican migrant, and Anglo American society.[10] While scholars have analyzed the causes of the El Paso incident from a variety of perspectives, including those of political ascendancy and public health regulation among Mexican Americans, all have failed to move beyond local or national boundaries to examine the event within its broader transnational context.[11] The historical transborder context of El Paso's ethnic Mexican population fundamentally shaped the ways in which they understood and strategically shaped their position as racialized subjects and citizens during a moment of intense bi-national diplomacy. El Paso was a critical transnational political hub for the staging and formation of newly emergent ethno-racial identities in the pre-World War II years.

This article examines the El Paso incident at interconnected local, national, and transnational levels. I begin the article with a close focus on the importance and relevance of El Paso, a border city at the crossroads of transnational economic and political change. I then widen the aperture and analyze how—in the years prior to the 1936 reclassification—the construction of national racial ideologies, economic and social relations, domestic politics, and foreign policies in Mexico and the United States shaped the seemingly bureaucratic decision by the El Paso city registrar. Next, I again sharpen the focus on the local dynamics of race formation in the border city and turn to a discussion of El Paso's emerging middle-class leaders as part of the so-called Mexican American generation, and the "Faustian bargains" they made with whites championing the dominant ideology of white supremacy while subordinating blacks, Asians, and Native Americans.[12] I conclude with a discussion of the enduring consequences of the reclassification and the legacy of transnational racial formation in the post-World War II era.

EL PASO AT THE CROSSROADS

El Paso's position as a strategic gateway for the growing transborder flow of revolutionary exiles, migrants, and capital in the first decades of the twentieth century made it a unique witness to the changing historical struggles over race and racism among the region's Mexican community.[13] The 1936 El Paso incident had national and transnational reverberations and implications, but it also occurred in and was shaped by its local contexts.[14] Highlighting the relevance of El Paso's frontier location in the reclassification case, a local paper noted that "[o]ther Texas cities have adopted the 'white-colored' classification including Latin-Americans with Negroes and Orientals, but none of them are border cities where the question assumes the importance it does in El Paso."[15]

The tensions and violence of the Mexican Revolution and U.S. military intervention in Mexico forced the inhabitants of the border city of El Paso to uniquely and acutely experience this transnational relationship. The city had served as a revolutionary hub for insurgents plotting to overthrow President Porfirio Díaz (1876–1911) and his successors. Francisco Madero's 1911 capture of Ciudad Juárez, Pancho Villa's 1916 attack on U.S. mining employees in Chihuahua and raid on Columbus, New Mexico (only 80 miles from El Paso), and U.S. General Pershing's subsequent "Punitive Expedition" into Mexico each forced Mexican and U.S. residents of El Paso to reconsider their relationship with and allegiances to their own countries. Many Mexicans left El Paso to fight in the Revolution while U.S. troops at the nearby Fort Bliss increased border surveillance.[16] Although Mexican migrants received exemptions, the 1917 and 1924 immigration acts in the United States increased restrictions of entry and imposed literacy requirements, a head tax, and visa fees. These changes, along with the formation in 1924 of the Border Patrol, with powers to conduct humiliating inspections and interrogations of migrants, made crossing the Ciudad Juárez/El Paso border "a painful and abrupt event permeated by an atmosphere of racism and control—an event that clearly demarcated one society from another."[17] Mexican women were particularly mistreated, as border guards often discriminated against single women attempting to cross into El Paso.[18]

The frontier city witnessed the industrialization of West Texas that was part and parcel of the continuing U.S. economic domination of Mexico initiated the previous century. In the first decades of the twentieth century, El Paso and its cross-border counterpart, Ciudad Juárez, were the most economically and politically important cities along the U.S.-Mexico line.

The bi-national urban area had the largest population between San Antonio, Texas, and Los Angeles, California. From 1881 and the arrival of the Southern Pacific Railroad to 1920 and the end of the Mexican Revolution, the border region became the destination of eight railroads linking it to markets deep into both countries. Escaping the ravages of the protracted revolutionary war and attracted to employment opportunities in the expanding agricultural and urban industries of the Southwest United States, hundreds of thousands of Mexicans migrated north through El Paso. Concrete symbols of U.S. imperial economic expansion, the train and its passengers transformed the small frontier region dominated by Anglo Americans into a thriving urban center with a majority ethnic Mexican population in a matter of decades.[19] In addition to the railroad itself, the area became home to the mining industry (notably the American Smelting and Refining Company, ASARCO in 1889) in addition to cattle farming and processing.

As the border economy expanded and men worked in factories and the service industry, El Paso city census records also indicate that a growing number of ethnic Mexican women and minors found employment as domestics and wage laborers, working for middle-class Anglo American families and in the city's laundries. In the post-World War I decade, women were also active in the city's nascent labor movement, in one case joining local and state organizers from the American Federation of Labor to establish a laundry workers' union.[20] Although some Anglo Americans, African Americans, and Asians provided basic labor for the expanding city and its services, their numbers remained small. Ethnic Mexicans supplied by far the largest numbers of El Paso's work force. Texas received over half of the early twentieth-century flood of Mexican migrants, many of whom entered through El Paso. By 1920, the West Texas city had more ethnic Mexicans than U.S.-born Anglo Americans and was second only to San Antonio in total number of Mexicans.[21] By 1930, El Paso's Mexican population had swelled to 68,476 or 56.9% of the population.[22]

The same economic expansion also enabled the development of a small but influential middle class of business owners among Mexicans. Located mostly in the Mexican barrio Chihuahita, ethnic Mexican small-scale entrepreneurs had restricted capital due to the paltry incomes of their working-class Mexican clients. Other business leaders arriving as political refugees from Mexico managed to transfer their relative wealth to the city.[23] However, despite the economic success of a small percentage of Mexicans, both citizens and non-citizens worked in the context of structural racial discrimination that sustained a two-scale wage system between whites and ethnic Mexicans. In addition to outward expressions of racial contempt, Anglo American elites tightly circumscribed the opportunities for economic advancement among Mexicans. As a result, Mexicans accounted for an average of only three percent of professional and managerial positions in the city in the pre-World War II years, the vast majority working as service workers and laborers.[24] When asked in an interview if there had been employment discrimination against U.S. citizens of Mexican background, Mike Romo, a longtime member of the League of United Latin American Citizens (LULAC), responded: "Very much, very much. However, [it was] not as bad as it was east of El Paso, like for instance in Pecos and Fort Stockton. But in El Paso we had quite a bit of discrimination." Commenting on the limited employment opportunities in the city, Romo added: "Well, if stores like Popular, Heyman Krupp, and the Elite Confectionary employed Mexican people, it was only for janitor service or dishwashers. They didn't employ them to wait on people."[25] Educational and living conditions were similarly racist. Mexican children attended poor-quality segregated schools, and most families lived along the border in overcrowded neighborhoods that lacked basic municipal services.[26]

The Raza Mexicana and White Mexicans

These daily experiences of racism and discrimination in 1936 El Paso grew out of centuries of colonial relationships and liberal racial ideologies imposed upon diverse populations in both Mexico and the United States. Leaders from both nations asserted a racial logic of white supremacy following imperial encounters with indigenous populations. Liberal philosophies that rested on citizenship rights and popular consent shaped post-Independence histories on either side of constantly changing borderlines. Although the colonial-era racial hierarchies ultimately endured, during the nineteenth century, the composition of "citizens" and definition of "people" "evolved along sharply different paths" in both countries.[27] While two percent of the population elites in the United States barely acknowledged American Indians, Mexico's nearly sixty percent indigenous population forced an entirely different racial dynamic. "Excluding that . . . percentage of the nation's population based on race," Anthony Mora explains, "would not have been possible. Mexico, therefore, came to depend much more heavily than did the US on cultural affiliation, itself modulated by economic class and social status, to determine full citizenship."[28] Starting in the mid-nineteenth century, Mexican migration to the United States intersected with that history to shape new racialized social and political arrangements. In the context of Mexico's post-revolutionary debates about indigeneity and mestizaje, Mexicans confronted in the United States a nativist racialized system that linked citizenship to whiteness. In this frame, middle-class ethnic Mexicans in El Paso fought to be categorized as white.

In order to divide and conquer the heterogeneous indigenous societies they encountered, and the subsequent addition of African slave populations, Spanish colonial elites fashioned a caste system of racial subtypes that placed purported blacks at the bottom and whites at the top of a social hierarchy.[29] After independence from Spain (1810–1821), Mexican elites struggled (unsuccessfully) to distance themselves from colonial-era race constructs while simultaneously promoting a Mexican version of liberalism that showcased a unified national mestizo race.[30] Later in the century, the liberal economic policies of President Porfirio Díaz that encouraged both foreign economic investment and a "civilizing" whitening of the population gave way to a protectionist re-definition of the nation during the Mexican Revolution.

After the battles of the Revolution came to a tenuous end in 1917, a new set of leaders—many of them *norteños* from the states bordering Texas— debated the "relationship between 'nation' and 'Indian' in Mexico that would lay the foundation of racial identity through the twentieth century."[31] By the time of the El Paso incident, competing claims on the significance of Indians in Mexico's modernization had developed. While many theorists seized on the mestizo or mixed race as an icon of racial and social integration, others viewed a mythologized Indian as more than a cultural icon but rather as the "very model of egalitarian politics, social conscience, and virtue."[32]

Supporters of the emergent "nationalization of the mestizo" rejected the notion of *indios* as impediments to modernity and national consolidation, and instead imagined them—integrated with a modernizing white European stock—as critical sources of resistance fundamental in protecting the nation-state from the pernicious encroachment of foreigners. During the period of the El Paso incident, two critical proponents of the cult of the mestizo, Manuel Gamio and José Vasconcelos, advocated two different but equally influential versions of racial citizenship.[33] Gamio looked to notions of acculturation as fundamental to "civilizing" and homogenizing Mexico's indigenous peoples. In his formulation, Vasconcelos turned the European notion of racial purity and superiority on its head and instead positioned the mestizo Mexican as part of a cosmic race (*raza cósmica*), which represented a final—instead of intermediary—step in a Darwinian hierarchal typology of species development.[34] Both Vasconcelos and Gamio also concerned themselves with protecting Mexico's "race" from the potentially deleterious effects of an Anglo-U.S. imperial presence in their country.[35] Mexican officials and race theorists (often one and the same) struck an ambivalent position between protecting the unique racial status of their citizens abroad and promoting the "civilizing" benefits of exposure to whites in the United States. They were, however, clear on the potential racial contamination of classifying their compatriots as "colored" and categorizing them alongside blacks and Asians.

Reflecting the prevailing popular and scholarly attitudes of the time, Vasconcelos in his writings also excluded blacks from his vision of a modern Mexico, viewing them as a "negative stain on racial progress." Although Afro Mexicans had played vital roles in the establishment and formation of Mexico since the colonial era, politicians and writers relegated them to a heroic colonial past, far from contemporary modernizing nationalist initiatives and discourses.[36] In the late nineteenth and early twentieth centuries, politicians ignored the enduring presence of Afro Mexican communities in coastal states such as Veracruz, Yucatán, and Oaxaca, and focused instead on what they perceived was the problem of the national integration of black immigrants. On the one hand, some progressive thinkers of the time argued that the settlement of blacks from the United States and Caribbean countries should be encouraged due to their diligent work ethic, technical skills, and demonstrated propensity to quickly assimilate into Mexican society. Matías Romero, the prominent Porfirian statesman, went so far as to proclaim that besides "Latino" migrants from southern Europe, blacks represented the best alternative, especially to work in the country's hot and humid coastal climates. On the other hand, conservative intellectuals, such as the historian Alberto Carreño, vehemently argued against the entry of blacks since, he argued, they could only morally and physically contaminate Mexico's racial mixture. This opposition to an increased Afro Mexican presence predominated among government officials and directly influenced policy. In 1927 the government officially prohibited the immigration of blacks, Syrians, Lebanese, Armenians, Palestinians, Turks, Arabs, and Chinese in order to "avoid the *mestizaje* with them because, in general, they cause the degeneration of the *raza*."[37] The struggles of the Depression caused Mexican elites to further subordinate the relatively small Afro Mexican population and continue to restrict immigration of foreign blacks to Mexico until 1935.[38]

Although anti-African American racism played roles in shaping Mexico's modern racialized discourses, a virulent Sinophobia that had developed starting in the late 1800s was the most forceful example of racist practice in Mexico and epitomized the transborder nature of racialization in the first half of the twentieth century. Mexicans, Mexican Americans, and Anglo Americans in both countries situated Chinese with African Americans in a subordinate racialized social hierarchy.[39] Taking advantage of their constantly shifting legal status, non-Chinese groups often used Chinese as convenient scapegoats for generalized economic and social problems.[40] Scholars have argued that anti-Chinese movements and legislation in Mexico allowed the increasingly muscular Mexican state to flex its centralized power from Mexico City.[41]

The movement and residence of the transborder Chinese population was shaped by anti-Chinese immigration campaigns and policies first in the United States and then in Mexico. While tens of thousands of Chinese fled the United States to Mexico following the 1882 Chinese Exclusion Act, others remained in the United States or crossed illegally from Mexico into the United States. As with its Mexican counterpart, United States government exclusion of Chinese, Erika Lee argues, helped craft a "new imperialist American assertion of national sovereignty over its borders and marked the extension of American immigration control beyond its own territory."[42]

By the mid-1920s, Chinese migrants from various socio-economic backgrounds lived in every Mexican state and comprised the second largest foreign ethnic minority in the country.[43] As president of Mexico in an extended rule from 1924–1934, Plutarco Calles increased pressure on the Chinese community in his home state of Sonora that forced Chinese migrants into other border states such as Chihuahua. Calles's cancellation of Mexico's 1899 friendship treaty with China in 1927 and the passing of the 1921 and 1928 migration laws further restricted the entry of Chinese into Mexico. In 1931, after decades of intimidation and violent repression, the Mexican government forcibly expelled most of the small but well-established Chinese population. According to José Trueba Lara, the expulsion of Chinese from Mexico strategically coincided with the deportation of Mexicans from the United States.[44]

Despite similar imperial and ideological beginnings, the historical construction of racial order and difference took on distinct contours in the United States. The unstable legal and racial status of Mexican residents in the United States emerged from historically constructed notions and legal practices that conflated nationality with race, or more specifically, citizenship with whiteness.[45] Those instabilities ultimately served to reinforce the white supremacist status of race in the United States.[46] Although initially excluded from legal

membership in the United States due to the 1790 federal law limiting naturalization to "free white persons," Mexicans gained access to de jure citizenship
following the colonial annexation of half of Mexico's territory during the
Mexican-American War (known in Mexico as *La invasión norteamericana*)
and the Treaty of Guadalupe Hidalgo in 1848, which granted citizen status to Mexicans living in the conquered territory of the newly defined U.S.
Southwest.[47] In the subsequent decades, life in El Paso and elsewhere in the
borderlands was characterized by increased economic and social relations
between Mexico and the United States. Race relations during this period
drew on nineteenth-century and older colonial notions equating Hispanic
peoples with the barbaric Black Legend.[48] These ideological constructions
helped whites in the United States to position Mexicans and later Mexican
Americans as an irredeemably atavistic and violent group, which in turn
fueled and legitimated racist practices against them.[49]

In the 1920s, the rapid expansion of the Mexican population in the
United States further added to the increasingly fluid racial and national
designations of the country's migrant population and became part of the
wider debates about racial identity throughout the country.[50] Whereas
racial and national identities had been separated for European migrants,
allowing them to retain distinct ethnic and racial characteristics, the ethnic
characteristics of Mexicans "became reified and naturalized as immutable
racial ones."[51] These perceptions by some Anglo North Americans exposed
the legal fiction of U.S. citizenship for Mexicans and enabled their de
facto subordination.[52] Unlike blacks, Mexican (and Asian for that matter)
migrants could be construed by Anglos as illegal, unassimilable racialized
others, permanent outsiders who, despite filling the critical labor demands
of expanding agricultural and industrialized economies, often lacked the
qualifications for naturalization.[53] Circumscribed by these raciological
structures, Mexican Americans, such as the community leaders in El Paso,
often adopted the dominant discursive and legal practice of being white.[54]
This strategy necessarily meant distinguishing themselves from the less
politically powerful groups of blacks, Asians, and Native Americans. In
his 1934 study of race relations in Nueces County, Texas, Paul Taylor
clearly illustrates this point:

> Thus Mexicans, who began their contacts with Negroes along the Texas
> border by befriending them, have been moved toward "Americanization"
> through their desire to protect, and also recently, to enhance, their own social
> position. In order to prove their American allegiance, Mexican Americans

proclaim upon occasion not only their patriotic military service, but their adoption of the race attitudes of the local white community, insofar as they apply to the black race beneath them.[55]

At the time of the El Paso incident, thinkers based in the eugenics movement coupled popular notions of racial hierarchy to scientific explanations. In contrast to their Mexican counterparts, most U.S.-based eugenicists rejected the neo-Lamarckian notion that favored a "soft" eugenics approach that considered the power that human will and the physical and cultural environment had in shaping genetic outcomes. Instead, race scientists based in the United States posited a "hard" Mendelian strain of eugenics that supported the view that race and behavior were genetically determined and thus linked to biological inheritance.[56] These racial/biological theories also helped shape ideas and legislation toward issues such as migration, racial intermarriage, sterilization, and "the decline of the white civilization by barbarians from within as well as without."[57] The Social Darwinist notion of the "survival of the fittest" failed to convince eugenicists, who turned their concerns to the survival of the unfit.

Intensified by the economic depression of the late 1920s and early 1930s, these racial ideologies, anxiety, and xenophobia found one manifestation in the 1930 United States federal census.[58] For the first and only time, the census listed Mexicans as a separate, non-white race under an imprecise definition of persons born in Mexico, or with parents born in Mexico, and who were "not definitely white, Negro, Indian, Chinese, or Japanese." Following these and other vague directions, census enumerators recorded over 1.4 million people of Mexican descent as "Mexican," or non-white, and only 65,986 as white.[59]

In that same year, 1930, in Texas, local legislators blurred the line between de jure and de facto segregation in the court case *Independent School District v. Salvatierra*. The case concerned the segregation of Mexican American students of Del Rio from "the school children of *all other white races* in the same grade." The Texas court of appeals ruled in favor of this creative designation that subordinated Mexican Americans as separate but equal in their relationship to whiteness. Districts throughout the state continued to segregate Mexican children because of language "difficulties" and other proxy determinants for race.[60] Events such as the 1930 census and Salvatierra court case further helped set the stage for the 1936 reclassification in El Paso.

It was in the context of these divergent racial claims on national membership in Mexico and the United States that the El Paso racial re-categorization caused such an international uproar. Three days after the event, Josephus Daniels, the Ambassador to Mexico, wrote an urgent letter to Cordell Hull, the U.S. Secretary of State, stating:

> Those protesting against this method of classification say this will be certain to bring about racial animosity along the border, and I am sure it will have very bad repercussions all over Mexico. Nothing offends a Mexican, or any other Latin American with Indian blood, more than being classified as colored, because they regard that as putting them in the same classification as negro.[61]

Despite his arbitrary hereditary distinction of Latin Americans, Daniels was right about the impact of the classification. In letters to newspapers, consular officials, and various government agencies in Mexico and the United States, Mexicans and Mexican Americans expressed their concern and contempt for the reclassification. Echoing the sentiments of other leaders in the city's middle-class Mexican American community, attorney George Rodriguez protested the announcement, arguing that "[t]he practice is contrary to all facts and classifications of anthropology and ethnology. . . . Latin Americans belong in the white race. Classification of Spanish-speaking people as colored will result in discrimination in foreign countries. . . . This thing goes further than Mexico. All South America is involved."[62]

In Mexico, some critics used the reclassification to assert their position within the federal government's dominant narrative of the "nationalization of the mestizo." In Monterrey, Nuevo León, the dominant urban and political center in Mexico's north and an industrial counterpart to El Paso, elites viewed their city as the vanguard of Mexico's industrial modernity.[63] Although emphasizing their whiteness, leaders and industrialists in the state capital took pride in their mestizo heritage. Celebrating the federal census that recorded the state of Nuevo León as twenty percent "white" and containing the smallest indigenous population in the republic, Governor Porfirio González boasted that "[t]here are no Indians in Nuevo León!"[64]

The editors of *El Porvenir*, a conservative and unabashedly pro-industry newspaper in Monterrey, promoted a narrative that proclaimed the uniqueness of the city and region and that united socio-economic classes in the face of an intrusive federal government led by President Cárdenas.[65] With strong ties to U.S. capital, city elites were troubled by the El Paso incident and the re-racialized depiction of their compatriots. One article in the paper called U.S. authorities "ignorant and unaware of the 'Mexican culture'" and accused them of a "failure to know our traditional history which shows the prestige of our race and our blood of unsuspected purity. The various social elements of this city felt themselves hurt in their racial pride at the contempt shown the Mexicans in El Paso."[66] Highlighting the importance and influence of neo-Lamarckian racial construction, the article added that "[m]en of high character and outstanding intelligence such as Lic. Vasconcelos and many others have fully described the greatness of our race and the vigor of our blood."[67] In conclusion, the article proclaimed added outrage in the face of the friendship the Mexican government has "always extended to the American people" and especially to Ambassador Daniels.[68]

A TALE OF TWO NATIONS

In addition to these transborder reactions to the 1936 El Paso incident, the broader political and economic contexts of the era—situated between a revolution, an economic depression, and a world war—further shaped the historical experience of the city's inhabitants. The growing numbers of Mexicans migrating to the United States in the first decades of the twentieth century prompted different and often ambivalent responses toward definitions of race and citizenship in both countries. Mexican migrants and revolutionary exiles linked the two countries and helped forge the unique transnational space of the border. In the face of national consolidation in the years following the Mexican Revolution, the departure of nearly 1.5 million Mexican citizens to the United States between the turn of the century and the start of the Great Depression in 1929 was the source of considerable concern in Mexico. Mexican officials expressed apprehension for the well-being of their fellow citizens crossing to *el norte*. Newspapers in Mexico warned of exploitative U.S. labor recruiters who would charge migrants exorbitant fees and then pay them desperately low wages. These concerns led the Chamber of Commerce in Ciudad Juárez, the major point of departure for El Paso-bound migrants, to suggest that the Mexican government limit the number of northward emigrants.[69]

Ambivalence was also a hallmark of immigration policy in the United States during the early decades of the twentieth century. On the one hand, the rapid economic development of the Southwest required Mexican labor. On the other, the related increased number of Mexican nationals north of the border drove many to fear for the potential contamination of the perceived race-based social and cultural purity of the United States. Some growers and politicians argued that the perceived infectious and corrupt characteristics of Mexican workers in the United States could be regulated. The laborers, they claimed, could be segregated from Anglo Americans, and their stay would only be temporary.

In the 1930s, the U.S. and Mexican governments simultaneously attempted to consolidate domestic rule by closing geographic frontiers and to build amicable foreign relations across those frontiers. The El Paso incident coincided with the implementation of President Franklin Roosevelt's "Second New Deal" administration and the recently crafted Good Neighbor Policy in the United States.[70] At the same time in Mexico, efforts to politically and culturally consolidate the nation in the post-Revolutionary years took form in President Lázaro Cárdenas's Six Year Plan. The heightened attention to and sensitive nature of Mexican and U.S. diplomatic relations during this period fashioned a unique context in which opponents to the reclassification announcement could strategically employ domestic and international pressures to their benefit.

In the United States, the 1930s represented the end of the "formative" era of modern borderlands history. In this period, especially following increasingly restrictive immigration legislation and the formation of the Border Patrol in 1924, historians Samuel Truett and Elliott Young argue that "the borderlands between nations . . . were finally starting to harden into the clearly marked boundaries that appeared on most national maps. For a while, the borderlands had seemingly become 'bordered' lands."[71] Starting in 1929, the Great Depression reinforced these political limits as increased economic anxiety and nativist sentiment fueled the deportation (repatriation) of close to half a million Mexicans, some of whom were U.S. citizens.[72] Borderlanders in El Paso and Ciudad Juárez directly witnessed this massive displacement when U.S. officials ushered hundreds of Mexicans out of the United States and through the Customs checkpoints separating the two cities.[73] In 1930, officials in Ciudad Juárez complained of being overwhelmed by the return of over one hundred deported Mexicans a day, arriving from various points in the United States. Despite Mexican federal- and state-sponsored assistance for the relocation of return migrants, many former emigrants returned to impoverished conditions in their hometowns, motivating them to try their luck again in Texas and elsewhere in the United States.[74] Although the Mexican government hoped to distribute the 400,000 return migrants throughout the republic, most returned to densely populated states such as Michoacán, Jalisco, and Zacatecas and did little to develop local agriculture.[75]

Despite this recent history of deportations and continued U.S. military intervention in Mexico throughout the years of the Revolution, by the 1930s, a strengthening détente had been reached between the two nations. Although some U.S. politicians longed for a return to the liberal economic policies of Porfirio Díaz, the Depression had forced each country's government to focus on models of socio-economic domestic intervention. Furthermore, in the pre-World War II years, the growing global threats of Japan and Germany obliged the United States to seek out Mexico as a strategic ally in the military defenses of the Western Hemisphere. Despite his anti-imperialist and staunch nationalist leanings, President Cárdenas was regarded by the United States as a strong partner in its Good Neighbor Policy and new non-interventionist policy in Latin America.[76] Under FDR's leadership, the U.S. government officially emphasized cooperation and trade rather than military force, to maintain stability in the hemisphere.

Civic leaders and residents in the United States and Mexico rhetorically framed the El Paso incident within the diplomatic context of the Good Neighbor Policy.[77] In a telegram to Cordell Hull, the Secretary of State and the Good Neighbor Policy's first ambassador at the 1933 Montevideo, Uruguay, conference, Servando Esquivel, President of Comité Cívico Mexicano in El Paso, at once praised and cautioned Hull about the reclassification. Esquivel wrote that "since [the] Montevideo conference you have been [the] highest exponent of [the] Good Neighbor Policy. [The El Paso] classification has caused general indignation among Latin Americans in the southwest. [I urge you to] rectify this unjustified blunder."[78]

In Mexico, hard on the heels of a bloody, protracted Revolution, President Lázaro Cárdenas worked to consolidate and centralize his rule among the states of the republic. Cárdenas implemented the designs of his corporatist state in the Six Year Plan (coinciding with the length of a Mexican presidential term). The Plan highlighted the role of an interventionist state, national development of industry by Mexicans themselves, socialist education, minimum wages, and collective bargaining rights for labor, and, in particular, it focused on agrarian reform and redistribution of land to the peasantry.[79] In 1938, Cárdenas nationalized Mexico's oil industry, taking it out of the hands of largely U.S.-owned companies, and by 1940, the president had designated forty-seven percent of all cultivated land as *ejido* or communally owned land. In this nationalist spirit, representatives from Mexico's senate requested that President Cárdenas file a formal protest against the El Paso reclassification. Local officials and citizens, especially in Mexico's northern states, but also in Mexico City and the Mexican Embassy in Washington, D.C., penned angry letters demanding compensation for "insult" against "not just Mexicans in the United States, but an entire race, an entire nation."[80]

Race in El Paso

Inhabitants of the border city understood, contextualized, and articulated at the local level the national responses in Mexico and the United States to the racial reclassification. Some scholars have argued that because of the city's relatively isolated, western location and its proximity to and social integration with Mexico, El Pasoans did not experience the same degree of racism prevalent elsewhere in Jim Crow Central and East Texas. In his explanation of the short-lived and limited influence of the Ku Klux Klan on the city in the early 1920s, El Paso historian Wilbur Timmons describes the "atypical Texas community" as an "isolated, semifrontier, middle class, bicultural [city], quite unlike the cities of the eastern part of the state."[81] Nevertheless, revolutionary unrest and oral history accounts reveal a different picture of the border city, one that illustrates a complex set of racial dynamics and prejudices.

Enduring memories of a "race riot" during the Revolution no doubt contributed to race tensions among the transborder populations. On January 10, 1916, Francisco Villa ordered the execution of sixteen mining engineers en route to a mine in Chihuahua. Angry relatives of the miners in El Paso, including soldiers from Fort Bliss, grew into a mob of nearly four hundred people and indiscriminately attacked ethnic Mexicans they encountered on the city streets. Although the local police managed to quickly stem the violence, the "rioting shattered the community that existed in El Paso and, in many ways, lapped over into Ciudad Juárez."[82]

In El Paso, the construction of racial attitudes toward Mexicans in the 1930s existed within transnational and local sociological and juridical contexts that transcended a "black-white paradigm" and included the presence of other racialized minorities, including blacks, Asians, and Native Americans.[83] In fundamental contrast to the totalizing nature of Jim Crow attitudes and policies toward African Americans during the era, the ambivalent and porous racialization of ethnic Mexicans left especially the lighter-skinned and wealthier among them far greater room for occupational and social mobility. The albeit deeply contested access to whiteness gave middle-class ethnic Mexicans, in general, a powerful practical incentive to resist being categorized as "colored" and therefore subjected to all of the outrages of a full-blown Jim Crow regime.

The racial terms "Anglo" and "white" were, of course, far from static and monolithic categories in 1930s Texas. As Neil Foley has explained, "[i]n reducing all whites of European descent into one category, the term *Anglo* thus fails completely to identify any single ethnic group." Texans used the terms "Anglo" and "Mexican" in opposition to one another.[84] The same, of course, was true with the categories of blacks, Asians, and Mexicans. Nevertheless, all of these "non-Anglo" groups often failed to differentiate amongst one another. Underscoring this point, Paul Taylor wrote in 1934: "In different parts of the United States the native-born of Mexican labor class descent carry different names. To Americans generally they are all 'Mexicans,' but among themselves and among Americans who know them better and distinguish, certain distinctive groups are recognized."[85] Conflating race with nationality, Anglo Texans often designated Mexican Americans and Mexicans simply as "Mexicans."[86]

El Paso's population understood and responded to the racial recategorization in the context of these historically constructed and politically charged conceptualizations of race in Mexico and the United States. The border city's ethnic Mexican and white populations situated Chinese and Native Americans with African Americans in a subordinate racialized social hierarchy. In an attempt to define the era's Mexicans and whites against the one-drop hereditary structure of an imagined black and Asian racialized opposition, Aurelia Phillips, the granddaughter of El Paso's former mayor, argued that

> [t]he Negro is a different race altogether. Even their bone structure is different. The Negro is black. They don't mix. Japanese and Chinese don't mix either. You marry a Chinese. You have Chinese children. You marry a Negro and you have Negro children. But the Mexicans, they're not a brown race. They are whites. You go to Mexico City and you'll never see so many blue-eyed blondes, not even here in El Paso.[87]

Unlike the cotton farming areas of Central Texas, El Paso was not home to a significant number of African Americans.[88] Some continued to reside in the city after initially arriving during the Civil War. In 1890, the census recorded 361 African American inhabitants growing to only about 800 in 1929.[89] Not until after World War II did the African American population begin to grow in size and percentage of the population.[90] When asked how blacks fit into El Paso society in the 1930s, Drusilla Nixon, wife of the prominent African American doctor Lawrence Nixon, responded: "Well, they didn't. They would have, but my husband used to say that if El Paso hadn't been in the state of Texas they wouldn't have had any segregation laws. But as it was we couldn't go to any shows and we, of course, couldn't go to any restaurants. . . . [Everything] was entirely separate."[91] Jim Crow was alive and well in El Paso, with schools, transportation, restaurants, and social establishments segregated during the 1930s. According to some black residents of the period, Ciudad Juárez served as a segregation-free refuge for black families to dine and view "picture shows." However, revealing the importance of class in race relations in Juárez, Drusilla Nixon pointed out that despite being generally "well treated . . . [in] some of the very exclusive places, I don't think we were accepted."[92]

The small Chinese population in El Paso also contributed to the racial discourse of the 1930s. The Mexican community's revulsion at being included with Chinese as another "non-white race" emerged from the often denigrated historical presence of Chinese in El Paso. The Chinese colony in El Paso, once active in the laundry business and gambling, began to decline during the Mexican Revolution, due to an increased regulation of Chinese migrants, the illegalization of gambling, and the absence of Chinese women.[93] El Paso officials complained of the expense of deporting Chinese back to Mexico. Between 1931 and 1933, 2,676 Chinese laborers were deported across the border back to Ciudad Juárez.[94] Nevertheless, by 1935, there were still enough Chinese children in El Paso to initiate Sunday school classes in the Baptist Chinese Mission, and in 1937, members of the "Chinese Colony," a group of four hundred merchants, marched in the annual Sun Carnival Parade, a public display of status in the city.

Native Americans in and around El Paso were few in numbers but played a significant role in the invented official history that relegated Indians to a heroic traditional past while celebrating a civilized, white, and modern present. Erasing their distinct identity and agency, local elites heralded the Tigua Indians of the region as the "oldest permanent settlers in Texas" who continued to celebrate their "quaint" traditions.[95]

City elites also strategically conflated hygiene with citizenship and used the lens of public health statistics to structure and control the city's complex racial and class divisions.[96] Integrated with the city politicians' raciological classification of El Paso's Mexican community was a specific concern for the "health" of the border city. Although not officially acknowledged, also at stake with the racial reclassification was a touristic representation of El Paso as a hygienic destination for the growing health resort industry. In celebrations surrounding the 1936 centennial celebrations of Texas independence from Mexico, city publications touted El Paso as a choice locale for rest and recuperation. An official flyer integrated notions of citizenship with public health, stating that "El Paso in recent years has become one of the leading tuberculosis healing grounds of the world, and thousands of persons afflicted with this disease have moved here to recover completely, and become so fond of the everlasting sunshine that they remain in El Paso to become useful citizens."[97] Within these contexts, political elites imagined that categorizing Mexicans—who suffered high infant mortality rates—in census records as "colored" would administratively reduce the southwestern city's high death rates of "white" infants.[98] Bolstering their case for segregating Mexicans, some municipal officials for years had considered Mexicans unable to be taught "proper" hygiene.[99]

The Mexican American Generation Responds

The city administration's recategorization tested El Paso's local race dynamics. On October 7, 1936, two days after the announcement, the city's middle-class ethnic Mexican population, mobilized by leaders of prominent Mexican American organizations including LULAC, opposed the proposal with a court injunction.[100] LULAC served as the political and organizational touchstone for the "Mexican American Generation," a term scholars have used to describe middle-class and elite ethnic Mexicans that emphasized the importance of U.S. citizenship, assimilation, and whiteness in their struggles for political and social power while strategically distancing themselves from poor immigrant Mexicans.[101] El Paso officials claimed that they had been responding only to a U.S. Bureau of the Census request for racial reclassification that had already taken place in Dallas, Fort Worth, Houston, and San Antonio.[102] Cleofás Calleros and other members of the El Paso Federation of Latin American Societies rallied against the "colored" classification and challenged the broader political motivations behind the announcement. In strong terms, Mexican American leaders argued that the "colored" classification placed them in the same inferior social category as African Americans, which "carries with it almost the complete negation of the person as a human being."[103] The leaders also argued their case with the fact that in 1934, Texas state officials had unsuccessfully attempted to disenfranchise Mexicans by classifying them as non-white.[104] Mexican American leaders feared that the 1936 reclassification would again threaten their voting rights and relegate Mexican Americans to the subordinate and segregated treatment experienced by the city's African Americans. In a letter to the El Paso Spanish-language paper *El Continental*, Ramón Zepeda pondered why, after previous innumerable "slurs and reprisals against the raza," had the community never protested. He went on to offer an answer:

> [B]ecause the early sporadic manifestations were against foreign Mexicans. Now the insult is directed towards Mexicans of American citizenship. . . . And what is the goal of this [racial reclassification]? . . . It concerns eliminating us from local politics; it entails the goal of segregating us from a society where increasingly our race is proving itself in the area of ideas and technologies and threatening, understandably, their way of life.[105]

Following the court case, Federation members lobbied for the commitment of local politicians to support El Paso's Mexican American community and categorize them as white. Aware of the voting power of the Mexican American community, all of the canvassed officials eagerly pledged their support.[106] The city health officer, Dr. T. J. McCamant, stated that although he felt that the race-based classifications would be useful in terms of public health, he quickly added that the incident had been a "misunderstanding" and that no one in the city government had ever intended actually to register Mexicans as "colored." The court ruled against the city officials, rescinded the classification, and the Mexican American community celebrated its victory.[107]

The involvement of LULAC and other similar organizations greatly aided the rapid resolution of the case. LULAC's presence also highlighted the pronounced socio-economic dimension of the conflict and its intersection with the construction of whiteness and privileged status for emergent middle-class Mexican Americans. Founded in Texas in 1929, LULAC had its roots in previous battles over race and citizenship status. In south Texas during the era of the Mexican Revolution, a group of Tejano rancheros struggled to restore the political and economic power they had lost to the expansion of Anglo American- and elite ethnic Mexican-owned industrial agriculture. Unlike their Tejano ranchero predecessors who drew ideological inspiration from Mexico *and* the United States, the founders of LULAC focused exclusively on the benefits of U.S. citizenship. "This was not because they had turned their backs on Mexican culture or customs," argues historian Benjamin Johnson, "but rather because what they had endured during the Plan de San Diego [rebellion] convinced them of the dangers of statelessness: that they risked becoming a people belonging to no nation at all."[108] Building on these past struggles and filled with nationalist pride as veterans of World War I, LULAC members sought to transform Mexicans into a generation of Mexican Americans, into respected citizens of the United States. As national boundaries (concrete, racial, and symbolic) became more rigid, the organization's members advocated for an inclusive social position as whites and committed "themselves to the American political and economic systems while emphasizing the responsibilities as well as the rights of American citizens."[109]

ENDURING CONSEQUENCES

The deceptively short-lived legal struggles between middle-class Mexican American organizations such as LULAC and the El Paso municipal government touched off a four-year transnational debate among groups and individuals in both Mexico and the United States. The recategorization incident was a window into the politics of racialization, citizenship, and state formation culminating with the 1940 decennial census and the advent of World War II. With significance beyond its local and regional contexts, the recategorization incident became a focal point for bi-national diplomatic exchange that ultimately hinged on the flow of migratory labor from Mexico to the United States. As was the case throughout most of the twentieth century, the simultaneous demand for Mexican migrant labor by U.S. industry and the turn of Mexican laborers to the United States for increased economic opportunity yielded an almost steady stream of south-to-north migration throughout the century.

Ongoing indignation over the El Paso reclassification was fueled in subsequent months and years by case after case of U.S. state agencies at the local, regional, and national levels competing over the definition and administration of racial taxonomies and record keeping.[110] Transnational debates around the El Paso case came to a head in 1939 with administrative preparations for the decennial census in the following year. The debates centered on whether or not people of Mexican descent should be classified as white. Opponents to the white-race designation for Mexicans included prominent officials such as Dr. Halbert L. Dunn, the Chief Statistician for Vital Statistics at the Bureau of Census in the Department of Commerce. Dunn was dismayed that Mexicans were categorized as white in the first place. He argued that the enumeration of Mexicans as white

> means the virtual destruction of the census of vital statistics so far as concerns their scientific use in determining certain facts in regard to health, length of life, birth rate and other important matters. . . . This is because there are fundamental biological differences between the average American and the average Mexican in the way in which they react to disease as well as great differences in the rate of multiplication.

Perhaps more important, Dunn added that "[f]rom the sociological and cultural standpoints, Mexicans are also different. The solution of many labor
problems throughout the Southwest depends upon a knowledge of their
numbers and geographic distribution." Finally, Dunn was "alarmed" that
continuing to classify Mexicans as white would force the Bureau to "extend
the white race designation to other peoples of Central and South America
with a 'preponderance of Indian blood.'"[111] Echoing Dunn's pronouncements, the two main opponents represented the health and labor industries.
Interested labor organizations notably included the federal departments of
labor, agriculture, and war, which required legible statistics to keep track
of Mexican sources of labor and military recruits so vital to the emergent
U.S. economy on the verge of a second world war.[112]

Solicited and unsolicited letters from government officials, university
professors, health agency directors, and private citizens from the United
States and Mexico inundated the Bureau of Census, arguing for and against
the white-race designation.[113] However, regardless of social and political
positions adopted, framing the debate within a white-dominant racial regime
only further reinforced a racist hierarchy. In one example, state Congressman Joe H. Eagle from Houston, Texas, rallied for his Mexican constituents
and complained that Mexicans descended "directly from the white Spanish
stock."[114] In the context of the Good Neighbor Policy, vigorous opposition to
the non-white racialization of "Mexicans" by the Mexican Secretary of Foreign Relations and other federal agencies in concert with Mexican American
organizations such as LULAC, U.S. officials re-categorized Mexicans in
the 1940 census as white unless "definitely Indian or of other non-white
race."[115] The census would continue to be a contested document of racial
and ethnic classification until the present day.

The El Paso case stood at the nexus of transnational racial formation in
the pre-World War II era and exemplified the ultimately abortive attempts
at racialized democracy. Both nations and their border hybrids never really
challenged the frame of white supremacy, but rather continued to debate
racial citizenship within a predetermined racist paradigm. The war and its
attendant political and economic demands increasingly interconnected the
two countries. The heightened strategic importance of the Good Neighbor
Policy, the bi-national Bracero Program (1942–1964) that provided temporary working visas for Mexicans in U.S. agriculture, and the entry of
hundreds of thousands of Mexicans and Mexican Americans into the U.S.
armed services intensified struggles around the relationship between race
and nation.[116] These debates continued to persist despite postwar claims of

racial democracy and "celebrations of rights, freedom, opportunity, and equality."[117] Through the lens of "border thinking" and a transnational focus, the El Paso incident allows us to view how racial regimes emerged in both countries and developed and endured along the border.

NOTES

I very much appreciate the careful readings and suggestions of Rick López, Ben Johnson, John Mckiernan-Gonzalez, Oscar Martinez, Curtis Marez, and two anonymous readers at the *JAEH* who made this a far better piece. I also appreciate the comments on an earlier version from fellow panelists and audience members at the Latin American Studies Association and the Organization of American History conferences. The assistance of Claudia Rivers at the University of Texas at El Paso (UTEP) archives and the hospitality of my *tios* José (*que en paz descansa*) and Ruth Velázquez, formerly of El Paso, Texas, helped me to complete my research.

1. In this article, I employ several different, albeit imperfect, racial and ethnic terms to describe the diversity of identities along the border. "Mexican" refers to citizens of Mexico either living in Mexico or as migrants in the United States. "Mexican American" refers to U.S. citizens of Mexican heritage. "Tejano" is a Texas resident of Mexican descent. "Ethnic Mexican" is an umbrella term that subsumes all of the above. Similarly, I use the terms "Anglo" and "Anglo American" interchangeably to identify individuals and groups outside of and in opposition to non-Anglo inhabitants of the region (i.e., ethnic Mexicans, blacks, Asians, and Native Americans). As I describe in the text below, these problematic terms existed in relational contexts often historically developed in opposition to one another.

2. Neil Foley, *Quest for Equality: The Failed Promise of Black-Brown Solidarity* (Cambridge, MA, 2010).

3. See discussion in Anthony Mora, *Border Dilemmas: Racial and National Uncertainties in New Mexico, 1848–1912* (Durham, NC, 2011), passim.

4. David G. Gutiérrez, "Migration, Emergent Ethnicity, and the 'Third Space': The Shifting Politics of Nationalism in Greater Mexico," *Journal of American History* 86, no. 2 (1999): 488.

5. Mora, *Border Dilemmas*; Raúl A. Ramos, *Beyond the Alamo: Forging Mexican Ethnicity in San Antonio, 1821–1861* (Chapel Hill, NC, 2008); Andrés Reséndez, *Changing National Identities at the Frontier: Texas and New Mexico, 1800–1850* (New York, NY, 2005).

6. David G. Gutiérrez, *Walls and Mirrors: Mexican Americans, Mexican Immigrants, and the Politics of Ethnicity* (Berkeley, CA, 1995); George Sánchez, *Becoming Mexican American: Ethnicity, Culture, and Identity in Chicano Los Angeles, 1900–1945* (New York, NY, 1993); Neil Foley, *The White Scourge: Mexicans, Blacks, and Poor Whites in Texas Cotton Culture* (Berkeley, CA, 1998). For references to migration in Mexican history, see Mary Kay Vaughn, "Cultural Approaches to Peasant Politics in the Mexican Revolution," *Hispanic American Historical Review* 79, no. 2 (May 1999): 301. One recently published history of Mexico laments that the historiography "lacks a sustained focus on the process of migration to and from the United States." Joseph M. Gilbert, Anne Rubenstein, and Eric Zolov, eds., *Fragments of a Golden Age: The Politics of Culture in Mexico since 1940* (Dur-

ham, NC, 2001), 18. Mexican academics have also devoted relatively little attention to the historical study of Mexican emigration and its part in the making of modern Mexico. For an extended discussion of the absence of Mexican migration in national historiographies, see Mark Overmyer-Velázquez, "Histories and Historiographies of Greater Mexico" in *Beyond la Frontera: The History of Mexico-US Migration*, ed. Mark Overmyer-Velázquez (New York, NY, 2011), xix–xlvi.

7. Although some works analyze select periods and themes of this protracted bi-national relationship, none provides an examination of transnational race formation. For examples, see Lawrence A. Cardoso, *Mexican Emigration to the United States, 1897–1931* (Tucson, AZ, 1980); Gilbert G. Gonzales and Raul A. Fernandez, *A Century of Chicano History: Empire, Nations, and Migration* (New York, NY, 2003); Jorge Durand, ed., *Migración México-Estados Unidos. Años veinte* (México, DF, 1991); Moisés González Navarro, *Los extranjeros en México y los mexicanos en el extranjero: 1821–1970* (México, DF, 1994); John Mason Hart, ed., *Border Crossings: Mexican and Mexican-American Workers* (Wilmington, DE, 1998); Rodolfo F. Acuña, *Corridors of Migration: The Odyssey of Mexican Laborers, 1600–1933* (Tucson, AZ, 2008); Manuel Ceballos Ramírez, *Encuentro en la frontera: Mexicanos y norteamericanos en un espacio común* (México, DF, 2001).

8. See the examinations of these two historiographic approaches in Erez Manela, "The United States in the World," in *American History Now*, ed. Eric Foner and Lisa McGirr (Philadelphia, PA, 2011), 201–20; and Gilbert M. Joseph, Catherine LeGrand, and Ricardo D. Salvatore, eds., *Close Encounters of Empire: Writing the Cultural History of U.S.-Latin American Relations* (Durham, NC, 1998).

9. Walter D. Mignolo, *Local Histories/Global Designs: Coloniality, Subaltern Knowledges, and Border Thinking* (Princeton, NJ, 2000). Quote from José David Saldívar, *Border Matters: Remapping American Cultural Studies* (Berkeley, CA, 1997), ix.

10. I follow the definition of transnationalism as a "social process in which migrants establish social fields that cross geographic, cultural, and political borders." *Towards a Transnational Perspective on Migration: Race, Class, Ethnicity, and Nationalism Reconsidered*, ed. Nina Glick Schiller, Linda Basch, and Cristina Blanc Szanton, *Annals of the New York Academy of Sciences* 645 (New York, NY, 1992), ix.

11. Mario T. García, "Mexican Americans and the Politics of Citizenship: The Case of El Paso, 1936," *New Mexico Historical Review* 59, no. 2 (1984): 187–204; Foley, *White Scourge*, 208; Ann Gabbert, "Defending the Boundaries of Care: Local Responses to Global Concerns in El Paso Public Health Policy, 1881–1941" (PhD diss., University of Texas at El Paso, 2006).

12. Neil Foley, "Becoming Hispanic: Mexican Americans and the Faustian Pact with Whiteness," in *Reflexiones 1997: New Directions in Mexican American Studies*, ed. Neil Foley (Austin, TX, 1998), 53–70.

13. Sanchez, *Becoming Mexican American*, 38–62.

14. Clare Sheridan underscores the importance of examining the construction of "racial and cultural orders" at the local level. Clare Sheridan, "Cultural Racism and the Construction of Identity," *Law and History Review* 21, no. 1 (Spring 2003): 207–09.

15. *El Paso Herald Post*, October 7, 1936: 3.

16. Mario T. Garcia, *Desert Immigrants: The Mexicans of El Paso, 1880–1920* (New Haven, CT, 1981), 172–96.

17. Sanchez, *Becoming Mexican American*, 59.

18. Vicki L. Ruiz, *From Out of the Shadows: Mexican Women in Twentieth-Century America* (New York, NY, 1998), 3–32.

19. On the U.S. imperial origins of Mexican migration to the United States, see Gilbert Gonzalez, "Mexican Labor Migration, 1876–1924," in *Beyond la Frontera*, ed. Overmyer-Velázquez, 28–50.

20. "El Paso, TX: Remite datos estadísticos sobre situación de la Colonia mexicana," in Secretaría de Relaciones Exteriores. Archivo Histórico Genaro Estrada, Mexico City (hereafter: SRE), IV-108–24; Mario T. García, "The Chicana in American History: The Mexican Women of El Paso, 1880–1920: A Case Study," *Pacific Historical Review* 49, no. 2 (May 1980): 315–37.

21. Garcia, *Desert Immigrants*, 36–37.

22. U.S. Department of Commerce, 14th Census, Abstract, p. 57; 15th census, population, 2, 67–73; El Paso, TX: Census Data, 1930 in C. L. Sonnichsen Special Collections Department, University of Texas at El Paso, Cleofas Calleros Papers, MS 231 (hereafter: CCP), Box 16, Folder 2.

23. Garcia, *Desert Immigrants*, 79–87.

24. Oscar J. Martínez, *The Chicanos of El Paso: An Assessment of Progress*, Southwestern Studies Monograph No. 59 (El Paso, TX, 1980), 140.

25. C. L. Sonnichsen Special Collections Department, University of Texas at El Paso, Oral History Collection (hereafter: OHC), Mike Romo, interview by Oscar J. Martinez, October 8, 1975.

26. Martinez, *Chicanos of El Paso*, 143–44.

27. Foley, *Quest for Equality*, 7.

28. Mora, *Border Dilemmas*, 32.

29. Magali M. Carrera, *Imagining Identity in New Spain: Race, Lineage, and the Colonial Body in Portraiture and Casta Paintings* (Austin, TX, 2003).

30. Claudio Lomnitz, *Deep Mexico Silent Mexico: An Anthropology of Nationalism* (Minneapolis, MN, 2001), 51.

31. Alexander Dawson, "From Models for the Nation to Model Citizens: Indigenismo and the 'Revindication' of the Mexican Indian, 1920–40," *Journal of Latin American Studies* 30, no. 2 (1998): 279.

32. Ibid., 284.

33. See detailed comparison of Gamio and Vasconcelos in Rick López, *Crafting Mexico: Intellectuals, Artisans, and the State after the Revolution* (Durham, NC, 2010), 127–37.

34. José Vasconcelos, *The Cosmic Race/La raza cósmica* (1925; Baltimore, MD, 1997).

35. Alexandra Minna Stern, "From Mestizophilia to Biotypology: Racialization and Science in Mexico, 1920–1960," in *Race and Nation in Modern Latin America*, ed. Nancy P. Appelbaum (Chapel Hill, NC, 2003), 194–95.

36. See discussions of this strategic neglect in Herman Bennett, *Colonial Blackness: A History of Afro-Mexico* (Bloomington, IN, 2009); and Ben Vinson III and Bobby Vaughn, *Afroméxico: Herramientas para la historia* (México, DF, 2004).

37. Stern, "From Mestizophilia to Biotypology," 38–42.

38. Bobby Vaughn and Ben Vinson III, "Unfinished Migrations: From the Mexican South to the American South: Impressions on Afro-Mexican Migration to North Carolina," in

Beyond Slavery: The Multilayered Legacy of Africans in Latin America and the Caribbean, ed. Darién J. Davis (New York, NY, 2007), 226. See also Gonzalo Aguirre Beltrán, *La población negra de México: Estudio etnohistórico* (México, DF, 1989).

39. Vasconcelos, *Cosmic Race/raza cósmica*, 20.

40. Grace Peña Delgado, "At Exclusion's Southern Gate: Changing Categories of Race and Class among Chinese Fronterizos," in *Continental Crossroads: Remapping U.S.-Mexico Borderlands History*, ed. Samuel Truett and Elliott Young (Durham, NC, 2004), 183–208. The sheer quantity of files in the SRE archives pertaining to Chinese migrants in Mexico reveals an overwhelming preoccupation with the perceived negative influences of Chinese and other Asian populations on Mexican society and culture. In particular, see material from the anti-Chinese committee in Torreon, in SRE, 15–28–22. Evelyn Hu-DeHart, "Racism and Anti-Chinese Persecution in Sonora, Mexico, 1876–1932," *Amerasia* 9, no. 2 (1982): 1–28; Robert Chau Romero, *The Chinese in Mexico, 1882–1940* (Tucson, AZ, 2010).

41. José Jorge Gómez Izquierdo, *El movimiento antichino en México (1871–1934): Problemas del racismo y del nacionalismo durante la Revolución Mexicana* (México, DF, 1991); Gerardo Rénique, "Race, Region, and Nation: Sonora's Anti-Chinese Racism and Mexico's Postrevolutionary Nationalism, 1920s–1930s," in *Race and Nation in Modern Latin America*, ed. Nancy P. Appelbaum, Anne S. Macpherson, and Karin Alejandra Rosemblatt (Chapel Hill, NC, 2003), 219–26.

42. Erika Lee, *At America's Gates: Chinese Immigration during the Exclusion Era, 1882–1943* (Chapel Hill, NC, 2003), 176.

43. Chau Romero, *Chinese in Mexico.*

44. José Trueba Lara, *Los chinos en Sonora: Una historia olvidada* (Hermosillo, Mexico, 1990).

45. Cheryl Harris examines the historical construction of a racialized legal system in the United States as a product of the entangled relationship between property and race. See "Whiteness as Property," *Harvard Law Review* 106, no. 8 (1993): 1713–14.

46. Michael Omi and Howard Winant, *Racial Formation in the United States from the 1960s to the 1980s* (New York, NY, 1994).

47. Gary Gerstle points out that the 1790 law remained in effect until 1952. *American Crucible: Race and Nation in the 20th Century* (Princeton, NJ, 2001), 4.

48. The Black Legend refers to a propagandist discourse elaborated by enemies of the Spanish Empire to demonize colonial-era Spaniards and their descendants as uncivilized and barbaric, exaggerating their mistreatment of indigenous peoples and non-Catholics. This trope continued into the modern era and was used as part of a racist discourse to discriminate against ethnic Mexicans in the United States.

49. Arnoldo De Leon, *They Called Them Greasers: Anglo Attitudes toward Mexicans in Texas, 1821–1900* (Austin, TX, 1983).

50. Matthew Pratt Guterl, *The Color of Race in America, 1900–1940* (Cambridge, MA, 2001).

51. Clare Sheridan, "'Another White Race': Mexican Americans and the Paradox of Whiteness in Jury Selection," *Law and History Review* 21, no. 8 (2003): 109–44; See also Mai Ngai, "The Architecture of Race in American Immigration Law: A Reexamination of the Immigration Act of 1924," *Journal of American History* 86, no. 1 (June 1999): 67–92.

52. Sheridan, "'Another White Race,'" 2.

53. Ibid., 5; and Nicholas De Genova, "Introduction: Latino and Asian Racial Formations at the Frontiers of U.S. Nationalism," in *Racial Transformations: Latinos and Asians Remaking the United States*, ed. Nicholas De Genova (Durham, NC, 2006), 1–22. Although the 1897 racial prerequisite case *In re Rodriguez* confirmed the 1848 ruling on citizenship status and for the first time vaguely designated Mexicans as "white," the ruling remained arbitrary and left Mexicans' "white" status open to debate. Subsequent rulings (e.g., *Morrison v. California* in 1933) continued to view Mexicans' status as "an unsettled question." In re Rodriguez, 81 F. 337 (W.D. Tex. 1897); Ian Haney López, *White By Law: The Legal Construction of Race* (New York, NY, 2006), 43–47.

54. In *Walls and Mirrors*, Gutiérrez carefully distinguishes the integrationist strategies of upwardly mobile Mexicans active in organizations such as LULAC from the efforts of working-class Mexicans to resist assimilation and form mutual aid and labor societies.

55. Paul Schuster Taylor, *An American-Mexican Frontier: Nueces County, Texas* (Chapel Hill, NC, 1934), 268–69.

56. Nancy Leys Stepan, *The Hour of Eugenics: Race, Gender, and Nation in Latin America* (Ithaca, NY, 1991).

57. Foley, *White Scourge*, 5.

58. Laura E. Gómez, *Manifest Destinies: The Making of the Mexican American Race* (New York, NY, 2007), 152.

59. Foley, "Becoming Hispanic," 61.

60. Steven H. Wilson, "Brown over 'Other White': Mexican Americans' Legal Arguments and Litigation Strategy in School Desegregation Lawsuits," *Law and History Review* 21, no. 1 (Spring 2003): 145–94; Carlos Kevin Blanton, "From Intellectual Deficiency to Cultural Deficiency: Mexican Americans, Testing, and Public School Policy in the American Southwest, 1920–1940," *Pacific Historical Review* 72, no. 1 (2003): 39–62.

61. National Archives II [hereafter: NAII], College Park, MD, 811.4016/215, p. 41.

62. *El Paso Herald Post*, October 6, 1936: 5, 42.

63. Alex Saragoza, *The Monterrey Elite and the Mexican State, 1880–1940* (Austin, TX, 1988).

64. *El Porvenir*, Monterrey, Mexico, June 17, 1926: 2, 42, quoted in Michael Snodgrass, *Deference and Defiance in Monterrey: Workers, Paternalism, and Revolution in Mexico, 1890–1950* (Cambridge, England, 2003), 10.

65. Ibid., 11–12, 115, 177.

66. *El Porvenir*, Monterrey, Mexico, October 16, 1936: 15, 43.

67. Members of LULAC and Mexican Americans in general had direct exposure to Vasconcelos and his writings. During this presidential campaign in 1928, Vasconcelos visited cities in Texas, including El Paso. Benjamin Johnson, "The Cosmic Race in Texas: Intermarriage, White Supremacy, and Civil Right Politics," paper presented at the Tepoztlán Institute for the Transnational History of the Americas Conference, July 2006.

68. *El Porvenir*, Monterrey, Mexico, October 16, 1936: 15, 43.

69. Oscar Martínez, *Border Boom Town: Ciudad Juárez since 1848* (Austin, TX, 1978), 74–76.

70. On the racialized practices of the New Deal, see, Tey Marianna Nunn, *Sin Nombre: Hispana and Hispano Artists of the New Deal Era* (Albuquerque, NM, 2001); Foley, *White Scourge*, 163–82; Alexandra Minna Stern, *Eugenic Nation: Faults and Frontiers of Better Breeding in Modern America* (Berkeley, CA, 2005), 115–49.

71. Samuel Truett and Elliott Young, "Making Transnational History: Nations, Regions, and Borderlands," in *Continental Crossroads*, ed. Truett and Young, 19–20.

72. On this period in Mexican-U.S. history, see works by Fernando Alanís Enciso, for example, "No cuenten conmigo: La política de repatriación del gobierno mexicano y sus nacionales en Estados Unidos, 1910–1928," *Estudios Mexicanos* 19, no. 1 (2003): 401–61. Examples of U.S. scholarship include Francisco Balderrama and Raymond Rodríguez, *Decade of Betrayal: Mexican Repatriation in the 1930s* (Albuquerque, NM, 1995); and Camille Guerin-Gonzalez, *Mexican Workers and American Dreams: Immigration, Repatriation, and California Farm Labor, 1900–1939* (New Brunswick, NJ, 1994).

73. "Consulado en El Paso: Deportados a México," SRE, IV-344–6, 1931; and Associated Press Report in CCP, MS 231, Box 15, Folder 8. See also *La Prensa*, March 19, 1931: 3, 44. One set of data indicates that during the deportation period, the Mexican population of El Paso (both citizens and non-citizens of the United States) decreased from 102,421 in 1930 to 96,804 in 1940. A different source shows a decline of Mexican Americans from 68,476 in 1931 to 55,000 in 1940. Martínez, *Border Boom Town*, 189n45.

74. "Datos estadísticos sobre situación colonia mexicana, April 28, 1930," in SRE, IV-524.5.

75. Fernando Saúl Alanis Enciso, "The Repatriation of Mexicans from the United States and Mexican Nationalism, 1929–1940," in *Beyond la Frontera*, ed. Overmyer-Velázquez; David Fitzgerald, "Inside the Sending State: The Politics of Mexican Immigration Control," *International Migration Review* 40, no. 2 (2006): 259–93.

76. Alan Knight, *U.S.-Mexican Relations, 1910–1940*, Center for U.S.–Mexican Studies, Monograph Series, 28 (San Diego, CA, 1987), 1–18.

77. See for example, "Telegram to Vice President John Garner," in CCP, Box 16, Folder 1.

78. NAII, 811.4016/216.

79. Mary Kay Vaughan, *Cultural Politics in Revolution: Teachers, Peasants, and Schools in Mexico, 1930–1940* (Tucson, AZ, 1997).

80. *El Paso Times*, October 20, 1936: 10; see examples of protest in CCP, Box 16, Folder 2.

81. W. H. Timmons, *El Paso: A Borderlands History*, 2nd ed. (El Paso, TX, 2004), 277; See also OHC, Chris P. Fox, interview by Leon C. Metz and Ed Hamilton, July 25, 1972; Shawn Lay, *War, Revolution and the Ku Klux Klan: A Study of Intolerance in a Border City* (El Paso, TX, 1985).

82. William Beezley and Colin MacLachlan, *El Gran Pueblo: A History of Greater Mexico* (Englewood Cliffs, NJ, 1994), 267–68.

83. Ariela Gross, "Texas Mexicans and the Politics of Whiteness," *Law and History Review* 21, no. 1 (2003): 195–205.

84. Foley, *White Scourge*, 8.

85. Taylor, *American-Mexican Frontier*, 241.

86. Foley, *White Scourge*, 8.

87. OHC, Aurelia Phillips, interview by Oscar J. Martinez, September 16, 1975.

88. David Montejano, *Anglos and Mexicans in the Making of Texas, 1836–1986* (Austin, TX, 1987); and Foley, *White Scourge.*

89. The population remained static in the early years of the twentieth century, remaining below two percent of the total population by 1920 and dropping to one percent in the early

1940s. OHC, Chris P. Fox, interview by Leon C. Metz and Ed Hamilton, July 25, 1972; and Drusilla Nixon, interview by Sarah E. John and Oscar J. Martinez, December 11, 1975.

90. OHC, Chris P. Fox, interview by Leon C. Metz and Ed Hamilton, July 25, 1972; Gabbert, "Defending the Boundaries of Care," 8, 357.

91. OHC, Drusilla Nixon, interview by Sarah E. John and Oscar J. Martinez, December 11, 1975.

92. Ibid.; and OHC, Leona Washington, interview by Charlotte Ivy, November 2, 1985.

93. Nancy Farrar, *The Chinese in El Paso*, Southwestern Studies Monograph No. 33 (El Paso, TX, 1972), 46.

94. "Consulado en El Paso: Listas de pasajeros chinos que se dirijen a México," SRE, IV-397-2, 1930; Julia Maria Schiavone Camacho, "Traversing Boundaries: Chinese, Mexicans, and Chinese Mexicans in the Formation of Gender, Race, and Nation in the Twentieth-Century U.S.-Mexican Borderlands," January 1, 2006. ETD Collection for University of Texas, El Paso. Paper AAI3214013, p. 135.

95. Texas Centennial Pamphlet, 1836–1936 in CCP, Box 71, Folder 4.

96. In her analysis of the impact of public health regimes on immigrant populations in late nineteenth- and early twentieth-century Los Angeles, Natalia Molina examines how "public health as an institution and a discourse evolved into a key site of racialization . . . and . . . came to exert an influence that extended far beyond the realm of health." *Fit to Be Citizens?: Public Health and Race in Los Angeles, 1879–1939* (Berkeley, CA, 2006), 4. This discourse built on late nineteenth-century definitions of the "modern" citizen and urban resident that relied on the construction and subsequent regulation of "normal and deviant" populations imagined along lines of race and ethnicity. See also Nayan Shah, *Contagious Divides: Epidemics and Race in San Francisco's Chinatown* (Berkeley, CA, 2001), 3–7; and Alan M. Kraut, *Silent Travelers: Germs, Genes, and the "Immigrant Menace"* (New York, NY, 1994).

97. *Texas 1936 Centennial Celebration: Official Publication*, El Paso City Council.

98. Cleofas Calleros, Press Release in CCP, Box 16, Folder 1; Gabbert, "Defending the Boundaries of Care," 420, 454.

99. García, "Mexican Americans and the Politics of Citizenship," 188.

100. "M. A. Gomez et al. v. T. J. McCamant, and Alex K. Powell, et al., District Court of El Paso County, Texas, Sixty Fifth Judicial District, 12 October 1936," in CCP, Box 77, Folder 18. In his oral interview discussing his experience of El Paso in the 1930s, Mario Acevedo recalls the collaborative opposition to the classification by Mexicans of all stripes: "Me acuerdo [que fue] una de las veces en que tanto el nacido aquí de origen nuestro, tanto el exiliado, todo el mundo de sangre mexicana, hablando a lo pelón, nos unimos," in OHC, Mario Acevedo 1900, interview by Cesar Caballero, April 9, 1973.

101. Mario T. Garcia, *Mexican Americans* (New Haven, CT, 1989), 1–3; Montejano, *Anglos and Mexicans*, 232; Zaragosa Vargas, *Labor Rights Are Civil Rights: Mexican American Workers in Twentieth-Century America* (Princeton, NJ, 2005), 63.

102. "Clasificación del Mexicano como de raza de color," in CCP, Box 16, Folder 1.

103. Servando Esquivel, *El Continental*, October 18, 1936: 5, 46.

104. "A los nuestros," in CCP, Box 16, Folder 2.

105. *El Continental*, October 11, 1936: 7.

106. "Federation of Latin American Societies," in CCP, Box 16, Folder 1.

107. CCP, Box 16, Folder 2.

108. Benjamin Johnson, "The Plan of San Diego Uprising and the Making of the Modern Texas-Mexican Borderlands," in *Continental Crossroads*, ed. Truett and Young, 292.

109. Craig A. Kaplowitz, *LULAC, Mexican Americans, and National Policy* (College Station, MD, 2005), 6.

110. See for example, "Treasury Department," in CCP, Box 16, Folder 2; and NAII, 811.4016/225.

111. NAII, 811.4016/236.

112. NAII, 811.4016/233 and 235.

113. For examples, see letters of support from Arizona, Colorado, and Houston, in CCP, Box 16, Folder 1.

114. NAII, 811.4016/221.

115. Gómez, *Manifest Destinies*, 152; Gross, "Texas Mexicans."

116. See for example, Thomas A. Guglielmo, "Fighting for Caucasian Rights: Mexicans, Mexican Americans, and the Transnational Struggle for Civil Rights in World War II Texas," *Journal of American History* 92 (March 2006): 1212–37; and the case of wartime bi-national labor organizing in El Paso and Ciudad Juárez, in Mario T. García, *Mexican Americans: Leadership, Ideology, and Identity, 1930–1960* (New Haven, CT, 1989), 188–90. The struggle over Mexicans' racial classification and division continued after the war. On May 3, 1954, just two weeks before the Supreme Court ruled in *Brown v. Board of Education*, the Court ruled on *Hernández v. Texas*, in which it condemned the "systematic exclusion of persons of Mexican descent" from state jury pools. Sheridan, "'Another White Race.'"

117. Daniel Martinez HoSang, *Racial Propositions: Ballot Initiatives and the Making of Postwar California* (Berkeley, CA, 2010), 2.

8

"Forget All Differences until the Forces of Freedom Are Triumphant": The World War II–Era Quest for Ethnic and Religious Tolerance

ROBERT L. FLEEGLER

IN NOVEMBER 1942, Louis Adamic, a public intellectual who wrote several books about the role of immigrants in American society, authored an article in the *New York Times Magazine* titled "No 'Hyphens' This Time." Adamic commented on the lack of punitive action against recent immigrants during the war: "So far in this war—aside from the campaign against the Japanese group on the Pacific Coast, which was old-time exclusionism hitched to a potentially serious military problem—there has been no great hue and cry about the 'foreigners.'"[1] He suggested that Americans were beginning to think anew about diversity:

> The result is the partial but continuing breaking down of the belief, held by many old-line Americans, that the great diversity of backgrounds in our population is a disadvantage to the United States as a nation. The gradual deterioration of this idea has apparently been enough to prevent anti-alien hysteria, in spite of considerable attempts not unrelated to Hitler's purposes to foment it.

To contemporary ears, Adamic's indifferent reference to the Japanese American internment may seem incongruous. Nevertheless, his comments reflect that while the U.S. government interned 120,000 Japanese Americans during World War II, the conflict accelerated the incorporation of "white ethnic" groups such as Jews, Italians, and other descendents of the great immigrant wave of 1882 to 1924 into a broader conception of American nationhood. Adamic went on to presciently note, "It is possible that a few decades hence historians will regard this fact as one of our biggest present slices of good fortune."[2]

Indeed, historians have often cited World War II as a key turning point in the acceptance of the Ellis Island–era immigrants. Most scholars agree that World War II accelerated the decline of nativism and the integration of immigrants from southern and eastern Europe and their children into

American society.[3] Wartime migrations of Americans to different regions played an important role as 27 million citizens left their homes and neighborhoods for employment in wartime industries or to join the military.[4] Many left homogenous, rural communities and urban ethnic neighborhoods where they had relatively little contact with people from different national and religious backgrounds.

The military experience brought disparate peoples into contact, as native-stock Americans and immigrants from various ethnic backgrounds fought and died together. In his 1944 book, *A Nation of Nations*, which detailed the contributions of virtually every immigrant group, Adamic wrote, "There is more getting together among Americans than ever before, more acceptance of people on the basis of their personal qualities regardless of background. This is especially true of the men in the services. There is nothing like being together in a foxhole, a bomber, or a submarine."[5] A *New York Evening Post* headline above the obituary of soldiers from March 25, 1943, sounded this same theme: "Their Names Are Alien But—Their Blood is All American."[6]

As a result of the changes wrought by the war, many remember World War II as a watershed in their acceptance as Americans. Paul Piscano, an Italian American architect, recalled that after the war, "The Italo-Americans stopped being Italo and started becoming Americans."[7] The Jewish American baseball player Hank Greenberg agreed:

> When you joined the Army, you became an American. When I broke into baseball, every time they wrote about me it had something to do with my ethnic background. When the war was over, the ballplayers were no longer referred to by their religion. I think it was an amazing change that took place.[8]

Of course, the inclusion of white ethnics came at the partial expense of other racial groups. While white ethnics fought together, African Americans and Japanese Americans fought in segregated units. Wartime propaganda, such as the platoon films, largely excluded African Americans from this new conception of American identity. Furthermore, government propaganda portrayed the Japanese enemy as a homogenous foe, sometimes using racialized rhetoric to compare them to apes and vermin.[9]

Wartime pluralism also revealed very important limits for white ethnics that scholars have tended to downplay. Before the war, educational and propaganda programs combined two different approaches. One, which I call "contributionism," emphasized the cultural and economic benefits that immigrants brought to American life. To a certain degree, it highlighted the differences between ethnic groups and stressed the disparate contributions they made to American society. This message suggested that the United States was a "nation of immigrants" enhanced by the gifts brought by the newcomers.

The radio program, *Americans All . . . Immigrants All*, which aired in 1938–39, illustrated the contributionist perspective. In an attempt to improve public attitudes toward immigrants, *Americans All* featured a weekly discussion of the accomplishments of groups such as Italians and Jews.[10] The press release for the show about Jews noted, "There is not one episode or crisis in our national history in which the Jews have not played a part."[11] The release revealed contents of the show, which included the Jewish role in the American Revolution, among other things: "Stirring episodes deal with the help given by Jews to George Washington; their heroic participation in the War between the States and the World War and the battle against disease of misery."[12]

In a similar vein, the American Common exhibit at the 1939–40 World's Fair in New York City displayed the cultural traditions of different groups every week. Opened for the 1940 season, the Common consisted of an open-air theater with six booths displaying arts and crafts from different ethnic groups. A pamphlet from the Department of Education of the New York World's Fair described the events planned at the Common: "During each week of the 1940 season it is expected that a different group will take over this special area. Here will be found native folk-dances, native art, and native food."[13]

The second philosophy, which I call the "tolerance and unity" school, focused on the need to treat individual citizens equally as well as the imperative for cooperation between all Americans, regardless of race or ethnicity. It diminished the differences between groups and focused on what individuals from diverse backgrounds shared in common. This school suggested that immigrants should be accepted as American citizens because, in the final analysis, they were little different from native-stock Americans. The universalist approach of this school neglected the varied heritages brought to the United States by different ethnic groups.

The World's Fair also illustrated the "tolerance and unity" school. During the week celebrating Hungarian Americans at the American Common, Frederick Sheffield, assistant United States commissioner to the exposition, explained it was important that ethnic groups work together "so that as a unit and as a nation it [United States] can put forth its very best efforts."[14] During an interfaith week, Monsignor Francis W. Walsh, president of the College of New Rochelle, declared, "Any one who seeks to divide America on purely religious grounds in matters purely economic, political, or social is a public enemy of America, and if he refuses to keep his pen dry he should be banished beyond the territorial limits of the United States."[15]

As a result of the need for national unity during the war, propaganda and educational efforts shifted significantly away from contributionism and toward the tolerance message. Many policy makers feared that the contributionist approach, by discussing the achievements of groups separately, only increased ethnic tensions. The onset of the conflict made cooperation a paramount concern as the country needed to work together to defeat Japan and Germany. Many feared a repeat of the nativist hysteria of World War I, when immigrants, and German Americans in particular, faced discrimination that hindered the war effort. During their blitzkrieg across Europe, the Nazis exploited divisions in France and other countries to speed their military victories. Japanese and German propagandists were hard at work trying to accomplish the same ends in the United States. The Office of War Information (OWI), created by FDR in 1942 to explain the war to the American people, was determined to fight these divisions by promoting an ideological view of the conflict as a battle for democracy and tolerance against fascism and intolerance.[16] Private organizations such as the American Jewish Committee (AJC) and the National Conference of Christians and Jews (NCCJ) adopted a similar strategy, merging the practical wartime need for unity with the idealistic interest of eliminating nativism. Motivated by the rise of Nazism abroad as well as the growth of anti-Semitism at home, Jewish groups often led these efforts.[17] An OWI official best summarized the approach of these groups: "By making this a people's war for freedom, we can help clear up the alien problem, the negro problem, the anti-Semitic problem."[18]

Wartime propaganda and its postwar counterpart emphasized that tolerance and cooperation represented an essential part of American identity. Various public and private organs labeled discrimination based on race, religion, and ethnicity as un-American and dangerous to the nation's stability and role as a world leader. To the proponents of this view, the war's goal was not merely to defeat the nation's military enemies, but to create a more tolerant society without racial, ethnic, and religious discrimination. Tolerance and "teamwork" were essential not only to victory in World War II, but also to the successful conversion to a peacetime economy and to fighting the Cold War. While not disappearing entirely, contributionism moved into the background as the wartime message broadened the definition of Americanism to include white ethnics while largely excluding African Americans and Japanese Americans. This evolution paved the way for a definition of national identity which suggested that the children and grandchildren of immigrants should be accepted, not because of the cultural benefits provided by a more diverse polity, but rather because these immigrants shared the same basic values and ideologies as native-stock Americans.[19]

FDR led the way in promoting the message of tolerance and national unity. As early as January 2, 1942, Roosevelt criticized employers who were firing loyal aliens, declaring that such actions were "engendering the very distrust and disunity on which our enemies are counting to defeat us."[20] In a fireside chat on February 23, 1942, FDR was explicit in directly connecting tolerance to the success of the war effort: "We Americans will contribute unified production and unified acceptance of sacrifice and effort. That means a national unity that can know no limitations of race or creed or selfish politics."[21] FDR continued to use the same rhetoric throughout the conflict. Campaigning in Boston on November 4, 1944, he declared that religious intolerance had no place in American life.[22]

Roosevelt's comments regarding tolerance did not usually extend beyond European immigrants, whom he viewed in a far more positive light than Asian immigrants. He repeatedly praised the achievements of eastern and southern European newcomers but offered no such remarks regarding Japanese or Chinese Americans. FDR evinced a long history of suspicion toward the Nisei and Issei communities dating back to the 1920s, which informed his support for the Japanese American internment.[23] Furthermore, when he announced the repeal of the Chinese Exclusion Act in 1943, Roosevelt made no comment on the contributions made by the Chinese American community to the war effort, merely saying that "an unfortunate barrier between allies has been removed" and that "the war effort in the Far East can now be carried on with greater vigor and a larger understanding of our common purpose."[24]

FDR often expressed an ideological view of the war's aims. "The United Nations are fighting to make a world in which tyranny and aggression cannot exist; a world based upon freedom, equality, and justice; a world in which all persons regardless of race, color or creed may live in peace, honor, and dignity," he declared on March 24, 1944.[25] Roosevelt repeated those sentiments in his Boston campaign speech, saying, "They [our soldiers] also are fighting for a country and a world where men and women of all races, colors and creeds can live, work, speak and worship—in peace, freedom, and security."[26]

Propaganda posters produced by the Office of War Information stressed the need for cooperation between racial and ethnic groups. One poster declared, "TEAMWORK among all nationalities, groups and creeds made America great. That same teamwork now will spread our victory."[27] Others read, "In Unity There Is Strength" and "Together for Victory."[28] Some posters equated bigotry with a lack of patriotism. One included a headline that said, "Our enemies' orders to their spies in the U.S.A," above a letter signed by Hitler, Mussolini, and Hirohito. The letter said, "Divide labor and management, turn class against class and spread religious hatred." The caption instructed citizens to "FIGHT un-American propaganda." Another urged, "Don't fall for ENEMY PROPAGANDA—Against our Government—Against Our Allies—Against Catholics, Jews, or Protestants." The poster said below, "Remember—Hitler and the Japs are trying to get us to fight among ourselves."[29]

Echoing this sentiment, one poster displayed the text of President Roosevelt's Executive Order 8802 of 1941 banning racial discrimination in military production. Another showed a number of people working on a tank with names that represented a cross section of ethnic groups, including Cohen, Lazzari, Kelly, and Dubois, with the caption, "Americans All." Below that, the poster paraphrased 8802: "It is the duty of employers and labor organizers to provide for the full participation of all workers without discrimination because of race, creed, color, or national origin."[30]

Although not the dominant message, traces of contributionism appeared in these images. One poster read, "This is America" in large letters with "Keep it Free" scrolled at the bottom. In between, it described the country as a "melting pot of liberty-loving people from all corners of the earth. People of different origins, faiths, cultures—all cemented together into one great nation by their passions for freedom." Another featured an immigrant saying, "I'm an Ellis Island American. I left the old country to be free—and nobody is going to take that freedom away. That's why I'm fighting on the production line—to help destroy the enemies of freedom. Let's keep'em rolling."[31]

The OWI delivered a similar message to foreign-language newspapers concerning their coverage of the war. At the time, future California U.S. senator Alan Cranston served as the chief of the Foreign Language Division of the OWI. In August 1942, he told a group of foreign language newspaper editors that their colleagues in underground newspapers overseas would ask them to: "Unite! Stand together against the forces of aggression. Forget all differences until the forces of freedom are triumphant. Print nothing that will divert attention from the all-important task of defeating the Nazis and the Fascists."[32]

Believing the foreign-language press was more susceptible to enemy propaganda, the OWI provided a list of recommendations for that press's coverage, which are especially helpful in discerning the priorities and rationales behind government propaganda efforts. The first recommendation emphasized the ideological nature of the war: "This is not a racial or a national war, but a war against dictatorship and for the freedom of people of every race, color, and creed." They also suggested that reporters minimize divisions between ethnic groups: "We must close our ranks against the common enemy, the Axis. Strife within groups in this country weakens our war effort." In practical terms, this meant avoiding any news stories "which tend to promote long-standing dissensions among Americans of different extractions. We must forget all differences until the forces of freedom are triumphant."[33]

Director Frank Capra's famous *Why We Fight* movie series contained similar messages. The films were a series of seven movies commissioned by the Pentagon to explain the reasons for the war. In episode 7, *War Comes to America*, which discusses religious life in America, the narrator says, "Churches. We have every denomination on earth. 60 million of us regularly attend. And nobody tells us which one we have to go to." As the narrator reads this statement, the images of several churches appear on the screen, as well as one of a synagogue. In this film, a synagogue is simply another "church" rather than a place of worship for people of a different religion. This rhetoric and imagery promoted tolerance for non-Christian faiths by implying that all religions are essentially the same.[34]

The short film, *The House I Live In* (1945), starring the young Frank Sinatra, expressed an almost identical point of view. Sinatra sees a mob of children attacking another young kid and asks them why they are picking on this one child. One of the children responds, "We don't like his religion," and another says, "Look mister, he's a dirty . . . "—but before he can complete his sentence, Sinatra cuts him off. The singer tells them that they are behaving like Nazis:

> Religion makes no difference. Except maybe to a Nazi or somebody as stupid. . . . God created everybody. He didn't create one people better than another. Your blood's the same as mine. Mine's the same as his. Do you know what this wonderful country is made of? It's made up of a hundred different kinds of people and a hundred different ways of talking and it's made up of a hundred different ways of going to church. But they're all American ways.[35]

Sinatra, like the narrator of the *Why We Fight* episode, reflects the universalist approach of wartime propaganda. Both Sinatra and Capra largely eschew discussing the disparate cultural contributions of various faiths; instead, they cite the similarities between different religions as the primary reason for religious tolerance.

Sinatra tells the children about the cooperation between Colin Kelly, a Presbyterian pilot, and Meyer Levin, his Jewish comrade, when they attacked a Japanese battleship after Pearl Harbor. "You think maybe they should have called the bombing off because they had different religions? Think about that fellas. Use your good American heads. Don't let anyone make suckers out of you," declares Sinatra. Ol' Blue Eyes concludes the film by singing, "The House I Live In," in which he celebrates the contributions paradigm, crooning, "All races and religions . . . That's America to me."[36]

Sinatra's performance of the "The House I Live In" also revealed that African Americans were excluded from the new definition of Americanism. One section of the song, which contained references to black civil rights, was excluded from the film. This version of "The House I Live In" spoke of "The words of old Abe Lincoln, of Jefferson and Paine, of Washington and [Frederick] Douglass, and the task that still remains!"[37]

Hollywood war films also featured themes of unity and cooperation.[38] Movies such as *Bataan* (1943), *Gung Ho* (1943), *Guadalcanal Diary* (1943), and *Pride of the Marines* (1945) showed soldiers from different groups working together to defeat the nation's enemies. Each of these "platoon" films had a variety of characters, usually including a southerner, a Jew, an Italian, and a native-stock American. Like *The House I Live In*, the films demonstrated the limits of the wartime message, as blacks rarely appeared, and Asians were nonexistent, except as Japanese villains. African American groups protested their limited presence in these movies; Walter White, head of the National Association for the Advancement of Colored People (NAACP), complained to OWI director Elmer Davis that "the Negro has been very largely confined in the films to comic or menial roles."[39]

These films downplayed the ethnic backgrounds of the various characters and presented a cross section of ethnic types that were obvious to people of the time. In *Pride of the Marines*, a gun with both a Star of David and a shamrock painted on it depicts the importance of cooperation. More often, the message is simply implied. The audience sees soldiers from different ethnicities and religions working together without prejudice hindering their efforts. "The diversity roster varied from one film to another," observed Gary Gerstle, "but the stock characters were the Anglo-Protestant, the Irish Catholic, and the eastern European Jew."[40]

Like other forms of wartime propaganda, the platoon films underscored the values Americans held in common. One of the first images in *Guadalcanal Diary* is of a Catholic priest leading an interfaith service on a navy ship. One of the soldiers says to another, "Say Sammy, your voice is OK." Sammy responds, "Why not? My father was a cantor in the synagogue."[41] The message is clear: people of all religions are working together to win the war.

As with many aspects of wartime propaganda, filmmakers manipulated the tolerance message to suit wartime needs. Whereas 1930s Hollywood movies had shown Chinese peasants exploited by Chinese warlords, the stereotypical characters changed following Pearl Harbor. Now viewers saw the Chinese peasants, who had become allies of the U.S., being exploited by Japanese warlords.[42]

The 1943 edition of National Brotherhood Week, which the National Conference of Christians and Jews (NCCJ) had started in 1934 to promote understanding between different religious groups, also reflected this perspective. Everett Clinchy, the president of the NCCJ, invoked the same ideas as the OWI posters in a CBS Radio address. Clinchy discussed American soldiers in their training camps: "Do you realize what goes on in these camps? They make teams. Yes, teams like basketball teams and baseball teams, only these are fighting for our country's big ideas." Like the Hollywood films, Clinchy praised the ethnic platoon. "Listen to the roll-call of the families which have relatives in the service along with yours and mine,—Anderson, Bonet, Fernandez, Garcia, Goldstein, Jones, Kelly, Palegolos, Wysocki . . . the men who know that we don't have to fear anybody as long as the nation ticks together like the wheels of a clock."[43]

The motto for Brotherhood Week 1943 was "Brotherhood: Democracy's Shield Against Intolerance and Oppression," a significant shift from the "Make America Safe For Differences" slogan of 1939. The literature instructed religious groups to have a priest, a minister, and a rabbi deliver the message of tolerance to their congregations, so that all major faiths were represented. Declaring that all forms of prejudice must be rejected, one such trio reiterated that the mission was "to proclaim and illustrate by acting at home these principles of justice, amity, understanding and cooperation among men of all religious persuasions and racial origins upon which human brotherhood depends and to commend them to the world."[44]

While emphasizing tolerance, Brotherhood Week did not entirely discard contributionism. Clinchy also asked rhetorically in his radio address, "What is the American Idea? It is the big idea that on a continent 3,000 miles wide people of 47 Old World nationalities have come to live together as one nation." He also noted that Americans can often be divided by religion and ethnicity and that these divisions did not necessarily present a problem. Clinchy elaborated, "The only danger is that each might build the walls of separation too high so that they do not know what their neighbors are thinking or doing and do not understand them or cooperate with them."[45] Differences were acceptable, he argued, as long as they were not too great.

I'm an American Day, a holiday started by the Justice Department in 1939 to celebrate immigration, offered a similar wartime message. This observance grew dramatically during the war, from two hundred participating communities in 1939 to five hundred in 1943.[46] Some observances were quite large, with 675,000 people attending the 1942 celebration in Central Park.[47] The Immigration and Naturalization Service (INS) published a guide, "Gateway to Citizenship," to the staging of these ceremonies in 1943. The celebration centered on an induction ceremony for new citizens, speeches on the meaning of being an American, and patriotic songs.

The speeches, editorials, and celebrations associated with the day offered familiar themes. "Hitler has moved heaven and earth to break our spirit by dividing us," thundered one 1943 speech editorial, adding that "His propagandists have tried to start American Catholics, Protestants and Jews quarrelling among themselves." Another speech, in 1944, celebrated the virtues of tolerance. "Real Americanism—the only Americanism any of us can accept without reserve—is based on respect for human beings, the conviction that the true worth of an individual has no relation to his birthplace, religion, or color."[48]

As with the platoon films, I'm an American Day's festivities revealed how African Americans could be excluded from the more expansive definition of American identity. While New York City mayor Fiorello LaGuardia asked Walter White to serve as a member of his holiday committee every year during the war, it seems likely that blacks played a less prominent role in many communities. Chester Gillespie, an attorney in Cleveland, wrote White before I'm an American Day 1942 to suggest an alternative version of the immigration celebration: "I believe Negroes all over the country should call May 17th 'I Am an American Too' day and in connection there—with huge mass meetings should be held. Such action seems necessary because the government has officially set Negroes apart from the American people."[49]

Still, some observers believed the tolerance message would eventually have implications for the status of American blacks. Most famously, Gunnar Myrdal's study, *An American Dilemma* (1944), suggested that the World War II –era ideology of the United States exposed the contradiction between American ideals and practices. Myrdal, a Swedish sociologist analyzing race relations in America, noted that the war required the United States to profess ideas of tolerance and equality to combat the fascist doctrines of the Nazis and the Japanese. "The Negro problem has taken on a significance greater than it ever had since the Civil War," concluded Myrdal. "The world conflict and America's exposed position as the defender of the democratic faith is thus accelerating an ideological process which was well under way."[50]

American education joined the fight for tolerance during the war. In 1944 the National Education Association, the nation's largest teachers' union, made "education for tolerance" a priority for that year. As with other groups, the intercultural education movement shifted from a contributionist approach to promoting unity and cooperation, as the Service Bureau for Intercultural Education became simply the Bureau of Intercultural Education.[51] "The basic idea upon which intercultural education rests is simple," declared the American Jewish Committee's (AJC) magazine in 1943: "It is that members of one culture group can be taught to get along with members of other groups within the framework of a democratic society."

Unlike the Americanization campaigns of the World War I era, intercultural education did not seek to eliminate group differences.[52] Instead, intercultural education exposed students to the cultures of different immigrant groups. Students visited ethnic restaurants and neighborhoods, prominent figures from different groups appeared at classrooms, and schools held joint celebrations of Christmas and Chanukah. These programs focused on the similarities between peoples. "Folk dances, folk music, historical pageants, and native costumes emphasize the 'sameness' of all people in their joys, sorrows, etc. rather than the 'strangeness' of different groups," according to the AJC.[53] A poster in one of the classrooms summarized this perspective: "America—A Nation of One People From Many Countries."[54]

The military also promoted tolerance in its ranks. Every week, the Orientation Section of the Information and Education Division, Army Service Forces (ASF), distributed a discussion outline on important issues. Groups of soldiers were supposed to discuss the topic for a minimum of an hour a week during a period called Army Talk.[55] The subject of Army Talk no. 70 for May 5, 1945, was prejudice, and the message was a familiar one. "The man who spreads rumors," ASF Manual M 5 declared, "particularly rumors about any group—racial, religious, or national is doing Hitler's or Tojo's work." The manual asked the soldiers why racial and religious discrimination was harmful. The army replied, "History has taught us that when we discriminate against one segment of people, we set a pattern that may be used against other groups."[56]

Army regulations also facilitated interfaith cooperation, as standard operating procedure required chaplains to accommodate the religious needs of soldiers from traditions different than their own. In fact, religious leaders actively participated in the rituals and celebrations of other faiths; in one case, an Episcopal minister conducted a Passover seder when no rabbi was available. It was very common for a priest, a rabbi, and a minister to lead jointly funeral services for fallen soldiers. Cooperation did not always come easily, of course, and sometimes these policies forced religious conflicts to the surface. Declaring that his faith did not recognize the legitimacy of other religions, a Catholic chaplain once refused to provide volunteers for a seder. As a whole, though, military protocol, like Brotherhood Week, buttressed the idea that the United States was a "Judeo-Christian nation."[57]

"Car cards" appeared in buses, subways, and streetcars during the war with the same theme. These cards featured various protolerance and anti-prejudice messages, such as, "If You Hear Anyone Condemn a fellow American Because of Race or Religion . . . Tel'em Off [sic]" and "We Fought Together . . . Let's Work Together." Another showed a child crying while saying, "I Am So An American!" The rest of the card responded, "You Bet, Sonny . . . No Matter What Your Race or Religion!"[58]

These messages were ubiquitous during the war. Dr. Samuel Flowerman, research director of the American Jewish Committee, noted in a speech at the Waldorf Towers on November 30, 1945: "You have seen full page ads, you have seen billboards, you have seen match folders driving home the unity message; Catholics, Protestants, and Jews having fought together and lived together and died together and the need for unity in the post-war period." He noted the breadth of these efforts: "On the radio more than 216 individual stations broadcast every day some message of unity. . . . Way over a quarter million books have been distributed in libraries, hoping that people will understand and people will change their own ideas and get them across to others."[59]

Flowerman's observation reveals how widespread the message of toler-ance and national unity had become during the conflict. At the same time, the contributionist message, which formed an equal part of prewar pluralism, no longer had the same prominence. As a result, the war brought about a liberalization of attitudes toward recent immigrants, but in a way that tended to play down their cultural and economic contributions. The message of wartime pluralism seemed to be that ethnic diversity was acceptable because everyone was very close to being the same.

Toward the end of World War II and in its immediate aftermath, govern-ment and private organizations began to emphasize that the tolerance essen-tial to winning the war was also vital to the survival of postwar America. They feared that nativism, while submerged during the war, lurked beneath the surface and that domestic bigots were poised to take advantage of any instability that might occur while the country returned to a civilian foot-ing. Jewish organizations again took a leading role as the American Jewish Committee, fearing that Nazi propaganda during the 1930s and 1940s had exacerbated ethnic divisions, advocated the cause of postwar pluralism:

> Today the time has come for informing the American people of the dan-
> gers to American life and to American prosperity which the animosities

resulting from this propaganda involve, and which will continue to use Hitler's methods to promote their own selfish methods.[60]

Appeals during Brotherhood Week offered similar warnings about the dangers of the postwar world. FDR's Brotherhood Week message for February 1945 suggested, "It is a solemn duty for us to keep our country free of prejudice and bigotry so that when our fighting men return they may find us living by the freedom for which they are ready to give full measure of devotion."[61] A speech-editorial for Brotherhood Week declared, "Though the battle moves in our favor, we can lose it even in victory. Though we win by arms, we shall all go down to destruction if the spirit of brotherhood dies."[62]

Progressive groups such as the AJC and the NCCJ were not the only organizations concerned about intolerance and disunity following the war. Eric Johnston, president of the U.S. Chamber of Commerce, a conservative business group, gave a speech stressing that prejudice hindered economic growth. The AJC paraphrased a version of his talk for distribution:

> True economic progress demands that the whole nation move forward at the same time. It demands that all artificial barriers erected by ignorance and intolerance be removed. . . . I repeat: Intolerance is poor economy. Prejudice does not pay. Discrimination is destructive. These are things that should be manifest to the American people if we are to counteract the pestiferous labors of race and hate-mongers.[63]

Johnston's belief that discrimination harmed prosperity would become a central theme after the war. He continued, "Let's not apologize for the amazing variety of our human material here in America. Let us rather glory in it as the source of our robust spirit and opulent achievements," adding that Americans need to be reminded that the country "receives more than it gives" from immigrants.[64]

Hollywood movies also began to highlight the need for tolerance in the postwar world. In *Pride of the Marines*, another multiethnic platoon is fighting on Guadalcanal. The movie revolves around Al Schmid, a soldier who is blinded while fighting for his life during the battle. After Schmid is wounded, he is sent to a military hospital to recover. He convalesces with a number of other wounded soldiers, who are concerned about their prospects in the postwar world.

Lee Diamond, a Jewish soldier who was wounded with Schmid, stresses the need to continue wartime cooperation. "One happy afternoon when God was feeling good, he sat down and he thought up a rich beautiful country, and he named it the USA. . . . Don't tell me we can't make it work in peace like we do in war. Don't tell me we can't pull together." The film reiterates the need for tolerance in postwar America. While on a train back to the East Coast to receive a medal, Schmid fears that his blindness will make him unable to obtain employment. Diamond tells him that a lot of people will have problems after the war. Schmid replies, "What problems have you got? You're in one piece ain't you. . . . When you go for a job there ain't nobody gonna say we don't have a use for ex-heroes like you." Diamond tells him that he could face discrimination as well: "There's guys that won't hire me because my name is Diamond instead of Jones. Cause I celebrate Passover instead of Easter. Don't you see what I mean. . . . You and me . . . we need the same kind of world. We need a country to live in where no one gets booted around for any reason."[65]

The war's conclusion did not relieve the anxieties of the protolerance coalition, as these groups continued to fear that ethnoreligious disunity and prejudice posed an imminent threat to the nation's social and political health. The Ad Council, an organization founded in 1942 to make public service announcements during the war, declared, "Our nation no longer has the supremely unifying cause of victory. The trend will be to stop pulling together, to stop working for the common good. Group clashes promise to be renewed, old hatreds revived; new war-born discords seem almost inevitable."[66] Some feared that unless wartime unity continued, the United States might undergo some kind of political cataclysm. The AJC added, "If the present system is allowed to proceed unchecked, it can undermine the American system. It may lead to revolution or dictatorship in which no cultural or economic group would be secure, in which freedom from fear and want would become a lost memory."[67] In his speech at the Waldorf Towers in November 1945, Flowerman warned the audience about the internal threat: "the war of machines and bullets has ended temporarily, not in all parts of the world, but the war of ideas has not even begun. We are just in the early stages of the war of ideas." Referring to domestic bigots, he said, "The enemy is not over there; the enemy isn't in the Pacific, the enemy is here."[68]

National Brotherhood Week's growing popularity exemplified the continuity with wartime themes as the NCCJ's summary of Brotherhood Week 1946 suggested it was the biggest and most successful ever: "It topped all previous years. Never was it more evident that Brotherhood Week has been taken over by the nation at large, and made it its own."[69] Equally revealing was the message for 1946. The slogan, echoing wartime propaganda, was "In Peace as in War TEAMWORK!" President Truman wrote a letter in support of the goals of Brotherhood Week, declaring, "The teamwork of the armed forces won the war. The spirit of teamwork should extend to our national life. As we united for victory, we must unite for peace."[70]

The week focused on the common bonds between Protestants, Catholics, and Jews. Three Supreme Court justices of different faiths, Felix Frankfurter, Harlan Stone, and Frank Murphy, stood on the steps of the Court for a newsreel in support of Brotherhood Week.[71] A radio roundtable between members of the three faiths emphasized the same idea. The Protestant said, "It's a strange thing, but what has become the burning necessity of modern times brings us back to the age-old teachings of the three religions we represent. The core of three religions is the brotherhood of men, under God."[72]

There were traces of the contributionist message that was central to the 1939 celebration. Frankfurter declared in a newsreel:

> The unfolding of our republic is the story of the greatest racial admixture in history. Of the 56 signers of the Declaration of Independence, 18 were of non-English stock. Foreign-born citizens from almost every land fought in the war for independence, helped to save the union, and in conspicuous numbers are found on the honor rolls of the two world wars.[73]

The NCCJ also suggested that schools produce plays illustrating the contributions of various groups to American life.[74]

The overriding message, however, focused less on contributions than intergroup cooperation. Truman's letter in support of Brotherhood Week 1947 reinforced this theme: "Democracy rests upon brotherhood. Justice, amity, understanding and cooperation among Protestants, Catholics, and Jews throughout the nation are cornerstones of our democracy. . . . With them we can maintain our national unity and keep up the teamwork needed in peace as in war."[75]

I'm an American Day followed a similar course after the conflict. The celebration continued its enormous growth, expanding from five hundred communities in 1943 to 1,100 communities by 1945.[76] In 1946 the Justice Department suggested a number of approaches for material to be published or broadcast on the day. They first emphasized the need to continue wartime unity during peacetime. Other suggestions included, "draw attention to the rich contributions to American thought and life, to her arts and science, by her foreign-born citizens" and "combat the doctrines that would divide and weaken this Nation by pitting one group of Americans against another."[77]

Unsurprisingly, the celebrations tended to be concentrated in states with significant immigrant populations. According to the INS, thirty-five states had at least one city with multiple I'm an American Day celebrations, and such observances were usually in large and medium-sized cities in the

Northeast and the Midwest. Boston, New York City, and Pittsburgh as well as other major metropolitan areas held festivities every year between 1939 and 1945. Smaller communities with diverse populations like Fort Wayne, Indiana, and Fall River, Massachusetts, observed the day at least five times in the same time frame. The fifteen states that did not feature cities with multiple celebrations were predominantly in the South and the West (See Figure 1).[78]

Minneapolis's observance of I'm an American Day 1947 provides an illustration of a typical community's celebration. The morning featured a music program followed by a talk by Mayor Hubert Humphrey and the presentation of certificates of citizenship to new arrivals to the country. With the certificates, the new Americans pledged to protect the Constitution and "to oppose all efforts to divide the American people and to sow the seeds of bigotry and prejudice among them."[79] Humphrey added, "The United States of America owes its greatness as a nation to the diversity of the peoples of all races and nationalities who have, over the generations, migrated to our shores."[80] Detroit's observance offered a similar array of events. In addition to a talk by the mayor, academics lectured the new

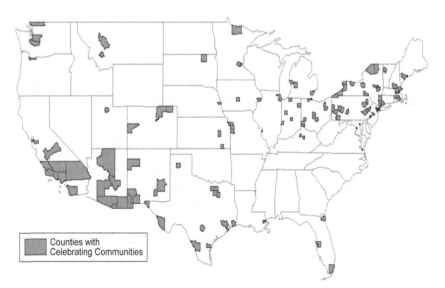

Counties with
Celebrating Communities

Figure 1. Communities Prominent in the Celebration of I'm an American Day, 1939–1945.
Source: "Roll-Call of Communities Prominent in the Observance of Citizenship (I Am an American) Day," U.S. Immigration and Naturalization Service, 1945.

Americans on the responsibilities of citizenship, including the necessity of voting.[81] Both celebrations included speeches and radio performances by people of various racial and ethnic groups.

Materials surrounding I'm an American Day repeatedly emphasized that Americans should not judge people on the basis of their race, color, or creed. One suggested editorial for 1947 exhorted, "Whenever a man is refused a job because of his parentage or religion; wherever a hooded gang can keep a man from voting; wherever folks are kept from speaking their minds without fear, American security is in danger."[82]

These festivals and holidays were only one of the ways organizations promoted the tolerance message. The American Jewish Committee's Department of Public Information sponsored the First American Exhibition on Superstition, Prejudice, and Fear. The exhibit, held at the American Museum of Natural History in New York in August 1948, contained an area known as the Hall of Prejudice. This section featured, among other things, a quiz called "How Much Do You Know About the Human Races?" The answers to the quiz demonstrated that every nation is an amalgamation of different races, and that the "strongest nation," the United States, contained the greatest mixture.[83] The exhibit also included illustrations from books like the *Races of Mankind*, by Ruth Benedict, which criticized theories of scientific racism. One sign in the exhibit said, "Judge a person for himself, not for His Color, Race or Creed."[84]

Hollywood also produced a number of films decrying bigotry in the immediate postwar years, most notably *Crossfire* (1947) and *Gentlemen's Agreement* (1947). These two films told very different stories about anti-Semitism but promoted the same message about the necessity of tolerance. In *Crossfire*, Robert Young and Robert Mitchum play a policeman and a military officer who investigate the murder of a Jewish man. In *Gentlemen's Agreement*, Gregory Peck portrays a reporter who pretends to be a Jew in order to write a story about anti-Semitism in America. Both films were nominated for the Academy Award for Best Picture in 1947, with *Gentlemen's Agreement* receiving the award. While the films discuss anti-Semitism, they also analyze the broader theme of the universal nature of prejudice and its overall dangers to society.

In both films, traditional anti-Semitic stereotypes are visible. During the war, there were persistent rumors that a disproportionate number of draft dodgers were Jews. In *Crossfire*, Montgomery (Robert Ryan), the soldier who turns out to be the killer, claims to have not met the victim, Joseph Samuels, until that evening. He tells Captain Finlay (Young), "Of course . . . seen a lot of guys like him." Finlay says, "Like what?" Montgomery responds, "Oh you know, guys that played it safe during the war. Scrounged around keeping themselves in civvies. Got swell apartments. Swell dames. You know the kind." Finlay replies, "I'm not sure that I do. Just what kind?" Montgomery elaborates, "Oh you know. Some of them are named Samuels. Some of them got funnier names."[85] In *Gentlemen's Agreement*, a coworker assumes that Phil Green (Peck) must have been in public relations rather than in the trenches during the war because he seems like a "clever guy."[86]

The films both stress the need to look beyond the more odious forms of anti-Semitism and examine the genteel prejudice that exists in America among people who do not consider themselves bigots. In *Gentlemen's Agreement*, Green's editor tells him he wants to get beyond the overt anti-Semites and root out "the people who would never attend an anti-Semitic meeting or send a dime to Gerald L. K. Smith."[87] In *Crossfire*, Finlay says, "This business of hating Jews comes in a lot of different sizes. There's the you can't join our country club kind. And you can't live around here kind. And yes, you can't work here kind. And because we stand for all of these we get Monty's kind. He's just one guy. We don't get him very often . . . but he grows out of all the rest." In both films, all forms of prejudice, even the most "harmless," are seen as equally threatening.

The movies emphasize the similarities between ethnic and religious groups. In *Gentlemen's Agreement*, Green's son asks him, "What are Jews anyway? I mean exactly." Green responds, "There are lots of different churches. The people who go to that particular church are called Catholics. Then there are people who go to other churches and they're called Protestants. And there others who go to still different churches and they're called Jews. Only they call their kind of churches synagogues or temples." This language echoes the approach of wartime films like *Why We Fight* and *The House I Live In*. Green adds, "You can be an American and a Protestant or a Catholic or a Jew. Religion is different from nationality." Green also reproaches his Jewish secretary for her shock when he reveals that he is a Gentile. In a variation on Shylock's "Hath not a Jew eyes" speech from Shakespeare's *The Merchant of Venice*, he declares, "Same face. Same eyes. Same nose. Same suit. Same everything. Here take my hand. Feel it. Same flesh as yours, isn't it? No different today than it was yesterday, Miss Wales. The only thing that's different is the word Christian."[88]

Along the same lines, *Crossfire* demonstrates that any kind of prejudice is the problem, not merely anti-Semitism. Finlay has to convince Leroy, a GI from Tennessee, to help him obtain evidence against Montgomery. Leroy says, "I don't see that this is any of my business anyway." Finlay asks, "Has Monty ever made fun of your accent?" Leroy replies, "Sure. Lots of times." Finlay says:

Why? He calls you a hillbilly doesn't he? Says you're dumb. He laughs at you because you are from Tennessee. He's never even been to Tennessee. Ignorant men always laugh at things that are different. Things they don't understand. They're afraid of things they don't understand. They end up hating them.

Finlay also tells Leroy that his grandfather was killed for being an Irish Catholic a century ago in Philadelphia. Perhaps reflecting the paucity of information about immigrants in history books, Finlay says, "That's history, Leroy. They don't teach it in school. But it's real American history just the same." He continues, "Thomas Finlay was killed in 1848 just because he was an Irishman and a Catholic. It happened many times. . . . And last night Joseph Samuels was killed just because he was a Jew." Further universalizing the experience of prejudice, Finlay concludes, "Hating is always the same. Always senseless. One day it kills Irish Catholics, the next day Jews, the next day Protestants, the next day Quakers, it's hard to stop, it can end up killing men who wear stripe neckties, or people from Tennessee."[89]

National civil rights organizations reiterated Finlay's message that all types of prejudice affected all minorities. At its national conference in 1947, the NAACP passed a resolution on racial and religious tensions, declaring that, "In defending the rights of Negroes, we recognize the fact that what happens to one minority group effects [sic] all the others," adding, "we must combat the continuing wave of anti-Jewish, anti-Semitic, anti-Oriental, anti–foreign born feeling in this country."[90] Rabbi Irving Miller, president of the American Jewish Congress, discussed similar themes when he addressed the NAACP convention of 1950: "Through the thousands of years of our tragic histories we should have learned one lesson and learned it well: that the persecution at any time of any minority portends the shape, quality and intensity of the persecution of all minorities."[91]

As Myrdal had predicted, the postwar period witnessed important advances for African Americans. Jackie Robinson broke the color line in major league baseball when he debuted for the Brooklyn Dodgers in 1947, and President Truman integrated the military in 1948. Public displays of virulent racism became less respectable as Mississippi senator Theodore Bilbo's blatantly bigoted rhetoric, which had largely gone unnoticed before the war, became a source of national controversy. Indeed, the Senate refused to seat Bilbo in 1947 because he had incited violence against black voters during his reelection campaign.[92]

The tolerance message remained visible in educational programs into the late 1940s. The Ad Council launched a campaign called "United America" in June 1946 to attack prejudice. According to the Ad Council's 1946–47 annual report, the campaign's "objective is to promote American unity by the lessening of inter-faith and inter-racial prejudices."[93] Like Brotherhood Week, the campaign echoed the wartime themes of unity, cooperation, and the dangers of prejudice and discrimination.

All of the 1949 ads concluded by emphasizing that tolerance was an essential element of American identity: "Make sure that you are not spreading rumors against a race or religion. Speak up, wherever you are, against prejudice, and work for better understanding. Remember that's what it means—to be a good American citizen."[94] One ad reiterated that rumors about different ethnic groups posed just as much danger to American unity today as they had during World War II, adding, "But perhaps we don't know that rumors are just as dangerous today as they were during the war. *Because*—rumors about other groups, other religions and other races always threaten our national unity—without which we cannot hope to survive."[95]

By this time, international themes were becoming more prominent in these programs, partly to counter Soviet propagandists who were attempting to use the discrepancy between American rhetoric and practice as a tool in the Cold War.[96] A radio spot for I'm an American Day in 1949 noted, "Today they [immigrants] join with their fellow-Americans in telling the world that it's great to live in a land where bigotry and discrimination are on the run, where human rights and brotherhood are on the rise, where there's equality, opportunity and justice for all."[97] John Sullivan, general chairman of Brotherhood Week 1950 and a former secretary of the navy, declared, "Our aims and our objectives are not limited to the creation of a more dignified and amicable life within our own borders, for we know beyond doubt that today the biggest question for the entire world is whether the human spirit is to remain free or is to be swallowed up by totalitarianism."[98] A speech from the Veterans of Foreign Wars (VFW), a conservative veteran's group, for Brotherhood Day 1949 echoed this sentiment: "The V.F.W. believes that [brotherhood] can be our effective answer to the communist and fascist enemies who foster DIS-unity among our own people in an effort to conquer the very foundation of American democracy."[99]

The VFW's involvement in the antidiscrimination campaign reveals how much this language became part of postwar American thought and rhetoric, if not practice.[100] Most of the programs promoting tolerance came from liberal organizations such as the NCCJ and AJC. The VFW's rhetoric for Brotherhood Week 1949, however, was virtually identical to that of the progressive groups. "Some of our people forget that American Protestants and Catholics, Gentiles and Jews, Japanese-Americans, Negroes and men of many other racial origins have fought shoulder to shoulder under one flag—the Stars and Stripes."[101]

World War II laid the groundwork for the greater inclusion of the descendents of southern and eastern European immigrants during the postwar period. Discrimination by no means disappeared in the immediate postwar years; anti-Catholic feeling continued to manifest itself in attacks by some observers on the "authoritarian" nature of Catholicism and its supposed incompatibility with American democracy.[102] Jewish groups remained very worried about the persistence of anti-Semitism. Nevertheless, poll after poll revealed that traditional forms of religious and ethnic prejudice were less virulent after 1945. The wartime message of tolerance and unity, however, facilitated this greater inclusion of white ethnics by emphasizing that these groups were little different from native-stock Americans or each other. The contributionist ideology, which focused more on the unique cultural benefits brought by these different groups, faded into the background. This message, however, would slowly gain strength during the 1950s and 1960s as Americans became increasingly appreciative of the cultural and economic assets provided by the "nation of immigrants."

NOTES

I would like to thank Andrew Huebner and Alan Petigny for their very helpful comments on this article. I would also like to thank Gabe Rosenberg for constructing the map.

1. *New York Times Magazine*, November 1, 1942.

2. Ibid.

3. David Bennett, *Party of Fear: From Nativist Movements to the New Right in American History* (New York, 1995), 285. Bennett wrote, "By war's end, nativism was all but finished." John Blum discussed the greater acceptance of Jews and Italians in *V Was for Victory: Politics and American Culture during World War II* (New York, 1976), 154, 175. He wrote, "More important, the President's order [ending the enemy alien status of Italians] marked the beginning of the end of Italian American separatism. As in the past, Italian Americans, like Irish or Polish or Scandinavian Americans, preserved much of their ethnicity, but henceforth, increasingly, they did so from choice rather than necessity." About Jews, he echoed this sentiment: "Nevertheless, wartime prosperity, the increasing geographic mobility of Americans, the homogenizing effects of shared dangers in battle, the essential contributions of Jewish refugee scientists, and the stunned reactions to the Nazi gas chambers, continued to facilitate for American Jews acceptance by the society in which they lived." These works and others like them have influenced books that synthesize extended periods of American history. Eric Foner concurred in *Story of American Freedom* (New York, 1998), 237. He wrote, "By the end of the war, the new immigrant groups had been fully accepted as ethnic Americans, rather than members of distinctive and inferior 'races.'"

4. Richard Polenberg, *One Nation Divisible: Class, Race, and Ethnicity in the United States since 1938* (New York, 1980), 54.

5. Louis Adamic, *A Nation of Nations* (New York, 1944), 5–6.

6. *New York Evening Post*, March 25, 1943.

7. Studs Terkel, *"The Good War": An Oral History of World War Two* (New York, 1984), 138.

8. *The Life of Hank Greenberg*, director Aviva Kempner (Fox, 1999).

9. John Dower, *War without Mercy: Race and Power in the Pacific War* (New York, 1986), 3–32. Some scholars have shown that the war did accelerate the acceptance of Chinese Americans, who were viewed in a more positive light because they were associated with an Allied government. See K. Scott Wong, *Americans First: Chinese Americans and the Second World War* (Cambridge, MA, 2005).

10. Nicholas V. Montalto, *A History of the Intercultural Education Movement, 1924–1941* (New York, 1982), 155–58. Montalto notes that program's designers hoped to prevent a repeat of World War I–era anti-immigrant hysteria and to help pave the way for the admission of European refugees fleeing Nazism.

11. Press release, 1 February 1939; *Americans All*, Promotion and Follow-Up; Records of Special Programs and Projects; Records Relating to Radio Programs, 1935–1941, Americans . . . All, Immigrants . . . All-Brave New World; Records of the Office of Education, RG 12; National Archives at College Park, Maryland (NACP henceforth).

12. "What the Recordings Are About," Promotion and Follow-Up; Special Programs and Projects; Records Relating to Radio Programs; Office of Education, RG 12; NACP.

13. "Teaching the New York World's Fair, No. 1," Century of Progress International Exposition—New York World's Fair Collection, Group 820, Box 38, Folder 5, Manuscripts and Archives, Yale University Library, Yale University, New Haven, Connecticut.

14. *New York Times*, July 7, 1940.

15. Ibid.

16. Allan M. Winkler, *The Politics of Propaganda: The Office of War Information, 1942–1945* (New Haven, CT, 1978), 1–6.

17. Leonard Dinnerstein, a leading authority on anti-Semitism, suggests that American anti-Semitism peaked during the war years. Dinnerstein, *Anti-Semitism in America* (Oxford, 1994), 105–49.

18. Polenberg, *One Nation Divisible*, 46.

19. Many scholars have discussed the drive for tolerance in the years before and during the war. For instance, see Philip Gleason, *Speaking of Diversity* (Baltimore, 1992), 153–88; Richard Steele, "The War on Intolerance: The Reformulation of American Nationalism," *Journal of American Ethnic History* 9 (Fall 1989): 9–35; Richard Weiss, "Ethnicity and Reform: Minorities and the Ambience of the Depression Years," *Journal of American History* 66 (December 1979): 566–85; and Nicholas V. Montalto, *A History of the Intercultural Education Movement, 1924–1941* (New York, 1982). For instance, Steele notes how the tolerance approach gained strength at this time: "It seems fair to conclude that by 1942 a more liberal view significantly challenged the bigotry that had long dominated public attitudes and national policy. The propaganda effort introduced the general public to ideals that had earlier captivated social scientists, educators, religious leaders, and others. In this process, however, it probably undermined any hope the cultural pluralists may have had for national acceptance of their vision of America" (Steele, "The War on Intolerance," 31). While each of these pieces dealt with part of this story, they did not follow the evolution of these ideologies from the war to the early postwar period. Thus, they do not show both the full shift away from contributionism and toward tolerance during and after World War II.

20. Franklin D. Roosevelt, *The Public Papers and Addresses of Franklin D. Roosevelt*, vol. 11 (New York, 1950), 6.

21. Franklin D. Roosevelt, *Nothing to Fear: The Selected Addresses of Franklin Delano Roosevelt* (New York, 1946), 321.

22. Franklin D. Roosevelt, *The Public Papers and Addresses of Franklin D. Roosevelt*, vol. 13 (New York, 1950), 398.

23. Greg Robinson, *By Order of the President: FDR and the Internment of the Japanese Americans* (Cambridge, MA, 2001).

24. Franklin D. Roosevelt, *The Public Papers and Addresses of Franklin D. Roosevelt*, vol. 12 (New York, 1950), 548. The Chinese Exclusion Act, passed in 1882, banned all Chinese immigration to the United States.

25. Ibid., 103.

26. Roosevelt, *Nothing to Fear*, 431–32.

27. OWI Poster, 44–PA-1869, Records of the Office of Government Reports, RG 44, NACP.

28. Ibid., 44–PA-414A; 44–PA-2151, NACP.

29. Ibid., 44–PA-1477; 44–PA-660, NACP.

30. Ibid., 44–PA-352, NACP.

31. Ibid., 44–PA-2049; 44–PA-165, NACP.

32. Address by Alan Cranston, Chief, Foreign Language Division, Office of War Information, before the Editors and Publishers of Foreign Language Newspapers in New York City, August 25, 1942, Speech Materials, Public Relations Files, 1940–54, Education and Americanization Files; Records of the Immigration and Naturalization Service (INS), Record Group 85; National Archives Building, Washington, D.C. (NAB henceforth).

33. Ibid.

34. *Why We Fight*, director Frank Capra (Special Service Division, Army Service Forces, 1942–44), episode 7.

35. *The House I Live In*, director Mervyn LeRoy (RKO, 1945).

36. Ibid.

37. The African American singer Paul Robeson often performed this version of the song. It is not exactly clear when he began to do so, but he must have started sometime after the summer of 1942, as the lyrics contain references to the Battle of Midway (June 1942). *Paul Robeson: The Original Recording of "Ballad for Americans" and Great Songs of Faith, Love, and Patriotism* (Vanguard, 1989 ed.). Robeson and the language of *"The House I Live In"* emerged from the Popular Front culture of the 1930s, when the alliance of the Communist Party with American liberals produced art and literature that promoted a pluralistic definition of citizenship. Eric Foner explained that the Popular Front suggested "ethnic and racial diversity was the glory of American society," adding that, "Museum exhibitions, murals sponsored by the Works Progress Administration, the federally sponsored 'people's theater,' and Hollywood films all rediscovered the American people and expanded its definition to include the new immigrants and their children, and even non-whites." See Foner, *Story of American Freedom*, 212.

38. See Thomas Doherty, *Projections of War: Hollywood, American Culture, and World War II* (New York, 1999), 139–48, for a thorough look at these films. See also Gary Gerstle, *American Crucible* (Princeton, NJ, 2001), 204–10. Gerstle observes how these films were one of the primary forces behind the image of the multiethnic platoons, which included white ethnics but excluded blacks.

39. "Letter from Walter White to Elmer Davis," NAACP Papers, Part II, Box A462, Folder 5, Library of Congress, Manuscript Reading Room, Washington, D.C. The OWI worked closely with Hollywood on the content of these films during the war.

40. Gerstle, *American Crucible*, 205.

41. *Guadalcanal Diary*, director Lewis Seller (Fox, 1943).

42. Richard Oehling wrote that during the war, "The warlords and soldiers simply had to be put into Japanese uniforms." See Oehling, "The Yellow Menace: Asian Images in Film," in *The Kaleidiscopic Lens: How Hollywood Views Ethnic Groups*, ed. Randall Miller (Englewood, NJ, 1980), 196–97. Reflecting the integration of the military, the combat films of the early 1950s featured a more multicultural cast. *Steel Helmet*, a Korean War film released in 1951, shows a unit with black and Nisei soldiers. *Go For Broke*, released the same year, portrayed the exploits of the all–Japanese American 442nd combat division during World War II.

43. "America's Big Idea," 2, National Conference of Christians and Jews Collection (NCCJ henceforth), Brotherhood Week 1943, Box 5, Social Welfare History Archives (SWHA henceforth), Elmer L. Andersen Library, University of Minnesota, Minneapolis.

44. "A Call to the Churches of America," NCCJ, Box 5, Brotherhood Week 1943, SWHA.

45. "America's Big Idea," 5, SWHA.

46. "Brief Suggestions on Citizenship Recognition Ceremonies for 'I'm an American Day Committees,'" INS, Holidays and Holydays, I'm an American Day, 1941–54, YIVO Institute for Jewish Research (YIVO henceforth), American Jewish Historical Society (AJHS henceforth), New York, N.Y.

47. "Letter from Walter White to Mayor LaGuardia," Papers of the NAACP, Part II, General Office File, 1940–55, Box A319, Folder 3, "I'm an American Day," 1941–49, Library of Congress, Manuscript Reading Room, Washington, D.C.

48. "I'm an American Day," 1944, 4, AJC Records, RG 347.17.10, Gen-10, Box 98, Holidays and Holydays, 1942–50, I'm an American Day, Articles, Editorials, and Speeches, YIVO, AJHS.

49. Papers of the NAACP, Part II, General Office File, 1940–55, Box A319, Folder 3, "I'm an American Day," 1941–49, Library of Congress, Manuscript Reading Room, Washington, D.C.

50. Gunnar Myrdal, *An American Dilemma: The Negro Problem and Modern Democracy* (New York, 1944), 997, 1004.

51. Stuart Svonkin, *Jews against Prejudice: American Jews and the Fight for Civil Liberties* (New York, 1997), 64. He wrote, "Whereas the Service Bureau under DuBois (1934–1941) had stressed the distinctive cultural contributions of particular racial and ethnic groups . . . the reconstituted bureau emphasized 'unity and understanding among all cultural groups,' a message specifically designed to fit wartime demands for social cohesion."

52. *American Jewish Committee (AJC) Reporter*, April 1944, 6.

53. *AJC Reporter*, May 1944, 6.

54. *AJC Reporter*, April 1944, 6.

55. *Common Ground*, Autumn 1945, 24. Louis Adamic edited this journal.

56. Ibid., 25, 28.

57. Deborah Dash Moore, *GI Jews: How World War II Changed a Generation* (Cambridge, MA, 2004), 118–55.

58. *Anti-Defamation League (ADL) Bulletin*, October 1952, 3.

59. Samuel H. Flowerman speech at Waldorf Towers, November 30, 1945, AJC Records, RG 16, DIS-15, Scientific Research Subject Files, General Subject Files, 1945–48, Blaustein Library (BL henceforth), New York, N.Y.

60. "Details of Plan," 1945, 2, AJC Records, RG 347.17.10, Gen-10, Box 168, Mass Media, 1944–48, Intergroup Relations, YIVO, AJHS.

61. "Brotherhood Week Is a Fighting Week," January 9, 1945, AJC Records, RG 347.17.10, Gen-10, Box 97, Holidays and Holydays, 1946–60, National Brotherhood Week, YIVO, AJHS.

62. Ibid. The files listed some items as potential speeches and some items as potential editorials for Brotherhood Week. It is not always clear which was which.

63. "Prejudice is Bad Business," 4, AJC Records, RG 347.17.10, Gen-10, Mass Media, Bigotry and Prejudice, Educational Kit—WWB, YIVO, AJHS.

64. Ibid., 4.

65. *Pride of the Marines*, director Delmer Daves (Warner Brothers, 1945).

66. "Program Information Exchange: Recommendation for an Advertising Campaign on American Unity," 1946, 1, AJC Records, RG 347.17, Gen-10, Box 14, Mass Media, Bigotry and Prejudice, Advertising and Public Relations, 1946–1951, YIVO, AJHS.

67. Ibid., 1.

68. Flowerman speech, 16, BL.

69. "Brotherhood Week in 1946," 1, NCCJ, Box 5, Brotherhood Week 1946, SWHA.

70. "Problem No.1 for Americans," NCCJ, Box 5, Brotherhood Week 1946, SWHA.

71. "Brotherhood Week in 1946," 4, SWHA.

72. "The Good World of the Future," 2, 11/14//45, AJC Records, RG 347.17.10, Gen-10, Box 97, Holidays and Holydays, 1945–59, Brotherhood Week, Radio and Television, YIVO, AJHS.

73. "U.S. Justices Plead for Tolerance," February 14, 1946, Universal Newsreels, RG 200, Vol. 19–47, NACP.

74. "Problem No. 1 for Americans," SWHA.

75. "Letter from Truman to Clinchy," NCCJ, Box 5, Brotherhood Week 1946, SWHA.

76. "'I'm an American Day,' a Fact Sheet for the Use of I'm an American Day Committees," INS, 1, AJC Records, RG 347.17.10, Gen-10, Box 98, Holidays and Holydays, 1941–54, I'm an American Day, YIVO, AJHS.

77. Ibid., 3.

78. Papers of the NAACP, Part II, General Office File, 1940–45, Box A319, Folder 3, "I'm an American Day," 1941–49, Library of Congress, Manuscript Reading Room, Washington, D.C.

79. "Memo from Minnesota Jewish Council," May 29, 1947, AJC Records, RG 347.17.10, Gen-10, Box 98, Holidays and Holydays, 1941–54, I'm an American Day, YIVO, AJHS.

80. Ibid.

81. "Eighth Annual Welcome to New Citizens," May 18, 1947, AJC Records, RG 347.17, Gen-10, Box 98, Holidays and Holydays, 1941–54, I'm an American Day, YIVO, AJHS.

82. "The Watchword is Vigilance," 1, May 18, 1947, AJC Records, RG 347.17.10, Gen-10, Box 98, Holidays and Holydays, 1942–50, I'm an American Day, Articles, Editorials, and Speeches, YIVO, AJHS.

83. "Memo on Exhibit on Superstition, Fear, and Prejudice," October 5, 1946, 5, AJC Records, RG 347.17.10, Gen-10, Box 14, Exhibits, Bigotry, and Prejudice, 49–61, YIVO, AJHS.

84. *AJC Reporter*, September 1948, 5.

85. *Crossfire*, director Ed Dmytryk (RKO, 1947).

86. *Gentlemen's Agreement*, director Elia Kazan (Fox, 1947).

87. Ibid. Gerald L. K. Smith was a populist, anti-Semitic demagogue during the 1930s and 1940s.

88. Ibid.

89. *Crossfire.*

90. "Resolutions Adopted by the National Conference of the NAACP, Washington D.C., June 28, 1947," Papers of the NAACP, Part I, 1909–1950, Reel 12, Group II/Series A/Box 40, 1947 Annual Convention, File: Resolutions, 0119, "Resolutions Adopted," Rhode Island College, Providence, RI.

91. "Address by Rabbi Irving Miller to the 41st Annual Convention of the National Association for the Advancement of Colored People, Boston, Massachusetts, July 21, 1950," Papers of the NAACP, Part I, 1909–1950, Reel 12, Group II/Series A/Box 148, File: Speeches (1–2), "Address of Rabbi Irving Miler," Rhode Island College, Providence, RI.

92. Robert L. Fleegler, "Theodore Bilbo and the Decline of Public Racism, 1938–1947," *Journal of Mississippi History* 68 (Spring 2006): 1–27.

93. "1946–1947 Ad Council Annual Report," AD Council Annual Reports, 1942–2000, Record Series 13/2/202, Box 1, Folder: Ad Council Annual Report, 1946–47, University of Illinois Archives (UIA henceforth), Urbana, IL. In 1949, the AD Council noted in an introduction to proofs of these ads that, "In the past few years newspapers in the United States have run thousands of ads which are especially prepared by volunteer advertising agencies."

94. "Proof of Ad Council Ads," Ad Council Historical File, 1942–97, Record Series 12/2//207, Box 7, United America (Anti-Prejudice, 1949), UIA.

95. "Do You Know a Rumor?—when you hear one," Ad Council Historical File, 1942–97, Record Series 12/2//207, Box 7, United America (Anti-Prejudice, 1949), UIA.

96. See Mary L. Dudziak, *Cold War Civil Rights: Race and the Image of American Democracy* (Princeton, NJ, 2000), and Thomas Bortelsmann, *The Cold War and the Color Line: American Race Relations in the Global Arena* (Cambridge, MA, 2001).

97. "I'm an American Day, 30 Second Spot," AJC Records, RG 347.17.10, Gen-10, Holidays and Holydays, 1945–49, I'm an American Day Radio and Television, YIVO, AJHS.

98. "Brotherhood for Peace And Freedom," Papers of the NAACP, Part II, Box A387, Folder 3, Library of Congress, Manuscript Reading Room, Washington, D.C.

99. "Letter from Mark Kinsey to Joseph J. Wolfson," January 12, 1949, AJC Records, RG 347.17.10, Gen-10, Holidays and Holydays, 1945–57, Brotherhood Week, Articles, Editorials, Speeches, YIVO, AJHS.

100. The notion of promoting tolerance to fight the Soviet Union in the Cold War would become even more prevalent in the 1950s. Virtually every public event regarding immigration and every political debate over immigration policy would stress the idea that intolerance hindered our ability to win the allegiance of the decolonizing world. See Robert Fleegler, "A Nation of Immigrants: The Rise of Contributionism, 1924–1965" (PhD diss., Brown University, 2005), 134–84.

101. Ibid.

102. For instance, Paul Blanshard, *American Freedom and Catholic Power* (Boston, 1949). Blanshard first put forth this argument in a series of articles in the *Nation* in 1948.

9

Romantic Crossings:
Making Love, Family, and Non-Whiteness in California, 1925–1950

ALLISON VARZALLY

"I'M SORRY IT IS ONLY A DOLLAR," Tommy Yoneda apologized in the note accompanying his donation to United China Relief, a social service agency dedicated to war-torn China, "but I am an evacuee here with my parents who are Americans, the same as I am. My daddy used to be a longshoreman in San Francisco, and he picketed together with thousands of Chinese and white people—although he is of Japanese descent." A young boy of mixed race, Tommy entered a Japanese internment camp just after the outbreak of World War II with his Jewish mother, Elaine, and Japanese father, Karl. In 1930s and 1940s California, Karl and Elaine had mingled with an eclectic mix of minority activists and participated in leftist organizations ranging from the Civil Rights Congress, Communist party, and International Labor Defense to the Filipino social club and Chinese Worker's Association. When Tommy learned from his parents of suffering among Chinese displaced and disoriented by conflict, he looked beyond his own difficult circumstances and ethnic roots to express his support. His empathy persisted after his mid-war release. As soon as Karl enlisted in the United States Army's Military Intelligence Service, Elaine secured her and her son's exit from Manzanar on the condition that Tommy remained in a Caucasian's custody. She begrudgingly accepted the terms, but not before voicing her objection: "If Tommy was to spend weekends or what have you with any of our Chinese, Filipino, or Negro friends," she asked the camp director, "would he be in violation of his right to be in Military Area No. 1?" Practicing the multicultural preferences of his mother, Tommy regularly associated with non-whites in his new home of Petaluma, California. As a Jew and Japanese at a time when both ethnic groups were subject to hatred and hostility, Tommy was doubly vulnerable. But rather than defend himself against anti-Semitic or anti-Japanese attacks, Tommy devoted his energies to countering the racist remarks of classmates "who were just terrible as far as the Negroes are concerned." Tommy's personal experiences of discrimination and his family's teachings made him appreciate and challenge the breadth of ethno-racial prejudice he observed.[1]

Although not typical of 1940s Californians, the multiethnic associations and sympathies of the Yonedas suggest the growing sense of connection and compatibility among non-whites in the second quarter of the twentieth century. Increasingly, minorities in the period perceived similarities in their histories and current conditions. Recognition of shared misfortune and a will to correct ethnic and race-based inequalities drew them together. This emerging sensibility among non-whites, hurried by the stresses of World War II, first developed out of local spaces and relationships. Between 1925 and 1950, the arrival of new immigrants and migrants accentuated the already impressive diversity of the state. Although many planned to live and work in ways that preserved their ethno-racial integrity, the very diversity of California and its patterns of prejudice frequently undercut these efforts. These non-whites mixed in churches, farms, schools, working districts, and neighborhoods because it was difficult not to. A host of unjust laws and practices that included restrictive housing covenants, alien land laws, employment discrimination, and school segregation pressed them into the same areas.[2] Intercultural families like the Yonedas sometimes resulted and hinted at the new and potentially subversive closeness of American minorities.

Proliferating works on whiteness have traced the complex process by which European ethnics acquired racial advantages. Typically, these works see whiteness as an identification defined by privilege and access. By exploiting political footholds, responding to overtures of established whites, and forgiving class differences, Italians, Poles, and Slavs lifted themselves into whiteness during the end of the nineteenth and first half of the twentieth century. As they assimilated, they revised and accepted a singular set of values and behaviors understood as "American." Also critical to their elevation were invidious comparisons they made between themselves and non-white groups: Asian, Mexican, and especially African Americans. Although whiteness studies provide critical insights into race formation, they have neglected the perspectives and experiences of non-whites. In most accounts, these latter groups appear as necessary foils or receptacles into which whites projected their submerged longings. The perceptions and actions of non-whites themselves remain obscured.[3]

Focusing upon the romantic and familial ties made among minorities, this article notes the emergence of "non-whiteness" in the second quarter of twentieth-century California. This contingent and fledgling social category appeared alongside and in contrast to whiteness, but was still independent enough to shape its own content and membership. In other words, those who became non-white were not simply cast out or denied the preferred status of white. They forged a new and admittedly fragile identification defined not by power and a single standard of inclusion (the glue holding together whites) but disadvantage and heterogeneity. Certainly, Jewish, African, Mexican, Chinese, Japanese, and Filipinos did not suffer the same set of discriminations. If one imagines whiteness and color as designations of social and political privilege spread across a spectrum, Mexicans and Jews held middling positions in late 1940s California, while those of African and Asian descent remained clearly on the side of color. Although the former groups enjoyed the legal designation of "white" and Jews would achieve greater socioeconomic and political standing through the 1950s and 1960s, Mexicans and Jews confronted barriers in employment, education, and housing that belied the fullness of their inclusion as whites. This was especially true for those who hailed from working class, multiethnic, urban environments. Moreover, their proximity to minorities encouraged them to define themselves as fellow outsiders. Non-white individuals overall did not forget or surrender distinct ethno-racial backgrounds in the period, but many borrowed from one another to create multiple and hybrid identities defiant of the mainstream. In doing so, they set a course of Americanization different from the more linear, unidirectional path traveled by those European ethnics who had preceded them.[4]

Among the social relationships that nurtured pan-ethnic sensibilities and collaborations among non-whites, those of dating youth, romantic partners, and spouses were especially important. These intimacies expressed a depth of connection missing from the typically more casual encounters of minority neighbors, shoppers, workers, or worshipers. They represent unique sites of engagement and change where one can read the larger meanings of social relations.[5] In the 1930s and early 1940s, minority youth eager to experience the gendered possibilities of other cultures periodically dated other non-whites. Although often short-lived, these relationships showcased the excitement of ethnic crossings and the generation's interest in multicultural contacts. Building upon and pushing beyond the more fleeting interactions of youth, non-white adults attempted formal, lasting relationships. Their commitments marked a deeper investment in a non-white sensibility and dealt a more powerful blow to established categories of ethnicity and gender. The stresses of war, namely Japanese internment and conflict in the Pacific, pushed these partners and their mixed race progeny to their breaking points. In keeping together the non-white families proved their longevity and helped weaken community resistance to cultural mixing. Changed postwar attitudes made possible the end of legalized marital discrimination in California.

Intimacies between minorities developed in distinct contexts and had separate meaning from those that linked whites and non-whites. Without idealizing or denying the play of power in inter-minority pairs, it is true that they usually met on more even ground. This leveled terrain existed in a landscape shaped by white privilege. As relative equals, non-white partners enjoyed more chances to compromise and negotiate their cultural differences. Alternatively, in white-minority partnerships, the pull of dominant white culture had usually forced non-white members to surrender much of their own. Although some exchange of habits and values occurred, marriage tended to whiten, assimilate, and socially elevate minorities in the first half of the twentieth century. At the same time, the power differential encouraged whites to exoticize potential and actual partners.[6] Yet, inter-minority matches had different consequences. Rather than sacrifice traditions and views for the sake of socioeconomic mobility and acceptance, such couples often believed they could preserve their distinctions within a cross-cultural setting. With the help of their multiethnic children, they consolidated rather than erased ethnic ties and social boundaries, coming together around a more multicultural version of Americanization.

OBSTACLES AND RESISTANCE

Close social relationships between non-whites did not happen easily. In the second quarter of the twentieth century, legal limits and popular thinking about race and ethnicity constrained the romantic choices of all Californians. Whites expressed the fiercest opposition and directed the greatest resources to suppressing interracial dates and the marriages that might and did result. However, minorities similarly objected to romantic pairings made with cultural outsiders. Prejudice, international politics, and concerns about the longevity of the ethno-racial group in a hostile American society motivated their separatism.

At the beginning of the twentieth century, white Americans persuaded by an ideology of white supremacy and fears about the state's growing heterogeneity tried to shore up ethno-racial boundaries. Influential scientific studies documented the danger of intermixing and portrayed mixed race individuals as anemic, sterile, and degenerate. White Americans for the most part accepted these views and condemned sex and love across the color line. In retreating from contact with minorities and stressing their own racial greatness, whites believed they were defending a national identity. As more immigrants and minority migrants arrived and mixing appeared more likely, whites turned to legal protections. The California legislature pushed through a series of anti-miscegenation laws prohibiting a white person from marrying "a Negro, Mulatto, or Mongolian." By 1933, further amendments had also blocked 'Malays' (Filipinos) and Japanese from legal unions with whites.[7]

Minorities objected to these prohibitions because they feared the narrowing of already limited civil rights. The most persistent challenges originated among Filipinos, an overwhelmingly male group who felt the restraints most acutely. By 1931, the Los Angeles Superior Court settled four cases brought by Filipinos about the legality of their unions with whites. Within the black community, leaders urged state governments to overturn marital restrictions because such rules disrespected black citizens, especially black women who were made vulnerable to unscrupulous white men. Under the existing regime, white men could coerce black women to become their mistresses, discard them at will, and bear no legal responsibility. Japanese, too, chafed under anti-miscegenation statutes. Marriages between Japanese men and women warranted brief, but celebratory mention in widely read, Japanese American newspapers such as the *Kashu Mainichi* and *New World Sun,* but the union of a Filipino man and a Japanese woman evoked longer and more poignant comment. Speculating about the racial origin of the woman's new husband—"the only chance for a Japanese to marry in this country is with Filipino, Chinese, or other Mongolian race. The gentleman in question is neither Siamese nor Chinese, so it leaves a margin for Filipino"—the article highlighted the untraditional marital practices forced upon the Japanese by a restrictive American social system. Sociologist, George Simpson, corroborated the bad feelings stirred up by marital limits, observing that Japanese and other minorities resented what reduced them to a separate, inferior category of citizenship.[8]

Despite these principled challenges to anti-miscegenation laws, most minorities preferred to pair with and have family members pair with one of their own. Concerns about ethnic longevity, inherited and learned prejudice, as well as conflicts abroad shaped these wishes. Among Chinese and Japanese immigrants, schemes for ranking and distinguishing among people that privileged Asians, relegated whites, and disparaged blacks were part of the ethno-racial baggage imported to their new home. Their prejudices against other groups only strengthened in a California setting where social standing was so closely correlated with race and ethnicity. Chinese elders frowned upon social contacts and matches made with non-Chinese, especially with blacks and Mexicans. The advice George Lew offered his children "to marry no blacks, no Mexicans," captured the majority's opinion.[9]

Motivated by more decisive notions of racial purity, Issei objected to intimate contacts with others. They even resisted inter-Asian matches. Local economic competition compounded political tensions associated with war in Asia. Japan's aggressive expansion in the region beginning in the early twentieth century strained relations among Filipinos, Koreans, Chinese, and Japanese in the United States who still felt passionately about events in their countries of birth. Reaction to the elopement of Felisberto Tapia (Filipino) and Alice Chiyoko (Japanese) exemplified the intense opposition brought to bear against inter-Asian couples.[10] Their romance precipitated a melee of kidnapping, boycotting, and protesting by the town's Filipinos and Japanese that ultimately forced the pair's separation. But like Chinese, Japanese reserved their strongest objections for pairings with Mexicans and blacks. In a survey measuring marital expectations, over 85 percent of this immigrant generation expressed their disapproval of marriages between Nisei and the two non-white groups. "Japanese married to [blacks] would be looked down upon by others," offered one participant in explanation of the general ethnic sentiment.[11]

As mixed race individuals themselves, Filipinos and Mexicans in California were usually more accepting of racial difference and mixture. The physical reality of so many mestizo individuals in Mexico and the Philippines worked against a strict doctrine of purity. So did political events such as the Spanish-American-Filipino War (1898) and Mexican Revolution (1910) that celebrated alternatives to the Eurocentric racism of Spaniards. Yet, these groups were not blind to color. Mexican citizens and political officials alike often referred to Chinese as dirty, diseased, and lustful, attitudes that prompted the persecution and eventual expulsion of Chinese merchants in the 1930s. In addition to Chinese, blacks and even North Americans sometimes confronted the antipathy of mestizos. These views shaded the perceptions of Mexican immigrants to the United States. When contemplating partners, Mexican American children and their protective parents considered factors of color and culture, privileging Mexican ancestry. Filipinos drew distinctions too. Although turn of the century mestizo nationalists downplayed ethnic distinctions and accented the essential sameness of Filipinos, ethno-racial thinking did not disappear altogether. Once in California, Filipino bachelors tended to accept interethnic relations more readily if they included whites or Mexicans rather than blacks or Japanese "colonizers."[12]

Blacks and Jews favored romances and marriages with co-ethnics too. For Jews, concerns about religious and racial integrity preached by rabbis and embraced by many community members discouraged branching out beyond the ethnic circle. With the exception of areas where few Jews resided, these minorities partnered with one another. So did African Americans. Although they confronted a relatively more relaxed racial climate in California, persistent social prejudice and their own racial pride discouraged interethnic intimacies.[13]

Given these preferences and prejudices, the intercultural romances and families attempted by minorities sometimes collapsed. Their relationships threatened to realign ethno-racial categories both they and their ethnic communities revered. As a result, even non-whites who admitted strong feelings for one another ended their relationships early and abruptly. The ill will of family, friends, and strangers as well as their own reservations weighed too heavily upon them.

The respective romances of Adele Hernandez (Mexican) and Harry Lem (Chinese) highlight how inter-minority couples could unravel under pressure. A young Los Angelino, Adele Hernandez (Chicana) began seriously dating a Jewish co-worker immediately after WWII. "I didn't think he was so good looking. He was not tall either," she admitted, but "I liked him quite a bit." Despite the pair's attachment, resistance from siblings and parents soon forced them apart. As Adele remembered, "At the time, especially with strict Jewish families, you didn't marry out of your faith." Aware of these conventions, Adele admitted that the affair "wasn't getting us anywhere" and called it off. The couple liked and loved one another, but not enough to defy divisive cultural norms. Harry Lem's associations with a series of black girlfriends during the 1930s underscored the weight and respect afforded ethnic prejudice. According to his sister, "Harry loved black women," and regularly brought African American dates to family dinners, a practice his mother, like most in her Los Angeles Chinatown community quietly abhorred. Although this Chinese American pursued black women, his relationships were always fleeting. Factors independent of external prejudice may have mattered, but so did the clear disapproval of family and neighbors. In repeatedly introducing his black companions to his parents and sibling, Harry demonstrated the importance he lent their opinions. When push came to shove, minorities who enjoyed intercultural dating and contemplated long-term commitments often chose the standards of their own ethnic group rather than risk ostracism.[14]

Anti-miscegenation laws and white supremacist notions limited inter-ethnic crossings, but so did the social practices and views of minorities. Concerns about civil rights in the abstract gave non-whites pause. Yet in general, they promoted co-ethnic dates and marriages in order to maintain familiar boundaries. Those who wandered beyond these boundaries were coaxed to return.

YOUTHFUL EXPERIMENTS

Despite these separatist expectations of parents and community, a small number of non-white adolescents dated across cultural borders. Their relationships expressed a frustration with familiar gendered experiences and a longing for new ones. Bending established rules about proper behavior and companions was appealing for young men and women. Although such crossings were uncommon, questioned and typically short-lived, they highlighted how some non-white youth managed their acculturation and pursued alternatives to standard assimilation. Their journeys mapped out a course for becoming non-white that if rarely traveled still indicated changing attitudes and customs of ethno-racial relations.

The heterogeneous character of their neighborhoods and schools promoted the mixing of non-white adolescents. Stepping out onto the bustling streets, sidewalks, and parks of their communities, youth struck up impromptu conversations that evolved into more planned encounters. This was the case in demographically eclectic urban districts—West Oakland, San Francisco's Fillmore, and Los Angeles' Boyle Heights—as well as rural areas—East Stockton, and the eastsides of such small towns in the Imperial Valley as Brawley and Calexico. Local institutions in these diverse areas—schools, temples, churches, YMCA chapters—brought youth together in classes, services and extracurricular activities. Thus, non-white youngsters had ample opportunity to mingle as they participated in classes, services, and extracurricular activities. Los Angeles' Roosevelt High, All People's Church and St. Patrick's Church, West Oakland's Technical High School, Sacramento's Trinity Church, San Franciso's Girls High School, and Berkeley's Plymouth Church were among these multiethnic spaces.[15]

Within these environments, those California teens who most consistently defied community opinion and dated ethnic strangers were alternatively known as "zoot suiters," "pachucos," or "yogores."[16] Few in number and more rebellious in attitude than most teenagers, these boys and girls designed a street-centered, oppositional youth culture defined by particularly permeable ethno-racial and gender lines. Although Chicanos represented the most visible and talked about participants, a wide variety of minority adolescents chose defiant styles and attitudes. As marginalized members of urban, immigrant, and working class communities, African, Mexican, and Asian Americans had reason to resent the conditions of their lives and similarly articulate their frustrations. Signature attributes of this mixed cohort included a style of speech and dress that pieced together varied cultural sources. Most visually dramatic, the so called zoot suit—long baggy pants in bright colors, an oversized jacket with padded shoulders, a wide brimmed hat, and metal chain that dangled down—had alleged origins among blacks in Harlem, New York as well Mexicans in urban Mexico. Hybridity defined speech as well as dress with Mexican and Japanese teens using phrases such as "slick chick' and 'so keen' lifted from black peers. In the internment camps, Charles Kikuchi (Japanese) noted the extroverted Nisei zoot suiters who spoke "the same jitterbug language with the same facial expression" that they had "copied from the Negroes."[17]

A willingness to participate in other cultures and socialize with other peoples characterized this cohort's attitudes about and practices of dating as much as a hybrid style. Typically, boys hoped to acquire or prove a more assertive masculinity. For a minority of Japanese youth, this meant copying the ways of blacks, Filipinos, and Mexicans who appeared appealingly more aggressive. Born in 1925, Lester Kimura grew up in Boyle Heights, Los Angeles, where he went "around with a lot of Mexican guys" with whom he regularly cut school and practiced petty thievery. He credited these associates for his lawlessness. Drawing the same conclusion, his distraught parents relocated the family with the hopes that a new environment and new friends would help reform their son. But Lester sought out and connected with Mexican boys who shared his rebellious pastimes in the new neighborhood. Being the only Nisei in a gang of fifteen Mexicans, gave him a sense of distinction and power; he cultivated his status as ethnic outsider by his cultural crossing.[18]

Multiethnic settings certainly complicated even as they enriched the identity making process for minority boys. A native of Stockton, Barry Shimizu played almost exclusively with Nisei boys in his early childhood, but expanded his friendship circle to include Mexicans and Italians as he aged. "I didn't drift away from my Nisei friends," Barry reported, "I was living right between Japanese and Mexican towns so I got to know both groups pretty well." Ethnic based cliques with distinct public profiles developed in high school, but Barry managed to move among them, reluctant to settle in with any single group. "I had three sets of friends that were all different" explained Barry, "and I couldn't make up my mind which was best for me." He admired Mexican boys who "were rugged characters," "bold and daring," "car crazy" African Americans who taught him how to play poker and stay out late, and finally the "quiet clean-cut" Nisei boys "who talked nice" and won the praise of teachers. In straddling ethnic groups and assuming behaviors deemed "un-Japanese," Barry was able to create the alternative self-definition he desired.[19]

One of the best ways to access and express a defiant masculinity, however, was by dating girls outside the ethnic group. Author Chester Himes told of black zoot suiters in the mid-1940s who propositioned "anyone of any race who is nice looking" from their perches on Los Angeles street corners. The youths distinguished themselves by their inclusive admiration of women as much as their forwardness. As a yogore himself, Charles Kikuchi regularly wooed those of non-Japanese descent. Born in Vallejo, California to Japanese immigrants, Charles had worked as a houseboy, graduated from San Francisco State University, and labored alongside Filipino farm workers before joining a mixed gang of San Francisco youth who called themselves "the Yamamoto garage gang." Writing in his diary the day after Pearl Harbor, he contemplated a visit to San Francisco's Chinatown "to chase girls." Jimmy Hong (Chinese) joked that Charles was not "allowed to screw Chinese girls anymore," unless he sported an "I Am Chinese" button. The friend's jab not only illustrated the shifting political climate, but the regularity of Charles' interethnic, romantic escapades. For Charles and others, the possibility of dating across ethnic lines only enhanced the thrill of the pursuit and their sense of themselves as daring young men.[20]

In their conflicted and varied responses to the brash masculinity of zoot suiters, ethnic girls displayed their own identity struggles. An exasperated Japanese parent in 1946 reporting on young women who socialized with yogores claimed that they went "out with anyone who can show them a good time" indifferent to whether these suitors were "Negroes, Mexicans, or hakujins." These girls' pursuit of fun and personal freedom flaunted ethnic notions of respectability. At a local dance held in the early 1940s, a young Nisei woman, Mariko, also frowned upon the intercultural intimacies of her peers. "Some of them [Japanese American men] brought cheap looking Caucasian women," she huffed, "I don't know where they picked them up." As troublesome to this young girl and her friends as the behavior of certain

Nisei boys, were the advances of Mexicans who "made a great play over Maudie Yamazaki," making the girl look "as cheap" as the Caucasians. But Maudie and "other girls like her" delighted in the dance and the attention of the Mexican suitors. The pleasure they took in ethnic crossing spotlighted the rift dividing communities of ethnic youth. Cross-cultural contacts with the opposite sex that enthused select teens separated them from a disapproving majority.

Filipino and Mexican women who dated Barry Shimizu in the early 1940s gained from their romances even as they scandalized peers. The girls enjoyed Barry's liberal spending and spirited personality. None of these relationships lasted very long as Barry soon concluded that these women "were not good anyway and were only interested in the money I had to spend on them." Rather than passive pawns of immoral men as critics claimed, these women advanced their own ambitions through interethnic dating. The chance to be shocking and unexpected in one's choice of men, to have a great time, and to be treated appealed to some ethnic girls who were as eager to find gender alternatives as the zoot suiting boys.[21]

However, most non-white girls defined their femininity in ways more consistent with ethnic norms than the aggressive, multiethnic practices of the zoot suiters. They eschewed associations with boys on the margins, a tendency that frustrated yogores like Tommy Hamada. Born and raised in San Francisco, by the early 1940s this discontented Nisei had distanced himself from "all those Japs in Frisco" whom he found "too damm Jappy." Nisei girls reciprocated his hostility, rallying around ethnic conventions they hoped to preserve. Hamada grumbled that these young women "were afraid to be seen with me because they thought it would hurt their reputation."[22] Indeed community standing mattered to many girls. Margarita Salazar (Mexican) of Boyle Heights maintained a careful distance from zoot suiters and their female companions in the 1930s. She looked upon the "drape pants, excessive makeup, and tight skirts" of the girls as unappealing and inappropriate. Her good neighborhood friend, Rose Echeverria Mulligan, echoed her discomfort, articulating the division between "straight" and rebel that ran through their Mexican American cohort. "We didn't talk to them" she explained of the girls who fraternized with pachucos, "we assumed that they would do anything the zoot suiters asked," a willingness she found surprising because "why would any girl dress like that or even be associated with anybody who didn't respect her?" For these young Mexican Americans, the sexuality practiced by such boys and girls—defined in part by active dating across cultural lines—was distasteful.[23]

The multiethnic and predominantly male environments of California, especially rural California, encouraged girls to be watchful and suspicious of other minority men. Given typical occupations of their parents—labor contractors or operators of boardinghouses, pool halls, and restaurants—they frequently grew up in the company of non-white bachelors. Regular contact with lonely and single young men often made young women feel vulnerable. In Oxnard during the mid-1930s, Nikki Bridges' Japanese father hired gangs of non-white men to harvest his strawberry crop. Nikki understood the dilemma restrictive legislation created for these laborers who "could never have a wife" and because of "anti-miscegenation law couldn't get married to Caucasians." But despite her appreciation of these restraints, Nikki avoided these men whom she perceived as aggressively sexual. Among the group were Koreans who appeared "a desperate group" and "very silent." Motoko Shimosaki agreed that non-white men were dangerous. During the mid-1930s, the Nisei helped her father operate a pool hall in rural Guadalupe, serving a primarily Mexican and Filipino clientele. Proximity and familiarity made her distrust rather than accept these men. She saw them as troublemakers who "went around murdering" and "seemed too sexist." Clearly, these bachelors violated her sense of how men should interact with women. In critiquing and distancing herself from them, she held out for a preferred set of gender relations.[24]

When the reluctance of girls to associate with non-white men clashed with the expectations of parents, generational tensions surfaced. Like many young Japanese Americans whose fathers contracted labor, Frances Nishimoto grew up among Filipino field hands. She could identify the exact moment at which she began hating these bachelors. "When I was ten years old," Frances explained, one of the workers "got fresh with me on the farm" and "I talked back to him." Frances refused to give the Pinoy a ride back to the house, an act that so angered her father, he slapped her and urged her not "to be nasty to the Filipinos because they are good workers." Despite his reprimand, Frances continued to distrust Pinoy because "they were desperate for a mate," and "always looking at girls funny." Kindly and regular interactions between daughters and non-white men were sometimes a business practice upon which fathers insisted. In these cases, they must have trusted their workers and clients, dismissing their daughters' feelings as foolish or selfish. But when girls like Frances continued to avoid contact with or disrespected minority men, generational conflict ensued. The business interests of parents could compromise the efforts of young girls to create and protect their own gendered sensibilities.[25]

Even though the same feelings of vulnerability did not condition their reactions to zoot suiters, non-white boys also designed identities in tension with their more eager multiethnic peers. George Yani who attended the post-internment dance described by Mariko deplored the "grotesque" and "sneering attitudes" of his yogore peers who behaved "worse than any Filipino groups." Having spent time in Seattle organizing Filipino cannery workers, he thought he had seen the extreme of male drunkenness and disorder until he witnessed the behavior of fellow Nisei who "were worse than any Filipino groups I have seen." Second generation James Sakoda confirmed these complaints about zoot suiters, juxtaposing his conservative upbringing in 1930s Boyle Heights with that of "rowdy" Nisei. His youthful "activities were pretty much circumscribed. We lived with the Mexicans but we really didn't get involved with them at all," Sakoda recalled. In sharp contrast "there was a bunch of Nisei" who "were less likely to be serious, more likely to go for group sports like football and basketball, and more likely to get in trouble." In a more formal and public condemnation in 1941, leaders of the Mexican American Movement (MAM)[26] accused pachucos "of giving Mexicans a bad name." They urged their rebellious brothers to follow a more traditional path of Americanization marked by education, citizenship and the dilution of Mexican traditions.[27]

Although the majority of youth found the repeated, bold crossings of zoot suiters off-putting, they did not eschew interethnic romance altogether. More cautiously and infrequently than the pachuco cohort, these non-white adolescents still dated or condoned dating cultural outsiders. If such intimate mingling constituted a less defining aspect of their identity and had a less defiant meaning, it still offered minority teens a way to escape into new gender roles and consider other forms of being American. Without erasing the prejudices of youth, such relations did pull non-white teens closer together than previous generations.

A developing sense of cosmopolitanism among second-generation teens made intercultural dating more acceptable. Increasingly, minority youth stressed the importance of mixing peoples and ideas in order to correct discrimination. Their own multiethnic mingling then became both a critique of and solution for ethno-racial tensions. At schools like Roosevelt High in pre-war Boyle Heights where no ethno-racial group could claim a numerical majority or monopoly of leadership positions, students celebrated the variety of backgrounds calling the institution "a crucible of all nations. Russians, Jews, Japanese, Mexican, Chinese, Negro," and insisting "all help to make their school the better for having been there." The front page of Roosevelt's newspaper on December 7, 1939 announced those chosen as "exceptional members" of the senior class by fellow students and faculty. The list of names suggested the breadth and depth of the school's cultural diversity: "Harry Adelman, Edward Condejas, Audrey Dineedn, Mosamori Kojima, Chiyo Morohe, Adolph Moskovits, Maria Luispa Pesquiera, Nellie Shuringa, Art Takemoto." Annual international days intended to educate students about the variety within their midst involved speeches, performances, and a parade of native costumes worn by students and teachers. Although a school which prided itself on being "truly a melting pot in the sense that students with different ideas and customs are melted together to form a better American," it also encouraged students to express pride in their native cultures and learn about each other." Perhaps, there was a superficial quality to the multicultural pageants at the high school, but the instinct to connect with other ethnic and racial groups was often genuine and originated among the students themselves.[28]

Outside the grounds of mixed schools, minority youth celebrated cultural pluralism as well. In the *Chinese Press* of 1941, Chinese American students pointed enviously at Hawaii where mixing between groups, including Japanese, Koreans, Filipinos, Chinese and Portuguese, appeared to happen so easily and completely. In noticing the social scene across the Pacific, the adolescents implied California could and should create similarly successful intercultural relations. Readers of the *Mexican Voice,* the mouthpiece of the youth organization, MAM, asserted the value of cosmopolitanism as well. The writers praised the hiring of diverse non-whites practiced by the University of California in 1938, including Chinese, Japanese, Mexican, and African Americans, as a model other institutions should emulate. In a short story within the same newspaper, four Chicano boys discussed their varied experiences of discrimination. The narrator's wistful insertion, "Here in our country we have Jews, Spaniards, Italians, Armenians, Chinese, Negroes and so forth and all of these persons yearn to be American and call themselves as such," implied both the continued injustice in American society and the simple goodness of its cosmopolitan population.[29]

Out of this cosmopolitan ethos, came a cautious endorsement of intercultural dating. In a mid-1930s series printed in the *New World Sun* Nisei urged their cohort to reach beyond the ethnic community. One writer chastised her readers for their "smug self-satisfaction" and "sense of superiority vis-a-vis other minorities." She advised the Nisei, "NOT to gossip if one dates with a Chinese, Nisei or any young person of any other nationality."[30]

Non-white Californians acted upon this advice and discovered appealing, new gender dynamics as they did so. Tamie Ihara, (Japanese) slipped the standards of her own ethnic group in the early 1940s when she befriended Sammy, "a cute Jewish boy" of her Boyle Heights hometown. In contrast to her Nisei boyfriend, "who was so bashful that he sent [her] a scarf for a Christmas present and he didn't put his name on it," Sammy was fun and "interesting." She liked how differently he behaved from the shy, boring Japanese Americans she typically dated. Overly familiar ethnic characteristics to Tamie appealed to Rose Mary Escobar as unexpected and unique. In the year before internment, this Oakland Chicana dated a Nisei neighbor whom she described "as a perfect gentleman." Both teens enjoyed interethnic romance as an escape from gendered conventions specific to their respective ethnic communities.[31]

Boys praised the novelty of intimacy with cultural outsiders too. At a San Francisco Chinatown dance in the early 1940s, Robert Vallangca (Filipino) accompanied a Chinese American friend. To ensure his admittance, he presented himself under the ethnic alias, "Ben Lee." Robert waltzed for the first time with a Chinese American girl. Although initially petrified by the girl's surprising request to dance, Robert/Ben soon relaxed and enjoyed her "heavenly" company. Given the reluctance of some Japanese and probably Chinese American girls to receive the advances of Filipino bachelors, Robert's posing allowed him to experience a warmer, friendlier set of interactions between the sexes. Adolescents like these may not have made interethnic dating as central a part of their social lives as the zoot suiters did, but they sought out such relations temporarily.[32] Thus, a handful of minority youth through the 1930s and early 1940s were romancing across ethnic boundaries and promoting hybrid, multicultural sensibilities as they did so. Most youth may not have departed from familiar cultural traditions, but those who tested new gender roles and familial traditions or approved of such testing sketched the outlines of a new collectivity that would be more fully realized in decades to come: non-white youth.

CONSENTING ADULTS

Youth defied conventions and explored other cultural traditions, but non-white adults in the period committed to and lived out multicultural lives. Though numerically few and frequently marginalized, these pairs recommended mixed race relationships to a skeptical public. Examining their romances enables us to uncover the process by which maverick individuals began to fashion non-whiteness out of intimate connections and as an alternative to monoethnic norms. In part, the long-term entanglements between men and women of distinct minority backgrounds precipitated out of legal limits, sex imbalances, and shared geography. The work and leisure of minorities brought them into close contact while a scarcity of co-ethnic women left men hungry for female attention. Given state restrictions and popular hostility, some of these bachelors shied away from white women and shimmied up to non-white women. Proximity and a longing for love and family drew minorities together.

California's peculiar demography forwarded matches among minorities. The maleness of state residents—most pronounced in migrant communities—structured romantic choices. Asians suffered particularly skewed sex ratios through mid-century. Among Chinese, men outnumbered women by 27 to 1 in 1920. The difference narrowed without disappearing through the century. In 1940 more than two times as many Chinese men as women resided in the western state. The Filipino community faced a similar imbalance. Between 1924 and 1929, women accounted for only 16 percent of the 24,000 Filipinos journeying to California. Even more male in composition than this immigrant flow, 99 percent of Asian Indians were men. Comparatively, the Japanese community enjoyed a more stable demography with women reaching roughly 42 percent of the population by 1940, but a gap clearly remained. Overall, these Asian men had the greatest reason to gripe about female companionship, but Mexican American men longed for more co-ethnic women too. In 1930 Los Angeles, the male to female ratio stood at 114 to 100. African and Jewish American men more often arrived with wives and families, but some traveled and lived alone.[33]

One of the practical consequences of this abundance of male minorities was intercultural marriage. Confronted with either singleness and childlessness or family and procreation, some bucked tradition and married across cultural lines. Although limited records make a precise accounting of interracial relationships extremely difficult, repatriation documents and remembered cases indicate that such marriages did occur. In surveys conducted of Chinese and Japanese Americans of California about their ethnic pasts, interviewees consistently acknowledged the presence of at least one mixed, minority couple in their neighborhood. Representative of such replies included William Chan's assertion, "a neighbor married a Mexican girl," Peggy Kanzawa's observation, "there were a few [Nisei] that were married to other nationalities," and finally Ida Lee's recollection, "a few Chinese men married colored and Mexican." Repatriation records also pull inter-minority couples out from the shadows of history. Filed by women hoping to regain citizenship lost after marriage to foreign men, these materials document the lasting commitment of non-white men and women. As examples, two black women, Marguerite Takeuchi and Bertia Morial, fell in love and resided in southern California with their respective husbands, immigrants from Japan and Mexico in the late 1930s.[34]

In one of the only published studies of intermarriage among minorities in the period, Constantine Panunzio offered more quantitative evidence of ethno-racial crossing. Between 1924 and 1933, she calculated Los Angeles' intermarriage rates. For Chinese males, 23 of 97 marriages were exogamous, for Filipino males, 701 of 1000. As further evidence of just how important sex ratios were to marital patterns, in the Japanese community where women proved more numerous, intermarriages happened infrequently. In sharp contrast to the figures for Chinese and Filipinos, only 27 of 1,163 Japanese marriages involved non-Japanese.[35]

Too few women encouraged non-white intermarriages, but so did the state's legal climate. As noted previously, miscegenation statutes banned marriages between whites and individuals deemed not white. Of the many states that legislated intermarriage, only North Carolina and Louisiana prohibited long term partnerships between non-whites, and only between African and Native Americans. Ironically, whites had most constrained their own marital freedom. A person of color could marry members of all ethno-racial groups provided he or she denied a white identity.[36]

The case pitting Gavino C. Visco against Los Angeles illustrated this opportunity. Although the court initially withheld a marital license from this Filipino man and his fiancee, Ruth Salas (Mexican), because the judge construed her as white, the pair successfully exploited the awkward, inconsistent character of rules against miscegenation. In proving a partial Indian descent, Ruth gained the status of non-white and was permitted to marry Gavino. This shedding of a white identity highlighted the more malleable racial status of Mexicans and a willingness to sacrifice privilege for love and family. California law classified Mexicans as white, a distinction many within the ethnic community dearly prized and defended because of the privileges it afforded. Unlike Asians, Mexican immigrants could naturalize and own land. Unlike blacks, they were less consistently segregated in housing and education. Thus, Ruth's decision to step away from rather than cling to the security of her marginal whiteness was a brave defense of minority rights and a challenge to white privilege. Yet whites paid little attention to

defiant crossings such as Ruth and Gavino's. As long as minority mixing did
not generate labor unrest, they policed only the color line that divided them
from non-whites. Thus, minorities had strong incentives to select non-white
rather than white partners. In fact, over 95 percent of Chinese intermarriages
in Los Angeles between 1924 and 1933, 74 percent of Japanese, 93 percent
of black, and slightly fewer than 50 percent of Filipino were contracted with
other non-whites.[37]

As much as imbalanced sex ratios and permissive laws, the proximity
of certain minority groups in the rural towns and urban neighborhoods of
California immediately before the war precipitated intercultural romances,
many of which paired the same ethnic groups. The same spaces that cultivated
romances among minority youth, engendered more lasting commitments.
Philip Vera Cruz, a Filipino who spent much of his time moving between farm
jobs in Delano, MacFarland, and Wasco, noted the importance of shared work
and location to the marriages between Mexicans and Filipinos so common in
the California valleys. As Japanese and Chinese laborers became rare subsequent to immigration restriction, growers had increasingly recruited the two
groups in the 1920s and 1930s. Vera Cruz observed that many of his countrymen "as a poor hard-working minority" married Mexican women "because
they often lived in the same area." Filipinos interviewed by sociologists
confirmed Cruz's statement, confessing that Filipinos typically befriended
Mexican women in taxi dance halls or farms. In fact, unlike Chinese and
Japanese men who favored Asian women when selecting mates, Filipinos
favored Mexicans. In Los Angeles County between 1924 and 1933, twenty-
six chose Mexican brides compared to only two Japanese and one Chinese.
Later studies confirmed the continuity of this preference. Sociologist Benicio
Catapusan concluded in the early 1930s that "most of the Filipino mixed
unions are Filipino-Mexican; some are Filipino-white, Filipino Mulatto, and
Filipino-Negro unions." A study based upon Los Angeles County marital
licenses, concurred, indicating that two-thirds ofFilipino men who married
between 1949 and 1959 chose Mexican American women."[38]

The coincidence of geography and labor produced such consistent pairings between other minority groups that distinctive, truly bicultural settlements emerged. Toiling in the southern California farm communities,
Mexican women and Asian Indian men frequently fell in love and married.
As Sikhs of peasant background restricted from bringing wives and children to California by the tightening of immigration laws, the men sought
out single, young females newly arrived from Mexico. Other examples of
biethnic spaces where all husbands belonged to one ethno-racial group

and all wives another appeared in rural California. In the border town of Calexico, Chinese men built lives with Chicanas and "pretty much assimilated into the local Mexican population," a local resident reported, while smaller concentrations of Mexican-Japanese families dotted the valley.[39]

The heterogeneity of certain urban neighborhoods similarly grounded the romantic entanglements of non-whites. While Asian men and Mexican women found romance in the fields where they labored, the work environments of cities brought sets of minorities together too. In 1940s Los Angeles, Garding Liu, a local resident, chairman of the city's Chinese Consolidated Benevolent Association, and amateur historian, noted the presence of Chinese-black couples. If not working or shopping in Chinese owned groceries or restaurants, black women met Chinese men as customers of their boarding houses. From everyday interactions evolved greater intimacies. Ordinary sightings of interracial couples in the multicultural Fillmore district, Boyle Heights, and West Oakland further illustrated the importance of place and population in inter-minority matches. These areas both encouraged and harbored mixed couples. Jews, Mexicans, Chinese, Japanese, blacks, and Filipinos who grew up there looked more favorably upon and likely felt more inclined to intermarry themselves. At the same time, mixed couples squeezed out of familiar ethnic areas found refuge in more diverse city sections and among like-families. Dorothy Siu recalled the four interracial families in her Los Angeles neighborhood, ostracized by Chinese, who banded together and organized special picnics. Rose Mary Escobar observed a similar social dynamic in pre-war Oakland. The polyglot composition of some California neighborhoods allowed support and anonymity impossible in most others.[40]

Encouraged by discrimination, demography, and diverse environments, select minorities suspended ethno-racial prejudices and embraced local opportunities for family and connection. Gender imbalances in labor and locale help explain the patterns in these ethnic partnerships. Although uncommon in the period, these non-white couples were important examples of the close social ties and creative collaborations possible among non-whites.

NEW AMERICAN FAMILIES:
ASCENDANT MOTHERS AND WIVES

More than the entanglements of youths, the bonds forged among minority men and women sharing space and discriminations expressed a mature commitment to becoming non-white, to blending multiple traditions. As they created their families, these couples faced much tougher negotiations of gender roles and relations with extended relatives. In many cases, the desire to perpetuate their cultures and the scarcity of women, forced men not only to pursue ethnic outsiders, but reluctantly adopt different gendered behaviors. These men found their own cultural expectations about the privileges of suitors and husbands—reinforced by observations of white patriarchy—bent by the competing ambitions of girlfriends and wives. Demographic advantage afforded women the luxury of intermarrying only when such matches appeared to improve their condition. In breaking away from their own ethnic communities and relatives, the wives gained significant influence.

In marrying cultural outsiders, non-white men and especially women wrestled familial control from their elders. New brides substituted their own marital ambitions for those of in-laws and parents. Winning this independence brought unaccustomed and uncomfortable discord into the lives of these young women. A contemporary sociologist reported that the family of a Nisei bride severed all contact with their daughter after she married a Filipino in the late 1930s. Although "quite unhappy about it," the woman accepted her isolation. Even when evacuation aggravated that separation from her native community, she remained with her husband and accepted the consequences of her break from ethnic convention. She expected that she would be taken with other persons of Japanese ancestry, but "was not even able to participate in the collective punishment the government was meting out to the Japanese."[41]

Blanche Corona (Jewish) weathered familial discontent and community resentment as she too realized her own desires. Blanche, whose Jewish family moved to West Los Angeles soon after her birth in 1920, met and married a Mexican American, Bert Corona, in the 1930s who shared her political interests and Los Angeles orientation. Blanche's family readily accepted the match, but his, especially his grandmother, actively objected. Bert's grandmother unexpectedly "confronted" Blanche one day soon after her nuptials. Although Blanche couldn't understand much Spanish," Bert recounted, "she definitely knew my grandmother wasn't happy." Blanche's own parents echoed the concerns of the elder woman, fearing their daughter's Jewish values and those of her Mexican husband would collide and ultimately divide the pair. In disregarding parental advice and pressure, Blanche expressed a different and independent understanding of marriage and cultural negotiation. So did Elaine Black Yoneda. A Jewish American of Russian parents who grew up in San Diego, Elaine met Karl, a Kibei[42] from

Glendale in Los Angeles. Elaine's mother opposed the marriage to a Japanese man, insisting the relationship "wouldn't look good" and "would never work out." To prove her point, she cited various cases of failed intermarriages she had learned about through gossip. By referring to local expectations and experiences, Mrs. Black showed the stake she put in community opinion. By marrying a Japanese man, Elaine showed how little that opinion mattered. She remained wedded to her own affections rather than accommodate the wishes of others.[43]

The breakdown of intergenerational controls could strengthen the position of minority women in intercultural marriages, but so could the more equitable footing of minority partners and their competing efforts to perpetuate endangered minority cultures. In white-minority families, spouses often agreed that offspring best accept the traditions and beliefs that would win them the privileges of whiteness. A dominant culture overwhelmed a more marginal one. But for inter-minority marriages the cultural choice was less clear and more negotiated. The recommendation one writer of the *New World Sun* offered a Japanese woman underscored the contested character and high cultural stakes of marriages between non-whites. In a 1936 special interest story about a Japanese woman who had recently married a Filipino, the author urged the new bride "to inject the culture of the Japanese and the education of American schools into your children," as if he feared the husband would win the battle over offspring. Recognizing the importance of parenting to the preservation of customs and beliefs, intermarried men aspired to be more active fathers; they lacked the security of those who married co-ethnic women and confidently watched a familiar transmission to the next generation. The assertions of non-white men, however, ran up against and wavered in the face of women's own childrearing strategies. Reluctant to surrender an authority assigned by ethnic communities and enhanced by the conflicted character of intermarriage, women pressed their views and often prevailed.[44]

The results of these marital contests highlighted the gains women might achieve through inter-minority relationships. Among Chinese-Mexican couples of Los Angeles, clashes over the gendered treatment of children and the involvement of extended family upset husbands. In 1940s Los Angeles, Garding Liu related the grievances of Chinese men bothered by the care of offspring. The men resented that their own preference for sons and disconnection from in-laws was largely ignored. In pre-war Punjabi-Mexican households of the Imperial Valley fathers sought to supervise and limit the dating practices of their progeny. But backed by Hispanic godmothers, wives successfully undercut these controls, allowing sons and daughters more freedom in courtship.[45]

The case of Sugar Pie De Santo further demonstrated the triumphs of mothers and frustrations of fathers in mixed, non-white families. Born and raised in San Francisco's multiethnic Fillmore district in the late 1930s and 1940s, Sugar Pie aspired to become a professional entertainer. Her Filipino father, though, forbade her singing at local nightspots and talent shows, construing such entertainment as inappropriate for a young girl. This specific prohibition and his general conservatism frustrated the young girl. Luckily for Sugar, her black mother supported her daughter's dreams and helped her sneak into clubs and choir practices without Mr. De Santo's knowledge. Mrs. De Santo consistently overruled her husband's stricter rules, a practice that made Sugar Pie and her siblings feel much closer to their mother and much "blacker" in their sensibilities.[46]

Disagreements with family, cultural distinctions and the relative balance of partners in mixed minority marriages may have made them more contested than most, but women frequently benefited. Without the expectation of assimilation or a common cultural script to structure their decisions, the negotiations among spouses were often more uncertain than those between white-minority or endogamous pairs. Both partners pushed competing, gendered views of family with the hopes of retaining and extending beloved legacies. Yet, women's traditional authority over children and relative detachment from intergenerational controls made them more likely victors.

NEW AMERICAN FAMILIES:
COMMON FAMILY VALUES

This female authority and the need to reconcile cultural differences set non-white families apart. But frequently, recognition of common habits and ideals that transcended ethno-racial lines distinguished them from white-minority pairs as well. The division of Californians into categories based upon race and ethnicity represented only one, artificial, and often unsatisfactory way minority individuals could organize themselves. Choosing to associate based upon other criteria of membership—appearance, politics, or culture—non-white men and especially women defied existing social hierarchies and assumptions that identities should be singular.

Non-white adults who partnered with ethnic outsiders sought a more permanent refuge from familiar gender regimes and cultural expectations than had young minority daters. Youth had enjoyed the freedoms of other ethno-racial groups, but non-whites who intermarried expressed deeper, gendered longings for cultural alternatives. In the 1920s, Mrs. Machida, a Chinese American of San Francisco, married a Japanese man who effectively removed her from a Chinese community she despised. Unlike the Japanese whom she admired as "more intelligent and better educated," Mrs. Machida faulted Chinese in the United States for their craftiness, disinterest in education, and conservatism. Most important, she denounced Chinese men's treatment of women. "They don't want them to be educated," she observed, "and when they get to a certain point the men make them stop because they are afraid their women will get the American idea of equality and they want to keep them nothing but chattel." Mrs. Machida escaped into a Japanese community whose gender relations she admired. Given ethnic preferences and sex ratios, Mrs. Machida's marriage represented a particularly bold transgression and statement against Chinese norms; more than their more numerous male counterparts, minority women like Machida unsettled communities by their crossings and won more control over their lives.[47]

There were other telling cases of frustrated women whose romantic decisions narrowed cultural and ethnic distance. In contrast to Mrs. Machida, a Japanese woman found a haven with a Chinese American husband who lived and operated a small market in Oakland. Mrs. Chew told police in 1942 "she didn't like Japs," and explained that she cut herself off from her Japanese family and community almost ten years earlier, never regretting her separation. The politics of the moment, namely growing American hostility towards Japan and its people informed this ethnic rejection, but her marriage marked a larger dissatisfaction with things Japanese and her simultaneous attraction to another Asian culture. Chinese gender roles were just different enough to appeal.[48]

Although distanced from their ethnic pasts, these Asian American women did not travel far. Communities relatively close in history, culture, and color attracted them. Though still rigid, the ethnic lines dividing Asians, which would bend readily in the postwar, were already relaxing in the pre-war. Individuals and families pointed to similarities in cultural heritage and racial ancestry. When asked about intermarriage in the years just before World War II, Los Angeles resident William Chew Chan (Chinese) referenced Chinese American neighbors who partnered with Mexican and Italian women. He differentiated these relationships from that of his own son who had married a Japanese girl. In insisting that "Japanese and Chinese [were] of same race," William indicated the relative closeness of Asian groups and the acceptability of their partnerships. Intermarriage rates underscored this trend. Asian ethnics who intermarried, especially women, showed a strong preference for Asian spouses over other minorities or even whites. Again, according to figures from Los Angeles between 1924 and 1933, 61 percent of Chinese who intermarried selected Japanese mates while 41 percent of Japanese men and 70 percent of Japanese women found love with Chinese partners.[49]

The lure of other minority cultures engendered unconventional mixed families as well as intermarriages. Born in 1926 to Mexican American parents, Guy Gabaldon spent most of his early youth in the neighborhood streets of Boyle Heights, running errands for bar girls, grabbing beers, and getting into trouble. At the age of twelve, he met and became fast friends with two Nisei brothers, Lyle and Lane Nakano, whom he admired for their honesty, studiousness, and respect for the law. "Fascinated by the tradition and customs," he began spending a lot of time at their home, learned the Japanese language, and eventually moved in with them, remaining for 7 years until their internment. Rather than resent his adopted second family, Guy's parents supported his closeness to the Nakanos and hoped he would mend his ways under their influence. Indeed, the Japanese Americans reshaped the young Mexican American's life. He admired and followed in the military footsteps of his surrogate brothers, Lyle and Lane, serving valiantly in the South Pacific where he used his language skills to capture enemy troops. The thoroughness of his cultural voyage further expressed itself in his transnational residence and intermarriage. After World War II, Guy married a Mexican woman of Japanese descent and split his time between Modesto, California and Saipan, Japan. In becoming a member of another family, Guy promoted the possibilities inherent in other minority cultures.[50]

As much as cultural escapism propelled inter-minority families and reorganized ethno-racial categories, so did the recognition of common traditions and physical features. According to Garding Liu, Chinese businessmen of the early 1940s Los Angeles often favored Mexican women as employees and romantic partners. "People from Mexico remind the Chinese of their own nationality," Liu asserted, "the women are vivacious, are small in size, have black hair, and remind in other ways of people from the Orient." These bachelors saw Chinese-like qualities in the bodies and behaviors of Mexican women, seeking out the familiar rather than the exotic. In discovering similarities between Mexicans and Chinese, the businessmen deliberately, and thoughtfully stretched ethnic definitions.[51]

After graduating from Los Angeles' Polytechnic high school in the late 1920s, Clarence Yip Yeu (Chinese) worked as a servant alongside other

Chinese Americans and blacks in the homes of wealthy whites. Clarence remarked that the two ethnic groups "got along nice," because African Americans "respected Chinese more than the white." This understanding fostered social intimacy beyond the confines of work as Chinese men visited black nightclubs and married black women. Yet, within the community he observed, black-Chinese marriages were less frequent than Mexican-Chinese ones. Clarence interpreted this pattern as evidence of color preferences among Chinese who perceived the skin tone of Mexican American women as closer to their own. They worried about physical likeness for the sake of their children as much as themselves. The offspring of Mexicans and Chinese "don't look so bad . . . so different," asserted Clarence. Although willing to disturb established ethnic categories by intermarrying, the Chinese men proceeded with a carefulness that showed their sensitivity to community prejudices. Despite the contentions of critics, their interethnic families were calculated rather than impulsive creations.[52]

As certainly as cultural or color concerns, political beliefs—especially the opposition to discrimination and racial prejudice—shaped non-white families. In the mid–1920s, 1930s and 1940s, progressive circles included those of diverse backgrounds who shared a frustration with the status quo, mingled comfortably, and embraced tolerance as a social ideal. In the mixed environment of labor unions and civil rights organizations, interracial marriages appeared more acceptable and customary. If one's friends and political allies were Mexican, Chinese, Jewish, and black, why not contemplate marriages with other minorities? Certainly, more progressive political positions did not break down traditional ethnic allegiances altogether, but they did loosen and refashion these loyalties into a semblance of non-whiteness.

The union of minority activists, Bert and Blanche Corona, exemplified the powerful pull of common politics and the subversive implications of minority marriages. A prominent Mexican American, Bert fought to improve the conditions of workers and immigrants. Growing up in Boyle Heights, he knew many Jewish families. In the late 1930s, he met his future wife, Blanche (Jewish) while both were picketing outside the North American Aviation Plant in Los Angeles. Blanche belonged to the Democratic Youth Federation and generally involved herself in progressive politics of the era. The couple soon fell in love and eloped. To Bert, his interracial marriage seemed unremarkable, a logical result of the company he kept and ideas he espoused. "In the labor and radical circles I was a part of, there was a good deal of interaction both political and social, among people of different racial and ethnic backgrounds. Our common commitments and struggles brought us together," he explained. Allegedly, racism and conflict took a back seat to the young peoples' struggle in the Popular Front.[53]

In addition, progressive politics grounded the marriage of Elaine and Karl Yoneda, the couple whose story opened this essay. Falling in love as they jointly pursued "labor, civil rights, and anti-fascist" activities, the pair married in 1935. Even during Karl's military service, Elaine carefully maintained their ties to non-white activists, demonstrating how much the partners valued the connections. In her almost daily letters to her husband, Elaine reported conversations with Paul Robeson (African American), Joe Hittleman and Sydney Rogers (Jewish), as well as Chinese American seamen. Her presence at meetings of the Japanese American Citizens League (JACL) and county-based groups dedicated to tackling anti-Semitism and "the Negro question," during World War II further displayed the multicultural world the Yonedas inhabited. Against this backdrop of interethnic mingling, their mixed marriage likely felt secure.[54]

Many minorities rejected existing ethno-racial rules about marriage and family. They chose spouses who complemented their own political ideals, color, and history or liberated them from confining cultural mores. These inter-minority couples reorganized identity and redistributed power between men and women. Within a landscape of separatism and prejudice, they located an intimacy born of being non-white.

WHAT ABOUT THE CHILDREN?

As those who literally embodied ethnic crossing, mixed minority children reshaped the meaning of American family and ethno-racial boundaries. Social scientists have noted the ability of bicultural individuals to select or combine parental cultures in contemporary America. Even though mixed race youngsters in the second quarter of the twentieth century faced a more rigid racial climate and decisive discrimination, they still aspired to more fluid and multiple identities. Their own bodies and experiences supported more flexible notions of race and a more multicultural version of Americanization; they departed singular ethnic traditions and moved towards more blended ones. In doing so, they often became mediators not simply between cultures as the pioneering 1930s sociologist Robert Park observed, but between parents and ethnic communities or relatives who had become estranged.[55]

Mixed race children were not without their detractors. By reminding communities and families of ethnic crossings many preferred to forget, they sparked animosity. Mary Matsuno, an orphan and internee, recalled how administrators struggled to place the less popular, less wanted "mixed bloods" with willing foster families. Unlike full-blooded Japanese who found a supportive environment within the camps, mixed race children suffered teasing and taunting. During his site inspection in January 1943, Dr. Tetsuya Ishimaru found the hostility so pronounced that he urged camp officials to intervene on behalf of the mistreated youngsters.[56]

Most children were aware of and disoriented by discrimination. Looking back upon their pre-World War II childhoods in the Imperial Valley, Punjabi-Mexicans recalled the bitter prejudices of teachers and students. The majority Mexican population at their mostly non-white school, pushed, shoved, mocked and generally made their lives unpleasant. Sociologists investigating Peter, a young boy of Mexican-Japanese descent in the late–1920s, reported the difficulties he faced as a mixed race child. Peter confessed that Mexican and especially Japanese peers bullied and called him "half-breed." His principal confirmed that "Peter was isolated in a certain sense," an isolation that extended beyond school grounds. Japanese who typically felt a sense of responsibility for fellow ethnics, a local Reverend reported, considered Peter an "outcast" because of his mixed status and denied him any protection or support. As worried family and friends had predicted, multicultural children met misunderstanding and antagonism.[57]

However, rather than tragic victims of ethno-racial prejudice, these sons and daughters softened community resistance to ethnic crossing, repairing the social position of their parents, and championing non-white families. In part, the relatively more relaxed ethno-racial views of minority groups made such reconciliation possible. Born in 1930, Peter Jamero spent his childhood and adolescence in rural Livingston where Filipino men regularly partnered and parented with Mexican, Japanese, and African American women. Rather than cast out, the spouses and mixed race children were easily folded into the community. We did not "quibble about whether you were one third or one quarter Filipino, you were just Filipino," emphasized Peter. Language, religion, and foodways rather than blood assured one's status as Filipino.[58]

Even among the more racially homogeneous Chinese population a limited tolerance for mixture, especially among the younger generation, existed. Students, who attended one Chinese language school in Los Angeles in the decade before World War II, remembered classmates who were part black and part Mexican. Their Chinese fathers wished to impart some of their culture to their multiethnic offspring. According to Allen Mock, these children blended easily among their peers and gained the begrudging acceptance of local Chinese. "Anybody that even has 1/8th or 1/16th blood of Chinese is considered Chinese," Allen explained, "Chinese are more accepting." At the outset, Chinese Americans might oppose intermarriages, but such views could mellow following the birth of children. Although more concerned about racial purity than most Filipinos, Chinese still considered cultural as well as biological criteria when setting group membership. Thus, more than whites, they could perceive the "Chineseness" of bicultural offspring. In allowing that these progeny could learn ethnic ways, the community lightened the pressures on inter-minority couples.[59]

Mixed race children eased pains between generations of the same family as well, healing wounds first inflicted when couples chose to become long-term partners. After San Francisco born Marshall Hoo (Chinese) married a Korean American in 1939, both his and her parents despaired. They feared their children were betraying their ethnic pasts and ungluing cohesive ethnic communities. Yet, their opposition waned. A rising number of intermarriages through the 1940s, common Asian ancestry, and the passage of time helped, but more important were the births of cute children. The grandparents learned to accept their in-laws as mothers and fathers of their grandsons and granddaughters. Even when parents had been relatively receptive to ethno-racial crossing, this tolerance deepened with the arrival of mixed race children. Dorothy Siu (Chinese) did not openly object when her son chose a Japanese American bride in mid-1940s Los Angeles, but she admitted feeling much closer to her daughter-in-law after the birth of three grandchildren. Lovable kids could improve relations with extended family, reducing the stresses upon partners and increasing the likelihood of a lasting relationship.[60]

The mere presence of these children diffused tensions between parents and their families or ethnic communities, however, so did their more deliberate challenges. As members by birth or adoption of mixed families, these offspring frequently became informal ambassadors of cross-cultural relationships and multicultural identities. On September 1944, the supervisor of the State Charities Aid Association, which collaborated with the agency responsible for managing the internment, the War Relocation Authority (WRA), reported a surprise meeting with a young Chinese American boy, Alva, in the foster care of a Nisei couple, Mr. and Mrs. Mori. The boy marched into the office of the agent unannounced to defend his new family, particularly their ambitions to adopt a Japanese baby. Alva had overheard the Moris express their fears that the welfare service "would not want to place a Japanese child with them," because "they were Japanese" and Alva was Chinese. Hoping to correct the organization's bias against mixed families, the boy insisted his caregivers "would love a Japanese child and that it would make no difference to him": in fact he eagerly anticipated a baby sister. Alva occupied a unique position from which he could explain the health and happiness of a family most Californians suspected because of its blended form. He could defend as well the advantages of living within two cultural traditions rather than squeezing into one. An agent's assertion that "the Moris are devoted to Alva and certainly have done a good job bringing him up," suggested the success of the young boy's persuasions.[61]

In maturing and marrying, mixed race children further validated committed cultural crossovers and non-whiteness. As individuals who embodied at least two distinct cultures, they traversed ethnic lines necessarily. These men and women might search out spouses with similarly hybrid backgrounds, but these matches proved difficult to make. More important, few considered ethno-racial heritage a critical variable in calculations about marriage. To see ethnicity and race as stable and meaningful categories defied the reality of their own lives. The marriage of Avery Diaz and Nami Nakashima highlighted the dynamics by which intercultural children perpetuated hybrid families. Although it was a "no-no to marry out of the race" Nami's Mexican American mother slipped across the United States border and made her wedding vows with a Japanese immigrant whom she had met in Los Angeles. Growing up in then rural Long Beach, the Japanese-Mexican girl observed firsthand the trials of a mixed marriage: her mother surrendered her citizenship and the support of her ethnic community when she married an Asian alien. But rather than seek a partner who matched her ethnic background, Nami chose Avery Diaz, a Chicano in 1939, a selection based upon mutual attraction and values rather than a consideration of racial pedigree. Local Japanese certainly looked upon this pairing as unusual, but not the couple. "I just loved her," Avery simply stated, a sentiment Nami echoed. Nami's unique perspective and ancestry subverted conventional marital practices and definitions of exogamy. With little effort or self-consciousness, she entered what outsiders tried to label a cross-cultural romance.[62]

Rather than perpetually mixed up and miserable, as families, ethnic communities, and even many social scientists of the period predicted, bicultural offspring of minorities could enjoy and promote multicultural identities. Taking advantage of more flexible ethno-racial ideas in non-white communities, they drew marginalized couples back into familial and ethnic networks. With their own marriages, these children committed still further to the promise of non-white families.

MARITAL AND WAR BONDS

Non-white families forged in the pre-war period were stressed and ultimately strengthened by the disruptions of World War II and its immediate
aftermath. Executive Order 9066 and heightened tensions between Asian
nations strained mixed couples already strained by the prejudices of families
and communities. In fighting to preserve their relationships at this historical
juncture, they defended the very possibility of ethnic crossing in a nation
still invested in ethno-racial segregation. As the crises of the era made intercultural marriages and children more public, ethnic communities felt new
pressure to acknowledge, if not condone them. Ultimately, the slow, subtle
shift in community attitudes accomplished by these couples contributed to
the end of marital discrimination. Their intimate relationships brought about
greater freedom for non-whites and greater acceptance for ethnic crossings
in postwar California.

As fighting in the Pacific accelerated, already tense relations among
Asian groups in the United States deteriorated. Anti-Japanese violence,
harassment, and boycotts in the late 1930s and early 1940s expressed the
rising resentment of local Chinese, Koreans, and especially Filipinos. So did
noisier objections to interethnic mingling published in ethnic newspapers.
In 1941 the *New Korea,* an English language newspaper read throughout
California, shared the alleged plot of the Japanese government to offer a
"reward to those Koreans who marry Japanese women," and reminded its
readership that "we certainly don't want their blood in our future generations." Similar fears increasingly circulated among Chinese Americans. The
Hawaii Chinese Journal scared its many mainland readers with its 1943
report that Japan would integrate conquered Asian peoples through forced
marriages with Japanese women.[63]

Within this hostile setting, mixed Asian couples fought to keep their
relationships alive and their respective communities from conflict. As those
in between or on the edges, they occupied a unique position from which
they might act as mediators. Throughout 1942, the press reported crimes
in varied California locales. In El Centro, owners shut down their shops
after Filipinos fired at two Japanese exiting a pool hall. A few days later, a
Filipino gunman shot an elderly Japanese couple in the same town. Meanwhile, San Francisco police questioned Filipinos armed with knives and
Los Angeles law enforcement arrested Filipinos for robbing and beating a
Japanese hotel porter. Other violent incidents allegedly perpetrated by Pinoy
included a drive-by shooting in Costa Mesa, a kidnapping in Gilroy, and

the breaking of shop windows in Stockton. Some of these cases may have been exaggerated, but they clearly indicate how much interethnic interactions had deteriorated. Yet, even though anger frayed most Filipino-Japanese interactions, more amicable interethnic relations prevailed in Pasadena. The community owed the relative peace to Chizu Sanada, the Nisei spouse of a Filipino. Japanese expressed shock and disappointment on first learning of the girl's marriage in the late 1930s. To avoid their censure, the young woman lived and socialized among Filipinos. Because "all the Filipinos knew her," and accepted her relationship with one of their own, a Nisei friend related, they "left the rest of the Japanese alone."[64]

Although a fictitious account of a Filipino-Japanese love affair during World War II, the short story, printed in the mainstream magazine *Good Housekeeping* in 1942, "Mary Osaka, I Love You," suggested as well how individual romances might promote interethnic rapprochement. Against the backdrop of war, a Filipino bus boy, Mateo, and the daughter of his Japanese employer, Mary, fall madly in love. Mateo's Filipino friends condemn the romance as a disgrace to the Filipino nation, propose dates with a more suitable Chinese girl, and even go so far as to rough him up. Mary encounters like resistance from her father who tosses her boyfriend out the door. Yet Mary and Mateo eventually ease hostilities between their ethnic groups. The leader of local Filipino realizes that "the girl is not Japanese, but an American of Japanese descent," a distinction that transforms her from enemy to friend. At the same time, Mary's father warms to his Filipino son-in-law after the bombing of Pearl Harbor, begging Mateo to forgive the cruelties Japanese have inflicted upon Filipinos and supporting Mateo's decision to enlist in the United States Army. In this story intended as morality play, inter-ethnic romance blurred ethnic difference and created patriotic Americans.[65]

However, even more than escalated tensions between Asian nations and Asian immigrants, internment stressed and changed mixed families. The WRA ordered that all persons of partial Japanese ancestry living on the West Coast abandon their homes for remote camps in more interior parts of the country. But this policy did not originally consider the non-Japanese spouses of evacuees or their mixed children. These relationships challenged the WRA's assumption that families were racially singular and conformed to standards of racial segregation. As the United States government realized the existence of such families, it elaborated its rules. Non-Japanese wives and husbands could choose to enter camps or remain outside. More complicated and shifting regulations governed the offspring of such couples.

Part-Japanese children with non-Japanese fathers could return to their homes, but those with Japanese fathers had to stay. The gendered distinction reflected the WRA's conviction that fathers more than mothers determined the political and cultural loyalties of the next generation.[66]

The existence of orphaned or abandoned part-Japanese offspring forced other policy contortions. The Japanese community supported three major orphanages before World War II: Maryknoll and Shonien (Japanese Children's Home) in Los Angeles, as well as the Salvation Army Home in San Francisco. Consistent with their belief that even the smallest fraction of Japanese blood compromised one's loyalty to the United States, authorities closed these establishments and relocated their residents to a specially created division of Manzanar, "Children's Village." To ensure no youth slipped through the cracks and violated their rules, officials investigated orphanage records for signs of Japanese ancestry and invited non-Japanese foster parents to turn over their charges.[67]

The reality of internment tested and focused new attention upon the progeny of and relationships between Japanese and non-Japanese; couples had to surrender their romances and families or make unprecedented sacrifices to maintain them. Some broke apart under the weight of internment, but many survived. Mixed race children faced new uncertainties and hostilities as well. For the families who chose to stay together despite wartime pressures, their varied, periodically dangerous strategies highlighted the injustice of internment and the arbitrariness of the American ethno-racial system.[68]

The government's decision to relocate Japanese proved too sudden and severe for some couples and families. Twenty-year-old Mio Jean Ikebuchi (Japanese) called off her wedding with Leonard Wan (Chinese) in 1942. Although she admitted feeling as passionately about her beloved as before the war, she feared that the thousands of Japanese at Santa Anita Assembly center would mistreat him. "I love Leonard too much to allow him to figure in anything that might prove painful," she explained. Internment tore apart established families as well as aspiring spouses. Rather than risk prosecution or the loss of personal freedom, a Mexican foster mother surrendered her Nisei children. In another case, authorities puzzled over how to handle Ronald Kamamoto, the six-month-old baby of a Japanese internee and his Mexican American wife. Police arrested the woman, Rael Kamamoto, after she abandoned the child on a San Diego street corner in 1943. Although they considered placing Ronald in camp with his father, in the end they concluded, "the man wasn't reliable" and admitted the baby into Children's Village.[69]

Other couples risked social ostracism, protecting the form and principle of mixed families. In 1942, Miyo Joan Kobuchi won approval to temporarily leave Santa Anita Assembly Center to marry her San Francisco based Chinese American boyfriend. Despite the obstacles of removal and separation the youths confronted, they chose to formalize their courtship rather than end it. Married couples entered the camps together, even though non-Japanese partners were under no legal obligation to do so and were usually unwelcome by fellow internees. To protect themselves from the hostilities of others, these wives and husbands disguised their identities. At Manzanar, Jeanne Wakatsuki noticed that one of her neighbors "was a tall, broad woman, taller than anyone in camp," who "walked erectly and wore an Aunt Jemima scarf around her head." Jeanne used to play with the adopted Japanese daughter of this distinctive woman and her Japanese husband. Only later did she realize that the woman was actually "half-black, with light mulatto skin, passing as Japanese in order to remain with her husband." Avery Diaz (Mexican) and Nami Nakashima (Japanese-Mexican) may not have altered their appearances, but they "mainly stayed together" once evacuated because they "stuck out like a sore thumb" within the "sea of Japanese faces." Nami and Avery discerned the whispered and indirect disapproval beneath the surface-level politeness of other evacuees.[70]

By accompanying loved ones, waiting patiently for their release, or committing more absolutely to intercultural relations outside the camps, minorities rejected the government's preference for ethnically homogeneous units. In the pre-war period, Milicio and Treba Jacoban (Filipino Americans) became deeply attached to their Nisei foster child. In the face of internment, rather than surrender the boy and dissolve their mixed family, they successfully undertook adoption proceedings and negotiated his permanent exemption from the camps. At the same time, Elaine Yoneda negotiated release from Manzanar while arguing the virtues of mixed families and friendships before WRA officials. Even for those men and women who opted to live apart and hoped for the brevity of internment, keeping children with their mothers preserved a semblance of family unity. Kim Pong Tom of Los Angeles remembered at least two Japanese women who brought their half-Chinese, half-Japanese kids into the camps while their husbands waited for their return.[71]

Other families practiced riskier, extralegal versions of family unity, testifying to the importance of their bonds. At times, Japanese partners violated Executive Order 9066, continuing to live with their spouses in California. This course of action defied the removal policy and its disregard for

intermarriages. In 1942, police arrested Ida Esteban, the young Nisei bride
of a Filipino, on their farm in Sunnyvale. She faced criminal charges as a
woman of Japanese descent for remaining in a prohibited zone. Authorities
also uncovered the attempted subterfuge of Mrs. Liwa Chew who had long
denounced her Japanese heritage and immersed herself in her husband's
Chinese American community. The *Hawaii Chinese Journal* noted her 1942
arrest in Oakland as the first Bay Area case in which "alien restrictions"
caused marital troubles.[72] Though not always deliberately or directly, the
struggle of mixed couples for family preservation defied conventions of
ethno-racial conformity and homogeneity; they implicitly defended the
right to cross ethnic lines in the United States.

Internment and general wartime anxieties shook up mixed race progeny
as forcefully as their parents, pushing questions of identity to the fore. For
Dennis Baumbauer internment taught him new lessons about his heritage.
After scrutinizing files kept by Japanese homes for children, authorities
concluded that Dennis' mother was part Japanese. They delivered Dennis
to Manzanar where he grappled with his new ethnic designation and the
surname, "Tojo," so suddenly thrust upon him. His fairer skin and taller
stature differentiated him from other internees and made him vulnerable.
Tommy Yoneda had realized his mixed background, but it assumed greater
importance once World War II erupted. His mother remembered, "the effects
of internment lasted." "Taunted with anti-Japanese and anti-Semitic insults,"
long after his release from the camps, Tommy felt pained and confused.[73]

War not only unsettled mixed race children, but opened new possibilities
for preferred identifications. One Filipino-black child previously viewed as
foreign and strange boldly proclaimed himself an "American." The morning
after the bombing of Pearl Harbor, he dropped by Daisy Satoda's (his Nisei
neighbor) house in Berkeley to offer his condolences. "Gosh, I'm sorry that
your country is at war with our country," the boy admitted, an expression of
empathy that actually made Daisy feel an outsider for the first time.[74] The
presence of Daisy and other Japanese Americans allowed the youth to enjoy
the status of insider despite his mixed parentage. He cleverly negotiated
new wartime confusions about nationality, race, and ethnicity for his own
advantage.

As wartime made mixed couples reluctant activists or mediators, and
exacerbated the identity issues of mixed race children, it simultaneously
forced ethnic communities to confront the phenomenon of intercultural
families. Mixed couples of the pre-war period who felt the disapproval of
their relatives and friends often moved to places and socialized in ways that

hid them from view. In keeping low profiles, they permitted ethnic groups to deny or forget their existence. But internment forced many of these couples into the public's line of vision. As a result, community opinion slowly shifted.

In the pages of the Japanese American press, mixed families were recast from social outcasts into compelling victims of injustice. Throughout 1942 and 1943, the *Pacific Citizen,* the newspaper read widely by Los Angeles' Japanese, empathetically depicted the struggles of Chinese, blacks and Filipinos married or related to Japanese. Among the stories shared were those of a Japanese American woman arrested when she attempted an unauthorized reunion with her Filipino husband, and an ebullient Nisei girl granted permission to marry her Chinese American beau. The sudden prominence of these pairs and families in the journal contrasted sharply with their near invisibility in the pre-war years. Their plight now served to dramatize the suffering of Japanese unfairly pushed from the West Coast.[75]

Internment brought mixed marriages to the attention of San Francisco's Filipinos as well. Miguel Ignacio, the secretary of the Filipino Community of San Francisco, Inc. joined forces with Ernest Besig of the American Civil Liberties Union in 1942 to consider the fate of Japanese partners of Filipinos. The men were surprised to learn about such unions in the middle of a combat zone. Together, they demanded a separate location for the Japanese wives of Filipino men, arguing that marriage effectively changed the ethnic status of these women. They were "no longer Japanese in the sight of Hirohito" and thus deserved special treatment.[76] In addition, the long history of inter-Asian tension made Besig and Ignacio fear for the safety of the wives. All this interest in the fate of Filipino-Japanese couples marked a noticeable transition in awareness from the pre-war. Rather than dismiss or disregard these men and women as the Filipino community had done before the crisis of evacuation, it moved slowly towards accepting responsibility for them.

The Chinese American community similarly took note of and appeared to soften its opposition to intercultural couples. Allen Mock recalled the protection extended a Japanese wife and her Chinese husband. The pair had created a comfortable, bicultural life for themselves inside Los Angeles' Chinatown in the early 1940s. "Their house was done up in traditional Japanese style, he speaks Chinese and Japanese, she speaks some Chinese and Japanese," described Allen. To make ends meet, they operated a small neighborhood barbershop servicing an almost exclusively Chinese clientele. Although authorities sought to locate and intern Mrs. Tien Gee in the months after the passage of Executive Order 9066, they failed in their endeavor. When a FBI agent arrived at their place of business and asked about Mrs. Tien Gee's whereabouts, customers unanimously denied knowing the woman. The duped official walked away unaware the couple had stood before him cutting hair. The willingness of Chinatown residents to encircle the Tien Gees underscored war's success in revising community attitudes about ethnicity and race, especially among Asian groups.[77]

In the postwar period, a non-white sensitivity and acceptance of cultural mixing deepened thanks to those intercultural families who survived the disruptions of war, the return of minority soldiers with Asian wives, and increased cases of interethnic adoption. Sociologists as well as ethnic and mainstream presses noted a new social phenomenon following World War II: a rise in mixed marriages. They were referring to the hundreds of minority servicemen who brought brides, many of them from Asia, home to the United States. Mixed race clubs like Los Angeles' "Club Miscegenation" sprouted up in the period to accommodate these unique couples. Marriages to ethnic insiders remained the preferred and commonplace arrangement through the late 1940s, but this standard began to ease.[78]

These newlyweds confronted significant barriers as they settled into postwar neighborhoods. Often ostracized by whites and non-whites alike, they socialized together while struggling to establish wider circles of acquaintances. In a study of black-Japanese spouses settled in Indianapolis, sociologists observed relationships and community dynamics that most likely characterized the California scene. Japanese war brides received chilly welcomes from established blacks and Japanese of the city who resented them. Different understandings of appropriate marital relations in part fed the bad feelings. According to the researchers, black women criticized the way Japanese women spoiled their men, and envied the kind treatment the foreign brides received. But the stresses of adjustment for these wartime lovers went beyond community disapproval. Following his tour of duty, Mr. Reyes (Mexican) brought his Japanese wife back to his hometown of San Francisco only to suffer humiliation and heartbreak. According to sociologists who interviewed Reyes, he had never dated an American girl, but enjoyed multiple Japanese girlfriends during his service overseas. The soldier explained "I can't talk to a girl or make friends with girls in the United States." However, although he believed his cultural crossing was a solution to long loneliness, his relationship proved short-lived. Allegedly, Mrs. Reyes became sexually promiscuous with several men, including the local grocer and a driving instructor. The dissolution of the marriage demonstrated the cultural strains inherent in the peacetime setting. The early bloom of romance faded as couples of strikingly different backgrounds faced the real, severe strains of everyday life in California.[79]

Despite these tensions, many Japanese women made successful matches and gained gradual acceptance by minority communities. In the Indianapolis cases, interracial friendships slowly evolved out of common church attendance and conversations begun in adjacent backyards. The ability of black servicemen to draw upon their own experiences of discrimination helped them relate to the troubles their wives faced. White GIs lacked the same sources for empathy and advice. Moreover, the black men believed their communities could eventually embrace them and their culturally diverse offspring. "I think that what we have done is a good thing and I think the U.S. Negroes will be proud of our children" one predicted, "imagine little Negro children who speak Japanese as a second tongue! I like to think of that."[80] This hopefulness called upon a tradition of relative racial tolerance among blacks.

Even if ambitions for full inclusion into minority communities were rarely realized, war brides and their husbands still raised the profile of mixed marriages and helped erode opposition to them. The *Los Angeles Sentinel,* a prominent black newspaper, reported in 1948 that the foreign wives of black GIs faced obstacles in their married lives, but fared "better than war brides of whites," who were more often "jilted and divorced." The newspaper emphasized the normalcy of these pairs who "are having no more or less trouble than any other young couple." *Ebony* magazine took a similarly respectful and supportive position in its multiple page spread on the life and marriage of Woodrow Strode (African American) and Luukialuanna (native Hawaiian). Born and raised in Los Angeles, Woodrow met and married his Hawaiian bride in 1938 while serving in the army. The pair later returned to southern California where Luukialuanna starred in Hollywood films and Woodrow anticipated a career with the Los Angeles Rams football team. *Ebony's* text and images portrayed the Strodes as attractive, blissfully happy, and enviably ordinary. The caption under the article's central photo encapsulated the endorsement of intermarriage: "Woody Strode and his lovely Hawaiian wife, Luukialuanna, peel clothes in hot weather and play cards on the floor." Rather than condemn this interracial marriage, the magazine encouraged acceptance by its black readership. As crossers of national as well as racial lines, these couples confronted challenges distinct from those of American minorities who intermarried. However, the positive, regular coverage of such matches revealed the local ethnic community's interest in and altered thinking about outmarriage generally.[81]

Like these marriages, an increase in intercultural children and adoptions, or at least heightened discussions about their existence or likelihood in the immediate postwar era, chipped away at resistance to mixed families. An apparent increase in the population of part-Japanese children marked the war's disorienting effect on Nisei Californians. Of 101 Japanese descent children relocated from community run homes to Children's Village at Manzanar in 1943, about 19 percent were of mixed race (defined as one-half or less Japanese), a much higher percentage than in the population at large. Sociologists studying the group noted "there were more very young than older of biracial ancestry," a pattern credited to "the strain of the months between the beginning of the war against Japan and the evacuation." The researchers further conjectured that the "greater acceptance of other races by sansei and nisei" and an acute desire to "overcome the limitations of race" at a time when race seemed so determinative, motivated their mixing.[82] Whatever the reasons, the ethnic boundaries of the Japanese community had been breached and postwar Japanese soon became aware of these breaches.

The ethnic press' heightened coverage of mixed race children and intercultural adoptions exposed these changing trends in sexual behavior and forced the Japanese and even the Chinese community to recognize mixing within their midst. A 1942 article in the *Pacific Citizen* sympathetically depicted the longing of a Japanese evacuee who reported "having no family of my own, but I adopted two Chinese orphans." The foster father humbly explained his desire to reunite with and continue the education of his sons. Using the story as further evidence of internment's injustice, the paper also implied the legitimacy of such interethnic families. More frequently, the media presented intercultural adoptions as problematic, but its accounts still made clear the softening of ethno-racial borders. A 1949 report listed Nisei children in Los Angeles orphanages needing foster care. Perhaps, in the interests of truthful advertising, it specified the racial background of the orphans: twelve pure Japanese, and six part Japanese. Many of these kids currently resided in black and Caucasian homes, even though the placement agencies preferred to match the race of the adopted and adopters.[83]

The clash between a desire for racial uniformity in families, and the growing reality of mixture shaped the postwar Chinese community too. The San Francisco based *Chinese Press* announced the availability in 1950 of "two full-blooded Japanese babies" and one "Chinese-Japanese girl" through the Alameda County Welfare Commission. These orphans had places in white foster homes, but the organization desired an "Oriental family" to become their permanent guardians. A related article printed one year earlier called "the tragedy of Chinatown," the failure of Chinese to take care of co-ethnic orphans. Histrionically, it depicted the fates of "Eugene who must live in a Negro home because his own people do not care" and "Rosie, who for the want of a home is forced to live with Caucasians.[84] The newspaper acknowledged the practice of interracial crossing, even as it recommended ethnic matching as a community value. Its definition, though, of what constituted an appropriate family was more capacious than in the pre-war. Although the paper critiqued black and white parents who cared for Asian American children, it protected the right of Chinese couples to adopt Japanese babies. In doing so it both forwarded and reflected the fading divisions between Asian ethnics. Real cases of mixed families showed the futility of efforts to preserve strict ethnic categories. Chinese Americans could no longer deny the changed composition of their group in postwar California.

A public dialogue about the consequences of intermixing wore down its opponents, but so did the more liberal marital practices of the second generation. These young adults helped change pre-war norms. They still favored marriages with cultural insiders, but this preference was less strongly felt and practiced. By the mid–1930s, some in the second generation were already criticizing prohibitions to intermarriage. Articles in the Nisei-centered newspaper of Los Angeles, *The New World Sun*, urged it readers to consider intermarriage "an individual problem and not condemn it generally" for fear that such condemnation meant "admitting the justice of the legal barriers that have been set up." In coupling the issues of racial discrimination and intermarriage, the authors sought to change community opinion. This cosmopolitan perspective seemed to strengthen through the 1940s as intercultural pairings, particularly those of Asian ethnics, became more common. Marge Ong recalled her Chinese American brother's marriage to a Korean immediately after World War II as the first of its kind in Los Angeles. Immigrating to the southern California city in the early 1920s, the Ongs raised their children to preserve Chinese culture and marry a person of Chinese descent. Yet when their youngest son selected a non-Chinese spouse, they welcomed the match. Marge confessed that her parents "would have disowned her" if she had attempted such a crossing, but because her brother was younger, "by then" her father "didn't mind so much," explaining to his wife that "she's oriental, we're Chinese, what's the difference?" The parental tolerance Marge found unexpected in the mid-1940s indicated the era's changing definitions of ethnic membership.[85]

These roomier notions of group-belonging enabled mixed, especially inter-Asian, couples to preserve ties to their own families. In 1946, as part of a series in which she chronicled her post-internment experiences in Los Angeles for the liberal leaning *Common Ground,* Mary Oyama wrote about a child's birthday party she attended. Hosted by two Nisei daughters with Chinese American husbands and Chinese-Japanese children, the event was relaxed and joyous. The Chinese American son-in-laws chatted amicably with their father-in-law as he proudly watched his seven grandchildren at play. In reporting this celebration and remarking upon the apparent contentment of the Issei, Oyama stressed that Asians could and were creating harmonious families in California. Reflecting back upon the ethnic attitudes and practices of Asian Americans in mid–1940s Los Angeles, Allen Mock agreed that those years marked a turning point: "The color line started to break and the Japanese girls were just as acceptable and pretty in my age group." Although Asian ethnics in Hawaii passed over the line much earlier, Mock stated, it took San Francisco and Los Angeles communities until the late 1940s and 1950s. As Chinese Americans increasingly married Nisei, they mellowed the objections of their parents. "What the heck at least it's an Oriental, they could have married a black or brown or whatever," Mock recalled as the growing sentiment of most first generation Asians, a sentiment that betrayed both the expansion of and continued limits upon ethnic affiliation. As certain color lines faded, others remained vivid.[86]

This gradual shift in social practice and attitudes grounded political action in the late 1940s. Changes in how non-whites thought about intercultural marriages crystallized as legal challenges to anti-miscegenation. In California the couple whose case rose through the court system and ultimately ensured full marital rights for non-whites were respectively of African and Mexican descent. Although her Mexican ancestry subjected her to the discrimination typical of minorities, Perez was legally white. Backed by the Catholic Interracial Council and St. Patrick's church of Los Angeles, which acknowledged their marriage, Andrea Perez and her black fiance, Sylvester Davis, fought to gain legal recognition. In *Perez v. Lippold* (1948), the Supreme Court ruled in Andrea and Sylvester's favor, striking down the anti-miscegenation statute as a violation of the equal protection clause.[87]

The man and woman who guaranteed freedom of marriage for non-whites were themselves non-white. As a woman of Mexican heritage, Andrea likely had mixed ancestors, yet she consistently described herself in marriage licenses and legal petitions as "unmixed." In doing so, she left the court no doubt about the applicability of the anti-miscegenation statute to her relationship; she used her privilege as a marginal white to challenge American racism. Perez and Davis's case suggests the willingness and ability of those on the border of whiteness to pull those positioned at a distance, closer. In 1932 another woman of Mexican descent, Ruth Salas, had exploited the flexibility afforded Mexicans within the American racial system; she denied a white identity so that she could marry a Filipino.[88] Andrea's self-designation—a more political act than Ruth's and one more deliberately intended to advance the interests of other minorities—suggested her personal courage. But it also spoke to the changed climate of opinion and practice in late 1940s California that nurtured such a direct and ultimately effective challenge.

Although intercultural marriages precipitated by *Perez v. Lippold* remained modest in number, non-whites interpreted the decision as a political victory for them all. Almost uniformly, the ethnic press gave the story positive coverage. "Few members of the minority racial groups have been affected by the law or are likely to be in the immediate future," the *Pacific Citizen* acknowledged, yet "its existence on the statute-books of California has been a blow at the dignity of the non-Caucasian population." *The California Eagle* and *Los Angeles Tribune* agreed. The former condemned as "racist" a brief issued by Los Angeles' Board of Supervisors supporting the miscegenation statute while the latter praised the Catholic Church for its participation in the suit.[89] More obliquely, the *Chinese Press* in 1949 supported the case's denouement by uncritically reporting eleven interracial marriages by Chinese that had since occurred in Los Angeles County. Non-whites celebrated the dismantling of discrimination that had begun from their own ranks. Political success born of common social experiences pointed the way towards future collaborations among non-whites and greater consciousness of interlocking lives.

CONCLUSION

Making love and family across ethnic lines, non-white Californians became unintended, even reluctant advocates of multiethnic lives. With varying enthusiasm, minority youth dabbled in other non-white cultures. Their brief romances not only introduced them to new gender roles and sexualities, but also celebrated ethnic crossing at a moment when separatism was the rule. Minority adults went even further. In the years leading up to World War II, a small number discovered and drew together because of common values and traits that transcended traditional cultural divisions. Rather than random, these pairings happened in repeated ways that expressed continued concerns about color, history, and background. Demography and power mattered too. Women took advantage of their scarcity and the more even power dynamic of minority pairs to press their own ambitions. Social climbing and relinquishing one culture for a more advantageous one did not structure minority interactions as they did white-minority relationships. As a result, men more often had to revise their romantic and familial scripts to accommodate competing female desires. The coming of mixed race children further consolidated these non-white families and the unique combinations of cultures they embodied.

The events of wartime put the relationships of non-white families to the test. Japanese internment and conflict among Asian nations prompted the tightening of ethnic and racial borders. To most Americans, separatism and segregation appeared the best defenses in a warring world. Mixed, non-white families who fought to remain together, however, rejected this strategy and became public proponents of ethnic crossing. Their very personal acts of affection and connection slowly changed community attitudes. As the postwar advanced, this mellowing of ethno-racial prejudice collapsed the legal supports behind marital discrimination.

Overall, these youthful daters, lifetime partners, and mixed race children expressed the growing closeness and cohesiveness of non-whites. Their relationships defied ethnic separatism and mainstream segregation, offering up an alternative identification based upon cultural belonging and compromise. A non-white sensibility certainly did not eclipse smaller, ethnic allegiances in the period. Jews continued to understand themselves and act as Jews, Chinese as Chinese, blacks as blacks, etc. However, recognition of linkage among minorities—exemplified in the making of non-white families— slowly developed. It is this awareness that echoes a more contemporary category of organization, "people of color," and reminds us of how multiple and shifting are ethno-racial allegiances in the American past.

NOTES

1. Statement to the Commission on Wartime Relocation and Internment of Civilians (undated) Box 3 *Elaine Black Yoneda Papers* Labor Archives, San Francisco State University; Letter to United China Relief, May 1, 1942, Folder 2, Box 8, *Karl Yoneda Collection* (Collection 1592) Department of Special Collections, Charles E. Young Research Library, University of California, Los Angeles.

2. For how whites segregated places of worship, see: Edwin B. Almirol, "Church Life Among Filipinos in Central California," in *Religion and Society in the American West*, ed. Carl Guarneri and David Alvarez (Maryland: University Press of America, 1987), 306; Fred Cordova, *Forgotten Asian Americans* (Demonstration Project for Asian Americans, 1983);

Gaston Espinosa, "Borderland Religion: Los Angeles and the Origins of the Latino Pente-costal Movement in the U.S., Mexico, and Puerto Rico, 1900–1945" (Ph.D. diss., University of California, Santa Barbara, 1999), 29. For a detailed account of school segregation, see Charles Wollenberg, *All Deliberate Speed: Segregation and Exclusion in California Schools, 1855–1975* (Berkeley: University of California Press, 1976), 27, 44–45, 73, 112. Social scientists of the period documented the residential convergence of non-whites in California neighborhoods. Charles Spaulding, "Housing Problems of Minority Groups in Los Angeles" *The Annals of the American Academy* (1946): 248; Eshref Shevky and Marilyn Williams, *The Social Areas of Los Angeles: Analysis and Typology* (Berkeley: University of California Press, 1949), 53; *Digest of Final Report: Housing Survey, City of Los Angeles* (Los Ange-les: Housing Authority of the City of Los Angeles, 1940), 19; San Francisco Department of City Planning, *The Population of San Francisco: A Half Century of Change, 1900–1950* (1954), 17–19; Oakland City Planning Department, *Oakland's Changing Community Pat-terns* by Bryce Young, 1961, 3; Earl Hansen and Paul Beckett, *Los Angeles: Its Peoples and Its Homes* (Los Angeles: The Haynes Foundation, 1944), 12; Davis McEntire, *Race and Residence* (Berkeley: University of California Press, 1960), 48; Far West Surveys, San Francisco. *San Francisco-Oakland Metropolitan Area: Population Report of White, Negro, and Other Races.* San Francisco, 1961; Leonard Austin, *Around the World in San Francisco: A Guide to Unexplored San Francisco* (San Francisco: Fearon, 1955), 63; City of Oakland, California, *Housing Authority Annual Report* (1940–1963); B. Shrieke, *Alien Americans: A Study of Race Relations* (New York: Viking Press, 1936), 36; Kathryn Cramp, *Study of the Mexican Population in Imperial County* (New York: Committee on Farm and Cannery Migrants, 1926), 15; Harold Wise, *Characteristics of the Low Rent Housing Market in Brawley, Holtville, Calexico, Imperial and Westwood, California* (Planning and Housing Research Associates, 1950), 23. More recent demographic studies confirm and elaborate early findings of neighborhood diversity. James Allen and Eugene Turner, *The Ethnic Quilt: Population Diversity in Southern California* (Northridge, California: Center for Geographical Studies, California State University, Northridge, 1997), 125–127; George Sanchez, *Becom-ing Mexican American: Ethnicity, Culture and Identity in Chicano Los Angeles, 1900–1945* (New York: Oxford University Press, 1993), 77; Marilyn Johnson, *The Second Gold Rush: Oakland and the East Bay in World War II* (Berkeley: University of California, 1993), 93; Alonzo Smith, "Blacks and the Los Angeles Municipal Transit System," *Urbanism Past and Present* (Winter/Spring 1981): 26.

3. So called "whiteness studies" have come under recent, heavy fire. Scholars acknowl-edge the concept's contributions: it crystallizes the long asserted notion that race is a social construction, debunks the romantic portrait of cross-race, working class solidarity, and reminds us that whites too are raced. However, many complain that whiteness is overused as an explanation of social phenomenon, that it is too often divorced from specific historical contexts, that its meanings are alternatively too elastic or too static, that it shifts attention away from racism by falsely balancing the racial identities of whites and blacks, that it cov-ers over other important lines of distinction (gender, religion, sexuality, politics, etc.), and that it ignores the views of non-whites. My work is in part an answer to these criticisms. It addresses concrete social relations at a specific moment in California history, privileges the perspectives and activities of groups deemed "unwhite," and stresses the contingent and flexible nature of a non-white sensibility. On the promises and pitfalls of whiteness studies, see Peter Kolchin, "Whiteness Studies: The New History of Race in America," *Journal of*

American History (June 2002): 154–173 and a symposium by six historians: "Scholarly Controversy: Whiteness and the Historian's Imagination," *International Labor and Working Class History* (no. 60, Fall 2001): 1–92.

4. On the shifting ethno-racial position of Jews, see Gary Gerstle, *American Crucible: Race and Nation in the Twentieth Century* (Princeton: Princeton University Press, 2001). On the postwar gains of Jews and other European ethnics see George Sanchez, "The Agony of Whiteness: How Jews Moved Out of the Eastside And What Difference That Makes For Race In Los Angeles," working paper, Autry Western History Workshop, Los Angeles, Calif., February 2003; Renee Romano, *Race Mixing: Black-White Marriages in Postwar America* (Cambridge, Mass.: Harvard University Press, 2003), 46; Karen Brodkin, *How Jews Became White Folks* (New Jersey: Rutgers University Press, 1998), 46.

5. Historians and sociologists have long noted the richness of meanings embedded in these kinds of relationships. Henry Yu traced the academic interest in interracial sex and marriage over the course of the twentieth century: "Mixing Bodies and Cultures: The Meaning of America's Fascination with Sex between 'Orientals' and 'Whites' in *Sex, Love, Race: Crossing Boundaries in North American History,* ed. Martha Hodes (New York: NYU Press, 1999), 446–458; *Thinking Orientals: Migration, Contact and Exoticism in America* (New York: Oxford University, 2000), 56–63.

6. Nineteenth-century marriages forged on the frontier of U.S. settlement between white American men and minority women were relatively balanced and mutually beneficial. Such dynamics became rarer as whites gained greater social, economic, and political authority. On the incidence and changing dynamic of such relationships, see Albert Camarillo, *Chicanos in a Changing Society: From Mexican Pueblos to American Barrios in Santa Barbara and Southern California, 1848–1930* (Cambridge, Mass.: Harvard University Press, 1979), 11, 69–71; David Montejano, *Anglos and Mexicans in the Making of Texas, 1936–1987* (Austin: University of Texas, 1987), 32; Deborah Moreno, 'Here the Society is United': Respectable Anglos and Intercultural Marriage in Pre-Gold Rush California," *California History* (Spring 2001): 3–17; Pablo Mitchell, "Accomplished Ladies and Coyotes" in *Sex, Love, Race,* ed. Martha Hodes, 334. Studies that suggest how white privilege defined marital relations and parental strategies through the twentieth century include, Rachel Moran, *Interracial Intimacy: The Regulation of Race and Romance* (Chicago: University of Chicago Press, 2001); Ruth Frankenberg, *White Women, Race Matters: The Social Construction of Whiteness* (Minneapolis: University of Minnesota Press, 1993); and Peggy Pascoe, "Miscegenation law, Court Cases, and Ideologies of 'Race' in 20th Century America" *Journal of American History* 83 (1996): 44–70.

7. Pascoe, "Miscegenation Law," in *Sex, Love, Race,* 467; Gary Nash, "The Hidden History of Mestizo America" *Journal of American History* 82 (December 1995): 941; Yu, "Mixing Bodies and Cultures," 458; Yu, *Thinking Orientals,* 58.

8. Nellie Foster, "Legal Status of Filipino Intermarriages in California," *Sociology and Social Research* 16 (May–June 1942): 449–450; Moran, "Interracial Intimacy," *Kashu Mainichi* (December 11, 1931); George Simpson, *Racial and Cultural Minorities: An Analysis of Prejudice and Discrimination* (New York: Harper and Brothers, 1953), 503; *New World Sun* (May 3, 1936); Paul Spickard, *Mixed Blood: Intermarriage and Ethnic Identity in Twentieth Century America* (Wisconsin: University of Wisconsin Press, 1989), 229.

9. Interview with George Lew by Beverly Chan (August 18, 1979) *Southern California Chinese American Oral History Collection (SCOHC)* (Collection 1688) Department of Spe-

cial Collections, Charles E. Young Research Library, University of California, Los Angeles. On the ethno-racial views Chinese and Japanese immigrants brought with them, see Frank Dikotter, *The Discourse of Race in Modern China* (London: Hurst and Company, 1992), 90, 131–136; Michael Weiner, "The Invention of Identity: Race and Nation in Pre-War Japan" in *The Construction of Racial Identities in China and Japan: Historical Contemporary Perspectives,* ed. Frank Dikotter (London: Hurst and Company, 1997), 135.

10. Throughout the essay, these parenthetical references specify ethno-racial background rather than nationality.

11. Arleen De Vera, "The Tapia-Saiki Incident" in *Over the Edge: Remapping the American West,* ed. Valerie Matsumoto (Berkeley: University of California Press, 1999), 206–209. Conclusions about Japanese marital attitudes based upon my analysis of 194 cases in "Issei Interview Survey," *Japanese American Research Project (JARP)* (Collection 2010) Department of Special Collections, Charles E. Young Research Library, University of California, Los Angeles. The results of this survey are used here to buttress conclusions about racial ideas drawn from earlier dated materials. I do not mean to suggest that Issei perceptions did not reflect the character of their experiences in the 1960s, but I believe Japanese ideas retained some consistency (if anything, opposition to intermarriage lessened) between 1925 and 1960.

12. Sanchez, *Becoming Mexican American,* 30. Spickard, *Mixed Blood,* 42, 353; Alan Knight, "Racism, Revolution, and Indigenismo: Mexico, 1910–1940" in *Idea of Race in Latin America, 1870–1940,* ed. Richard Graham (Austin: University of Texas, 1990), 95. For more about the racial aspects of Filipino nationalism, see John Schumacher, *The Propaganda Movement: 1880–1895, The Creators of Filipino Consciousness, The Makers of Revolution* (Solidaridad Publishing, 1973); Michael Salman, *The Embarrassment of Slavery: The Controversies over Bondage and Nationalism in the American Colonial Philippines* (Berkeley: University of California Press, 2001), 10–19; and Antonio Pido, *The Filipinos in America: Macro/Micro Dimensions* (New York: Center for Migration Studies, 1986). For works that suggest the comfort of Filipino immigrants with intermixing, see Barbara Posadas, "Mestiza Girlhood," in Asian American Women United of California, *Making Waves: An Anthology by and About Asian American Women* (Boston: Beacon Press, 1989); Barbara Posadas, "Crossed Boundaries in Chicago: Pilipino American Families Since 1925" in *Unequal Sisters: A Multicultural Reader in U.S. Women's History,* ed. Ellen DuBois and Vicki Ruiz (New York: Routledge, 2000); and Paul Spickard, "Injustice Compounded: Amerasians and the Question of Multiethnic Identity," *Journal of American Ethnic History* (Spring 1986), 5–22.

13. Spickard, *Mixed Blood,* 353.

14. Interview with Betty Wong Lem by Jean Wong (April 5, 1979) *SCOHC*; Interview with Adele Hernandez Milligan by Sherna Berner Gluck (1983), *Rosie the Riveter Revisited: Women and the World War II Experience,* Oral History Resource Center, Special Collections, California State University, Long Beach. Harry's consistent choice of black women hints at the possibility of exoticism.

15. "In Furtherance of Unity," *Now: The War Worker* (May 1944); "The Race War that Flopped," *Ebony* (July 1946); Interview with Japanese American Minister, (August 1943) Reel 74 *Japanese American Evacuation and Resettlement Records (JAERR)* BANC MSS 67/14c, Bancroft Library, University of California, Berkeley.

16. These were the varied names used to designate the youth. The term "pachuco" originated and circulated most widely among Mexican Americans. "Yogore" had roots and wide

currency among Japanese Americans, many of whom used it as a slur. For scholarly works on this defiant, youthful cohort see: Paul Spickard, "Not Just the Quiet People: The Nisei Underclass," *Pacific Historical Review* (1999): 78–94; Douglas Henry Daniels, "Los Angeles Zoot: Race 'Riot,' The Pachuco and Black Music Culture," *Journal of Negro Culture* (1997): 201–220; Eduardo Obregon Pagon, *Murder at the Sleepy Lagoon: Zoot Suits, Race and Riot in Wartime Los Angeles* (Chapel Hill: University of North Carolina Press, 2003); Luiz Alberto Alvarez, "Power of the Zoot: Race, Community and Resistance in American Youth Culture, 1940–1945" (Ph.D. diss., University of Texas, Austin, 1999).

17. Cecil Wan remembered the presence of Chinese zoot suiters on San Francisco street corners. Author's Interview with Cecil Wan (April 19, 2001); Chester Himes, Carey McWilliams, and Emory Bogardus emphasized the diverse participation in zoot culture. Emory Bogardus, "Gangs of Mexican American Youth," *Sociology and Social Research* (September 1943); Chester Himes, *Black on Black: Baby Sister and Selected Writings* (New York: Doubleday and Company, 1973), 220–221. Beatrice Griffith, *American Me* (Boston: Houghton Mifflin Company, 1948), 51. According to one Mexican American, pachucos "were carrying on habits and traditions of their land of origin." Unsigned statement, Folder 10, Box 4, *Sleepy Lagoon Defense Committee Papers* (Collection 107) Department of Special Collections, Charles E. Young Research Library, University of California, Los Angeles; Beatrice Griffith, "The Pachuco Papers" *Common Ground* (Summer 1997).

18. Interview with Lester Kimura by Charles Kikuchi (September 1944) Reel 78 *JAERR.*

19. Interview with Barry Shimizu, (August 1944) Reel 78 *JAERR.*

20. Chester Himes, *Black on Black: Baby Sister and Selected Writings* (New York: Doubleday and Co., 1973), 224; Charles Kikuchi, *The Kikuchi Diary: Chronicle From an American Concentration Camp* (Urbana: University of Illinois Press, 1973), 44.

21. A Japanese term used to identify white Americans; Interview with George Yani by Charles Kikuchi (November 1943) Reel 77 *JAERR.*

22. Interview with Barry Shimizu, *JAERR*; Interview with Rose Echeverria Mulligan by Sherna Berger Gluck (1983), *Rosie the Riveter Revisited: Women and the World War II Experience,* Oral History Resource Center, California State University, Long Beach; Interview with Tommy Hamada by Charles Kikuchi (October 1944) *JAERR.*

23. Interviews with Rose Echeverria Mulligan and Margarita Salazar McSweyn by Sherna Berger Gluck (1983), *Rosie the Riveter Revisited.*

24. Interview with Nikki Bridges by Eric Saul (November 23, 1985) "Women Oral History" *Oral History Project* National Japanese American History Society; Interview with Motoko Shimosaki by Charles Kikuchi (September 22, 1944) Reel 78 *JAERR.* For more general accounts of young ethnic women in California, see Valerie Matsumoto, "Redefining Expectations: Nisei Women in the 1930s," *California History* (Spring 1994): 63–65; Yicki Ruiz, *From Out of the Shadows: Mexican Women in Twentieth Century America* (New York: Oxford University Press, 1998); Judy Yung, *Unbound Feet: A Social History of Chinese Women in San Francisco* (Berkeley: University of California Press, 1995).

25. Interview with Frances Nishimoto by Charles Kikuchi (December 13, 1943) Reel 73 *JAERR;* Nisei, Ch Am (the name is reproduced as it appears in the record) also held herself aloof from the Filipino customers who borrowed money from her father at an Oakland gambling establishment. She had trouble explaining the source of her anti-Filipino feelings, but maintained them through much of her life. Interview with Ch Am by Charles Kikuchi (1943) Reel 74 *JAERR.*

26. This organization dedicated itself to the successful integration of Mexican Americans. Its more leftist critics accused members of rejecting or denying Mexican traditions.

27. Interview with George Yani by Charles Kikuchi (November 1943) Reel 75 *JAERR;* "Negroes Prove Worth Despite Historical Tale of Opposition," *Mexican Voice* (Spring 1993); James Sakoda Interview with Art Hansen, August 9–10, 1988, in Art Hansen, ed. *Japanese American WWII and Evacuation Oral History Project Part III: Analysts* (Munich: K.G. Saur, 1994).

28. "Brotherhood in Roosevelt" *Rough Rider* (March 26, 1942); "Chosen as Ephebians" *Rough Rider* (December 7, 1939); "Roosevelt—A Melting Pot" *Rough Rider* (October 3, 1940); "Hawaii Melting Pot Theory Probed by Chinese" *California Chinese Press* (April 11, 1941).

29. "Hawaii Melting Pot Theory Probed by Chinese" *California Chinese Press* (April 11, 1941); Editorial, *Mexican Voice* (October/November 1938); Manual de La Raza, "Four of Us" *Mexican Voice* (Winter 1941). The narrator of the story did not distinguish between whites and non-whites per se, grouping together those most on the margins (Chinese, "Negroes," "Spanish") with those much closer to the center (Italians, Armenians). Such a blurring of distinctions was consistent with his message of inclusiveness. It also represented a clever way for non-whites to gain advantage by claiming solidarity with those of more elevated socioeconomic positions.

30. "Go Adventuring for Friendships" *New World Sun* (March 17, 1936); "Nisei Should Not Be Prejudiced" *New World Sun* (July 25, 1936).

31. Interview with Tamie Ihara by Charles Kikuchi (July 1943) *JAERR;* Author's Interview with Rose Mary Escobar (March 8, 2001).

32. Robert Vallangca, *The First Wave* (San Francisco: Strawberry Hill Press, 1977), 63–66.

33. Sucheng Chan, *Asian Americans: An Interpretive History* (Boston: Twayne Publishers, 1991), 10–14, 17–23; Karen Isaksen Leonard, *Making Ethnic Choices: California's Punjabi Mexican Americans* (Philadelphia: Temple University Press, 1992), 23.

34. Other Asian American interviewees remembered inter-minority marriages. For more examples see: Survey results 0700202, 763204, 725201, 796205, 183204, *JARP;* "Women Oral History Transcripts" *Oral History Project (OHP)* National Japanese American Historical Society (NJAHS); *Southern California Chinese American Oral History Collection (SCOHC)* (Collection 1688) Department of Special Collections, Charles E. Young Research Library, University of California, Los Angeles; Sample interviews cited: Interviews with Ida Lee by Beverly Chan (July 29, 1980), and with William Chew Chan by Suellen Chung (January 7, 1980) *SCOHC,* Interview with Peggy Kanzawa by Kiku Funabiki, (February 8, 1989) "Women Oral Transcripts" *OHP,* NJAHS; "Application to Take Oath of Allegiance to United States under Act of June 25, 1936, as Amended and Form of Such Oath" 246-R1236 and 246-R1526 *Repatriation Documents,* National Archives, Laguna Niguel.

35. Constantine Panunzio, "Intermarriage in Los Angeles, 1924–1933" *American Journal of Sociology* 47 (March 1942). Although Panunzio's work does not cover the entirety of the time period under review in this paper, 1925–1950, it indicates general patterns of intermarriages that likely persisted through mid-century. These limited statistics as well as remembered and recorded cases of intermarriage underscore the existence of mixed marriages and hint at the presence of others. Given the indifference of whites to relations among minorities, such pairings appeared less regularly in mainstream sources. At the same time, embarrassment about interracial intimacy in minority communities discouraged members

from speaking about or publicly acknowledging known cases. The recovered evidence, therefore, likely understates mixed marriages and progeny. But if not besides the point, counting is secondary to the analysis of this work. Even the limited sample of committed relationships in this study demonstrates the mechanisms by which minorities fashioned families that defied traditions of separatism and discrimination.

36. Louisiana Constitution (1920), art. 220; North Carolina *Consolidated Statutes* (1927), sec. 2495; John D'Emilio and Estelle Freedman, *Intimate Matters: A History of Sexuality In America* (New York: Harpers & Row, 1988), 93. In the summary opinion of the case that would eventually overturn the state's anti-miscegenation law, the judge cleverly extended the logic of the statute to challenge white privilege: "It might be concluded therefore that section 60 is based upon the theory that the progeny of a white person and a Mongolian or Negro or Malay are inferior or undesirable, while the progeny of members of other different races are not . . . Furthermore there is not a ban on illicit sexual relations between Caucasians and members of the proscribed races. Indeed it is covertly encouraged by race restrictions on marriage." *Perez v. Lippold,* 32 Cal 2d 711 (1948).

37. Foster, "Legal Status of Filipino Intermarriages," 449; percentages calculated from Panunzio, "Intermarriage in Los Angeles," 694–699.

38. Lillian Galerdo and Theresa Quilenderino, "Filipinos in a Farm Labor Camp" in *Asians in America: Selected Student Papers,* ed. David Mar and Joyce Sakai (Asians in American Research Project: University of California Davis, 1970), 53–60; Craig Scharlin and Lilia V. Villanueva, eds., *Philip Vera Cruz: A Personal History of Filipino Immigrants and the Farmworkers Movement* (Los Angeles: UCLA Labor Center, Institute of Industrial Relations, and UCLA Asian American Studies Center, 1992), 53; Karen Leonard, "Intermarriage and Ethnicity: Punjabi Mexican Americans, Mexican Japanese, and Filipino Americans," *Explorations in Ethnic Studies* 16 (July 1993):149, 152; Panunzio, "Intermarriage in Los Angeles," 695; John Burma, "Interethnic Marriage in Los Angeles, 1948–1959," *Social Forces* (December 1963): 159; Benicio Catapusan, "Filipino Intermarriage Problems in the United States," *Sociology and Social Research* (January–February 1938): 267.

39. Interview with Allen Mock by Jean Wong (December 12, 1980) *SCOHC*; Karen Leonard, *Making Ethnic Choices,* 69.

40. Garding Liu, *Inside Los Angeles Chinatown* (United States, 1948), 154–156; Interview with Dorothy Siu by Jean Wong (January 12, 1979) *SCOHC;* Author's Interview with Rose Mary Escobar (March 8, 2001).

41. Daily Reports from Santa Clara County Reel 108 (July 1946) *JAERR.*

42. Kibei is the term for someone of Japanese descent, born in the United States and sent to Japan for his or her secondary education.

43. Mario Garcia, *Memories of Chicano History: The Life and Narrative of Bert Corona* (Berkeley: University of California Press, 1994), 130; Interview with Elaine Black Yoneda by Lucy Kendall (May 21, 1977).

44. Buddy Ono, "She Married a Filipino," *New World Sun* (May 3, 1936).

45. Rachel Moran noted the ability of white parents to extend their racial privileges to their mixed race children. Non-white spouses tended to embrace this transmission. Moran, *Interracial Intimacy,* 157; Karen Leonard reported how Hispanic wives challenged, often successfully, the marriages their husbands had proposed between their offspring and either local Punjabi pals or Indian women abroad. Most members of the second generation managed to choose partners that pleased them. Leonard, *Making Ethnic Choices,* 149, 154–156.

46. Author's Interview with Sugar Pie De Santo (February 16, 2001).

47. Interview with Mrs. Machida by Chloe Holt (July 2, 1924) *Survey of Race Relations Records,* Hoover Institution Archives.

48. "Japanese Wife of Oakland Chinese Arrested as Alien" *Hawaii Chinese Journal* (July 16, 1942).

49. Panunzio,"Intermarriage in Los Angeles," 694, 698; Interview with William Chew Chan by Suellen Cheng (January 7, 1980) *SCOHC.*

50. Interview with Guy Gabaldon by Ruchika Joshi (July 25, 2000) *U.S. Latino and Latina WWII Oral History Project,* volume 2, (Fall 2000) School of Journalism, University of Texas, Austin.

51. Liu, *Inside Chinatown,* 157.

52. Interview with Clarence Yip Yeu by Suellen Cheng (April 24, 1980) *SCOHC.*

53. Garcia, *Memories of Chicano History,* 130.

54. Letter to Karl from Elaine (August 11, 1943) Folder 7, Box 3 *Elaine Black Yoneda Papers.*

55. Historians such as Paul Spickard asserted that multiracial individuals had little opportunity to choose identities for themselves until well after the civil rights movement of the 1960s. Prior to that decade, most accepted socially ascribed, monoracial identities. Paul Spickard, "The Illogic of American Racial Categories," in *Racially Mixed People in America,* ed. Maria Root (Newbury Park: Sage Publications, 1992), 165. Echoing the early twentieth-century thinking of Robert Park who depicted biracial children as likely cosmopolitans, Lise Funderburg and Rachel Moran have noted greater tolerance and attraction to "dualism" in the desires and attitudes of mixed race individuals. Lise Funderberg, *Black, White, Other: Biracial Americans Talk about Race and Identity* (New York: William Morrow and Co., 1994), 197; Moran, *Interracial Intimacy,* 158; Kathleen Odell Korgen, *From Black to Biracial: Transforming Racial Identity Among Americans* (Westport, CT: Praeger, 1998), 78; Spickard, "The Illogic of American Racial Categories," 165.

56. Tetsuya G. Ishimaru, Report on the Children's Village of Manzanar Relocation Project (January 1943) and Levine, "Children in Residence—Japanese Children's Home" (March 31, 1942) *Children's Village Project Materials,* Compiled by Art Hansen, Oral History Program, California State University, Fullerton.

57. Life History of Peter by William C. Smith (1924) *Survey of Race Relations Records,* Hoover Institution Archives; Statement to the Commission on Wartime Relocation and Internment of Civilians (undated) Box 3 *Elaine Black Yoneda Papers;* Leonard, *Making Ethnic Choices,* 132; Levine, *A Fence Away,* 7.

58. Author's Interview with Peter Jamero (August 10, 2000).

59. Interview with Allen Mock by Jean Wong (December 13, 1980) *SCOHC.*

60. Interview with Dorothy Siu by Jean Wong (December 12, 1979) *SCOHC;* Interview with Marshall Hoo by Beverly Chan (May 24, 1980) *SCOHC.*

61. Letter to Ralph Merritt from Marion Brainerd (September 1, 1944) *Children's Village Project Materials.*

62. Levine, *A Fence Away,* 7.

63. "150,000 Japanese Girls Will be Married Off" *Hawaii Chinese Journal* (June 3, 1943); "Matrimony by Bribery" The *New Korea* (April 10, 1941).

64. Interview with Chizu Sanada by Charles Kikuchi (September 1944) Reel 78 *JAERR;* "Filipinos Run Amok, Murder U.S. Japanese" *Rafu Shimpo* (January 2, 1942); "Gilroy

Farmers Face Stiff Prison Sentence for Attack" *Pacific Citizen* (July 2, 1942); "Imperial Valley Merry-Go Round" *Philippines Mail* (January 13, 1942); Miscellaneous Newspaper Clippings (December 1941) Reel 17, *JAERR;* Ben Ijima's Diary (August 25, 1942) Reel 17, *JAERR.*

65. John Fante, "Mary Osaka, I Love You," *Good Housekeeping* (October 1942).

66. "Statement of JACL, (September 15, 1949) Box 74, *John Anson Ford Collection,* The Huntington Library, San Marino, California; Helen Elizabeth Whitney, "Care of Homeless Children of Japanese Ancestry during Evacuation and Relocation" (M.A. Thesis, University of California, Berkeley, 1948), 22.

67. Risa Hirao and Professor Boskey, *Orphans of Manzanar: The Story of Children's Village* (September 1998) *Children's Village Materials;* Statement of JACL (September 15, 1949) *John Anson Ford Collection.*

68. Whitney, "Care of Homeless Children of Japanese Ancestry," 30–34, 50–51.

69. "Nisei Girl Postpones Wedding to Chinese Until End of War" *Pacific Citizen* (July 16, 1942); Letter to Ralph Merritt from T.G. Ishimaru (February 1, 1943) and Memorandum to William Ball from Paul Vernier (June 5, 1945) *Children's Village Materials.* A 1945 statistical study of the marriages of Los Angeles County Japanese uncovered some evidence of intermarriages dissolved soon after the bombing of Pearl Harbor. Leonard Bloom, Ruth Riemer, and Carol Creedon, *Marriages of Japanese-Americans In Los Angeles County: A Statistical Study* (Berkeley: University of California Press, 1945), 19–20.

70. Jeanne Wakatsuki, *Farewell To Manzanar* (Boston: Houghton Mifflin Company, 1973), 35; Levine, *A Fence Away,* 7, 65, 119.

71. Statement to the Commission of Wartime Relocation and Internment of Civilians (undated) Box 3 *Elaine Black Yoneda Papers;* Interview with Kim Fong Tom by Beverly Chan, Box 18, *Southern California Chinese American Oral History Collection (SCOHC)* (Collection 1688) Department of Special Collections, Charles E. Young Research Library, University of California, Los Angeles; Levine, *Fence Away,* 219.

72. Memorandum to William Ball by Paul Vernier (June 5, 1945) *Children's Village Materials;* "Nisei Girl, Wife of Filipino Held" *Pacific Citizen* (July 9, 1942); "Japanese Wife of Oakland Chinese Arrested as Alien" *Hawaii Chinese Journal* (July 16, 1942) .

73. Oral Histories of Petaluma Jewish Community (December 15, 1977) Folder 3, Box 4 *Elaine Black Yoneda Papers.*

74. Interview with Dwight Nishimura by Daisy Uyeda Satoda (June 30, 1985) Box 3, *OHP,* NJAHS; Risa Hirao and Professor Boskey, *Orphans of Manzanar: The Story of Children's Village* (September 1988) *Children's Village Materials.*

75. A sampling of such stories from the *Pacific Citizen:* "Nisei Girl, Wife of Filipino Held" (July 9, 1942); "WCLA Plays Cupid to Chinese-Japanese Pair" (1942); "Japanese Evacuee Supports Adopted Chinese Children" (December 24, 1942); "Chinese American Gets Into Difficulties Over Nisei Experience" (March 4, 1943); "Nisei Girl Arrested on Return to Evacuated Area" (August 4, 1943); "Japanese American Woman, Wife of Chinese, Receives Permission to Return Home" (December 4, 1943).

76. Arthur Caylor, "Behind the News with Arthur Caylor" *San Francisco News* (April 18, 1942).

77. Interview with Allen Mock by Jean Wong (December 13, 1980) Box 47, *SCOHC.*

78. Cloyte Larsson, ed. *Marriage Across the Color Line* (Chicago: Johnston Publication Co., 1965): 62–65; "War Brides of Colored GI's Fare Very Well" *Los Angeles Sentinel*

(March 13, 1948); "Intermarriage" *New World Sun* (March 4, 1936); Interracial social clubs sprouted up throughout the nation soon after WWII. In 1948, twenty-three mixed couples of Los Angeles formed Club Miscegenation to promote a sense of respectability and offer a supportive social space. Romano, *Race Mixing,* 142.

79. Larsson, *Marriage Across the Color Line,* 62–65. George DeVos, "Personality Patterns and Problems of Adjustment in American-Japanese Intercultural Marriages" (Master's Thesis, University of California, Berkeley, 1959).

80. Larsson, *Marriage Across the Color Line,* 63.

81. "War Brides of Colored GI's Fare Very Well" *Los Angeles Sentinel* (March 13, 1948); "Negroes Come Back to Pro Football" *Ebony* (1946).

82. Helen Elizabeth Whitney, "Care of Homeless Children of Japanese Ancestry during Evacuation and Relocation" (Master's Thesis, University of California, Berkeley, 1948), 66. Her conclusions were based upon interviews and reports of the War Relocation Authority.

83. "Seek Foster Homes for Nisei Children in Los Angeles Area" *Pacific Citizen* (September 10, 1949); "Japanese Evacuee Supports Adopted Chinese Children" *Pacific Citizen* (December 24, 1942).

84. "Unwanted Children: A Chinese Tragedy" *Chinese Press* (December 16, 1949); "Children for Adoption" *Chinese Press* (April 28, 1950).

85. "Intermarriage" *New World Sun* (March 4, 1936); Interview with Marge Ong, *(SCOHC).*

86. Mary Oyama, "A Nisei Report from Home" *Common Ground* (Winter 1946); Interview with Allen Mock by Jean Wong (December 13, 1980) *SCOHC.* As another example of growing comfort with inter-Asian matches, Vangie Buell's (Filipina) parents looked most favorably upon her Chinese dates whom they perceived as more culturally familiar than black and Mexican men. Author's interview with Vangie Buell (May 24, 2000).

87. *Perez v. Lippold,* 32 Cal 2d 711 (1948).

88. Foster, "Legal Status of Filipino Intermarriages," 449.

89. "Decision Declares Interracial Marriage Prohibition Violates Equal Protection Guarantee" *Pacific Citizen* (October 2, 1948); "County Acts on Racist Brief in Davis-Perez Case" *California Eagle* (October 23, 1947); "Eleven Los Angeles Chinese Intermarry in Year" *Chinese Press* (October 14, 1949).

10

An Unintended Reform: The 1965 Immigration Act and Third World Immigration to the United States

DAVID M. REIMERS

SCHOLARS, POLITICIANS AND JOURNALISTS who talk of a recent wave of new and different immigrants usually identify the 1965 amendments to the McCarran-Walter Act of 1952 as a crucial turning point in immigration history. They note that since 1965 Hispanics, South and East Asians, Middle Easterners and non-Hispanic Caribbean migrants dominate the immigration statistics. The leading sending nations in 1979, for example, were all Third World and illustrate the changes since 1965.[1]

Except for Mexico, these countries had not been known for exporting large numbers to the United States; yet they now outnumber European immigrants. In 1979, Great Britain, Germany and Ireland—traditional leading sources for American immigration—sent only a few thousand people. In that year Great Britain recorded 13,907 entrants; Germany, 6,314; and Ireland only 982. Even Italian and Greek immigration, notable in the decade after the passage of the 1965 Act, began to fall in the mid-1970s.[2]

Although racist voices, so common early in the twentieth century, are largely muted today, this new immigration prompts uneasiness. Richard Lamm, governor of Colorado, himself the grandson of immigrants, recently declared, "Immigration is another of the ideas which served us well in times past, but which hurt us in the decade of the 1980s. It is out of control, and the effects penetrate every layer of society."[3] In apparent agreement, Theodore White, in his best selling *America in Search of Itself* (1982) blamed the 1965 law for changing "all previous patterns, and in so doing, probably changed the future of America." The Act, he wrote, "was noble, revolutionary—and probably the most thoughtless of the many acts of the Great Society. It conceived of America as being open to the world, its sources of fresh arrivals determined not by those already here, but by the push and pressures of those everywhere who hungered to enter."[4]

Journal of American Ethnic History
Fall 1983, Vol. 3, No. 1, pp. 9–28

TABLE 1   Immigration from Leading Sending Nations in 1979

Nation	Number 1965	Number 1979
Mexico	37,969	52,096
The Philippines	6,093	41,300
China, Taiwan and Hong Kong	4,769	30,180
Korea	2,165	29,348
Jamaica	1,837	19714
India	582	19,708
Dominican Republic	9,504	17,519

Source: Unpublished data furnished by the Immigration and Naturalization Service.

Certainly the 1965 Act was in part responsible for the changing patterns of immigration, but White's assertion of that law's conception is wide of the mark. Congress did not intend to make radical changes in immigration patterns when it amended the McCarran-Walter Act, nor did the lawmakers mean to increase immigration substantially. Rather the 1965 Act culminated the efforts of reformers to increase immigration only slightly and to eradicate discrimination against Southern and Eastern Europeans and to a much lesser extent against Asians. At the same time, Congress intended to make immigration more restrictive. The legislators for the first time imposed a ceiling on the Western Hemisphere, which was meant to curtail rising immigration from Mexico and Central and South America. In addition Congress established what it thought were tighter labor controls on potential immigrants. Finally, by providing for refugees in the 1965 law, the legislators hoped to limit the power of the President to admit refugees by executive action.

The basic problem for post-World War II immigration reformers and liberals was the national origins quotas and the Oriental Exclusion Act enacted during the 1920s. Those restrictions practically eliminated immigration from Asia and sharply curtailed it from Southern and Eastern Europe.[5] Of the approximately one hundred fifty thousand permitted from Europe, Great Britain, Germany and Ireland were entitled to about two-thirds of the total. During and immediately after the war Congress modified some laws, including repealing Chinese exclusion in 1943, granting India and the Philippines a quota in 1946 and passing the War Brides Act in 1945.[6] These changes enabled some Asian immigrants to come to the United States, though not many. The new China quota was only one hundred five and those for India and the Philippines, one hundred. Asian women who were previously ineligible for admission became eligible because of the War Brides Act as amended. About six thousand to seven thousand entered from Japan and China under this law though most war brides were German, English, Italian or French.[7] Yet these modest changes were a straw in the wind of things to come.

More pressing as an issue was the European refugee situation. Jewish and some liberal organizations searched for a way to admit survivors of the Holocaust and other peoples uprooted by the devastation of World War II. As Leonard Dinnerstein has shown in his careful study of the Displaced Persons (DP) Acts of 1948 and 1950, after a sometimes bitter and prolonged struggle, Congress finally permitted approximately four hundred thousand displaced persons to enter the United States.[8]

During the debates over the DP Act practically no thought was given to Third World refugees. A few representatives and senators unsympathetic to the DP measure suggested that reformers were inconsistent in their concern about European displaced persons and refugees when so many other uprooted peoples existed in Palestine, India and China. On rare occasions DP opponents also suggested that if European refugees were admitted then a precedent might be established to admit non-Europeans. Sen. James Eastland (D.-Miss.), long a foe of immigration, told his colleagues that if the United States admitted European DPs "how can we deny special consideration to persons who have been displaced throughout the world? No one can deny the compelling humanitarian reasons which will be advanced to obtain special consideration for millions of unfortunate displaced victims of the war in China, or approximately 10,000,000 Pakistanian displaced persons in the partition with India, or approximately 1,000,000 Palestinian persons displaced in the Palestine war."[9]

But these scare tactics of suggesting that hordes of non-Europeans might seek entrance convinced no one, and Congress debated which Europeans would get preference and whether or not the DP law of 1948 was anti-Semitic.[10] Admission of non-Europeans was not an issue.

While the DP Act represented a hard won victory for the admission of many Southern and Eastern Europeans, the McCarran-Walter Act of 1952, passed over President Harry S. Truman's veto, did not. That Act reaffirmed the national origins quotas that attempted to preserve the Northern and Western European domination of immigration patterns. Thus Great Britain-Northern Ireland alone still had almost half of the quota slots, and combined with other Northern and Western European countries, had about two-thirds.[11]

The McCarran-Walter Act moderately liberalized immigration for Third World Asian nations. At the urging of Rep. Walter Judd (R.-Minn.), formerly a missionary to China, Congress created a large geographical triangle in the Far East which covered most of South and East Asia. This area was called the Asia-Pacific Triangle and nations within it were granted quotas, usually 100. Congress also permitted all Asians the right of naturalization, which it had already granted to Chinese, Indians and Filipinos. This was a limited victory, for total immigration allowed from Triangle nations was only 2000. Moreover, persons of one-half or more Asian ancestry born and living outside the Triangle, such as in the nonquota Western Hemisphere countries, had their immigration counted against the Asian nation of their parents' birth not the nation of their birth. Thus persons of Japanese parentage born in Peru who wanted to migrate to the United States had their number subtracted from Japan's small quota of only 185.[12]

This racial, discriminatory provision was not the only curb on Third World immigration in the McCarran-Walter Act. Prior to its passage in 1952, persons from British possessions in the Western Hemisphere entered under the large British quota, but the Act placed a limit of 100 on all colonies. When this proposal first appeared in Congress in 1949 as part of the measure designed to admit Asians and grant them naturalization rights, Rep. Adam Clayton Powell, Jr., (D.-N.Y.) said he favored granting Asians the right of naturalization and immigration but that a worldwide quota of 100 for colonies would reduce immigration of black West Indians. It was proper to "remove an injustice to orientals," but why "bring in the West Indies," he asked. Powell attempted to separate these issues but his motion failed.[13] When Congress finally incorporated the Asia-Pacific Triangle into the 1952 Immigration and Nationality Act, the limit of 100 on colonies, including those in the British West Indies, carried and thus led to a reduction in West Indian migration to the United States.

Following passage of the 1952 law, liberals, led by Sen. Herbert Lehman (D.-N.Y.) and Hubert Humphrey (D.-Minn.) and Rep. Emanuel Celler (D.-N.Y.), suggested various ways to modify the national origins system. These included pooling unused quotas and using more flexibility for the admission of refugees.[14] Yet the liberals lacked strength in the 1950s, and when immigration was loosened, as it was, special laws for refugees were passed by Congress, influenced by foreign policy or humanitarian considerations. In 1953 the legislators passed the Refugee Relief Act that admitted another two hundred thousand refugees outside the quotas. A law in 1957 admitted several thousand additional nonquota persons and cancelled mortgaged quotas under the DP Act. Under that Act nations were permitted to mortgage one-half of their future annual quotas in order to admit persons above their small national origins quotas. Thus some countries like Estonia, Latvia and Lithuania had mortgaged one-half of their annual places for generations. The cancellation of these mortgages freed more places each year for additional immigrants.

In 1958 Congress permitted entry of the victims of volcanic eruptions in the Azores and Dutch-Indonesians who had been expelled by the Indonesian government. Following the abortive Hungarian Revolution of 1956, President Dwight D. Eisenhower invoked the parole power of the 1952 law to admit thousands of Hungarian "Freedom Fighters." The provision used by the President and his attorney general was originally intended for individuals and not classes of immigrants like Hungarian refugees, but Eisenhower established an important precedent by employing it for the Hungarians.[15]

The special legislation of the 1950s was European-oriented, but a few persons in Congress did begin to suggest what Eastland had feared a few years earlier; namely, that humanitarian and Cold War arguments could be used to open the door for non-Europeans as well. During the debates over Eisenhower's proposals in 1953 to admit additional refugees to relieve overcrowding among America's European allies, several congressmen called for a broader world view. Walter Judd insisted that Asians be included in the legislation and several Arab-American organizations argued that provision should be made for Palestinians. Congress responded favorably and the final 1953 Refugee Act included several thousand Asians and Near Easterners.[16]

In response to the United Nation's declaration of 1960 as World Refugee Year, Congress passed the Fair Share Law to permit a few thousand more European refugees to enter. Sen. Hiram Fong (R.-Hawaii) persuaded his colleagues to include forty-five hundred Hong Kong Chinese refugees in the bill. He told the senators that, although he knew the primary function of the Fair Share Law was to liquidate the program of refugee camps in Europe, can "we convince the man in the Far East and the man in the Middle East that this is the fact? Back of this argument is the thought that he is not wanted; that he is not as good as the refugee from Europe. This is not only a reflection on the refugee, but it will be regarded by all those of the same ethnic group that they are not wanted; that they are not as good as the people of Europe."[17] Although the Senate accepted Fong's amendment, the House rejected it, and the final bill omitted the Chinese. However, in 1962 President John F. Kennedy invoked the parole power to admit over fifteen thousand Chinese refugees from Hong Kong.[18]

Repeated special legislation for displaced persons, Cold War refugees and other groups and the use of the parole power enabled hundreds of thousands to enter outside the regular national origins quotas. By the early 1960s two-thirds of immigrants were nonquota. Of these about half were from the Western Hemisphere which had no quotas. The balance included some Asians but mostly Europeans. That the national origins system was not working as intended gave further ammunition to reformers in their quest to replace it with a nondiscriminatory policy. A Senate committee supporting the 1965 amendments commented:

> The performance of the Congress in the field of immigration in the post-war period has been far more generous and sympathetic than adherence to the national origins system alone would allow and the failure of that system to maintain the flow of immigrants in the pattern contemplated is the result of the special legislation which has been responsive to the demand in those cases where a strict application of the quota provision would have resulted in undue hardship. . . . The system of national origins concept has been significantly modified during that time as the result of the enactment of special legislation.[19]

While supporters of change insisted that the system needed to be discarded because it did not work, some defenders of the 1952 national origins quotas, like Sen. Sam Ervin (D.-N.C.), suggested that since Congress had responded in the past to emergencies and would continue to do so in the future, a change in the basic law was unnecessary.[20]

The unworkability of the McCarran-Walter Act was not the only issue at stake in the 1965 amendments. Liberals wanted the very concept of national origins scrapped. They regarded national origins quotas as discriminatory and insulting to America's allies. By the early 1960s the climate appeared ripe for such a change. Accompanying the successes of the Civil Rights movement and following the sweeping victory of Lyndon Johnson in 1964, reformers now possessed the votes to affect changes.[21]

President Kennedy originally sent his suggestions for alteration of the McCarran Act to Congress in July 1963, but other pressing issues delayed passage of the bill until September 1965. The Kennedy-Johnson proposals called for the immediate abolition of the Asia-Pacific Triangle, a gradual elimination of the national origins quotas, and a new system to admit immigrants on the basis of their occupations or family ties in the United States. For the Eastern Hemisphere a total of 165,000 was proposed with no nation having more than 10 percent of the total. "Immediate" family members—defined as spouses, minor children and parents of United States citizens—were to be admitted above these numerical limits. Because countries like Great Britain and Ireland had not fully utilized their quotas in recent years and because the Administration wished to see parents of United States citizens added to the numerical exempt list, immigration was expected to increase about 50,000 annually.

Congress eventually altered these suggestions and made the Act more restrictive than the Administration originally desired. As finally enacted, each nation in the Eastern Hemisphere received a maximum of 20,000 places, exclusive of the "immediate" family members noted above, on a first come, first served basis. A maximum of 170,000 was reserved for the Eastern Hemisphere, exclusive of immediate family members. Immigrants were admitted on a preference system with those having family ties in the United States receiving 74 percent of the places. Only 20 percent were for those with special skills, talents or occupations needed in the United States. The largest preference category allowed 24 percent of the slots for those who were brothers and sisters of United States citizens. The remaining 6 percent, or 10,200 places, were for Eastern Hemisphere refugees. Congress hoped that by providing for refugees that special laws or the executive's use of the parole power would no longer be required.

The original Kennedy-Johnson plan emphasized skills, talents and occupations more than the final bill with its greater orientation toward family unification. The congressional changes, largely the work of Rep. Michael Feighan (D.-Ohio), who chaired the powerful immigration subcommittee, softened the impact of reform.[22] Because the prospective immigrants needed close family ties in the United States, Congress thought that recent patterns of immigration would be maintained. Numerous representatives and senators made this point. Emanuel Celler, for example, told his colleagues, "There will not be, comparatively, many Asians or Africans entering this country. . . . Since the people of Africa and Asia have very few relatives here, comparatively few could immigrate from those countries because they have no family ties in the U.S."[23]

The Administration and its congressional allies argued that the major impact of the changes would be to ease barriers in Southern and Eastern Europe where backlogs in Greece, Italy and Poland were high and quotas low. As for Asian nations and the repeal of the Asia-Pacific Triangle, they predicted that only a few thousand would come in annually. In 1964 Attorney General Robert Kennedy told the House subcommittee on immigration, "I would say for the Asia-Pacific Triangle it [immigration] would be approximately 5,000, Mr. Chairman, after which immigration from that source would virtually disappear; 5,000 immigrants would come in the first year, but we do not expect that there would be any great influx after that."[24] Although Administration officials differed in their estimates, most were similarly low, such as Attorney General Nicholas Katzenbach's figure of 6,000 the next year.[25] At the same time, they insisted, because of foreign policy needs and because of the desire to end discrimination in immigration law, it was necessary to abolish the national origins quotas and the Asia-Pacific Triangle.

These predictions about how family unification would not modify Asian immigration substantially might have eased the fears of some congressmen, but they made the Japanese American Citizens League (JACL) unhappy. While supporting the reforms, JACL agreed that family unification would not benefit Asians much because the Asian-American population was so small. JACL concluded, "Thus, it would seem that, although the immigration bill eliminated race as a matter of principle, in actual operation immigration will still be controlled by the now discredited national origins system and the general pattern of immigration which exists today will continue for many years yet to come."[26]

In addition to abolition of national origins quotas and the Asia-Pacific Triangle one other reform deserves note. When Jamaica and Trinidad and Tobago gained independence in the early 1960s, their 100 quota established in 1952 remained in effect. Other nations in the Western Hemisphere had no quotas and the reformers wanted to end this inequity. The matter was not controversial because it seemed reasonable for all independent nations in the Western Hemisphere to be placed on the same footing. Yet it should be emphasized that in this case, as in others, the reformers underestimated potential immigration from these two new Caribbean countries. Thus the Administration was once again insisting that immigration would not change much but symbolic reforms were important.

President Johnson caught much of the flavor of the debate and changes in the law when he signed the bill at the base of the Statue of Liberty in October 1965. The President said:

> This . . . is not a revolutionary bill. It does not affect the lives of millions. It will not reshape the structure of our daily lives, or really add importantly to either our wealth or our power.
>
> Yet it is still one of the most important acts of this Congress and of this Administration.

> For it does repair a very deep and painful flaw in the fabric of American
> justice. . . .
> The days of unlimited immigration are past. But those who come will
> come because of what they are—not because of the land from which they
> sprung.[27]

The *Wall Street Journal* also summed up much of the debate when it noted the major change was shifting from national origins to a family unification system. "This had more emotional appeal and, perhaps more to the point, insured that the new immigration would not stray radically from the old one."[28]

In order to "repair a deep and painful flaw," as the President put it, concessions had to be made. Emphasizing family unification over occupations was one concession. Another was the institutionalization of tight Labor Department controls over those coming under the occupational preferences and placing the power of certification in the Department of Labor which was considered to be sympathetic to the demands of labor unions. Under the old law, foreign labor was subject to exclusion when the Secretary of Labor said sufficient American workers existed in that prospective immigrant's occupation or that the employment of the alien would adversely affect the wages and working conditions of American workers. The Secretary of Labor enforced this exclusion loosely. The Assistant Secretary of Labor, Stanley H. Ruttenberg, told a congressional committee in 1968, "Under the old provision, the Department of Labor was able to prevent undue competition with U.S. workers and adverse effects on their wages and working conditions only on rare occasions. From 1957 to 1965, only 56 certifications of availability of American workers or adverse effect were issued, and more than half of these were limited to employment with one employer in one city."[29]

Under the Feighan bill, "this procedure is substantially changed. The primary responsibility is placed upon the intending immigrant to obtain the Secretary of Labor's clearance *prior* [italics author's] to the issuance of a visa."[30] As finally passed, the certification applied to immigrants from the Western Hemisphere as well, unless they were immediate family members of American citizens or those accompanying immigrants with certification. The purpose of this change was to keep out the skilled and semiskilled workers who might compete with union members, and on the whole for Europeans and Asians the Labor Department tended to be generous only with special occupations such as doctors, nurses, engineers and scientists. Immigrants from the Western Hemisphere coming with less skilled occupations, such as domestics, were more successful in obtaining certification. For example, in the first few years of the new law's operation, about one-half of Jamaican migrants entering with occupations were classified as household workers.[31]

Framers and supporters of the 1965 Act assured their colleagues that the law's provisions on labor rules were being made more restrictive. Even though total immigration was expected to increase by about fifty thousand a year at most, Rep. Leonard Farbstein (D.-N.Y.) noted:

> There has been a lot of loose speculation by conservative and right-wing spokesmen about how this bill will somehow cause a worsening in the unemployment situation in the United States. Visions are conjured up of unwashed Hottentots taking jobs away from good wholesome American types. I say this is a lot of hot air, and I have the evidence to back it up. For one thing, it is on the record that this bill will require the Secretary of Labor to make an affirmative finding that any alien seeking to enter the United States as a worker will not adversely affect the wages and working conditions of the United States worker. Secondly, the labor unions, who more than anyone would be concerned if a worsening employment situation were to result, overwhelmingly favor the bill.[32]

If labor controls became more restrictive than in the past and were designed to keep out competitive workers, of greater importance was the ceiling for the Western Hemisphere, which became the major issue in the debates. As a concession for passage of the bill, opponents of ending national origins managed to include a numerical ceiling for the first time on the Western Hemisphere. The Administration and most reformers opposed such a ceiling and at first narrowly defeated it in the House. But in the Senate Everett Dirksen (R.-Ill.) and Sam Ervin, both of whom favored the ceiling, had considerable leverage as members of the subcommittee controlling immigration. Supporters of the ceiling generally avoided racist arguments when glancing at migration from Mexico and Central and South America. Rather they talked of the population explosion in Latin America and the recent growth of immigration from that region as reasons for a numerical limit and said that if a ceiling existed for the Eastern Hemisphere, then one should be established for the Western too.[33] The Senate majority report, for example, concluded:

> Not only is the Committee concerned with the volume of immigration, but it has difficulty with reconciling its decision to eliminate the concept of an alien's birth determining the quota to which he is charged with the exemption from the numerical limitation extended to persons born in the

Western Hemisphere. To continue unrestricted immigration for persons born in the Western Hemisphere countries is to place such aliens in a preferred status compared to aliens born in other parts of the world which the committee feels requires further study.[34]

Opponents of the ceiling said that other controls such as those requiring Labor Department certification or keeping out people apt to become public charges or subversives would suffice to regulate the flow from south of the border and that imposition of a ceiling would offend America's Latin American neighbors.[35] In the end, to achieve a consensus bill, the Johnson Administration accepted the ceiling of 120,000 for the Western Hemisphere, clearly a victory for immigration restriction and the price paid to end the Asia-Pacific Triangle and national origins quotas. As Sen. Jacob Javits (R.-N.Y.), a liberal on immigration and a member of the Senate subcommittee on immigration, said, "We all understand that the bill is a package deal. . . . Without such a package, we would not have had a bill in the Senate."[36]

As intended and expected, immigration patterns from Europe changed as the 1965 law went into effect. Eastern and Southern European nations began to overtake the Northern and Western European countries as leaders in European immigration to America. The most notable increases were Italian, Greek and Portuguese. Italy's 1952 quota was less than 6,000 but now Italy could send 20,000 not including immediate family members, and Italy became the leading European sending nation and for a decade after 1965 averaged over 20,000 per year. As Italian and Greek immigration grew that of Great Britain and Germany fell. The reformers had intended to ease the restrictions by the use of a family unification system and those drafting the law knew that many of these newcomers would be siblings of American citizens. Indeed, in the first decade after passage of the 1965 Act Europeans dominated the preference category for brothers and sisters.

By the mid-1970s the backlog of those awaiting visas in Greece and Italy eased and immigration began to drop from those nations. In the case of Portugal, pressure for migration remained strong and many Portuguese still came to the United States. Overall, however, European immigration began to fall after 1965. In that year Europe sent 113,424 people to America, primarily from Northern and Western Europe, and in 1979 only 60,845.[37]

While desiring to ease restrictions on Southern and Eastern Europe by abolishing their small national origins quotas, Congress had also intended to limit Western Hemisphere immigration by the imposition of the 120,000 ceiling and Labor Department controls that applied to all, except immediate family members, in that hemisphere. Although Canadian immigration dropped, elsewhere in the hemisphere it rose, in some cases dramatically. From 1970 to 1979 nearly two million persons emigrated from the Western Hemisphere. In 1978 it reached a decade high of 262,542 or more than double the ceiling enacted in 1965 and imposed the next year.[38] Clearly the ceiling worked imperfectly. Why has this happened?

Certainly the pressures for immigration have been enormous. Congress worried about this pressure and population growth, hence the imposition of the ceiling. Yet even the legislators might have underestimated the desire to come to America. For example, experts told Congress that a "small increase" of about five to seven thousand persons would come in from Jamaica and Trinidad and Tobago after those countries had their quota of one hundred lifted. Yet these two nations together sent about twenty-five thousand to the United States in 1979.[39] Of course the lawmakers could not be expected to predict precisely the effect on West Indian immigration when Great Britain tightened its controls on immigration at virtually the same instant that the United States eased its regulation. Nor could the Congress foresee accurately the social and economic conditions in Mexico and the Caribbean and their impact on immigration. Nations in the Caribbean Basin that have been sending large numbers of persons to the United States are victimized by poverty, unemployment and underemployment and high population growth. Moreover, because of the impact of television, radio, American goods and capital, and cheap transportation these people are aware of considerably higher wages paid in the United States. For many, of course, American friends and relatives also relate the good news about a better life in the United States and help them immigrate.[40]

These pressures for emigration alone do not totally explain the phenomenon, for if the 120,000 ceiling were strictly enforced, immigration would be less than it has been. This is not to deny the effect of the ceiling since 1965. The Immigration and Naturalization Service (INS) noted the first year after the new law was fully in effect that because so many wanted to enter a waiting list developed and caused immigration to drop: "In 1969, there were 129,045 special immigrants admitted, a reduction of 17 percent from the 1968 figure of 155,308."[41] Waiting lists continued to develop in the 1970s, especially in Mexico; hence the new law did reduce immigration from what it might have been without the 1965 restrictions. At the same time, however, immigration from the Western Hemisphere exceeded the 120,000 limit as noted above.

One reason for the increase was the refugee situation in Cuba. The Senate committee reporting the 1965 Act noted the new refugee provisions and indicated that executive action, such as use of the parole power, should be limited in the future: "Inasmuch as definite provision has now been made for refugees, it is the express intent of the committee that the parole provisions of the Immigration and Nationality Act, which remain unchanged by this bill, be administered in accordance with the original intention of the drafters of that legislation. The parole provisions were designed to authorize the Attorney General to act only in emergency, individual, and isolated situations, such as the case of an alien who requires immediate medical attention and not for the immigration of classes or groups outside of the limit of the law."[42]

President Johnson, on the very day he signed the new act, ignored this intent of Congress. In agreeing to the bill, he added that the American door was open to all Cuban refugees who wished to escape Castro's communist state, and hundreds of thousands eventually did so after 1965.[43] In 1980 President Jimmy Carter invoked the parole power again in admitting another 130,000 Cubans and Haitians.[44]

The position of Cubans remained unclear until Congress passed legislation in 1966 to permit them to adjust their status to regular immigrants. Yet, if paroled refugees became immigrants and had their numbers counted against the Western Hemisphere ceiling, then the ceiling would still have been effective in keeping out others. That was precisely INS's policy from 1968 to 1976. But in the fall of 1976 the Justice Department directed INS to permit Cuban refugees to be counted above the Western Hemisphere ceiling. Furthermore, federal court decisions handed down in 1978 and 1979 held that 144,999 places charged against that ceiling from 1968 through 1976 should be made available retroactively to others in the Western Hemisphere.[45]

Cuban refugees alone do not account for the entire increase after 1965. Congress in 1929 allowed spouses and minor children of American citizens to enter without regard to quotas, a practice continued under the 1952 McCarran-Walter Act. As noted, in 1965 the legislators added parents of United States citizens to the quota exempt list. Experts predicted that these immediate family members would run about 40,000 to 50,000 yearly and enable the hemispheres to exceed their numerical limits and individual countries in the Eastern Hemisphere to surpass their 20,000 limit. However, these numbers grew, especially after 1972, and were double that estimate from 1965 to 1975.[46] In 1978 immediate family members topped 125,000, the vast majority of whom were Third World people from Asia or the Western

Hemisphere. The next year immediate family members increased again, to over 138,000. Most hailed from Asia, Mexico or Central and South America.[47]

While immigration from the Western Hemisphere grew steadily it would have no doubt been even greater without the controls imposed by Congress. An important aspect of immigration from the Caribbean and Mexico involves those who arrive without legal documents. Perhaps lacking family ties or unable to receive Labor Department certification, they enter illegally to work either temporarily or permanently in the United States. How many undocumented aliens now live here is a subject of constant debate and speculation. While no one knows for certain, the Census Bureau, after reviewing various studies, said in 1980 that the number might be between three and one half to five million. Most experts do agree about one thing: the vast majority of these people are from the Caribbean countries or Mexico.[48]

Given the relative ease of getting into the United States from these areas, the pressures for emigration, the economic restrictions involved with obtaining a visa from 1968 to 1977, and the availability of low paying jobs in the United States, it is not surprising that so many chose to migrate north in search of opportunity. In the case of Mexico, the ending of the Bracero Program in 1964, which permitted entry of temporary workers between 1942 and 1964, nearly coincided with the passage of the 1965 Immigration Act; hence many former braceros who could not gain legal entry simply crossed the border anyway.[49] By the late 1970s INS was apprehending about one million undocumented aliens, mostly along the United States–Mexico border where the agency concentrated its resources.[50]

Some Asian immigrants in the first years after 1965 continued to enter as nonquota immigrants as they had done before 1965, as spouses and children of American citizens, especially United States servicemen. But the 1965 preference system made possible new Asian immigration. For example, because of the shortage of doctors, nurses, scientists and engineers, highly educated (sometimes in the United States) East Asians at first obtained Labor Department certification to immigrate to America. Once here, as resident aliens, they used the preference category for spouses and children of resident aliens to bring in their families. They also saw the advantages of becoming citizens quickly, for as new citizens they could sponsor their brothers and sisters or bring in immediate family members as nonquota immigrants. Hence, Asian immigration grew slowly but steadily after 1965 largely because of initial use of occupational categories. As the 1970s progressed, because of rapid naturalization of Asians and the use of the family preference system and the migration of nonquota immediate family members, Asian immigration grew rapidly. The table below illustrates the trend.[51]

As the table and trend make clear it was not always necessary to have a large population present in the United States in 1965 for groups to develop immigrant networks under the new system.

Of course, some of the South and East Asian increase had little to do with the new law, for among those arriving after 1975 were over one-half million refugees from Indochina, chiefly Vietnamese but also Cambodians and Laotians. From 1965 to 1975 only thirty thousand Asians entered under the refugee provision of the 1965 Act; the vast majority after 1965 were paroled by the executive branch and sanctioned by special acts of Congress after the fall of the American-backed government in Saigon in 1975.[52] These large admissions of refugees above the numbers allocated by the refugee preference finally prompted Congress to pass the 1980 Refugee Act which increased the "normal flow" of refugees to fifty thousand and permitted the President to admit others if he deemed it in the national interest. Both Presidents Carter and Ronald Reagan allowed hundreds of thousands of others to enter, beyond the fifty thousand limit.[53] The law also liberalized rules for those already in the United States temporarily to apply for asylum.

But whether as refugees, nonquota immediate family members or regular preference system immigrants, immigration from Asia grew rapidly, especially after 1972. At the time the law was passed Asian immigration mounted to 20,683 or about 5 percent of the total. By 1979 it reached 189,193, over 40 percent of the total. Altogether 1.5 million Asians immigrated to the United States in the 1970s.[54]

The substantial increases in immigration from Third World nations will continue in the near future unless the United States drastically changes its immigration policy. The largest backlogs of those awaiting visas are in Mexico, the Philippines, China and Korea, all Third World countries.[55]

TABLE 2   Asian Immigration

Year	Nonquota Immediate Family Members	Occupational Preferences	Spouses and Children of Resident Aliens	Brothers and Sisters of United States Citizens
1968	15,800	17,729	6,688	6,307
1972	29,585	24,758	19,364	11,985
1978	45,064	16,607	31,468	46,422

Source: Annual reports of INS, 1968 and 1972 and *Statistical Yearbook, 1978*

Now that the Western Hemisphere has a preference system and now that countries such as Columbia, Jamaica, Mexico, Korea, the Philippines, India and the Dominican Republic have sizable populations in the United States, they have the necessary kinship networks to bring in their families under the 1965 law. Moreover, the federal government recently granted separate quotas for China and Taiwan.

Of course, political turmoil, such as that occurring in Cuba in 1959 or Vietnam in 1975, can create large pools of refugees and lead to the influx of immigrants into the United States. Some of the world's explosive situations are in the Caribbean area, such as El Salvador. Since the liberalization of the refugee law in 1980 the number of persons already in the United States on a temporary basis requesting asylum has grown from twenty-five hundred to over one hundred thousand. Practically all of these people come from a Third World nation.[56] If refugees win their struggle in the courts (as in the case of Haitians) or are granted asylum by the government, and become resident aliens and eventually citizens they will be able to use the family unification procedures to sponsor their countrymen.

Because of the importance the law gives to family unification and the seemingly ever present refugee situation, Labor Department certification has not proven especially effective in controlling immigration from the Third World. Most immigrants work within a few years of their arrival, but they come here under the family preference categories or as refugees and not through the Labor Department certification system. Since the 1965 law went into effect only about one-tenth of the immigrants entered with certification, often the highly skilled and educated Third World elites but also household workers from the Caribbean. Immigrants generally come to work but do not bother with certification as there are other ways of getting into the United States. And if they cannot obtain admission through the front door, they enter without documents.

In sum, in 1965 the Administration and Congress by abolishing the national origins quotas and the Asia-Pacific Triangle and by adding parents of United States citizens to the nonquota list, projected a slight increase in immigration and a modest liberalization of policy. At the same time, the lawmakers did not intend to make radical changes and certainly did not foresee present day immigration patterns and volume. Indeed, the 1965 policymakers intended the law to be more restrictive as well as more liberal; hence they provided for tight Labor Department controls, a ceiling for the Western Hemisphere and a family unification system which was thought to keep immigration on its most recent paths. Clearly they did not see how the new law would work, nor could they predict the fairly generous response of the United States to the post 1965 refugee crisis, both of which have brought about a fundamental shift in historic immigration patterns to the United States.

NOTES

The author wishes to thank Leonard Dinnerstein and Fred Binder for their helpful comments. A grant from the American Philosophical Society assisted the research. A different version of this paper was presented to the American Civilization seminar at Columbia University in September 1981.

1. Unpublished data furnished by the Immigration and Naturalization Service (INS). Many observers have also pointed to the increase in immigration. Immigration averaged about 325,000 annually in the 1960s, but in the last five years has averaged over 500,000. Over 800,000 arrived in 1980.

2. Data from unpublished records of INS and annual reports of INS. Italians averaged over 21,000 from 1966 to 1976 and Greeks about 18,000. By 1979 Italian immigration had fallen to 6,174 and Greek to 5,090.

3. *Newsweek,* 12 April 1982, p. 50.

4. Theodore White, *America in Search of Itself* (New York, 1982), p. 363.

5. Robert Divine, *American Immigration Policy, 1924–1952* (New Haven, 1957), chap. 2 and Marion Bennett, *American Immigration Policies: A History* (Washington, D.C., 1963), chaps. 5–7.

6. Bennett, *American Immigration Policies,* pp. 71 and 73–75 and Divine, *American Immigration Policy, 1924–1952,* pp. 146–54.

7. *Annual Report of INS,* 1948, pp. 14–15.

8. See Leonard Dinnerstein, *America and the Survivors of the Holocaust* (New York, 1982).

9. U.S., Congress, Senate, *Congressional Record,* 28 February 1950, 96: 2476.

10. See Dinnerstein, *America and the Survivors,* especially chaps. 6–7, 9.

11. An excellent study of the McCarran-Walter Act is Marius A. Dimmitt, "The Enactment of the McCarran-Walter Immigration Act of 1952," (Ph.D. diss., University of Kansas, 1970).

12. Proponents of Asian immigration feared Congress would reject it if persons of Asian ancestry living in the Western Hemisphere were permitted to enter as nonquota immigrants, hence the racial ancestry provision controlling this possible immigration. See the comments of Walter Judd in United States, Congress, House, Subcommittee on Immigration and Naturalization of the Committee on the Judiciary, *Providing for Equality Under Naturalization and Immigration Laws,* Hearings, 80th Cong., 2d sess., 1948, p. 8. See also the statement of Sen. Pat McCarran (D.-Nev.) on the Asia-Pacific Triangle in U.S., Congress, Senate, *Congressional Record,* 22 May 1952, 98: 5765.

13. U.S., Congress, House, *Congressional Record,* 1 March 1949, 95: 1683.

14. Reformers wanted to place Great Britain and Ireland's unused quotas into a general pool to be used by nations with oversubscribed quotas such as Italy and Greece. They also

wanted to change the basis for determining quotas from the 1920 to the 1950 census which would have given Southern and Eastern European nations larger quotas. The liberal critique of national origins quotas can be found in William S. Bernard, ed., *American Immigration Policy: A Reappraisal* (New York, 1950) and especially in President Truman's commission on immigration: President's Commission on Immigration and Naturalization, *Whom Shall We Welcome?* (Washington, D.C., 1953).

15. Bennett, *American Immigration Policies,* pp. 204–205. See also Arthur A. Markowitz, "Humanitarianism versus Restrictionism: the United States' and the Hungarian Refugee," *International Migration Review,* 7 (Spring 1973): 46–58. In 1958 Congress passed legislation to permit the Hungarian parolees to adjust their status to resident aliens.

16. For the groups admitted under the 1953 refugee act see Administrator of the Refugee Relief Act of 1953 as amended, *Final Report* (Washington, D.C., 1958). For Judd's comments on the Eisenhower proposal see United States, Congress, Senate, Subcommittee of the Committee on the Judiciary, *Emergency Migration of Escapees, Expellees and Refugees,* Hearings, 83rd Cong., 1st sess., 1953, pp. 83–95. For the critique of liberal church leaders and Arab-American groups see ibid., pp. 115–16, 295–96 and 305–306.

17. U.S., Congress, Senate, *Congressional Record,* 1 July 1960, 106: 15400.

18. Abba Schwartz, *The Open Society* (New York, 1968), pp. 139–50.

19. United States, Congress, Senate, Committee on the Judiciary, *Immigration and Nationality Act Amendments,* S. Rept. 748, 89th Cong., 1st sess., 1965, p. 13. One expert concluded the national origins system "was dead" by 1964. Marion Bennett, "The Immigration and Nationality (McCarran-Walter) Act of 1952, as amended to 1965," *Annals of the American Academy of Political and Social Science: The New Immigration,* 367 (September 1966): 136.

20. Senator Ervin eventually supported the 1965 reforms to abolish national origins quotas, but he was their most persistent defender during the Senate hearings.

21. The Democratic majority in the House was 295 to 140 and 68 to 32 in the Senate. Committees responsible for immigration contained majorities favoring the abolition of national origins quotas and the Asia-Pacific Triangle. One of the key obstacles to reform was removed when Francis Walter (D.-Pa.), who chaired the House subcommittee on immigration, died in 1963. He was replaced by Michael Feighan, who after some hesitation, favored doing away with the national origins system.

22. The best discussion of the 1965 amendments can be found in William S. Stem, "H.R. 2580: the Immigration and Nationality Act Amendments of 1965—A Case Study," (Ph.D. diss., New York University, 1974). See also Charles Keely, "The Immigration Act of 1965: a Study of the Relationship of Social Science Theory to Group Interest and Legislation," (Ph.D. diss., Fordham University, 1970); Jethro K. Lieberman, *Are Americans Extinct?* (New York, 1968) and Sen. Edward Kennedy (D.-Mass.), the floor manager of the amendments, "The Immigration Act of 1965," *Annals: The New Immigration,* pp. 137–49. Abba Schwartz, who played a key role in drafting the original proposals, has told his story in *The Open Society.*

23. U.S., Congress, House, *Congressional Record,* 25 August 1965, 111: 21758. See also the comments of the representatives of the American Legion in Deane and David Heller, "Our New Immigration Law," *American Legion Magazine,* 80 (February 1966): 6–9 and 41, which argued that recent patterns of immigration would be maintained under the new law. By 1965 few organizations still favored the McCarran-Walter Act.

24. United States, Congress, House, Subcommittee No. 1 of the Committee on the Judiciary, *Immigration,* Hearings, 88th Cong., 2d sess., 1964, p. 418.

25. United States, Congress, House, Subcommittee No. 1 of the Committee on the Judiciary, *Immigration,* Hearings, 89th Cong., 1st sess., 1965, p. 14.

26. U.S., Congress, Senate, *Congressional Record,* 20 September 1965, 111: 24503.

27. *Weekly Compilation of Presidential Documents,* 1 (11 October 1965): 364–365.

28. *Wall Street Journal,* 4 October 1965. Of the three major national news journals, *Newsweek, Time* and *U.S. News and World Report,* only the last saw much potential change in immigration and even it underestimated the future shifts.

29. United States, Congress, House, Subcommittee No. 1 of the Committee on the Judiciary, *Immigration,* Hearings, 90th Cong., 2nd sess., 1968, p. 111. See also Stem, "H.R. 2580," pp. 167–68, 111–12 and 121–25 and Frank H. Cassell, "Immigration and the Department of Labor," *Annals: The New Immigration,* pp. 107–108.

30. Subcommittee No. 1, Hearings, 1968, p. 111.

31. An excellent discussion of Jamaican immigration can be found in Nancy Foner, "Jamaican Migrants: A Comparative Analysis of the New York and London Experience," Paper presented to the New York University Research Program in Inter-American Affairs, September 1982. Data on West Indian immigration is derived from the annual reports in INS.

32. U.S., Congress, House, *Congressional Record,* 25 August 1965, 111: 21770.

33. S. Rept. 748, pp. 17–18; U.S., Congress, House, *Congressional Record,* 24 August 1965, 111: 21573–77; ibid., 25 August 1965, pp. 21760–62, 21770–73 and 21808–12.

34. S. Rept. 748, pp. 17–18.

35. U.S., Congress, Senate, *Congressional Record,* 10 September 1965, 111: 25657–59 and ibid., House, 25 August 1965, 111:21762, and S. Rept. 748, p. 59.

36. U.S., Congress, Senate, *Congressional Record,* 30 September 1965, 111: 24704. No preference system was included in the limit for the Western Hemisphere. In 1976 Congress added a modified preference system for that hemisphere and two years later created a worldwide ceiling of 290,000 with a uniform preference system and a 20,000 per country limit, excluding immediate family members.

37. Unpublished data from INS.

38. Ibid.

39. United States, Congress, House, Subcommittee No. 1 of the Committee on the Judiciary, *Immigration,* Hearings, 89th Cong., 1st sess., 1965, pp. 15, 45. For the 1979 figures data furnished by INS.

40. For a discussion of the knowledge of the United States abroad see United States, Departments of Justice, Labor and State: Interagency Task Force on Immigration, *Staff Report* (Washington, D.C., 1979).

41. *Annual Report of INS,* 1969, p. 3.

42. S. Rept. 748, p. 17.

43. *New York Times,* 4 October 1965.

44. Congress had passed a new refugee act in April 1980, but the President preferred to use the parole power to admit the Cubans and Haitians.

45. *Interpreter Releases,* 53 (27 September 1976): 322–23 and ibid., 56 (23 August 1979): 419.

46. Interagency Task Force, *Staff Report,* pp. 176–88.

47. *Statistical Yearbook of INS,* 1978, p. 8 and *Annual Report of INS,* 1979, pp. 7 and 9. For estimates on the nonquota numbers see the statements of Administration officials in U.S.,

Congress, Senate, Subcommittee on Immigration and Naturalization of the Committee on the Judiciary, *Immigration,* Hearings, 89th Cong., 1st sess., 1965, pp. 12–15 and 105–307. Nonquota immigrants were mainly immediate family members, but Congress did allow others, such as ministers, to enter outside the numerical limits.

48. The literature on undocumented aliens is vast. For the Bureau of the Census study, see United States, Department of Commerce, Bureau of the Census, "Preliminary Review of Existing Studies of the Number of Illegal Residents in the United States" (January 1980). See also Ellen Sehgal and Joyce Valiet, "Documenting the Undocumented: Data Like Aliens are Elusive," *Monthly Labor Review,* 103 (October 1980): 18–21 and General Accounting Office: Report to Congress by the Comptroller General, *Illegal Aliens: Estimating their Impact on the United States* (Washington, D.C., 1980).

49. For a good discussion of Mexican migration see Wayne A. Cornelius, *Mexican Migration to the United States: Causes, Consequences and U.S. Responses* (Cambridge, Mass., 1978), especially pp. 17–18.

50. *Annual Report of INS,* 1978, p. 17.

51. Data derived from annual reports of INS, 1968 and 1972 and *Statistical Yearbook,* 1978.

52. The refugee quota for the Eastern Hemisphere was only 10,200 from 1968 to 1978. In 1978 when Congress created a worldwide system it increased to 17,400 throughout the world.

53. Carter permitted 168,000 Indochinese and 130,000 Cubans and Haitians to enter in 1980. The Reagan Administration admitted another 120,000 refugees during its first year in office. In the fall of 1981 the Reagan Administration announced cuts in the number of refugees for 1982, but the figures could still go as high as 120,000. *New York Times,* 19 September 1981.

54. Unpublished data furnished by INS and annual reports of INS.

55. Select Commission on Immigration and Refugee Policy, *U.S. Immigration Policy and the National Interest* (Washington, D.C., 1981), p. 146.

56. *Bergen (County) Record,* 30 June 1982.

11

Queering Mariel: Mediating Cold War Foreign Policy and U.S. Citizenship among Cuba's Homosexual Exile Community, 1978–1994

JULIO CAPÓ JR.

IN DECEMBER 1980, twenty-year-old Wilfredo Nuñez Pinilla sat in an unfamiliar and foreign United States military camp, uncertain of where he would reside in the coming days. Pinilla, like so many others, fled the Communist nation of Cuba in 1980 during the controversial Mariel boat-lift exodus. The United States welcomed nearly 125,000 Cubans that year, many of whom were former convicts and deemed mentally unstable by Fidel Castro's government. As a homosexual, Pinilla was among the Communist nation's "undesirables" given permission to leave his homeland and granted admission by the United States to settle on its soil.[1] In 1980, however, the Immigration and Naturalization Service (INS) regarded homosexuality as grounds for exclusion from the United States.

One might imagine that the gay and lesbian Marielitos, or Cubans who entered the United States from Cuba's Mariel harbor, would aim to conceal their homosexuality to better their chances of being admitted into the United States. Pinilla, however, openly expressed and practiced his homosexuality on the military base where he was temporarily housed. In fact, several internees at Fort Chaffee in western Arkansas knew Pinilla as one of the many cross-dressing homosexuals at the enclave who had a penchant for hair care and fashion. Homosexuality may have officially been grounds to exclude one from entering the U.S., and consequently from achieving American citizenship, but most homosexual Marielitos like Pinilla had a different experience.[2] In fact, the evidence suggests the U.S. did not deport a single Marielito solely based on his or her homosexuality.[3]

While some recent scholarship has explored the effects of sexuality in shaping American immigration policies, very little has addressed the tension between the Cold War imperative of welcoming anti-Communist exiles and the immigration policy of barring homosexuals.[4] The growing and fairly nascent field of queer migration studies has demonstrated how

Figure 1. A queer Marielito points to a sign, written in Spanish, posted outside one of the housing barracks at Fort Indiantown Gap in Pennsylvania, where unclaimed male Marielitos were housed. The warning, which sought to suppress ostentatious homosexual behavior and male effeminacy, translates to: "Important Warning: By order of Colonel Melnyk, it is categorically prohibited to dress up in women's clothing, use makeup, eye shadow, lipstick and other such things. Whoever is caught committing immoral acts, either inside or outside the barracks, shall be imprisoned by the military police. Military General Staff." Photo by Patsy Lynch © 1979~2009.

Figure 2. A group of queer Marielitos pose for a picture outside their barracks at Fort Indiantown Gap. One man wears rag curlers in his hair, while another dons a bedsheet around his body that serves as a makeshift dress. This demonstrates a direct rejection of the military orders prohibiting the men in transition from partaking in behavior traditionally associated with women—such as hair care and dressing in women's clothing. Photo by Patsy Lynch © 1979~2009.

sexual identities and behavior (i.e., "performances") have been interpreted, negotiated, and even compromised to achieve the goals of a particular state. In turn, research has also shown how (homo)sexuality has altered national objectives in complex and often converging ways.[5] Susana Peña's important work on the Mariel community has demonstrated how Cuba and the United States perceived the homosexual Marielitos and their individual gay "performances" in distinct and sometimes overlapping ways. In particular, she notes how each government's "state gaze" on Mariel's homosexual community focused on different elements of gender transgression. Peña argues that each government construed the existence of "obvious gays" as part of their national agenda. During the Mariel boatlift, male effeminacy facilitated an exile's purge from Cuba, while the United States interpreted such behavior as a cause for alarm.[6]

This article utilizes a number of sources—including articles from the national, local, and gay press; government documents; and autobiographical accounts—to explore how anti-Communism and the persecution of homosexuals in late Cold War America played out simultaneously and altered immigration policies in Cuba and the United States. It reintroduces the gay press into the larger narrative of the 1980 Mariel boatlift so as to view the exodus through a queer lens. The essay suggests that the gay press—and, in turn, the homosexual community in the U.S.—played a vital role in mobilizing queer resistance and support for the Marielitos. It also further explores the often-overlooked treatment of female homosexuals during the Mariel crisis. The essay ultimately analyzes the relationships that existed among immigration, nationality, and sexuality by examining the experiences of these Cuban exiles. In particular, it examines the role of the Refugee Act of 1980 in regulating and facilitating the homosexual Marielitos' fate in the U.S. In doing so, it complicates the "state's gaze" on homosexuality as the U.S. negotiated its larger national goals of anti-Communist rhetoric in response to the Mariel boatlift. The evidence suggests that the United States drastically shifted its long-standing antihomosexual stance on immigration and citizenship to reconcile its position as a refuge for those fleeing Cuban Communism.

The third major wave of Cuban migration to the United States following the 1959 Revolution began in April 1980 as an airlift that caused great humiliation for Fidel Castro's regime.[7] Just weeks before the Mariel boatlift began, nearly eleven thousand Cubans flocked to the Peruvian embassy in Cuba in hopes of receiving political asylum and fleeing the Communist nation. On April 16, 1980, Cuba completed negotiations with Peru and several other countries, including the United States, to permit an airlift that would purge the political refugees from the island. Castro conveyed a powerful ideological message shortly after to avoid further embarrassment and avert a potential domestic crisis. He maintained that those who fled were enemies of the revolution and insignificant to the sustainability of Cuba's revolutionary project.[8] Four days after the airlift began, the Cuban government announced that it would allow anyone who wanted to leave the island to do so. After suspending the short-lived airlift, Castro opened up the port of Mariel and urged U.S. émigrés to pick up their relatives and others who wanted to leave Cuba. Less than a month later, over one thousand boats had made the trip to Mariel and returned to the United States with more than thirteen thousand Cuban refugees.[9]

In response to Castro's opening of Mariel harbor, President Jimmy Carter famously said that he welcomed the refugees with "an open heart and open arms."[10] While the U.S. Coast Guard and the INS maintained that those who violated U.S. immigration laws would be liable to corresponding fines, President Carter and his administration faced an unprecedented situation and applied lax rules to those who entered the country. Following much scrutiny and the potential for what appeared to be an uncontrollable situation, however, the U.S. Coast Guard was urged to enforce the U.S. policy of allowing only those with valid permits or visas to enter the country. Some in the United States continued to risk the penalties of

Figure 3. Marielitos aboard a boat anxiously look to the American coast, anticipating their arrival at Key West, Florida, in early May 1980. The Coast Guard Cutter *Diligence* can be seen in the background, ushering the boat to its destination. Miami News Collection, Historical Museum of Southern Florida, 1981–099–89.

illegally chartering Cuban refugees into the U.S. until Castro officially closed Mariel on September 25. By then over 124,000 Cubans had made their way into the U.S.[11]

PURGING CUBA'S "LUMPEN" COMMUNITY

On May 1, 1980, a defiant Fidel Castro stood at the José Martí Revolution Square in Havana and delivered a speech at the International Workers' Day Rally offering an ideological explanation for the ongoing Mariel boatlift. He pitted Cuban revolutionaries against rightists and "Yankee imperialism." He boosted public morale and assured his audience that those who left from Mariel, those he referred to as the "lumpen," were an affront to Cuba and its revolutionary ideals. Above all, he attempted to shatter the allegations that the Marielitos were anti-Communist dissidents. Instead, he argued that those who accepted the exiles, chiefly the United States, were "doing an excellent sanitation job."[12] Castro accused the "Yankee press" of spinning the story and trying to pass the Marielitos off as dissidents. Instead, he maintained, "There is lumpen there in that embassy. . . . They do not know what the word dissidence means, they would not know the meaning of this word." Castro argued that the "imperialist press" was depicting the situation as such to further its battle "against socialism, against communism, against the Cuban revolution."[13]

Castro insisted that the Marielitos were of no good use to Cuba and its ongoing revolution. In doing so, he suggested that the exiles were anti-revolutionaries. "He who has no revolutionary genes, he who has no revo-lutionary blood. . . . We do not want them; we do not need them."[14] Later in his May 1 speech, Castro referred to the homosexuals among the Marielitos as part of Cuba's "lumpen" community. "But the large majority of the people there were of that kind: lumpen. Some limp wrists [*flojito*]."[15] The crowd laughed, and Castro continued: "Some shameless creatures who had been covering up. . . . The committees [for the Defense of the Revolution] know it better than anyone . . . those managed to slip through. By the way, they are the ones that produce the most irritation. Those who cover up."[16]

Research demonstrates, as the above quotes suggest, that the Mariel boatlift was a clear episode of the Castro regime's "institutionally pro-moted homophobia."[17] Ian Lumsden has argued that the boatlift was a stra-tegic and "explicitly homophobic campaign by the government" to purge Cuba of homosexuals.[18] Some American reports written from Havana also demonstrate that the Mariel boatlift was regarded as an attempt to purge homosexuals from the island. One article reported the social harassment inflicted on a family after Cuban officials notified them that a charter boat had arrived in Mariel to take them away. The father defended himself to the media and the Cuban people. He argued that although his family had filed papers to leave the island, its members were not like some of the other "scum" who wanted to leave the island through Mariel. "In my family, we are moral people. We are not prostitutes or homosexuals."[19] In an attempt to mend its reputation, this Cuban family detached itself from the exile community Castro referred to as "lumpen," including Cuba's homosexual community.

Castro constantly referred to the Marielitos as "lumpen," a version of the Marxist term "lumpen proletariat," which further explains the "criminal" and counterrevolutionary stigma he attributed to the exile community. He drew on Marxist-Leninist theory that defined the lumpen proletariat as the "scum of the depraved elements of all classes, which established headquarters in the big cities."[20] In this regard, the Castro regime regarded the lumpen proletariat—which included homosexuals—as counterrevolutionary individuals who did not represent the diligent, virile, and altruistic proletarian man. Homosexual "lumpen" openly flaunted their sexuality and could not properly contribute to the Cuban Revolution because they lacked the "revolutionary genes" to which Castro referred. In fact, an effeminate homosexual appeared to be the very antithesis of the workingman's masculine image as defined by the ideals of the Cuban Revolution.

In Cuba, "revolutionary morality" relied on heterosexual and normative expressions of sexuality and gender, such as male masculinity. Nonnormative representations of gender threatened the ideals of the Cuban Revolution of 1959. The Cuban press revealed the regime's institutionalized homophobia in April 1965, the year Cuba began forcing its "counter-revolutionaries"—including homosexuals—to work in forced labor camps as part of its Military Units to Aid Production (UMAP) program. This program aimed to rehabilitate individuals the regime perceived as problematic and unproductive, including Castro's "lumpen" community. It was then that the Havana periodical, *El Mundo*, published a report that exposed Cuba's growing gay subculture. The Cuban press believed the prevalence of homosexuality in Havana was an urban or big-city phenomenon. The periodical further associated homosexuality with urban capitalism by noting "that the virility of our peasantry does not permit that abominable vice."[21] To the Castro regime, homosexuality represented a sexually expressive culture that manifested itself in individual indulgence and hedonism, assets it attributed to capitalists and the bourgeoisie. Moreover, the surreptitious behavior that homosexuals engaged in—the "covering up," in Castro's words—carried with it the taint of subversion, hidden as it was from the eyes of the state and the Comités de la Defensa de la Revolución (CDRs; Committees for the Defense of the Revolution). The report noted that the once-clandestine homosexual community could not further the principles of the Cuban Revolution: "No homosexual represents the revolution, which is a movement of he-men."[22] The Castro government largely based its institutionalized homophobia on the notion that homosexuals, particularly effeminate men, represented the antithesis of Cuba's virile machismo and hyper-masculine "Revolutionary" man.

The expulsion of homosexuals from Cuba—and the public condemnation that homosexuals were enemies of the revolution and potential risks to the state—poses an interesting parallel to the pre-Stonewall United States. The purging of American homosexuals from the federal government in the 1950s, for example, over fears that they posed a risk to the state as morally weak characters vulnerable to Soviet influence and blackmail, demonstrates another context in which a state attempted to ferret out and regulate covert sexuality to advance its own political agenda and ideology—in this instance, Cold War anti-Communism.[23] In a mirror image of this stance, the antirevolutionary views that the Castro regime believed homosexuals represented were the byproducts of the dynamics between gender and sexual politics and its relationship to the state.

Indeed, the hangover from the "Lavender Scare" of earlier decades greeted gay Cubans when they reached the U.S. The U.S. gay community's fear that the Marielitos would not be admitted into the United States did not subside once the Cubans reached Key West, at the southern tip of Florida. The American gay press perpetuated the concern that Marielitos—particularly gay Marielitos—would be refused admission into the U.S. and sent back to Cuba. *Gay Community News*, a Boston gay newsmagazine, reported in June that "some observers remain skeptical about administration promises that homosexuals will not be sent back to Cuba."[24] The case for sending homosexual Marielitos back to Cuba was far more complex than the gay press often revealed. While homosexuality remained official cause for barring an alien from the country, the status of "criminal" also played a major role in permitting or barring a Cuban from residing in the U.S. Under the regime of Fidel Castro, the definition of "criminal" was often at odds with American definitions of criminality. The alien's "criminality" was ultimately a relative term in the American context. An officer stationed at Fort McCoy revealed that Marielitos suspected of being "hardened criminals" were sent to federal correctional institutions. They were held in these facilities until the Justice Department heard their case and determined their fate in the U.S.[25]

Although the press reported that a high percentage of those who entered the United States through Mariel were hardcore felons, recent scholarship estimate that less than 4 percent had committed serious felonies in Cuba.[26] Most of the people whom the American government deemed serious felons were taken to the Federal Correctional Institution in Talladega, Alabama, pending further investigation. The media heavily focused on these felons and the estimated fifteen hundred mentally and physically disabled people who were also sent to the United States. However, as María Cristina García has noted, the media coverage overshadowed the reality: about 80 percent of the Marielitos did not have a criminal past. Nevertheless, an estimated twenty-six thousand of the Cubans had criminal records upon entering the United States.[27]

Although some Marielitos were deemed criminals in Cuba, the United States may not have categorized the immigrants as such on American soil. Many Marielitos, for example, had been arrested under petty theft charges—many times for stealing food to feed their starving families. In the United States, the case for a Jean Valjean–type character was far more sympathetic, considering the well-documented social conditions Cubans endured under Communism (including rationed foods). One of the "criminal" Marielitos, for example, told American authorities he had served nearly ten years in prison in Cuba for stealing a cow to feed his family. Upon making this confession to immigration officials in the U.S., he spent nearly a year and a half in an American detention center pending further investigation.[28]

The case for criminalized homosexuality in Cuba is equally complex. Although homosexuality was not an official crime in Cuba by 1980, many homosexuals in the island were often arrested for seemingly arbitrary "social crimes." This too mirrors the way local police forces treated homosexuals in the U.S. during the pre-Stonewall era that preceded the gay liberation movement.[29] Nonnormative gendered men and women—including the more effeminate gays and masculine lesbians—were often charged with "crimes against society" as a result of their behavior and identity. Until 1979, Cuba's Penal Code was based on Spanish law that criminalized homosexuality. That law "imposed a prison sentence of up to six months or an equivalent fine upon anyone who 'habitually engaged in homosexual acts,' who 'sexually propositioned someone,' or who created a 'public scandal' by 'flaunting' his homosexuality in public."[30] In both Spain and Cuba, the Ley de Peligrosidad, or the Law of Dangerousness, left homosexuals vulnerable to "preventative detention."[31] Cuba enacted a new Penal Code that officially decriminalized homosexuality in 1979. The Ley de Peligrosidad Social, or the Law of Social Dangerousness, did not list homosexuality as a direct offense; however, homosexuality fell under the jurisdiction of this law. The law criminalized those who defied "the norms of socialist morality" and broadly defined the offense as "the exploitation or practice of socially reprehensible vice."[32]

Several gay Marielitos recounted stories of being arrested and harassed by Cuban officers because they congregated with other homosexuals or because they acted in an effeminate manner. Vladimir Martinez, a nineteen-year-old who worked as a dancer at a nightclub in Cuba, revealed: "We were discriminated against because we are gay. The police were always mistreating us, they would beat us; they would throw us in jail."[33] Another Marielito, named William, said he was jailed and put on trial three days later. During that trial, William claimed: "They told lies about me. They said that I dyed my hair, that I painted my fingernails; that I ran around in extravagant fashion."[34] Another man, named Jorge, recalled walking to the Coppelia ice cream shop—a common gathering place for homosexuals in Havana—when a police officer asked for his identification papers and then used a white handkerchief to wipe the young man's face. In doing so, he learned that Jorge was wearing makeup. The officer then, according to Jorge, proceeded to "pummel" him. Jorge recalled other instances in which policemen arrested him under the category of "social dangerousness" for wearing sandals while on his way to the beach and another time for wearing bright orange pants—markers the Cuban government associated with ostentatious effeminacy.[35] These instances of alleged effeminate behavior constituted social deviancy in Communist Cuba and, as a result, the afore-mentioned men were deemed criminals under Cuba's Penal Code.

Contemporary sources, including autobiographical accounts, confirm institutionalized and social homophobia in Cuba. Reinaldo Arenas, the late prolific gay writer of the autobiography *Before Night Falls* (Sp. 1992; Eng. translation, 1993), was among those who came to the United States during the Mariel exodus. While waiting to receive an exit permit to leave Cuba, Arenas remembered seeing a poster that read: "Homosexuals, get out; scum of the earth, get out."[36] Reports demonstrate that homosexuals were encouraged to leave.[37] Arenas recalled how his identification as a homosexual hastened the process of receiving permission to leave the country: "Since the order of the day was to allow all undesirables to go, and in that category homosexuals were in first place, a large number of gays were able to leave the

Island in 1980."[38] There is evidence that many of those that came to the U.S. via Mariel forged fictional records as criminals—identifying themselves as burglars, murderers, rapists, and even CIA agents—to leave Cuba.[39]

Arenas and other sources corroborate that some Cubans also pretended to be homosexuals to better their chances of being granted leave. One man recalled his mother advising him to feign being a homosexual in front of the Cuban military review panel that distributed exit permits. The teen followed his mother's advice and in response to the young man's queer "performance," an officer who recognized the teenager as the son of his friend, noted: "I didn't know that the family of my distinguished friend . . . included faggots. Let him go away!"[40] Arenas also noted that obtaining an exit permit was easy for him once Cuban investigators determined he was a "true" homosexual (he argues that "active," sexually penetrating homosexuals were sometimes not considered homosexual by the investigators; sexually "passive" men, however, were allowed to leave). Arenas claimed that the Cuban government asked him to sign a document acknowledging that he opted to leave Cuba on his own accord and because he did not fall in line with the revolution.[41]

Some sources also suggest that the Cuban government purged imprisoned homosexuals from the island during the Mariel boatlift. During a congressional subcommittee hearing that addressed how the U.S. would deal with the exodus, congressmen asked a Marielito named Juan Carlos how many homosexuals were on the boat that brought him from Mariel to Key West. Juan Carlos, who served several sentences in Cuban prisons for theft, estimated that about 30 of the 120 people who came on his boat were homosexual. He also noted how Cuban officials asked many prisoners, presumably including the incarcerated homosexuals, to leave the country. He also claimed that officials threatened the prisoners with more years behind bars should they refuse to leave the island during the exodus.[42] Other reports also indicate that the Cuban state threatened homosexual "criminals" with more years in prison if they did not leave through Mariel.[43]

Other accounts prior to the Mariel boatlift demonstrate how Cuba's institutionalized homophobia may have prompted Cuban homosexuals to find innovative ways to exit the island. There is some evidence that gay Cubans used the regime's African adventures to escape the island. Cuba, serving in its capacity as the custodian and main proponent of Communism in the West, involved itself in African affairs as early as the 1960s in Algeria. It continued its missions in Africa in subsequent decades. In particular, Cuba was heavily involved in fighting for the Communist cause in Angola and Ethiopia. As a result, Cuban "volunteers" were deployed to Angola beginning in 1975.[44] In 1978 Cuban vice president Carlos Rafael Rodriguez noted how Cuba's civilian contingents in Africa "looked like a kind of correctional institution." According to him, Cuba's international missions to promote Communism in Africa were filled with "delinquents, undesirables, homosexuals—even Jehovah's Witnesses." The vice president noted that the presence of such "undesirables" in Angola was a "distortion" of Cuba's purposes abroad. He also suggested, however, that the deployment was an effective way for "undesirables" to flee persecution on the island: "Some people falsified their papers or exchanged papers with comrades so that they could go."[45] The vice president's reports demonstrate how homosexuals in Cuba sought to leave the island and found innovative ways of achieving this. The risks of combat in a foreign continent and the potential repercussions of falsifying military records may have even outweighed the prospect of remaining in the homophobic Cuban state.

Personal accounts of the lesbian experience in Castro's Cuba were scant in the gay press. One reporter for the *Advocate*, one of the most popular national gay publications in the United States, conducted an investigative report on the homosexual community being housed at Fort Indiantown Gap. In this article, the reporter revealed that lesbian Marielitas shared two distinct barracks in the camp with other female refugees who worked as prostitutes in Cuba. He noted, however, that lesbians refused to leave the barracks and talk to the media.[46] Interviews with gay men, however, provide glimpses of the lesbian experience in Cuba. Vladimir Martinez recalled that many of the dancers he worked with at the nightclub in Cuba were lesbians, although he remembered how they "had to closet themselves." He noted how "some wanted to dress as men, to wear hats and to wear pants all the time, but they couldn't do that. They had to act like 'women' all the time."[47] A twenty-five-year-old gay journalist recalled similar experiences with his lesbian friends in Cuba. "If there were two or three of them on the street, whatever policeman didn't happen to like them could throw them in the patrol car and take them off to jail where they would stay until the next morning."[48] The accounts suggest that lesbians in Cuba were—like gay men—criminalized for their homosexuality outside the parameters of civil law.

Reports from gay men at the U.S. military bases reveal that many lesbians came in the exodus, but that it was difficult to determine exactly how many because the sexes were segregated in these transitional environments.[49] Scholars have deduced that lesbians came in much smaller numbers than the gay men who fled Cuba in 1980. Statistics also show that men represented the vast majority—almost 70 percent—of the over 124,000 Marielitos.[50] Some have even linked this phenomenon to the "fuller integration of women into Cuban society and the increased status and freedom enjoyed by lesbians, as women, under the revolution."[51] Assessing the advances of feminism and women's rights in socialist Cuba, however, has proven to be far more complex and paradoxical than the above statement suggests. Scholarship has demonstrated how Castro's government defined the women's rights movement in Cuba within the regime's interpretation of the Marxist-Leninist model. In this regard, "advances" in Cuban feminism were often negotiated and restricted to best suit the principles of the Cuban Revolution.

Sources indicate that lesbians were doubly oppressed in socialist Cuba: they were discriminated against as homosexuals and, as women, were often seen as second-class citizens living in a society that privileged heteromasculinity. In August 1960, Fidel Castro created the Federation of Cuban Women (FMC). In part, he did this to indoctrinate women as vital members of the Cuban Revolution and, on the surface, to address gender equality. The FMC seems to have been primarily occupied with mobilizing women into a revolutionary consciousness.[52] Although the FMC formally accepted any woman into its organization, contemporary reports demonstrate how some FMC members found ways to keep lesbians out of the Federation.[53] In some instances, active FMC members would spy on a suspected lesbian to determine whether she was a homosexual. One Cuban lesbian recalled how she tried to fool the government, revealing the numerous steps she took to dispel rumors of her homosexuality. According to her, she always took extra precaution to appear feminine. In particular, she was sure to always apply makeup. This woman also noted that she joined both the FMC and a CDR to avoid appearing suspicious. She also claimed that lesbian couples would sometimes invite a gay male couple to go out with them in public. In public areas, the homosexual couples would swap partners to appear like two heterosexual couples. Once they had reached a "safe spot," the partners would swap once again, so that the homosexual couples would be reunited.[54]

It is unknown just how many Marielito homosexuals entered during the boat lift. María Cristina García has estimated that about one thousand homosexuals entered the United States during the exodus. Some contemporary media reports provided seemingly exaggerated estimates, with a number of them estimating that as many as twenty thousand homosexuals may have been purged from Cuba during the episode. Deducing the exact number proves nearly impossible. Considering the sensitivity of the subject matter and the political reprisal that a homosexual Cuban potentially faced in 1980, it is most likely that the number exceeded one thousand.[55]

QUEER MARIELITOS AND CHANGES
IN U.S. COLD WAR FOREIGN POLICY

Timing was crucial for the Marielitos who entered the United States in 1980. On March 17, 1980, a month before Fidel Castro announced he would open Mariel harbor, President Carter signed the Refugee Act of 1980.[56] The Act changed the definition of "refugee" to eliminate the "geographical and ideological restrictions contained in the prior law."[57] The Act discarded what Congress perceived as a bias in immigration policy that favored aliens who fled a Communist regime. "There is no reason why an individual fleeing Communism should any more be presumptively considered a refugee than an alien escaping a right-wing dictatorship," the House Subcommittee on Immigration asserted.[58] Following much criticism of its previous policies, the U.S. adopted the definition of a refugee established by the international community, particularly as defined by the 1951 United Nations Convention Relating to the Status of Refugees and its successor, the 1967 Protocol Relating to the Status of Refugees.[59] The new law defined "refugee" as an individual fleeing "persecution on account of race, religion, nationality, membership in a particular social group, or political opinion" in an effort to remove the anti-Communist Cold War rhetoric that had dominated past U.S. policies.[60] U.S. policymakers responsible for the 1980 Refugee Act noted that determining refugee and asylee status based on an anti-Communist foreign policy appeared to be anachronistic and innately discriminatory; also, it ultimately made the U.S. seem insincere about its human rights initiatives. The Mariel exodus, however, demonstrated that the Cold War and the ideological battle against Communism were far from over. Mariel severely tested the newly passed Act and inadvertently helped revert refugee and asylee policies in the U.S. back to Cold War terms. The Reagan administration found ways to continue its anti-Communist foreign policy, which privileged refugees from Communism within the limitations of the Refugee Act of 1980.[61]

The executive and the legislative branches passed the measure entirely unaware that a mass exodus from the United States' Communist neighbor to the south would soon challenge it. Before the Act was passed, Cubans were commonly regarded as an exception to the immigration rule, since they were fleeing a regime deemed politically, socially, and economically oppressive. During a hearing held by a House of Representatives subcommittee on the Mariel exodus and the immigration of several thousand Haitians during 1980, a government official noted how the Refugee Act of 1980 altered the treatment of Cuban immigrants: "Until the beginning of the crisis, Cubans were welcomed in our tradition as a haven for the victims of Communist repression."[62] Prior to the passage of the Refugee Act, the United States policy privileged providing refugee and asylee status to individuals fleeing countries that were politically or ideologically deemed inimical to the U.S. American policy and was particularly shaped in Cold War terms, so that refugee or asylum seekers hailing from Communist nations—including Cuba, Cambodia, Vietnam, and the Soviet Union—were more easily admitted into the U.S. On the other hand, Haitian refugee and asylum seekers, for example, were often denied admission. The U.S. defined them as economic rather than political refugees/asylees. This policy partially stemmed from the United States' historical policy of privileging nationals from Communist countries while opting to spare its ideological allies, such as Haiti, the humiliation of its citizens being granted refuge.[63]

The political discourse that followed the Mariel exodus tested the United States' commitment to humanitarianism and anti-Communist sentiment. The Refugee Act of 1980, which partially amended the McCarran-Walter Act of 1952, required presidential and congressional approval for designating refugee status. Under this new act, the executive and legislative branches would meet once a year to determine annual refugee admissions, including whether an emergency existed that would warrant an increase in the suggested quota of fifty thousand for admitted refugees. To win approval then, potential refugees would have to demonstrate that their refugee status was premised on "special humanitarian concern to the United States."[64] Since Carter and Congress had made no such suggestion for the Cubans specifically, on May 2 the government ruled that the guidelines of the Refugee Act of 1980 would not permit designation of the Marielitos as refugees. They would instead be judged on a case-by-case basis. The Carter administration was under considerable pressure to admit them, however, especially since the president had publicly welcomed the Cubans into the country. As a result, on June 20 the Cubans and Haitians who entered the U.S. during the Mariel period were granted a special classification that facilitated their admission to the country as "Cuban-Haitian entrant (status pending)."[65] The Mariel exodus thus helped perpetuate the practice of treating Communist Cuba as an exception to U.S. immigration policy.

After the Marielitos were allowed to physically enter the United States, the next major cause of contention was whether they would be allowed to *stay* there. This was of particular concern for the homosexual Marielitos. The INS fostered a consistent official policy—through many manifestations from 1917 to 1990—of excluding homosexuals from entering the U.S.[66] Immigration policy in the U.S. consistently reflected the political atmosphere of the period in which it was drafted and implemented. A product of McCarthyism and overall fears of Communism, the McCarran-Walter Act integrated language that reflected fears and concerns over national security, family stability, and sexual deviancy. It is in this context that a holdover from the American "Lavender Scare" of the 1950s—or the era's residual attitude that linked political fears of Communism to social anxieties over homosexuality—greeted homosexual Marielitos.

The INS historically consulted with the Public Health Service (PHS) to provide the medical language that reflected existing psychiatric concerns with immigration. While homosexuality was never listed as ground for exclusion, immigration laws, made in consultation with the PHS, broadly excluded homosexual aliens under psychiatric clauses. The McCarran-Walter Act, for example, barred aliens who exhibited a "psychopathic personality" or "mental defect."[67] The Act's policy of denying U.S. citizenship on the premise of one's homosexuality was contested in the U.S. Supreme Court case *Boutilier v. INS* (1967). Despite the liberal Supreme Court decisions of the late 1960s and early 1970s—as seen with the *Loving v. Virginia* decision of 1967 that invalidated laws against interracial marriage—six out of nine justices ruled in favor of upholding the McCarran-Walter Act's policy of barring homosexuals and, as a consequence, the notion that homosexuality was a mental illness.[68]

Well-mobilized gay and lesbian grassroots organizations began surfacing in the United States following the Stonewall Riots of 1969, the event that in many ways sparked the gay liberation movement. One of the first major accomplishments of this movement came in 1973, when lobbying efforts contributed to the decision of the American Psychiatric Association (APA) to decategorize "homosexuality" from its list of mental disorders. While this was a major success for gays and lesbians, the PHS did not immediately follow suit, thus potentially leaving homosexuality in place as a grounds for exclusion.[69]

Months before thousands of Cubans sought refuge at the Peruvian embassy, legislation had been proposed in Congress to amend the anti-homosexual implications of the McCarran-Walter Act. In January 1980,

Senator Alan Cranston, a Democrat from California, introduced a bill to amend section 212(a)(4), the Act's exclusionary clause that barred homosexual aliens from entering the country.[70] Earlier, the INS had temporarily suspended enforcing that portion of the Act on August 2, 1979, immediately following Surgeon General Julius Richmond's recommendation that homosexuality no longer be deemed a "mental disease or defect."[71] As a result, PHS physicians were instructed to stop their investigations to decipher whether an alien seeking entry to the United States was homosexual. The PHS's temporary procedure came six years after the APA declassified homosexuality as a mental illness.

Since the antihomosexual policy remained in the McCarran-Walter Act, however, the INS and Justice Department could continue to cite the Act as just cause for refusing homosexual Marielitos from entering the United States. Following months of extensive media coverage on the Marielitos' fate in the U.S., political and public discourse began to question Americans' commitment to human rights. On May 2, 1980, *The Sentinel*, a gay periodical based in San Francisco, reported that the Carter administration had granted special waivers to the gay Marielitos which would allow them to enter the U.S. despite the INS policy of barring homosexuals. Stuart Eisenstadt, the chief of Carter's Domestic Policy Staff, noted that the administration was working with the INS so that the Cubans "would be eligible to have a waiver on humanitarian grounds on a case by case basis."[72] *The Sentinel* commented that "Washington observers" believed that the Carter administration had offered the waiver to avoid international embarrassment by denying oppressed individuals who were fleeing a Communist regime sanctuary in the U.S.: "The decision to act now in the case of the Cuban refugees appeared due as much to an effort to avoid international embarrassment if the United States should turn back refugees who reached this country as it was an effort to assuage American gay concern."[73]

With the whole world watching, the issue of what to do with the homosexual Marielitos tested the authenticity of the administration's anti-Communist and humanitarian platform. Should the federal government deny entry to the homosexuals, the administration would run the great risk of appearing inconsistent, contradictory, and even hypocritical in its condemnations of oppressive regimes and political systems. However, the gay Cubans' fate appeared to be sealed when the government announced it would not classify the Marielitos as "refugees." Following the decision to designate the group as "entrants," the future of the homosexual Cubans was once again unclear. *The Sentinel* reported on the matter on June 13,

1980, noting that Carter had missed his opportunity to ensure that the homosexuals would be allowed to stay in the U.S.: "White House officials also conceded that the planned 'waiver' for gay Cubans had fallen by the wayside in the face of Presidential inaction on the status of the Cubans. They suggested that sufficient time remained to address any actual problems after they arise, and said the Justice Department had no plans to take actions against gay Cubans."[74]

In late June 1980, *Gay Community News* stated that the Mariel situation was grounds for federal exception, and that the Carter administration had urged a waiver of the INS policy that would exclude homosexuals from entering the United States. The administration made this change in practice "on humanitarian grounds," although the policy remained unchanged in writing.[75] Later in July, the Carter administration stated that it would support Senator Cranston's bill allowing gay and lesbian foreigners to enter the U.S. without restriction. A special assistant to President Carter commented that the reversal of position stemmed from "the President's human rights policies and the nation's responsibilities to be consistent with our immigration expectation of other countries."[76] In the end, however, Cranston's bill failed to receive strong support from the Carter administration and lobbyists and, as a result, it died soon after.[77]

Figure 4. Gay Community News, a Boston-based lesbian and gay weekly newspaper, featured this image throughout its extensive coverage of the Mariel boatlift. The image depicts gay Marielitos en route to the U.S. It features the pink triangle, a gay rights symbol, suggesting that the American reception of the purged Cuban homosexuals was an extension of gay pride and success. Rob Schmieder, *Gay Community News*, August 2, 1980, 1.

In addition, some officials, including Assistant Secretary of State for Human Rights Patricia Derian, noted how barring homosexuals from entering the United States was inconsistent with the Helsinki Accords of 1975 that surfaced in the midst of détente international politics. While the international political effects of these agreements have been well-documented, Helsinki also affected domestic human rights issues in the U.S.[78] Derian relayed to the Justice Department her concern that the current policy of excluding homosexuals was incongruent with the pact. She noted that the Accords promoted goodwill and international human rights and were signed by the Soviets, the United States' ideological enemy. In response to the Carter administration's allegations, the Justice Department reported that it too would support the proposed bill to amend the exclusionary sections of the McCarran-Walter Act.[79]

On September 9, 1980, the Justice Department officially announced its ruling on whether it would uphold its policy of barring homosexual aliens from entering the U.S.[80] The Department concluded that it had "the legal obligation to exclude homosexuals from entering the United States, but it will be done solely upon the voluntary submission by the alien that he or she is homosexual."[81] Thus, ironically, under this proto–"don't ask, don't tell" policy, the explicit professions of homosexuality necessary to leave Cuba became potential grounds for exclusion on the other side of the Florida straits.[82] Following the approval of the Carter administration, the Justice Department instructed the INS to forego the questioning of an alien's sexuality. The new policy would consider barring a homosexual only if he or she made "an unsolicited, unambiguous oral or written admission of homosexuality."[83] One's mannerisms, form of dress, or possessing "gay" paraphernalia, such as a gay pride button or literature, would no longer warrant further investigation. In addition, if a third party at the scene identified an individual as a homosexual, the INS would have to undertake a "secondary inspection." This would warrant having an official ask the suspected individual if he or she was a homosexual. In regard to the third-party exclusionary clause, the INS noted that "the likelihood of a third-party stating that an alien is homosexual is remote."[84]

The policy had a direct effect on the majority of the homosexual Marielitos, even though it was officially enacted only two weeks before Castro closed Mariel harbor. A final handwritten note in the press release that announced this change of policy read: "Pre-June 19 homosexuals will not be affected."[85] This suggests that the new change in policy would be applied to those who entered the United States after June 19, thereby easing the process for Marielitos who had yet to enter the U.S. The decision also facilitated the pending status of homosexual Marielitos in the United States. Although the Justice Department had been considering this initiative for over a year—long before Mariel had even opened—the ultimate change in policy appears to have been the product of great political pressure that stemmed largely from the publicity and worry over the homosexual Marielitos. The decision seems to have been a compromise of sorts, one that would address the "emergency" issue of the large group of homosexual Marielitos who entered the country that year without subjecting the McCarran-Walter Act—or the Refugee Act, for that matter—to further congressional scrutiny. The change in policy was not carried over into any change in the legislation. The decision was, then, ultimately an informal change in practice. While some gay groups across the country celebrated this advance in the treatment of homosexual aliens, others expressed disappointment and argued it fell short of securing equal treatment through formal legislation. In its report on the matter, *The Bay Area Reporter*, a San Francisco gay periodical, referred to this policy as a "Carter Cop-Out," noting what it perceived as a half-attempt at humanitarianism and equality.[86]

THE QUEER MARIELITOS' CONTRIBUTION TO THE U.S. GAY RIGHTS MOVEMENT

Although there appears to be no evidence that homosexual Marielitos were denied entry into the U.S as a result of their sexuality, past research demonstrates that the state interpreted sexual behavior and "performance"— such as the ones described above—in different and often ambiguous ways.[87] In November 1980, two months after the new policy was implemented, British gay activist Carl Hill challenged it. He openly professed his homosexuality to INS officials upon entering the U.S. As a result, they required him to attend an exclusion hearing. Although the case saw several appeals, the ultimate decision noted that the INS could not exclude a suspected homosexual from entering the U.S. without an official diagnosis from a qualified medical examiner that the individual had a sexual or mental deviancy—which remained the official means of exclusion. The PHS, however, had recently clarified that homosexuality would not constitute such a deviancy. The Hill case provided a new precedent, although it would not be applied in the same fashion throughout the country. According to the Hill decision, an INS officer could not rely on his or her own interpretations of what constituted a "homosexual."[88] As a result, courts determined the fate of suspected alien homosexuals who qualified for exclusion under the new policy.

This complicated the exclusion process and facilitated the admission of alien homosexuals into the U.S. Although some courts interpreted the policy differently and regarded its flexibility as contradictory to the formal legislation, advances in the U.S. gay rights movement also led to more court victories and new favorable decisions for foreign homosexuals.[89] Gay American activism helped change past cultural and social assumptions about homosexuality and, as a result, the courts' interpretation of the new policy. The policy remained quite ambiguous until the passage of the Immigration Act of 1990. In order to pursue an exclusionary hearing under that Act, officials had to provide a diagnosis that the alien was mentally or physically ill and, as a result of that illness, a potential threat to society.[90] Although this was a major step forward from the previous decade of legal ambiguity, the Act also paved the way for future contentious interpretations of the law—such as in cases of aliens living with HIV or AIDS.[91]

A number of international embarrassments and crises—including the Iranian takeover of the American embassy in Tehran and the taking of several dozen hostages, the Soviet invasion of Afghanistan, and the Mariel boatlift—played a role in President Carter's defeat in the presidential election of 1980. The Republican candidate, Ronald Reagan, won the presidency in a decisive election. During his campaign for the presidency, Reagan was highly critical of many of Carter's policies and decisions. Although Reagan backed Carter's decision to allow the Cuban exiles to enter the United States, he condemned the way it was carried out. Carter was often accused of being an ineffective president for not enforcing U.S. immigration laws and barring the Cuban exiles from entering the U.S. During his presidential campaign, Reagan adamantly supported the plight of the Marielitos. In a debate, he argued that the "fear that some of the wrong people might be coming here," referring to the allegations that Marielitos were Castro's "undesirables," was insufficient reason to "shut off the rescue mission."[92] Reagan's reference to the exodus as a "rescue mission" demonstrated what he perceived as an American initiative to aid anti-Communist dissidents. Reagan maintained this policy throughout his presidency, ultimately undermining the objective of the Refugee Act of 1980 to disassociate the term "refugee" with "anti-Communism." This shift facilitated the Marielitos' residency in the U.S., even though Castro had closed Mariel harbor by the time Reagan took office.

In February 1981, the Select Commission on Immigration and Refugee Policy, established by Congress in 1978, recommended that no changes be made to the McCarran-Walter Act and its subsequent amendments that excluded some aliens from entering the United States—namely Communists and homosexuals. The Commission unofficially commented on its recommendation in media reports. It argued that passing any amendments would be difficult in a conservative Congress.[93] In addition, recent immigrant quandaries had tainted public perceptions of immigration. In this regard, the Mariel boatlift stood out as an example of failed immigration policy. However, the American Association for the Advancement of Science and the American Association of University Professors, along with the Association of the Bar of the City of New York, all favored amending the immigration policy. They argued that the reputation of the United States as a free nation would be undermined by upholding such policies: "Our reputation for allowing expression free from unnecessary governmental restraint will continue to be tarnished by these anachronistic remnants of a fearful era."[94] As the Cold War was thawing out following predominantly successful détente politics and Soviet concessions, the organizations argued that the Cold War–motivated legislation no longer was relevant to contemporary society.

In the mid-1980s, a homosexual Marielito severely tested the new U.S. definition of "refugee," as indicated by the Refugee Act of 1980. In the case *In re Toboso-Alfonso,* the courts for the first time considered homosexual persecution as a cause for refugee status under the Refugee Act of 1980. The applicant, a man named Fidel Armando Toboso-Alfonso, entered the U.S. in June 1980 during the Mariel boatlift. Toboso-Alfonso, like the majority of Marielitos, was granted an extended parole. His parole was terminated in 1985 and he was subsequently forced to appear in exclusion hearings. Since he was already residing in the U.S., he applied for asylum before an Immigration Judge (IJ) in Texas. The IJ noted that as a homosexual, Toboso-Alfonso was eligible for asylum under the 1980 Refugee Act, which extended refugee/asylee eligibility to applicants who were persecuted members of a "particular social group." The INS, however, found gaps in the argument and appealed the ruling. As a result, Toboso-Alfonso's case would be heard before the highest immigration court, the U.S. Board of Immigration Appeals (BIA). Five years after the IJ's ruling, Toboso-Alfonso would have to demonstrate the "clear probability" that he would be persecuted in his native Cuba as a result of his homosexuality.[95]

Toboso-Alfonso argued that government officials had harassed and persecuted him in Cuba as a consequence of the state's institutionalized homophobia—much as other homosexual Marielitos had revealed in interviews with the gay press years before (and described earlier in this essay).

Toboso-Alfonso provided substantial evidence—including testimonials from other homosexual Marielitos conducted by gay media—to demonstrate that homosexuals "form a particular social group in Cuba and suffer persecution by the government as a result of that status."[96] Ultimately, the BIA agreed with the IJ and discredited the INS's argument that granting Toboso-Alfonso asylum would "be tantamount to awarding discretionary relief to those involved in behavior that is not only socially deviant in nature, but in violation of the laws or regulations of the country as well."[97] The BIA's decision to grant Toboso-Alfonso asylum stemmed from its belief that homosexuals in Cuba were not necessarily criminalized as a result of homosexual actions, per se. Rather, it argued that state-led negative repercussions were rooted in one's "status of being a homosexual." In particular, the Mariel exodus was used as evidence for institutionalized homophobia in Cuba: "The record indicates that rather than a penalty for misconduct, this action resulted from the government's desire that all homosexuals be forced to leave their homeland."[98]

The Toboso-Alfonso case provides further evidence for how Marielitos effectively challenged immigration and refugee policy in the United States. Attorney General Janet Reno established that ruling as the new precedent for refugee/asylum cases in 1994, four years after the BIA's decision in the Toboso-Alfonso case.[99] Reno formally established the ruling as the new law of the land and supported the BIA's decision in the case, ultimately changing—at least statutorily—the role of (homo)sexuality in shaping immigration and refugee politics in the United States. In response to Reno's affirmation, openly gay U.S. representative Barney Frank (D-MA) noted how this decision allowed homosexuals "to argue that they can be considered a member of a particular social group which is targeted by their government for persecution."[100] The homosexual community that entered the U.S. during the Mariel boatlift had far-reaching effects on American foreign policy, particularly in regards to immigration, refugee, and asylee status. In this regard, the American "state gaze" on homosexuality benefited alien homosexuals as the U.S. sought to defend—at least in the courts—Cuban homosexuals from that regime's "state gaze."

It is clear that government officials feared that the U.S. policy of excluding gay and lesbian aliens on the basis of their homosexuality was incongruent with the human rights initiative the Carter administration promoted to the international community, including the Soviet Union. To avoid appearing insincere about its commitment to human rights in the midst of an ideological war against Communism and socialism, the Carter administration was forced to embrace a policy—albeit on a more temporary, emergency basis than subsequently—that would allow homosexuals to enter the United States without restriction. The political discourse that surfaced following the Mariel boatlift eventually facilitated a change in the federal government's policy of barring homosexuals from entering the United States. While the clause that excluded homosexuals from entering the country remained in the law until the passage of the Immigration Act of 1990, the Carter administration's informal change in practice forged a new precedent which established that homosexuality was no longer deemed a mental illness. In addition, the change also suggested that the notion of an exclusionary clause premised on one's sexuality was contradictory to the administration's own international human rights initiative and the anti-Communist ideology it advanced in the late Cold War. The Marielitos played a significant role in the propaganda schemes of both Cuba and the United States. The homosexual communities from both countries ultimately benefited from these schemes, or the ideological messages, that both governments conveyed. They were allowed to leave Cuba as a result of their homosexuality and, in turn, allowed to remain in the U.S. because they fled a Communist nation. As a result, the Refugee Act of 1980 served to facilitate their stay in the United States. The homosexual Marielitos continued to influence U.S. immigration, refugee, and asylee procedures—easing the long-standing antigay policies of the U.S.—years after the Cuban government purged them from the island.

NOTES

The author would like to thank Alex Lichtenstein, Darden A. Pyron, Sherry Johnson, Aurora Morcillo, Horacio N. Roque Ramírez, John J. Bukowczyk, William B. Turner, Danny Mermel, and the two anonymous reviewers for their valuable comments and support.

1. Paul Heath Hoeffel, "Fort Chaffee's Unwanted Cubans," *New York Times*, December 21, 1980.

2. Ibid.

3. Susana Peña, "'Obvious Gays' and the State Gaze: Cuban Gay Visibility and U.S. Immigration Policy during the 1980 Mariel Boatlift," *Journal of the History of Sexuality* 16, no. 3 (September 2007): 514.

4. For more on how sexuality shaped immigration laws and policies in the United States, see Lauren Berlant, *The Queen Goes to Washington City: Essays on Sex and Citizenship* (Durham, NC, 1997); Margot Canaday, "'Who is a Homosexual?': The Consolidation of Sexual Identities in Mid-Twentieth Century American Immigration Law," *Law and Social Inquiry* 28 (Spring 2003): 351–87; Margot Canaday, "Building a Straight State: Sexuality and Social Citizenship under the 1944 G.I. Bill," *Journal of American History* 90, no. 3 (December 2003): 935–57; Brad Epps, Keja Valens, and Bill J. Gonzalez, eds., *Passing Lines: Sexuality*

and Immigration (Cambridge, MA, 2005); Eithne Luibhéid, ed., "Queer/Migration," GLQ: A Journal of Lesbian and Gay Studies 14, nos. 2–3 (2008): 169–424; Eithne Luibhéid and Lionel Cantú Jr., eds., Queer Migrations: Sexuality, U.S. Citizenship, and Border Crossings (Minneapolis, 2005); Eithne Luibhéid, Entry Denied: Controlling Sexuality at the Border (Minneapolis, 2002); Marc Stein, "Boutilier and the U.S. Supreme Court's Sexual Revolution," Law and History Review 23, no. 3 (Fall 2005): 491–536; William B. Turner, "Mirror Images: Lesbian/Gay Civil Rights in the Carter and Reagan Administrations," in Creating Change: Sexuality, Public Policy, and Civil Rights, ed. John D'Emilio, William B. Turner, and Urvashi Vaid (New York, 2000), 3–28; and William B. Turner, "Lesbian/Gay Rights and Immigration Policy: Lobbying to End the Medical Model," Journal of Policy History 7, no. 2 (Spring 1995): 208–25.

5. Eithne Luibhéid, "Queer/Migration: An Unruly Body of Scholarship," GLQ: A Journal of Lesbian and Gay Studies 14, no. 2–3 (2008): 169–90.

6. Peña, "'Obvious Gays.'"

7. For more on the Mariel boatlift, see David W. Engstrom, Presidential Decision Making Adrift: The Carter Administration and the Mariel Boatlift (Lanham, MD, 1997); María Cristina García, Havana USA: Cuban Exiles and Cuban Americans in South Florida, 1959–1994 (Berkeley, CA, 1996), chap. 2; Alex Larzelere, Castro's Ploy—America's Dilemma: The 1980 Cuban Boatlift (Washington, DC, 1988); Alejandro Portes and Alex Stepick, City on the Edge: The Transformation of Miami (Berkeley, CA, 1993), chap. 2; and Emily H. Skop, "Race and Place in the Adaptation of Mariel Exiles," International Migration Review 35, no. 2 (Summer 2001): 449–71. For more on Mariel's homosexual entrants and community, see Lourdes Arguelles and Ruby B. Rich, "Homosexuality, Homophobia, and Revolution: Notes toward an Understanding of the Cuban Lesbian and Gay Male Experience, Part I," Signs 9, no. 4 (Summer 1984): 683–99; Lourdes Arguelles and Ruby B. Rich, "Homosexuality, Homophobia, and Revolution: Notes toward an Understanding of the Cuban Lesbian and Gay Male Experience, Part II," Signs 11, no. 1 (Autumn 1985): 120–36; Peña, "'Obvious Gays'"; and Susana Peña, "Visibility and Silence: Mariel and Cuban American Gay Male Experience and Representation," in Queer Migrations: Sexuality, U.S. Citizenship, and Border Crossings, ed. Eithne Luibhéid and Lionel Cantú Jr. (Minneapolis, 2005), 125–45.

8. García, Havana USA, 54–61.

9. Engstrom, Presidential Decision Making, 86–89; García, Havana USA, 54–61.

10. Milt Freudenheim and Barbara Slavin, "The World in Summary," New York Times, May 11, 1980.

11. García, Havana USA, 66–68.

12. Fidel Castro, "Speech by Cuban President Fidel Castro at International Workers' Day Rally Held at José Martí Revolution Square, Havana," May 1, 1980, Castro Speech Database: Speeches, Interviews, Articles: 1959–1996, Latin American Network Information Center (LANIC) (University of Texas at Austin), http://www.lanic.utexas.edu/project/castro/db/1980-/19800501–1.html (accessed March 26, 2008).

13. Ibid.

14. Ibid.

15. Ibid.

16. Ibid.

17. Ian Lumsden, *Machos, Maricones, and Gays: Cuba and Homosexuality* (Philadelphia, 1996), 78. For more on the treatment of homosexuality in modern Cuba, see Arguelles and Rich, "Homosexuality, Homophobia, and Revolution, Part I"; Arguelles and Rich, "Homosexuality, Homophobia, and Revolution, Part II"; Emilio Bejel, *Gay Cuban Nation* (Chicago, 2001); Brad Epps, "Proper Conduct: Reinaldo Arenas, Fidel Castro, and the Politics of Homosexuality," *Journal of History of Sexuality* 6, no. 2 (October 1995): 231–83; Marvin Leiner, *Sexual Politics in Cuba: Machismo, Homosexuality, and AIDS* (Boulder, CO, 1994); Abel Sierra Madero, *Del otro lado del espejo: La sexualidad en la construcción de la nación cubana* (Havana, 2006); Rafael Ocasio, "Gays and the Cuban Revolution: The Case of Reinaldo Arenas," *Latin American Perspectives* 29, no. 2 (March 2002): 78–98; José Quiroga, *Tropics of Desire: Interventions from Queer Latino America* (New York, 2000); Lois M. Smith and Alfred Padula, *Sex and Revolution: Women in Socialist Cuba* (New York, 1996), 172–76; and Allen Young, *Gays under the Cuban Revolution* (San Francisco, 1981).

18. Lumsden, *Machos*, 80.

19. Jo Thomas, "Behind Barred Doors in Havana, Would-Be Émigrés Wait in Fear," *New York Times*, May 2, 1980.

20. Friedrich Engels, *The Peasant War in Germany*, 3rd ed. (New York, 2000), xii.

21. Paul Hofmann, "Cuban Government Is Alarmed by Increase in Homosexuality," *New York Times*, April 16, 1965.

22. Ibid.

23. For more on the persecution of homosexuals by the United States federal government, see John D'Emilio, "The Homosexual Menace: The Politics of Sexuality in Cold War America," in *Passion and Power: Sexuality in History*, ed. Kathy Peiss and Christina Simmons (Philadelphia, 1989), 226–40; and David K. Johnson, *The Lavender Scare: The Cold War Persecution of Gays and Lesbians in the Federal Government* (Chicago, 2004).

24. David Morris, "Gay Cuban Refugees Here: Where Do Feds Send Them?" *Gay Community News*, June 21, 1981.

25. Ibid.

26. García, *Havana USA*, 65.

27. Ibid., 64–65.

28. Reginald Stuart, "3 Years Later, Most Cubans of Boatlift Adjusting to U.S.," *New York Times*, May 17, 1983.

29. For more on the 1969 Stonewall Riots and their effect on the gay liberation movement, see John D'Emilio, *Sexual Politics, Sexual Communities: The Making of a Homosexual Minority in the United States, 1940–1970* (Chicago, 1983); Martin Duberman, *Stonewall* (New York, 1994); David Eisenbach, *Gay Power: An American Revolution* (New York, 2006); John Howard, *Men Like That: A Southern Queer History* (Chicago, 1999); Charles Kaiser, *The Gay Metropolis: The Landmark History of Gay Life in America since World War II* (New York, 1997); and Marc Stein, *City of Sisterly & Brotherly Loves: Lesbian and Gay Philadelphia, 1945–1972* (Chicago, 2000).

30. Lumsden, *Machos*, 82.

31. Ibid. Spain achieved significant advances in gay rights following the death of authoritarian ruler Francisco Franco (r. 1939–1975) and the implementation of the Constitution of 1978. For more on homosexuality in modern Spain, see Victoriano Domingo Loren, *Los*

homosexuales frente a la ley: Los juristas opinan (Barcelona, 1978); Fernando Olmeda Nicolas, *El látigo y la pluma: Homosexuales en la España de Franco* (Madrid, 2004); and Gema Pérez-Sánchez, *Queer Transitions in Contemporary Spanish Culture: From Franco to la Movida* (Albany, NY, 2007).

32. Lumsden, *Machos*, 83.

33. David Morris, "Cuba's Gay Refugees Starting Over," *Gay Community News*, October 25, 1980.

34. Ernie Acosta, "Thousands Seek Sponsors: Gay Refugees Tell of Torture, Oppression in Castro's Cuba," *The Advocate*, August 21, 1980.

35. Daniel Shoer-Roth, "Invited to Leave by the Government, Gays and Lesbians—and a Few Pretenders—Took The Opportunity to Start New Lives," *Miami Herald*, April 23, 2005.

36. Reinaldo Arenas, *Before Night Falls*, trans. Dolores M. Koch (New York, 1993), 280.

37. Thomas, "Behind Barred Doors."

38. Arenas, *Before Night Falls*, 281.

39. García, *Havana USA*, 63.

40. Shoer-Roth, "Invited to Leave."

41. Arenas, *Before Night Falls*, 281. Past scholarship has demonstrated that the label "*maricón*" was most commonly identified with an effeminate and sexually passive gay man. In Cuba, as in many other Latin American countries, the *maricón* was perceived as a far greater social threat than the "*bugarrón*," or the more masculine and active man who often penetrates or receives oral sex from another man but does not identify himself as a homosexual and has sexual relations with women. Often, the penetrator was not deemed—socially or politically—a homosexual at all.

42. U.S. Congress, House of Representatives, Committee on the Judiciary, *Caribbean Migration: Oversight Hearings before the Subcommittee on Immigration, Refugees, and International Law of the Committee on the Judiciary, House of Representatives*, 96th Cong., 2nd sess., May 13, June 4, 17, 1980, 65–67.

43. *Matter of Toboso-Alfonso*, United States Board of Immigration Appeals, March 12, 1990, UNHCR Refworld, http://www.unhcr.org/refworld/docid/3ae6b6b84.html (accessed March 20, 2009).

44. For more on Cuba's missions in Africa, see Piero Gleijeses, "Moscow's Proxy? Cuba and Africa, 1975–1988," *Journal of Cold War Studies* 8, no. 4 (Fall 2006): 98–146; Piero Gleijeses, *Conflicting Missions: Havana, Washington, and Africa, 1959–1976* (Chapel Hill, NC, 2002).

45. Strobe Talbott, "'Comrade Fidel Wants You,'" *Time*, July 10, 1978.

46. Acosta, "Thousands Seek Sponsors."

47. Morris, "Cuba's Gay Refugees."

48. Ibid.

49. Ibid.; Hoeffel, "Fort Chaffee's Unwanted Cubans."

50. García, *Havana USA*, 68.

51. Arguelles and Rich, "Homosexuality, Homophobia, and Revolution, Part I," 695.

52. Smith and Padula, *Sex and Revolution*, 36–37.

53. Ibid., 173; Haidy G. Möller, "Los homosexuales en la Cuba actual," *Mariel: Revista de literatura y arte* 2, no. 5 (Spring 1984): 13.

54. Möller, "Los homosexuales."

55. García, *Havana USA*, 65; Peña, "'Obvious Gays,'" 507; Arguelles and Rich, "Homosexuality, Homophobia, and Revolution, Part II," 128.

56. For more on the Refugee Act of 1980, see Carl J. Bon Tempo, *Americans at the Gate: The United States and Refugees during the Cold War* (Princeton, NJ, 2008); Peter H. Koehn, *Refugees from Revolution: U.S. Policy and Third-World Migration* (Boulder, CO, 1991); and Norman L. Zucker and Naomi Flink Zucker, *Desperate Crossings: Seeking Refuge in America* (Armonk, NY, 1996).

57. U.S. Congress, House of Representatives, Committee on the Judiciary, *Caribbean Migration*, 2.

58. Ibid.

59. The Harvard Law Review Association, "Immigration Law. Asylum. Ninth Circuit Holds That Persecuted Homosexual Mexican Man with a Female Sexual Identity . . . *Hernandez-Montiel v. INS,* 225 F.3d 1084 (9th Cir. 2000)," *Harvard Law Review* 114, no. 8 (June 2001): 2569.

60. Quotation in Bon Tempo, *Americans at the Gate*, 9–10.

61. Ibid.

62. U.S. Congress, House of Representatives Committee on the Judiciary, *Caribbean Migration*, 259.

63. Bon Tempo, *Americans at the Gate*, 1–10; Juana María Rodriguez, *Queer Latinidad: Identity Practices, Discursive Spaces* (New York, 2003), 84–88.

64. García, *Havana USA*, 229.

65. Ibid.

66. Turner, "Lesbian/Gay Rights," 208–9.

67. Ibid., 208–11.

68. For more on the Boutilier case, see Stein, "Boutilier."

69. Turner, "Lesbian/Gay Rights," 208–11.

70. "Cranston Bill Seeks Halt to Immigration Ban," *The Sentinel*, January 25, 1980.

71. Turner, "Lesbian/Gay Rights," 217–18.

72. Larry Bush, "Gay Cubans Win Waiver," *The Sentinel*, May 2, 1980.

73. Ibid.

74. "Cuban Gays Lose Waiver," *The Sentinel*, June 13, 1980.

75. Morris, "Gay Cuban Refugees Here."

76. "Carter Supporting Change in Anti-Gay INS Laws," *Gay Community News*, July 5, 1980.

77. Turner, "Lesbian/Gay Rights," 219.

78. For more on the Helsinki Accords' effects on domestic and international politics and their connection to human rights, see William G. Hyland, *Mortal Rivals: Understanding the Hidden Pattern of Soviet-American Relations* (New York, 1987), 114–19; Daniel C. Thomas, "Human Rights Ideas, the Demise of Communism, and the End of the Cold War," *Journal of Cold War Studies* 7, no. 2 (Spring 2005): 111–12; and Daniel C. Thomas, *The Helsinki Effect: International Norms, Human Rights, and the Demise of Communism* (Princeton, NJ, 2001), chaps. 1–2, 4.

79. "Carter Supporting Change."

80. Donnel Nunes, "Rules on Immigration by Homosexuals Eased," *Washington Post*, September 10, 1980; Robert Pear, "U.S. Bars Exclusions of Homosexual Aliens in Most Circumstances," *New York Times*, September 10, 1980.

81. Letter from the Department of Justice, 9/9/1980, Folder "Homosexuals (File No. 2),"
Box 22, Records of the Cuban-Haitian Task Force (hereafter CHTF), Jimmy Carter Library
(hereafter JCL), Atlanta, GA.

82. My reference to "don't ask, don't tell" is separate from the American military's 1993
policy that excludes homosexuals who openly profess their sexuality from serving in the
U.S. armed forces. Although distinct and unrelated, both of these policies require (homo)
sexual discretion as part of the state mandate. They also provide further evidence of sexual
discriminatory patterns at the federal level. For more on the U.S. military's 1993 "Don't
Ask, Don't Tell" policy, see Aaron Belkin and Geoffrey Bateman, eds., *Don't Ask, Don't
Tell: Debating the Gay Ban in the Military* (Boulder, CO, 2003).

83. Telegraphic Message from David Crossland, Acting Commissioner of the INS,
9/8/1980, Folder "Homosexuals (File No. 2)," Box 22, Records of the CHTF, JCL.

84. Ibid.

85. Ibid.

86. "INS Will Bar Admitted Gays," *Bay Area Reporter*, September 11, 1980.

87. Peña, "'Obvious Gays,'" 510–12.

88. Bill Ong Hing, *Defining America through Immigration Policy* (Philadelphia, 2004),
86–89.

89. William N. Eskridge, *Dynamic Statutory Interpretation* (Cambridge, MA, 1994),
54–55.

90. Turner, "Lesbian/Gay Rights," 219–20.

91. Eithne Luibhéid, *Entry Denied*, 26–27; Timothy F. Murphy, *Ethics in an Epidemic:
AIDS, Morality, and Culture* (Berkeley, CA, 1994), 131–33.

92. Howell Raines, "Reagan Says Carter's Effort to Halt Cuban Refugee Boats Is Inhu-
mane," *New York Times*, May 17, 1980.

93. Robert Pear, "No Changes Sought on Excluding Aliens," *New York Times*, February
1981.

94. Ibid.

95. *Matter of Toboso-Alfonso*.

96. Ibid.

97. Ibid.

98. Ibid.

99. Chuck Stewart, *Homosexuality and the Law: A Dictionary* (Santa Barbara, CA, 2001),
155–56.

100. David Johnston, "Ruling Backs Homosexuals on Asylum," *New York Times*, June
17, 1994.

12

"Couch Potatoes and Super-Women": Gender, Migration, and the Emerging Discourse on Housework among Asian Indian Immigrants

VIBHA BHALLA

IN APRIL 1991 a letter written by Ms. Subbi Mathur and titled "Couch Potatoes and Super-Women" appeared in *India Abroad*, the first newspaper of the expatriate Indian community in the United States.[1] A quasi-humorous piece of writing, the letter focused on the household division of labor within Indian immigrant families in the U.S. and particularly noted Indian immigrant wives' increasing workload as a consequence of migration. The letter portrayed Indian women's transformation into "super-women," who were continuously juggling increasing work at home along with their paid work. In sharp contrast, the letter labeled Indian immigrant husbands as "couch potatoes," or indolent men, who seemed oblivious to their wives' increasing household responsibilities, remained glued to their couches, and did not participate in household chores. The letter stated:

> Indian husbands rule the household from their couches (any resemblance to a couch potato is entirely incidental) through most of their married and child-rearing years, without much ado about anything . . . Indian women living abroad inherit duties of both worlds. Most hold decent jobs. . . .
>
> After putting in a "man(!)day's" work, Indian women muster fresh energy to perform the menial tasks without which a house stops being a home. . . . In spite of the multitude of gadgets, the workload of Indian wives here is more demanding than that of their counterparts in India who have less amenities but more household help. . . . Not having the immediate family's support, raising children becomes a lonely job filled with daily anguish and self-doubt. An Indian husband watches his wife with a condescending and philosophical air while she struggles with the daily trials and tribulations of "their" offspring. . . . While they are trying their best not to fly away in a super-women costume, the ever patient Indian husband waits for his dinner, relaxing on a couch, while enriching his mind with news around the world on all television channels.[2]

This characterization of Indian immigrant husbands as couch potatoes was rather surprising, since men in India, husbands or not, rarely participated in everyday domestic tasks; the strict separation of spheres dictated by Indian cultural norms deemed domesticity as woman's domain and economic responsibilities as the male realm. Despite its drollness, the critical undertones toward Indian immigrant husbands reflected a new desire, at least in this letter's author, for male assistance in household chores, a remarkable development since it was contrary to Indian cultural practices. What was amazing was that this letter was not unique in displaying changing expectations towards male participation in domestic tasks; it was, in fact, part of the fourth round of an exchange occurring since 1978 among the expatriate Indian men and women in the "Letters to the Editor" pages of *India Abroad*. Indian immigrant wives in the U.S. were increasingly voicing their complaints about their escalating domestic responsibilities and displaying new expectations for their spouses to ease their growing domestic chores. Implicit in their complaints and their simple wish for male participation in household tasks lay the seeds of overturning age-old Indian family norms as they applied to male and female responsibilities and, ultimately, determined their gendered identities.

Indian women's complaints that their household burden had increased as a consequence of migration and their attempts at transforming traditional male-female identities in the domestic division of labor are not unique. Literature on immigrant families has amply documented family as a key site where immigrant men and women struggle to renegotiate gendered responsibilities and power.[3] Families, Nancy Foner points out, are gendered, cultural units that undergo transformation after migration, and this development is particularly noticeable among first-generation immigrants.[4] Foner argues that the constant interaction between three variables—culture, structure, and agency—are instrumental in altering relationships within immigrant families. The structural conditions immigrants encounter in the host country, especially their relationship to the labor market, is pivotal in bringing about changes within families. The inability of immigrant men to find work in the U.S. forces women to enter the labor force and becomes the central factor in transforming gender relationships. Women's greater participation in the waged labor force strikes at the heart of gendered identities within families that traditionally view men as primary economic providers. Along with women's economic contributions to sustain the family economy, the cultural influences of the host society also affect immigrant families. Immigrants, Foner argues, are active agents who constantly act upon changing circumstances. Migration's dislocations provide women with new opportunities to renegotiate power and recreate family patterns that are favorable to them.[5]

Along with Foner, other works on immigrant families have also located them as arenas of conflict where immigrant men and women struggle. In doing so, these studies have also drawn attention to the particularities of a given migration stream, as well as to noneconomic factors that strengthen women's position within families. Pierette Hondagneu-Sotelo's study of Mexican families highlighted the role of female networks in renegotiating gender relationships.[6] Nazli Kibria's work on Vietnamese immigrant families further emphasized the salience of noneconomic factors and demonstrated the vital role played by the gender imbalance within the Vietnamese community in transforming family relationships.[7] Kibria also argued that women selectively challenged particular aspects of family structure to benefit their position and rarely challenged patriarchy.[8]

A large majority of the studies on immigrant families have focused on working-class families. Since the passage of the Immigration and Naturalization Act of 1965, many skilled, professional immigrants have migrated to the United States, and this migration stream includes professional women. Our knowledge of the issues that shape the struggles of middle-class immigrant families and the ways in which women's skilled, professional work shapes their domestic responsibilities after migration remains sketchy. How does migration affect the workings of immigrant families where both men and women occupy equivalent positions in the professional work force? The family experiences of Indian immigrants in the U.S. allow us insights into the ways class and women's professional work shape domestic practices after migration.

This article documents the emerging public discourse on the domestic division of work between Indian men and women in the United States as it emerged through approximately forty readers' letters written to the expatriate Indian newspaper *India Abroad* from 1978 to 1992. These letters highlight the gendered nature of Indian settlement and help us examine the issues confronting Indian immigrant families in the U.S. and their role in transforming women's activities within Indian families. The article argues that migration's adversity forced Indian wives to carve out new gender identities. As Indian women began moving away from Indian traditions that defined the domestic arena exclusively as woman's domain, they began propagating new identities that argued for principles of shared domestic responsibility with men. These letters indicate that the loss of class privileges, especially the loss of domestic help, as a result of migration, strongly influenced women's desire to redistribute domestic tasks. However, in the call for redefining male-female domestic roles lay issues of gender, class, and identity. While women were attempting to preserve their class privileges, they were also trying to move away from their primary and traditional identities as wives and mothers and preserve dual identities as wives and as workers.

Gendered identities are shaped by class, and the letters clearly reveal the women's middle-class origins. Along with the reference to "household help," pointing to middle-class women's privilege of employing women to take care of their domestic responsibilities, the use of the term "man(!)day's work" suggests a comparison of woman's paid work to male work. It also draws attention to middle-class women's entrance into the professional work force, which was increasing since India's independence in 1947. The command of English as evident in Ms. Subbi Mathur's letter further implied privileged upbringing since middle- and upper-class families commonly provided their children with English education. These new, dual identities as wives and workers were permanent, and women intended to reproduce them in their daughters; these identities are also particular to Indian immigrants in the U.S.

To draw conclusions on the basis of forty letters may seem rather ambitious, since the letters have their limitations. They are not part of any comprehensive study, nor do they constitute a substantial sample either of the Indian community or of Indian immigrant women. The letters do not provide background details of their writers, their paths of migration, the relationships of letter writers to the labor market, or the economic inequities between men and women within families. Despite these limitations, the letters are an important source and provide a foothold from which to explore the private workings of the Indian families. The impromptu nature of these letters, the issue-based engagement among complete strangers, and the diverse voices of Indians across the United States represented in them provide new insights into the problems encountered by Indian women in the early phase of post-1965 migration. Most importantly, the developing discourse on the topic of women's problems seen in these letters helps us historicize this issue and detail the transformations that occurred within Indian families in the U.S. during this period.

This article further argues that *India Abroad* played a vital role in mediating this gendered conflict. Its "Letters to the Editor" page emerged as a site where immigrant men and women began to thrash out publicly their private struggles. The newspaper in particular provided Indian women across the United States a space to form a women's community to strategize and to organize, or perhaps at least to imagine, forms of domestic resistance. The exigency of women's problems and the women's consequent determination to change the prevalent male-female relationship vis-à-vis domestic work is evident from the frequent discussions of this issue by women writing to *India Abroad*. Women increasingly wrote letters to the newspaper drawing attention to their domestic concerns, a notable development given the fact that they rarely wrote letters to the newspaper; these letters also brought to the fore other women's issues that were rarely reported in the newspaper. This article further contends that the public nature of this debate demonstrated a keen desire for transformation not only at the level of the individual family but throughout the Indian community.

Large-scale Indian migration to the United States began with the passage of the Immigration and Naturalization Act of 1965. In 1970 there were 172,132 Indians in the United States, a population that increased to 286,120 in 1980 and 815,447 in 1990.[9] As Indians migrated under the labor certification provisions of this act, the consequent migration was very selective, resulting in the settlement of a highly educated and professional Indian community, primarily as engineers, scientists, and physicians. Even Indian women were disproportionately employed in specialized skills. In 1980 more than half of the Asian Indian population in the U.S. was employed in managerial and professional specialty occupations; among women, more than one-third of those employed were in managerial occupations.[10] In 1990, 49 percent of Indian men and 35 percent of Indian women were in professional and managerial work.[11]

Studies on Indian immigrants have noted the development of more egalitarian gender relations within Indian families after arrival in the United States with greater male participation in domestic work, although the degree and nature of this participation varied among families.[12] These studies suggest that the professional nature of women's work, the distance from the immigrants' Indian homes, and the subsequent social isolation in the U.S. brought about a closer relationship between Indian husbands and wives. A recent work by Sheba George on Indian nurses from the state of Kerala has added new dimensions to our knowledge of the domestic redistribution of work within immigrant families. Like other researchers, George found transformations occurring within Indian families and also noted the uneven degree of change within families. She found that the largest transformation occurred in families where women became the primary earners and concluded that the paths of migration and immigrants' resultant relationship to the U.S. labor market played a central role in shaping this transformation. The need for nurses in the United States resulted in many women's emergence not only as primary migrants but also as primary economic providers, since their spouses often encountered problems in locating work. This economic role reversal and the shift work of nurses emerged as the central factors in the redistribution of domestic responsibilities and in increased male participation in domestic tasks.

George, using Arlie Hochschild's conceptual framework and terminology of "gender ideologies" and "gender strategies," argues that redistribution of domestic responsibilities did not necessarily entail ideological transformations among men and women. Transformations in gender ideologies are usually accompanied by ideological shifts in the understanding of new male and female roles within individuals and their families. These are permanent changes and probably are reproduced in subsequent generations. Gender strategies, however, are "plans of actions that individuals adopt to reconcile their gender ideology with their lived reality."[13] George argues that the redistribution of work within Keralite immigrant families was part of a gendered strategy to deal with the larger structural problem of the male inability to find work and did not signify a transformation in the cultural ideologies of the families. She found that families where men remained the primary economic providers continued the traditional gendered division of household work.[14]

The letters from *India Abroad* further illuminate these dynamics. *India Abroad* was the first newspaper of the Indian immigrant community in the United States, commencing publication in New York City in 1970, first as a monthly, then a fortnightly in 1972, and becoming a weekly in 1973. The primary purpose of the newspaper was to provide the growing Indian immigrant community in the U.S. with news of India. However, as the Indian settlement became permanent, the paper's contents began changing to incorporate issues pertinent to the Indian community in the U.S. Readers began voicing their problems of settlement through the "Letters to the Editor" page and its special column titled "Reflections on Life Abroad," or in the "Life and Leisure" section of the newspaper. It was in the "Letters to the Editor" page that Indian men and women began informing the larger Indian community of their domestic problems and engaged other men and women of that community in a discussion about the need for role transformation in domestic labor. The first letter and the resultant interactions among Indian men and women on this issue appeared in 1978, roughly a decade after the commencement of large-scale Indian immigration to the United States. The second letter appeared in 1983, the third debate opened in 1988, and a fourth exchange, of which Ms. Mathur's letter was a part, started in 1991.

WOMEN'S PERSPECTIVES

The first letter to provoke a discussion on domestic issues in *India Abroad*, interestingly enough, was written by an American woman who was married to an Indian. Writing in 1978, S.S., the initials by which the author identified herself, censured Indian husbands for not helping their wives in household chores. She wrote that

> In almost every home that I have visited I have had the misfortune to meet a terrible M.C.P. i.e. "Male Chauvinist Pig." This all supreme gent will sit in the living room and virtually order his wife—who may herself be a qualified doctor or professional—to get everything from an ash tray to dinner. And while the men intellectually gossip about their newest car, the poor "domestic help" will be frantically trying to save the honor of all great women of Indian mythology by finishing the dishes before the guests leave. . . . At this rate the Indian woman will never be liberated—not even in the United States.[15]

S.S.'s letter portrayed the gendered division of work within Indian homes in the U.S. and bemoaned the continuation of Indian domestic practices within Indian immigrant homes. Furthermore, the letter writer indicated migration's ill effects on working women. The loss of domestic help pushed even professional women to perform domestic tasks that in India were done by the hired help. S.S.'s desire to initiate domestic changes within Indian homes aimed not only to alleviate her Indian sisters' domestic burden, but also to pave the way for Indian families' immersion into American culture. S.S.'s motivation, while individualistic, reminded one of the "Americanization" movement of the early decades of the twentieth century, although her context and language was particular to the decade of the 1970s. Her language, especially the use of words like *male chauvinist pig*, *domestic help*, and *liberation* suggests the influence of the women's liberation movement of the 1970s, where liberation, among other things, included liberation from housework for women, given the fact that U.S. men and women shared domestic tasks.

S.S.'s attempt to cross cultural boundaries and form a bond of sisterhood with Indian women failed miserably, as other letters revealed that Indian immigrants overwhelmingly rejected her recipe of liberation and assimilation. All of the letter writers, with one exception, opposed S.S.'s attempts to initiate changes within Indian families.[16] Women particularly defended Indian gendered norms and the prevalent division of work within Indian homes, emphasizing cultural differences in the internal working of Indian and American households and rejecting adaptation to American ways of life. "American values," wrote one respondent, "do not always fit comfortably into the patterns of Indian homes. . . . What disturbed [S.S.] . . .about Indian women may not be disturbing to the Indian women."[17] Defending Indian men's lack of participation in domestic chores, the writer further stated, "we do not blame them, for they are not accustomed to helping in certain things."[18]

S.S.'s attempts to connect the domestic division of labor with the larger issues of women's liberation and assimilation into American culture did not seem to impress Indian women at all, since those who responded to her revealed a strong disapproval of liberation as well as of American women. Women's liberation emerged in these letters as a negative notion fraught with conceptions of neglected homes and broken marriages, frightening for women who held marriage as sacrosanct. Elaborating on this theme, one letter writer stated: "The situation of the Indian wife with all its shortcomings seems stabler than the intolerable dilemma we might be forced into by choosing to be 'liberated.' How would Indian men accept so-called liberated wives and neglected homes? The risk of finding out seems rather great, for we might lose our husbands."[19] Linking the stability of Indian marriages to their ability to follow the traditional division of work, the author further stated: "If you want to see a happy man and a happy marital life, you may have to make the man happy and leave him the way he wants to be and not try to change him to what you want him to be."[20]

While S.S. was trying to liberate Indian women from domestic tasks, an Indian woman, by drawing attention to the wage differentials between men and women in the U.S. labor force, questioned the very notion that American women were liberated. Furthermore, highlighting the issue of domestic abuse, the writer also pointed to the problems plaguing the liberated American homes. She wrote, "I think it is a piece of misguided (however well intentioned) advice to suggest a stay in the U.S. as a recipe for liberation."[21] Another woman, pointing to the issue of legal rights, informed S.S. that India's Hindu Code gave women legal equality with men whereas in the U.S. the ERA had not passed as yet.[22]

The sole letter that supported S.S.'s viewpoint was from an Indian woman who displayed new expectations from marriage. Marriage, she wrote, was a "participatory relationship" between men and women and, consequently, men and women shared responsibilities in all aspects of life, including onerous domestic chores. Expressing a firm belief that American marriages were egalitarian in nature, she implored Indian men to learn from their American counterparts. "One does not degrade oneself by offering a helping hand," she reminded the Indian men.[23] This writer, however, did not contextualize the need for male participation in domestic work in relation to working women or their problems.

The first kitchen debate clearly became mired in nationalistic tones where Indian values prevailed over U.S. ideals. Indian women and men, with one exception, presented a united front, stating their intent to continue traditional Indian domestic arrangements in the United States and opposing the adoption of U.S. domestic practices. The letters presented a picture that all was well in Indian homes, and S.S's attempts were viewed as interfering and reflecting her own ethnocentric notions and presumed cultural superiority. Consequently, little emerged in this debate about Indian immigrant women's increasing domestic workload or whether, indeed, professional women were performing the work of servants as S.S. had suggested in her letter.

If the first debate upheld Indian cultural values, the second began five years later in 1983 with another letter to the editor from an Indian woman bemoaning the startling changes occurring within Indian families in the United States due to the transgression of traditional Indian male-female roles. In an attempt to stall these revolutionary changes, she wrote to *India Abroad* to remind women of Indian family norms as they applied to the division of work at home. She wrote,

> I am ashamed of people who have changed their lifestyle after coming to the United States. Back in India I used to see wives worshipping their husbands. On the other hand I see housewives and those who are working make their husbands do cooking, cleaning and looking after the children. I would rather commit suicide than ask my husband to change my own kids' diaper. Sometimes the wives work and help their student-husbands pay tuition fees. The husbands no longer remain husbands because of this. They go down in esteem and when they have to do housework, they resent it.
>
> If the husband wants to work it is fine, but the wives should not ask them to help them. After all, I do not think ladies should forget their own culture.[24]

In stark contrast to the 1978 exchanges, this letter suggested that a rapid change was occurring within Indian homes. Migration had altered traditional notions of male-female identities within marriage, resulting in the ability of men in some families, especially student families, to be the sole economic providers, allowing women to be the domestic caretakers.[25] Economic marginalization, the erosion of the male's role as economic provider in the U.S., and the subsequent participation of women in the work force to support their family were instrumental in blurring male-female identities. Consequently, new domestic arrangements were emerging within dual-income families where women were seeking paid work to support their family economy and were seeking male help in daily domestic tasks. These changes, the author suggested, were accompanied by increasing domestic tensions within Indian homes.

Although this letter was in the same vein as were the vast majority of letters written in 1978 and advocated the continuation of traditional family roles between men and women in the United States, women's responses to this letter were startlingly different and pointed to changing expectations. Women now expected men to share the domestic tasks, and they provided their rationale for their viewpoints.[26] For the first time, working women documented a considerable increase in their domestic workload since their migration and revealed their problems in attempting to juggle paid work and domestic responsibilities. They also confessed living a life in which they were continually tired. "A lot of us combine two jobs, one outside the home and one inside. . . . Perpetual exhaustion was not asked for by any woman who married a man and went abroad," stated one writer.[27] "A wife's job is never done," wrote another.[28] In addition to carrying on their traditional domestic responsibilities, women also noted the additional responsibilities of outdoor work like mowing the lawn and gardening, which in India were considered male tasks. Furthermore, pointing to the blurring of public and private responsibilities, another letter writer asked: "How many women take the responsibility of grocery and other shopping by driving around in India as they do here . . . ?"[29] Letters particularly complained of the absence of hired and family help. "After all we do not have servants at our beck and call as our sisters do in India," wrote one woman.[30] "There are no servants, and there are no relatives to help," noted another.[31] In view of their escalating domestic work, women expressed a desire for their husbands' assistance in order to ease their domestic responsibilities. The arguments they put forth can be divided into four categories.

The first argument that justified male participation in domestic work viewed men as taking over some domestic responsibility to make up for the absence of domestic servants. "A working woman gets home tired after a hard day's work as much as the husband does. It will be cruel on the part of the husband to relax and watch television when she starts cooking, feeding the children and cleaning up—without any help from anyone," wrote one woman.[32] While agreeing with the initiator of this debate that domestic tensions within Indian immigrant families were on the rise, women unequivocally rejected her claim that male participation in household work caused marital problems. One letter writer suggested that, on the contrary, it was women's increasing domestic work that contributed to increasing family stress and that, consequently, male help in household tasks would alleviate such tensions within families. "Cooperation," argued one reader, "strengthens marriages."[33] The writer further stated: "A marriage is not so fragile that it results in divorce merely because the male partner takes out the garbage or cooks a meal."[34] Demonstrating awareness that their solution went against Indian cultural norms, women justified their request by extolling the principle of the dignity of work.

The second argument came from a woman who claimed to be modern and progressive and had new expectations for marriage. Marriage, according to her, was as an institution "based on concepts of equality," and she expected partnership from her spouse in all spheres of family life, including onerous domestic tasks.[35] These companionate marriages, the author argued, brought a closer relationship between husbands and wives and resulted in happy marriages, unlike the traditional Indian marriages that, she argued, were akin to a slave-master relationship. To support her point, she referred to studies and surveys.[36] Given the fact that the majority of Indian marriages were arranged and based on a relationship where men wielded more power, these companionate marriages and the close relationship they entailed between husbands and wives emerged as an important argument justifying male work at home. It should be stated that the notion of companionate marriages was within the framework of changing expectations among women in India and was not related to the adoption of U.S. practices.

The transformation in the traditional norms of marriages as a consequence of migration became the basis for the third argument. Migration, a letter writer argued, had altered certain sacrosanct canons of Indian marriages. "Traditionally," wrote a reader, "an Indian woman married for economic security and a tacit understanding that she would raise the family and do the household work."[37] In the U.S., however, she noted, these time-honored practices were changing, and in some families women were emerging as the primary economic providers of their families. She wrote, "I have noticed that a good number of Indian immigrants [mostly men] go to India and marry physicians just to protect themselves from possible future unemployment."[38]

The author was referring to the complex interaction of gender, work, and the particularities of Indian migration, whereby a disproportionate number of female physicians were migrating through arranged marriages.[39] Given the high earnings commanded by physicians in the United States, these marriages resulted in economic role reversals, with women becoming the primary economic providers for their families. The writer put forth the notion that economic role reversals justified domestic role reversals. She wrote that "in cases like this, can one blame the wives if they make demands on their husbands? . . . It is time to redefine marriage and its obligations, if we want this trend to be reversed."[40] While this letter alluded to families where women were the primary breadwinners, it did not state whether similar role transformations should occur in marriages where women were working but were not the primary breadwinners.

The fourth and final argument for change was rooted in the need for Indian immigrants to instill new values in their children. As the Indian settlement became permanent, women argued that domestic practices within Indian families needed to change for the sake of their children. This was a revolutionary argument, since it signified a clear break from Indian family traditions and underscored women's unwillingness to reproduce cultural values as they related to male and female identities within Indian homes. Women did not expect their daughters to be solely responsible for domestic concerns; they also wanted their sons to be trained in household chores. Therefore, they wanted the fathers to work at home and set examples for their children. "We try to instill the best of both cultures in our children, and we hope they will learn from examples set by their parents and choose the right path," wrote a woman.[41] This ideology was also shaped by class expectations. Indian families expected their children, sons as well as daughters, to be educated and professionals. Along with women, a fourteen-year-old girl joined the forum and threatened not to marry an Indian man if he did not help with her professional aims: "Even though I am only 14, I have big career plans for the future. And if that means not marrying an Indian chauvinist, I am willing to sacrifice that with no regrets at all."[42]

The letters of 1983, unlike those of 1978, clearly demonstrated migration's ill effects on working women. Migration selectivity had resulted in a presence of a disproportionate number of highly educated and professional Indian men as well as women in the United States. Moreover, the exigencies of migration, coupled with the desire of many to attain middle-class status, also resulted in Indian women's entry into the paid world, resulting in a large pool of Indian immigrant working women in the U.S. In presenting their problems, these women were also exhibiting their class consciousness and their loss of class privileges. Migration had removed these working women's class privileges, and in the U.S. they had the added responsibility of performing servants' work as part of their wifely duties in addition to their new tasks acquired in the U.S., such as yard work, grocery shopping, and driving children around for their various activities. Facing downward mobility, these women were asking for a redistribution of domestic work to maintain their class position, even if it entailed changing age-old Indian traditions. These letters contextualized Indian women's domestic problems within the daily realities of Indian immigrant women's lives and were bereft of notions of assimilation, liberation, and becoming American.

Although these letters reflected for the first time a strong desire among working women for change in domestic arrangements, they also revealed that little real change had occurred in Indian homes in the U.S.. The maximum change noted was an understanding by men of women's plight, without an accompanying change in men's domestic roles. A woman wrote that "even though my husband does not know cooking, he sends out for pizza, and even though he hates cleaning, he will do it off and on."[43] Cooking remained woman's prerogative; men who cared resorted to ordering takeout.

The slow pace of change in the redistribution of work at home resulted in yet another letter in 1988 drawing attention once again to the double bind facing Indian working women in the U.S. Titled "Super Woman Balances Career, Family," the letter, for the first time, characterized the Indian immigrant woman as a "super woman" and located immigrant women's problems to India and its cultural norms.[44] The author pointed to contradictions between contemporary women's lives and their historical representation. Despite the reverence accorded to strong Indian women in Indian mythology and history, women in modern India were expected to be subservient and identified primarily in their roles as wives and daughters. Consequently, educated, middle-class, working women in India, whose numbers were rapidly increasing, faced an identity crisis since their labor force participation in India occurred without redefining women's traditional household responsibilities, and their identity remained rooted in their domestic roles.

This contradiction between women's traditional domestic roles and their new realities as working women, the author argued, migrated to the United States and became the root cause of Indian immigrant women's problems. Women's labor force participation in the U.S. increased without any corresponding relief from their increased domestic responsibilities. Rather than addressing women's problems, the author argued, migration added new responsibilities for women, especially of reproducing Indian cultural traditions. This additional responsibility, the author continued, put pressure on women to follow the traditional separation of roles between men and women, although there were differences in the ways it affected professional and nonprofessional working women. Professional women were expected to demonstrate that having a successful career had not "turned their heads" and that they were prepared to meet the demands of the family, just like the traditional wife in India, despite the absence of hired help in the U.S. Women who were working at low-paying jobs faced a different kind of pressure; their jobs were seen as secondary to their household responsibilities as well as to their spouses' work. "The husband reaches the conclusion that because the work she does is not important, she is not subject to the same fatigue and tensions that he is. Hence, she ought to be able to juggle her household chores and her career with ease," wrote the author.[45] This letter writer not only wanted changes in the domestic division of work but also wanted women to have a say in family financial matters, an area that was traditionally a male preserve.[46]

The letters of 1988 by and large followed the rationale established by women in 1983, especially women's lack of expectations that the traditional separation of spheres between men and women would continue in their children's lives. A woman wrote,

> One had to consider what kinds of examples are being set for kids. Those who are being raised in a home where Mom and Dad are equally comfortable in doing any task, domestic or financial, will face less hang-ups in the future. They will have fewer stereotypes to deal with. They will know that there is nothing wrong in Dad changing a diaper and cleaning house, or Mom working and mowing the lawn.[47]

While discussing concrete ways to alleviate women's problems, one letter revealed a major attitudinal shift and a move away from Indian traditions in some women. For the first time, a writer reproached Indian women, arguing that women's problems were of their own making because of their inability to make choices between their work and domestic responsibilities. First, she asked women to stop trying to recreate their mothers' homes, which, she stated, were based on an array of hired help ranging from "maid, dhobi, cook, and at times a gardener."[48] Second, she asked women to stop feeling guilty if they wanted to give precedence to their paid work, relegating their household responsibilities to a secondary concern. In addition, the author also asked Indian women to emulate American women's example: "When American women entered the workforce certain changes followed. Instead of cooking women bought food. In my opinion there is nothing wrong in using this as a model."[49]

This new rationale for change suggested that the professional nature of women's work allowed women a considerable reduction in their domestic burdens. Comparing women's work to men's work, a writer stated that women held responsible jobs, which "demand[ed] their time, energy, and physical and mental effort."[50] Giving precedence to her paid work, she advocated reducing women's cooking responsibilities as a way of alleviating women's problems. Complaining that even "westernized Indian men," a term used to denote cosmopolitan Indian men, remained Indian when it came to food habits, she asked those men either to participate in domestic work or to change their food habits and lower their expectations from women with regards to cooking.[51] Another writer, seeking new alternatives that were suited for the Indian immigrant families in the U.S., recommended that Indian women forget about the way homes were run in India. "The only way to do this is to forget what used to be the way of things back home," she wrote.[52]

The final debate started in 1991 after a male reader commented on the blissful state of Indian wives in the U.S. He wrote: "The Indian wife in America, I think, is perhaps the luckier of the human species. Thanks to the miracle of microwave and other modern gadgets, her household chores are done with alacrity."[53] Along with the benefits of modern gadgetry ubiquitous in American homes, the author also pointed to Indian immigrant husbands' transformation in the U.S. into "genial husbands" who shared domestic burdens with their wives. Describing men's work, he wrote: "In most households, he is the one who does the income tax or talks to the broker about family finances or pays all the monthly bills or keeps the car running or mows the lawn or calls the plumber or takes the children to the baseball game."[54]

Disputing the contention that modern gadgets either eased their domestic responsibilities or reduced the time spent on it, a woman wrote: "Believe me it has not been easy trying to perform well in everything one wants to do, even with modern gadgets and microwave ovens."[55] Household gadgets, noted another writer, were a necessity and not a luxury, as men generally believed.[56] Documenting the time spent on domestic chores, a writer noted: "In an average week we put in 35–40 hours in the office, 10–15 hours behind the wheel commuting, running errands, shopping and taking the children to school, and 20–25 hours cooking, cleaning, washing clothes and running the household."[57] In addition to these daily chores, the writer also documented women's additional responsibilities in the United States, especially those relating to running ethnic and community institutions. She stated, "We are the ones who play a major role in child rearing and many social and community functions and give emotional support and under-standing to our loved ones."[58] Referring to other additional responsibilities, especially those related to child rearing in the U.S., another woman wrote, "Indeed with easy access to cars, the burden of grocery shopping and rushing back from work to bring home an ailing child from the day-care, attending PTA meetings rests on the wife's shoulders. . . . The workload of the 'genial' husbands," she wrote, consists of "playing the chauffer for the family, meeting occasional plumbing needs or filing the income tax once a year," for which he prides himself.[59] Although agreeing that Indian husbands in the U.S. worked more in their homes than did their counter-parts in India, she stated that it was usually at the insistence of the wife, given Indian men's penchant for watching football on TV and "leaving the wife to tackle the much heavier domestic ball."[60] Furthermore, the author derided the initiator of this debate for comparing men's occasional or annual domestic tasks to women's daily household responsibilities. "But it is the wife who wakes at the crack of dawn, prepares the family breakfast, feeds the children and readies them for school, and helps her husband to find his tie—all while getting herself organized and ready for a long day ahead," she noted.[61]

Although a large majority of letters by women discussed ways to allevi-ate their condition and cautiously sought new domestic arrangements, this debate brought forth a new argument. A writer argued that women had the power to change their lives, giving individual woman the agency to override cultural traditions. Stating that women and not culture dictated women's responsibilities, she asked women to take action and demand change. The author also criticized women writers who were creating an impression that Indian woman "will have to carry the heavy burden of raising children and household chores."[62] She wrote that "we women play a big part in making our destinies. It is not karma that makes our marriage what it is. If working women do not expect and extract more from the men they are married to (or plan to marry), they will end up with . . . [a] 'genial husband.'"[63] Showing signs of change in her marriage, this writer documented her husband's work, stating that it ranged from "child-care responsibilities, grocery shopping, mopping and vacuuming the floor to picking up the child from day-care, to little expectation from his wife in terms of cooking; he did not have a problem ordering pizza."[64]

It was within this context—women demanding changes in domestic arrangements—that Ms. Subbi Mathur wrote the letter titled "Couch potatoes and Super-women" in 1991. Her letter reiterated the old theme of Indian women's increasing workload in the United States. Her description of Indian men as lazy and helpless, dependent upon their wives, was somewhat new. It demonstrated that a segment of Indian women had given up hopes of changing their husbands' behavior. Her letter, however, also implied that the emergence of the super-women phenomenon was a way for women to deal with their daily realities and an indicator that Indian women continued to follow traditional Indian ways, taking care of domestic chores along with the new responsibilities that befell them. It also suggested that women had given up on their men and reconciled themselves with the idea of taking complete household responsibility.

MEN'S PERSPECTIVES

Along with women, men also actively participated in these domestic debates. In fact, in the earlier forums, men wrote more frequently than women. However, with each forum, the increase in women's participation was accompanied by a marked decrease in male letter writing. The men, with one exception, wanted the continuation of the domestic arrangements that prevailed in India.

In the first debate, spurred by S.S.'s letter, men and women were united in opposing her plans of liberating Indian women. Voicing sentiments similar to Indian women, a letter by a male writer stated: "Indian women do not care about Women's lib, but about the happiness and oneness of the family."[65] Another man, redefining liberation as rooted in Indian women's domestic roles, argued that Indian women were liberated. The Indian family system, he wrote, might seem male dominated to an outsider; in reality, women wielded real power within their homes. He wrote that "it is really the Indian woman who is the guiding force behind her family. She pulls and manipulates the strings and reins of social customs, home finances, and the destiny of the entire family. . . . Indian women may seem subservient and submissive but in reality they are the uncrowned captains of the family ship."[66] This definition of liberation propagated the continuation of the domestic division of work between men and women as it existed in India.

In subsequent debates, new rationales emerged to support the continuation of traditional domestic arrangements. A writer argued that women's domestic responsibility should continue not for just cultural reasons but for practical ones. Women, after all, were "experts in cooking, cleaning and looking after children."[67] Letters also cited Hindu philosophy to support the traditional separation of family responsibilities. A writer argued that "in the Hindu religion, man and wife are considered two wheels of a cart. Both have to share equal responsibilities and try to live in harmony instead of competing with each other. Let men do their duties of providing financial support and let women do rearing of family. This is our ancient tradition and it has worked for thousands of years."[68] Showing a lack of understanding of the changing world around him in which working women were becoming common, the author of this letter suggested that women's outside work was acceptable as long as it supported the family's economic needs. Becoming career oriented, however, was not acceptable, since it implied competition with their husbands. This letter writer viewed careerism in women as a sign of adapting to American practices and as the root cause of tension. "In order to qualify themselves to earn more wages, Indian women began to compete with their husbands and became career oriented. . . . One has to sacrifice family life, in order to go out and earn money. . . . More family disappointments, more disruption in routine life and more arguments with their husbands. This is a perfect groundwork for broken marriages," he wrote.[69] Male letter writers' continued support of traditional ideologies revealed that working women were seen as an anathema. Their letters also revealed a disconnection between the new reality of professional and working Indian women within the Indian community and their Indian ideologies.

There was, however, one exception to this male discourse. A male writer taking umbrage at women's complaints noted that men were increasingly beginning to share in domestic chores. Agreeing with women that "the extent of work required in a home is much greater in the U.S.," the writer rejected the notion that women, especially professional women, took their domestic responsibility seriously. He wrote: "I would very much like to meet the physician who runs home to cook. I do not know any woman who took cooking seriously. As a matter of fact, I admire the man who can manage to make her do that. I am personally sick and tired of eating pizza, Chinese food and spaghetti and meatballs. I look forward to the summer when I can barbecue."[70] He also disagreed with the characterization of men as chauvinists and sexists or the view that men did not work at home. He wrote: "Of all the people I know, no man, repeat, no man sits down and watches the tube while the wife is breaking her back over the stove."[71] His letter documented his extensive responsibilities at home:

> Painting, repairing appliances, gardening, lawn-mowing, snow-shoveling, fall-cleanup; car repairs and maintenance; swimming pool service; bathe kids and put to bed; read to kids and help with homework; take kids to sitter and doctor; stay home when kids are sick; clean up after dinner; serve when we have company and clean up; iron shirts and vacuum. The men I know do similar amount of work, some do grocery and laundry but not some of the above chores. I always joke, "A man's work is never done."[72]

This letter revealed that male domestic responsibilities, as with women's, increased in the United States with regard to tasks that had been completed by hired help in India, or in regard to tasks that were particular to American homes, such as snow shoveling, fall cleanup, and swimming pool service. Interestingly, the letter showcased the fact that this change was occurring within the homes of professionals and that some Indian women preferred their work and were relegating their domestic responsibilities, especially the onerous task of cooking, to a secondary status. The rapid blurring of male and female roles occurring at least within some families of professionals was further revealed when the writer expressed a desire for women to share responsibilities in areas that were traditionally the male preserve, especially financial matters. He complained that "in spite of all the MBA's, work experience and decision-making, I have not met any who will take responsibility of making and tracking investments. They will not invest the family money in the market, certificates of deposits, mutual funds or other instruments. They just want the freedom to have the credit cards to go shopping with and not worry where the money is coming from."[73]

This letter was extraordinary because it revealed some women's movement away from their conventional domestic responsibilities. These professional women were according primacy to their paid work. It is not clear how representative this family was among Indian immigrants, since this letter did not generate any response from the readers of *India Abroad*.

GENDER, MIGRATION, AND CHANGING IDENTITIES

These letters, in detailing women's problems, document the growing realization among women that Indian gendered norms as they applied to domestic tasks were not feasible in the United States. In tracing the emerging discourse on housework, these letters inform us about the larger issue of recreating Indian gendered identities in the U.S. The early letters high-lighted women's increasing household responsibilities since migration and emphasized the loss of class privileges as a result of the absence of domestic help in the U.S., a fact noted by various studies on Indian immigrants.[74] Moreover, the letters documented women's additional domestic responsi-bilities after migration. Child care now incorporated driving children to various extracurricular activities and domestic tasks also now incorporated yard work and grocery shopping. In addition, Indian immigrants' attempts to maintain the Indian way of life in the U.S., along with the emergence of home as the bastion of resistance against the dominant culture, meant that women had new responsibilities as cultural reproducers.[75] Furthermore, new community responsibilities of maintaining and sustaining Indian ethnic and religious institutions also fell on women.[76] Finally, works on Indian immigrants accentuate a new development occurring within the Indian com-munity that adversely affected women. In trying to carve out a homogenous Indian identity, Indian institutions, especially religious institutions, began redefining women's identities in traditional restrictive terms as housewives and as family caretakers who subsumed their individual identity for the greater good of the family.[77] This new representation of women's iden-tities was particularly disturbing for working women, since it created a deep disconnect between their lived realities and the emerging gendered expectations.

It is within this larger context of Indian settlement that women's attempts to recreate new gendered identities need to be analyzed. The propagation of principles of shared domestic responsibilities reflected a desire of Indian women to move away from traditional identities as wives and as mothers and to carve out new dual identities as wives and as workers, a phenomenon that had not emerged in India with middle-class women's entry into the labor force.[78] Consequently, women's entry into the work world did not increase male contributions to domestic tasks in India.[79] Migration selectivity and the presence of disproportionate numbers of young professional women who demonstrated more affinity toward their careers than their domestic work were central factors in this emerging discourse, since these women com-pared their employment with men and concluded that their jobs demanded as much attention as did men's work. *Man day's work* and *responsible jobs* were some of the terms used in the letters to signify the nature of their work. They represented a new type of Indian women, who—although they were termed derogatorily as "careerists" in one letter—took pride in their work and did not assign negative connotations to "careerism." While not questioning their household responsibilities, they wanted a balance between their work and their family identities without feeling guilty about neglecting some of their domestic responsibilities.

The transformation of the domestic division of work, Nazli Kibria argues, is based upon the balance of power between men and women and their access to resources.[80] Parminder Bhachu's work on Indian immigrant women in Great Britain points to independent women's transformative power.[81] While the extent of support among women for change, the details of women's economic contributions to their families, and the economic role of the men are unknown, what is evident is that professional women started a new discourse on the need for change within families. The professional nature of their work in the United States became a central factor in their argument for transformation. Not keen on taking on the multiple domestic responsibilities that were coming their way, they exhorted women not to be passive victims nor to blame their karma for their situation but, instead, to establish their own cultural norms suited to their needs rather than be held hostage by the dictates of Indian culture. While professional women were at the forefront in seeking these changes and their letters were the most vocal in demanding that the allocation of domestic work be based on revised premises, it should be noted that the consequences of their efforts would surely have trickled down to all Indian families.

However, the letters also demonstrate a diversity of attitudes among women and some women's resistance to change. The letter writers to *India Abroad* can be classified into three categories: the traditionalists, the pragmatists, and the modernists. The traditionalists accepted the prevalent male and female identities and were highly uncomfortable with changes occurring within Indian immigrant families. Studies indicate that this group even included professional women, who gave up their professions after migration and became transitional workers in order to take care of their family, in particular to take on child-rearing responsibilities.[82] These studies also note women's ambivalent attitudes towards these changes, documenting their unhappiness over having to give up their work or having accorded primacy to their spouses' work. The second group, the pragmatists, wanted a middle ground and were strategizing ways to reconcile their working and domestic identities, necessitated by their inability to perform both roles to the best of their abilities. While hesitant to completely overhaul the domestic division of labor, they seemed unwilling to let their daughters carry similar domestic burdens. The third group constituted the modern, progressive women, primarily professional, who demonstrated new egalitarian expectations of companionate marriages and openly rejected the notion that women were responsible for domestic tasks. Their identity, as it was shaped in India, was not solely in domestic terms.[83]

Three factors clearly indicate progressive women's aspirations for permanent change. First, mothers did not want to reproduce for their daughters those Indian cultural norms that pertained to domestic responsibilities. In fact, women's first rationale for men to participate in household tasks was so that the men would become a role model for their children and teach their sons that men also worked at home. Studies of Indian immigrants, however, paint a complex picture regarding this matter. While a large majority of the studies contend that Indian women were reproducing Indian cultural identity in their daughters, it should be noted that the retention of Indian cultural traditions was in relation and opposition to dominant American cultural practices regarding sexuality; the women were attempting to control daughters' sexuality, given Indian families' opposition to dating and premarital sex.[84]

Indian families, as Jean Bacon's study has highlighted, were not homogenous; individual family dynamics, the sacrosanct values of a given family and their notion of Indian identity to be transmitted to the second generation, varied considerably across families.[85] Moreover, studies also document that while mothers were inculcating messages of cultural normativity and appropriate gender behavior, they were also encouraging their daughters to become professionals, were training their children in new gender ideology, bent family rules for their daughters, encouraged them to be economically independent, and essentially wished better lives and more egalitarian relationships for their daughters than they had experienced in their own family relationships.[86] Sangeeta Gupta has noted the complexity of mothers' attempts to socialize their daughters. She stated that daughters received implicit and explicit messages from mothers about Indian culture, allowing the daughters to negotiate their own beliefs and behavior reflecting their gender and cultural identities. Studies of second-generation Indian women also point out that these women were redefining gender boundaries and creating their own understanding of what it meant to be Indian by reconciling their cultural norms with their lived realities. In family relationships these young women expected equality and expected men to equally share domestic tasks; Gupta, however, noted that male expectations were not as quick to change.[87]

The second argument which suggests that women wanted permanent change is based on the fact that women seemed dissatisfied even with "genial" husbands who claimed that they shared in domestic tasks but who did not do an equal share. Pointing to the inequity of prevalent work distribution, the women expressed wishes for a more equitable division of work.[88] A case in point was the narrative of a stay-at-home mother whose unhappiness with her husband's domestic contribution was clear in her statement, "I don't want to be grateful for the crumbs."[89]

Third, the very public nature of the debate is a firm indicator of women's desire to transform gender identities within the Indian community. The success of family struggle, Nazli Kibria argues, is dependent upon its visibility, and the discussions in *India Abroad* provided women's cause a visibility. Women seemingly devised a two-pronged strategy: to initiate changes at home within their individual families, and also to discuss the issue in the Indian community at large through the pages of *India Abroad*. Narratives of individual successes and personal alternatives provided others with options and strategies to employ within their own homes; documentation of changes in the immigrant newspaper also emerged as a way to legitimize individual gains.

These letters also showcase the centrality of *India Abroad* in mediating women's concerns. Its "Opinion/Letters to the Editor" page (formerly "Letters to the Editor" page) provided Indian men and women a space to voice their concerns. By taking their personal struggles to public spaces, women not only changed the discourse within the Indian community but also in *India Abroad*, which, until then, had ignored women's issues.[90] *India Abroad* essentially became a place where women organized domestic resistance. Although Madhulika Khandelwal has pointed out that in New York City, with one of the largest concentrations of Indian immigrant population in the United States, public discussions on women's concerns were beginning to take place, for the majority of Indian women, living in the isolation of their homes, the immigrant newspaper was the only avenue for discussion and provided a forum where strangers from across the country bonded through letters.[91] Letters generated support groups, creating a community of women united by their common concerns.

The issue of housework, although begun as an issue of assimilation, was in no way related to women's desire to adapt to American cultural practices or to assimilate into mainstream American society. These letters clearly documented Indian women's negative views on liberation as well as of American women. Moreover, the language of the letters was bereft of the language of feminist discourse; women used language and means that were within their cultural context. Letters were rarely confrontational. They cajoled, respectfully asked, slowly prodded, and even pleaded with men to understand their plight; only later did they demand.[92] Although women were not using the language of feminism, they were displaying the behavior of liberated women and a common understanding of their situation.

India Abroad, while it provided women space to voice their concerns, also wielded editorial power in selecting letters or curtailing these debates. Current events further limited readers' input in matters of importance to the community. A case in point was the abrupt ending of the "couch potatoes" debate soon after the publication of Ms. Mathur's letter. The political turmoil in India as a result of the assassination of the then Prime Minister Rajiv Gandhi completely transformed the content of the newspaper and its letters for months to come. Despite such limitations, these letters clearly indicate that a section of Indian women was unwilling to perpetuate their domestic responsibilities as defined by Indian gendered norms, and that they were collectively taking new steps to define a new identity for Indian women. These letters also indicate that becoming a "super-woman" was a forced phenomenon and an unwelcome development that women were beginning to resist. Women's attempts to transform "couch potatoes" into working men at home indicated ideological changes, new relationships between men and women, and a new Indian domestic culture that was more egalitarian. How successful they were in effectuating these new domestic ideologies within their homes and those of their children remains to be explored. What is important is that Indian immigrant women were attempting to carve out new identities as Indian women in America, individually and collectively.

> We learned,
> in this country, to stand straighter,
> speak up for what we want.
> And what we want is this: for us and our daughters,
> India *and* America,
> the best of both together[93]

NOTES

I would like to thank Rob Buffington, Eithne Luibhéid, Tim Messer-Kruse, Leslie Moch, Susana Peña, and the two anonymous readers for their helpful comments. In addition, I would like to thank the members of the "Sexuality and Border" writing cluster of the Institute for the Study of Culture and Society at Bowling Green State University.

1. Ms. Subbi Mathur, "Couch Potatoes and Super-Women," *India Abroad*, April 26, 1991, 3.
2. Ibid.

3. Numerous studies have focused on tensions within immigrant families that occur after migration. Some of these are Maria Patricia Fernandez-Kelly and Anna Garcia, "Power Surrendered, Power Restored: The Politics of Home and Work among Hispanic Women in Southern California," in *Women in Politics in America*, ed. Louise Tilly and Patricia Guerin (New York, 1991), 130–49; Evelyn Nakano Glenn, *Issei, Nissei, War Bride: Three Generations of Japanese American Women in Domestic Service* (Philadelphia, 1986); Sherri Grasmuck and Patricia Pessar, *Between Two Islands: Dominican International Migration* (Berkeley, CA, 1991); Pierette Hondagneu-Sotelo, *Gendered Transitions: The Mexican Experience of Immigration* (Berkeley, CA, 1994); Nazli Kibria, *Family Tightropes: The Changing Lives of Vietnamese Americans* (Princeton, NJ, 1993); and Pierette Hondagneu–Sotelo, ed., *Gender and U.S. Immigration: Contemporary Trends* (Berkeley, CA, 2003).

4. Nancy Foner, "The Immigrant Family: Cultural Legacies and Cultural Changes," *International Migration Review* 31, no. 4 (Winter 1997): 961–74.

5. Ibid., 961–74.

6. Hondagneu-Sotelo, *Gendered Transitions*.

7. Kibria, *Family Tightropes*, 112–21.

8. Ibid., 108–43.

9. *Census of Population: General Social and Economic Characteristics* (Washington, DC, 1980), T-79; *Census of Population: General Social and Economic Characteristics* (Washington, DC, 1990), T-105.

10. *Census of Population: General Social and Economic Characteristics* (Washington, DC, 1980), T-163.

11. *Census of Population: General Social and Economic Characteristics* (Washington, DC, 1990), T-110.

12. See Madhulika Khandelwal, *Becoming American, Being Indian: An Indian Immigrant Community in New York City* (Ithaca, NY, 2002); Prema Kurien, "Gendered Ethnicity: Creating a Hindu Indian Identity in the United States," in *Gender and U.S. Immigration*, ed., Hondagneu-Sotelo, 151–73; Prema Kurien, *Kaleidoscopic Ethnicity: International Migration and the Reconstruction of Community Identities in India.* (New Brunswick, NJ, 2002); Padma Rangaswamy, *Namasté America: Indian Immigrants in an American Metropolis* (University Park, PA, 2000); Sheba George, *When Women Come First: Gender and Class in Transnational Migration* (Berkeley, CA, 2005); Aparna Rayaprol, *Negotiating Identities: Women in the Indian Diaspora* (Delhi, India,1997); and Arpana Sircar, *Work Roles, Gender Roles, and Asian Indian Immigrant Women in the United States* (Lewiston, NY, 2000). The majority of these works, however, do not explore the factors that motivated these changes. Consequently, it appears that changes within Indian families occurred as a natural progression without any accompanying tensions.

13. George, *When Women Come First*, 77–117.

14. Ibid., 19–38.

15. S.S., "Disgusting," *India Abroad*, February 10, 1978, 10.

16. In a period of three months, seventeen people responded to S.S.'s letter. These included four women, nine men, and four persons who chose to remain anonymous by signing their letters with initials.

17. Mrs. A. Q. Hoque, "Indian Wives," *India Abroad*, March 17, 1978, 10.

18. Ibid.

19. Ibid.

20. Ibid., 14.

21. Meera Mitra, "Indian Wives," *India Abroad*, March 17, 1978, 14.

22. Shailaja Kambli, "Indian Wives," *India Abroad*, March 25, 1978, 14.

23. S.T., "Indian Wives," *India Abroad*, March 17, 1978, 14.

24. Kumari Kalpana R. Jhakur, *India Abroad*, December 2, 1983, Life & Leisure section, iv.

25. During the decades of the 1970s and the 1980s, there were a considerable number of Indian students in the U.S. According to *Open Doors: Report on International Educational Exchange* (New York, 1975), in the academic year 1974–75, there were 9,660 students from India in the U.S.; a decade later, the number was 14,610.

26. Eight people responded to this letter and, in contrast to the first debate, six were written by women.

27. U. Radhakant, "Not So Fragile," *India Abroad*, December 22, 1983, Life & Leisure section, iv.

28. Sundari Ramachandran, "Cooperation the Key," *India Abroad*, December 22, 1983, Life & Leisure section, iv.

29. U. Radhakant, "Not So Fragile."

30. Ibid.

31. Raj Prasad, "Family Link Enhanced," *India Abroad*, January 27, 1984, Life & Leisure section, iv.

32. Sundari Ramachandran, "Cooperation the Key."

33. U. Radhakant, "Not So Fragile."

34. Ibid.

35. Pooja Mahajan, "On Team Spirit," *India Abroad*, December 22, 1983, Life & Leisure section, iv.

36. Ibid.

37. Sarojini Reddi, "Blame the Men," *India Abroad*, December 22, 1983, Life & Leisure section, iv.

38. Ibid.

39. Occupations are gendered. According to Joanna Liddle and Rama Joshi, *Daughters of Independence: Gender, Caste, and Class in India* (London, 1986), 72–73, in independent India, the medical profession, along with teaching and social work, were considered suitable professions for women, resulting in many middle-class women becoming physicians. Many of these female medical professionals migrated to the United States through arranged marriages.

40. Sarojini Reddi, "Blame the Men."

41. U. Radhakant, "Not So Fragile."

42. Ina Hathi, "Help the Women."

43. U. Radhakant, "Not So Fragile."

44. Farhat Biviji, "Superwoman Balances Career, Family," *India Abroad*, January 22, 1988, 3.

45. Ibid.

46. Ibid.

47. Latha Kumar, "Choices, Not Clichés," *India Abroad*, March 4, 1988, 3.

48. Sunita Saxena, "Choices for Working Indian Women," *India Abroad*, February 26, 1988, 3.

49. Ibid.

50. Sharmila Nambiar, "A Wife's View on Wifehood," *India Abroad*, March 15, 1988, 3.

51. Ibid.

52. Ammini Murthy, "Working Couples Can Play Fair and without Conflict," *India Abroad*, March 15, 1988, 3.

53. P. Ramanathan, "A Husband's View of Wifehood," *India Abroad*, January 11, 1991, 3.

54. Ibid.

55. Ammini Murthy, "Working Couples," 3.

56. Sharmila Nambiar, "A Wife's View," 3.

57. Ammini Murthy, "Working Couples," 3. A study by Krishnendu Ray, "Meals, Migration, and Modernity: Domestic Cooking and Bengali Indian Ethnicity in the United States," *Amerasia Journal* 21, no. 1 (1988): 105–27, is the only work that I have come across which offers insights into the Indian immigrant—or, to be more specific—the Bengali immigrant kitchen, its foods, and the ways food habits were changing as a result of migration.

58. Ammini Murthy, "Working Couples," 3.

59. Sharmila Nambiar, "A Wife's View," 3.

60. Ibid.

61. Ibid.

62. Marita Gonzalves, "Men Who Share the Chores," *India Abroad*, May 3, 1991, 3.

63. Ibid.

64. Ibid.

65. Jayant Shah, "Indian Wives," *India Abroad*, March 17, 1978, 14.

66. M. P. Patel, "Indian Wives," *India Abroad*, March 25, 1978, 14.

67. Dharam Jit Jigyasu, "Woman's Place," *India Abroad*, December 22, 1983, Life & Leisure section, iv.

68. G. Modi, "How to Break Up a Marriage," *India Abroad*, February 19, 1988, 3.

69. Ibid.

70. Viresh Sharma, "Who Says Husbands Do No Housework," *India Abroad*, February 19, 1988, 3.

71. Ibid.

72. Ibid.

73. Ibid.

74. Sangeeta R. Gupta, ed., *Emerging Voices: South Asian American Women Redefine Self, Family, and Community* (Walnut Creek, CA, 1999); Khandelwal, *Becoming American, Being Indian;* Johanna Lessinger, *From the Ganges to the Hudson: Indian Immigrants in New York City* (Boston, 1995); Kurien, "Gendered Ethnicity," 151–73; Rangaswamy, *Namasté America*; George, *When Women Come First*; Rayaprol, *Negotiating Identities*; Sircar, *Work Roles, Gender Roles, and Asian Indian Immigrant Women in the United States;* and Sathi S. Dasgupta, *On the Trail of An Uncertain Dream: Indian Immigrant Experience in America* (New York, 1989), all emphasize the absence of domestic help and the substantial increase in women's domestic work.

75. Sonia Shah, "Three Hot Meals and a Full Day at Work: South Asian Women's Labor in the United States," in *A Patchwork Shawl: Chronicles of South Asian Women in America*, ed. Shamita Das Dasgupta (New Brunswick, NJ, 1998), 206–22.

76. See Kurien, "Gendered Ethnicity," 151–73. Maxine P. Fisher, *The Indians of New York City: A Study of Immigrants from India* (Columbia, MO, 1980), 61, 62, and 66 also details

the elaborate meals that were served to hundreds of people at Indian community events, religious, cultural, and social.

77. Shamita Das Dasgupta, "Introduction," in *A Patchwork Shawl,* 1–7; Sayantani Das Gupta and Shamita Das Gupta, "Women in Exile: Gender Relations in the Asian Indian Community in the United States," in *Asian American Studies: A Reader,* ed. Jean Ye-wen and Min Song (New Brunswick, NJ, 2000), 324–37; Anannya Bhatacharjee, "The Habit of Ex-nomination: Nation, Women, and the Indian Bourgeoisie," *Public Culture* 5, no. 2 (Fall 1992): 19–44; Kurien, "Gendered Ethnicity," 151–73; Margaret Abraham, *Speaking the Unspeakable: Marital Violence among South Asian Immigrants in the United States* (New Brunswick, NJ, 2000), 9–15, 19–23.

78. The emergence of middle-class women in the Indian work force was a relatively new phenomenon that became more common after India's independence in 1947. The following works provide insights into the lives of Indian middle-class women after independence: Carol Chapnick Mukhopadhyaya and Susan Seymour, ed., *Women, Education, and Family Structure in India* (Boulder, CO, 1994); Joanna Liddle and Rama Joshi, *Daughters of Independence: Gender, Caste, and Class in India* (London, 1986); Rhoda Lois Blumberg and Leela Dwarki, *India's Educated Women: Options and Constraints* (Delhi, India,1980); and B. R. Nanda, ed., *Indian Women from Purdah to Modernity* (New Delhi, India, 1976).

79. G. N. Ramu, "Indian Husbands: Their Role Perceptions and Performance in Single- and Dual-Earner Families," *Journal of Marriage and the Family* 49, no. 4 (November 1987): 903–15.

80. Kibria, *Family Tightropes,* 22–23.

81. Parminder Bhachu, "Identities Constructed and Reconstructed: Representations of Asian Women in Britain," in *Migrant Women: Crossing Boundaries and Changing Identities,* ed. Gina Buijs (Oxford, 1993), 99–118.

82. Sunil Bhatia, *American Karma: Race, Culture, and Identity in the Indian Diaspora* (New York, 2007), 100–11; Khandelwal, *Becoming American, Being Indian,* 123–34; Arpana Sircar, *Work Roles, Gender Roles, and Asian Indian Immigrant Women in the United States,* 135–48, 215–22; Dasgupta, *On the Trail of an Uncertain Dream,* 131–87.

83. My research on Indian immigrants in metropolitan Detroit indicates that many professional women were encouraged by their families to focus on their professional education; consequently, they did not know how to cook.

84. Sharmila Rudrappa, "Disciplining Desire in Making the Home: Engendering Ethnicity in Indian Immigrant Families," in *The Second Generation: Ethnic Identity among Asian Americans,* ed. Pyong Gap Min (Walnut Creek, CA, 2002), 85–112; Bandana Purkayastha, *Negotiating Ethnicity: Second-Generation South Asian Americans Traverse a Transnational World* (New Brunswick, NJ, 2005), 87–116; Karen Isaksen Leonard, *The South Asian Americans* (Westport, CT, 1997), 145–68; Karen Leonard, "The Management of Desire: Sexuality and Marriage for Young South Asian Women in America," in Gupta, ed., *Emerging Voices,* 107–19.

85. Jean Bacon, *Life Lines: Community, Family, and Assimilation among Asian Indian Immigrants* (New York, 1996).

86. See Purkayastha, *Negotiating Ethnicity,* 87–116; Bacon, *Life Lines,* 75–201. Manisha Roy, "Mothers and Daughters in Indian American Families: A Failed Communication?" in Dasgupta, ed., *A Patchwork Shawl,* 97–110, highlights the pressures Indian parents put on their children to become professionals.

87. Sangeeta R. Gupta, "Walking on the Edge: Indian American Women Speak Out on Dating and Marriage," in Gupta, ed., *Emerging Voices*, 120–45; Diya Kallivayalil, "Gender and Cultural Socialization in Indian Immigrant Families in the United States," *Feminism and Psychology* 14, no. 4 (November 2004): 535–59.

88. Khandelwal, *Becoming American, Being Indian*, 123–34; Anju Jain and Jay Belsky, "Fathering and Acculturation: Immigrant Indian Families with Young Children," *Journal of Marriage and the Family* 59, no. 4 (November 1997): 873–83; Sudha Sethu Balagopal, "The Case of the Brown Memsahib: Issues That Confront Working South Asian Wives and Mothers," in Gupta, ed., *Emerging Voices*, 146–68; Raji Swaminathan, "Relational Worlds: South Asian Immigrant Women Talk about Home/Work," in *Immigrant Women of the Academy: Negotiating Boundaries, Crossing Borders in Higher Education*, ed. Mary V. Alfred and Raji Swaminathan (New York, 2004), 89–104.

89. Balagopal, "The Case of the Brown Memsahib," 146–68.

90. Rashmi Luthra, *Coverage of Women's Issues in the Indian Immigrant Press: A Content Analysis*, Women in International Development Series, Working Paper no. 138 (East Lansing, MI, 1987).

91. Khandelwal, *Becoming American, Being Indian*, 133.

92. Maria Mies, *Indian Women and Patriarchy: Conflicts and Dilemmas of Students and Working Women in India* (New Delhi, India, 1982), argues that Indian women are rarely confrontational; instead, they negotiate delicately within the system.

93. Chitra Banerjee Divarkaruni, "We the Indian Women in America," in *Contours of the Heart: South Asians Map North America*, ed. Sunaina Maira and Rajni Srikanth (New York, 1996), 268–70.

13

Malls of Meaning: Building Asian America in Silicon Valley Suburbia

WILLOW LUNG-AMAM

CALIFORNIA'S SILICON VALLEY OFTEN CALLS to mind a land-scape of white-collar office parks and manicured research campuses filled with young dot-com boomers and self-made millionaires.[1] Much of the writings on this vast suburban region likewise have tended to concentrate on the area as a breeding ground for invention, innovation, and entrepreneurship—home to America's creative class and the pioneers of the digital revolution.[2] This narrative, however, fails to acknowledge the diversity of people and places behind the region's storied image. In a place often measured by the number of start-ups and venture capitalists, the lives of other residents and communities, especially those on the margins, frequently have gone unnoticed.

Addressing this gap, several scholars have offered alternative accounts that spotlight the contributions of and the conditions suffered by women, minorities, immigrants, the poor, and others who have long existed in the Valley's shadows.[3] While not a prominent part of the writings about the region, such stories are not difficult to locate on the ground, as the expansion in information technology has gone hand in glove with vast demographic changes. Over the past half-century, as Silicon Valley's population has swelled to accommodate a booming innovation economy, it also has shifted from majority-white to majority-minority. Asian immigrants have been among the region's largest and fastest-growing groups (see table 1).

Asian immigrants began arriving in Silicon Valley in record numbers after the passage of the historic 1965 Immigration and Naturalization Act, otherwise known as Hart-Celler. The act opened the floodgates to Asian immigration by lifting restrictive quotas from non-European countries and instituting new policies aimed at family reunification and at attracting skilled labor.[4] Chinese from Hong Kong and Taiwan as well as Filipinos were particularly prominent among initial migrants. In the Valley, they later were joined by a rush of political refugees from Indochina, particularly Vietnam, who arrived in several successive waves after the Fall of Saigon in 1975 and throughout the 1990s. By then, the Valley was also welcoming large numbers of skilled immigrants from mainland China and India (see table 2).[5] The region's mild climate, extant Asian American community, and perhaps

Table 1: Santa Clara County Population by Race,* 1970–2010

	1970		1980		1990		2000		2010	
White*	1,003,989	94.3%	1,030,659	79.6%	1,035,029	69.1%	905,660	53.8%	836,616	47%
Asian American	35,237	3.3%	101,922	7.9%	261,574	17.5%	430,095	25.6%	570,524	32.0%
Hispanic	129,010	12.1%	226,288	17.5%	307,113	20.5%	403,401	24.0%	479,210	26.9%
African American	18,090	1.4%	42,835	3.3%	55,365	3.7%	47,182	2.8%	46,428	2.6%
Other	7,489	0.7%	119,655	9.3%	316,243	9.7%	299,648	17.8%	328,074	18.4%
Total	1,193,815		1,521,359		1,975,324		2,085,986		2,260,852	

Source: U.S. Census. *All groups include those of Hispanic origin for comparisons across time.

Table 2: Santa Clara County, Population of Asian Americans by Ethnic Group, 1970–2010

	1970		1980		1990		2000		2010	
Chinese/Taiwanese	7,817	25.1%	22,745	23.7%	65,924	25.8%	115,781	27.1%	152,701	27.0%
Vietnamese	—	—	11,156	11.6%	54,739	21.5%	99,986	23.4%	125,695	22.2%
Filipino	6,728	21.6%	28,229	29.5%	59,963	23.5%	76,060	17.8%	87,412	15.5%
Indian	4,048	13.0%	5,187	5.4%	19,675	7.7%	66,741	15.6%	117,596	20.8%
Other Asian	12,596	40.4%	28,499	29.7%	54,733	21.5%	68,203	16.0%	82,062	14.5%
All Asians	31,189		95,816		255,034		426,711		565,466	

Source: U.S. Census.

most importantly, wealth of new job opportunities for both high- and low-skilled workers made it a favored destination for various Asian migrants in the late twentieth and early twenty-first centuries.

Within only a few decades, the Asian American population boomed around Silicon Valley and within certain neighborhoods and cities in particular. Asian immigration changed many cauliflower fields, orange groves, and

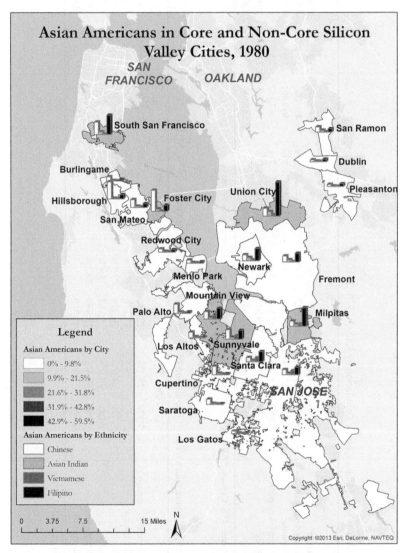

Figure 1: In 1980, Asian Americans could be found in limited numbers throughout many Silicon Valley communities. Image by the author.

predominately white middle-class suburbs into areas with Asian American majorities, and otherwise remapped the social geography of the region (see figs. 1 and 2). And while scholars have begun to take note of Asian Americans' important contributions to the region's economy and culture of innovation,[6] there is yet little research about what this tectonic demographic shift meant in the neighborhoods, on the streets, and in the everyday places of Valley life.

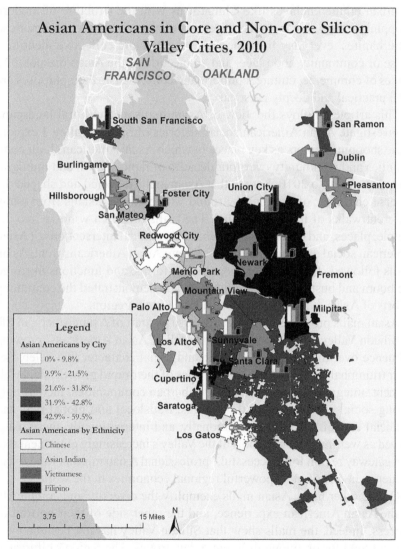

Figure 2: By 2010, Asian Americans were fully embedded in many Silicon Valley municipalities, including several Asian American-majority towns in the region. Image by the author.

This article uses Asian malls[7] as a lens to investigate multiple narratives of Asian American place-making in Silicon Valley. In other centers of Asian American suburban life, scholars have studied these malls' unique spatial qualities, functions, and ownership mechanisms, and their sometimes contentious politics of reception.[8] Elsewhere, I have argued that these malls counter many negative stereotypes and assumptions about suburban shopping malls and their social meanings.[9] By mixing many traditional functions of urban ethnic enclaves like Chinatowns with the structure of modern shopping centers, Asian malls reflect and reinforce many Asian American suburbanites' everyday life practices, personal and collective identities, sense of community and place, and connection to the Asian diaspora. As places of commerce, culture, comfort, and convenience, their purposes are both practical and deeply personal.

This article employs the view of Asian malls as a cultural landscape to investigate Asian American social histories of Silicon Valley. I explore these shopping centers as key places in which Asian Americans built communities and community over four decades of rapid growth and immigration, from 1970 to 2010. I argue that Asian malls reflected and shaped the diverse character of the places around which ethnic Asians from many different walks of life congregated. The malls offered a window into the people, places, and processes that defined the critical intersections of Asian American social and community life. Where Asian Americans went, Asian malls followed. Their diverse geographies, forms, and functions mirrored the boom and bust cycles of immigration and demonstrated the continuing efforts of Asian Americans to make a home in the region.

Asian malls provide a varied and diverse portrait of Asian American life in Silicon Valley. On the one hand, they tell of Asian Americans' growing influence over the region's economic and social character that celebrates their triumphal stories. These include tales of their rapid growth and development, integration within exclusive suburban communities, increasingly strong social and professional networks, translocal and global ties, and financial capital.[10] Regionally, nationally, and internationally, these malls served as well-regarded symbols of the Valley's increasingly prominent role as a gateway region for "successful," professional Asian migrants and Asian influence in one of most powerful regional economies in the world.

On the other hand, Asian malls exemplify the diversity and complexity of the Asian American experience, and the other side of their portrait of success. Indeed, the malls show that Silicon Valley has not been an even playing field for or among different Asian groups. The region's bifurcated labor system has distributed financial capital unevenly across racial and ethnic groups, exacerbating Asian Americans' social and spatial stratification. Asian malls expose the deepening fissures between those within low- and highly skilled groups (especially between Vietnamese and Chinese Americans) and the continued struggles of many to carve out a meaningful place for themselves in this highly dynamic and increasingly competitive region.

The tales of Silicon Valley life that Asian malls present are part of a much broader Asian American suburban story. The work of many suburban scholars has steadily eroded the classic portait of suburbia as the exclusive home of the white middle-class and elites by exposing a diversity of suburban faces, spaces, and experiences.[11] Asian Americans' suburban narratives have been most extensively documented in the literature on "ethnoburbs," a term coined by geographer Wei Li to describe the emergence of multi-ethnic, largely immigrant enclaves on the urban periphery. As Asian Americans have moved to the suburbs at unprecedented rates over the last half-century, scholars have shown ethnoburbs as particularly important spaces for inquiries into the dynamics of their social and political incorporation, racial and ethnic identities, electoral politics, ethnic economies, transnational networks, residential mobility, and assimilation.[12] Existing research focuses particular attention on the political nature of Asian immigration in suburbia, and how Asian Americans have negotiated their new lives in suburbs socially and economically.

This article roots an investigation of Asian Americans' everyday life within particular spaces and places in Silicon Valley. It provides a place- and community-based community perspective on a region of growing scholarly interest. Southern California's San Gabriel Valley has historically been the epicenter of research on ethnoburbs, particularly Monterey Park, which Timothy Fong notably referred to as "America's first suburban Chinatown."[13] And while many of the characteristics of Monterey Park remain salient to Silicon Valley, as Wei Li and Edward Park have pointed out, "techno-ethnoburbs" like the Valley are distinct from other varieties, including the "L.A.-type ethnoburbs."[14] The Valley's high-tech economy has helped to shape the dynamics of Asian American community formation as well as their ethnic economies and development histories. As high-tech suburbs increase in number and geographic range—from Austin, Texas, and Research Triangle Park, North Carolina, to the outskirts of Boston, Phoenix, and Denver—Asian malls poignantly speak to the ways in which newcomers to emerging immigrant destinations are remolding the landscape to reflect their own needs, desires, and dreams.[15]

EAST SAN JOSE'S EMERGENCE
AS A WORKING-CLASS MECCA (1970–1989)

The year 1970 did not mark the beginnings of Asian American community life in the Santa Clara Valley. Rather, it signaled a turning point from Asian Americans' integration in the area's rural economy to their embeddedness within its growing high-tech economy. Forced out of Gold Rush-era mining camps because of anti-Asian sentiments, many Chinese Americans worked alongside Japanese Americans to clear the Valley's chaparrals for farmland and build the San Francisco and San Jose Railroad and the transcontinental railroad in the mid-nineteenth century. Later, these groups mixed with Filipino Americans and other migrant laborers in the salt mines, nurseries, canneries, and packing sheds that were the backbone of the region's thriving agricultural economy, for which it became well known as the "Valley of the Heart's Delight."[16] Up until 1970, when many of the cannery and agricultural jobs dried up, Asian Americans of various nationalities maintained small but viable communities around San Jose's historic Chinatown and Japantown and in various backwater regions, like Alviso near San Jose, where they were able to purchase homes and land.[17]

But by the 1970s, the area was in the midst of a dramatic tranformation, exemplified by its now popular name "Silicon Valley." Facilitated by post-Cold War alliances between industry and university research, Stanford University engineering professor and later provost Frederick E. Terman, the so-called "father of Silicon Valley," pioneered efforts to pair talented university researchers and engineers with the needs of emerging industries to create a "community of technical scholars." Within the region's growing number of white-collar office parks and research campuses, a unique culture of competition, collaboration, and innovation emerged.[18] Between 1960 and 1980, Valley companies broke new ground on some of the most important technological milestones of the modern era—microelectronics, the semiconductor, and the personal computer.

Drawn by new employment opportunities, Asians from around the United States and abroad flocked to the Valley after 1970. Between 1970 and 1990, the Asian American population in Santa Clara County grew from less than four percent to nearly eighteen percent of the total population—a jump of over four hundred percent. Many of these first-wave migrants joined the ranks of the Valley's low-skilled employment sector (see table 3). Within the region's "barbell economy," work was, and continues to be, concentrated at the top and bottom. Jobs in the latter tier required little skill or English

Table 3: Santa Clara County Population of Asian Americans Employed in Technology-related Occupations by Ethnicity, 1970–2010

		Chinese	Japanese	Filipino	Asian Indian	Korean	Vietnamese	Other Asian
1970	High tech	900	900	200	0	100	0	0
	Professional/Management	800	1,200	0	0	0	0	0
	Low-skilled/Service	3,400	6,300	3,000	0	100	0	0
1980	High tech	2,700	1,500	900	1,000	500	1,300	0
	Professional/Management	1,900	1,800	1,200	800	600	300	0
	Low-skilled/Service	4,100	7,300	11,000	700	2,800	2,500	0
1990	High tech	10,423	2,938	3,405	3,618	1,029	5,334	645
	Professional/Management	8,500	4,449	5,786	1,997	2,025	2,499	412
	Low-skilled/Service	15,033	8,853	27,313	4,856	4,789	17,411	824
2000	High tech	25,253	3,649	6,402	19,510	2,334	10,917	1,446
	Professional/Management	17,266	5,534	9,140	8,325	3,164	7,537	1,207
	Low-skilled/Service	21,477	6,085	32,381	9,036	5,741	36,228	649
2010	High tech	33,635	2,068	5,730	30,097	4,499	12,620	235
	Professional/Management	26,713	5,605	14,885	14,244	7,737	11,416	838
	Low-skilled/Service	23,826	4,231	30,497	8,542	4,825	41,058	172

Data Source: Steven Ruggles, J. Trent Alexander, Katie Genadek, Ronald Goeken, Matthew B. Shroeder, and Matthew Sobek. Integrated Public Use Microdata Services: Version 5.0 [Machine-readable database]. Minneapolis: University of Minnesota, 2010. Data recoded. For a full list of occupations that comprise each occupational category, see http://tinyurl.com/lpgkcr3.

language. Companies often gave Asian Americans preferential treatment over other racial minorities for these positions, as racial segregation was often deployed to manage the labor force and suppress wages. Racial stereotypes depicting Asian Americans as compliant and hardworking made their labor particularly attractive.[19] By 1988, they made up the Valley's largest contingent of assembly workers, comprising about forty-four percent of all operatives.[20] Initially, many of these positions were held by those of Japanese, Chinese, and Filipino descent, but as lower-income Vietnamese migrants arrived in the Valley after 1980, they came to dominate the low-skilled labor sector.[21]

Asian Americans' early class and occupational schisms were reflected in their geographies. The working classes and the poor, including large numbers of Filipino and Vietnamese Americans, tended to cluster in "South County," the area of Santa Clara County stretching all the way south to Gilroy and north into Milpitas, whose core was in San Jose. San Jose is a vast suburban area—the largest by land area in the Bay Area—built on the backs of municipal leaders' aggressive postwar annexation campaigns. As the Valley's economy grew, city officials courted the rush of new jobs and residents, but often found the city playing second fiddle to its "North County" neighbors. In exclusive suburbs like Palo Alto, Santa Clara, and Mountain View, high-end office parks and research campuses thrived. By underwriting generous tax incentives and subsidies to high-tech companies, these suburbs tended to attract the more prestigious among them and their higher-income workers.[22] By contrast, San Jose's relatively inexpensive housing, land, infrastructure, labor, and taxes were more amenable to computer component manufacturing facilities and their blue-collar workers, including not only large numbers of Asian Americans, but also Latinos and, to a lesser extent, African Americans.[23]

While residing in many neighborhoods throughout the city, Asian Americans tended to cluster in East San Jose. With its mix of apartments and modest single-family homes, East San Jose was a working-class suburban area that provided a range of affordable housing options for newly arrived immigrants. Its generous industrial land offered easy access to manufacturing jobs (which also made the neighborhood among the most polluted in the region),[24] and its strip malls provided affordable retail space for small immigrant businesses. While many early Southeast Asian American businesses got their start in downtown, where disinvestment had left a large number of vacancies and cheap rents,[25] the commercial heart of the Asian American community migrated with its residents to East San Jose.

Figure 3: Grand Century Mall in East San Jose was Silicon Valley's first Asian mall. Built in 1982 in the heart of San Jose's Vietnamese community, the mall was a popular destination for many of East San Jose's working-class Asian Americans in the 1980s. Photo by the author.

Silicon Valley's first Asian malls were the most visible symbol of East San Jose's burgeoning Asian American community. By 1982, Grand Century, a 150,000-square-foot enclosed shopping center stood at the corner of Story and McLaughlin roads, in the heart of the area's Vietnamese American community (see fig. 3). That same year, construction began on Lion Plaza, a 105,000-square-foot center about three miles away in a slightly more upscale, but still largely working-class neighborhood more heavily populated by Chinese Americans, including many who had fled with their Vietnamese compatriots from the wars in Indochina (see fig. 4). Like other Asian malls in Southern California's San Gabriel Valley, Vancouver, and elsewhere, East San Jose's shopping centers offered a fairly standard mix of stores. Various mom-and-pop shops sold jewelry, herbal medicine, Asian-language CDs and books, as well as services like acupuncture, massage, travel, real estate, and banking. But the clear focus was food. Both Lion Plaza and Grand Century centered around pan-Asian food courts in addition to their various restaurants, cafés, and bakeries. Lion Plaza's name, in fact, derived from its anchor, Lion Market, a 27,000-square-foot Asian supermarket that was, at the time, the largest in Northern California. These

Figure 4: Lion Plaza was located in a more heavily Chinese neighborhood than was Grand Century, but likewise served a cross section of Asian Americans from various ethnic and class backgrounds around the region. Photo by the author.

malls stuck out in the landscape of otherwise seemingly standard suburban strip malls. Both welcomed visitors with lucky lions and large fountains, wishing patrons and businesses luck and prosperity.

These malls were pan-Asian, ethnically diverse spaces that reflected the character of the Asian American community in San Jose during the period. Lion Plaza, which was well-known as a Vietnamese American hub, also served as headquarters to *World Journal*, one of the largest Chinese language newspapers in the United States, as well as a twenty-four-hour Vietnamese and Chinese broadcasting station. The mall also paid homage to Chinese National leader, Dr. Sun Yat-sen, for whom its international food court was named.[26] With a slightly more Southeast Asian bent, Grand Century reflected a shared space for its diverse clientele and the desires of its developers—Alan Wong, an immigrant from Hong Kong, and his wife and his father-in-law, Lap Tang, who were both immigrants from Vietnam.

These malls also served as important meeting spaces for Asian Americans from around the region. Their customers came from the adjacent neighborhoods as well as many more distant communities. Though built as neighborhood-style shopping centers, early Asian malls tended to have wide geographic appeal.[27] On Friday and Saturday nights, they were overrun with customers who crowded into their parking lots, stores, and restaurants with family and friends. By the mid-1990s, both malls had built additions to accommodate increasing demand. And by the end of the decade, Lion Plaza developer Jerry Chen estimated that the mall attracted about five thousand shoppers daily on the weekends and half that number during the week.[28] Noting the large number of Asian elderly immigrants who regularly gathered at the center, one *San Jose Mercury News* reporter referred to Lion Plaza as "the new village green." "This is a place where no one makes a rendezvous, yet everyone comes," explained a seventy-six-year-old Vietnamese man.[29] For many immigrants, these malls not only provided products and services from their home countries, but also served as "a home away from home" that connected them to their new communities in the Valley and those they left behind. These functions were reinforced by mall design. At Lion Plaza, Jerry Chen explained that having customers hang out at the mall was part of its design intent.[30] With ample seating, late night hours, flexible management, and active programming of cultural and community events, Lion Plaza and Grand Century secured their reputations as the centers of early Asian American life in the region.

These malls supported the continued concentration of Asian American residents and businesses in East San Jose. In the surrounding neighborhoods, Asian Americans were quickly buying many of the homes. Capitalizing on these trends, Chen constructed a 272-unit gated apartment complex, Lion Villas, adjacent to Lion Plaza. Among immigrants, especially elders, who tended to have limited English-language proficiency and transportation options, the complex was popular. Asian American-owned businesses followed suit, and the area around Lion Plaza saw a rush of new Asian shopping center development in the mid-1990s. King Plaza was the fourth Asian mall built near Lion Plaza in late 1980s and early 1990s, and was constructed amidst protest from the Lion Plaza Business Association, whose members likely feared the encroaching competition. Similarly, Story Road became home to at least four new or converted Asian malls—all located within a two-block radius of Grand Century. Early Asian malls bolstered these important intersections of Asian American settlement and their emerging ethnic economies.

As Asian immigrants concentrated in the South Bay after 1970, particularly within the suburban area of San Jose, Asian shopping centers comprised the centerpieces of their early multi-ethnic, working-class neighborhoods. Regardless of class, ethnicity, or even city of residence, these malls were important spatial markers of Asian Americans' burgeoning sense of themselves as a community. With the building of these malls, Valley residents no longer (or at least not nearly so often) returned to central city ethnic enclaves for goods and services or to connect with others like themselves. By 1990, Santa Clara County had surpassed San Francisco County as the dominant gateway for new immigrants in the Bay Area, with the largest absolute concentration of immigrants of any city.[31] Silicon Valley's Asian malls emerged as new centers of commerce and community around which Asian Americans from various ethnic and national origins fostered their social networks and cultural practices, and claimed their place in the region.

SAN JOSE'S MIDDLE-CLASS, HIGH-TECH ASIAN IMMIGRANT COMMUNITY (1990–1995)

About six miles north of Lion Plaza in San Jose lies Berryessa, a suburban neighborhood that by the early 1990s had become another hub of Asian American life. Berryessa adjoins the "Golden Triangle," a popular name for the white-collar industrial district that attracted some of San Jose's earliest and most well-known high-tech companies, including Cisco Systems and Ford Aerospace. Though modest in comparison to the lush research campuses found in many North County suburbs, the Golden Triangle marked an important departure from San Jose's traditional role as a blue-collar employment center. Likewise, Berryessa's stately Mediterranean-style single-family homes and modern apartment complexes, constructed atop former apricot and prune orchards, offered a more pastoral and picturesque setting than many neighborhoods in East San Jose.

Berryessa was home to many of Silicon Valley's first Asian American engineers, researchers, and other high-tech professionals, including many immigrants who had come directly from overseas on professional visas, as well as those who arrived on F-1 student visas and were enrolled in U.S. academic programs. Preference given to educated immigrants under the 1965 Hart-Celler Act boosted the occupational profile of Asian Americans, particularly as new arrivals from Hong Kong and Taiwan entered the professional ranks. Unlike Filipino and Vietnamese immigrants who had fled deteriorating economic and political conditions abroad, Chinese immigrants from these more prosperous Asian nations often arrived in the United States seeking better jobs and educational opportunities, as well as greater political stability and freedom. In the Valley, these highly skilled Asian immigrants frequently encountered the "bamboo ceiling" in seeking management positions,[32] but broke new ground as scientists and engineers. For instance, in 1965, only forty-seven scientists and engineers in the United

States had emigrated from Taiwan, whereas two years later, the number had increased to 1,321.[33]

In 1990, Asian immigration received an even larger boost with the passage of a new immigration act designed to attract high-skilled laborers. It tripled annual quotas for professional employment-based visas from 54,000 to 140,000 and initiated the H-1B, a work visa that permitted migrants with "special skills" to work in United States for six years with the option of pursuing a green card. The initial cap on new H-1B visas was set at 65,000. Silicon Valley companies were prime beneficiaries of the program, as the bulk of visas went to computer-related occupations. Policies promoting skilled immigration coincided with mainland China's opening up to greater immigration and trade, improved foreign relations with India and China, and booming new economies in both countries that helped to produce larger numbers of highly trained professionals. By 1990, approximately one-third of the engineers and scientists in Santa Clara County were foreign-born— and of those, almost two-thirds were Asian. Fifty-one percent of these were from China, including Hong Kong and Taiwan, and twenty-three percent were from India.[34]

Two Asian malls were built in Berryessa in the 1990s to accommodate the neighborhood's swelling Asian immigrant—and particularly Taiwanese—population: Pacific Rim Plaza I in 1991 and its sister project, Pacific Rim Plaza II, in 1994. Both were built by T. Chester Wang, CEO of Pacific Rim Financial Corporation. Pacific Rim I was a 75,000-square-foot center developed on a 7.5-acre lot at the corner of Lundy and Murphy avenues. In partnership with his brother Stanley, Wang completed the second 46,000-square-foot project kitty-corner to the first.

These two malls reflected Asian Americans' increasingly professional status and their more middle-class lifestyles. For instance, as opposed to the various traditional Asian architectural elements of East San Jose's malls, both Pacific Rim I and II were designed as more contemporary American shopping centers that were nearly indistinguishable from others in the area, except for their Asian-language signage. Like the middle-class homes that surrounded them, the two malls seemed to reflect Asian Americans' desire to quietly blend into this previously white suburban neighborhood—all but erasing their outward symbols of difference. Pacific Rim's parking lots were larger and the stores less crowded than those in East San Jose's malls. They included fewer mom-and-pop stores and more established chains like the popular Filipino bakery, Goldilocks, a global brand that by 1999 had over a hundred stores in Asia, the United States, and Canada.[35] At Pacific Rim

I, the popular Taiwanese American-owned 99 Ranch Market served as its main anchor. Launched in Los Angeles in 1984, 99 Ranch (or Tawa) was a rapidly expanding Asian supermarket chain in Southern California and the largest in the United States (see fig. 5). Compared to Lion Supermarket, which catered to more working-class Southeast Asians,[36] 99 Ranch appealed to the tastes of its largely Taiwanese immigrant middle-class customers. At 99 Ranch, the prices were higher, reflecting its higher quality of products, selection, and ambience. As one Asian mall developer put it, if shopping at Lion's is like shopping at Ross (a discount clothing store), then shopping at 99 Ranch is like shopping at Macy's.[37]

The location of 99 Ranch at Pacific Rim was an important measure of Silicon Valley's status among established Asian American businesses and developers in the early 1990s. While Jerry Chen opened Lion Supermarket out of frustration from being unable to attract a major Asian supermarket to Lion Plaza, Wang's success at drawing 99 Ranch to Pacific Rim Plaza was hard-won and well recognized. Many Asian mall developers knew his story well. As several recounted, when Wang first approached the company to serve as the anchor tenant, he was told by 99 Ranch officials that they were too busy expanding in Southern California and were not yet convinced

Figure 5: Berryessa was one of most popular neighborhoods for Silicon Valley's first generation of high-tech Asian immigrants. Pacific Rim Plaza I became home to the region's first 99 Ranch Market, which was especially popular among the neighborhood's growing middle-class Taiwanese American population. Photo by the author.

of their success in Northern California. Wang's persistence and the growing evidence of the Asian American market in the area, however, convinced the company to take a chance. They signed a franchise agreement with Wang to open Northern California's first 99 Ranch Market. After securing a strong anchor tenant, the rest of the center came together quickly. Wang received nearly seven hundred applications for the twenty-eight retail slots, many of them Southern California businesses seeking to capitalize on 99 Ranch's popularity in the Valley's relatively untapped market.[38] These malls helped solidify Silicon Valley's reputation as an important gateway for Asian immigrants, businesses, and financial capital.

Like previous malls, Pacific Rim I and II marked—as well as helped to create—vibrant centers of Asian American community life. By 1994, the neighborhood was what one *San Jose Mercury* reporter called the "most Asian neighborhood in the city," based on surrounding census tracts in which Asian Americans were in the majority.[39] Further reinforcing this role, Asian American developers and real estate agents streamed new residents into the neighborhood, highlighting the proximity of homes to Pacific Rim I and II, and particularly 99 Ranch. Conversely, they streamed new businesses into the malls by calling attention to the area's demographics. Fresh off his success at Lion Villa, Jerry Chen began work on Berryessa Villa, a residential complex of 117 town homes and garden apartments about a half-mile away from Pacific Rim I, which opened in the same year. The project used feng shui principles to align homes, and its streets referenced popular places in China and Taiwan with names likes Peking Drive, Shanghai Circle, Hong Kong Drive, and Taipei Drive.[40] "It's just like living in Taiwan," explained one Villa resident, who said she particularly enjoyed that her mother could walk safely to nearby shopping centers.[41]

Pacific Rim's design facilitated its community function. Pacific Rim II was planned as a town square that included a community center, post office, and medical center oriented around an amphitheater-like open space. Its retail center connected to Starlight Court, an eighty-four-unit townhouse and apartment complex with street names like Star Jasmine and Morning Star Court, which, like those at Berryessa Villa, were meant to appeal to Asian immigrants. By designing housing and retail around the idea of community, developers took advantage of what was happening in their malls every day. Their customers used them as social spaces to meet and hang out with friends and family. These malls created spaces for Asian Americans to come together to develop shared bonds and identities, and the innovative designs supported their desires to do so.

The popularity of early Asian malls was indicative of Asian Americans' rapid rise in number, capital, and influence over the shape and character of Silicon Valley communities, especially those in the city of San Jose from the 1970s through the mid-1990s. As malls located at the important intersections of established and emerging Asian American communities, they became markers and harbingers of change as well as important spaces of everyday life for Asian Americans around the region. At the same time, these malls reflected the increasingly different niches that Asian Americans played in the Valley's economy. In both their designs and locales, they signaled a social and spatial sorting that was dividing Asian Americans by class, ethnicity, and locality—a process that would reach new heights by the end of century.

BOOMING ASIAN AMERICAN SUBURBANIZATION IN THE DOT-COM ERA (1995–2000)

The explosion of information technology in the latter half of the 1990s that became known as the "dot-com boom" had an unprecedented effect on Asian immigration in Silicon Valley. Between 1995 and 2000, over 168,000 new jobs were created in Santa Clara County—more than had been produced in the previous fifteen years of a thriving high-tech economy.[42] Arguing that there were insufficient American-born employees to fulfill these jobs, Silicon Valley companies pressed Congress for extensions to the H-1B program. In 1998, the American Competitiveness and Workforce Improvement Act was passed, significantly increasing the number of visas for skilled workers. By 2001, Congress had tripled the initial H-1B cap from 65,000 to 195,000. Silicon Valley companies placed ads in overseas trade journals and newspapers and otherwise used the visas to aggressively recruit foreign-born workers, especially those from Asia. Between 1997 and 2012, Chinese and Indians received over half of all H-1B visas, with the vast majority (forty-eight percent) going to Indians, whose education system had shifted in the 1980s and 1990s to train more engineers.[43] By 1998, Chinese and Indian immigrants ran about one-fourth of the Valley's high-tech businesses. Between 1995 and 1998, they employed around 58,000 people and were responsible for roughly one-third of all start-ups.[44] And in 2000, among all the high-tech workers in the region, thirty-nine percent were of Asian descent.[45]

Not coincidentally, Asian malls also underwent their most significant growth period during the Valley's boom years, particularly in North County. Three suburbs saw the bulk of new Asian American residents and Asian malls—Milpitas, Fremont, and Cupertino. Prior to the introduction of high tech, these communities had significant working-class populations. Milpitas was in fact the subject of Bennett Berger's famous 1960 study on blue-collar auto workers in suburbia.[46] But, by 2000, these suburbs were fully embedded in the new high-tech economy and more middle- and upper-middle-class. Slow- and no-growth policies adopted in the most exclusive Valley cities like Palo Alto were pushing residents and high-tech businesses into other North County suburbs with room to grow.[47] Many welcomed, if not courted, such opportunities with tax breaks and subsidies for new development. These communities offered an abundance of relatively affordable homes, easy access to Silicon Valley jobs, good schools, and small but extant Asian American populations. For Asian Americans who had secured their fortunes during the boom years, these up-and-coming suburbs were particularly attractive alternatives to neighborhoods in San Jose, offering better schools, bigger houses, and safer, quieter communities.

Their appeal was further heightened by new Asian mall development. In Milpitas, a suburb just north of the Berryessa neighborhood, which in 2000 became the first Asian American-majority city in the Bay Area, two major Asian malls were built in the late 1990s. City Square, a 100,000-square-foot mall anchored by Lion Supermarket, opened in 1995 followed by Milpitas Square only a couple months later. In Fremont, a city abutting Milpitas's northern border, Northgate Shopping Center began to transition when 99 Ranch opened as the anchor store in 1995. Mission Square, a center affectionately known to patrons as "Little Taipei," opened in Fremont three years later. On the other side of the Bay, the opening of Marina Foods marked the transition of a small Cupertino strip center into a new Asian mall in 1991, and six years later, the revitalized Cupertino Village opened with 99 Ranch as the anchor. These new malls signaled Asian Americans' increasing prominence in these once largely white suburbs.[48]

It was not only the pace and range of Asian mall development that characterized the dot-com era, but also their new scale and prominence. While previous malls had been built largely in the style of neighborhood strip centers, some newer malls resembled regional shopping centers.[49] In 1995, the 165,000-square-foot Milpitas Square became the largest Asian mall in Northern California. It sat at the interchange of two major highways and directly in front of a high-tech campus that later became home to many major public companies, including Quantum Corporation, LSI Corporation, Sybase, SanDisk, Sun Microsystems, and Cisco Systems. The mall included over 1,100 parking spaces and the five-hundred-seat Mayflower Restaurant, the largest restaurant in Milpitas and an outpost of its popular

San Francisco parent company. On opening day, Mayflower celebrated with an elaborate display of fireworks, drumming, and dancing that attracted about two hundred onlookers, including such prominent guests as the Congressional representative for San Jose, the state assemblywoman, Santa Clara county supervisor, and then mayor Pete McHugh.[50] Months later, ten thousand people gathered in the rain for the official opening of Milpitas Square, which included speeches by then state treasurer Matt Fong, and the new mayor Henry Manayan, the first directly elected mayor of Filipino ancestry in the continental United States.[51] The important political figures that descended on Milpitas Square served as a tacit acknowledgment of Asian malls' critical role in the Asian American community. Politicians understood that if they wanted to reach their Asian American constituents, they had to go to the mall. With larger Asian malls came a larger voice of Asian Americans in regional politics.

While many new immigrants and even second- and third-generation Asian Americans continued to frequent their local malls, regional centers like Milpitas Square also served a slightly different function. As Lion Plaza and Grand Century demonstrated, Asian malls had always served consumers well beyond their neighborhoods, but centers like Milpitas Square greatly expanded their reach. According to Philip Su, while most of Milpitas Square's weekday visitors were Asian American engineers and researchers from nearby high-tech companies and families from the surrounding suburbs, on the weekends, the center also regularly drew customers from over fifty miles away in San Francisco and Oakland. John Luk, President of GD Commercial, a brokerage company specializing in Asian malls, identified Milpitas Square as important in driving a reverse commuting pattern wherein Asian Americans began leaving central city ethnic enclaves like San Francisco's Chinatown to head south to Asian malls in Silicon Valley.[52]

Like its predecessors, Milpitas Square quickly became a popular weekday and especially weekend gathering space for ethnic Asians from around the region—a regular "third space" as well as a prominent destination for cultural and religious holidays, weddings, and other special occasions.[53] While it did not actively integrate the housing or community center concept employed in earlier Asian malls, it maintained their vital social and cultural functions. Milpitas Square was regularly visited by international dignitaries, political candidates, and even Taiwanese pop stars like Richie Jan and A-Mei Chang.[54] It was a meeting space for the Asian diaspora locally, and increasingly translocally and globally, reflecting how many of them were beginning to think about their communities across regional and national borders.[55]

This new scale of mall-building was aided by a network of Asian American developers and other real estate professionals, who, much like Asian malls themselves, came of age during the dot-com era. Prior to building the $25 million Milpitas Square, Philip Su was a seasoned developer, best known for his work on San Gabriel Square, the largest Asian mall in Southern California. By 2000, Su was but one among many successful Asian mall developers, most of whom had emigrated from Hong Kong or Taiwan. They included Jerry Chen; Alan Wong, developer of both Grand Century and Union City's El Mercado Shopping Center; Peter Pau, CEO of Sandhill Properties, who developed Cupertino Village; Chester and Stanley Wang, developers of Pacific Rim I and II as well as Fremont's Northgate Shopping Center; Ray Tong of Pacific General Construction, the developer of Fremont's "Little Taipei" who also worked with Wang on Pacific Rim I; Terry Kwong, who developed both City Square in Milpitas and Pacific East Mall in Richmond; and John Luk, who brokered many of these projects. This emerging class of real estate professionals promoted a new science of Asian malls by collaborating on projects, sharing best practices in development, tenant marketing, and management, as well as information about emerging opportunities. Groups like the Chinese American Real Estate Association and the Silicon Valley Chapter of the Asian American Real Estate Association facilitated these professional networks. They helped developers to keep watchful eyes for new markets and take advantage of them when they emerged. John Luk explained the increasingly commonsense rule for those in the business of Asian malls—once an area got to be around thirty to forty percent Asian, it was time to build a mall.[56] Developers' shared knowledge base, networks, and increasing financial resources intensified the rate of expansion and competition for new mall development.

While continuing to serve the practical tastes of many Asian Americans for relatively inexpensive goods and services, new Asian malls also reflected the fortunes that the Valley's boom years brought to many. By 2000, Asian Americans' median household income in Santa Clara County exceeded that of whites—over $82,000 versus $76,000. This further broke down along ethnic lines. Taiwanese, Chinese, and Indians had median incomes exceeding $90,000, and Vietnamese, just over $68,000. In Milpitas Square, many stores catered to Asian Americans' newfound wealth including Chong Hing Jewelers, a popular high-end jeweler founded in Los Angeles; Atelier Collection, a boutique offering exclusive Italian brands; and a branch of Charles Schwab Investment Management company that employed Chinese-language brokers.

Taken together, the scale, sophistication, and popularity of Asian malls signaled that Silicon Valley no longer needed to prove itself as an important marketplace for Asian-oriented goods and services. By the mid-1990s, 99 Ranch CEO Roger Chen was actively working with experienced developers like Philip Su and Peter Pau to scout out locations for expansion. Likewise, Silicon Valley developers were no longer regularly traveling to Southern California and San Francisco to court new businesses—the businesses were coming to them. At least half the original tenants at both Milpitas Square and Cupertino Village were established businesses that had migrated from Southern California, and many were well-known restaurants and stores from downtown San Francisco and Oakland.[57] Further, the popularity and prominence of both centers allowed developers to command rents well beyond the market for retail space in the area. By 2006, the success of Cupertino Village was so well established that Pau sold it to KIMCO, the nation's largest shopping center real estate investment trust, at a healthy profit. As Philip Su explained, Asian malls during the dot-com years went from being thought of as "second-class centers" to "major players in the commercial marketplace."[58]

Interestingly, the developers who profited most from these ventures often appeared to be concerned as much about building community as the structures themselves. Most developers with whom I spoke discussed their projects in somewhat personal terms. One reported that building an Asian mall was her way of giving back to the community to which she owed her success.[59] She spent time mentoring, nurturing, and growing several of the businesses in her center, even providing loans or partnering with businesses to help them succeed. In their own ways, developers recognized and supported their malls' vital community and cultural roles. By building spaces that fostered their customers' sense of place, belonging, and identity, these immigrant entrepreneurs often fostered that same sense within themselves—and, not coincidentally, made a healthy profit.

While focusing attention on Silicon Valley as a popular and important place for Asian Americans, Asian malls also simply made suburbs like Milpitas, Fremont, and Cupertino more convenient and desirable places to live. As more malls were built, these suburbs better reflected Asian immigrants' desires for both the comforts of their home countries and the conveniences of suburban American life. Dan, an immigrant from Taiwan who moved to Fremont in the mid-1980s, explained how the city rapidly changed after he arrived, in ways that made him and his wife feel increasingly at home.[60] They had a Chinese-language newspaper delivered to their door, maintained all the television stations that they used to have in Taiwan, and because of the large number of Asian malls built nearby, ate out regularly in Chinese restaurants and shopped at Asian supermarkets. By the end of the decade, many Asian Americans (much like Asian American businesses) had stopped looking north to San Francisco or south to the San Gabriel Valley. Instead, they found the nexus of their social and cultural lives in the South Bay suburbs, and more particularly, within the Asian malls that increasingly dotted the landscape.

DIVERSIFICATION, EXURBANIZATION, AND GLOBALIZATION OF THE ASIAN MALL (2000–2010)

After 2000, Silicon Valley faced challenging times. First came the dot-com bust that resulted in many layoffs of both high-tech and low-wage workers. Then, the 2008 financial crisis hit, leaving even more unemployed. Many high-tech Asian migrants were forced to return to their home countries, especially H-1B workers who were unable to remain in the United States without an employer sponsor. Immigration was further restricted by Congress's 2003 downgrade on new H-1B visas to the original cap of 65,000.[61] With thriving technology sectors abroad in places like Bangalore, India; Chengdu and Dalian, China; and Hsinchu, Taiwan, many immigrants were lured back to their home countries for better employment opportunities.[62]

Asian immigration slowed, but continued at a steady pace during the first decade of the twenty-first century. Between 2000 and 2010, the Asian American population in Santa Clara County increased by thirty-two percent, to around 565,000. Particularly prominent in the new wave of high-tech migrants were Chinese mainlanders and Indians, who by the early 2000s, were the two most populous Asian American nationalities. The Indian population grew the fastest of any Asian ethnic group in the county, increasing by more than seventy-six percent to around 118,000 residents.

Though large in number, however, Indian Americans and other Asian ethnic groups, including Koreans and Japanese Americans, were not as quick to build ethnic malls as Chinese, Taiwanese, and Vietnamese Americans. While developers proposed several Indian malls, none were actually built by 2010. That same year, however, Filipino Americans broke new ground with the opening of Seasons Marketplace in Milpitas, the first Bay Area shopping center in which the majority of businesses were Filipino American-owned.[63] The mall was anchored by Seafood City, the nation's largest Filipino supermarket chain, which advertised itself as a "home away from home" for Filipinos in the United States.[64] Seasons was an important symbol of Filipino American success and identity, underscored by the attendance of various Milpitas government officials, including the mayor, at the opening ceremonies, and more poignantly, by a visit from the Phillipines' newly minted President Benigno S. Aquino III soon thereafter. But Seasons also exposed Filipino Americans' struggles to make their presence felt in the region. While Filipino Americans had long been among the most populous Asian groups in the Valley, they had few places that catered to their specific needs and tastes. As one reporter suggested, the question that many asked about Seasons was simply "What took so long?"[65] Among the challenges facing Filipino, Indian, Korean American, and many other ethnic mall projects were the lack of major anchor tenants, established businesses to serve as satellite stores, and a network of real estate professionals with know-how and connections.

While not fully reflective of Asian Americans' vibrant ethnic diversity, Silicon Valley Asian malls grew and diversified in other ways. In the mid-1980s, Asian Americans in the Valley in search of co-ethnic camaraderie or products from Asia had few choices but to head to Grand Century or Lion Plaza. But, by 2010, they had plenty of options. In Milpitas, Fremont, and Cupertino—all of which were, by 2010, Asian American-majority suburbs—competition for new Asian malls was fierce. In one five-mile stretch of Warm Springs Boulevard between Fremont and Milpitas were five Asian malls. In Cupertino, Asian malls had become so widespread by 2012 that when 99 Ranch announced their plans to take over a Lucky Supermarket at the McClellan Square, *The Cupertino Courier* reported that many residents felt frustrated by the changeover because Lucky was "one of the last non-ethnic, non-specialty supermarkets in Cupertino."[66] These malls came in increasingly diverse forms. In addition to the standard Asian mall configuration, developers were also testing out "destination dining" malls composed almost exclusively of Asian eateries; Asian medical office complexes, sometimes built adjacent to Asian malls; and malls focused on the needs of Asian American students with test prep courses, pre-schools, music instruction, table tennis, Chinese- and other Asian-language instruction, ballet and traditional Asian dances, and other afterschool and academic enrichment activities. Some even ventured into other ethnic markets. At least one major developer, who believed that the Asian mall market had gotten too tight, shifted his focus to Latino malls. For developers who had stuck through the hard times, increasing competition pushed them to be ever more sensitive to the needs of their customers. As they did so, their malls came to better reflect the diverse character of the community itself.

The concentration of Asian American residents and competition for Asian malls in the most popular Silicon Valley suburbs pushed development even further out. In the early 2000s, Asian American population growth in many Tri-Valley communities like Dublin, Pleasanton, and San Ramon began to mirror that of Fremont, Milpitas, and Cupertino during the dot-com heyday. These exurbs were dominated by white middle-class residents, but had amenities that were becoming harder to find in the Valley's inner-ring suburbs—lots of land, new homes, low crime rates, research parks, abundant open space, and new shopping centers. These factors combined to make the region among the most rapidly expanding in the Valley generally, but especially among Chinese and Indian American high-tech workers. Between 2000 and 2010, the Asian American population, as a percentage of the overall population, in San Ramon and Pleasanton doubled from fifteen to thirty-four percent, and eleven to twenty-three percent, respectively. Dublin's Asian American population quadrupled from just over three thousand to over twelve thousand, making up nearly a quarter of all city residents. Signaling this shift, both Pleasanton and San Ramon welcomed large Asian supermarkets, and Dublin became home to the Tri-Valley's first Asian mall.

Completed in 2007, Dublin's 52,000-square-foot Ulferts Center embodied the increasingly prosperous and cosmopolitan lifestyles of high-tech immigrants, even more so than Asian malls built during the dot-com era. By 2010, Indian, Chinese, and Taiwanese American median household incomes in Santa Clara topped $100,000 and were the highest among all ethnic groups in the region. Built adjacent to Dublin's high-tech industrial park, the mall courted these customers. Advertised as an elite center that brought "globally inspired lifestyle and international cuisine" to the region, it was anchored by Ulferts Furniture, a high-end Hong Kong-based store specializing in European-inspired furniture, and it featured a 2,500-square-foot "signature" dining room with state-of-the-art multimedia capabilities.[67] Its modernist and minimalist aesthetic appealed to many *nouveau riche* high-tech workers. Fitted with ironclad siding, the center's focal point was a stainless steel abstract sculpture designed by world-renowned artist Aries Lee. This modern, upscale center was smaller but no less exclusive than others where Ulferts Furniture typically located in Hong Kong. Their siting in Dublin was a global nod to Asian Americans' prosperity in the region.

Malls built during the decade also exposed the increasingly transnational ties held by Asian mall developers, brokers, businesses, and patrons as well as the importance of Silicon Valley as a site for international investment. Dublin's center was the second Asian mall built by the Hong Kong-based Ulferts Furniture company in the Valley (their first completed in 1998 in Milpitas, less than a mile from Milpitas Square). Seasons was the first North American project of Ayala Land, Inc., one of the top real estate development companies in the Philippines. And in 2012, The Torgan Group, Canadian developers who previously had built Pacific Mall in Toronto, one of the largest Asian malls in North America, proposed to convert McCarthy Ranch in Milpitas, the Valley's twenty-fifth largest shopping center, into an enclosed Asian mall. The new center was to include 450 small retail condominium units and a twelve-story, 240-room hotel, presumably to accommodate the increasing flow of international investors and professionals regularly arriving from around the Pacific Rim. Peter Pau and other Asian mall developers capitalized on this trend, expanding their businesses to include services for EB-5 visa recipients, or what David Ley termed "millionaire migrants."[68] These are immigrants eligible to obtain citizenship for starting a business that creates ten or more jobs or those making an investment of $1 million or more in the United States. John Luk opened offices in Shanghai, Beijing, Hong Kong, and Guangzhou to tap foreign companies wishing to expand their holdings.[69] Many Silicon Valley-based Asian mall developers also began working on projects in Asia. As Philip Su pointed out, however, developers could not directly apply the formulas abroad that they had perfected in the Valley.[70] In China, for instance, Walmart was a more popular anchor than Asian grocers—forcing many to rethink what they meant by "Asian mall."

While many new malls reflected the cosmopolitan lifestyles enjoyed by some Asian Americans, others underscored that such prosperity was not shared by all. Indeed, they helped to expose the swelling class and ethnic divide that had deepened among Asian Americans over the years, especially during the Valley's economic downturn. Low-wage workers were among those most affected by the high-tech bust, as increasing outsourcing and contract work resulted in higher rates of layoffs, wage suppression, and wage inequality. In Santa Clara County, the median household income of Vietnamese Americans rose less than five percent to just above $72,000 during the decade compared to twenty-six percent for all Asian Americans. Between 1990 and 2010, Vietnamese American incomes dropped from eighty-four to sixty-nine percent of Asian Americans' median household income. These strains were compounded by the Valley's rising real estate values, which made the region among the most expensive places in the world to live.[71] In the face of such shifts, once-shared multi-ethnic spaces became more mono-ethnic, and the social and spatial divide between the haves and have-nots widened.

While prosperous Chinese and Indian Americans solidified their presence in middle- and upper-middle-class suburban and exurban communities during the decade, many Vietnamese Americans continued to cluster in working-class areas of the Valley like East San Jose. By 2010, San Jose was widely recognized as the "political capital" of the Vietnamese community in the United States, and its Vietnamese population, which numbered over 93,000, was the largest of any city outside of Vietnam. But, while thriving as a destination and symbolic home for many Vietnamese Americans, East San Jose's Asian malls showed signs of decline and disinvestment that reflected their struggles. The poor condition of many aging shopping centers was often cited in residents' and politicians' calls for renewal and revitalization of the area. This effort was catalyzed in 2007 by the city's designation of the four blocks of Story Road, the site of the Valley's first Asian mall, as "Little Saigon." Signs along Highway 101 directed visitors to this stretch of shopping centers that had grown to include over two hundred Vietnamese-owned businesses. "Little Saigon" banners lined the streets, inviting patrons to stay and shop. While commodifying and exoticizing Vietnamese culture, the designation simultaneously celebrated Vietnamese American success and signaled new opportunities for investment. Hoping to capitalize off the trends, Lap Tang, one of the original developers of Grand Century, completed construction of a 256-unit mall in the adjacent lot in 2007. He called the new mall Vietnam Town—one of the several proposed names for the area.[72] Five years later, the majority of the project was vacant (see fig. 6). And in 2013, the property was sold at a foreclosure auction to a Singapore-based investor. While overseas investment in East San Jose's Asian malls pointed to the area's integration within the larger global economy, it also underscored the area's relative economic vulnerability in the region.

The designation of Story Road as "Little Saigon" also reflected the new ethnic makeup of East San Jose. Many higher-income Filipino and Chinese American residents and businesses had moved out, and others were not moving into the area at the same rates as they once had. At Lion Plaza, many Chinese American businesses were turned over to Vietnamese Americans. Over the years, the multi-ethnic character of the neighborhood became more defined by Vietnamese Americans and Latinos than Chinese and Vietnamese

Figure 6: Since the mid-1970s, Vietnamese immigrants have continued to entrench themselves in East San Jose. San Jose's designation of a section of Story Road as "Little Saigon" in 2007 and development of new shopping centers like Vietnam Town marked the neighborhood's importance to Vietnamese Americans and served as a tool of neighborhood redevelopment and revitalization. Photo by the author.

Americans. This shift was evident in a shopping center proposal by Frank Jao (often described as the "Asian Donald Trump" because he purportedly owned about forty-five percent of the malls in Southern California's "Little Saigon" in Westminster).[73] Proposed in 1999, the mall was to be located at the intersection of King and Story roads, less than two miles from both Lion Plaza and Grand Century. In 1990, this area was about seventy-four percent Latino and twenty percent Vietnamese American.[74] Plans called for an open-air shopping center with hundreds of small booths for taquerias, noodle shops, and zapaterias designed to "bridge the cultural and commercial divide between the Vietnamese and Latino communities."[75] But the proposed mall also revealed the difficulties of bringing such disparate groups together—it never moved beyond the planning stages.

Hit hard by the dot-com bust and rising cost of living in the Valley, low-income and working-class Vietnamese Americans and other Southeast Asian Americans, alongside many African Americans and Latinos, were being pushed to the margins of the Valley altogether. Communities like Tracey and Stockton in San Joaquin County—exurban regions so far from the core of the Valley that they were not, by most accounts, considered part of the Bay Area—and cities as far north as Sacramento in the Central Valley saw dramatic gains in their Southeast Asian American populations. These communities had, on the whole, fewer public services, longer commutes, and higher rates of poverty and foreclosure than many in the Valley.[76] Between 2000 and 2010, the Vietnamese American population in the Greater Sacramento Area grew by fifty-eight percent to nearly thirty thousand—faster than Asian Americans on the whole and any other ethnic group in the region. Lower real estate costs, the reduced competition for businesses, and the increasingly strong Southeast Asian American consumer base in these areas allowed Asian businesses to thrive as they once did in East San Jose. In South Sacramento, Stockton Boulevard became a new Southeast Asian American business haven flanked by four Asian malls that opened or converted during the decade. In 2010, the area was officially dubbed "Little Saigon" like its predecessor over 100 miles to the south.[77] "It's growing out of control out there," observed Paul Vu, the San Jose-based investor of Vietnamese heritage who developed Pacific Rim, one of the area's anchor malls. "Everybody is migrating from the South Bay."[78]

By 2010, the transformation of Silicon Valley from a landscape of cauliflower fields, apricot orchards, and white middle-class suburbs to the hub of Asian American life in Northern California was complete. Four decades of Asian mall growth had helped transform once-fledgling destinations for new Asian migrants into primary immigrant gateways. Between 2000 and 2010, while Santa Clara County's Asian American population grew by 140,000, San Francisco added only 28,000 new Asian American residents. And while Chinatowns in San Francisco and Oakland were struggling to survive amidst what one *Contra Costa Times* reporter called a long process of "bleeding restaurants to suburbs," Silicon Valley came of age and thrived as a destination for new Asian American residents and businesses.[79] Among a more wealthy and educated generation, inner city urban enclaves no longer served as their primary centers of everyday life. Rather, their lives revolved around their suburban residences, workplaces, and Asian malls. But the story of Asian American life emerging on the urban edge was complicated, diverse, and increasing economically and spatially stratified. In the Valley, as elsewhere, it is a story that continues to be written within the Asian mall.

• • •

Asian malls have much to offer scholars who are attempting to revise the Silicon Valley story and other suburban narratives to include marginalized groups, perspectives, and places. These landscapes embody their constituents' diverse meanings, values, identities, cares, concerns, aspirations, desires, and struggles. They mirror Asian Americans' roles as place-makers, who have transformed suburbia's social and cultural life and its built forms, functions, and meanings. By looking carefully at Asian malls and the people, processes, and everyday practices that help to produce and sustain them, stories about Asian American communities that have long remained hidden become visible.

In Silicon Valley, these malls proved critical to the ways in which Asian Americans built community and established a sense of place. These shopping centers drew diverse communities together, claimed and marked the important intersections of their everyday lives, symbolized Asian American success, provided vehicles to wealth and opportunity, facilitated vital local, translocal, and global connections, and simply made the Valley into a place where it is, as one resident explained, "easy to be Asian."[80] Critically, Asian malls also represented the struggles that divided Asian Americans by class, nationality, and ethnicity, and offered a sobering portrait of how inequality and segregation have shaped Asian American social and community life.

Narratives of Asian American suburban community life are constantly changing—spanning generations, vast regions both at home and abroad, and many different groups. Built environments like Asian malls, however, serve as a repository for such stories—reflecting the ways different groups give landscapes meaning and transform them into living, breathing, and valued places. In both form and function, Asian malls have continually adapted to the diverse needs, aspirations, and tastes of their Asian American constituents and have actively reflected back their dynamic character.

To provide a fuller picture of Asian Americans' dynamic community life, more narratives of important suburban cultural landscapes like Asian malls are needed. Asian Americans are now, as they have been since at least 1990, the most suburban of all racial minority groups.[81] And just as Chinatown's streets, stores, tenements, gambling dens, laundries, and family associations once provided a lens into Asian Americans' lives in cities like San Francisco and New York, today, Asian malls in Silicon Valley and elsewhere do the same. As Aiwha Ong observed, "Chinatown is for the old immigrant; 99 Ranch is for the new."[82] These malls, found in suburbs around the nation, serve as important spaces to study how Asian Americans continue to build vibrant places and lives in a rapidly changing landscape.[83]

Unfortunately, the trends in suburban poverty and the increasing social divide that Asian malls exposed in Silicon Valley are also not unique. As scholars increasingly turn their attention to suburban poverty and what historians Becky Nicolaides and Andrew Wiese called "suburban disequilibrium,"[84] Asian malls give insight into the lived experience of communities negatively affected by the global economy and the processes shaping the new geographies of poverty, particularly within high-tech communities. The conditions of inequality across various Asian ethnic groups in the Valley should raise considerable concern about the ongoing production of unjust geographies and the increasing invisibility of these groups as they are pushed farther to the fringes.

In telling the stories of Asian Americans and others overlooked in the dominant suburban narratives, scholars will need to seek out other sites. This study showed the limits of any given space to tell the tales of multiple groups. The history of Asian malls in the Valley has largely excluded the perspectives of Indians, Koreans, Japanese, and other Asian and non-Asian groups, while privileging the voices of immigrants from China, Hong Kong, Taiwan, and Vietnam. Historical scholarship is ripe for explorations into other types of quotidian landscapes—parks, schools, sidewalks, community centers, single-family homes, and the like. At such a dynamic time in suburbia's evolution, these landscapes have much to say about how different groups are actively making—and have historically made—a home, a community, and a meaningful life within suburban regions.

NOTES

The author wishes to acknowledge Becky Nicolaides, Carol McKibben, and Eric Porter for their commentary on different iterations of this article as well as the research support of Emma Boundy and David Boston.

1. Silicon Valley is comprised of various municipalities throughout the San Francisco Bay Area that host high-tech companies and their employees. The cities that constitute the core of the Valley are subject to various definitions. The maps in figures 1 and 2 of this article include the primary cities as presented by the Silicon Valley Regional Center, http://www.siliconvalleyeb5.com/silicon-valley/cities/ (accessed March 30, 2014).

2. See, for instance, James C. Williams, "Frederick E. Terman and the Rise of Silicon Valley," *International Journal of Technology Management* 16, no. 8 (1998): 751–60; Leslie Berlin, *The Man behind the Microchip: Robert Noyce and the Invention of Silicon Valley* (New York, 2005); and Randall Smith, *The Prince of Silicon Valley: Frank Quattrone and the Dot-Com Bubble* (New York, 2010).

3. See David N. Pellow and Lisa Sun-Hee Park, *The Silicon Valley of Dreams: Environmental Injustice, Immigrant Workers, and the High-Tech Global Economy* (New York, 2002); Glenna Matthews, *Silicon Valley, Women, and the California Dream: Gender, Class, and Opportunity in the Twentieth Century* (Redwood City, CA, 2003); Stephen J. Pitti, *The Devil in Silicon*

Valley: Northern California, Race, and Mexican Americans (Princeton, NJ, 2004); Ted Smith, David Allan Sonnenfeld, and David N. Pellow, eds., *Challenging the Chip: Labor Rights and Environmental Justice in the Global Electronics Industry* (Philadelphia, PA, 2006).

4. The Act allocated all countries an equal quota of twenty thousand visas per year and set up a preference system whereby seventy-four percent of visas were granted for family reunification, twenty percent for skilled labor and professionals, and six percent for political refugees.

5. For a brief history of the push and pull factors affecting Chinese immigration in the San Francisco Bay Area, see Bernard P. Wong, *Ethnicity and Entrepreneurship: The New Chinese Immigrants in the San Francisco Bay Area* (Upper Saddle River, NJ, 1998). For accounts of Vietnamese refugees' settlement in San Jose, see James M. Freeman, *Hearts of Sorrow: Vietnamese American Lives* (Redwood City, CA, 1989). For an account of Filipino immigration history in the San Francisco Bay Area, see Benito Vergara, *Pinoy Capital: The Filipino Nation in Daly City* (Philadelphia, PA, 2008).

6. See various writings by AnnaLee Saxenian on the Valley's Asian American entrepreneurs, including *The New Argonauts: Regional Advantage in a Global Economy* (Cambridge, MA, 2006); and Wong, *Ethnicity and Entrepreneurship*.

7. These malls have been variously referred to in the literature as "Asian malls," "Chinese malls," "Vietnamese malls," and "Asian-themed malls." I have chosen to use the term "Asian malls" because those discussed here have been built largely to serve Asian immigrants of different nationalities.

8. See Peter S. Li, "Ethnic Enterprise in Transition: Chinese Business in Richmond, B.C., 1980–1990," *Canadian Ethnic Studies* 24, no. 1 (1992): 120–38; Mohammad A. Qadeer, "Ethnic Malls and Plazas: Chinese Commercial Developments in Scarborough, Ontario" (working paper, Centre of Excellence for Research on Immigration and Settlement, 1998); Shuguang Wang, "Chinese Commercial Activity in the Toronto CMA: New Development Patterns and Impacts," *Canadian Geographer* 43, no. 1 (1999): 19–35; Chuenyan David Lai, "A Study of Asian-Themed Malls in the Aberdeen District of City of Richmond, British Columbia" (working paper, Vancouver Centre of Excellence for RIIM, 2001); Lucia Lo, "Suburban Housing and Indoor Shopping: The Production of the Contemporary Chinese Landscape in Toronto," in *From Urban Enclave to Ethnic Suburb*, ed. Wei Li, 134–54; and Joseph Wood, "Making America at Eden Center," in *From Urban Enclave to Ethnic Suburb*, ed. Wei Li, 23–40.

9. See Willow Lung-Amam, "Not Your Typical Suburban American Mall: The Vibrant Life of Asian Malls in Silicon Valley," in *Making Suburbia: New Histories of Everyday America*, ed. John Archer, Paul J. P. Sandul, and Katherine Solomonson (Minneapolis, forthcoming). Notable histories of the American shopping center have been written by historians such as Howard Gillette, Lizabeth Cohen, and Richard Longstreth. See Howard Gillette, Jr., "The Evolution of the Planned Shopping Center in Suburb and City," *Journal of the American Planning Association* 51, no. 4 (1985): 449–60; Lizabeth Cohen, "From Town Center to Shopping Center: The Reconfiguration of Community Marketplaces in Postwar America," *American Historical Review* 101, no. 4 (1996): 1050–81; and Richard Longstreth, *City Center to Regional Mall: Architecture, the Automobile, and Retailing in Los Angeles, 1920–1950* (Cambridge, MA, 1998).

10. Archival data sources for this article include city planning, design, and development documents from various municipalities in Silicon Valley and local, regional, and national

newspaper archives. United States census data and Geographic Information Systems software mapping helped to identify demographic patterns across both space and time. This work is also informed by in-depth interviews with seven Asian mall managers, developers, owners, and brokers; sixty-five semi-structured interviews with Asian mall store owners, employees, and customers; and site visits to thirty-five malls in eleven cities throughout the Valley conducted between 2009 and 2012.

11. A summary of works in the "new suburban history" is provided by Kevin M. Kruse and Thomas J. Sugrue, eds., *The New Suburban History* (Chicago, 2006); and Becky M. Nicolaides and Andrew Wiese, eds., *The Suburb Reader* (New York, 2006).

12. See, for example, Hsiang-Shui Chen, *Chinatown No More: Taiwan Immigrants in Contemporary New York* (Ithaca, NY, 1992); Timothy P. Fong, *The First Suburban Chinatown: The Remaking of Monterey Park, California* (Philadelphia, PA, 1994); John Horton, *The Politics of Diversity: Immigration, Resistance, and Change in Monterey Park, California* (Philadelphia, PA, 1995); Peter Kwong, *The New Chinatown* (New York, 1996); Leland T. Saito, *Race and Politics: Asian Americans, Latinos, and Whites in a Los Angeles Suburb* (Urbana, IL, 1998); Wei Li, ed., *From Urban Enclave to Ethnic Suburb*; Wei Li, *Ethnoburb: The New Ethnic Community in Urban America* (Honolulu, 2009); and Wendy Cheng, *The Changs Next Door to the Díazes* (Minneapolis, 2013).

13. Fong, *First Suburban Chinatown*.

14. See Wei Li and Edward J. W. Park, "Asian Americans in Silicon Valley: High-Technology Industry Development and Community Transformation," in *From Urban Enclave to Ethnic Suburb*, ed. Wei Li, 119–33.

15. Notable work, however, has been done recently on "techno-ethnoburbs." See, for example, Wei Li and Lucia Lo, "Highly-Skilled Indian Migration in Canada and the US: The Tale of Two Immigration Systems" (International Migration and Diaspora Studies Working Paper Series 4–6, 2009); Wei Li and Lucia Lo, "New Geographies of Migration? A Canada-U.S. Comparison of Highly Skilled Chinese and Indian Migration," *Journal of Asian American Studies* 15, no. 1 (2012): 1–34; and Emily Skop, *The Immigration and Settlement of Asian Indians in Phoenix, Arizona 1965–2011: Ethnic Pride vs. Racial Discrimination in the Suburbs* (Lewiston, NY, 2012).

16. For an early history of Japanese and other Asian American agricultural laborers in the Valley, see Timothy J. Lukes and Gary Y. Okihiro, *Japanese Legacy: Farming and Community Life in California's Santa Clara Valley* (Cupertino, CA, 1985). For a history of Asian Americans in San Francisco and throughout the West, see Charlotte Brooks, *Alien Neighbors, Foreign Friends: Asian Americans, Housing, and the Transformation of Urban California* (Chicago, 2009).

17. Because of its lack of racial covenants, Alviso was an area that historically served as the home of various waves of new immigrants, including Puerto Ricans, Japanese, Chinese, and Mexicans. The area, however, had few streetlights or paved roads until the mid-1950s. For further historic and contemporary perspectives on Alviso, see Pitti, *Devil in Silicon Valley*; and Aaron Calvin, "The Borders of Ciitzenship: The Politics of Race and Metropolitan Space in the Silicon Valley" (PhD diss., University of Michigan, Ann Arbor, 2012).

18. For regional histories of Silicon Valley, see John M. Findley, *Magic Lands: Western Cityscapes and American Culture after 1940* (Berkeley, CA, 1993); Margaret P. O'Mara, *Cities of Knowledge: Cold War Science and the Search for the Next Silicon Valley* (Princeton, NJ, 2005).

19. Regarding racial segregation in the early Silicon Valley labor force, see Karen J. Hossfeld, "Divisions of Labor, Divisions of Lives: Immigrant Women Workers in Silicon Valley" (PhD diss., University of California, Santa Cruz, 1988); and Edward Jang-Woo Park, "Asian Americans in Silicon Valley: Race and Ethnicity in the Postindustrial Economy" (PhD diss., University of California, Berkeley, 1993).

20. Park, "Asian Americans in Silicon Valley."

21. The working conditions in these jobs were difficult and frustrating. They were often temporary jobs, offering few legal protections, hazardous working conditions, and little opportunity for upward mobility. For further discussions about the working conditions of minorities, immigrants, and women in the Valley, see Pellow and Park, *Silicon Valley of Dreams*; Matthews, *Silicon Valley, Women, and the California Dream*; and Pitti, *Devil in Silicon Valley*.

22. For discussion of the politics of place in North County and South County in Silicon Valley history, see Philip J. Trounstine and Terry Christensen, *Movers and Shakers: The Study of Community Power* (New York, 1982); AnnaLee Saxenian, "Silicon Valley and Route 128: Regional Prototypes or Historic Exceptions?," in *High Technology, Space, and Society*, ed. Manuel Castells, Urban Affairs Annual Reviews Series 28 (Beverly Hills, CA, 1985), 81–105; and Everett M. Rogers and Judith K. Larsen, *Silicon Valley Fever: Growth of High-Technology Culture* (New York, 1984). For a broader perspective on the politics of suburbanization in the Bay Area that produced such fragmentation and exclusion in the postwar era, particularly the politics of suburban tax policy, see Robert O. Self, *American Babylon: Race and the Struggle for Postwar Oakland* (Princeton, NJ, 2003).

23. For a history of African Americans in Silicon Valley, see Herbert G. Ruffin II, *Uninvited Neighbors: African Americans in the Silicon Valley, 1769–1990* (Norman, OK, 2014).

24. See the discussion of environmental justice battles in Silicon Valley in Pitti, *Devil in Silicon Valley*.

25. Freeman, *Hearts of Sorrow*.

26. Maya Suryaraman, "Lion Plaza Roars with Life for San Jose; Asian Community: Shoppers Drawn to Tully Strip by Familiar Products, Culture," *San Jose Mercury News*, December 5, 1990: 4.

27. Anonymous, interview by Willow Lung-Amam, December 1, 2011.

28. K. Oanh Ha, "Bridging the Commercial Divide; New Shopping Center in San Jose Will Blend Latino and Asian Tastes, Revitalize Blighted Area," *San Jose Mercury News*, July 26, 1999: 1E.

29. De Tran, "The New Village Green Strip Malls Emerging as Ethnic Crossroads: Ethnic Shopping Centers Provide Piece of Home to Bay Area's Immigrants," *San Jose Mercury News*, April 5, 1998: 1B.

30. Tran, "New Village Green."

31. Audrey Singer, "The Rise of New Immigrant Gateways: Historical Flows, Recent Settlement Trends," in *Redefining Urban and Suburban American: Evidence from Census 2000*, ed. Alan Berube, Bruce Katz, and Robert E. Lang (Washington, DC, 2004), 41–86.

32. AnnaLee Saxenian, "Silicon Valley's New Immigrant Entrepreneurs" (working paper, Center for Comparative Immigration Studies, University of California, San Diego, May 1, 2000).

33. Shirley L. Chang, "Causes of Brain Drain and Solutions: The Taiwan Experience," *Studies in Comparative International Development* 27, no. 1 (1992): 27–43.

34. Saxenian, "Silicon Valley's New Immigrant Entrepreneurs."

35. Goldilocks, "Milestones," http://www.goldilocks-usa.com/milestones (accessed May 12, 2014).

36. Shortly after starting Lion Supermarket, Chen sold the company to the Trans, a Chinese-Vietnamese family, who grew the market to include five Bay Area stores.

37. Anonymous, interview by Willow Lung-Amam, July 7, 2011.

38. Sherri Eng, "The Taste of Success; Asian Shopping Centers Often Anchored by Popular Groceries, Are Expanding While Others Struggle," *San Jose Mercury News*, November 7, 1993: 1E.

39. Ken McLaughlin, "Feeling of Home Draws S.J. Asians to Neighborhood," *San Jose Mercury News*, August 23, 1994: 1B.

40. Chen went on to construct Lion Estates, a $60 million development of ninety-seven high-end single-family homes in San Jose, also built using feng shui principles and marketed largely to Asian Americans.

41. McLaughlin, "Feeling of Home," 1B.

42. This figure is from a report by the Association of Bay Area Governments, in "Jobs vs. Homes: Econ 101 Explains the Insane Prices, but Other Cities besides San Jose Need to Work Harder on New Housing Opportunities," *San Jose Mercury News*, August, 7, 2000: Editorial section, 10B.

43. These numbers are based on analysis of data from the U.S. Department of State.

44. Saxenian, "Silicon Valley's New Immigrant Entrepreneurs," 7.

45. Dan Nakaso, "Asian Workers Now Dominate Silicon Valley Tech Jobs," *San Jose Mercury News*, November 30, 2012, http://www.mercurynews.com/ci_22094415/asian -workers-now-dominate-silicon-valley-tech-jobs.

46. Bennett M. Berger, *Working-Class Suburb: A Study of Auto Workers in Suburbia* (Berkeley, CA, 1960).

47. By 1975, around 84,000 people commuted daily to Sunnyvale, Palo Alto, Mountain View, and Santa Clara from outlying cities. Quoted in Findley, *Magic Lands*, 156.

48. Other smaller suburban communities also saw the arrival of Asian malls during the period. Though not as prestigious or large as many of those in Milpitas, Fremont, and Cupertino, the malls served as evidence of the growth of Asian Americans across a broad swath of Silicon Valley suburbia. In Newark, a small and largely working-class city made into an island by its borders with Fremont, the opening of Asian supermarkets marked the transition of two existing shopping centers in the mid-1990s: 99 Ranch Market in the dilapidated Lido Faire Shopping Center and Lion Supermarket in a small enclosed mall that took on the familiar name of "Lion Plaza." Union City, a slightly more upscale suburb adjoining Fremont's northern border, welcomed its first Asian mall in 2000 in the half-vacant El Mercado Shopping Center.

49. For distinctions in neighborhood and regional mall forms, see Longstreth, *City Center to Regional Mall*; and Dolores Hayden, *Building Suburbia: Green Fields and Urban Growth, 1820–2000* (New York, 2009).

50. Steve Johnson, "Big Eatery Opens in Milpitas," *San Jose Mercury News*, August 4, 1996: 1B.

51. Corey J. Lyons, "Milpitas Square Draws 10,000 for Grand Opening under Rainy Skies," *Milpitas Post*, November 21, 1996: Business section.

52. John Luk, interview by Willow Lung-Amam, September 29, 2011.

53. The term "third space" here refers to informal public gathering spaces. Urban sociologist Ray Oldenburg has written extensively about the importance of these places for community and public life. See, for instance, *The Great Good Place* (New York, 1991).

54. Vanessa Hua, "Asian Sensations: Pop Fads from across the Pacific Rim Finding an Enthusiastic Market Here," *San Francisco Chronicle*, November 27, 2002: B1.

55. See, for instance, works on Asian Americans' transnational identities and place-making, including Shenglin Chang, *The Global Silicon Valley Home: Lives and Landscapes within Taiwanese American Trans-Pacific Culture* (Stanford, CA, 2006); and Shenglin Elijah Chang and Willow Lung-Amam, "Born Glocal: Youth Identity and Suburban Spaces in the U.S. and Taiwan," *Amerasia Journal* 36, no. 3 (2010): 29–52.

56. Katherine Conrad, "Broker Thrives by Straddling Two Worlds," *Silicon Valley/San Jose Business Journal* 28, no. 1 (April 16, 2010): 12.

57. Philip Su, interview by Willow Lung-Amam, November 29, 2011; and Anonymous, telephone interview by Lung-Amam, October 9, 2012.

58. Su, interview by Lung-Amam, November 29, 2011.

59. Anonymous, telephone interview by Lung-Amam, October 9, 2012.

60. Dan [pseudonym], interview by Lung-Amam, May 15, 2009.

61. There have been, however, several exemptions to the law that have allowed for the extension of additional visas. These include exemptions for applicants with master's-level or higher degrees, all university or government employees, and foreign-born students graduating from U.S. universities.

62. Saxenian, *New Argonauts*.

63. Seafood City Supermarket, "Seafood City Featured on CBS," http://seafoodcity.com/html/news.html#null (accessed October 25, 2013).

64. Seafood City Supermarket, "About Us," http://www.seafoodcity.com/html/aboutUs.html (accessed October 25, 2013).

65. Seafood City Supermarket, "Seafood City Featured on CBS."

66. Matt Wilson, "Cupertino; Ranch 99 Market to Take Over Location of Former Lucky Supermarket," *Cupertino Courier*, September 20, 2012, http://www.mercurynews.com/ci_21596679/cupertino-99-ranch-market-take-over-location-former.

67. Ulferts Center, Dublin, "About Us," http://www.ulferts.com/dublin/aboutus.php (accessed October 25, 2013).

68. David Ley, *Millionaire Migrants: Trans-Pacific Life Lines* (West Sussex, Eng., 2010).

69. Sharon Simonson, "Cupertino Square Tries New Team," *Silicon Valley/San Jose Business Journal* 26, no. 23 (October 3, 2008): 1.

70. Su, interview by Lung-Amam, November 29, 2011.

71. In 2013, *Forbes* reported that the Silicon Valley had the two most expensive ZIP codes in the United States, with median home prices of more than $5.4 million. See Morgan Brennan, "Silicon Valley Dominates 2013 List of America's Most Expensive ZIP Codes," *Forbes*, October 16, 2013, http://www.forbes.com/sites/morganbrennan/2013/10/16/the-complete-list-americas-most-expensive-zip-codes-in-2013/ (accessed April 10, 2014).

72. This naming brought international attention to San Jose's Vietnamese community. The controversy centered on Madison Nguyen, the city's first Vietnamese American council member elected under the promise of getting a name for the area. Nguyen's support for the name "Saigon Business District," however, was opposed by many Vietnamese residents and

businesses owners, who called Nguyen a traitor, organized rallies for "Little Saigon," and initiated a recall campaign.

73. Thuy-Doan Le, "Sacramento, Calif., Retail Project Inspires Asian American Developers," *Sacramento Bee*, November 14, 2004, http://www.highbeam.com/doc/1G1–124700216.html.

74. Ha, "Bridging the Commercial Divide," 1E.

75. Ibid.

76. For more on the suburbanization of poverty and foreclosures in the Bay Area, see Alex Schafran, "Origins of an Urban Crisis: The Restructuring of the San Francisco Bay Area and the Geography of Foreclosure," *International Journal of Urban and Regional Research* 37, no. 2 (2013): 663–88.

77. Cathleen Ferraro, "Developer Hopes Sacramento, Calif., Asian Retail Center Will Dominate Niche," *Sacramento Bee*, September 4, 1999.

78. Quoted by Le, in "Sacramento, Calif."

79. Angela Woodall, "Eatery End: A Sign of Changing Tastes: End of Silver Dragon Restaurant Is Another Sign That Oakland's Chinatown Is Facing a Redefining Moment If It Wants to Survive," *Contra Costa Times*, March 15, 2012: 1A.

80. Anonymous, interview by Willow Lung-Amam, Februrary 7, 2011.

81. Based on 1990–2010 U.S. Census Data analyzed in William H. Frey, "Melting Pot Cities and Suburbs: Racial and Ethnic Change in Metro America in the 2000s," Metropolitan Policy Program at Brookings, *State of Metropolitan America*, May 4, 2011: 10, http://www.brookings.edu/~/media/research/files/papers/2011/5/04%20census%20ethnicity%20frey/0504_census_ethnicity_frey.pdf.

82. Quoted by Patricia Leigh Brown, in "In California Malls New Chinatowns Booming: Asian-American Shops Serve as Cultural Centers," *International Herald Tribune*, March 25, 2003: 7.

83. The website *Asia Mall*, http://www.asiamall.com (accessed May 20, 2008), estimates that there are approximately 140 Asian malls in the United States.

84. Becky M. Nicolaides and Andrew Wiese, "Suburban Disequilibrium," *New York Times*, April 6, 2013, http://opinionator.blogs.nytimes.com/2013/04/06/suburban-disequilibrium/ (accessed October 25, 2013). On the suburbanization of poverty, see William H. Lucy and David L. Phillips, *Confronting Suburban Decline: Strategic Planning for Metropolitan Renewal* (Washington, DC, 2000); Bernadette Hanlon, *Once the American Dream: Inner-Ring Suburbs of the Metropolitan United States* (Philadelphia, PA, 2010); and Elizabeth Kneebone and Alan Berube, *Confronting Suburban Poverty* (Washington, DC, 2013).

14

The Politics of Expulsion: A Short History of Alabama's Anti-Immigrant Law, HB 56

RAYMOND A. MOHL

IN JUNE 2011, THE REPUBLICAN-CONTROLLED Alabama legislature passed a tough immigration law, known as House Bill 56 (or HB 56) that endorsed a policy of expulsion of undocumented immigrants from the state. One of several state anti-immigrant laws enacted around the same time, HB 56 targeted Latinos, hoping to make life so difficult for them that they would "self-deport." The U.S. Congress has persistently failed to pass some type of immigration reform to deal with the twenty-first-century surge of Mexican and Central American border crossers. Democrats insisted on a "path to citizenship" for undocumented workers, but Republicans wanted tighter border controls and a means of reducing the number of illegal immigrants, mostly Latinos, in the United States. The impasse in Congress opened the door for states to take action. Tea Party Republicanism surged during the 2010 midterm elections, putting Republican politicians in control of many southern state legislatures. Nativist fears of large numbers of ethnically different newcomers, especially over job competition and unwanted cultural change, sometimes referred to as "cultural dilution," provided political cover for politicians who sought to control and regulate immigration within state borders, but also to push illegal immigrants out. Conservative Republicans, according to historian-journalist Mike Davis, had been promoting anti-immigrant policies since the 1990s. As Davis noted in his book, *No One Is Illegal* (2006), "the Far Right has sought to mobilize against immigrants (and a guest-worker program) on the grounds that it 'dilutes American culture' and 'burdens' the social welfare system. This racist component is omnipresent in the media and interlocks neatly with the more acceptable economic alarmism." The intensity of the political war over immigration only got worse as the first decade of the twenty-first century ended. In the severity of its 2011 immigration law, Alabama became the "poster boy" for recent American nativism. The state's harsh, aggressive, and discriminatory anti-immigrant policy also brought back memories from a half-century earlier, when state-sponsored racial discrimination targeted African Americans.[1]

POLITICS AND THE NEW NATIVISM

Demographic change after 2000 helped to promote the new politics of expulsion in Alabama. The 2010 Census revealed some 186,000 Hispanics in Alabama, not a huge number compared to Latino migration to other southern states such as Georgia, North Carolina, and Virginia. Politicians and local media emphasized the 145 percent increase since 2000, when Alabama's Latinos numbered 75,800, ignoring the fact that statistical increases over time are magnified when beginning with a small base number. Latinos had been coming to Alabama in relatively small numbers since the late 1980s, following passage of the federal Immigration Reform and Control Act of 1986. That law legalized over three million Mexican and other Latinos nationwide, some of whom eventually found their way to southern states, primarily for work in agriculture, poultry, construction, and manufacturing. Small towns in north Alabama especially seemed overwhelmed by the newcomers in the years after 2000. In places like Albertville, Collinsville, and Russellville, Latinos pumped new life into local economies and provided an essential and dependable labor force; they also made up 30 percent or more of the population of those towns in 2010. The seemingly sudden demographic transformations of life and culture in small-town Alabama created racial tensions in a southern state familiar with such matters. Latinos made up only 3.9 percent of the total state population in 2010, but right-wing politicians exaggerated the immigrant impact. Republican rhetoric especially raised fears of a "minority-majority" future in some parts of the state. In the public discourse over HB 56, racial issues became linked with immigration concerns, and the Republican racial vocabulary conflated all Latinos with illegal immigrants. As Fred L. Hammond, a Unitarian minister in Tuscaloosa, complained in a public letter to Alabama Governor Robert Bentley in June 2011, "the Legislature is assuming that all Spanish speaking citizens are undocumented," and thus HB 56 "targets anyone whose first language is Spanish and who looks like they come from south of the border."[2]

In Alabama, the run-up to the 2008 presidential election unleashed a vehement public discussion about illegal immigrants, and especially the growing number of Latinos in the state. Political leaders at several levels argued that immigrants drained state and local social services, crowded public schools, depressed wages, and deprived American citizens of jobs. Politicians generally mentioned cultural distinctions rather than race or ethnicity in public discussion of immigration, but it was clear that they had targeted the state's growing urban and rural Latino communities. In 2007, as the surge of nativism intensified, the state legislature formed the Alabama Patriotic Immigration Commission, charged with holding hearings around the state and reporting on the extent and impact of illegal immigration. Commission town hall meetings in various cities drew raucous crowds of Alabamians demanding crackdowns on illegal immigrants and tougher national immigration policies. The Commission's report to the state legislature in January 2008 recommended numerous punitive policies against undocumented immigrants, many of which ultimately found their way into Alabama's HB 56. State legislators Scott Beason of Gardendale and Micky Hammon of Decatur, later sponsors of the HB 56 legislation, served on the Commission and helped shape its final report.[3]

This official effort by the Alabama legislature launched a more aggressive campaign against Latino immigrants. In early 2008, Republicans lawmakers began drafting anti-immigration bills and pushing for English-only driver's license exams. Several Alabama cities increased penalties for unlicensed drivers, thought to be mostly Latinos; a few cities enacted ordinances limiting the number of unrelated people who could live in a house or mobile home (a common living arrangement for young, single, male Latino workers). By 2008, racial profiling and police harassment of Latinos in Alabama, especially in small towns and rural areas, was on the rise. Also in 2008, in the U.S. Congress, Alabama Senator Jeff Sessions challenged emerging Republican and Democratic presidential candidates to "commit" to a series of policies that would curb illegal immigrants and deal harshly with those already residing in the United States. Over the next few years, Sessions became a powerful national voice for pushing undocumented immigrants out of the United States. At every level of government, Alabama's elected officials seemed primed to take punitive action against Latino immigrants.[4]

Nativist hostility toward immigrants persisted and intensified nationwide over the next few years, especially after the emergence of Tea Party Republican groups in 2009. Moreover, the Congressional logjam on immigration reform encouraged states to step in with their own policy solutions. By 2010, a flurry of new state laws initiated the long-discussed crackdown on immigrants. Arizona's tough immigration law provided the model for Alabama and other states. Passed in April 2010, the Arizona law, known as SB 1070, expanded police powers in arresting suspected undocumented immigrants, prohibited hiring and otherwise assisting immigrants, and denied social services and other state benefits to undocumented people. The Arizona anti-immigrant law was especially notable because it introduced the concept of "attrition through enforcement," the idea that states had inherent police powers to arrest immigrant law violators who would then be subject to federal deportation proceedings. Persistent application of such a policy, it was believed, would also encourage illegal immigrants "to leave on their own." In 2010, Arizona State Senator Russell Pearce, a strong backer of SB 1070, contended that the law "will not change a thing for lawful citizens. It simply takes the handcuffs off law enforcement and allows them to do their job." By contrast, Chris Newman, legal director of the National Day Laborer Organizing Committee, argued that SB 1070 "criminalizes undocumented status," and "effectively mandates racial profiling." The Arizona law prompted pro-immigrant demonstrations around the nation and a boycott movement against the state, but it also encouraged other states, including Alabama, to consider similar legislation.[5]

Behind the scenes, hard-line conservative Republican politicians and organizations mobilized anti-immigrant action in some cities and numerous state legislatures. A key player in this movement was Kris Kobach, a Kansas attorney and politician who had worked in President George W. Bush's Justice Department and later helped draft the Arizona law that included "attrition through enforcement" provisions. In 2006, Kobach played a major role in crafting an immigration-control ordinance for Hazelton, Pennsylvania, which was later overturned in the courts. He also traveled to many Republican strongholds in southern and western states, helping conservative politicians draft legislation, similar to that of Arizona, which, Kobach argued, would survive legal challenges. The idea of attrition, later labeled "self-deportation," was central to Kobach's anti-immigrant legal strategy.[6]

Kobach had deep connections with the politically conservative Federation for American Immigration Reform (FAIR). For several years, Kobach worked as an attorney for FAIR's legal wing, the Immigration Reform Law Institute. Since the 1990s, FAIR had been pounding the drum for state action aimed at controlling undocumented immigrants. In 1994–1995, for instance, backed by conservative foundations and think tanks, FAIR supported the successful campaign in California for Proposition 187, a new nativist effort denying public services and schooling to undocumented immigrants and their children. After much media attention and considerable litigation, Proposition 187 was overturned in the courts and never enforced. The Southern Poverty Law Center (SPLC) in Montgomery, a defender of immigrant legal rights, named FAIR a "nativist hate group."[7]

During an early visit to Alabama in 2007, Kobach spoke at a conference of the Eagle Forum of Alabama, a self-described "conservative think tank."

At that time, Kobach met state legislator Scott Beason, who was already promoting bills in the legislature on immigration control. The Kobach-Beason relationship ultimately led to Alabama's immigrant law HB 56 in 2011. Kobach was also meeting with Alabama city officials, including city councilman Chuck Ellis of Albertville, regarding possible local ordinances targeting illegal immigrants. A small town in northeast Alabama, Albertville had a large population of Latino immigrants, mostly working in agriculture and poultry plants. While the immigration wars were heating up in Alabama, federal immigration reform legislation, especially efforts to create an amnesty program or some other path to citizenship for the undocumented, languished in a divided Congress. However, Congress did provide funds for new border controls, the construction of seven hundred miles of a border fence, and over twenty thousand additional border agents; deportations during the Obama administration surged to an astonishing 400,000 in 2012. Nevertheless, these border controls did not satisfy right-wing politicians at the state level. The issue of 11 to 12 million undocumented immigrants in the United States remained unresolved, creating an opening for state action. At the same time, many state legislators recognized that federal courts, and probably the U.S. Supreme Court, ultimately would be compelled to render legal decisions on controversial state immigration laws.[8]

The skirmishing over immigration that stemmed from the punitive Arizona law and the anti-immigrant hysteria promoted by conservative Republicans during the 2010 midterm elections encouraged Alabama politicians to pursue the enactment of a tough, restrictive immigration law. Nativist fears intensified once the 2010 census numbers were released, with subsequent demands for legislative action to protect Alabama workers from low-wage immigrant competition. Moreover, the Republican Party had achieved super-majorities in both houses of the Alabama legislature for the first time in more than a century. Republican legislator Robert Bentley ascended to the governorship in the 2010 election, completing the Republican political trifecta in Alabama. In December 2010, the *Birmingham News* commented on what every Alabamian already knew: "White Democrats Vanishing in State." The political stage was set, with Kobach and Beason waiting in the wings with their draft anti-immigration bills.[9]

HB 56 AND ITS CONSEQUENCES

In June 2011, with wide majorities, the state legislature passed, and Governor Bentley signed HB 56, euphemistically titled the Beason-Hammon

Alabama Taxpayer and Citizen Protection Act. However, Kris Kobach played a key role in selling the legislators on his "attrition" strategy and in drafting the final bill approved by state lawmakers. As Hammon stated, HB 56 was designed "to attack every aspect of an illegal alien's life . . . so they will deport themselves." Among its thirty provisions, the law made it a crime for undocumented immigrants to reside in the state of Alabama. Local police were authorized to perform traffic checks of suspected illegal immigrants and arrest those without proper documents. The law prohibited any financial or other transactions between illegal immigrants and government agencies or private individuals, such as employers and rental agents. Immigrants without papers were to be denied access to medical care, social services, utility hook-ups, and public universities. The law demanded that employers check the legal status of their workers through a federal program called E-Verify, with employer sanctions and fines for those who did not comply. It also criminalized sheltering undocumented immigrants or transporting them to work, church, school, grocery stores, medical facilities, or other destinations. The legislature provided no funding for implementing any of these HB 56 provisions, essentially leaving enforcement to local police and other agencies.[10]

One final provision of HB 56, unique to Alabama, had ominous implications. Section 28 of the law required public schools to verify the legal status of their students, although it did not deny public education to immigrant children. This section of the law was drafted by Michael Hethmon, Kobach's colleague at FAIR's Immigration Reform Law Institute. Unlike Kobach, Hethmon avoided the public spotlight, but worked closely with him on drafting state, county, and city immigration laws and ordinances. Hethmon held strongly nativist views, fearing a future "minority-majority" America, and he promoted the idea of "self-deportation" to prevent cultural dilution and maintain the nation's white majority. Thus Hethmon emphasized the importance of keeping immigrant children out of public schools. The "discriminatory intent" of Section 28 of HB 56 was obvious, as a federal judge subsequently concluded. The requirement to document the number of immigrant children in schools, Hethmon later admitted to a journalist, was part of a long-term plan. He hoped states would gather statistical data that could be used to support a legal challenge to a 1982 U.S. Supreme Court decision in *Plyler v. Doe* that guaranteed public education to undocumented immigrant children. *Plyler v. Doe* was a 5–4 decision, and, the thinking went, might be overturned by a slightly more conservative Court. The ultimate goal of Hethmon's strategy was to deny public education to undocumented immigrant children. Alabama's Republican legislators endorsed Hethmon's idea of immigrant checks in schools as another means of creating a climate of racial fear and uncertainty in Latino communities, with the purpose of driving them out of Alabama.[11]

The HB 56 immigration law was stunning in its hostility and aggressiveness toward immigrants, and its consequences were immediate. Latinos across the state pulled their children from schools and abandoned their jobs in agriculture, poultry, construction, landscaping, restaurants, and service industries. They packed up cars and pickups with their belongings and disappeared into the night, when they were less likely to be stopped by police. In HB 56, there was no account made for "blended" families in which one spouse held citizenship, or of undocumented immigrants with children who were native-born American citizens. All were equally targeted as undesirable minorities. Few Latinos returned to Mexico, but large numbers moved to nearby southern states with more immigrant-friendly policies, such as Texas, Tennessee, Arkansas, North Carolina, and Florida. Many also remained, living in difficult circumstances under the radar of enforcement agencies. As Mary Bauer, an attorney with the SPLC, stated in Congressional testimony in December 2011, "Alabama is suffering a humanitarian crisis that hearkens back to the bleakest days of our racial history." Some editorialists gave the form of racial discrimination in HB 56 a new label with an old meaning: "Juan Crow." Wade Henderson, head of the Leadership Conference of Civil and Human Rights (a national coalition of over 200 civil rights organizations dating back to 1950), blasted HB 56 in a June 2011 *Los Angeles Times* interview: "This draconian initiative signed into law this morning by Governor Robert Bentley is so oppressive that even Bull Connor himself would be impressed." Connor, of course, was the public safety director in Birmingham who unleashed police attacks, with dogs and fire hoses, on school children demonstrating for Civil Rights in 1963. Responding to the legislature's action, religious groups—Methodist, Baptist, Episcopalian, Lutheran, and Catholic—issued a statement that the hostile provisions of HB 56 ran counter to biblical teachings and "the Christian spirit of compassion." Little compassion was on display in the state legislature, however. Instead, conservative Alabama legislators seemed fiercely proud of what they had done, even "bragging" about their role in giving Alabama the strongest immigration-control law in the land. Nevertheless, despite the political posturing, it soon became evident that the main purpose of HB 56 was to encourage undocumented immigrants and their families to "self-deport." Micky Hammon, one of the sponsors of HB 56 in the legislature, articulated that objective, as reported by the *New York Times* in June 2011: "We really want to prevent illegal immigrants from coming to Alabama and to prevent those who are already here from putting down roots." Within weeks, it appeared that HB 56 had at least partially accomplished that goal.[12]

The attack on Latino immigrants through Alabama's HB 76 had other consequences. As immigrants abandoned jobs in Alabama, employers in construction, agriculture, poultry, and other businesses struggled to find new workers. In places such as Hoover, a Birmingham suburb, Latino pick-up day laborers disappeared from established hiring spots; businesses that handled money transfers to Mexico were running out of customers. In small towns in north Alabama, groceries and restaurants that catered to Latinos were losing both customers and employees. In April 2011, tornadoes roared through Tuscaloosa and nearby towns, causing enormous physical destruction. Two months later, after HB 56 became law, local construction firms engaged in rebuilding reported losing large numbers of key workers in roofing, house framing, drywall, concrete work, and landscaping. Jay Reed, president of the Alabama Associated Builders and Contractors, in an October 2011 interview with the *Birmingham News*, lamented the loss of undocumented as well as legal immigrants in the construction industry. Contractors were unable to meet their deadlines because, Reed stated, "there simply isn't a pool of individuals ready and willing to work on our job sites." Farmers across the state who relied on immigrant labor found few replacements and faced enormous losses from unpicked crops rotting in the fields. Alabama had a high unemployment rate during the Great Recession, peaking at 10.5 percent in December 2009 and averaging 9.7 percent between July 2009 and January 2011. The sponsors of HB 56 repeatedly stated that they expected out-of-work American citizens to replace departing immigrants, but that never happened. A state program launched by Governor Bentley in October 2011 to link unemployed Alabamians with farmers needing laborers was a complete failure. Facing low pay and hard labor, the few hundred Americans hired under this program barely lasted a single day. Around the same time, Alabama Agricultural Commissioner John McMillan suggested a backup plan. As reported in the *Christian Science Monitor*, McMillan wanted the state "to force residents receiving unemployment benefits to take farm-labor jobs or risk losing their benefits." A few weeks later, McMillan came up with a new idea—using nonviolent state prison inmates as voluntary backup farm laborers. Farmers were doubtful, and neither plan was implemented. Despite legislative assurances to the contrary, agriculture, construction, and

poultry jobs in Alabama had become "immigrant jobs," physically demanding and low-paid work that Americans shunned. Unemployed white-collar
workers, retail clerks, or skilled craftsmen simply were not ready to start
picking and packing tomatoes, peppers, onions, or sweet potatoes in the
steamy Alabama summer.[13]

In January 2012, at the height of the HB 56 controversy, University of
Alabama economist Samuel Addy released a "cost–benefit analysis" of
Alabama's immigration law. The results were stunning. Addy identified
numerous ways in which Alabama would suffer economically as a consequence of HB 56. These included: (1) the costs of implementation,
enforcement, and anticipated litigation; (2) greater "inconveniences" for
citizens and businesses; (3) reduced opportunities for economic development;
and (4) "the economic impact of reduced demand as some immigrants leave
and therefore no longer earn and spend income in the state." For Addy,
this last economic consequence was most important. Addy estimated that
between forty thousand and eighty thousand undocumented immigrants
would depart, causing job losses in sectors serving immigrants and economic
losses for businesses patronized by immigrants. Collectively, Addy estimated
that HB 56 would reduce Alabama's gross domestic product by $2.3 billion
to $10.8 billion for each year the law was in effect. Admittedly, Addy's study
was based on imprecise data—no one knew the exact number of Latinos who
had left the state—but the idea that Latinos contributed several billion dollars
annually to the state's economy did get considerable media attention.[14]

Addy's economic forecast seemed to be playing out across the state. In
the small towns in north Alabama where many Latinos lived and worked, tax
collections for local governments and schools began shrinking. In enacting
HB 56, the legislature ignored these expected economic consequences. The
law's architects were not happy with Addy's report, some calling it "baloney."
It is telling, however, that the legislature never considered commissioning its
own independent economic study of possible outcomes or, later, challenging
Addy's conclusions. Supporters of HB 56 continued to contend that denying
work to Latino immigrants made jobs available to American workers, that
HB 56 was actually a "jobs-creation" bill, a typical Republican mantra at
the time. Alabama Congressman Mo Brooks typified this way of thinking
in a speech on the floor of the U.S. House of Representatives: "Evict all
illegal aliens from America and immediately open up millions of jobs for
unemployed Americans." In an interview with a reporter in 2013, State
Senator Scott Beason also emphasized the jobs-creation benefits of HB 56:
"Some of the pointy heads [a nod here to former Alabama Governor George

Wallace, who often denigrated professors, intellectuals, and government bureaucrats as "pointy heads"] can say that they don't see it statistically, but I've had normal people, everyday people, seek me out at restaurants, Walmart, wherever and thanking me for helping them and their families." Brooks, Beason, and others relied on opinion, anecdote, and "talking points" because they had nothing else. Several economists and business groups in Alabama contended that no factual evidence supported the positions advanced by Brooks and Beason. By the end of 2011, when tens of thousands of Latinos had abandoned their jobs in poultry, agriculture, landscaping, construction, and service occupations, few unemployed Alabamians rushed in to replace them. In a September 2012 editorial, the *Birmingham News* challenged state officials "to come forward with evidence showing HB 56 had put people back to work." The self-described "job creators" in the legislature never responded.[15]

THE LEGAL ROLLBACK

Opposition to HB 56 quickly led to legal challenges. Diverse organizations such as the SPLC, the American Civil Liberties Union, various church groups, and the Hispanic Interest Coalition of Alabama (a Birmingham-based organization of Latino professionals that represented and lobbied for Latino immigrants) filed lawsuits in federal district court. Generally, they argued that HB 56 violated the supremacy clause of the U.S. Constitution that designated matters of immigration as a federal responsibility. Their briefs also contended that HB 56 violated the unlawful search and seizure clause and the equal protection clause, respectively, of the Fourth and Fourteenth Amendments to the U.S. Constitution. The U.S. Justice Department also challenged HB 56 on constitutional grounds. In August 2011, U.S. District Court Judge Sharon Blackburn temporarily blocked implementation of the law while she reviewed the case. Blackburn's subsequent ruling on September 28, 2011, upheld most of the key sections of HB 56 and rejected arguments that Alabama's action intruded on federal authority or constitutional rights. Opponents of HB 56 expressed serious concern that Blackburn did not rule against local police authority to "stop-check" drivers' immigration status, which they considered a form of racial profiling. However, Blackburn did block implementation of a few HB 56 provisions: undocumented immigrants could still seek work (but employers were required to use E-Verify), and they could attend state universities if admitted and if they paid out-of-state tuition. Harboring, transporting, or renting to undocumented people could no longer be criminalized by the state. Beyond that, Blackburn's ruling upheld the most repressive sections of HB 56 and represented a clear victory for the state legislature and supporters of the nation's toughest immigration law.[16]

Judge Blackburn did not end the battle over immigration in Alabama. In the wake of the Blackburn decision, Alabama's agricultural and industrial interests, desperately in need of workers, sought "relief" from the legislature in the form of exceptions to the law. Latinos began a new exodus from the state. Protests, demonstrations, boycotts, and prayer marches opposing HB 56 picked up steam around the state, including rallies at important Civil Rights sites in Montgomery and Birmingham. Pro-immigration activists descended on Alabama, social workers and community organizers who networked with local groups in support of immigrants confused by the new law and its implications. Reminiscent of the 1960s Civil Rights battles, anti-immigrant spokespersons labeled these new community activists "outside agitators," perhaps forgetting that they had their own chief outside agitators, Kris Kobach and Michael Hethmon, who wrote the HB 56 legislation.[17]

Diverse organizations and agencies joined the call for blocking enforcement of HB 56. For instance, the Alabama Coalition for Immigrant Justice (ACIJ), a "grassroots network" of local organizations founded in 2006 by the Greater Birmingham Ministries and "galvanized" by passage of HB 56, took a leading role in these activities supporting Alabama's immigrant communities. Union leaders, agricultural and construction groups, poultry interests, and mobile home park owners publicly opposed the law. The Southern Poverty Law Center, Human Rights Watch, and the national AFL-CIO published detailed reports on the devastating social and humanitarian consequences of HB 56 for Hispanic families and communities. Business organizations, such as the Birmingham Business Alliance, worried about the effect of HB 56 on economic development in the state. Mayors and police officials expressed concerns about unfunded enforcement mandates draining municipal budgets. The U.S. Department of Justice sent several lawyers to Alabama to monitor potential violations of civil liberties and civil rights. The *Birmingham News*, the *New York Times*, and other newspapers editorialized on the emergence of a new Alabama civil rights movement focused on immigrant rights. In November 2011, the National Day Labor Organizing Network held a three-day workshop in Albertville that discussed ways of organizing and empowering local communities to "fight back" against those who targeted immigrants.[18]

Responding to pushback by HB 56 opponents, some Alabama politicians, including Governor Bentley and Attorney General Luther Strange, began backing off, suggesting that the law might need some "tweaking" to make it less "complicated." Bentley had not changed his views on illegal immigration in Alabama, but he seemed especially concerned about the damage to the state's image and the potential loss of foreign investment. Those concerns were magnified in late 2011 when, in two separate incidents, local police at checkpoints arrested German and Japanese auto executives without valid Alabama driver's licenses; Mercedes-Benz and Honda both had large auto plants in Alabama, attracted by tax incentives, infrastructure support, and favorable state economic development policies. The arrests subjected Bentley and the state generally to embarrassment and ridicule.[19]

Meanwhile, opponents of HB 56, including the U.S. Department of Justice and numerous plaintiffs, had turned to the 11th U.S Circuit Court of Appeals. In October 2011, the Appeals Court granted a temporary injunction blocking immigration status checks for newly enrolled public school students, a clear rebuke to Michael Hethmon, who drafted that provision of HB 56. The injunction also suspended the criminalization of immigrants without alien identification documents. A month later, the same court blocked still another section of HB 56—this one a provision that required proof of citizenship or legal status in applying for annual mobile home registrations. Significant numbers of Latinos in rural areas and small towns lived in mobile home parks. Following the court's ruling, a Southern Poverty Law Center news release noted that the decision endorsed its key legal argument against HB 56: "The court found that there was substantial evidence that the law was adopted with discriminatory intent against Latinos," and that Alabama's legislators "conflated race and immigration status." In March 2012, the Appeals Court enjoined additional sections of HB 56. This legal decision blocked the HB 56 prohibition of business transactions by illegal immigrants with state and local governments. It also reversed the HB 56 provision that denied Alabama citizens, rental agents, car salesmen, and others the right to enter contracts with undocumented immigrants. With most of its harsh provisions now blocked by various courts, HB 56 was, the *Birmingham News* reported, "a shadow of the 72-page measure" enacted in June 2011. As news of the various court decisions circulated in Alabama's immigrant communities, some Latinos began "trickling back" to the state.[20]

In May 2012, with overwhelming Republican majorities, the state legislature finally passed and Governor Bentley signed HB 658 revising the original immigration law. However, instead of moderating the harsh intent of the original law, the Republicans "doubled down" by adding a few new punitive provisions. For instance, HB 658 required that the names of all undocumented immigrants arrested for any state violation be published on Alabama's official state website. The new law, the *Los Angeles Times* wrote, had no "useful purpose" except "to shame immigrants." With HB 56 mostly blocked by legal action and HB 658 not yet in effect, all awaited the U.S. Supreme Court's pending decision on Arizona's anti-immigrant law, which was widely expected to have immediate implications for Alabama and other states that passed tough laws regulating and restricting undocumented immigrants.[21]

The Arizona decision was not long in coming. On June 25, 2012, by a 6–2 vote, the Supreme Court handed down its decision overturning almost every section of Arizona's immigration legislation. The Court affirmed federal authority over immigration matters, but it also let stand the authority of Arizona law enforcement officials to check the immigration status of drivers stopped for traffic infractions or other criminal offenses. Immigrant advocates had been deeply critical of the Arizona law's "stop-check" provision, which they argued permitted racial profiling. Thus the Court's decision on this matter provided the state with some limited control over illegal immigration, but its implementation would always be controversial and could be subject to further litigation. More significantly, the Court slapped down the rest of Arizona's SB 1070. Immigrants without papers were no longer subject to arrest or "unnecessary harassment," and illegal immigrants seeking work were no longer considered criminals. With only the "stop-check" exception, the Court de-criminalized undocumented immigrants. The Supreme Court's Arizona decision essentially decimated the law that served as a model for Alabama legislators. The Arizona decision also represented a powerful reprimand to the legal team of Kobach and Hethmon that had shaped immigration legislation in both states. Linda Greenhouse, a *New York Times* reporter who covered the Supreme Court, concluded that the Arizona decision was "a major reaffirmation of federal authority."[22]

The Supreme Court had ruled, but the immigration battles in Alabama persisted. In the aftermath of the Arizona decision, both sides claimed a victory of sorts. However, disagreement and confusion over enforcement of stop-check details in Alabama and elsewhere left legislators, police officials, pro-immigrant groups, and especially immigrants themselves struggling for clarity and guidance. Latino immigrants began returning to Alabama, but fear and intimidation persisted for many. Some claimed that racial profiling and housing discrimination intensified; others reported that immigrant children had been taunted and bullied at school. Thousands of protestors, led by church groups and the Alabama Coalition for Immigrant Justice, regularly marched and demonstrated in Montgomery, the state capital, especially during the first half of 2012, when the legislature was meeting and drafting the HB 658 revision. In April 2012, several hundred Alabama church leaders rallied outside the Statehouse in Montgomery, challenging the "xenophobic and racist" immigration restrictions imposed on Latino newcomers by the legislature. Big farmers, landscapers, and construction firms still had trouble finding workers with proper documents. Desperate for workers, poultry plant managers in some small towns had already hired labor brokers to recruit Haitians, Eritreans, Asians, and Puerto Ricans with legal documents to cut and process chickens. It was no secret that some Alabama legislators sought to de-racialize the labor force in small-town Alabama. However, the big corporate poultry companies had little concern for the race or nationality of their workers as long as the disassembly lines kept moving and the profits kept rolling in. The Supreme Court had spoken, but immigration issues remained contested.[23]

By July 2012, lawyers for the state of Alabama and for pro-immigrant groups were back in the courtroom of the 11th U.S. Circuit Court of Appeals. Each side sought new rulings on the few remaining sections of HB 56 in light of the Supreme Court's Arizona decision. In August, the Appeals Court issued a sweeping ruling blocking almost all of HB 56's thirty provisions. In particular, the court invalidated Section 28 of HB 56 requiring immigration verification of new students enrolling in Alabama's public schools. This requirement, the court determined, violated the equal protection clause of the Fourteenth Amendment. The court also blocked any remaining provisions in HB 56 regarding contracts and registrations. However, the court allowed immigrant document checks during traffic stops, but agreed to consider future challenges to that section of the law. Most tellingly, the Court of Appeals blasted the Alabama legislature for its willful attack on immigrants. As the court decision stated: "We are convinced that Alabama has crafted a calculated policy of expulsion, seeking to make the lives of unlawfully present aliens so difficult as to force them to retreat from the state."[24]

The anti-immigration campaign sputtered to a conclusion in November 2013 with a final settlement between plaintiffs and the state of Alabama. Approved by U.S. District Court Judge Sharon Blackburn, the settlement permanently blocked all of the most punitive sections of HB 56. Only the provisions requiring employers to use E-Verify during the hiring process and permitting document checks during traffic stops remained. Advocates and opponents of HB 56 each claimed vindication. Unapologetic, state legislators Hammon and Beason contended that the campaign against illegal immigrants was worth the sizeable costs to the state and its economy. Dis-ingenuously, they argued that keeping undocumented workers out of the labor force through E-Verify was always the most important provision of the law, somehow forgetting their relentless effort to prevent Latinos from "putting down roots" and to push them completely out of Alabama. And who could forget Alabama Congressman Mo Brooks's angry rant at a July 2011 town hall meeting in Decatur? Brooks made national headlines when he said that, when it came to getting rid of illegal Latinos, "I would do anything short of shooting them." Conservative Republican politicians tried to put the best face on the legal outcome, but remained committed to the hard-line anti-immigrant position. By contrast, opponents of HB 56 saw the legal settlement as a victory for the constitutional rights of immigrants, as well as for fairness and diversity in Alabama. Acerbic columnist John Archibald of the *Birmingham News* had the last word: for Archibald, the effort to drive Latinos out of Alabama "was just another big waste."[25]

THE POLITICS OF EXPULSION

For Alabama's Republican politicians, the policy of Latino expulsion seemed a potentially effective political strategy in a very conservative south-ern state. It was a policy that appealed to xenophobic fears of racial diversity, cultural change, and economic competition. The anti-Latino campaign in Alabama may have made sense to hard-right politicians and those who voted for them, but it was a misguided policy from the very beginning. Latinos made up a very small percentage of Alabama's total population—3.9 percent in 2010—and an even smaller proportion—0.5 percent—of public school students. In fact, new Latino migration to Alabama and other southern states began to decline dramatically in 2008, a consequence of the deep economic recession in the United States at the time, which discouraged new migration. By 2012, according to demographers at the Population Reference Bureau, "net immigration levels from Mexico are estimated to have reached zero in recent years." Ironically, the nativist hysteria that lay behind HB 56 culminated at the very time that new migration had virtually ceased.[26]

The nativist political discourse was off base in other ways, as well. Young, second-generation Latinos were quickly assimilating into American main-stream culture, largely through public school and college attendance, popular culture, and social media. Furthermore, according to immigration and labor specialists, American workers had little to fear from Latino economic or job competition except at the low end of the labor market. The biggest threat to

Alabamians' jobs came from deindustrialization in textile, apparel, carpet, furniture, plastics, and electronics manufacturing—jobs lost to overseas production in a globalizing economy over the past few decades. As in the nation generally, a mismatch developed between jobs lost in those sectors and the newer skilled positions opening up in automotive manufacturing, medical research, higher education, information technology, and other fields that were reshaping Alabama's economy in the twenty-first century. Latinos in agriculture and poultry were not stealing American jobs, but were doing the low-paid, backbreaking labor that American workers avoided. Kevian Deravi, an economics professor at Auburn University in Montgomery, weighed in on this jobs discourse in an August 2011 interview that minimized the impact of Latino workers in the total state labor market. Deravi estimated there were about 120,000 undocumented Latino workers in Alabama, but that was just a tiny proportion—about 6.3 percent—of the state's 1.9 million workers. As Deravi concluded, the state legislature "took a sledgehammer to hit a gnat." Nevertheless, conservative Republican rhetoric hammered home these false fears about race, culture, and jobs at every opportunity for more than a decade.[27]

Collectively labeling Mexicans and Central Americans as "illegal" provided the cover of respectability for the policy of Latino expulsion. The Alabama legislature, newly controlled by Republicans, and influenced by Tea Party activists and conservative organizations such as FAIR, latched onto the idea of state regulation of immigration. It was also a policy of state-sponsored racial discrimination, which raised ugly memories of the bad old days in Jim Crow Alabama. Congressional failure to address immigration reform and the problem of undocumented immigrants encouraged states such as Alabama to move into the policy vacuum. The result was HB 56, a "race-based attack on Latinos." As in the Civil Rights Era, Alabama rejected federal authority and pursued a policy of discrimination—a conclusion that was easily, and often, drawn by immigrant supporters and independent observers such as journalists, and eventually by federal judges. The restrictive Arizona immigration law provided a model, but Alabama officials, working with Kris Kobach and Michael Hethmon, pushed beyond Arizona to create the nation's most extreme immigrant-control legislation— Alabama was "Arizona on steroids," suggested immigration scholar Michael A. Olivas. Proud of their lawmaking accomplishments, Alabama legislators gained extensive media attention and support on the radical right. However, they gave little thought to the impact of HB 56 on real people—children, families, entire communities—or to the predictable consequences for the economic interests that relied on Latino labor. For state legislators Beason, Hammon, and the others, HB 56 was all about making a political statement and taking a stand against unwanted racial change in Alabama.[28]

The HB 56 legislation brought nativism and xenophobia into the political mainstream in Alabama. As anthropologist Chris Kyle has written, "the feeding frenzy among [conservative Republican] red states to see who could be the most nativist was an important element of the historical moment that HB 56 represented." That historical moment also involved a presidential election campaign in which Republican candidate Mitt Romney endorsed an immigration policy of "self-deportation." Not surprisingly, Kris Kobach served as an "informal" Romney campaign advisor on immigration issues. The U.S. Supreme Court has now spoken on the unconstitutionality of punitive and discriminatory state and local immigration laws targeting specific racial or ethnic groups. But the Court itself is badly divided on ideological grounds, and the radical right is gearing up to reshape the federal judiciary through appointments and lobbying. The U.S. Congress is gridlocked on the subject of federal immigration reform, with most Democrats supportive and most Republicans opposed. A February 2014 national poll conducted by the Pew Research Center revealed that 46 percent of Americans support "a path to citizenship" for undocumented immigrants. Nevertheless, the radical right seems to be able to control the media debate and to prevent Congress from taking action. The Supreme Court outlawed the policy of expulsion, but the persistence of nativist thinking in places where it counts, such as in state legislatures and the Republican-controlled House of Representatives, means that a politics of inclusion may be difficult to achieve anytime soon.[29]

NOTES

1. Mike Davis, "The Right Wing Calls the Shots," in *No One Is Illegal: Fighting Racism and State Violence on the U.S.-Mexico Border*, by Justin Akers Chacón and Mike Davis (Chicago: Haymarket Books, 2006), 237–47 (quote: 237).

2. Yanyi K. Djamba, Theresa C. Davidson, and Terance L. Winemiller, "The Hispanic Population in Alabama," Center for Demographic Research, Auburn Montgomery Outreach, May 2012; Kevin R. Johnson, "Sweet Home Alabama? Immigration and Civil Rights in the 'New' South," *Stanford Law Review* [online], December 5, 2011, http://www.stanfordlawreview .org/online/sweet-home-alabama; Fred L. Hammond to Robert Bentley, June 3, 2011, http://serenityhome.wordpress.com/2011/06/03/uu-alabama-ministers-send-gov-bentley -message-on-HB56. For earlier studies of Latino immigration to Alabama, see Raymond A. Mohl, "Latinization in the Heart of Dixie: Hispanics in Late-Twentieth-Century Alabama," *Alabama Review* 55, no. 4 (October 2002): 243–71; Raymond A. Mohl, "Globalization and Latin American Immigration in Alabama," in *Latino Immigrants and the Transformation of*

the U.S. South, ed. Mary E. Odem and Elaine Lacy (Athens: University of Georgia Press, 2009), 51–69. For key studies that provide historical background and global context for Latino migration to Alabama and the American South, see Douglas S. Massey, Jorge Durand, and Nolan J. Malone, *Beyond Smoke and Mirrors: Mexican Immigration in an Era of Economic Integration* (New York: Russell Sage Foundation, 2002); Kathleen C. Schwartzman, *The Chicken Trail: Following Workers, Migrants, and Corporations across the Americas* (Ithaca, NY: Cornell University Press, 2013); and Mark Overmyer-Velázquez, ed., *Beyond la Frontera: The History of Mexico-U.S. Migration* (New York: Oxford University Press, 2011).

3. Walter Bryant, "Panel Says Immigration Laws Must Be Enforced," *Birmingham News*, July 15, 2007; "Immigration Panel to Hold Hearing," *Birmingham News*, January 9, 2008; Mike Cason, "Hundreds Gather, Call for Immigration Crackdown," *Birmingham News*, January 11, 2008. For the Commission's final report, see "Joint Interim Patriotic Immigration Commission Report," January 10, 2008. On the rise of a new nativism in recent years, see Juan F. Perea, ed., *Immigrants Out! The New Nativism and the Anti-Immigrant Impulse in the United States* (New York: New York University Press, 1996); David M. Reimers, *Unwelcome Strangers: American Identity and the Turn against Immigration* (New York: Columbia University Press, 1998); Peter Schrag, *Not Fit for America: Immigration and Nativism* (Berkeley: University of California Press, 2010). Contemporary nativists can draw on a long anti-immigrant tradition in the United States. See, especially, John Higham, *Strangers in the Land: Patterns of American Nativism, 1860–1925* (New Brunswick, NJ: Rutgers University Press, 1955); David H. Bennett, *The Party of Fear: From Nativist Movements to the New Right in American History* (Chapel Hill: University of North Carolina Press, 1988); Ellis Cose, *A Nation of Strangers: Prejudice, Politics, and the Populating of America* (New York: William Morrow, 1992); Tyler Anbinder, "Nativism and Prejudice against Immigrants," in *A Companion to American Immigration*, ed. Reed Ueda (Malden, MA: Blackwell, 2006), 177–201.

4. Phillip Rawls, "English-Only Driver Exam Support High," *Birmingham News*, January 27, 2008; Kent Faulk, "Cities Increasing Penalties for Unlicensed Drivers," *Birmingham News*, January 27, 2008; David White, "House Panel OKs Illegal-Immigrant Benefit Ban," *Birmingham News*, May 8, 2008; Southern Poverty Law Center, "Racial Profiling by Law Enforcement Is Constant Threat," in *Under Siege: Life for Low-Income Latinos in the South*, principal author Mary Bauer (Montgomery, AL: Southern Poverty Law Center, 2009), 16–24, https://www.splcenter.org/sites/default/files/d6_legacy_files/downloads/UnderSiege.pdf; Mary Ondorff, "Sessions Quizzes Candidates on Immigration," *Birmingham News*, January 25, 2008. A prelude of things to come, significant hostility toward Latino immigrants emerged as early as 1990, when 88 percent of statewide voters approved an "official English" amendment to the Alabama Constitution. See Raymond Tatalovich, *Nativism Reborn: The Official English Language Movement and the American States* (Lexington: University Press of Kentucky, 1995), 182–85, 194–224; William Branigin, "As Hispanic Numbers Rise, Some Say No to Spanish," *Birmingham News*, February 7, 1999.

5. Kevin O'Leary, "Arizona's Tough New Law against Illegal Immigrants," *Time*, April 16, 2010, http://content.time.com/time/nation/article/0,8599,1982268,00.html (quotes); Randal C. Archibold, "Arizona Enacts Stringent Law on Immigration," *New York Times*, April 23, 2010, http://www.nytimes.com/2010/04/24/us/politics/24immig.html?_r=0; Pew Hispanic Center, "Hispanics and Arizona's New Immigration Law," Fact Sheet, April 29, 2010, http://www.pewhispanic.org/2010/04/29/hispanics-and-arizonas-new-immigration-law; Rick Su,

"The Overlooked Significance of Arizona's New Immigration Law," *Michigan Law Review* 76 (2010), http://www.michiganlawreview.org/assets/fi/108/su.pdf; Kristina M. Campbell, "The Road to S.B. 1070: How Arizona Became Ground Zero for the Immigrants' Rights Movement and the Continuing Struggle for Latino Civil Rights in America," *Harvard Latino Law Review* 14 (Spring 2011): 1–21; Kris W. Kobach, "Obama's Lawlessness on Immigration," *Human Events*, July 7, 2010, http://www.humanevents.com/article.php?i=37913. For the origins of the policy of "attrition through enforcement," see Kris W. Kobach, "State and Local Authority to Enforce Immigration Law: A Unified Approach for Stopping Terrorists," Center for Immigration Studies, June 2004, http://cis.org/StateEnforcement -LocalEnforcement; and Mark Krikorian, "Downsizing Illegal Immigration: A Strategy of Attrition through Enforcement," Center for Immigration Studies, May 2005, http://cis.org/ ReducingIllegalImmigration-Attrition-Enforcement. For a deeper history and analysis of the origins and impact of the Arizona law, see *Latino Politics and Arizona's Immigration Law SB 1070*, ed. Lisa Magaña and Erik Lee (New York: Springer, 2013), especially chap. 8, by Luis F. B. Plascencia, "Attrition through Enforcement and the Elimination of a 'Dangerous Class,'" in *Latino Politics*, ed. Magaña and Lee, 93–127.

6. Kobach, "State and Local Authority"; Kris W. Kobach, "Attrition through Enforcement: A Rational Approach to Illegal Immigration," *Tulsa Journal of Comparative and International Law* 15, no. 2 (2008): 153–61; Julia Preston, "Lawyer Leads an Immigration Fight," *New York Times*, July 20, 2009, http://www.nytimes.com/2009/07/21/us/21lawyer.html; Leah Nelson, with Evelyn Schlatter, and Heidi Beirich, "When Mr. Kobach Comes to Town: Nativist Laws and the Communities They Damage," Southern Poverty Law Center, January 29, 2011, https:// www.splcenter.org/20110130/when-mr-kobach-comes-town-nativist-laws-and-communities -they-damage; Suzy Khimm, "Kris Kobach, Nativist Son," *Mother Jones* (March/April 2012), http://www.motherjones.com/politics/2012/03/kris-kobach-anti-immigration-laws -sb-1070; George Talbot, "Kris Kobach, the Kansas Lawyer behind Alabama's Immigration Law," *Mobile Press-Register*, October 16, 2011.

7. On FAIR, see Jean Stefancic, "Funding the Nativist Agenda," in *Immigrants Out!*, 119–35; Reimers, *Unwelcome Strangers*, 46–54; Southern Poverty Law Center, "Anti-Immigrant Groups," Intelligence Report, Spring 2001 (see also https://www.splcenter .org/fighting-hate/intelligence-report/2015/active-anti-immigrant-groups); Heidi Beirich, "Federation for American Immigration Reform's Hate Filled Track Record," Southern Poverty Law Center, *Intelligence Report* 128, Winter 2007, https://www.splcenter.org/fighting -hate/intelligence-report/2007/federation-american-immigration-reform%E2%80%99s-hate -filled-track-record; Heidi Beirich, "Nativist Lawyer Kris Kobach Plays Dumb about His Employer's Racism," Southern Poverty Law Center Report, February 23, 2012, https:// www.splcenter.org/hatewatch/2012/02/23/nativist-lawyer-kris-kobach-plays-dumb-about -his-employer%E2%80%99s-racism. On Proposition 187 in California, see Marcelo M. Suárez-Orozco, "The Need for Strangers: Proposition 187 and the Immigration Malaise," *MultiCultural Review* 4, no. 2 (June 1995): 17–23, 56–58; Robin Dale Jacobson, *The New Nativism: Proposition 187 and the Debate over Immigration* (Minneapolis: University of Minnesota Press, 2008); Gebe Martinez, "Learning from Proposition 187: California's Past Is Arizona's Prologue," *American Progress Report*, May 5, 2010, https://www.americanprogress .org/issues/immigration/news/2010/05/05/7847/learning-from-proposition-187/; Jason DeParle, "The Anti-Immigration Crusader," *New York Times*, April 17, 2011, http://www .nytimes.com/2011/04/17/us/17immig.html?pagewanted=all; Robert Suro, *Strangers among*

Us: Latino Immigrants in Changing America (New York: Alfred A. Knopf, 1998), 107–16; Peter Schrag, *Paradise Lost: California's Experience, America's Future* (New York: New Press, 1998), 229–34, 255–56.

8. Walter Bryant, "Panel Says Immigration Laws Must Be Enforced," *Birmingham News*, July 15, 2007; Talbot, "Kris Kolbach, the Kansas Lawyer"; "Great Profile of Author of AL Immigration Law, Kris Kobach, in the Press-Register," Eagle Forum of Alabama, October 17, 2011, http://www.alabamaeagle.org/2011/10/17/great-profile; Tina Ford to Raymond A. Mohl, e-mail message, September 3, 2010. Tina Ford was an anti-immigrant activist in Birmingham working with Kobach, Ellis, and other city leaders on immigration restriction legislation.

9. Val Walton, "Hispanic Residents Up 161% in Area," *Birmingham News*, February 25, 2011; Phillip Rawls, "White Democrats Vanishing in State," *Birmingham News*, December 14, 2010; Kim Severson, "Southern Lawmakers Focus on Illegal Immigrants," *New York Times*, March 25, 2011, http://www.nytimes.com/2011/03/26/us/26immig.html.

10. For the full text of HB 56, see https://legiscan.com/AL/text/HB56/id/321074. For journalistic and other commentary on HB 56, see Julia Preston, "In Alabama, a Harsh Bill for Residents Here Illegally," *New York Times*, June 3, 2011, http://www.nytimes.com/2011/06/04/us/04immig.html; Eric Velasco, "Immigration Law Draws Praise, Scorn," *Birmingham News*, June 10, 2011; Stephen M. NeSmith, Jr., "Our Economy Needs Illegal Immigrants," *Birmingham News*, June 12, 2011; Greg Garrison, "Immigration Law Called 'Meanest' in US," *Birmingham News*, June 16, 2011; "Immigration Angst," *Birmingham News*, June 23, 2011; Patrik Jonsson, "Alabama Immigration Law Faces Legal Challenge: Can It Survive?" *Christian Science Monitor*, July 8, 2011, http://www.csmonitor.com/USA/Politics/2011/0708/Alabama-immigration-law-faces-legal-challenge-Can-it-survive/Arizona; Paul Harris, "Tensions Rise as Latinos Feel under Siege in America's Deep South," *Guardian*, August 20, 2011, http://www.guardian.co.uk/world/2011/aug/21/racist-immigration-law-in-deep-south; Patrik Jonsson, "Alabama Life Already Changing under Tough Immigration Law," *Christian Science Monitor*, September 29, 2011, http://www.csmonitor.com/USA/2011/0929/Alabama-life-already-changing-under-tough-immigration-law; George Talbot, "Alien Law Author Proud of Success," *Birmingham News*, October 16, 2011; Diane McWhorter, "The Strange Career of Juan Crow," *New York Times*, June 16, 2012 (includes Hammon quotation), http://www.nytimes.com/2012/06/17/opinion/sunday/no-sweet-home-alabama.html.

11. Campbell Robertson, "Critics See 'Chilling Effect' in Alabama Immigration Law," *New York Times*, October 27, 2011, http://www.nytimes.com/2011/10/28/us/alabama-immigration-laws-critics-question-target.html; Wendy Feliz, "Restrictionist Lawyer Reveals Long-Term Assault on Immigrant Children," Immigrant Impact, October 28, 2011, http://www.immigrationimpact.com/2011/10/28/restrictionist-lawyer-reveals-long-term-assault-on-immirant-children; Jeremy B. Love, "Alabama Introduces the Immigration Debate to Its Classrooms," *Human Rights* 38, no. 4 (2011): 7–10, http://www.americanbar.org/publications/human_rights_magazine_home/human_rights_vol38_2011/fall2011/alabama_introduces_the_immigration_debate_to_its_classrooms.html; Greg Varner, "Attorney General Strange Admits Ulterior Motive of Section 28 of HB 56," December 8, 2011, http://keatingsdesk.wordpress.com/2011/12/08/attorney-general-strange-admits-ulterior-motive; Mary Bauer, "Court Cites Discriminatory Intent behind Alabama's Anti-Immigrant Law," Southern Poverty Law Center, December 13, 2011, https://www.splcenter.org/news/2011/12/14/court

-cites-discriminatory-intent-behind-alabamas-anti-immigrant-law; David A. Fahrenthold, "Self-Deportation Proponents Kris Kobach, Michel Hethmon Facing Time of Trial," *Washington Post*, April 24, 2012, http://www.washingtonpost.com/politics/2012/04/24/gIQAe6lheT_story.html; John Caniglia, "Controversial Lawyer Michael Hethmon Debates Immigration Policy at Cleveland State University," *Cleveland Plain Dealer*, May 12, 2012, http://www.cleveland.com/metro/index.ssf/2012/05/controversial_lawyer_debates_i.html. FAIR had opposed the *Plyler v. Doe* decision and had been concerned about rising numbers of immigrant children in schools since at least 2002. See FAIR, "Immigration Issues: School Overcrowding (2002)," October 2002, http://www.fairus.org/issue/school-overcrowding. For a legal history of the *Plyler* case, see Michael A. Olivas, *No Undocumented Child Left Behind: Plyler v. Doe and the Education of Undocumented Schoolchildren* (New York: New York University Press, 2009).

12. Margaret Newkirk, "Hispanics Flee Alabama's Immigration Law," *Bloomberg Businessweek*, June 28, 2011; Mark Guarino, "Hispanics Leave School in Face of Alabama's Tough Immigration Law," *Christian Science Monitor*, October 1, 2011, http://www.csmonitor.com/USA/2011/1001/Hispanics-leave-school-in-face-of-Alabama-s-tough-immigration-law; AFL-CIO, "Crisis in Alabama: Investigating the Devastating Effects of HB 56," December 15, 2011, http://www.aflcio.org/content/download/4366/46493/alabama.pdf; Human Rights Watch, "No Way To Live: Alabama's Immigrant Law," December 2011, http://www.hrw.org/sites/default/files/reports/us1211ForUpload_1.pdf; Mary Bauer, "Testimony before Congressional Ad Hoc HB 56 Hearing," December 21, 2011, http://dreamact.info/forum/showthread.php?t=25797; Southern Poverty Law Center, "Alabama's Shame: HB 56 and the War on Immigrants," 2012, https://www.splcenter.org/sites/default/files/d6_legacy_files/downloads/publication/Alabamas_Shame.pdf; Garrison, "Immigration Law Called 'Meanest,'"; Kent Faulk, "Church Leaders File Statements in Court on Immigration Law," *Birmingham News*, August 19, 2011; Brian Lyman, "Catholic League Criticizes Illegal-Immigration Law," *Montgomery Advertiser*, August 30, 2011. On Juan Crow, see McWhorter, "Strange Career of Juan Crow"; David Person, "'Juan Crow' Law Alive in Alabama," *USA Today*, November 1, 2011, http://usatoday30.usatoday.com/news/opinion/forum/story/2011-11-01/alabama-illegal-immigration-law/51031138/1; Jennifer E. Brooks, "'No Juan Crow!,'" *Southern Cultures* 18, no. 3 (Fall 2012): 49–56. For Henderson quotation, see Richard Fausset, "Alabama Enacts Anti-Illegal Immigration Law Described as Nation's Strictest," *Los Angeles Times*, June 10, 2011, http://articles.latimes.com/2011/jun/10/nation/la-na-alabama-immigration-20110610. For Hammon quotation, see Preston, "In Alabama, a Harsh Bill." On "bragging," see Kevin Johnson, "Alabama Highlights Civil Rights Concerns in State Immigration Law," http://jurist.org/forum/2011/11/kevin-johnson-alabama-immigration.php. On the role of church groups in fighting HB 56, see also Angie Wright, ed., *Love Has No Borders: How Faith Leaders Resisted Alabama's Harsh Immigration Law* (Birmingham, AL: Greater Birmingham Ministries, 2013).

13. Kim Chandler, "Farmers, Builders Worried about Law," *Birmingham News*, October 2, 2011; Campbell Robertson, "After Ruling, Hispanics Flee an Alabama Town," *New York Times*, October 3, 2011, http://www.nytimes.com/2011/10/04/us/after-ruling-hispanics-flee-an-alabama-town.html; Rick Jervis and Alan Gomez, "Tough Immigration Law Raises Fears in Alabama," *USA Today,* October 19, 2011: A1; "Val Walton, "Where Have All the Day Laborers Gone?," *Birmingham News*, April 3, 2011; Jay Reeves, "Hispanic Students Exit Schools," *Birmingham News*, October 1, 2011; Roy L. Williams, "'I Have Said Over and Over,

When Alabama Works, Alabama Wins,'" *Birmingham News*, October 9, 2011 (interview with Jay Reed); Jay Reeves and Alicia A. Caldwell, "Few Americans Taking Immigrants' Jobs in Alabama," *Twin Cities*, October 21, 2011, http://www.twincities.com/ci_19160035; Jonsson, "Alabama Life Already Changing" (McMillan quote); Dan Rivoli, "Alabama Immigration Law: Worker-Strapped Farm Groups Doubt Prison Remedy," *International Business Times*, October 7, 2011, http://www.ibtimes.com/alabama-immigration-law-worker-strapped-farm -groups-doubt-prisoner-remedy-322016; Elizabeth Dwoskin, "Why Americans Won't Do Dirty Jobs," *Bloomberg Business*, November 9, 2011, http://www.bloomberg.com/bw/ magazine/why-americans-wont-do-dirty-jobs-11092011.html; Paul Reyes, "A State without Mexicans?," *Mother Jones*, September 28, 2011, http://www.motherjones.com/ politics/2011/09/hb-56-alabama-immigration-law. On Alabama's unemployment rates, see Kathleen Gabler, "The Great Recession: 18 Months Before, During, and After," Center for Business and Economic Research, University of Alabama, Tuscaloosa, 2011.

14. Samuel Addy, "A Cost–Benefit Study of the New Alabama Immigration Law," Center for Business and Economic Research, University of Alabama, Tuscaloosa, January 2012; "Immigration Law: A Steep Price to Pay," *Economist*, February 2, 2012, http:// www.economist.com/blogs/democracyinamerica/2012.02/immigration; Elizabeth Dwoskin, "Alabama's Immigration Law Could Cost Billions Annually," *Bloomberg Business*, February 14, 2012, http://www.bloomberg.com/bw/articles/2012–02–14/alabamas-immigration-law -could-cost-billions-annually. An earlier panel of economists meeting at Samford University in Homewood, a Birmingham suburb, also predicted that HB 56 would cause serious economic consequences for Alabama. Martin Swant, "Panel: Law Would Hurt State's Economy," *Birmingham News*, July 21, 2011. In March 2012, demographers at Auburn University at Montgomery and the University of Alabama at Tuscaloosa suggested a different economic argument for immigration: that Alabama's aging population needed the infusion of new immigrant replacements in the workforce to prevent a decline in the state's economy, especially the service sector. See Tim Lockette, "Immigrants Needed in State, Experts Say," *Birmingham News*, March 12, 2012.

15. "Phony 'Baloney,'" *Birmingham News*, February 2, 2012; Sarah Peters, "GOP Rep Says Removing Illegal Immigrants a US Jobs Program," The Hill, September 20, 2011, http://thehill.com/blogs/floor-action/house/182845-house-republican-says-getting-rid-of -illegals-a-us-jobs-program (for Brooks quotation); James Lewis, "HB 56 Hurts Alabama's Economy More Than It Helps," *Birmingham News*, October 9, 2011; Mike Cason, "Despite Legal Settlements, Immigration Debate Goes On," *Birmingham News*, November 3, 2013; Mike Cason, "HB56 Two Years Later: Settlement Takes Bite out of Alabama's Immigration Law," November 3, 2013, http://blog.al.com/wire/2013/11/hb56_two_years_later_constitut .html (for Beason quotation); "Not a Jobs Bill," *Birmingham News*, September 9, 2012.

16. Jonsson, "Alabama Immigration Law Faces Legal Challenge"; "HICA Files Lawsuit Challenging House Bill 56 Anti-Immigration Law," HICA News and Updates, July 8, 2011, http://www.hispanicinterest.org/news/hica-files-lawsuit-challenging-house-bill-56-anti -immigration-law/; "A Constitutional Assault," *Birmingham News*, July 31, 2011; Kent Faulk, "Justice, Bishops Sue over State Law," *Birmingham News*, August 2, 2011; Daniel Altschuler, "Alabama HB 56: Which Way Will the Ruling Lean?," *Americas Quarterly*, August 26, 2011, http://www.americasquarterly.org/node/2844; Brian Lawson and Kent Faulk, "Judge Delays Ruling on Immigration Law," *Birmingham News*, August 30, 2011; James Lewis, "HB 56 Hurts Alabama's Economy More Than It Helps," *Birmingham News*, October 9, 2011. On

Judge Blackburn's ruling, see Alan Gomez, "Parts of Alabama Immigration Law to Go Forward," *USA Today*, September 29, 2011, http://usatoday30.usatoday.com/news/nation/story/2011-09-28/alabama-immigration-law/50589580/1; Campbell Robertson, "Alabama Wins in Ruling on Its Immigration Law," *New York Times*, September 28, 2011, http://www.nytimes.com/2011/09/29/us/alabama-immigration-law-upheld.html; Brian Lawson, "Judge Halts Parts of Immigration Law," *Birmingham News*, September 29, 2011; Julianne Hing, "Profiling Legal! Court Upholds Alabama Immigration Law," *ColorLines*, September 29, 2011, http://colorlines.com/archives/2011/09/alabamas_anti-immigrant_hb_56_upheld.html.

17. Roy L. Williams, "State Industries Seek Immigration Law Relief," *Birmingham News*, September 30, 2011; Martin Swant, "Immigration Law Hits State Produce Industry," *Birmingham News*, September 30, 2011; Robertson, "After Ruling, Hispanics Flee"; Kim Chandler and Roy L. Williams, "Businesses, Schools Feel the Hispanic Boycott," *Birmingham News*, October 13, 2011; Jeremy Gray, "DOJ: Report Issues in Immigration Law," *Birmingham News*, October 14, 2011; Dawn Kent, "Immigration Law Foes Rally Blacks, Latinos," *Birmingham News*, October 28, 2011; Charles J. Dean, "Immigration Protesters Rally at Civil Rights Site," *Birmingham News*, November 13, 2011; Jay Reeves, "Activists Stream into State to Unravel Immigration Law, " *Birmingham News*, November 4, 2011.

18. Levana Saxon, "How the Fight against Alabama's Anti-Immigrant Law Transformed a Community," *YesMagazine*, February 17, 2014, http://www.yesmagazine.org/peace-justice/no-longer-afraid-how-the-fight-against-alabama; Ashley Hayes, "Human Rights Watch Criticizes Alabama Immigration Law," *CNN*, December 14, 2011, http://www.cnn.com/2011/12/14/us/alabama-immigration-report/index; Mary Orndorff, "US on Watch for Immigrant Rights Violations," *Birmingham News*, November 17, 2011; "Standing in the Schoolhouse Door [Editorial]," *New York Times*, November 5, 2011, http://www.nytimes.com/2011/11/06/opinion/sunday/standing-in-the-schoolhouse-door.html; "Alabama Immigration Law Foes Hold 3-Day Meeting to Organize Immigrants, Plot Course to Overthrow Law," November 3, 2011, http://blog.al.com/wire/2011/11/alabama_immigration_law_foes_h.html; Elizabeth Brezovich, "Immigration Workshop Wraps Up in Albertville," *Birmingham News*, November 7, 2011.

19. Ed Pilkington, "Alabama Red-Faced as Second Foreign Car Boss Held under Immigration Law," *Guardian*, December 2, 2011, http://www.theguardian.com/world/2011/dec/02/alabama-car-boss-immigration-law.

20. Dawn Kent, "Foreign Investment Worries Grow," *Birmingham News*, November 22, 2011; Frances Coleman, "Is This How We Say Thanks to Our Foreign Investors?," *Mobile Press-Register*, November 20, 2011; Michael Tomberlin, "Bentley: 'Simplify' Immigration Law," *Birmingham News*, November 8, 2011; Brian Lawson, "Immigration Law Parts Blocked," *Birmingham News*, October 15, 2011; "Eleventh U.S. Circuit Court Rules on Injunction of Alabama Immigration Law," Ballotpedia, October 2011, http://ballotpedia.org/Eleventh_U.S._Circuit_Court_rules_on_injunction_of_Alabama_immigration_law. For Judge Thompson's ruling on mobile home registrations, see Alan Gomez, "Judge Takes Another Bite out of Ala. Immigration Law," *USA Today*, November 25, 2011: 03A; Southern Poverty Law Center, "Alabama's Anti-Immigrant Law Dealt Yet Another Major Blow," December 12, 2011, http://www.splcenter.org/get-informed/news/alabama-s-anti-immigrant-law-dealt-yet-another-major-blow; Bauer, "Court Cites Discriminatory Intent." On the March 2012 Appeals Court decision, see Kate Brumback, "Challenges to AL and GA Immigration Laws in Court," *Miami Herald*, February 29, 2012; Brian Lawson, "Federal Appeals Court

Questions Both Sides," *Birmingham News*, March 3, 2012; Brian Lawson, "Provisions of Immigration Law on Hold," *Birmingham News*, March 9, 2012; Jay Reeves, "Immigrants Trickling Back into State Despite Crackdown," *Birmingham News*, February 20, 2012.

21. Kim Chandler, "Rewrite to Make Bill More 'Enforceable,'" *Birmingham News*, March 26, 2012; "HB 56 Redux," *Birmingham News*, March 27, 2012; Kim Chandler, "HB 56 Hearing Draws Opponents," *Birmingham News*, April 12, 2012; Campbell Robertson, "Alabama Gets Strict Immigration Law as Governor Relents," *New York Times*, May 18, 2012, http://www.nytimes.com/2012/05/19/us/alabama-gets-strict-immigration-law-as-governor-relents.html; "Alabama's Bad Road on Immigration [Editorial]," *Los Angeles Times*, May 24, 2012, http://articles.latimes.com/2012/may/24/opinion/la-ed-alabama-immigration-20120524.

22. O'Leary, "Arizona's Tough New Law"; Archibold, "Arizona Enacts Stringent Law"; John Schwartz and Randal C. Archibold, "A Law Facing a Tough Road through the Courts," *New York Times*, April 27, 2010, http://www.nytimes.com/2010/04/28/us/28legal.html; Adam Liptak, "Blocking Parts of Arizona Law, Justices Allow Its Centerpiece," *New York Times*, June 25, 2012, http://www.nytimes.com/2012/06/26/us/supreme-court-rejects-part-of-arizona-immigration-law.html; Adam Liptak, "Court Splits Immigration Law Verdicts; Upholds Hotly Debated Centerpiece," *New York Times*, June 26, 2012: A1, A12; Fernanda Santos, "In Arizona, Confusion on Ruling on Migrants," *New York Times*, June 26, 2012, http://www.nytimes.com/2012/06/26/us/in-arizona-confusion-on-immigration-law-ruling.html; Linda Greenhouse, "D-Day," *New York Times*, June 27, 2012, http://opinionator.blogs.nytimes.com/2012/06/27/d-day/. For a legal analysis of the battle over Arizona Law S.B. 1070, see Kristina M. Campbell, "The Road to S.B. 1070: How Arizona Became Ground Zero for the Immigrants' Rights Movement and the Continuing Struggle for Latino Civil Rights in America," *Harvard Latino Law Review* 14 (Spring 2011): 1–21, http://ssrn.com/abstract=1911435.

23. Mary Bauer, "Do I Look Illegal?," *Birmingham News*, March 4, 2012; "Alabama Immigration Laws Become New Focus of Selma Civil Rights March," *Fox News Latino*, March 4, 2012, http://latino.foxnews.com/latino/news/2012/03/04/alabama-immigration-laws-become-new-focus-selma-bridge-civil-rights-march/; Kay Campbell, "Alabama Faith Leaders Urge Repeal of HB 56," http://www.al.com/living/index/ssf/2012/04/repeal_hb_56.html; Jeremy Gray, "DOJ Faults Immigration Law," *Birmingham News*, May 5, 2012; Pamela Constable, "Alabama Law Drives Out Immigrants but Also Has Unexpected Consequences," *Washington Post*, June 17, 2012, https://www.washingtonpost.com/local/alabama-law-drives-out-illegal-immigrants-but-also-has-unexpected-consequences/2012/06/17/gJQA3Rm0jV_story.html; Alan Gomez, "Hispanics Feel Harassed under Alabama's Immigration Law," *USA Today*, July 21, 2012, http://usatoday30.usatoday.com/news/nation/story/2012-07-21/arizona-immigration-law-alabama/56394360/1; Brian Lawson, "Alabama's Immigration Law: Clearer Police Guidance Sought," *Birmingham News*, July 3, 2012; Kim Chandler, "Report: More Racial Profiling after State Immigration Law," *Birmingham News*, August 29, 2012; Karen Tumlin and Richard Irwin, *Racial Profiling after HB 56* (Los Angeles: National Immigration Law Center, 2012), http://www.immigrationresearch-info.org/report/other/racial-profiling-after-hb-56; Ana Rodriguez, "Day Laborers Protest, Say They Have Right to Seek Work," *Birmingham News*, August 22, 2012; countrycat, "Scott Beason's Signature Legislation Brings in a Whole New Set of Immigrants," Left in Alabama, September 26, 2012, http://www.leftinalabama.com/diary/10131/scott-beasons-signature-legislation-brings-in-a

-whole-new-set-of-immigrants; Margaret Newkirk and Gigi Douban, "Africans Relocate to Alabama to Fill Jobs after Immigration Law," *Bloomberg*, September 24, 2012, http://origin -www.bloomberg.com/apps/news?pid=conewsstory&tkr=6PP:GR&sid=avf3JcQpp_GY.

24. Campbell Robertson and Julia Preston, "Appeals Court Draws Boundaries on Alabama Immigration Law," *New York Times*, August 21, 2012, http://www.nytimes.com/2012/08/22/ us/appeals-court-limits-alabamas-immigration-law.html; John Winograd, "Alabama Ruling Yet Another Rebuke to State Immigration Laws," Immigration Impact, August 21, 2012, http://immigrationimpact.com/2012/08/21/alabama-ruling-yet-another-rebuke-to-state -immigration-laws/. For the full text of the Court's decision, see *United States v. Alabama*, August 20, 2012, http://caselaw.findlaw.com/us-11th-circuit/1609747.html ("expulsion" quotation on p. 10 of text).

25. Cason, "Despite Legal Settlements"; Brian Lawson, "DOJ Suit Blocks Much of Alabama's Immigration Law," *Birmingham News*, November 27, 2013; Brian Montopoli, "Rep. Mo Brooks: I'll Do 'Anything Short of Shooting' Illegal Immigrants," *CBS News*, July 13, 2011, http://www.cbsnews.com/news/rep-mo-brooks-ill-do-anything-short-of-shooting -illegal-immigrants/; John Archibald, "State's Fight over Immigration Law Was Just Another Big Waste," *Birmingham News*, November 1, 2013.

26. "Don't Look Now, but Mexican Migration Is Slowing Dramatically," *USA Today*, July 15, 2011; Mark Mather, "What's Driving the Decline in U.S. Population Growth?," Popula-tion Reference Bureau, 2012, http://www.prb.org/Publications/Articles/2012/us-population -growth-decline-aspx; Julia Preston, "Mexican Immigration to U.S. Slowed Significantly, Report Says," *New York Times*, April 23, 2012. http://www.nytimes.com/2012/04/24/us/ mexican-immigration-to-united-states-slows.html?_r=0.

27. On the globalizing economic trends that contributed to job losses in Alabama as well as Latino migration for low-wage work, see Schwartzman, *Chicken Trail*, especially chaps. 1–3. For the interview with Deravi, see George Talbot, "Alabama's Law of Unin-tended Consequences," August 24, 2011, http://blog.al.com/live/2011/08/alabamas_law_of_ unintended_con.html.

28. Keith Rushing, "Alabama's HB56 Shows Racism Still Part of State Culture," *Huff-ington Post*, October 4, 2011, http://www.huffingtonpost.com/keith-rushing/alabamas -immigration-law_b_992801.html. For the "race-based" quotation, see Southern Poverty Law Center, "Alabama's Anti-Immigrant Law Dealt Yet Another Major Blow," December 11, 2011, https://www.splcenter.org/news/2011/12/12/alabama%E2%80%99s-anti-immigrant -law-dealt-yet-another-major-blow. For the "Arizona on steroids" quotation, see Michael A. Olivas, foreword to Ediberto Roman, *Those Damned Immigrants: America's Hysteria over Undocumented Immigration* (New York: New York University Press, 2013), xi.

29. Chris Kyle to Raymond A. Mohl, e-mail message, February 19, 2014; Patrik Jonsson, "America's Red-Blue Divide Widens on Illegal Immigration," *Christian Science Monitor*, June 20, 2011, http://www.csmonitor.com/USA/Politics/2011/0620/America-s-red-blue -divide-widens-on-illegal-immigrants. On the Kobach alliance with Mitt Romney on the issue of "self-deportation," see Antonio Alarcón, "Do-It-Yourself Deportation," *New York Times*, February 1, 2012, http://www.nytimes.com/2012/02/02/opinion/do-it-yourself-deportation .html; Jefferson Morley, "Kobach's Radical Agenda," *Salon*, June 6, 2012, http://www.salon .com/2012/06/06/the_kobach_agenda; Julia Preston, "Republican Immigration Platform Backs 'Self-Deportation,'" *New York Times,* August 23, 2012, http://thecaucus.blogs.nytimes .com/2012/08/23/republican-immigration-platform-backs-self-deportation/; Alex Byers,

"Romney Adviser Files Immigration Suit," Politico, August 23, 2012, http://www.politico.com/story/2012/08/romney-adviser-files-immigration-suit-080069; Richard Wolf, "Justices' Jabs Reveal Ideological, Partisan Splits," *USA Today*, May 12, 2014, https://www.google.com/search?q=Richard+Wolf%2C+%E2%80%9CJustices%E2%80%99+Jabs+Reveal+Ideological+Rifts%2C&ie=utf-8&oe=utf-8; Adam Liptak, "The Polarized Court," *New York Times*, May 10, 2014, http://www.nytimes.com/2014/05/11/upshot/the-polarized-court.html; Muzaffar Chishti and Faye Hipsman, "Republican Congressional Leaders Shelve Immigration Reform for 2014," Migration Policy Institute, http://www.migrationpolicy.org/article/republican-congressional-leaders-shelve-immigration-reform-2014. For the Pew Research Center study, see Elise Foley, "Most Americans Support Legal Status for Undocumented: Poll," February 12, 2014, *Huffington Post*, February 27, 2014, http://www.huffingtonpost.com/2014/02/27/immigration-poll_n_4867345.html.

15

American Muslims and Authority: Competing Discourses in a Non-Muslim State

KAREN LEONARD

INTRODUCTION

How do American Muslims define and attempt to follow Islamic law, or *shari'a*? They are not living in an Islamic state, or even in a state dominated by Muslims, yet political spokesmen and specialists in Islamic law are attempting to define the nature of Islamic authority and determine its force in the U.S. This essay first reviews the contours of the American Muslim community and then outlines the problems associated with the understanding and practice of Islamic law in the U.S. Third, it delineates contests over sources of authority between American Muslim spokesmen trained in modern professions and more traditionally trained Islamic scholars. The contestants are chiefly Muslims, but after September 11, 2001, others have played roles in defining the legal and political landscape for American Muslims as well; that is the fourth part of the essay. This last development has brought Islamic scholars to the fore, challenging the claims to authority of the new spokesmen. It has also signaled important shifts, probably lasting ones, in the patterned interactions among American Muslims and between Muslims and others in America. While the focus here is kept on Islamic law and jurisprudence as sources of authority, other sources of authority are clearly emerging in the American context.

AMERICAN MUSLIM DIVERSITY

Muslims are an increasingly important part of the socio-political landscape in the U.S., and they are not only numerous[1] but come from many backgrounds. The number of African American Muslims is quite substantial, some 30% to 42% of American Muslims, and the number of European-American converts is growing. Historically, Arabs were the next most numerous group and formed the earliest Muslim American organizations. Arabs began immigrating at the end of the nineteenth century, but Christians were the great majority among them until recently. The growth of Islam in America has come chiefly through post-1965 immigrants, with South Asian Muslims arriving and becoming one of the three major groups.[2]

In studies done of Muslims in the U.S. in the 1970s and 1980s, the emphasis was still on Arabic-speaking Muslims based on the East Coast and in the Midwest. However, a group of highly educated Pakistanis in upstate New York loomed large in one important study, and it was found to be the most "conservative" in beliefs and practices.[3] The demographic shift in sources and numbers of Muslim immigrants after 1965 signaled an interruption in a perceived pattern of steady Muslim "assimilation" or adaptation to American society, and Islam and Muslims have begun claiming a place in American religious and political life.

Arab and South Asian Muslims are the largest immigrant groups. The Arabs are far more diverse in terms of national histories (and colonial pasts), coming from Lebanon, Egypt, Syria, Palestine, Iraq, Jordan, Morocco (and, in smaller numbers, from Tunisia, Algeria, Libya, Saudi Arabia, Kuwait, Bahrain, Yemen, and other Persian Gulf states). South Asian Muslims are almost all from three countries, India, Pakistan, and Bangladesh, with a largely shared subcontinental history, most recently of British colonial rule. At the present time, first-generation South Asian Muslim Americans are taking a conspicuous lead in the formulation of American Muslim political discourse.[4] Although diverse in terms of national backgrounds, languages, and religions, these immigrants are relatively homogeneous in terms of socio-economic class. A highly educated group,[5] its members are fluent in English, most of them having been educated in that language since childhood.

South Asian Muslims have some advantages in the national political arena. Indian Muslims, Pakistanis, and Bangladeshis share a heritage of political struggle with white or colonial rulers; Indian Muslims are accustomed to being in the minority, now, in Hindu-majority India. South Asian Muslims also, to different degrees, come to the U.S. with experience in democratic politics. This contrasts with Muslims from many Middle Eastern countries who have little or no experience with democratic processes. South Asian Muslims are better positioned than Arab Muslims with respect to the American media and the general public, since American foreign relations with South Asia are less politically charged than those with the Middle East and its Muslims. Some of the prejudice suffered by Arab Americans[6] is less easily triggered by South Asian Muslim leadership.

South Asian and Arab Muslims dominate the national leadership of Muslim organizations, relating somewhat uneasily to African American Muslims. Mosques are the most prominent sites of religious activity. Because Islam has no centralized clergy and mosques operate independently of each other and because mosque-attendees are only 10–20% of American Muslims,[7] Muslim political developments should not be equated with what is going on in the mosques. Yet one can generalize that, while Arabic-speakers tend to have greater proficiency in Arabic and *infiqh* and *shari'a* (jurisprudence and Islamic law), so that they may dominate in many mosque functions and in teaching the young (Arabic lessons, the first reading of the Qur'an), it is the recent South Asian professional immigrants who have been fuelling both the building of local mosques and the regional and national mobilization of Muslims on religious and political issues.[8]

ISLAMIC LAW IN THE AMERICAN CONTEXT

The importance of context is stated well by the anthropologist Talal Asad:

> Islamic religious, legal, and political ideologies do not have an essential significance which moulds the minds of believers in a predictable way. They are part of changing institutions, and of discourses which can be, and often are, contested and *re-constituted.* To understand the authoritative limits of such contestation one must focus on religious discourses within specific historical situations, and not on a supposedly original Islamic ideology. Because it is the way in which 'the word of God' is reproduced, and the [political] situation to which it is addressed, which together determine its force, and not the lexical and syntactic forms of the sacred text considered in isolation.[9]

Leading scholars like Khaled Abou El Fadl, Professor of Islamic Law at UCLA, and Taha Alalwani, President of the Fiqh (Islamic jurisprudence) Council of North America and head of the Graduate School of Islamic and Social Sciences,[10] urge that the context should strongly shape decisions about Muslim practices in America. Abou El Fadl, who now has several books and many articles published, stresses the search for authoritative findings, not the pronouncement of ahistorical authoritarian edicts.[11] An American Muslim lawyer, Anver Emon, emphasizes this process of searching in his foreword to the second edition of Khaled Abou El Fadl's important work *onfiqh* in North America:

> The Divine Will's categorizations of human actions (Shari'a) must be strictly distinguished from the human endeavor of understanding those categorizations and the Divine Will (fiqh). . . . With the multiplicity of opinions and their seemingly relative validity, does this mean there is no single answer to an issue of Islamic law? . . . The distinction between fiqh and Shari'a exists because of the limited capacity of the human intellect to know the Absolute absolutely. . . . The only burden on humanity is to engage in the process of inquiry and analysis.[12]

The historical experiences of Muslims certainly testify to variance despite adherence to certain basic teachings of Islam. There was an identifiable "core" Islamic way of thinking and acting in seventh-century Arabia, yet Islam is not a religion with a single, hierarchical structure of authority. There was a core text, the *Qur'an,* an evolving set of collected traditions, the *Hadith,* and an evolving body of law, the *Shari'a,* but those Arabian Islamic beliefs and practices have both influenced and been influenced by the places to which they were subsequently taken.[13] Islam moved to new and different places and confronted older religions, conquering or coexisting with them and their non-Muslim adherents. Without centralized institutions governing clergy or mosques, Islam has developed differently within regions of the Middle East, Central, South and Southeast Asia, China,[14] and elsewhere, and such situated interactions shape the diverse ways in which it is practiced throughout the world.[15] Even in Saudi Arabia, Islam's birthplace, Islamic beliefs and practices have been reshaped over time.[16]

American versions of Islam are being formulated in an ongoing dialogue with other members of American society. Some post-1965 immigrant Muslims had hoped to avoid an "Americanization" of Islam, such as they saw occurring among earlier Muslim immigrants and among contemporary Muslim Americans.[17] However, new versions of Islam are being constituted from "American" ways of being Muslim and from other ways, as long as Muslim immigrants keep coming, of being Muslim. These emerging constructions of self and community are being partially shaped by the debates over who should represent and interpret Islam in America.[18]

Muslims in America come from many places and represent many strands of Islam. The "Muslim community" in America, like Islam itself, is not monolithic, and differences or tensions within it are influencing the emerging versions of Islam. With respect to religious law, pluralism has long been characteristic and accepted. There are four main Sunni (mainstream or orthodox) schools of law, the Maliki, Shafi'i, Hanafi, and Hanbali, and a leading Shi'i school, the Ja'fari, all represented among American Muslims. In addition to the Sunni and Shi'i traditions, there are smaller Shi'i groups like the Ismailis and Zaidis, and sects like the Ahmadiyyas and Druze whose Islamic identity is contested. Then there are the Sufis, whose charismatic leaders teach mystical strands of Islam; the Sufis are from very diverse backgrounds but many are European-American converts.[19]

The problems associated with the understanding and practice of *shari'a* and *fiqh* in America derive partly from the scarcity of specialists in Islamic law and partly from the emergence of new spokesmen, men not well-schooled in Islamic civilization and law but well-credentialed in modem professions. The current leaders of national-level Muslim organizations working towards a unified Muslim community in the U.S.[20] are primarily well-educated immigrant professionals of South Asian and Arab background. While some *imams* in mosques and scholars of *fiqh* continue to exemplify high standards of Islamic learning, those in leadership positions in many mosques and in the increasingly powerful political coalitions are typically medical doctors, engineers, and other professionals. (There are a few African American scholars of *shari'a* and *fiqh,* but they have only recently engaged the immigrants, as will be seen.)

These new spokesmen have changed the inward foci of national-origin communities and reached out to other Muslims and the American public, advocating citizenship and participation in mainstream politics and abandoning a stance that had assumed only temporary residence in the U.S. As they built major organizations and institutions with professional staffs and bureaucratic procedures, the new leaders began defining the community in ways that emphasized their own role and marginalized spokesmen and groups less like themselves. Without classical training in Islamic history and law, it is they who have stepped forward, speaking, authoritatively and publicly on legal issues ranging from citizenship and voting to marriage and family law. As legal scholar Khaled Abou El Fadl says, "In the United States the field of *sharia* is flooded with self-declared experts who inundate our discourses with self-indulgent babble and gibberish . . . those who are unable to differentiate . . . the fundamentals of Islam from its particulars."[21]

CONTESTS OVER AUTHORITY
AMONG AMERICAN MUSLIMS

Muslim mobilization in the U.S. involves consideration of Islamic legal discourses and practices. The field of *fiqh* is being developed in the American context, but who should be authorized to develop it and authorized by whom? Is the U.S. *dar ul Islam* (the place or abode of Islam) or *dar ul harb* (place of war),[22] and if the latter, must Muslims migrate from it? If they remain, are they bound by the laws of the non-Muslim host state or not? As recently as 1986, national Muslim leaders advocated residing only temporarily in *dar ul-kufr,* or the place of unbelievers (the U.S.). But by the end of that same year, the Islamic Society of North America (ISNA), the leading North American Muslim activist association, took a position favoring citizenship and participation in mainstream politics in the U.S.[23]

The active role of Muslims in modern American politics encourages other legal designations, such as *dar ul aman* (place of order) and *dar ul 'ahd* or *dar ul sulh* (place of alliance or treaty). The latter terms reflect usages in South Asia and the new South Asian American leadership,[24] just as older references invoked Islamic movements in the Arab world like the Salafiyya and the Ikhwan and Arab American leadership.[25] American Muslim discourse now includes explicit discussions about the compatibility of Islam and democracy[26] and Islam and human rights. Proponents of democracy argue that the selection of the *caliph* (the political head of the *ummah,* abolished by Turkey's Ataturk in 1924) was not based on hereditary principles, and they promote the institution of the *shura* or "mutual consultation" council as analogous to democratic institutions in the West. ISNA helped form a national Islamic *shura* or representative council on religious issues, and the presidency rotated annually between the heads of ISNA and ICNA (Islamic Council of North America) and two African American leaders (W. D. Muhammed of Chicago and Imam Jamil Al-Amin of Atlanta).[27] ISNA's National Fiqh Council, however, has not been accepted as authoritative by all immigrant Muslim scholars, and it has been criticized by African American Muslims for being "overwhelmingly composed of naturalized Muslims," men who know little about U.S. family law and inheritance rights.[28] There are regional experiments with *shuras* as well, often focusing initially on practices.[29]

Both Abou El Fadl and Alalwani, the *fiqh* scholars invoked above, disapprove of the application of Islamic legal decisions made elsewhere to the contemporary American context and encourage *fiqh* scholarship in the U.S.[30] Alalwani rebuts the opinion of a scholar who maintained that it was unlawful for Muslims to hold citizenship in non-Muslim states by noting that this decision was specific to North Africa during Muslim struggles against French colonialism. He also rebuts an opinion holding that, since the U.S. is *dar al-kufr* and *dar al-harb,* Muslims can disobey U.S. laws and regulations, arguing that wherever Muslims find the freedom to practice Islam is *dar ul-Islam* and *dar ad-daw 'ah* (place of calling), a place where the laws must be obeyed and the message of Islam should be spread.[31] Abou El Fadl is particularly eloquent in a despairing critique of the pronouncements by *fiqh* specialists who met for three days in Detroit in November of 1999 as the "Sharia Scholars Association of North America." Although "[h]alf of the thirty-eight or so scholars have never lived in the U.S., the vast majority have never stepped foot in an American court room, and at least half live under corrupt and oppressive governments," these men issued a double-spaced thirteen-page set of opinions on major issues facing Muslims in North America.[32]

Yet, while *fiqh* and *sharia* have historically played central roles in defining Muslims and Islamic communities, they are arguably of declining importance in the U.S. The Wahhabi puritanical strand of Islam, so strongly associated with Saudi Arabia today and promoted elsewhere, erases reliance on these classical schools of law, not least in the U.S. with its dearth of Islamic legal scholars and traditions. Speaking of the *Qur'an* and *Hadith,* the sources of Islamic law, Abou El Fadl says:

> my books, in this context—you are so foreign, so marginal. . . . Here, in this time and place, you are fossilized showpieces. . . . Yet, I know that you are eternal and immutable because you speak forever. But you are contextual because it is the people that read you who must speak to the age, the people that read you who must transform through you into a book for our new age and new place.[33]

Who is reading and interpreting Islam and Islamic law in the U.S. context? The new spokesman and new kinds of media (print, radio, TV, videocassettes, and the Internet) have reinvigorated Islamic discourse, developing a wider role and mainstream audience for Islam. The more numerous and less observant Muslims, presumably beyond the reach of what is being said in mosques, are being reached through the new political organizations and popular Muslim media. Reaching the masses means "presenting Islamic doctrine and discourse in accessible, vernacular terms"; as elsewhere, American Islamic discourse has "become reframed in styles of reasoning and forms of argument that draw on wider, less exclusive or erudite bodies of knowledge."[34]

Thus men with educational qualifications in medicine, engineering, architecture, and business have emerged as major spokesmen for and about Islam in America. Immigrant doctors and engineers publish short general books intended for English-reading Muslim and non-Muslim audiences.[35] This is even a point of criticism with respect to leadership within mosques, as the "present leadership" is characterized as having medical, business, or computer technology training rather than "knowledge and wisdom."[36] Modern technology has reinforced the authority of the new spokesmen, producing "an increasing laicization among Muslims and a weakening of the competence of the 'ulama.'"[37] These confident new spokesmen have, however, produced a landscape devoid of respect for the schools and methods of Islamic legal scholarship.[38]

Abou El Fadl's view is borne out by two recent social science studies of Muslims in America. In April 2001, a highly-publicized national survey of mosques was released, undertaken and sponsored by some among the new spokesmen. In defining their survey population, they omitted some Shi'i (the Ismaili followers of the Aga Khan), the Ahmadis (until recently accepted as Muslims in the U.S.)[39] and the Nation of Islam (Louis Farrakhan's group). Defining a mosque as any organization that sponsored Friday prayers and other Islamic activities, the survey included young Muslim groups on campuses but overlooked the numerous, largely African American Muslim groups in American prisons.[40] One of the findings of the study was that those who attend mosques place the traditional schools of law at the very bottom of the list in terms of "sources of authority in the worship and teaching" of their mosques. Those who answered the questions posed by the survey, presidents and members of mosque boards of directors and *imams,* felt that the teachings of a particular *madhhab* or school of law were of little or no importance (52%), somewhat important (25%), very important (18%), or absolutely foundational (5%). Their preferred sources of authority (absolutely foundational) were the Qur'an (95%), Sunnah of the Prophet (90%), the teachings of the righteous *salaf* (elders) (16%), the teachings of great scholars of the past (10%), human reasoning and understanding (10%), and the teachings of certain recent Muslim leaders and scholars (7%).[41]

The first systematic poll of American Muslims designed to cover participation in public life included a section on religious practices. The poll was commissioned by the Project MAPS (Muslims in the American Public Square) and conducted by Zogby International in November and December

of 2001. This section covered the self-identified Muslim respondent's relationship with the mosque, conversion issues, the importance of religion in
one's life, and interactions between the mosque and politics. But this poll
made no attempt to ascertain sectarian affiliation within Islam or views of
sources of religious authority.[42]

Before September 11, 2001, the stance of these western-educated political leaders of American Islam was overwhelmingly optimistic, proclaiming
that American Muslims would play a major role in the "reconstruction"
of the United States. Thus one man wrote that Muslims could make "an
essential contribution to the healing of America" by becoming more visible
and ceasing to "cast doubt on the compatibility of Islam, democracy and
human rights." Indeed, he, like many others, felt that American Muslims
also would play a special role in leadership of the international Muslim
ummah. Arguing that Muslims in North America had a "head start" over
those in Europe, since most already were or were becoming citizens and
could participate in public life, he said:

> Muslims all over the world are looking with high expectations toward the
> Ummah in the United States and Canada. Its dynamism, fresh approach,
> enlightened scholarship and sheer growth is their hope for an Islamic
> Renaissance worldwide. Perhaps the mujaddid of the 15th Islamic cen-
> tury and the second millenium of the common era will be an American
> Muslim, insha Allah.[43]

Muqtedar Khan, a young Indian American Muslim political scientist, wrote
euphorically:

> "But internally, it [the U.S.] is the most Islamic state that has been opera-
> tional in the last three hundred years. Internally, it is genuinely seeking to
> aspire to its ideals and the growing cultural, material and religious health
> of American Muslims is the best testimony to my claim. This debate, the
> existence of a Muslim public sphere where Muslims can think freely to
> revive and practice Islam is its gift to Muslims. Something unavailable in
> most of the Muslim world."[44]

A Pakistani American physician echoed this, adding "All that we need is
unity among Muslims."[45]

CHANGES AFTER SEPTEMBER 11, 2001

Then came the tragedy of September 11, 2001, and evidence that the
World Trade Center explosions had been triggered by Islamic extremists.

The trajectory along which American Muslims were moving has changed dramatically, with significant implications for the contests over authority. Earlier tendencies on the part of American Muslim spokesmen and political organizations to narrow the boundaries of the community, de-emphasize the interpretative breadth of Islamic law, and emphasize foreign policy issues at the expense of domestic ones have been reversed. The new tendencies are being strongly shaped by non-Muslim politicians and the media in the U.S., in an interaction between American Muslims and the state that is, perhaps paradoxically, drawing Muslims more closely into national political life while drawing more widely on the religion's rich, long-standing traditions of humanistic and legal scholarship.[46]

American Muslims were initially silent, hoping that Muslims had not been responsible for the murderous attacks, but President Bush began meeting with Muslim religious leaders almost immediately[47] and visited the leading mosque in Washington. But it was not one of the new spokesmen, the political leaders, whom President Bush chose to stand on the White House lawn with him on September 20. It was Shaykh Hamza Yusuf, an American convert and charismatic teacher about Islam and Islamic law, who stood there as one of six religious leaders and the only Muslim to meet privately with the President that day, lamenting that "Islam was hijacked on that September 11, 2001, on that plane as an innocent victim."[48] A clear pattern emerged as the White House and the American media learned more about American Muslim leaders and organizations. Scholars and others outside the Muslim political organizations were called upon to speak publicly about the true meaning of *jihad*, Islamic views of terrorism, and similar topics, while the leaders of American Muslim political organizations found themselves on the defensive.[49]

Shaykh Hamza Yusuf, a white American convert[50] to Islam in his early forties who co-founded and directs the Zaytuna Institute in the San Francisco Bay area,[51] was arguably the leading figure. His words about hijacking Islam were repeatedly quoted and his views welcomed by the President, the media, and the American public. Young American Muslims, many of them already his fans, circulated his interviews and speeches more than any others on e-mail. In an interview published September 16, Hamza Yusuf called the World Trade Center attackers:

> enemies of Islam . . . mass murderers, pure and simple. . . . I think that the Muslims—and I really feel this strongly—have to reject the discourse of anger. Because there is a lot of anger in the Muslim . . . world about the oppressive conditions that many Muslims find themselves in . . . we have

to move to a higher moral ground, recognizing that the desire to blame
others leads to anger and eventually to wrath, neither of which are rungs
on a spiritual ladder to God. It's times like these that we really need to
become introspective.

Answering the reporter's questions about the meanings of *jihad,* martyrdom,
and suicide in Islam, he ended by saying, "If there are any martyrs in this
affair it would certainly be those brave firefighters and police that went in
there to save human lives and in that process lost their own." His words
resonated widely with the American public.[52]

Shaykh Hamza, in a CBC radio interview on September 23, invoked
his training in Arabic and Islamic law as he talked about his September
20 meeting with President Bush. He had told the President that "Infinite
Justice" was a poor choice of name for the American military operation
against terrorism, and that "crusade" evoked similarly negative reactions
among Muslims. The President told him that "the Pentagon doesn't have
theologians and they're the ones that name these things," and he said the
name would be changed.[53]

Shaykh Hamza's views about contemporary spokesmen for Islam were
clearly related to the contest for authority among competing spokesmen for
Muslims in America.

> Islam has very few scholars at very high levels. Most of the brilliant
> students in the [M]iddle East now go into medicine and engineering, . . .
> they don't go into philosophy . . . almost every one of these terrorists
> that are identified . . . you will not find amongst them anyone who did
> his degree in philosophy, in literature, in the humanities, in theology . . .
> [brilliant students are] only studying the physical sciences to the neglect
> of what makes us human, which is humanity, is poetry, is literature, as
> well as philosophy and theology. . . . I think the Muslim world really has
> to stop blaming the West for its problems . . . it's the easy way out, it's
> not a Qur'anic world-view . . . we all need to really look in the mirror
> . . . the Muslims need to become introspective and . . . the West needs to
> understand. . . . I came out of the enlightenment tradition and I still believe
> in the best of the enlightenment tradition and I think that Islam confirms
> and enhances that tradition. . . .[54]

Shaykh Hamza Yusuf, born Mark Hanson and with strong Sufi tendencies,[55]
has never been centrally engaged in American Muslim political organizing
(although he has often been a featured speaker at national conventions).
A charismatic speaker with a following like that of a rock star's among

second-generation American Muslims, the Shaykh has produced numerous, widely-circulated videos and cassettes. His public appearances, often
with Siraj Wahaj (a popular African American Muslim speaker), generate
enthusiastic audiences and fill stadiums. Already well known, he was "fast
becoming a world figure as Islam's most able theological critic of the suicide hijacking," according to a story in *The Guardian*. The story asserted
that "Many Muslims find his views hard to stomach, but he is advising the
White House on the current crisis" and reported that his detractors dubbed
him a "collaborator," Bush's "pet Muslim."[56] Hamza Yusuf told the British
reporter that Muslims should return to their "true faith," stripped of violence,
intolerance, and hatred. He declared:

> Many people in the west do not realise how oppressive some Muslim
> states are—both for men and for women. This is a cultural issue, not an
> Islamic one. . . . I think the way Muslims are allowed to live in the west is
> closer to the Muslim way. A lot of Muslim immigrants feel the same way,
> which is why they are here . . . if they are going to rant and rave about the
> west, they should emigrate to a Muslim country. The good will of these
> [western] countries to immigrants must be recognised by Muslims. . . .[57]

He remarked again on the backgrounds of the nineteen terrorists, the consistent feature being, in his view, that they were educated in the sciences
rather than the humanities.

Others who spoke out and were highlighted in the mainstream U.S.
media were Professor Ali Asani, Professor Khaled Abou El Fadl, Sheikh
Muhammad Hisham Kabbani, and Professor Muqtedar Khan. Asani, an
Islamic Studies professor at Harvard and a member of the Aga Khan's Shi'i
community (one of the groups excluded from the 2001 study of American
mosques), criticized American Muslim spokesmen for having used incendi-
ary language in private while speaking of peace to the American public.

> Even when there are disagreements within the Muslim community about
> extremism, they will project to the outside that we are all monolithic and
> peaceful . . . [but now, the more extreme leaders have gone] on alert. They
> realize that they are part of the problem, that the Sept. 11 incident can be
> the result of this kind of thinking they have been propagating for so many
> years.[58]

Asani was also quoted in a lead editorial in the *Los Angeles Times*. He
praised American pluralism as essential to the true spirit of the Koran, as
undermining "exclusivist" and repressive versions of Islam.[59] He voiced the
"general concern among Muslim intellectuals about how not only CAIR

but some of these other organizations are claiming to speak in the name of the Muslim community, and how they're coming to be recognized by the government as spokespeople for the Muslim community in the U.S."

Khaled Abou El Fadl, already introduced here, has been controversial in Muslim community circles.[60] Known for his independent views, particularly about women in Islam,[61] he had published a piece entitled "Terrorism is at Odds With Islamic Tradition" in the *Los Angeles Times* on August 22;[62] he was turned to after September 11, giving talks locally, appearing on CNN, and writing powerful indictments of Muslim leadership.[63] Trained in both Islamic and American law (at Cairo's Al Azhar, the University of Pennsylvania, Yale, and Princeton), Abou El Fadl talked about the "crumbling of the Islamic civilization [that] has removed the established institutions to seriously challenge the extremists. . . . Extremist theology is a combustible brew of puritanism, ethical and moral irresponsibility and rampant apologetics."[64] Long a critic of the science-trained new spokesmen for American Muslims, Abou El Fadl was admiringly profiled in January 2002 in the *Los Angeles Times*.[65]

Others turned to after September 11, Sheikh Muhammad Hisham Kabbani and M. A. Muqtedar Khan, illustrate not the background in classical legal training so much as the diversity and broader range of spokesmen;[66] the former leads a Naqshbandi Sufi group with a strong U.S. following,[67] and the latter is a young Indian-origin Ph.D. in political science from Georgetown, who did have a career as an unofficial *mufti* (legal scholar), but on the Internet and along innovative rather than classical lines.[68]

The media attention given to Islam and American Muslims has foregrounded not only Islamic legal scholars but issues of Islamic law, as an amusing, but fundamentally serious, e-mail from "an American" illustrates. The writer expressed resentment at "being bombarded by some instruction from the media on how I should 'understand' Islam." A few lines from this lengthy epistle give the idea:

> [I]t's been over a month . . . and there seem to be hundreds of TV talk-show hosts, news people, Islamic experts, roaming Imams, and Muslim clerics who keep telling me how I should get acquainted with the 'real' Muslim world of the Koran, Hadith and the Sunna and how these terrorist guys who pulled off the 9111 attacks don't really represent the actual Islamic faith . . . why should I be the target audience. . . . If I have it right, all the people who did this were Muslims. . . . I mean I already know what they did was wrong as do most honest Americans, so why are you telling me? . . . Tell them about the religion! Yes, tell the Muslims . . . that they have

it backwards and inside out. . . . So please, to all the media types and so-called Islamic experts—stop giving me your line on how these guys have hijacked a religion . . . [then 7 questions are posed, like, why not *a fatwa* on the hijackers, when one was put out on Salman Rushdie who only wrote a book that got it wrong?]. . . . I'm still not sure if I'm considered a non-believer that Muslims should live in peace with or if I am an infidel that should be killed for my corrupt life style, or my religious belief . . . there are but two possibilities: in the least, either the majority of Muslims aquiecese [sic] to the 'hijacking' of their religion, or at worst, they give tacit approval to the murderous actions the Islamic terrorists have done in the name of Allah.[69]

Some American Muslims have managed to see the events of September 11 as an opportunity. As one man wrote, "American Muslim leaders have gotten more media time than we could have ever imagined in our wildest dreams."[70] Copies of the Qur'an were sold out in bookstores all over the U.S., and many Islamic centers and mosques held open houses. Others, however, saw September 11 as a major setback for Islam in America.[71]

With all the conflicting reports and opinions being bandied about, the contest for authority goes on. American Muslim organizational leaders have tried to seize center stage again, only to attract media attention to some of their earlier rhetoric.[72] The outgoing president of ISNA, Muzzamil Siddiqi, led a memorial service at the Washington National Cathedral; as President Bush said later, "He did a heck of a good job, and we were proud to have him there."[73] Reporters did research and raised questions about Siddiqi's earlier remarks in public speeches.[74] The rhetoric designed for private and known audiences of co-believers, rhetoric designed to instill pride and a sense of mission, sounded very different when moved into a public arena and read by a wider audience.

American Muslims previously uninvolved in political organizing were galvanized into action, newly concerned with Islamic law and its implementation in the U.S. One new organization, led by medical men and other professionals, formed to combat extremism and implicitly accused leaders of earlier organizations of condoning extremism and doing a disservice to American Muslims.[75] A debate began about what is being said in American mosques, and by whom. Were the "traditional," foreign-born *imams* in American mosques or the western-educated members of the boards of directors that run the mosques more "immoderate" in their views before September 11? One writer argued that the "moderate" members of the boards should hire only American-educated *imams* "who are fluent in English and are voices of moderation, who can talk to the media . . . and who can sustain a constructive dialogue with Americans from all walks of life. . . ."[76] But others criticized the members of the boards of directors who employed *imams*: "board members, who are usually educated in various fields like medicine, engineering, computers, and so on, do not have adequate knowledge of Islam . . . they will not allow their imams to make independent statements." This writer advocated training young people in American schools to become both *imams* and board members.[77]

Events in 2003 and 2004 have intensified conflicts centered on Islamic law and its interpretation in the U.S. What began as a so-called "gender *jihad*" in the 1990s has led to a "progressive Muslim" movement in the twenty-first century. This has, in some ways, furthered a deepening division between immigrant Muslims and indigenous African American Muslims. Ironically, the gender *jihad* initially featured leading figures from both immigrant and indigenous Muslim backgrounds. African American women are prominent among the Muslim feminists writing about Islamic law and jurisprudence. Amina Wadud, an African American Muslim and an Islamic Studies professor, called in her book, *Qur'an and Woman* (1999),[78] for a radical and continual rethinking of the Qur'an and *hadith,* asserting that much now considered divine and immutable *shari'a* is the result of a long, male-dominated intellectual process. Another African American Muslim, Gwendolyn Zoharah Simmons, writes of the growing number of Muslim women scholars and activists "seeking to separate Islam, the religion, from culture, tradition, and social mores . . . at times bringing to the foreground the interpretations of earlier sects or groups in Islam who were labeled heterodox and their views dismissed."[79] The gender *jihad,* then, could work across sectarian boundaries.

The gender *jihad* is an important strand in an emerging cosmopolitan Islam in the U.S., one that is being produced by *fiqh* specialists and other scholars of Islam. This strand is best exemplified by a volume edited by Omid Safi and published in 2003, *Progressive Muslims.* The fifteen contributors are almost all now teaching in the U.S. but many are immigrants, and their academic degrees come from all over the world. Four are American converts, two of them African American women. In the volume, Kecia Ali and Moosa Ebrahim go further than Wadud and Simmons in questioning the patriarchial basis of Islamic law. Another and even more controversial element in the progressive Muslim movement involves open discussions of gender and sexuality. This has been initiated most conspicuously by the new website Muslimwakeup.com (it was preceded by a few gay and lesbian

Muslim websites). The fall of 2004 saw the formal establishment of the Progressive Muslim Union of North America.[80] The website (progressive-muslims.com) lays out its principles. These explicitly recognize as Muslim "anyone who identifies herself or himself as "Muslim," including those whose identification is based on social commitments and cultural heritage," and affirm "the equal status and equal worth" of all human beings, regardless of religion, gender, race, ethnicity, or sexuality."

The progressive movement is not just academic; it is beginning to have an impact on the national immigrant-led organizations that it has been actually attacking. The changes in the American political landscape after 9/11 have pushed the national Islamic and Muslim political organizations into the paths pioneered by the academic progressives. A leading national political organization, the Muslim Public Affairs Council (MPAC), made progressive Islamic thought the theme of its 2004 convention in Long Beach and invited some of the academics in the *Progressive Muslims* volume to speak; MPAC also has published an issue of its journal, *The Minaret*, focused on progressive Islam and Muslims and advocating moves in that direction. Even the more religiously oriented and conservative ISNA, in its journal *Islamic Horizons*, started a three-part series on its own history with a focus on the role of Muslim women in nurturing the Muslim Student Association (MSA) and its development into ISNA.[81]

There have also been deepening conflicts between immigrant Muslims and African American Muslims, and these are reflected both organizationally and in contests over sources of authority. African American leaders split off in 2001 from the immigrant-led Sunni Muslim groups to establish a new organization called MANA, the Muslim Alliance of North America.[82] Turning away from the national immigrant-led organizations because of their failure to reflect the concerns of indigenous Muslims, their focus on overseas agendas, and their efforts to become part of the dominant or white mainstream culture, MANA's leaders want to maintain a critical stance toward American society. MANA defines "indigenous" as "anyone who is native to America, including second generation immigrants."[83]

This African American Muslim initiative is also reflected in academic battles over Islamic law and jurisprudence. A respected African American Muslim scholar of Islamic law (and MANA board member), Sherman Jackson,[84] has publicly attacked Khaled Abou El Fadl, the latter now linked to the progressive Muslim academics. Jackson claims Abou El Fadl and other immigrant intellectuals are buying into white America's claims to "false universalisms" and are overlooking the justifiably different African American interpretations of Islam and African American needs for social justice. Jackson writes explicitly about doctrinal interpretations not shared by immigrant and black Muslims and calls for different versions of Islam tailored to constituencies strongly marked by race, class, and histories within the nation. Accusing immigrant Muslims like Abou El Fadl of being "American Muslim romantics" who try to appease the dominant culture by presenting an acceptable "universal" and progressive version of Islam, he sees them as presenting only a part, a specifically Middle Eastern "East's truth," as the whole in order to preempt views that lie outside the boundaries of their imagination or experience. Asserting that the Prophet Muhammad was sent for all peoples, at all times and in all places, and that there are not only New and Old World realities but different realities within the New World, Jackson sees Islam's pluralistic legal traditions as enabling interpretative communities to adapt Islam to their circumstances. If American Islam is to be truly pluralistic, he writes, "it will have to be bold and vigilant in its refusal to ignore or jettison any of these histories and experiences in favor of appeals to a false universal, no matter how chic, powerful, or expedient the latter may be."[85]

CONCLUSION

The boundaries of Muslim America and the numbers of authoritative spokesmen for American Muslims have been steadily expanding since September 11, 2001, and differences once suppressed have become open. The leaders of the American Muslim political organizations no longer are recognized by the American government or the public as the only spokesmen for American Muslims. There are pressures on the political spokesmen even from their own followers to broaden their constituencies by generation and gender and to put greater emphasis on American values, training, and domestic political issues.[86] Post-9/11 spokesmen and women for Islam speak for and represent a wider range of Islam's sectarian, intellectual, artistic, and legal traditions than do the political spokesmen. The gender *jihad* and a progressive Muslim movement have grown greatly in importance, interacting in interesting ways with organizational and legal challenges to immigrant Muslims from indigenous, primarily African American, Muslims.

These developments are taking place in the context of growing tensions between the goals of American Muslims and those of the political leaders of the U.S. In 2005, American Muslims and the leaders of American Muslim political organizations face many challenges and American, not Islamic, law is probably of more concern. National American Muslim groups like CAIR and MPAC increasingly allege violations of the civil rights of Muslims and Arabs, and there clearly have been such violations. Concern about profiling by religion and/or national origin has grown steadily.[87] The legal issues with which American Muslims are now most concerned are also of concern to many other Americans, as the Patriot Act and other measures threaten the civil liberties of all.

NOTES

1. Islam is poised to displace Judaism and will be second to Christianity in the number of its adherents in the United States. For the varying population estimates, from 1 to 8 million, see Karen Isaksen Leonard, *Muslims in the United States: The State of Research* (New York, 2003) 4, 147 (note 1).

2. One breakdown puts African Americans at 42%, South Asians at 24.4%, Arabs at 12.4%, Africans at 6.2%, Iranians at 3.6%, Southeast Asians at 2%, European Americans at 1.6%, and "other" at 5.4%. Another breakdown puts "Americans" at 30%, Arabs at 33%, and South Asians at 29%. The first is Fareed H. Nu'man, *The Muslim Population in the United States: A Brief Statement* (Washington, D.C., 1992); and the second is Ilyas Ba-Yunus and M. Moin Siddiqui, *A Report on the Muslim Population in the United States* (New York, 1999).

3. Yvonne Yazbeck Haddad and Adair T. Lummis, *Islamic Values in the United States: a Comparative Study* (New York, 1987) point to this conservatism in numerous places, e.g., 30–33, 123–24, 127. They saw considerable adaptation among earlier immigrants.

4. Karen Leonard, "South Asian Leadership of American Muslims," in Yvonne Haddad, ed., *Muslims in the West: From Sojourners to Citizens* (New York, 2002), 233–49.

5. In the 1990 U.S. Census, the immigrants from India had the highest median household income, family income, and per capita income of any foreign-born group, and they also had the highest percentage with a bachelor's degree or higher and the highest percentage in managerial and professional fields. Karen Isaksen Leonard, *The South Asian Americans* (Westport, Conn., 1997), 77–78. Since 80% of South Asians in the U.S. are from India and Pakistan, and about 90% of these are from India, the Asian Indian census data is quite relevant. Among Indian immigrants in the 1990 census, 10% were medical doctors and 17% were engineers. Iranian Muslims, also highly-educated and sharing many of the attributes of South Asians, are overwhelmingly secular in their orientation. See Mehdi Bozorgmehr, "Internal Ethnicity: Iranians in Los Angeles," in *Sociological Perspectives* 40, no. 3 (1997): 387–408, which reports that only 5% are religiously observant "always and often" and 95% are so "occasionally and never" (chart, 398). Also, Iranians are Shi'i, the minority sect within Islam and within American Islam as well.

6. Edward Said, *Covering Islam,* 2d ed. (1981; New York, 1997).

7. For the estimate, no longer accepted as accurate but without an accepted replacement, see Haddad and Lummis, *Islamic Values,* 8.

8. In the leadership of many mosques, too, South Asians are becoming prominent. Yvonne Yazbeck Haddad, "At Home in the Hijra: South Asian Muslims in the United States," in Howard Coward, John R. Hinnells, and Raymond Brady Williams, eds., *The South Asian Religious Diaspora in Britain, Canada, and the United States* (New York, 2000).

9. "Ideology, Class and the Origin of the Islamic State," *Economy and Society* 9, no. 4 (November 1980): 465.

10. Abou El Fadl, from Kuwait but educated in Egypt, is the Omar and Azmeralda Alfi Distinguished Fellow at UCLA's Law School. Alalwani, of Iraqi origin, has headed the Fiqh Council since 1986, when ISNA upgraded and expanded its thirty-year-old Fiqh Council. He is also president of the School of Islamic and Social Sciences (SISS).

11. Abou El Fadl first became known for his columns in *The Minaret*. Published by the Islamic Center of Southern California, this is one of the four leading American Muslim journals according to Sulayman Nyang, "Islam in America: a Historical Perspective," *American Muslim Quarterly* 2, no. 1 (1998): 10–11. Khaled Abou el Fadl, "The Authoritative and the Authoritarian," *The Minaret,* May 1997, 43, cites earlier jurists who explain that the purpose of a *Sharia* inquiry is not to reach the right result but the inquiry, the search for the ruling, "a life consumed by the search for the Divine Will."

12. Khaled M. Abou El Fadl, *The Authoritative and Authoritarian in Islamic Discourses: A Contemporary Case Study* (Austin, Tex., 1997), 10–11. The third edition is now out, with a lengthy new introduction and postscript. See *And God Knows His Soldiers: The Authoritative and Authoritarian in Islamic Discourses* (New York, 2001).

13. Talal Asad, *The Idea of an Anthropology of Islam* (Washington, D.C., 1986), 7, 14.

14. See the pathbreaking work by Maria Jasachok, *A Mosque of One's Own: On Being Muslim, Hui, and Woman in Contemporary China* (Richmond, Surrey, 2001).

15. See John Bowen, for example, on legal, moral, and social applications of Islamic texts in Indonesia: *Muslims through Discourse: Religion and Ritual in Gayo Society* (Princeton, N.J., 1993), 8.

16. Talal Asad, *Genealogies of Religion* (Baltimore, 1993), 208–14.

17. For earlier immigrants, see Barbara C. Aswad and Barbara Bilge, *Family and Gender Among American Muslims: Issues Facing Middle Eastern Immigrants and Their Descendants* (Philadelphia, 1996); Earle H. Waugh, Sharon McIrvin Abu-Laban, and Regula Burckhardt Qureshi, eds., *Muslim Families in North America* (Edmonton, 1991); Yvonne Yazbeck Haddad and Jane Idleman Smith, eds., *Muslim Communities in North America* (Albany, 1994); Mehdi Bozorgmehr and Alison Feldman, eds., *Middle Eastern Diaspora Communities in America* (New York, 1996). For the contemporary scene, see Yvonne Yazbeck Haddad and John L. Esposito, *Muslims on the Americanization Path?* (Atlanta, 1998); Jane I. Smith, *Islam in America* (New York, 1999).

18. See Talal Asad, "Modern Power and the Reconfiguration of Religious Traditions," *Stanford Humanities Review* 5, no. 1 (1996): 5 (http://www.stanford.edu/group/SHR/5-1/text/asad.html).

19. Marcia K. Hermansen, "In the Garden of American Sufi Movements: Hybrids and Perennials," Peter B. Clarke, ed., *New Trends and Developments in the World of Islam* (London, 1997), 155–78.

20. See Leonard, *Muslims in the United States,* Appendix II, for a chart of these organizations.

21. Khaled Abou El Fadl, "Setting Priorities," *The Minaret,* April 1998, 41. Others have described these new spokesmen as "boss Muslims" or "professional Muslims."

22. The secular Muslim scholar, Bassam Tibi, argues that globalization has swept all Muslims into an international state system that renders discussion of *dar ul Islam,* or "the abode of Islam," obsolete. Defining secularization as an inevitable part of social evolution

towards functional differentiation in modern society, Tibi says it will allow for the development of Islam as a religious ethic, a "civil theology." A political scientist born in Damascus
and living in Germany, Tibi uses Middle Eastern and North African materials and advocates
a secularization of Islamic religion, theology, and culture. Bassam Tibi, *The Crisis of Modern
Islam: a Preindustrial Culture in the Scientific Technological Age,* tr. Judith von Sivers (Salt
Lake City, 1988), xiii–xiv, 130–31, 148.

23. Larry Poston, *Islamic Da'wah in the West: Muslim Missionary Activity and the
Dynamics of Conversion to Islam* (New York, 1992), 32, citing an *Islamic Horizons* 15, no.
3 (May–June 1986) article by Dr. Muzammil Siddiqi, "Muslims in a Non-Muslim Society,"
22; for ISNA's initiative, see Steve A. Johnson, "Political Activity of Muslims in America,"
111; Sulayman S. Nyang, "Convergence and Divergence in an Emergent Community: A
Study of Challenges Facing U.S. Muslims," 247, both in Yvonne Yazbeck Haddad, ed., *The
Muslims of America* (New York, 1991).

24. One Indian American Muslim political scientist explains that since there is no explicit
declaration of war against Islam, the U.S. cannot be *dar ul harb,* and since there are no
specific treaties with resident Muslims, it cannot be *dar ul sulh.* He concludes that most
American Muslims believe the U.S. to be *dar ul aman* (as India, in fact, is categorized by
Muslims there). Mohommed A. Muqtedar Khan, "Muslims and Identity Politics in America,"
in Yvonne Yazbeck Haddad and John L. Esposito, eds., *Muslims on the Americanization
Path?* (Atlanta, 1998), 115, 118–19. Indian Muslim discourse has become increasingly
relevant since in both India and the U.S. Muslims are a minority in a secular state, very
concerned with secular pressures, with interrelations among Muslims, and interrelations
among religions Kenneth Cragg, *The Pen and the Faith: Eight Modern Muslim Writers and
the Qur'an* (London, 1985), 3–4.

25. In the 1980s, discussions within developing Muslim organizations revolved around
issues centered outside the U.S., and most American Muslim national leaders opposed Muslim participation in American politics or gave it only qualified support. Reflecting the Middle
Eastern origins of most leaders then, internal conflicts focused on Sunni-Shi'i differences
heightened by the Iranian Revolution of 1979 and the Iran-Iraq war, or Salafiyya versus
Ikhwan-ul-Muslimeen (that is, Reformist/Fundamentalist versus Muslim Brotherhood) and
intra-Ikhwan-ul-Muslimeen differences linked primarily to politics in Saudi Arabia, Egypt,
and the Gulf states. Johnson, "Political Activity," 111–24.

26. A new Center for the Study of Islam and Democracy (CSID) was formed in 2000
in Washington, D.C., as a membership-based nonprofit organization. See www.islam
-democracy.org. The Chair, Ali Mazrui, is also the Director of the Institute of Global Cultural
Studies at SUNY-Binghamton, and the Vice-Chair, John Esposito, is Director of the Center
of Muslim-Christian Understanding at Georgetown University.

27. *The Minaret,* August 1995, 22, and *The Orange Crescent* 18, no. 2 (February/March
1993) report the 1993 forming of this council, which was thought to include 65% of all
mosques in North America. Al-Amin's (the former H. Rap Brown's) arrest for murder in
2000 and recent conviction and W. D. Muhammad's reported withdrawal from the *shura* in
2000 put this arrangement in jeopardy. The National Fiqh Council was under reconstitution
in 2004, and women and Shi'i were being added.

28. Aminah Beverly McCloud, *African American Islam* (New York, 1995), 126–27.

29. *Shuras* typically try to set common dates for all mosques and Islamic centers for
Ramadan. South Asian and Arab-based congregations often differ on which day to offer

the Id prayers ending the Ramadan month of fasting. Some use Saudi Arabian sightings of the moon to determine the timing of observances in North America; others use local sightings. Some set the prayers for the day after the day of Arafat, others set them by sighting of the moon. Fifty-six member mosques and affiliated groups in southern California formed a *shura* in 1995, and twenty-six Islamic centers agreed on a common date for Id prayers in December of 1995. *Los Angeles Times,* January 20, 1996, B4. A common date for Id was still not being practiced in 2004.

30. Alalwani heads SISS, the School of Islamic and Social Sciences, first established as the International Institute of Islamic Thought (IIIT) by Dr. Ismail R. al-Faruqi and others in 1981 in Washington, D.C. In 1996, it moved to Herndon, West Virginia, and was reshaped as SISS with a small campus in Leesburg, Virginia. It offers an M.A. in Islamic Studies (an American-style graduate program) and in Imamate Studies. Christopher A. Furlow, "Islam, Science, and Modernity: From Northern Virginia to Kuala Lumpur," paper presented at the American Anthropological Association meeting, Chicago, 1999. It trains *imams* for the U.S. armed forces and has offered to train *imams* for Louis Farrakhan's Nation of Islam.

31. See Alalwani's examples of misapplied *fatwas* in Abu Amal Hadhrami, "Muslim Americans Need Own Outlook," *Islamic Horizons* 29, no. 1 (Jan.–Feb. 2000): 48–53. See also Abou El Fadl, "Striking a Balance."

32. Khaled Abou El Fadl, "The Page," *The Minaret,* January 2000, 41–42. Their opinions were the product, he says, of "oil-nourished plutocracy" (the remark points to the rising tensions between American and "foreign" forms of Islam).

33. "Conference of Books Revived," *The Minaret,* August 1996, 23.

34. Dale F. Eickelman and Jon W. Anderson, eds., *New Media in the Muslim World: The Emerging Public Sphere* (Bloomington, 1999), 12.

35. Examples of Eickelman and Anderson's "new people" include the physicians Dr. Hassan Hathout, *Reading the Muslim Mind* (Plainfield, Ind., 1995), and Dr. Shahid Athar, *Reflections of an American Muslim* (Chicago, 1994).

36. Aslam Abdullah, "Expectations from American Muslim Institutions and Leadership," *Pakistan Link,* Oct. 16, 1998, 14. He also wants social and behavioral science and management skills, not political maneuvering and wealth in those who run the Islamic centers and mosques.

37. Cragg, *The Pen,* 9.

38. Abou El Fadl, *And God Knows the Soldiers,* 1–42, lays this out forcefully.

39. C. Eric Lincoln found that, in 1960, "the Ahmadiyah were generally accepted as a legitimate sect of Islam." *The Black Muslims in America* (Boston, 1961), 221. Whether or not the Ahmadis consider their founder a Prophet is contested, and there are differences among Ahmadis too, who were declared non-Muslims in 1974 in Pakistan after the third of three court cases. The two earlier decisions, based on the same body of textual material as the third, did not find them unorthodox, and the third decision was reached only under extreme political pressure. Tayyab Mahmud shows the political forces behind all three decisions. "Freedom of Religion and Religious Minorities in Pakistan: a Study of Judicial Practice, *Fordham International Law Journal* 19, no. 1 (Oct. 1995): 40–100.

40. Ihsan Bagby, Paul M. Perl, Bryan T. Froehle, "The Mosque in America: A National Portrait," April 26, 2001, released through CAIR (Council on American-Islamic Relations), Washington, D.C. For the definitions and exclusions, Ihsan Bagby, personal communication, June 26, 2001. Project MAPS (Muslims in American Public Square), based at the Center for

Muslim-Christian Understanding at Georgetown University with an advisory board of leading academics, is also undertaking a national survey of Islamic centers, mosques, schools, and organizations.

41. Ihsan Bagby, Paul M. Perl, Bryan T. Froehle, *The Mosque in America: A National Portrait. A Report from the Mosque Study Project* (Council on American-Islamic Relations: Washington D.C., 2001), 28. Page 1 describes the respondents and other background information about the survey, which is the Muslim part of a denominational survey project coordinated by the Hartford Institute for Religious Research.

42. The questionnaire and interview results can be found at www.projectmaps.com/PMReport.htm. The method was to create a phone list by matching the zip codes of 300 randomly selected Islamic centers (from a list that omitted Nation of Islam and Ahmadi mosques) against local telephone exchanges, then identifying common Muslim surnames from the local telephone books and calling them. If the person answering identified him- or herself as Muslim, the interview proceeded. An additional sample of African American Muslims was taken in person at several (named) urban locations to compensate for their Anglo-American or non-Muslim surnames, to achieve a weighting for African Americans of 20% of the American Muslim population (many would consider this an underestimate).

43. Murad Wilfried Hofmann, "Muslims in the Next Millenium," *Islamic Horizons* (January/February 1999), 20–22. Hofmann is a retired German diplomat to Algeria and Morocco, with a Munich University doctorate in jurisprudence.

44. Mohommed A. Muqtedar Khan, "Muslims and American Politics: Refuting the Isolationist Arguments," *American Muslim Quarterly* 2, nos. 1–2 (1998): 68.

45. Orner Bin Abdullah, then President of the APPNA (Association of Pakistani Physicians in North America), said, "the U.S. Constitution and the Bill of Rights were knowingly or unknowingly based on the Islamic principles of equality and justice for all . . . [thus there is] a great similarity between the success of America, especially in science, medicine and technology, with the success that was achieved by the Muslims of Baghdad, Cordoba and Istanbul . . . in this country, Muslims have the opportunity to practice Islam as it should be practiced because there is no government edict to restrict religion, nor is there sectarian control over belief. . . ." Orner Bin Abdullah, "Eyes on the Muslim Future in America," *Pakistan Link,* August 18, 1995, 27.

46. See Karen Leonard, "American Muslims Before and After September 11, 2001," *Economic and Political Weekly* (Mumbai), June 15, 2002, for a fuller treatment of this topic.

47. Bush had been slated to meet with American Muslim leaders at 3 p.m. on September 11, with several of those I have termed the "new spokesmen." See Leonard, "American Muslims," for details.

48. Peter Ford, "Listening for Islam's Silent Majority," *Christian Science Monitor,* Nov. 5, 2001. On that very day, September 20, FBI agents showed up at Hamza Yusuf's house to question him about a talk he had given September 9 in which he had criticized the U.S. and said "this country has a great, great tribulation coming to it." His wife told them he was with the President, and they found she was correct. He had been the only Muslim invited to pray with the President, sing "God Bless America," and endorse the plans for military action. Hanna Rosin and John Mintz, "Muslim Leaders Struggle With Mixed Messages," *Washington Post,* Oct. 2, 2001, A16.

49. American Muslim leaders were caught in a situation that was difficult from the beginning and continues to be so. Proclaiming their loyalty to the U.S. and tempering their previ-

ously strong and outspoken criticisms of U.S. foreign policy, they have been confronted with the American bombing of Afghanistan, then the worsening situation in Israel and Palestine, and then uncertainties about the next targets of the "war on terrorism."

50. The respected scholar of Islam, John Esposito, told American Muslims that they had to put forth more women and young people who speak accentless American English to articulate their community's message. "Unless you tap the next generation, you are not going to make it through the next few months," he said, suggesting that, by using representatives who speak English as Americans do, Muslims would avoid appearing as though they were a predominantly foreign group. "Muslims Urged to Work on Improving Image," *Los Angeles Times,* Oct. 7, 2001, cited in CAIR Islam-Infonet American Muslim News Briefs of that date. Esposito was a speaker at a fundraising banquet for the Council on American-Islamic Relations, Los Angeles, Oct. 6, 2001.

51. A convert to Islam at age seventeen, Hamza Yusuf (42 in 2001) is the son of two academics, his father a professor of the humanities; he has studied with leading Islamic scholars in Algeria, Morocco, and Mauritania.

52. Richard Scheinin, "Expert Says Islam Prohibits Violence Against Innocents," *San Jose Mercury News,* Sept. 16, 2001.

53. Shaykh Hamza Yusuf also said that what Americans were now feeling "has been business as usual for Lebanese people, Palestinian people, Bosnian people," and when the reporter immediately asked about Israeli people, his answer was sympathetic: "Certainly the fear element is there for Israeli people . . . there are still a lot of Jewish people alive who remember the fear and terror of what happened in Europe. . . ." Interview transcribed by Jamillah Karim and sent to me via e-mail, Oct. 9, 2001. In Arabic, he said, "Infinite Justice" is an attribute of God and Muslims would consider using that phrase almost a proclamation that America was God.

54. Ibid.

55. Sufism, the mystical strand of Islam, increasingly has been attacked in the U.S. by post-1965 immigrant professionals.

56. Jack Sullivan, "Imam Hamza Yusuf: 'If you hate the west, emigrate to a Muslim country,'" *The Guardian,* Oct. 8, 2001 (the day Yusuf was to meet with religious leaders at the House of Lords in London).

57. Ibid.

58. Hanna Rosin and John Mintz, "Muslim Leaders Struggle With Mixed Messages," *Washington Post,* Oct. 2, 2001, A16. The story cites talks by Shaykh Hamza Yusuf and Muzammil Siddiqi before September 11 that had included apocalyptic warnings; Siddiqi could not be reached for comment for the *Post* story, but defended himself later by more fully contextualizing his remarks in CAIR Islam-Infonet and other venues.

59. *Los Angeles Times,* Oct. 10, 2001, B12.

60. He was a featured columnist for *The Minaret,* but it would not always publish his pieces. The Islamic Center of Southern California, which initiated MPAC and publishes *The Minaret,* is one of the most successful interethnic Islamic congregations in the U.S. and its new spokesmen make a self-conscious effort to formulate and represent an American Islam.

61. These are laid out in all his books, but see especially his *Speaking in God's Name: Islamic Law, Authority and Women* (Oxford, 2001).

62. *Los Angeles Times,* Aug. 22, 2001, B13.

63. "Derangements," *The Minaret,* special edition, Oct. 2001, 11; "When God Asks the Child," *The Minaret,* November/December 2001, 11.

64. Teresa Watanabe, "Extremists Put Own Twist on Faith," *Los Angeles Times,* Sept. 24, 2001, A13.

65. Teresa Watanabe, "Battling Islamic 'Puritans,'" *Los Angeles Times,* Jan. 2, 2002, A1.

66. For more on them, see Leonard, "American Muslims, Before and After September 11, 2001."

67. Kabbani is the representative in the U.S. of a sect based in Cyprus. He strove for ascendancy in American Muslim politics in the late 1990s, and he had been successful in presenting an individualistic and moderate form of Islam to Americans. But in 1999 Kabbani alienated the Sunni mainstream immigrant leaders by branding 80% of the American Muslim population "extremists" in a speech to the U.S. Secretary of State's Public Forum. Roundly condemned, he had been boycotted ever since by all major American Muslim groups. He was immediately called upon by the mainstream media after September 11.

68. While still a student, Khan was "the Cyberspace Mufti." "The Internet has made everyone a *mufti* [legal advisor] . . . [opening up] a variety of opinion . . . [it is] the globalization of the *mufti*." A self-described "more liberal voice," he gave advice that was no doubt controversial, reportedly saying, about homosexuality, that, while there certainly cannot be gay pride parades in mosques, "Clinton's 'Don't Ask, Don't Tell' is a perfectly Islamic solution." About premarital sex, he said "remember that Allah is all-forgiving, especially to those who repent sincerely (this is in case you have already been naughty)." Emily Wax, "The Mufti in the Chat Room: Islamic Legal Advisers Are Just a Click Away From Ancient Customs," *Washington Post,* July 31, 1999, C1.

69. I got this e-mail October 27 from a friend in Pakistan, and efforts to track down its author and source failed. The full-length message captures the mix of anger, ignorance, and intelligent questioning on the part of many Americans.

70. Nayyer Ali, M.D., "Winners and Losers," *Pakistan Link,* Nov. 2, 2001. He included President Bush, Pakistan, and Islam among the winners, India and Israel's right-wing among the losers, and Afghanistan as still unclassified. Addressing the Organization of Islamic Conference (OIC) in Qatar on October 10, the head of the American delegation said, "At no other time has the Muslim community in America been more effective in working with the American government." Dr. Jamal Barzinji, board member, American Muslim Council, and director, International Institute of Islamic Thought; full text in *Islamic Horizons,* January/February 2002, 56.

71. Dr. Ghulam M. Haniff said, "The dastardly act occurred just when Muslims were beginning to make inroads into the mainstream. . . . The Muslim community in America will be under the gun for a long time. . . . The future looks bleak and uncertain." Haniff, "WTC Tragedy: A Major Setback for Islam," *Pakistan Link,* Oct. 26, 2001, CL6. Two weeks later, he saw opportunities. "Muslims must stand up, assert their identity and not only accommodate to life in America but become champions of liberty and justice." Ghulam M. Haniff, "American Islam at a Turning Point," *Pakistan Link,* Nov. 9, 2001, CL4.

72. The most thorough story is Jake Tapper, "Islam's Flawed Spokesmen: Some of the Groups Claiming to Speak for American Muslims Find It Impossible to Speak Out Against Terrorist Groups," *Salon,* Sept. 26, 2001. He implicates CAIR and the AMC as having been tacitly supportive of extremist groups.

73. The President said this at the September 26 meeting with Muslim leaders, according to CAIR Islam-Infonet, Sept. 26, 2001.

74. Hanna Rosin and John Mintz, "Muslim Leaders Struggle With Mixed Messages," *Washington Post,* Oct. 2, 2001, A16. Siddiqi's statement that, "If you [the U.S.] continue doing injustice, and tolerate injustice, the wrath of God will come," was taken out of context (the Palestinian struggle for justice in the Middle East), he argued in a letter to the *Post* responding to the story, reproduced in CAIR Islam-Infonet, Oct. 5, 2001. See also Solomon Moore, "Fiery Words, Disputed Meaning," *Los Angeles Times,* Nov. 3, 2001, B20, for more on Siddiqi, Hamza Yusuf, Abdurahman Alamoudi of CAIR and the AMC, Nihad Awad of CAIR, and Sheikh Kabbani's spiritual mentor.

75. Mahjabeen Islam, M.D., "An American Muslim's Perspective," *Pakistan Link,* Nov. 16, 2001, CL3; and see http://www.usmae.org.

76. Hasan Zillur Rahim, "Silence of the Imams—Muslim Clerics Must Challenge Extremist Views," *India-West,* Oct. 26, 2001, A5. Rahim is a software consultant and was editor of *Iqra,* an Islamic magazine, from 1986–1999.

77. Zahir Ahmed (Chair, Islamic Research and Publications), "Mosques not Controlled by Imams," letter to *India-West,* Dec. 28, 2001, A6.

78. It was first published in Malaysia in 1992, where Wadud has been active, and then translated and published in Indonesian (1994) and Turkish (1997), evidencing the global reach of the gender *jihad.* Wadud taught in Kuala Lumpur's International Islamic University for three years and participated in Malaysia's influential "Sisters in Islam" group. See Jane Idleman Smith, *Islam in America* (New York, 1999), 201–2, for a brief biography.

79. Gisela Webb, ed., *Windows of Faith: Muslim Women Scholar-Activists in North America* (Syracuse, N.Y., 2000), 205.

80. The Progressive Union, inaugurated November 15 (Eid Monday), is led by Iranian-American Omid Safi, the editor of the *Progressive Muslims* volume, and three others (Egyptian-American Ahmed Nassef, the co-founder and editor of Muslimwakeup.com; Arab-American Sarah Eltantawi, who left her post as communications director of MPAC to hold the same post for the new group; and Hussein Ibish, Lebanese-American former Communications Director for the American-Arab Anti-Discrimination Committee (ADC).

81. *Islamic Horizons,* May/June 2003. This growing liberal, moderate, or progressive movement wherever it manifests itself is under attack from immigrant Muslim conservatives, of course, one of whom (Abid Ulla Jan 2002) calls it "neo-mod" and as harmful to Islam as America's "neo-cons."

82. Powerful African American Sunni Muslims were involved in planning this since 1999, with Jamil Al-Amin (the former H. Rap Brown) in Atlanta and Imams Siraj Wahaj and Talib Abdur-Rashid in New York; they conferred with other indigenous leaders, including Shaykh Hamza Yusuf. After Jamil Al-Amin's arrest in 2000, MANA was formally inaugurated in February of 2001. Its head is Siraj Wahaj, Sunni imam of the Al-Taqwa mosque in Brooklyn and a very charismatic speaker; other leaders include Ihsan Bagby, long a key insider in ISNA, and imams in Cleveland, Detroit, Ann Arbor, New Haven, and North Carolina.

83. http://www.mananet.org/about.asp.

84. Jackson has published on Islamic law but is now turning to African American Islam more specifically; his book, *Islam and the Black American: Looking Toward the Third Resurrection* (Oxford, 2005), is a major new interpretation of African American Islam.

85. Sherman A. Jackson, "Islam(s) East and West: Pluralism between No-Frills and Designer Fundamentalism," 112–35, in Mary L. Dudziak, ed., *September 11 in History* (Durham, N.C., 2003), 132. Jackson would use Islamic legal traditions to justify polygyny (to ease black women's poverty), Islamic punishments for adultery (when it destroys and impoverishes black families), violence (in the face of the overwhelming and unjust state power exercised by Israel against the Palestinians), and affirmative action (rather than reliance on Islam's commitment to equality).

86. Thus a widely-circulated piece by an American Muslim political scientist advises first-generation immigrants to redefine a Muslim American agenda, with a focus on issues in the U.S. and a more adequate reflection of the concerns of African American Muslims. Pointing out that Pakistani and Indian Muslims differ on Kashmir, he urges that "those . . . who feel compelled to pursue national or ethnic agendas should be free to do so through separate national or ethnic associations and lobbies." Himself a first-generation immigrant from India, Ayoob does not seem to envision the second generation taking leadership yet. Mohammed Ayoob, "How to Define a Muslim American Agenda," *New York Times,* Dec. 29, 2001.

87. Asma Gull Hasan, "First Betrayed by the Hijackers, Then by the Americans," *Pakistan Link,* Nov. 2, 2001, CL3, expresses the outrage of young American-born Muslims who feel suspicion and discrimination directed against them.

The University of Illinois Press
is a founding member of the
Association of American University Presses.

_____

University of Illinois Press
1325 South Oak Street
Champaign, IL 61820-6903
www.press.uillinois.edu